Caged Champions:
Colorful Firsts in U.S. Sports, 1855 - 2023

BOOKS by LARRY LESTER

THE NEGRO LEAGUES BOOK
with Dick Clark

THE NEGRO LEAGUES BOOK, VOLUME 2:
THE PLAYERS, 1862-1960
with Wayne Stivers

BLACK BASEBALL'S NATIONAL SHOWCASE
The East-West All-Star Game, 1933-1953
Reprinted in 2020, Expanded Version 1933-1962

BLACK BASEBALL IN KANSAS CITY
with Sammy J. Miller

BLACK BASEBALL IN DETROIT
with Sammy J. Miller and Dick Clark

BLACK BASEBALL IN CHICAGO
with Sammy J. Miller and Dick Clark

BLACK BASEBALL IN PITTSBURGH
with Sammy J. Miller

BASEBALL'S FIRST COLORED WORLD SERIES
1924 Meeting of the Hilldale Giants and the Kansas City Monarchs

RUBE FOSTER IN HIS TIME
On the Field and in the Papers with Black Baseball's Greatest Visionary

BLACK BASEBALL IN NEW YORK CITY
An Illustrated History, 1885 – 1959

Book Store

Caged Champions:
Colorful Firsts in U.S. Sports, 1855 - 2023

by Larry Lester

with a foreword by Dr. Brian Carroll

Published by NoirTech Research, Inc.
Copyright 2024 by NoirTech Research, Inc.
All Rights Reserved

For permission to reproduce selections from this book, contact:
NoirTech Research, Inc.
P.O. Box 380146
Kansas City, MO 64138
LarryLester42@gmail.com

ISBN: 978-1-7344944-4-0
ISBN: 978-1-7344944-5-7 eBook

African American Athletes, 2. Baseball, 3. Basketball, 4. Billiards, 5. Bowling, 6. Boxing, 7. Car Racing, 8. Cycling, 9. Football, 10. Golf, 11. Hockey, 12. Horse Racing, 13. Olympics, 14. Rodeo, 15. Swimming, 16. Tennis, 17. Track and Field, 18. Rule Changes

Printed in the United States of America
Seventh printing – Revised afterword

Book Cover Design: Artrocity from 99Designs

www.LarryLester42.com
@LesterLester42 – Instagram
LarryLester42 – LinkedIn
@LarryLester42 - X

Corrections and additions are welcomed.

Dedicated to my daughter:
Marisa Nikol Lester
1982 – 2021

In Memory of . . .

Shu'aib Abdul-Latif
Matthew Ajibade
Angelo Albano
Grady Alexis
Julian Alexander
Clinton Allen
Jerriel Da'Shawn Allen
Lawrence Allen
Louis Allen
Tom Allen
Wendell Allen
Javier Ambler
Derrick Ambrose Jr.
Jerry Lee Amie
Anthony Anderson
Edward Anderson
James Craig Anderson
Martin Anderson
Orion "Owen" Anderson
Tanisha Anderson
William Anderson
Brian Edmund Andrew
Ahmaud Arbery
Henry Argo
Deandre Armstrong-Starks
George Armwood
Anthony Ashford
Alonzo Ashley
Jimmy Atchison
Aaron Bailey
Leonard Bailey Jr.
Walter Bailey
Chance David Baker
Jordan Baker
William Baker
Ricky Ball
Frazier Baker
Roy Banks
Willie Ray Banks
Orlando Barlow

Mark Barmore Jr.
Herman Barnes
Anton Barrett Sr.
Erdman Bascomb
James Bauduy
Robert Beal
Tony Bean
Ronald Beasley
Daniel Bell
Sean Bell
Tedock Bell
John Bennett
Leonard Bennett
George Bibins
La'Vante Biggs
Ontario Billups
Frisco Blackwood
Allan Blanchard
Sandra Bland
Tonia Blanding
Thurman Blevins
Carolyn Sue Boetticher
Glen Boldware
Leroy Boyd
Rekia Boyd
Tarika Boyd
Mose Bozier
Emantic Fitzgerald Bradford Jr.
Thomas Hency Brewer Sr.
Willie Wallace Brewster
Dakota Bright
Rumain Brisbon
Keith Briscoe
James Brisette
Allen Brooks
Rayshard Brooks
Robert Brooks
William Brooks
Benjamin Brown
Corey Brown

Curtis Brown
Devin Brown
James Brown Jr.
Leonard Brown
Michael Brown Jr.
Niecey Brown
Joe Brown
Patterson Brown
Rebecca Brown
Robert Brown
Thomas Brown
Tyrone Brown
William Brown
Deondre Brunston
Henry Bryant
Jashon Bryant
Garfield Burley
Antonio Butler
George Bush
Sam Bush
Michael Byoune
James Byrd Jr.
Marcella Byrd
Damien Cameron
Aaron Campbell
Herman Canty
Mariam Carey
Angela Michelle Carr
Kiwane Carrington
Bonita Carter
Sam Carter
Philando Divall Castile
Wendell Celestine Jr.
Kenneth Chamberlain Sr.
Martin Chambers
Joseph Chandler
James Chaney
William Chapman II
Johnnie Mae Chappell
The Charleston #9

Dewayne Chatt
Michael Carpenter
Keith Childress Jr.
Henry Choate
Alexia Christian
Jamar Clark
James Clark
John William Clark
Mark Clark
Stephon Clark
Dominique Clayton
Elias Clayton
Steve Clemons
Avery Cody Jr.
Fred Coker
Bilal Dashawn Colbert
Trevon Cole
Sharonda Coleman-Singleton
John Coley
Addie Mae Collins
Darrick Collins
Robert Collins
Walter Collins
Malcolm Comeaux
J. L. Compton
Townsend Cook
Carl Cooper
Howard Cooper
James Cooper
Khiel Coppin
Henry Corbin
Emmanuel Cosbey
Rufus Council
Maurice Leroy Cox
Dennis Crawford
John Crawford III
Tyree Crawford
Stanton L. Crew
Johnnie Cromartie
Terence Crutcher
Michelle Cusseaux
Vernon F. Dahmer Sr.
William Dalton
D'Koy Dancy
Ben Daniels
John L. Daniels Jr.
Jonathan Myrick Daniels
Lige Daniels
Henry Darley
Keith Daughtry
Dan Davis
Jake "Shake" Davis
Jordan Russell Davis
Robert Joseph Davis
Shantee Davis
Vernard Davis
Donta Dawson
Leonard Deadwyler

Michael Lorenzo Dean
Henry Hezekiah Dee
Norris Dendy
Jeffrey Dennis
Henry Denson
Robert Dentmond
Egbert David Dewgard
Amadou Diallo
Ronnie Diamond
Will Dibrell
Jack Dillingham
Richard Dillon
Broderick Dixon
Charles Dixon Sr.
Michael Donald
Patrick Dorismond
Reginald Doucet
Lucille Douglas
Demetrius DuBose
Samuel DuBose
Román Ducksworth Jr.
Henry Duncan
Horace Duncan
Quarius Dunham
Willie Earle
Albert Easley
Jordan Edwards
Willie Edwards Jr.
Jesse Eley
Michael Ellerbe
Manuel Ellis
Eugene Ellison
Frank Embree
Miguel Espinal
Silas Esters
Randolph Evans
Ronald Evans
Medgar Evers
Lizzie Durr
Damon Lamont Falls
Flint Farmer
DeAunta Farrow
Darren Faulkner
Dominic Felder
Malcolm Ferguson
Jonathan Ferrell
Castenego Ficcarotta
Justin Fields
Magruder Fletcher
George Floyd
Janisha Fonville
Ezell Ford
Joseph Forrest
Eric Daniel Foster Jr.
Ronell Foster
Thomas P. Foster
Isaiah Fountain
Shereese Francis

Leo Frank
Mannix Franklin Sr.
Terrance Franklin
Shelly M. Frey
William Furr
Hattie Gainer
Korryn Gaines
Lloyd Gaines
Nathaniel Levi Gaines
Peter Matthew Gaines
Jerrald De-Shaun Gallion
Cjavar Galmon
Jonny Gammage
Antonio García Jr.
Edward Garner
Eric Garner
Simeon Garnett
Paul Gaston
George Gay
James Gerth
Philip Lafayette Gibbs
Lionel Gibson
Stanley Gibson
Nease and John Gillespie
Raymond Gilmer
Thomas Gilyard
Brendan Glenn
Roy Glenn Jr.
Clifford Glover
Henry Glover
William Godley
Andrew Goodman
Augustus Goodman
Casey Goodson Jr.
Joseph Gordon
Joseph Gould
Robert Graetz
Ramarley Graham
Oscar Grant
Maurice Granton Jr.
Freddie Gray
Kimani Gray
Annette Green
James Earl Green
Malice Green
William Green
Charles Greenlee
Dennis Gregory
Brianna Grier
D'ettrick Griffin
Michael Griffith
Deron Grimmitt
Lejoy Grissom
Bobby Gross
Paul Guihard
Dejuan Guillory
Akai Gurley
Melvin Guy

Aaren Gwinn
LaTanya Haggerty
Lavall Hall
Lee Hall
Robert "Bobby" Hall
Dontre Hamilton
Samuel Ephesians Hammond Jr.
Fred Hampton Sr.
Lamont Harmon
Donald Harp
James Harper
Robert Harper
Darnisha Harris
Eric Harris
Nathaniel Harris
Robert D'Lon Harris
Ernest Harrison
John Hartfield
Tyrone Hawkins
Yusef Hawkins
Kobe Heisler
Alexander Henderson
Amaree'ya Henderson
John Eric Henderson
Mark Henderson
Daniel Kenneth Henry
Heather Heyer
Nicholas Heyward Jr.
Christopher Hicks
Kevin Hicks
Andre Maurice Hill
Anthony Hill
Robert Hillard
Luther Holbert
Richard Holtz
Sam Hose
Mardio House
Frank Howard
William Howard
Willie James Howard
Marquis Hudspeth
Edward Lamont Hunt
Cynthia Graham Hurd
Robert James Hutton
Fred Ingraham
Rosa Lee Ingram
Eddie Irizarry
David Jackson
Elmer Jackson
Jimmy Lee Jackson
Jerry Jackson
Luther Jackson
Roosevelt Jackson
Susie Jackson
Wharlest Jackson
Michael Patrick Jacobs Jr.
John Henry James
Kendra James

Will James
Guy Jarreau Jr.
Botham Jean
Atatiana Jefferson
Dan Jenkins
Arthur Johnson
Charquissa Johnson
Clyde Johnson
Dion Johnson
James Johnson
Matthew Johnson
Trevon Johnson
Aiyana Jones
Betty Jones
Corey Jones
Derrick Jones
Henry Lee Jones Jr.
Jesse Levelt-Everett Jones
Juan Markee Jones
Lamontez Jones
Malik Jones
Nathaniel Jones
Prince Jones
Ralkina Jones
Robert Jones
Roy Lee Jones
Virgil Jones
William Jones
Xavier Jones
Derrick Jordan
David Joseph
India Kager
Jaahnavi Kandula
William Keemer
Edward Kemp
Isaac Kemp
Ami "Whit" Ketchum
Garfield King
Adrena Kitt
Bruce Klunder
Michael Knight
Félix Kumi
Robert Lacey
Ernest Lacy
Anolt Joseph Laguerre Jr.
Cameron Lamb
Ethel Lee Lance
Edward Lang
Berry Lawson
James Leatherwood
Anthony Lee
Euel Lee
General Lee
George Wesley Lee
Herbert Lee
John Lee
Quintonio Legrier
William Leonard

John LeRoy
Rufus Lesseur
Clifford Lewis
Robert Lewis
Warren Lewis
Henry List
Viola Liuzzo
Trey Antuan Lively
Clement Lloyd
Rita Lloyd
Amir Locke
Eric Logan
Robert V. Logan
Manuel Loggins Jr.
William Lomax
Elijah Parish Lovejoy
Dexter Luckett
Charleena Lyles
Donovan Lynch
Patrick Lyoya
Eddie Lee Macklin
Ronald Madison
Edward Mallet
Asshams Pharoah Manley
George Mann
Joseph Mann
Kenneth Marion
Michael Lee Marshall
Howard Eugene Martin
Trayvon Martin
Kevin Bruce Mason
Kevin Matthews
Larry Daniel Matthews
Lorenzo Matthews
Anthony Merisier
Arther McAfee Jr.
Frederick Devon McAllister
David McAtee
Jermaine McBean
Renisha McBride
Spencer McCain
Christopher McCorvey
Willie McCoy
Sammie McCullough
Kendric McDade
Jeremy McDole
LaQuan McDonald
Arthur McDuffie
Isaac McGhie
Francis McIntosh
Natasha McKenna
Michael Wayne McKnight Jr.
Elijah McLain
Tom McLain
Keith Harrison McLeod
Genie McMeans Jr.
Denise McNair
George Meadows

Lawrence Meyers
Christopher Middleton
Delano Herman Middleton
Depayne Middleton-Doctor
Charles Mitchell
Christopher D. Mitchell
Luther H. Mitchell
Robert Mitchell
Cedric Jamal Mifflin
Amos Miller
Arthur Miller Jr.
Philip Miller
Seay Miller
Willie Miller
Jack Mingo
Paul Monroe
Stephanie Montague
Bobby Moore
Brandon Moore
Charles Eddie Moore
DeCarlos Moore
Harry and Harriette Moore
Jason Moore
Kayla Moore
Oliver Moore
Oneal Moore
Will Moore
William Lewis Moore
Eddie Moss
Charlie Mack Murphy
Cornelius Murray
Earl Murray
Willie Murray Jr.
Robert Murtore
Don Myrick
Claude Neal
Anthony Nelson
Laura and L. D. Nelson
Randy Nelson
Samuel Nelson
Gabriella Nevarez
Tyre Nichols
Michael Noel
Sherron Norman
Eleanor Northington
Charles William Orebo
Christopher A. Okamoto
Roger Owensby Jr.
Paul O'Neal
Rubén Ortega
Irvo Otieno
Philip Pannell
Dante Parker
Mack Charles Parker
Benjamin Payne
Larry Payne
Alfred Peachlum
George Washington Peck

Lemuel Penn
James Jahar Perez
Dyzhawn Perkins
Frankie Ann Perkins
Richard Perkins Jr.
Julius "July" Perry
Harold Phillips
Charmene Pickering
John Pickett
Baron Pikes
Clemente C. Pinckney
Darius Pinex
Eugene Pitchford
Eric Pitt
Woodrow Player III
Michael Pleasance
Dennis Plowden
Aubrey Pollard
Leslie Prater
Jonathan Price
Junior Prosper
Daniel T. Prude
Tyrea Pryor
Michael Pugh
Gilbert Quinn
Sydney Randolph
Eric Reason
James Joseph Reeb
Dreasjon "Sean" Reed
Joseph Reed
Sam Reed
Andrea Nicole Reedy
Charles Reese
Clayde Reese
John Earl Reese
Jeremiah Reeves
Franklyn Reid
Jerame Reid
Kurt Reinhold
Tamir Rice
George Richard-Meyers
John Richards
Roy Lee Richards
Bunk Richardson
Joseph Richardson
Levonia Riggins
Gregory Riley
Joseph Riley
James Rivera Jr.
Thomas Rivers
Marcus Roach-Burris
Raymond Robair
Carole Robertson
Chad Robertson
Albert Robinson
Dick Robinson
Darius Robinson
Emery Robinson

Jamarion Robinson
Johnny Robinson
Kevin Robinson
Shatona Robinson
Tony Robinson Jr.
Torrey Lamar Robinson
Bernard Rogers
Christopher Rogers
Deravis Caine Rogers
Mario Romero
Calin Evonte Roquemore
Ernest Roquemore
Charles Roundtree Jr.
Antwon Rose II
Aura Rosser
Desmond Rudolph
John D. and Charles Ruggles
Craige Ruise Jr.
Carnell Russ
Robert Russ
Timothy Russell
James Rutledge
Michael Sabbie
Najier Salaam
Aquan Salmon
Donnie Sanders
Jonathan Sanders
Tywanza Sanders
Marquintan Sandlin
Ernest Sayon
Bothem Sean
Demarcus Semer
Michael Schwerner
Antronie Scott
Dane Scott Jr.
James T. Scott
Keith Scott
Ligon Scott
Marie Scott
Sal Saran Scott
Walter Scott
Jacob Servais
Errol Shaw
Matthew Shepard
Michael Sherard
Thomas Shipp
William Shorter
George and Ed Silsbee
Bennie Simmons
Daniel L. Simmons
John Simms
Allen Simpson
James Sims
Richard Sims
Yvonne Smallwood
Marquez Smart
Anthony Smashum
Alonzo Smith

Alphonso Smith	Breonna Taylor	Melvin Watkins
Abram Smith	Che Taylor	Shawn Watson
David Smith	Christian Taylor	Joe Watts
Denver Smith	Donald Taylor	Brandon Webber
Eric Smith	James Taylor	Erson Alexander Welchen
Henry Ezekial Smith	John Taylor	Cynthia Wesley
Jaffort Demont Smith	Recy Taylor	Tyrone West
Justin H. Smith	Fred Temple	Jordan West-Morson
Lamar "Ditney" Smith	Justin Tiegen	Bernard Whitehurst Jr.
Marshall Smith Jr.	Andre DeMon Thomas	Christopher Whitfield
Michael Smith	Christopher Thomas	William J. Whitfield
Parnell Smith	Danny Ray Thomas	Ben Chester White
Sylville Smith	Ernest Thomas	Phillip White
Ted Smith	Leonard Thomas	John H. Wilkins
Tony Bernard Smith Jr.	Terrill Thomas	Accelyne Williams
Vincent Smith	Simmont Donta Thomas	Arthur R. Williams
Winston Smith	Timothy Thomas	Cletis Williams
Yvette Smith	Myra Thompson	Courtney Williams
John Snowden	Windy Gail Thompson	Davinian Williams
Eloise Spellman	Jesse Thornton	Derek Williams
Kionte Desean Spencer	Will Thrasher	Elbert Williams
William Spencer	Charles Thurber	Eugene Williams
Robert Warren Spike	Haki Thurston	Malissa Williams
Alberta Spruill	Emmett Till	Matthew Williams
Rubin Stacy	Willie Sherman Tillman	Melvin Williams
Aiyana Stanley-Jones	Clarence Triggs	Mike Williams
William Stanley	Henry Truman	Perry Williams
Timothy Stansbury	Mary Truxillo	Roy Jean Williams
Dontrell Stephens	Brownie Tuggles	Yvette Williams
John W. Stephens	Willie Turks	Janet Wilson
Alton Sterling	Mary Turner	Joseph Wilson
Cordelia Stevenson	Pamela Turner	Mack Wilson
Lloyd D. Stevenson	Raynette Turner	Shawn Wilson
Darrius Stewart	Benjamin Uwumarogie	Tarika Wilson
Michael Stewart	Donald "D.J." Venable	Joe Winters
Troy Stewart	Ariston Waiters	George Witherell
Dwight Stiggons	Eugene Walker	Isaac Woodard
Marcellis Stinnette	Jayland Walker	Mack Woodfox
George Stinney Jr.	Shem Walker	Ellis Woodland
James Stokes	Reginald Wallace	Alteria Woods
Ryan Stokes	Tom Waller	Leonard Woods
Braylon Stone	Corey Ward	Charles Wright
Dontaze Storey Jr.	Cornelius Ware	Cleo Wright
Vivian Strong	David Antjuan Ware	Daunte Wright
Kenneth Strother	Virgil Lamar Ware	William Wright
Deon Studiemyer	Lloyd Warner	Diante Yarber
James Sullivan	Cornell Warren	Kemp Yarborough
Darrell Swain	Patrick Lynn Warren	Lester Steven Yarbrough
George Talbert	Brandon Washington	Arthur Young
Frank Tanner	Domonick Washington	Sammy Leamon Younge Jr.
Darius Tarver	Jesse Washington	Ousmane Zongo
Preston Tate	Steven Washington	

Say their names out loud. Silence will not end systemic racism and injustice.
Otherwise the status quo suggests that this list of names will only grow.

"Until the killing of Black men, Black Mothers' sons, becomes as important to the rest of the country as the killing of a White Mother's son, we who believe in freedom cannot rest." – Ella Baker

Table of Contents

Introduction: The Trophy Cage vi
Foreword by Brian Carroll, Ph. D. vii
Cage 1NE: Champion Timeline 9
Cage 2WO: Baseball Champions 113
Cage 3HREE: Basketball Champions 151
Cage 4OUR: Boxing Champions...199
Cage 5IVE: Football Champions..206
Cage 6IX: Golf Champions 248
Cage S7VEN: Hockey Champions...253
Cage 8IGHT: Horse Racing Champions 259
Cage 9INE: Olympic Champions 264
Cage 10EN: Rodeo Champions 280
Cage E11VEN: Tennis Champions 281
Cage 12ELVE: Other Caged Champions 287
Cage 13HIRTEEN: Roadblocks, Rules & Protests 295
Afterword...315
Bibliography 316
Index 320

v

Introduction: The Trophy Cage©

Somewhere in a dark dusty corner of a decaying building,
Stands a tall mahogany veneered trophy case surrounded with glass,
Trimmed in gold with a story to be told.
> Behind the glass roadblock are rows of bronze trophies
> Meekly echoing the triumphs of sporting exploits,
> Their cups overflowed with tears of neglect,
> One by one they vainly beckon to share their glorious past with the masses.

Quarantined from society's mainstream,
They are outlawed into the cage,
Meanwhile, their metal bodies precariously vibrate,
To emit a siren's welcome, only to be ignored by those who pass.
> Over time, once glittered with achievement,
> The trophies became tarnished with neglect.
> Their brass bodies pitted from daggers of racism,
> While off-color remarks smudge their once shining exterior.

Trophy after trophy, dusty with untold stories,
That once gleamed with excitement,
Are now quietly spirited away, one by one.
> While they are only a shadowy remembrance of a once bright life,
> The remaining cups thirst for visitors,
> As they plead to surrender their countless stories.

From dawn to dusk, they stand tall,
Reaching skyward for acceptance,
Absorbing the elements from a blind society,
Never to see the light of recognition.
> Unable to penetrate the glass barrier,
> The trophy cups become empty of ambition.
> One by one, randomly,
> They crumble before their next confession.

Their achievements are visible, yet unseen behind the glass façade,
As they are never touched with accolades from the sporting gods.
> Who has the keys to this dark dungeon?
> Who will discover these caged trophies?

And expose their unheralded glory?
Or will they live in an everlasting purgatory?

Foreword by Brian Carroll, Ph. D.

A few years ago, I researched the city of Savannah's complex civic forgetting of its principal role in Georgia's slave trade and in enslaving the nameless millions of African slaves shipped to its port. A city so proud of its Southern charms and traditions, Savannah has but one monument acknowledging slavery, a memorial absent of any enslavers and of any individual names at all. Ambiguous and, sadly, accessible to touristic teenagers whose amusement park thrill ride treatment of the memorial both profane and vandalize it, the monument is as much an enactment of forgetting as it is one of remembrance. By remembering so little, the monument forgets almost everything.

To tour Savannah's plantation museums and historical homes is to learn the progeny, construction, and value of their many furnishings – a Victorian settee in mahogany or Louis XIV armoire with inlays – but to learn virtually nothing of the enslaved upon which those estates' fortunes were made. Sure, occasionally, a long-time "servant" might get a photo on the wall, perhaps with her first name: Bessie the cook or Cuffee the foreman. Instead of discussing "slaves," these show homes provide tourists with information about "servants." Thus, visitors to Savannah are encouraged to "learn" and perpetuate an inaccurate, mystified understanding of the importance of the institution of slavery and the city's central role in its propagation without learning a single name or biography of the enslaved. Recovery of history begins with names, dates, and places.

His entire career, and a prolific career it has been, Larry Lester has sought to discover, reveal, chart, and place into historical context the people of Black baseball history, beginning with their names. Only by naming them can they even exist, at least in a historical sense. The very minimum requirement for consideration and remembrance, after all, is a person's name. He has labored to give (back) these athletes their identities, their statistical achievements, and, in some cases, a place in the National Baseball Hall of Fame. With his leadership, alongside chief project coordinator Dr. Jeremy Krock, of the Negro Leagues Baseball Grave Marker Project, Lester has also labored to make sure that these baseball men get the honor of being named in death, as well, so many of them still in unmarked graves. The problem of unmarked graves traces its origin to the fact that far too much history is white-centric, valorizing white ways of organizing the world and, by default, erasing any significant contribution of Black Americans. This is the dominant narrative to which this book serves as counter-memory. How many people know of Babe Ruth and Ty Cobb? How many of those same people know of Moses Fleetwood Walker and Rube Foster?

The Black narrative presents a history of struggle and resistance against brutality, resilience in the face of injustice, and dignity in the face of inhumanity, as this book helps to make manifest. An awful lot of people would rather not be confronted by that. Lester steps into this void regularly, frequently, with passion and conviction, affirming in this case the heroes of American sporting endeavors by acknowledging their names and places in the larger American sporting narrative. Many of these names and dates belong to people who etched those names and dates into history only after a long struggle and against seemingly impossible odds. Some merely happened upon their "first" status. A few would rather not be marked or known as "the first." For all three sorts, this book humanizes the subjects of its entries by personalizing them, by giving them names, identities, and histories, and by speaking to their individual achievements.

A name, a voice, and place in the foreground in American history are among the gifts Lester gives (back) to the pantheon of pioneers enshrined in this roster of human achievement, a roster sure to be updated as the great recovery project of Black history continues. As a collection of entries, a curated population of sports heroes, Lester's book centralizes the indispensable role of these pioneers in American sports over time. Often segregated physically, socially, then in history and history writing, these names, these people, these athletes can now re-join the larger American sporting narrative to which they always belonged. This book is an acknowledgement of the contributions these athletes made to sports and through those sporting endeavors to American society at large.

By placing these sporting figures and these Black sporting endeavors, leagues, and organizations in the foreground where they deserve to be, unavoidably shifted to the background, however, are the suffering and great personal cost many of these athletes paid so that elite Whites might enjoy their wonderful lives – owners, managers, even fans and spectators. Thus, this de facto "hall of fame" points to the contradictions of the American dream denied to so many Black Americans, including Black American athletes for so long, because though this book is expansive, its number of Black athletes is relatively modest. This modesty is a testimony to the long-fingered legacy of slavery, segregation, and race discrimination in all walks of American life for the entirety of American history. As the historian Simon Schama said in a critique of the TV phenomenon and pseudo-historical *Downton Abbey*, "History's meant to be a bummer, not a stroll down memory lane." But, make no mistake, this book and its many heroes are a celebration and not a dirge. As a custodian of the past, a discoverer and preserver of discrete facts, Lester furnishes readers with history, memory, "firsts," and stories that should be told, even shouted from the rooftops.

Brian Carroll, Ph. D.
Author of *A Devil's Bargain: The Black Press and Black Baseball, 1915-1955* (Routledge, 2015) and *When to Stop the Cheering: The Black Press, The Black Community, and the Integration of Professional Baseball* (Routledge, 2006), professor of communication, and a prolific Black press and sports historian.

ACKNOWLEDGEMENTS

Forever grateful to:
Lisa Lisa Feder - Aesthetic Analyst
John Graf – Fabulous Fact Checker
Rev. Tony Curtis Henderson – Spiritual Savant
Sam Lacy – Pioneer Advisor
Hisayo Nishimaru – Editor Supreme
Philip Ross – He was there!
Fay Vincent – Magnificent Mentor
& Andrew Spurgeon "Doc" Young

Cage 1NE: Champion Timeline

1855
"The color of the skin is in no way connected to the strength of mind or intellectual powers."
– Benjamin Banneker, *Banneker's Almanac*, 1796

The *Newark Daily Mercury* reports the first known game between two colored baseball teams, the St. John's and the Union Clubs. The game is played in East Orange, N.J. No score is reported.

1857
"If you turn a blind eye to racism, you become an accomplice to it." – Oprah Winfrey

Major White League baseball's first recognized African American baseball player, Moses Fleetwood Walker is born in Mt. Pleasant, Ohio.

1859
The *New York Anglo-African* prints the first known box score between two Black teams. The Henson Base Ball Club of Jamaica (New York) defeats the Unknowns of Weeksville, 54 to 43, in Jamaica, Long Island.

1860
"Change comes from listening, learning, caring and conversations." – Gwen Ifill

Brooklyn Excelsiors become the first African American baseball team to tour the U.S.

1866
"I was motivated to be different in part because I was different." – Donna Brazile

Abe Hawkins becomes the first African American jockey to win the Jerome Handicap, riding "Watson" and to win the Travers Stakes, riding "Merrill."

1867
"An America that looks away is ignoring not just the sins of the past but the sins of the present and the certain sins of the future."
- Ta-Nehisi Coates

The National Association of Base Ball Players (NABBP) votes to exclude Black players and their teams from membership, stating "any club which may be composed of one or more colored persons" will be barred. The NABBP reason was "If colored clubs were admitted there would be in all probability some division of feeling, whereas, by excluding them no injury could result to anyone."

1869
"Amnesia gets in the way of atonement in America." – Michele Norris

The Philadelphia Pythians become the first Black team to defeat an all-White squad, defeating the cross-town rival City Items, 27-17. The *New York Clipper* reports, "The prejudices of race are rapidly disappearing. A week or two ago we chronicled a game between the Pythians (colored) and Olympics (white) clubs of Philadelphia. This affair was a great success, financially and otherwise."

1870
"Do not look the other way, do not hesitate. Recognize that the world is hungry for action, not words.
Act with courage and vision." – Nelson Mandela

Viro "Black Sam" Small makes his wrestling debut at Owney's Bastille in New York, making him the first known African American wrestler in the U.S.

Ed Brown, or "Brown Dick," becomes the first African American jockey to win the Belmont Stakes, riding "Kingfisher."

Raleigh Colston becomes the first African American jockey to win the Kenner Stakes, riding "Enquirer."

Colorful Firsts in U.S. Sports

1872

An ideology that would become the motto of the Negro National League, founded by Rube Foster in 1920, was defined by Frederick Douglass at the Colored Men's National Convention in New Orleans, Louisiana. At Mechanics Hall on April 14th, Douglass spoke for the ages: "The Republican Party is the ship, all else is the sea." The delegates add, "Owing our political emancipation in this country to Republican legislation, to which all other parties and political shades of opinion were unjustly and bitterly opposed, we would be blind to our prospects and false to our best interests did we identify ourselves with any other organization."

1875

Thirteen of 15 jockeys in the inaugural Kentucky Derby are African Americans. William Lakeland (riding "Ascension") and Cyrus Holloway (on "Enlister") are the only White jockeys. Oliver Lewis rides "Aristides" to the winner's circle. Black jockeys win 15 of the first 28 Derbies.

1876

Nat Love or "Deadwood Dick" becomes the first known African American rodeo champion.

Charles A.C. Smith from Macon, Ga. claims the title of the first World Colored Heavyweight Champion. Known as "The Black Thunderbolt" he stood 5-foot-11 and weighed upwards of 230 pounds.

1877

Billy Walker rides "Baden-Baden" to victory in the Kentucky Derby and he becomes the first African American jockey to win the Dixie Handicap, riding "King Fargo."

1878

John W. "Bud" Fowler is the first known African American professional baseball player when he plays for the Live Oaks from Lynn, Mass., of the International Association. He pitches a 3-0 shutout over the Tecumseh Club of London, Ontario.

Cuba forms its first baseball league. It is called the Cuban League and operates until 1961.

1879

"I am not asking you as a white person to see yourself as an enslaver. I'm asking you as an American to see all of the freedoms that you enjoy and see how they are rooted in things that the country you belong to condoned or actively participated in the past."

- Ta-Nehisi Coates

Isaac Murphy becomes the first African American jockey to win the Clark Handicap, riding "Falsetto."

1880

George Lewis rides "Fonso" to victory in the Kentucky Derby.

Milton Young is the owner of several Kentucky Derby horses. His horse "Bancroft" finishes 3rd in the 1880 Derby, "Getaway" finishes 5th in the 1881 Derby, "Lost Cause" finishes 13th in the 1882 Derby, "Once Again" finishes 3rd in the 1889 Derby and "Ten Booker" finishes 3rd in the 1885 Derby.

Haiti-American Frank Hart, known as "The Negro Wonder or Black Dan," becomes the first Black world record holder in the 19th century sport of pedestrianism. Born Fred Hichborn, Hart is also the first Black athlete depicted on a sports card, trading card or tobacco-card set, when he appears in Thomas H. Hall's 1880 "Between the Acts & Bravo Cigarettes" card set, N344.

1881

"Your ordinary acts of love and hope point to the extraordinary promise that every human life is of inestimable value."

– Desmond Tutu

Moses Fleetwood Walker, an African American catcher for the Cleveland Whites, is not allowed to play against the Eclipse in Louisville, Ky. In 1884, the Louisville Eclipse and Walker's new team the Toledo Blue Stockings would join the American Association, a designated major league, obliging integrated play on the diamond.

Isaac Murphy becomes the first African American jockey to win the Saratoga Cup, riding "Checkmate."

1882

Babe Hurd rides "Apollo" to victory in the Kentucky Derby.

John Stoval becomes the first African American jockey to win the Kentucky Oaks, riding "Katie Creel." He would repeat the next year at the Kentucky Oaks, riding "Vera." Stoval is also the first African American winner of the Spinaway Oaks, riding "Miss Woodford" and the first to win the Alabama Stakes, riding the "Belle of Runnymede."

Billy Walker becomes the first African American jockey to win the St. Louis Derby, riding "Monogram."

George "Old Chocolate" Godfrey wins the first Colored Heavyweight Championship of America by knocking out Charles Hadley in round six. The referee John L. Sullivan, had refused to fight Godfrey at Bailey's Arena in South Boston, in 1881.

1883
"Truth is powerful, and it prevails." – Sojourner Truth

John Stoval becomes the first African American jockey to win the Clipsetta Stakes, riding "Eva S."

Isaac Murphy becomes the first African American jockey to win the first Latonia Derby, riding "Leonatus."

The *Toledo Daily Blade*, March 15, reports that the executive committee of the Northwestern League meets at Toledo's Boody House to consider "a motion … by the representative from the Peoria, Ill., club that no colored player be allowed in the league." This motion is made to ban mulatto Moses Fleetwood Walker from playing. After a hostile discussion, the motion is defeated, allowing Walker to play.

Shep Trusty of the Philadelphia Orions becomes the first player to pitch, catch and hit a home run in the same game. His Orions defeat the hometown Hartville Club of Philadelphia, 12 to 10.

A colored women's baseball team from Philadelphia, called the Dolly Vardens start play.

Cap Anson of the Chicago White Stockings refuses to play the Toledo Blue Stockings if Moses Fleetwood Walker takes the field. Anson pouts in the *Toledo Daily Blade*, "We'll play this here game, but won't play never no more with the nigger in."

1884

Isaac Murphy becomes the first Black jockey to win the Latonia Cup riding "Harry Gilmore," and the first to win the American Derby riding "Modesty." Murphy riding "Buchanan," also wins his first of three Kentucky Derbies.

John Stoval becomes the first African American jockey to win the U.S. Hotel Stakes, riding "Kosciusko."

George Withers becomes the first African American jockey to win the Great Western Handicap, riding "Boatman."

Moses Fleetwood Walker, catcher, becomes the first recognized African American to play in the white-centric major leagues with the Toledo Blue Stockings of the American Association.

1885
"It Is easier to build strong children than fix broken men" – Frederick Douglass

Erskine Henderson rides "Joe Cotton" to victory in the Kentucky Derby and in the Tennessee Derby.

Tiny Williams becomes the first African American jockey to win the Flatbush Stakes, riding "Charity."

Ed West becomes the first African American jockey to win the Tennessee Oaks, riding "Ida Hope."

The *Utica Morning Herald* reports a colored umpire, Jacob Francis from Syracuse, "umpired the game to the complete satisfaction of both teams." The game is between the Syracuse Stars and the Providence Grays of the New York State League.

The Cuban Giants are organized by Frank P. Thompson, head waiter at the Argyle Hotel in Babylon, N.Y., to become the first salaried professional Black team in the U.S. The players earn from $12 to $18 a week.

1886
"In the darkest moments I can still find peace." – Marian Anderson

George Stovey wins 16 of the 49 games won by the Jersey City Skeeters (or Jerseys) in the Eastern League.

Frank Grant, second baseman for the Buffalo Bisons in the International League becomes its first African American player. The next season other African American players Moses Fleetwood Walker, Robert Higgins, William J. Renfroe, George Stovey and Bud Fowler join Grant.

The Southern League of Colored Base Ballists is founded with roughly 19 teams based in Florida, Tennessee, Georgia, Louisiana, Alabama and South Carolina. The teams are: Athletic Baseball Club - Jacksonville, Fla; Boardways (or Boards) Baseball Club - Savannah, Ga.; Callathumpians Baseball Club - Tallahassee, Fla.; Chattanooga Baseball Club - Chattanooga, Tenn.; Clipper Baseball Club - Jacksonville, Fla.; Daisy Cutter Baseball Club - Fernandina, Fla.; Eclipse Baseball Club - Memphis, Tenn.; Eureka Baseball Club - Memphis, Tenn.; Fox Hunter Baseball Club - Macon, Ga.; Fultons Baseball Club - Charleston, S.C.; Garden Lilies Baseball

Colorful Firsts in U.S. Sports

Club - Palatka, Fla.; Lafayette Baseball Club - Savannah, Ga.; Macedonia Baseball Club - Jacksonville, Fla.; Montgomery Baseball Club - Montgomery, Ala.; Pensacola Baseball Club - Pensacola, Fla.; Roman Cities Baseball Club - LaVilla, Fla.; Tallapoosa Baseball Club - St. Augustine, Fla.; The Georgia Champions' Baseball Club - Atlanta, Ga.; and the Union Baseball Club - New Orleans, La. The league folds in August, naming the Memphis Eclipse as unofficial league champion.

Peter "The Black Prince" Jackson becomes the first African American to win a national boxing crown, when he becomes the Australian Heavyweight champion.

1887

"The prospect of organizing this league meets with the hearty approval of every person as something that should have been done long ago, so that our people could have been on the same footing as whites so far as baseball is concerned."
– Walter S. Brown, owner of the Pittsburg[h] Keystones, *Sporting Life*, 27 October 1886.

The National Colored Base Ball League (NCBBL) is organized. The original teams are the Boston Resolutes, Philadelphia Pythians, New York Gorhams, Pittsburg[h] Keystones, Baltimore Lord Baltimores, Louisville Falls City, Washington Capitol Citys and the Cincinnati Browns. The Washington and Cincinnati franchises would not play this season. The league folds in May.

George Stovey signs with Newark of the International League and joins catcher Moses Fleetwood Walker to form the first African American battery in White professional baseball. Stovey wins 33 games against 14 losses for the fourth-place Newark Little Giants. Cap Anson refuses to allow his National League Chicago White Stockings to play against the Newark Little Giants because African American pitcher George Stovey is on the roster.

The New York Times publishes a letter written by several White players entitled "A Color Line in Baseball" on Sept. 12. The letter addresses Chris von der Ahe, a German immigrant and owner of the St. Louis Browns: "Dear Sir, We, the undersigned members of the St. Louis Baseball Club, do not agree to play against negroes (sic) (Cuban Giants) tomorrow. We will cheerfully play against white people at any time, and think, by refusing to play, we are only doing what is right, take everything into consideration and the shape of the team is in at present."

Isaac Lewis rides "Montrose" to victory in the Kentucky Derby. "Montrose" is bred in Kentucky at Col. Milton Young's McGrathiana Stud farm.

Isaac Murphy becomes the first African American jockey to win the First Special, riding "Volante," and the first Black jockey to win the Hyde Park Stakes, riding the "Emperor of Norfolk."

Anthony Hamilton becomes the first African American jockey to win the Gazelle Stakes, riding "Firenze."

1888

The International League, which has eight Black baseball players, formally decides to sign no more African Americans as another "Gentlemen's Agreement" is mandated.

Isaac Murphy becomes the first African American jockey to win the Dwyer Stakes, riding the "Emperor of Norfolk;" the Second Special, riding "Kingston;" and the Swift Stakes, again riding the "Emperor of Norfolk."

Pike Barnes becomes the first African American jockey to win the Flash Stakes, riding "Princess Bowling;" the Futurity Stakes, riding "Proctor Knott;" and the Latonia Oaks, riding "Lavinia Belle." Barnes compiles a record 206 wins this season.

1889

"The more you know your history, the more liberated you are." – Maya Angelou

George "Spider" Anderson becomes the first African American jockey to win the Preakness, riding "Buddhist" to an eight-stride win at the Pimlico Race Course in Baltimore, Md.

Anthony Hamilton becomes the first African American jockey to win the Brooklyn Handicap, riding "Exile."

Pike Barnes becomes the first African American jockey to win the Champagne Stakes, riding "June Day." Barnes wins 170 races this year.

Catcher Moses F. Walker for the Syracuse Stars becomes the International League's last Black player, until Jackie Robinson joins the Montreal Royals of the Brooklyn Dodgers organization in 1946.

1890

"Racism, which leaves a shadow on one's sense of accomplishment, can make one feel like a perpetual outsider."

– Alvin Ailey

William Henry Lewis and William Tecumseh Sherman Jackson become the first African American players on a White college football team as members of the Amherst squad.

George Jewett becomes the first African American to play varsity football at the University of Michigan. Jewett was an Ann Arbor High School star in both football and track.

Isaac Murphy wins his second Kentucky Derby riding "Riley" and is the first African American to win the Tidal Stakes, riding "Burlington," and the first African American jockey to win the Suburban Handicap, riding "Salvator."

Pike Barnes becomes the first African American jockey to win the Belmont Stakes, riding "Burlington," and the first Black jockey to win the Ladies' Handicap, riding "Sinaloa II."

Monk Overton becomes the first African American jockey to win the Chicago Derby, riding "Prince Fonso."

Spider Anderson becomes the first African American jockey to win the Eclipse Stakes, riding "Sallie McClelland."

Anthony Hamilton becomes the first African American jockey to win the Juvenile Stakes, riding "St. Charles" and the Toboggan Handicap, riding "Fides."

The Chautauqua Tennis Club of Philadelphia is founded. The African American organization hosts its first interstate tournament in 1898.

George Dixon claims the World Bantamweight Championship in 1888 and was officially considered the champion after knocking out Nunc Wallace of England in 18 rounds on 27 June 1890. He was a Black Canadian professional boxer and the first Black world boxing champion in any weight class, while also being the first ever Canadian-born boxing champion.

1891

"Sometimes, I feel discriminated against, but it does not make me angry. It merely astonishes me. How can any deny themselves the pleasure of my company?" – Zora Neale Hurston

Moses Fleetwood Walker receives U.S. patent #458,026 for an exploding artillery shell.

Isaac Murphy wins a third Kentucky Derby, riding "Kingman," and becomes the first jockey to win three Derbies. He is also the first jockey to win back-to-back Derbies.

Anthony Hamilton becomes the first African American jockey to win the Lawrence Realization, riding "Potomac."

President Benjamin Harrison becomes the first sitting U.S. president to attend an interracial game and witness the New York Big Gorhams (colored) defeat the Cape May team from New Jersey.

1892

Fifteen-year-old Alonzo Clayton rides "Azra" to victory in the Kentucky Derby.

Anthony Hamilton becomes the first African American jockey to win the Grand Trial Stakes, riding "Chiswick."

William Henry Lewis, a center from Harvard University, is named the first African American All-American in college football. Lewis later serves 12 years as a football coach at Harvard.

The first collegiate football game is played between two historically Black colleges. In Salisbury, N.C., Livingstone College host Biddle University (now Johnson C. Smith University) from nearby Charlotte. Biddle wins 4-0. The game was played on a snow covered, converted cow pasture. This event is referred to as "The Birth of Black College Football."

1893

Saddle horse trainer and equestrian showman, Tom Bass invents the Bass Bit. The horse bit with hinges, prevents pain to the horse's mouth during training. The Bass Bit is still used today.

Willie Simms rides "Comanche" to first place in the Belmont Stakes.

1894

The Jockey Club is formed to regulate and license all jockeys. One by one, African American jockeys are denied their license renewals. By 1911 all Black jockeys are unemployed. See Marlon St. Julien.

Willie Simms rides "Henry of Navarre" to first place in the Belmont Stakes.

Colorful Firsts in U.S. Sports

Jerry Chorn becomes the first African American jockey to win the Burns Handicap, riding "Lissak."

1895

"Nothing is ever said or written about drawing the color line in the [National] League. It appears to be generally understood that none but whites shall make up the League teams, and so it goes." - *Sporting Life*, 29 June 1895

The Page Fence Giants out of Adrian, Mich., are organized by John "Bud" Fowler and Grant "Home Run" Johnson. Future Hall of Famer Sol White and ace pitcher George Wilson join the team and they compile a won-lost record of 118-36-2 against all levels of competition, which included two games against the Cincinnati Reds.

The Colored Hockey League of the Maritimes (CHL) is founded by four Black Baptist leaders James Borden, James Robinson Johnston, James A.R. Kinney and Henry Sylvester Williams in Halifax, Nova Scotia, Canada. It predates the National Hockey League (NHL) by 32 years. Its rule book is *The Bible*. The *Acadian Recorder* reports the Halifax Stanleys as CHL champions.

Major Taylor wins his first significant cycling competition, when he becomes the only rider to finish a 75-mile road race near Indianapolis.

Fifteen-year-old James "Soup" Perkins rides "Halma" to victory in the Phoenix Hotel Stakes. Three days later, Perkins rides "Halma" to victory in the Kentucky Derby. Perkins is America's winningest jockey this year with 192 wins.

1896

Willie Simms rides "Ben Brush" to victory in the Kentucky Derby and also wins the Wither Stakes, riding "Handspring."

Anthony Hamilton becomes the first African American jockey to win the Metropolitan Handicap, riding "Counter Tenor."

Isaac B. Murphy, jockey, dies of pneumonia at age 36. Murphy won 34.5% of his races, a standard no jockey has since met.

William Henry Lewis, former All-American collegian, writes the *Primer of College Football*, the first book of its kind. The volume is published by *Harper & Brothers* and serialized in *Harper's Weekly*. In 1911 he is among the first African Americans to be admitted to the American Bar Association.

After setting an unofficial world record in the one-fifth of a mile race and beating the one-mile time on the Capital City Track in Indianapolis, cyclist Major Taylor is banned from this venue.

In the second U.S. Open golf tournament, John Shippen becomes the first African American professional golfer to participate. Shippen finishes fifth in the 36-hole event.

1897

Willie Simms becomes the first African American jockey to win the Brighton Handicap, riding "Ben Brush," and the Tremont Stakes, riding "Handball."

Eugene M. Gregory suits for the Harvard freshman baseball team, becoming the first Black ballplayer at the collegiate level.

1898

"The best way to fight poverty is with a weapon loaded with ambition." – Septima Clark

Major Taylor is declared national cycling champion with 121 total points from 21 first-place victories, 13 second-place berths and 11 third-place showings. Taylor uses the Sager chainless bicycle, and in the process becomes the first Black athlete sponsored by the Sager Gear Company of Rochester, New York

Alonzo Clayton becomes the first African American jockey to win the California Handicap, riding "Traverser."

Willie Simms wins his second Kentucky Derby, riding "Plaudit." He is the only African American jockey to win the Preakness, riding "Sly Fox."

1899

Danny McClellan pitching the first recorded perfect game by an African American pitcher against the Penn Park Athletic Club of York, Pa., champions of the Tri-State League, is well known in 1903. Recently, Tony Kissel and Wayne Stivers found an earlier no-hitter in 1899. It was pitched by William Selden of the Cuban Giants on July 9 against the Bordentowns, a team in the Middle States League. Selden strikes out three and walks two batters, en route to a 2-0 win. A full account of the game is reported in the *Trenton Daily True American*.

African American dentist Dr. George Grant is issued U.S. patent #638,920 for inventing the golf tee. Grant was only the second African American to graduate from Harvard Dental School and later the first African American professor at Harvard.

Tom Bass is credited with developing the American Royal, a rodeo and livestock and horse show, in Kansas City, Mo.

William Hipple "Hippo" Galloway becomes the first African American hockey player with Woodstock of the amateur Central Ontario Hockey Association. Galloway would later play third base for the Cuban Giants and Cuban X-Giants baseball teams.

Major Taylor wins the world one-mile championship in Montreal, Canada, defeating Boston rival Tom Butler. Taylor becomes the first African American world champion athlete.

1900

"Never forget that we were enslaved in this country longer than we have been free. Never forget that for 250 years black people were born into chains-whole generations followed by more generations who knew nothing but chains."

- Ta-Nehisi Coates

Major Taylor becomes the U.S. Sprint champion in bicycle racing for the second consecutive year.

The Cuban League welcomes the addition of an all-Black team, the San Francisco B.B.C., which wins the pennant in its first season.

Mace Montgomery from Georgetown University becomes the first African American Olympic delegate, as a trainer.

Frank Armstrong becomes Cornell University's first Black graduate. During his final year at Cornell, Armstrong serves as captain of the school's baseball team.

French soccer player Constantin Henriquez de Zubiera becomes the first Black athlete to compete at the modern-day Olympics, which launched four years earlier in 1896. The Haitian-born rugby player was also the first person of color to earn an Olympic gold medal when the French team wins the first Rugby Olympic Tournament.

1901

"Defining myself, as opposed to being defined by others, is one of the most difficult challenges I face." – Carol Moseley Braun

Jockey Jimmy Winkfield, riding "His Eminence," wins his first Kentucky Derby.

Willie Simms becomes the first African American jockey to win at the Annual Champion Stakes, riding "Mid of Harlem."

Baltimore Orioles manager John McGraw passes Columbia Giants second baseman, Charlie Grant, off as a Native American named Chief Tokohama. Before the start of the season, Chicago White Sox president Charlie Comiskey exposes the ploy.

1902

Jimmy Winkfield, riding "Alan-a-Dale," wins his second consecutive Kentucky Derby. He is the first jockey to win back-to-back Derbies since Isaac Murphy (1890-91). He also becomes the first African American jockey to win the Crescent City Derby, riding "Lord Quez."

Harry "Bucky" Lew, a forward with Pawtucketville (Mass.) Athletic Club in New England becomes the first African American professional basketball player.

Joe Gans knocks out Frank Erne in the first round to become the first native-born African American to win a world lightweight championship.

1903

"It is a peculiar sensation, this double-consciousness, this sense of always looking at one's self through the eyes of others, of measuring one's soul by the tape of a world that looks on in amused contempt and pity."

– W.E.B. Du Bois, *Souls of Black Folk*

Danny McClellan pitches the first recorded perfect game by an African American pitcher, against the Penn Park Athletic Club of York, Pa., champions of the Tri-State League.

Rube Foster of the Cuban X-Giants strikes out 18 Philadelphia Giants to best St. Louis Browns Fred Glade's major league record of 15 whiffs in a game.

Willie Hicks becomes the first African American jockey to win the Matron Stakes, riding "Armenia."

Tommy Knight becomes the first African American jockey to win the Cincinnati Trophy, riding "Paris."

1904

"You can either stand up and be counted or lie down and be counted out!" – Maggie L. Walker

Aaron Brown becomes the first native-born African American to win the welterweight boxing title.

Colorful Firsts in U.S. Sports

1904 is the last year that the Colored Hockey League is considered a professional entity. Some notable teams from the CHL include the Africville Sea-Sides, Amherst Royals, Charlottetown West End Rangers, Dartmouth Jubilees, Dartmouth Victorias, Halifax Diamonds, Halifax Eurekas, Halifax Stanleys, Hammond's Plains Mossbacks, Truro Victorias, and the Truro Sheiks. Many team names reflect the struggle for freedom faced by the players' ancestors and their hope for equality and recognition.

Charles W. "Black Cyclone from Wooster" Follis becomes the first professional football player with the Shelby Blues of the Ohio League. Follis, a halfback, and Branch Rickey were teammates on the amateur Shelby Athletic Association in 1902 and 1903.

George Coleman Poage, in St. Louis, Mo., places third in both the 200- and 400-meter hurdles to win Olympic bronze medals. He becomes the first African American to win a medal in the Summer Olympics Games.

In Dayton, Ohio, Woody Hedspath or Headspeth, becomes the first Black cyclist to establish a new "Hour Record". The "Hour Record" is the longest distance cycled in one hour on a bicycle from a stationary start. It is considered one of the most prestigious records in cycling.

At the Cheyenne Frontier Days in Wyoming, Bill Pickett demonstrates his pioneer bulldogging technique of bringing a steer to its knees by sinking his teeth into the animal's upper lip or nose and releasing both his hands. The event later becomes known as steer-wrestling.

1905

Bob Marshall from the University of Minnesota is chosen for the Walter Camp's All-American football team.

Harvard and Boston University scholar William Clarence Matthews is the only known Negro player in professional baseball as a shortstop with Vermont's Northern League. Matthews passes the bar in 1908 and is appointed special assistant to the U.S. district attorney in Boston. He also serves from 1920 to 1923 as legal counsel to Jamaican political activist Marcus Garvey.

Future heavyweight boxing champion Jack Johnson organizes a semi-pro baseball team called the Johnson's Pets. Johnson plays first base.

1906

"I have found no better way to avoiding race prejudice than to act with people of other races as if prejudice did not exist."
– Jack Johnson

Harry "Bucky" Lew forms his own basketball team, "Buck Lew's Traveling Five" playing around the New England area.

Eddie Martin, with the Halifax Eurekas in the Colored Hockey League, is the first player to use the slapshot, according to historians George and Darril Fosty.

William Freihofer, who owns a chain of bakeries in Philadelphia organizes the International League of Independent Professional Base Ball Clubs. The original teams were the Cuban X-Giants, Philadelphia Quaker Giants (later replaced by the Philadelphia Giants), Cuban Stars of Havana, Havana Stars (later replaced by the Wilmington Giants of Delaware) and the Philadelphia Professionals with primarily a White roster. After 40 scheduled games, the Philadelphia Giants are declared winners of the Freihofer Cup.

Charles "Doc" Baker, a halfback, joins the Akron Indians who become the Akron Pros in 1920, a charter member of the American Professional Football Association (later renamed the National Football League in 1922). Raised in the Akron Children's Home, he is known as the second professional African American football player.

1907

"Only mediocrity escapes criticism." - John Steinbeck

The Smart Set Athletic Club of Brooklyn, managed by J. Hoffman Woods, creates the first independent African American basketball team. Nicknamed the "Grave Diggers" for their tendency to bury opponents, the team would win the first two Colored Basketball World's Championships in 1907-08 and 1908-09.

The Alpha Physical Culture Club of Harlem, founded by Jamaica-born brothers Conrad and Gerald Norman creates the Olympian Athletic League, a Black club basketball league. Better known as the Alpha Big Five, it is America's first all-Black athletic club.

King Solomon White, captain of the Philadelphia Giants, authors *The History of Colored Base Ball*. The first book written about African Americans in baseball, includes 57 rare images and chapters written by Andrew "Rube" Foster and Grant "Home Run" Johnson, on pitching and batting, respectively.

1908

"Each of us must earn our own existence. And how does anyone earn anything?
Through perseverance, hard work and desire." – Thurgood Marshall

Jack Johnson knocks out Tommy Burns in Sydney, Australia, to become the world's first African American heavyweight champion (1908-15). The fight lasts 14 rounds after being stopped by the police in front of more than 20,000 spectators.

Major Taylor, in Paris, sets world records in the Quarter Mile (25.4 seconds) and in the Half Mile (42.2 seconds) in cycling competition.

The University of Vermont names its first African American captain of a basketball team, Fenwick Watkins. After graduating from Vermont, Watkins coaches football, basketball, and baseball at Fargo College in Fargo, N.D, where he also leads the athletic program.

Major White League baseball's first recognized African American baseball player in 1884, Moses Fleetwood Walker authors *Our Home Colony: A Treatise on the Past, Present and Future of the Negro Race in America*. In his writing, Walker expresses defeat and urges Black people to leave the U.S. in search of better opportunities in Africa.

The Independent Pleasure Club of Orange, N.J., is created and managed by Nelson Frye. Upon defeating the Alpha Big Five and the Smart Set it is awarded the unofficial 1913 Colored Basketball Championship of New Jersey.

Jimmy Lee becomes the first African American jockey to win the Great American Stakes, riding "Sir Martin," and the National Stallion Stakes, again riding "Sir Martin."

John Baxter "Doc" Taylor Jr. becomes the first African American to win an Olympic team gold medal, as member of the 4x400-meters relay in London.

1909

Educator Booker T. Washington's son E. Davidson and C.G. Kelly create the first faculty tennis club at Tuskegee Institute.

Edwin B. Henderson creates the Washington (DC) 12 Streeters basketball team with students from Howard University. Sponsored by the Twelfth Street Colored Y.M.C.A., the team wins the 1909-10 unofficial Colored Basketball World Championship title with an undefeated season.

Matthew Henson, explorer, becomes the first man to reach the North Pole. He served as Admiral Robert Peary's navigator and craftsman during the Arctic expedition.

Cumberland Posey Jr. becomes the first colored student-athlete at Penn State. He plays on the freshman and varsity basketball teams and the freshman baseball team in 1910.

Pete Hill and Bruce Petway become the first African American players included in the Cabañas Cuban baseball card set.

1910

"We cannot stand still; we cannot permit ourselves simply to be victims." – W.E.B. Du Bois

Walter Speedy, known as the "Father of African American Golf in Chicago," leads a group suing the city of Chicago for the right to play in a city-sponsored tournament. The Chicago City Amateur Tournament began in 1904 to showcase golf's champion players at Jackson Park. However, tournament organizers excluded African Americans from playing on the public facility.

In the "Fight of the Century," former undefeated heavyweight champion James J. Jeffries comes out of retirement to challenge heavyweight champion Jack Johnson. Reno, Nevada odds had Jeffries as a 10–7 favorite, but he losses in 15 rounds on a TKO. The outcome of the fight triggers race riots across the country. Many states ban the showing of the Johnson-Jeffries film.

A colored female baseball club, the St. Louis Black Broncos is organized by Conrad Kuebler.

Leland Giants catcher Bruce Petway, playing for the Havana Reds in Cuba, is reported by the *La Lucha* newspaper, of throwing out American League batting champion Ty Cobb of the Detroit Tigers on several occasions. Cobb vows to never take the field against Black players.

On Feb. 22 the *Altoona Tribune (PA)*, shares editorial thoughts from future Hall of Fame pitcher Cy Young. "The little brown men of Japan are planning an invasion of the U.S. A baseball attack. They are planning to attack the American and National League teams. Among the tribes they will attempt to subdue is the White Sox. Also the Detroit Tigers. The players are students of Kelo (sic, Keio) University. If they succeed, a regular invasion will follow, and we will have unpronounceable names on every club." Young continues, "Baseball belongs to this country. Its supremacy in baseball will never be threatened. And for the very good reason that while some of the athletes of other nations may imitate and even equal our ball players in one department of the game, they cannot excel in all. Take the Japanese athlete. He can't hit worth a hurrah." Young also adds, "A Jap can't pitch. There is one reason for this, of course. That reason is that they can't grip the ball. The hands of the Japs are very small." Young did not forget the Cuban players, "That reason does not hold good with the Cuban. Yet their pitchers are a bad lot. They have no curve ball, and, of course, use little headwork."

In the Feb. 12 issue of the *Sporting News*, future Hall of Fame pitcher Cy Young makes this statement. "They (the Japs) are like the Cubans – too small to be big players . . . That's the trouble with all foreigners. Base ball will always be an American game." After Young's death in 1955, starting in 1956, the Cy Young Award is given annually to the best pitcher in the American and National Leagues.

The Spartan Athletic Club of Brooklyn (N.Y.), perhaps the first all-Black women's basketball team, is organized by President Bernadine Harris. Sister Mary Harris is team captain and manager, with Sidney Jackson coaching. The Spartan Girls were the sister squad to the Smart Set Athletic Club of Brooklyn.

Cumberland Posey forms an all-Black basketball team, the Monticello Athletic Association in Pittsburgh. The team defeats the Howard University team, 24-19, to claim the unofficial 1911-12 World's Colored Basketball Championship.

Major Aloysius Hart organizes an all-Black basketball team in Harlem, called the New York All Stars. Their home court is the Manhattan Casino in Harlem. The All Stars are led by Ferdinand Accooe, Charles Scottron and Charles "Mule" Bradford, a baseball pitcher with the Philadelphia Colored Giants of New York.

1911

Andrew "Rube" Foster, considered the "Father of Black Baseball" organizes the Chicago American Giants.

Henry McDonald from Haiti becomes the first Black player for the Rochester Jeffersons of the New York Professional Football League. The halfback plays with the team until 1917.

Cuban Armando Marsans debuts in the white-centric major leagues with the Cincinnati Reds, playing centerfield and first base. He later plays for the St. Louis Browns and the New York Yankees before joining the Cuban Stars of the Eastern Colored League in 1923.

1912

"It's no disgrace to be Black, but it's often very inconvenient"
– James Weldon Johnson, *The Autobiography of an Ex-Coloured Man*.

The Monticello Athletic Association basketball team, led by Cum Posey capture the consensus Black national championship, 1911-12.

Howard Porter Drew becomes the first African American to hold the world record for the 100-yard dash. The media calls him the "Negro Speed Marvel," the "Colored Flyer," the "Negro Dash Man," and the "Crack Colored Sprinter" but the title first given to Drew is one still used today, "World's Fastest Man."

1913

"You must never be fearful about what you are doing when it is right." – Rosa Parks

Golfer John Shippen finishes fourth in the U.S. Open. Because of his light complexion he passes for White in a tournament that excludes African Americans.

Will Anthony Madden legally incorporates the St. Christopher Club of New York, Inc., soon to be known as the Incorporators basketball team. The team defeats Howard University and the Alpha Physical Culture Club of Harlem to claim the unofficial colored championship.

Cumberland Posey Jr. forms a new basketball team, the Loendi Big Five, named after the prestigious Loendi Social Club in Pittsburgh, Pa. The club was known for its social group the FROGS, an acronym for Friendly Rivalry Often Generates Success, the light-skinned elites of Black society.

1914

Bill Pickett stars in a silent film called *The Bull-Dogger* advertising his techniques of steer-wrestling.

The Ideal Tennis Club is founded in Harlem, N.Y. Founding members of the Ideal Club are instrumental in the formation of the American Tennis Association (ATA).

1915

"Freedom is a precious thing, and the inalienable birthright of all who travel this earth." – Paul Robeson

Paul Robeson and Fritz Pollard become the first African American football players at Rutgers and Brown Universities.

Gideon "Charlie" Smith, a tackle, becomes the first African American player for the Canton Bulldogs of the Ohio League. Smith plays one game and is the last African American to play professional football exclusively prior to the formation of the National Football League in 1920. Smith becomes professor of physical education and head football coach at Hampton Institute in 1921.

Solomon W. Butler is the first African American to quarterback a team for all four years of college at the University of Dubuque in Iowa. Sol Butler earns 12 varsity letters in football, basketball, baseball and track, and participates in the 1920 Belgium Olympics. In 1926, the all-White New York Giants refuse to play the Canton Bulldogs with Butler as its quarterback.

The Pittsburgh Scholastics Basket Ball Club, pre-cursor to the famous Loendi Big Five, is organized by fitness trainer Hunter Johnson. Johnson is credited with training long jumper DeHart Hubbard, a gold medalist in the 1924 Olympics.

1916

Fritz Pollard, running back from Brown University, becomes the first African American to play in the Rose Bowl. Pollard is also the first African American football player at Brown. He becomes the first African American, who plays a backfield position, named to Walter Camp's All-American team. See 1892, when William Henry Lewis, a lineman, is selected to the All-American squad.

Mabel Fairbanks becomes the first African American and Native American member of the U.S. Professional Skating Association (USPSA). She later coaches Olympians Scott Hamilton, Tai Babilonia, Randy Gardner and Kristi Yamaguchi.

The American Tennis Association (ATA) is organized in Washington, District of Columbia, to promote tennis play among African Americans. Organizing officials include Dr. H.S. McCard, Dr. William H. Wright, Dr. B. M. Rhetta, Ralph V. Cook, Dr. Henry Freeman, John F. N. Wilkinson, Tally Holmes and others.

Despite cancellation of the Berlin Olympics, Henry Binga Dismond receives a gold medal for tying Ted Meredith's world record of 47.4 seconds in the 400-meter race. See Archie Williams, 1936.

The son of an Irish-English mother and an African-French-Native American father, Jimmy Claxton pitches two games for the Oakland Oaks of the Pacific Coast League. Recorded as a mulatto in the 1910 census, Claxton appears on No. 25 of the 143-card set by Zee-Nuts, becoming the first Black player with an American baseball card.

Alex Pompez's Cuban Stars, with José Méndez and Cristóbal Torriente, become the first Negro League franchise to visit Puerto Rico.

1917

"It isn't where you came from, it's where you're going that counts." – Ella Fitzgerald

The American Tennis Association (ATA) holds its first tournament. At its first championship in Baltimore at Druid Hill Park, Tally Holmes wins the Men's Singles, and Lucy Diggs Slowe wins the Women's Singles. Diggs Stowe becomes the first African American woman to win a major sports title.

Shortstop Jesús "El Tigre" Velásquez from Arecibo becomes the first dark-skinned Puerto Rican to play in the U.S.

1918

"We usually see things not as they are but as we are." – Louise Beavers

Fred "Duke" Slater becomes the first African American football player at the University of Iowa.

The YWCA establishes the Colored Branch of the Young Women's Christian Association, in Philadelphia, the first of its kind in the nation.

The ATA hosts its second tennis tournament in New York City on the Ideal Tennis Courts. Tally Holmes repeats as Men's Singles winner, and Mae Rae wins the Women's Singles event.

1919

"Color is fact. Race is a social construct." – Isabel Wilkerson

Fritz Pollard joins the Akron Indians (later the Pros) independent football team.

Colorful Firsts in U.S. Sports

1920

"We Are the Ship, All Else the Sea." – from the letterhead of the Negro National League's stationery

The first Black professional baseball league to survive a full season, the Negro National League of Professional Baseball Clubs, is established by Andrew Rube Foster, J. L. Wilkinson, Tenny Blount, C. I. Taylor and others. The principal stockholders are Willie Foster, Rube Foster, J. L. Wilkinson, Russell Thompson and Walter M. Farmer. The charter teams are the Indianapolis ABCs, Dayton Marcos, Detroit Stars, St. Louis Giants, Kansas City Monarchs, Chicago Giants, Chicago American Giants and the Cuban Stars based in Cincinnati.

Moses Fleetwood Walker receives U.S. patent #1,328,408 for a film end fastener for motion picture film reels, U.S. patent #1,348,609 for an alarm for motion picture film reels and U.S. patent #1,345,818 for motion picture film reel.

Willie Green, third baseman for the Chicago Giants faces pitcher Ed Rile of the Indianapolis ABCs in the first game of the newly formed Negro National League. The ABCs beat the Giants, 4-2, before an estimated 8,000 fans.

Pete Hill of the Detroit Stars hits the first home run in the newly formed Negro National League, against the Cuban Stars from Cincinnati.

Oscar Charleston of the Indianapolis ABCs against the Cuban Stars West is the first player to hit for the cycle in the Negro National League, going 4-for-5 with four RBIs.

The Cuban Stars of the Negro National League put the first all-Latino major league lineup on the field, in a May 9 doubleheader against the Indianapolis ABCs. The lineup in the first game includes, Eufemio Abreu (catcher), Bernardo Baro (centerfield), Valentine Dreke (leftfield), Marcelino Guerra (first base), Mike Herrera (third base), José LeBlanc (pitcher), Cando López (second base), Herman Rios (shortstop), and Faustino Valdés (rightfield).

Cuban Mike Herrera is an infielder for the Cuban Stars of the Negro National League later plays for the Boston Red Sox in the American League in 1925 and 1926. In 1928, he returns to the Eastern Colored League to play for the Cuban Stars.

The NAACP's *The Crisis* magazine reports that Harry J. Walker, a Negro, is the official announcer for World Series games at Cleveland's League Park. The Cleveland Indians of the American League defeat the Brooklyn Robins of the National League, five games to two.

Several professional football players, including Fritz Pollard (with the Akron Pros), and Robert "Rube" Marshall (Rock Island [Ill.] Independents), make their debut in the new American Professional Football Association (APFA), later to become the NFL.

The Loendi Big Five, managed by Cumberland Posey win the Colored Basketball World Championships, the first of four consecutive seasons from 1920 to 1923.

1921

"All of us are Black first, and everything else second." – Malcolm X

Football star Frederick Wayman "Duke" Slater from the University of Iowa is named Most Valuable College Player.

George "Papa Bear" Halas, head coach of the Chicago Staleys, refuses to play the Akron Pros unless they drop quarterback and running back Fritz Pollard from its team.

Jay Mayo "Inky" Williams, a wide receiver, becomes the first African American player for the NFL's Hammond (Ind.) Pros and the Canton (Ohio) Bulldogs. Williams is also known for starting the Chicago Record Company, releasing jazz, blues and gospel records on the Black Patti label. In 2004, he was posthumously inducted into the Blues Hall of Fame.

The Baltimore Black Sox Bloomer Girls baseball team start play.

Bill Gatewood of the Detroit Stars pitches the first no-hitter in the Negro National League. He shuts out the Cuban Stars from Cincinnati in a 4-0 win.

The first Black-owned golf course of nine-holes, the Shady Rest Golf & Country Club, is created in Scotch Plains, NJ. The *Pittsburgh Courier* reports the "club house ranks with the best." Activities include golf, tennis, horseback riding and skeet shooting. Notable celebrities at the country club include W.E.B. Du Bois, Count Basie, Ella Fitzgerald, Duke Ellington, Billie Holiday and Cab Calloway. Notables athletes include Ora Washington, Lula Ballard, Althea Gibson, Ted Rhodes, Bill Spiller and Joe Louis, an avid golfer.

Champion Timeline

1922

"You never really understand a person until you consider things from his point of view, until you climb into his skin and walk around in it." - Atticus Finch in *To Kill A Mockingbird*

Tackle Duke Slater becomes the first African American lineman in the National Football League as a member of the Rock Island Independents. Slater earns his law degree in 1928 and practices law as a Chicago attorney. In 1948, he is elected to the Cook County Municipal Court, becoming just the second African American judge in Chicago.

George Halas, now head coach of the renamed Chicago Bears, refuses to play the Milwaukee Badgers unless they drop African American players Fritz Pollard, Paul Robeson and Duke Slater from the team.

John Andrew Shelbourne, a running back, becomes the second African American player for the Hammond (Ind.) Pros of the NFL.

Alexander McDonald Williams, owner of the Pittsburgh Keystones, builds Central Amusement Park. The park is bordered by Humber on the northside, Junilla on the eastside, Hallett on the southside and Chauncey on the westside. It becomes the first Black-owned ballpark in the Negro National League.

Jim Jeffries from the Indianapolis ABCs becomes the first pitcher to win more than 20 games in a season in the Negro Leagues.

The Commonwealth Big Five basketball is formed by brothers from the Bronx, Edward and Roderick "Jess" McMahon Sr. The "Commons" become the first all-Black professional team in America. See 1923, New York Rens.

Jack Johnson, boxing heavyweight champion, receives U.S. patent #1,413,121 for a wrench.

Joseph Bartholomew designs the Pontchartrain Golf Course.

The Springfield Tennis Club is organized at St. John's Congregational Church in Springfield, Mass. Practices are held at Forest Park and Pratt Field.

1923

"We've been called colored, Negro, black, everything . . . Why can't we just be free?" – Paul Mooney

Running back Richard "Dick" Hudson, aka "Super Six," becomes the first African American to play for the Minnesota Marines in the NFL.

The New York Rens, named after the team's home court, the Renaissance Ballroom and Casino in Harlem, become America's first Black-owned all-Black professional basketball team. They are owned by Robert L. Douglas from St. Kitts, British West Indies.

Earl Brown becomes a member of the Harvard University baseball team.

The Mutual Association of Eastern Colored Clubs, better known as the Eastern Colored League, is created by postal worker Ed Bolden, owner of the Hilldale Athletic Club. Charter members include Hilldale, the Bacharach Giants, the Brooklyn Royal Giants, the Cuban Stars (East), the Lincoln Giants of New York, and the Baltimore Black Sox.

Cuban pitcher Pedro Dibut hurls for the Cuban Stars of the Negro National League. The next season he pitches for the Cincinnati Reds in the white-centric major leagues. He is a member of the Cuban Baseball Hall of Fame.

1924

"These players are as fine as any White players I've encountered," - White umpire Daniel J. McDevitt, after the first Colored World Series.

The first Colored World Series is played between the Kansas City Monarchs and the Hilldale Club from Darby, Pa. The Monarchs win the 10-game series, five games to four with one tie. Arguably the most dramatic World Series ever played, as each team reeled off three wins in a row, four games were decided by a single run and five games are won in the final inning.

Jesse "Nip" Winters of the Hilldale Club pitches the first no-hitter in Eastern Colored League competition. Winters defeats the Harrisburg Giants, 2-0.

In the second game, Nip Winters for the Hilldale Club pitches the first shutout in Negro World Series history. Winters throws a four-hitter in a 11-0 win over the Kansas City Monarchs.

In the third game, Newt Joseph, third baseman for the Kansas City Monarchs, becomes the first player to hit a home run in the Colored World Series. Joseph hits a two-run homer over the centerfield fence in Baltimore's Maryland Baseball Park, off of Red Ryan of the Hilldale Club.

Cuban pitcher Oscar Estrada with the Cuban Stars of the Eastern Colored League later plays for the 1929 St. Louis Browns in the white-centric major leagues.

Colorful Firsts in U.S. Sports

DeHart Hubbard becomes the first African American to capture an individual gold medal at the Paris Olympics. Hubbard long jumps 24 feet, 5 inches.

Earl Johnson becomes the first African American long distance runner to medal in the Olympic Games. In Rome, Johnson wins a bronze medal in the 10,000-meter race.

The annual Gold and Glory Sweepstakes, a 100-mile race on a one-mile dirt track at the Indiana State Fairgrounds is started by mechanic and race-car driver Charlie "the Negro Speed King" Wiggins. The inaugural event draws approximately 12,000 fans.

1925

"The Old Negro we must remember was a creature of moral debate and historical controversy. His has been a stock figure perpetuated as an historical fiction partly in innocent sentimentalism, partly in deliberate reactionism."

- Alain Locke, *The New Negro*

The U.S. Colored Golf Association is founded in Washington, District of Columbia. It is renamed the United Golfers Association (UGA) in 1929. At the time, the Professional Golfers Association has an article in its by-laws stating that it is "for members of the Caucasian race." When this by-law is repealed in 1961, the United Golfers Association eventually disbands.

The National Capitol Country Club for African Americans is formed in Washington, District of Columbia. It is known as a semi-social, semi-athletic club, whose membership includes men and women.

Fritz Pollard, a halfback, is the first and only Black player for the Providence Steam Rollers of the NFL.

The colorless American Basketball Association is organized and adopts a Jim Crow policy to exclude men of color.

The Hilldale Club from Darby, Pa. wins the Colored World Series, defeating the Kansas City Monarchs, five games to one in the best of a nine-game series.

The all-Black Wichita (Kan.) Monrovians of the Colored Western League face off against the local Ku Klux Klan No. 6 team at Wichita's Island Park. To avoid favoritism, the game is officiated by two Irish Catholics. The Monrovians win 10 to 8 with no violence reported by the local newspapers.

1926

"And now White editors are beginning to regard Negroes as interesting novelties, like white elephants or black roses. They'll print practically anything our coloured writers send in." - Carl Van Vechten, *Nigger Heaven*

On the final day of the playoff series in the Negro National League, Willie Foster for the Chicago American Giants wins both games against the Kansas City Monarchs while pitcher Wilber "Bullet" Rogan, takes a loss in both games. Their pitch counts are not available.

In the Negro World Series, Claude "Red" Grier for the Bacharach Giants pitches a no-hitter against the Chicago American Giants, the first in Negro League series play. It is the first World Series no-hitter in major league baseball history.

José "Gacho, Chico" Torres, an outfielder, is the first Puerto Rican to play in the organized Negro Leagues with the Newark Stars of the Eastern Colored League.

The Savoy Big Five, based in Chicago, are managed at Wendell Phillips High School by Dick Hudson (fullback for the Minnesota Marines and the Hammond Pros of the NFL). The team includes founder Tommy Brookins, Bobby Anderson, Inman Jackson, Lester Johnson, Joe Lillard (running back of the Chicago Cardinals), Randolph Ramsey and Walter "Toots" Wright. They split a two-game series with George Halas's Chicago Bruins.

Tiger Flowers becomes the first African American boxer to capture the middleweight title by defeating Harry Greb in New York City.

Duke Slater signs with the Chicago Cardinals and becomes the first African American to play for a current NFL franchise.

The United Golfers Association (UGA) is formed by Robert Hawkins in Mass. It replaces the earlier U.S. Colored Golf Association founded in 1925. It will serve the Black golfing community for the next four decades.

1927

"Accomplishments have no color." – Leontyne Price

The New York Globetrotters play its first game on January 7 in Hinckley, Illinois, before 300 fans.

The first Negro baseball team to play in Japan, the Philadelphia Royal Giants, owned by Lonnie Goodwin, visits the Far East. Catcher and sometimes pitcher Biz Mackey becomes the first player to hit a home run at Jingu Stadium, home of the Yakult Swallos.

Champion Timeline

1928

"An athlete must have ability to reach the top, but many who have ability and who do not live clean lives never have and never will be champions for obvious reasons." – Mayor Taylor

Cyclist Major Taylor self-publishes his autobiography, *The Fastest Bicycle Rider in the World.*

The Chicago American Giants of the Negro National League add numbers to their jerseys, one year before the New York Yankees and the Cleveland Indians do the same.

John Beckwith of the Homestead Grays becomes the first Black player to hit three home runs in a game off an active White major league pitcher, Rube Walberg of the Philadelphia Athletics. The Grays defeat the American League All-Stars, 12-10.

Walter Green, of Chicago, starts the Savoy Colts, a women's basketball team, managed by Dick Hudson. Their roster includes guards E. Williams, Blanche Winston, Corrine Robinson, forwards Lula Porter, Virginia Willis, H. Williams and famed Philadelphia tennis star Ora Washington at center.

The Chicago Black Hawks, an all-Black team, is organized by Dr. Albert C. Johnson and Fritz Pollard, who also serves as quarterback, running back and coach. The Black Hawks primarily play against White teams around Chicago.

1929

"Why hate when you could spend your time doing other things?" – Mariam Makeba

Sherman "Jocko" Maxwell, 22, becomes the first African American sports broadcaster, hired by WNJ (later WNJR), known as the "Voice of Newark." Later in life, he announces games for the Newark Eagles, winners of the 1946 Negro World Series. In 1971, he publishes *Great Black Athletes* by Snibbe Publications.

Emilio "Milito" Navarro, a shortstop, is the first Puerto Rican to bat more than .300 (.317) in the Negro Leagues as a member of the Cuban Stars of the American Negro League.

James "Cool Papa" Bell hits three inside-the-park home runs at Aida Park, in Cienfuegos, Cuba.

The Germantown Hornets, in Philadelphia, are formed by the YWCA Branch of Colored Girls and Women. The Hornets basketball team included Ora Washington, Lula Ballard, Louise Penn, Lil Fountainé, Helen Laws and Evelyn Manns.

The *New York Daily News* reports that the University of Georgia football team will not play the New York University Violets if quarterback Dave Myers is allowed to take the field. Despite protest from the NAACP, Myers is benched as the Violets beat the Bulldogs 27-19.

1930

"Not everyone likes chocolate ice cream." – Nipsey Russell

The Kansas City Monarchs play its first game under their portable lighting system in Enid, Okla., against the local college. This is six seasons before the first night game is played in the National League at Crosley Field in Cincinnati, Ohio in 1935.

Dexter Park, former home field for the Brooklyn Royal Giants of the Eastern Colored League, in Queens becomes the first ballpark in New York with installed stadium lights. Ebbets Field, home of the Brooklyn Dodgers, will not have a lighting system until 1938.

For the first time in history, two Negro League teams play at Yankee Stadium. The event sponsored by the Brotherhood of Sleeping Car Porters draws 20,000 fans who watch the New York Lincoln Giants and the Baltimore Black Sox split a pair. The Giants win the first game 13-4, with the Black Sox winning the nightcap 5-3. Baltimore's Rap Dixon hits three home runs and the Giants' Chino Smith has two round trippers and a triple.

The Tribune Girls are sponsored by the *Philadelphia Tribune* newspaper. The players come from two Black female basketball teams, the Philadelphia Quick Steppers and the Germantown Hornets. Inez Patterson from the Quick Steppers becomes coach and player of the team. Two tennis players from the YWCA Colored Branch in Germantown, Ora Washington and Lula Ballard become standout hoopsters.

Dave Willoughby Myers, an undrafted guard and quarterback from New York University, is the first African American to play for the Staten Island Stapletons in the National Football League (NFL). The next season he plays for the NFL's Brooklyn Dodgers.

Eddie Tolan becomes the first person officially credited with running the 100-yard dash in 9.5 seconds.

Duke Slater becomes the first lineman, Black or White, to make seven All-Pro teams.

Colorful Firsts in U.S. Sports

1931

"Racism is a scholarly pursuit, it's taught, it's institutionalized." – Toni Morrison

George Gregory Jr. captain and center for the Columbia University basketball team from 1928 to 1931, becomes the first African American to gain All-American honors. Despite opposition from the dean, athletic director and the coach, teammates vote him captain.

1932

Ted Radcliffe of the Pittsburgh Crawfords catches Satchel Paige in the first game of a doubleheader, for a 4-0 win. He pitches the second game and wins 6-0. Radcliffe becomes the first professional baseball player to pitch and catch a game in the same day.

The *Washington Post* reports the first night baseball game ever played at Griffith Stadium. The Washington Pilots and the Pittsburgh Crawfords of the East-West League play before 4,000 fans under the portable Klieg lighting system. Nine years later, the American League Senators would play its first night game on 28 May 1941.

Gus Greenlee, owner of the Pittsburgh Crawfords, builds Greenlee Park. He installs a permanent overhead lighting system, making it one of the first parks in the country to offer nighttime baseball.

Chicago American Giants outfielder Turkey Stearnes captures the "Quadruple Crown" in the Negro Southern League, as leader in doubles, triples, home runs and stolen bases. No other player in any league has duplicated this feat.

Joe Lillard is the first Black quarterback, and the only person of color, on the Chicago Cardinals of the NFL. Lillard also plays for the Harlem Globetrotters, Chicago Hottentots and Savoy Big Five basketball teams. And a pitcher and outfielder for the Brooklyn Royal Giants, Gilkerson Colored Giants, Cincinnati Tigers and Chicago American Giants baseball teams.

Robert "Pat" Ball files a motion and is granted court injunction allowing him to play in the Philadelphia Public Links Golf Tournament.

Louise Stokes and Tidye Pickett become the first African American women to be on the U.S. Olympic team. However, the track stars remain on the sideline and are not allowed to participate.

Eddie Tolan becomes the first African American sprinter to win gold medals in the Los Angeles Olympics, in both the 100- and 200-meter dashes. He set a world record of 10.3 seconds in the 100-meters and an Olympic record of 21.2 seconds in the 200-meters.

1933

"What you see is what you'll get." – Flip Wilson, comedian

The Negro Leagues play its first East-West All-Star game in Comiskey Park. Future Hall of Famer Willie Foster pitches the only complete game in major league All-Star history.

George "Mule" Suttles of the Chicago American Giants hits the first home run in East-West All-Star competition. Suttles hits a two-run homer off of Sam Streeter of the Pittsburgh Crawfords in the fourth inning.

Elzie Cooper is the first African American to play any sport or win a varsity letter at Northern Illinois University (NIU). He lettered in baseball, basketball and football. Cooper is inducted into the NIU Huskies Hall of Fame in 1983.

Ray Kemp with the Pittsburgh Pirates and Joe Lillard with the Chicago Cardinals are released, leaving the National Football League exclusively white.

The American Association Football League (AAFL) and the Pacific Coast Football League, both minor leagues, open its doors to African American athletes. The AAFL consists of five teams from New York state (Mt. Vernon Cardinals, Brooklyn Bay Parkways, New Rochelle Bulldogs, Staten Island's Stapleton Buffaloes and the White Plains Bears) and three teams from New Jersey (Orange Tornadoes, Paterson Panthers and the Passaic Red Devils). The AAFL operates until 1941, as America enters World War II.

1934

"Honey, eighty percent of the people could care less about your problems,

and the other twenty percent are glad that you have them." – Jackie "Moms" Mabley, comedian

From 1934 to 1945, African American players are banned from the newly re-organized National Football League, which is divided into two divisions and adds three new teams this season.

The "Caucasian-only" clause is added to PGA's constitution. The discriminatory clause is removed in 1952.

Ralph Metcalfe, from Marquette University, becomes the first sprinter to win the 200 meter dash in the NCAA Men's Outdoor

Track and Field Championship three consecutive years. His times were 20.3 in 1932, 20.4 in 1933 and 20.9 seconds in 1934. In 1971, Illinois House of Representative Metcalfe co-founded the Congressional Black Caucus.

Mabray "Doc" Kountze becomes the first African American sportswriter to receive a press pass to Fenway Park.

Charlie Wiggins, posing as a janitor to circumvent Jim Crow laws, is hired by Indy car driver Bill Cummings to tune his car. Cummings wins the Indianapolis 500 and sets a track record.

Harrison "Honey" Fitch becomes University of Connecticut's first African American basketball player. In a game against the U.S. Coast Guard Academy, due to a tradition "that no Negro players be permitted to engage in contests at the Academy." Fitch warms up with the team, but coach John Heldman does not play him.

1935

"Know thyself, believe in God, and dare to dream." – John Salley

Slim Jones of the Philadelphia Stars becomes the first pitcher to hit a home run in East-West All-Star competition, when he slams one off Ray Brown from the Homestead Grays.

At the Big Ten championships in Ann Arbor, Mich., Jesse Owens sets or equals four world records in the same day: 9.4 seconds in the 100-yard dash; 26 feet, 8¼ inches in the long jump; 20.3 seconds in the 200-yard dash and 22.6 seconds in the 200-yard hurdles.

Joe Louis is the first African American winner of the *Associated Press'* Athlete of the Year.

Herschel "Rip" Day, an African American athletic promoter from Harlem organizes the New York Brown Bombers professional football team, which would play until 1942. Fritz Pollard is named coach.

John Henry Lewis becomes the first African American boxer to win the light-heavyweight title.

Jerome Heartwell "Brud" Holland becomes the first African American football player at Cornell University. He achieved gridiron first-team All-American honors in 1937 and 1938. After receiving bachelor's and master's degrees from Cornell, he earned his doctorate from the University of Pennsylvania. Dr. Holland later became president of Delaware State College.

Ora Washington becomes the first African American woman to win seven consecutive tennis titles in the ATA (American Tennis Association), from 1929 to 1935, and was undefeated from 1924 to 1936.

1936

"Powerful people never educate powerless people in what they need that they can use to take the power away from powerful people. It's too much to expect. If I was in power, I would not educate people in how to take my powers away."

– John Henrik Clarke

Jesse Owens wins four gold medals at the Berlin Olympics and becomes the first African American on a Wheaties cereal box, back side. His victories helped dispel Nazi-based myths about Aryan supremacy.

Joe Louis becomes the first African American voted Fighter of the Year by *Ring* magazine.

John Woodruff becomes the first African American to win the 800-meters race in the Olympics.

Archie Williams becomes the first African American to win the 400-meters race in the Olympics.

Eugene Payton, a hurdler, is the first African American to earn a letter at Southern Illinois University.

John F. Terry becomes the first African American U.S. Olympic weightlifter. In 1939, he set a world record for the deadlift with 600 pounds, considered enormous for his bodyweight of only 132 pounds.

In Berlin, Chicago native Tidye Pickett, 5-foot-2, becomes the first African American woman to compete in the Olympics. becomes the first African American woman to compete in the Olympics. She represents the United States in the 80-meter hurdles but fails to medal when she breaks an ankle in the semi-finals. Pickett went on to serve as principal at Cottage Grove Elementary School in East Chicago Heights for 23 years. Upon her retirement in 1980, the school is named in her honor.

Louise "The Malden Meteor" Stokes, along with Tidye Pickett become the first African American women selected to the U.S. Olympic team. Stokes, a sprinter, fails to medal. She is honored in the Massachusetts Hall of Black Achievement.

Wilmeth Sidat-Singh becomes the first African American athlete at Syracuse University. He plays on both basketball and football teams.

Big Dave DeJernett from integrated Indiana Central University becomes the first African American collegiate athlete to sign with a professional basketball team, the New York Rens.

1937
"The road to success runs uphill." – Willie Davis

Joe Louis defeats James J. Braddock and becomes the heavyweight champion of the world.

Roy Campanella starts his professional baseball career with the Washington Elite Giants.

Willie Wells returns after five days following a beaning from spitball pitcher Bill Byrd. Wells appears at the plate with a modified construction hat. It is the first known instance of a player donning a "hard" hat -- four years before the Brooklyn Dodgers used padded inserts in their headgear in 1941. Charlie Muse, traveling secretary for the Pittsburgh Pirates, is credited as the inventor of the batting helmet. In 1952, the Pirates became the first white MLB team to wear hard helmets.

The Radcliffe brothers, Chicago American Giants' Alec (3b) and Cincinnati Tigers' Ted (c), become the first siblings to appear in the same East-West All-Star Game.

Homer Harris, an end, becomes the first African American captain of a Big Ten Conference football team, with the University of Iowa.

Football coach Eddie Hurt at Morgan State College devises the four-man defensive front, a first. Later, in 1943, his Bears team goes undefeated, untied and unscored upon. Hurt also coaches track & field and basketball.

The Pennsylvania Open is the first interracial tournament sponsored by a private organization, the Eastern Golf Association.

Lowell Steward, a childhood friend of Jackie Robinson, becomes the first Black captain of the Santa Barbara State College Gauchos basketball team. He guides the Gauchos to the semifinals of the 1941 NAIA Division I Men's Tournament but is not allowed to play because of his race. Steward later became a member of the Tuskegee Airmen and receives the Distinguished Flying Cross, and the Congressional Gold Medal.

William "Dolly" King, as a member of the Long Island University basketball team, becomes the first African American to play in the national AAU tournament.

The Wake Robin Golf Club, Washington, District of Columbia's first Black female golf organization is founded.

1938
"Facts set properly forth, will tell their own story."
-- Carter G. Woodson, *Negro History Bulletin*, 1938

The Tuskegee Institute organizes the first intercollegiate golf tournament for African Americans. Alfred Holmes wins the first tournament.

Nell Dodson, of Minneapolis, becomes the first female sports editor in the U.S. when hired by the *Baltimore Afro-American* newspaper.

Pitcher Chet Brewer becomes the first African American player to enter the Mexican League.

Josh Gibson is the first Negro Leaguer to appear on the cover of the NAACP's *The Crisis* magazine.

New York Yankee outfielder Jake Powell says in a radio interview on WGN Chicago that as a police officer during the off season, he keeps in shape by "cracking niggers over the head with his nightstick" as he walks his beat in Dayton, Ohio. Powell gets a 10-day suspension by Commissioner Kenesaw Mountain Landis.

The Chicago Brown Bombers organized by Fritz Pollard integrate the Northwest Football League, which lasted two and a half seasons, 1936-1938.

Quarterback Wilmeth Sidat-Singh of Syracuse and end Jerome "Brud" Holland of Cornell become the first African Americans invited to play for the College All-Stars against the New York Giants. Because of Sidat-Singh's light complexion and last name, he was thought to be Hindu. Both his parents were African American. After the death of his father, Elias Webb (a pharmacist), his mother Pauline married Samuel Sidat-Singh from India, who adopted Wilmeth.

Henry Armstrong defeats Lou Ambers at Madison Square Garden to win the lightweight championship, making him the only fighter to hold world championships in three divisions (lightweight, featherweight and welterweight [126 to 147 pounds]), simultaneously.

Henry Armstrong appears on the cover of *Newsweek* magazine.

Joe Louis defeats German boxer Max Schmeling in a rematch of their 1936 fight. Because of Hitler's disdain for Blacks, the fight becomes a political arena between democracy and Nazism. Louis strikes a blow for democracy, easily defeating Schmeling in the first round.

1939

"Color is not a human or a personal reality; it is a political reality." – James Baldwin

Running back Kenny Washington of UCLA leads the nation with 1,370 total yards gained. Of the 664 players nominated for All-American by *Liberty Magazine*, Washington is the only player named on every ballot. Washington is not drafted into the lily-white NFL.

The *Chicago Defender* reports "We have yet to find another single coach in the history of (college) football that has had the guts to play three of our race at one and have four on the squad." UCLA football starts Jackie Robinson and Kenny Washington in the backfield and Woody Strode at offensive and defensive end. Ray Bartlett is a wide receiver. The Bruins compile a 6–0–4 record (5–0–3 conference), finish in second place in the Pacific Coast Conference.

Langston Golf Course and Driving Range opens in Washington, District of Columbia. The golf course is named after John Mercer Langston, a Virginia congressman and Howard University Law School dean.

The National Negro Bowling Association (NNBA) is created by Joe Louis and others, in Detroit, Mich., because of restrictive clauses by the American Bowling Congress (ABC) and the Women's International Bowling Congress (WIBC) of non-Caucasians. In 1944, the NNBA is renamed The National Bowling Association (TNBA). In 1950, both the ABC and WIBC removed its discriminatory clauses. In 1947, *Ebony* magazine in its "Bowling Boom" article called bowling the top sport in the Black community.

Joe Louis defeats John Henry Lewis to retain his heavyweight championship. This is the first time in boxing history that two African Americans fight for the title. Louis is the winner by a TKO in the first round.

In Chicago, the New York Rens (Independent) defeat the Oshkosh All-Stars (NBL) in the first World Professional Basketball Tournament, 34-25. Their record for the year was 122 wins against seven defeats. The Harlem Globetrotters take third place.

Clarence "Puggy" Bell of the New York Rens is named MVP of the first World Professional Basketball Tournament.

Pop Gates plays in the first World Professional Basketball (WPB) Tournament. By 1949, he would become the only player to play in all 10 WPB tourneys.

The Negro Leagues played two East-West All-Star games, one in New York and the other in Chicago. This was 20 years before the white-centric major leagues would play two All-Star games in the same season. In 1959, the first major league baseball All-Star game is played at Forbes Field in Pittsburgh and the second game at Los Angeles' Coliseum. In 1942, three East-West All-Star games are scheduled but the third game, in Memphis, is rained out.

To stop a losing streak, owner Horace Stoneham of the New York Giants hires a 13-year-old Black youth, Cecil Haley as a mascot. Players can rub Cecil's head for good luck. The National League is still without any Black players.

1940

"We Black folk, our history and our present being, are a mirror of all the manifold experiences of America. What we want, what we represent, what we endure is what America is. If we Black folk perish, America will perish."

– Richard Wright, *Native Son*

The Harlem Globetrotters defeat George Halas' Chicago Bruins (NBL), 31-29, to capture the World Professional Basketball Championship in Chicago Stadium. Sonny Boswell of the Harlem Globetrotters is named MVP of the World Professional Basketball Tournament.

Jack Wilson, a bantamweight boxer, is the first African American to fight the main event at Hollywood Legion Stadium, when he defeats Tony Chavez.

Running back Louis Montgomery, Boston College's first African American player, is not allowed to make the trip to the Cotton Bowl due to segregation sanctions. In 1941, he made the trip to the Sugar Bowl in New Orleans but is not allowed to play. In 2012, Boston College retires his No. 21.

James "Cool Papa" Bell becomes the first Mexican League player to win the Triple Crown. He leads the circuit in batting average (.437), home runs (12) and RBIs (79), as well as triples (15) and runs scored (119). The fenceless outfields in Mexico aid this speedster.

Colorful Firsts in U.S. Sports

1941

"Yet, coming of age in the early twentieth century, when Jim Crow was at its cruelest, he [Paige] never had the chance to become all that he could have been."
– Isabel Wilkerson

Before the ban on segregated seating was lifted in 1944 at Sportsman's Park in St. Louis, the Kansas City Monarchs, with Satchel Paige on the mound, play the Chicago American Giants before an interracial crowd of 19,178 on the Fourth of July. Average attendance per game for the Cardinals was 8,229 and for the Browns 2,289.

Kansas City Monarchs Catcher Frank Duncan Sr. and pitcher Frank Duncan Jr. become the first father and son and the first father-and-son battery, to play for the same team, in the same year. This is 50 years before the Ken Griffey family make ancestral history.

Francisco "Pancho" Coimbre becomes the first Puerto Rican to play in the East-West All-Star game at Chicago's Comiskey Park.

John McLendon begins his basketball coaching career with the North Carolina College (now North Carolina Central University).

Jack Roosevelt Robinson becomes the first athlete to letter in four sports for the UCLA Bruins: baseball, basketball, football and track.

Eddie Robinson, Grambling State football coach, defeats Tillotson 37-6 for the first of his 408 wins.

Joe Louis becomes the first African American to appear on the cover of *Time* magazine.

1942

"I don't give a damn what others say. It's okay to color outside the lines." – Jimi Hendrix

Salvador "Chico" Hernández debuts with the Chicago Cubs as a catcher. In 1945, he joins the Indianapolis Clowns of the Negro American League.

Reece "Goose" Tatum joins the Harlem Globetrotters and soon drafted into the Army. Bob Karstens becomes the first White player to sign a contract with the Harlem Globetrotters. Karstens is credited with the Magic Ball pregame routine.

Before male students went off to fight in World War II, causing suspension of the football program for two seasons, Eddie Robinson's Grambling Tigers go undefeated, untied and unscored on.

1943

"Nothing is easy to the unwilling." – Nikki Giovanni

Alec and Ted Radcliffe become the first brothers to represent the same team, the Chicago American Giants, in the East-West All-Star classic.

The Homestead Grays defeat the Birmingham Black Barons in the Negro World Series, four games to three.

Rudolph "Rocky" Robeson, for the North Carolina College for Negroes (now North Carolina Central University) becomes the first African American hoopster to break a national college record, when he scores 58 points against Shaw University of Raleigh NC to break Stanford forward Hank Luisetti's record of 50 points set in 1938.

The Washington Bears, composed almost entirely of former N.Y. Rens, including John Isaacs, Pop Gates, Tarzan Cooper, Dolly and Sonny Woods capture the fifth annual World Professional Basketball Tournament in Chicago, defeating Wisconsin's Oshkosh All-Stars, 43-31.

Washington Bears (originally the Lichtman Bears) defeat the Oshkosh All-Stars (NBL) in the invitation-only World Professional Basketball Tournament. The undefeated Bears win all 41 games this season.

1944

"The most common way people give up their power is by thinking they don't have any." – Alice Walker

John McLendon coaches the first integrated game in the South, North Carolina College of Negroes versus Duke's Navy Medical School, in Durham, N.C. McLendon's Eagles win by a score of 88 to 44. It is the first collegiate basketball contest where Blacks and Whites compete on the same floor. This Sunday morning match has remained a secret for several decades.

Jessie Abbott becomes first women's track coach at Tennessee State University.

Staff Sgt. Joe Louis and Sgt. Walker Smith (Sugar Ray Robinson) are jailed at Camp Sibert, Alabama, for refusal to observe Jim Crow laws on the post. After participating in a camp show they enter the white section of the bus station to place a phone call for a taxi. There was no phone in the colored section. The camp was commanded by Gen. Haig Shekerjian, an Armenian-American, who ordered their release after several hours.

Ohio State University defensive lineman Bill Willis becomes the first African American to start in a College All-Star football game.

Gene Derricotte, a running back and kick return specialist, is the first Black player for the University of Michigan Wolverines football team.

Forward Bill "Bumps" Melvin becomes the first African American on Canisius College's basketball team.

The *New York Amsterdam News* reports that in a game against the New York Cubans, in Ebbets Field, on July 2, Satchel Paige "pulled all his usual tricks, such as loading the bases deliberately and then retiring the side without a run."

The Homestead Grays repeat as World Champions defeating the Birmingham Black Barons again in the Negro World Series, four games to one.

The St. Louis Cardinals and St. Louis Browns lift its policy of restricting Negroes to the bleachers and pavilion at Sportsman's Park. According to the local press, "Negroes now may purchase seats in the grandstand." Sportsman's Park was the last white-centric major league ballpark with a Jim Crow section. The black folks-only right field pavilion was covered by a screen preventing the catch of a home run. In 1927, the screen was removed when the Yankees played the Browns. That season Babe Ruth hit four of his 60 home runs into the pavilion, only 310 feet from home plate.

1945

Baseball in its time has given employment to known epileptics, kleptomaniacs, and a generous scattering of saints and sinners. A man who is totally lacking in character has often turned up to be a star in baseball. A man whose skin is white or red or yellow has been acceptable. But a man whose character may be of the highest and whose ability may be Ruthian has been barred completely from the sport because he is colored. – Sam Lacy, *Baltimore Afro-American*, 10 November 1945

The Cleveland Buckeyes defeats the Homestead Grays in four straight games to win the Negro World Series.

Charles "Benny" Jones becomes the first African American basketball player for the Dayton (Ohio) University Flyers. Jones later becomes business manager for heavyweight boxing champion Ezzard Charles.

Wally Triplett becomes the first African American football player in Penn State University history. He is also the first African American to start and earn a letter (1946).

In a letter to Lee MacPhail, American League President, dated 29 October 1945, Connie Mack, manager and president of the Philadelphia Athletics, writes, "It was a great disappointment to me to see that Branch Rickey had signed a negro (sic) for his Montreal Baseball Club. If all Major League Club owners would just let Branch have the negroes (sic), feel that we would all be better off in the long run."

New York Mayor Fiorello La Guardia forms a committee, to study segregation in baseball and, ultimately, pressure the New York teams to sign Black players. Yankee executive Larry MacPhail responds in part, "There are few, if any, negro (sic) players who could qualify for play in the major leagues at this time. A major league player must have something besides natural ability . . . In conclusion: I have no hesitancy in saying that the Yankees have no intention of signing negro (sic) players under contract or reservation to negro (sic) clubs."

1946

"The only thing new in the world is the history you do not know!"

- Newly elected President Harry S. Truman

The All-America Football Conference (AAFC) is organized by Arch Ward, the sports editor of the *Chicago Tribune*. The league would last but four seasons.

The Cleveland Browns sign running back Marion Motley and defensive lineman Bill Willis as the AAFC's first African American players. Each player's seasonal salary is $4,000, of which 75% was to be paid semi-monthly. The balance of 25% would be paid after the last game.

Cleveland quarterback Otto Graham sets up over the center with feet parallel, but one foot slightly behind to push off faster to get away from defensive player Bill Willis in practice. Other pro teams soon pick it up and call it the "Bill Willis Step."

An all-Black league, the Virginia Negro Football League is organized. The teams include the Richmond Rams (champions), Norfolk Brown Bombers, Newport News Lighthearts and the Portsmouth Swans.

UCLA products Woody Strode (end) and Kenny Washington (running back) are the first African Americans in the NFL, joining

Colorful Firsts in U.S. Sports

Dan Reeves' newly relocated Los Angeles Rams from Cleveland. Washington is the first Black player to score a rushing touchdown in the NFL.

Cleveland Abbott becomes the first Black person to be a member of the U.S. Olympic Committee. As head coach of the Tuskegee Golden Tigers, 1923 to 1954, he became the first Black coach to win 200 games (206-99-27), which included six undefeated seasons. Abbott is a member of least 10 collegiate Halls of Fame.

Former UCLA running back Jackie Robinson makes his minor league debut, as a second baseman, with the Montreal Royals in Canada.

Manny McIntyre (left wing) and brothers Herbie (center) and Ossie (right wing) Carnegie become the first Black players for the Sherbrooke Randies of the semi-pro Quebec Provincial League. This first all-Black line in pro hockey, is known as "The Black Aces." Manny, born as Vincent Churchill McIntyre, becomes the first Black Canadian to sign a professional baseball contract. He joins Quebec's Sherbrooke Canadians of the Borden League, an affiliate of the St. Louis Cardinals, as a shortstop and appears in 30 games.

Bill and Marcella Powell are the first African Americans to design, build and own a golf course. The nine-hole Clearview Golf Course, located in East Canton, Ohio, opens in 1948 to all races. In 1978, the second nine holes are added. The Powells often said, "The only color that matters is the color of the greens."

Leon Day of the Newark Eagles pitches the only Opening Day no-hitter in Negro league history and the second in major league history, following Cleveland Indian Bob Feller's no-hitter in 1940. Day defeats the Philadelphia Stars, 2-0.

The Newark Eagles with Monte Irvin, Larry Doby and Leon Day defeat the Kansas City Monarchs in seven games to capture the Negro World Series title. In the process, Effa Manley, co-owner of the Newark Eagles, becomes the first female in the Negro Leagues, whose team wins the World Series.

In Game six of the Negro League World Series, against the Kansas City Monarchs, Monte Irvin, for the Newark Eagles, becomes the first player to hit two home runs in a game.

Roy Campanella makes his affiliated baseball debut on May 8, with the Nashua Dodgers in the Class B New England League. The future three-time National League MVP goes 3-for-4 with a two-run homer.

Don Newcombe and Roy Campanella form the first all-Black battery to integrate White baseball in the 20th century with the Nashua (NH) Dodgers in the Class B New England League. Newcombe, whose victory at Pawtucket on the third day of the 1946 season makes him the first African American pitcher to win a game for an integrated professional baseball team.

The Continental Basketball Association is the first professional basketball league to hire Black players. The Hazleton (Pa.) Mountaineers sign Bill Brown, Zach Clayton from the New York Rens and John Isaacs from the Washington Bears.

The Basketball Association of America (BAA) is organized by Walter A. Brown of Boston. Brown creates the Boston Celtics this year and originates the NBL All-Star game in 1951, played in Boston. Brown is credited for drafting Chuck Cooper the first African American into the NBA.

John McLendon of North Carolina College co-founds the Central Intercollegiate Athletic Association (CIAA) Tournament with Talmadge Hill (Morgan State), John Burr (Howard University) and Harry Jefferson (Virginia State). The first games are played at Washington District of Columbia's Turner Arena. CIAA tournament becomes a showcase for future NBA players, such as Sam Jones, Earl Monroe, Cleo Hill, Ricky Mahorn, Charles Oakley and Ben Wallace.

Manny McIntyre and brothers Herbie and Ossie Carnegie become the first Black hockey players in the Quebec Provincial League when they join the Sherbrooke team.

1946-47, The NBA outlaws zone defenses to speed up play. Zone defenses are reinstated in the National Basketball Association during the 2001-02 season.

1947

For me, baseball's finest moment is the day Jackie Robinson set foot on a major league field for the first time. . . . I'm most proud to be an American, most proud to be a baseball fan when baseball has led America rather than followed it. It has done so several times, but this is the most transforming incident.
- John Thorn, official historian for major league baseball

Buddy Young of the University of Illinois becomes the first African American to score a touchdown in the Rose Bowl.

Running and defensive back Bert Piggott, receiver Ezzrett "Sugarfoot" Anderson and center John Edward Brown become AAFC Los Angeles Dons' first African American players.

Running and defensive back Bill Bass becomes the AAFC Chicago Rockets' first African American player.

Running back Buddy Young becomes the AAFC New York Yankees' first African American player.

Running back Elmore "Pepper" Harris becomes the AAFC Brooklyn Dodgers' first African American player.

Chester Pierce, senior tackle for Harvard, becomes the first African American collegian to perform against White players on a Southern collegiate field, Scott Stadium in Charlottesville, Va., against the University of Virginia.

John Edward Brown from North Carolina Central University becomes the first African American football player from a historically Black college to play professional football when he joins the Los Angeles Dons of the AAFC as a center. Tank Younger from Grambling State is usually recognized as the first, in 1949, with the NFL Los Angeles Rams. Marion Motley attends South Carolina State College (now Chaflin University) in 1939 before transferring to the University of Nevada to play varsity football.

Horace Gillom, punter for the Cleveland Browns, records the highest hang time in game history with 5.5 seconds. *Sports Illustrated* writer Dr. Z votes him to the All-Time Browns team in 1999.

Before the start of the season Cleveland Indians owner Bill Veeck hires Louis Jordan Jones, a Black public relations man, to ". . . prepare the black segment of Cleveland for the arrival of a Black ballplayer, unnamed [Larry Doby]." Jones was a highly visible force in the community who, among other claims to fame, had been singer Lena Horne's first husband. Larry Doby joins the Cleveland Indians, becoming its first African American player.

Jackie Robinson, with the Brooklyn Dodgers, becomes the first African American in modern times to play in the re-integrated major leagues and wins the newly created Rookie of the Year Award by the *Sporting News*.

Jackie Robinson becomes the first African American to lead the National League in Stolen Bases with 29. Black National League players dominate this statistic category for the next 40 years, not winning in 1948 when Richie Ashburn steals 32 bases and in 1952 when Pee Wee Reese steals 30 bases.

Jackie Robinson becomes the first African American baseball player to appear on the cover of *Time* magazine.

Dan Bankhead becomes the first African American pitcher in the re-integrated major leagues as a member of the Brooklyn Dodgers. He homers in his first plate appearance but does poorly on the mound. In 3 1/3 innings of relief, he gives up 10 hits and six earned runs to the Pittsburgh Pirates.

Hank Thompson, a second baseman, becomes the first African American to integrate the St. Louis Browns.

Willard Brown, an outfielder, joins Hank Thompson in a game against the Boston Red Sox, marking the first time two African Americans appear in the same American League lineup.

Willard Brown becomes the first African American ball player to hit a home run in the American League, a pinch-hit, inside-the-park homer in a win over the Detroit Tigers.

Willard "Home Run" Brown becomes the only baseball player to hit home runs in the Negro Leagues (Kansas City Monarchs) and in the American League (St. Louis Browns) in the same season.

Althea Gibson wins the first of 10 straight (all-Black) American Tennis Association (ATA) National Championships, a title that began in 1917.

The first official basketball game between Black and White collegiate teams is played between Wilberforce University and Bergen College of New Jersey at Madison Square Garden. Wilberforce wins 40-12.

Don Barksdale, of UCLA, becomes the first African American basketball player to be named to the consensus All-American team. He makes the second squad.

Bill Garrett becomes the first African American to play on the Indiana University basketball team and the first to regularly start on a Big Ten Conference team. In 1951, the 6-foot-3 center becomes the third African American drafted into the NBA by the Boston Celtics in the second round, 16th pick.

The New York Cubans, with Luis Tiant Sr. and Minnie Miñoso, win the Negro World Series by defeating the Cleveland Buckeyes, four games to one.

1948

"The distorting lens of caste can cloud the senses, make the dominant group willing to deprive itself of the benefit of talents outside its ranks, allow the gifts to those from groups deemed inferior to languish, as it did with Satchel Paige, to keep the castes separate or to uphold the fiction that all talent resides within one favored group."

– Isabel Wilkerson, *Caste*

The U.S. military integrates its service baseball teams.

Colorful Firsts in U.S. Sports

Bill Veeck signs 42-year-old Satchel Paige, on his birthday, to a Cleveland Indian's contract. Paige goes 6W-1L for the season.

Satchel Paige becomes the first African American pitcher in the American League and the first African American to actually pitch in a World Series game. Pitcher Dan Bankhead for the Brooklyn Dodgers was used as a pinch runner in the 1947 World Series.

The Cleveland Indians become the first major league (American League) baseball team with Black players to win a World Series, with outfielder Larry Doby and pitcher Satchel Paige.

In the fourth game of the 1948 World Series, Cleveland Indians pitcher Steve Gromek defeats the Boston Braves, 2-1 with the help of Larry Doby's home run. The local Cleveland paper, *The Plain Dealer* snaps a photograph of Doby and Gromek hugging and smiling in the locker room to the discontent of many. In his Hall of Fame acceptance speech, Doby fondly remembered that picture: "That was a feeling from within, the human side of two people, one black and one white. That made up for everything I went through. I would always relate back to that whenever I was insulted or rejected from hotels. I'd always think about that picture. It would take away all the negatives."

Roy Campanella makes his Minnesota debut in a Memorial Day twin-bill between the St. Paul Saints and the Minneapolis Millers (with a game in each team's home park). Campanella becomes the first African American player in the American Association, a AAA league. Campy is later joined by pitcher Dan Bankhead from the Memphis Red Sox.

According to *Howe News Bureau*, Artie Wilson hits .402 for the Birmingham Black Barons of the Negro American League and becomes the last .400 hitter in major league baseball history.

Audrey "Mickey" Patterson (Tyler) becomes the first African American female to win an Olympic medal, a bronze in the 200-meters, just days before Alice Coachman wins her gold medal in the high jump.

Alice Coachman (Davis) wins a gold medal in the high jump, clearing 5-foot-6 1/8, becoming the first African American woman to win an Olympic gold medal. She is the only American woman to win a gold medal in track and field this year.

Bill Rhodman becomes the first bowler to score a perfect 300 game in The Negro Bowling Association (TNBA).

John Davis of Brooklyn, N.Y., becomes the first African American heavyweight lifting champion in the Olympics.

Nell Dodson, one of the first female sports editors in the country, becomes the first African American admitted to the Minneapolis College Women's Club, by a vote of 588-129.

Herb Carnegie becomes the first African American hockey player to receive a tryout with an NHL team, the New York Rangers. The Rangers only offer him a contract to play in their minor league system. He was posthumously inducted into the Hockey Hall of Fame in the Builder Category in 2022.

Margaret Matthews (Wilburn) becomes the first female to broad jump more than 20 feet (20 feet, 1 inch).

Don Barksdale becomes the first African American to play on the U.S. Olympic basketball team.

The NAIB (later the NAIA) admits the first African American player, Clarence Walker from coach John Wooden's Indiana State Teachers College team to its tournament. Walker becomes the first African American player to participate in a national college basketball championship at any level.

Harrison "Bones" Dillard becomes the first athlete to win both the 100-meter sprint and 100-meter high hurdles in Olympic competition.

Running back Joe Perry and tackle Robert Mike become the San Francisco 49ers's (AAFC) first African American players.

Wally Triplett and Dennie Hoggard, Jr. become the first African Americans to play in the Cotton Bowl. Triplett catches the tying touchdown in Penn State's 13-13 tie with Southern Methodist University, who discourage the Nittany Lions from bringing African American players to the game.

Melvin Groomes, a halfback, and Bob Mann, an end, become the first African American players for the NFL's Detroit Lions.

Emlen Tunnell, a defensive back, becomes the first African American to play for the New York Giants of the NFL.

Willie Mays starts his professional baseball career with the Birmingham Black Barons. The Homestead Grays win the last Negro World Series title defeating Mays and the Birmingham Black Barons, four games to one.

Outfielders Fabiola Wilson and Gloria "Lovie" Dymond are the first ladies to play for the minor league New Orlean Creoles in a game against the Nashville Cubs in the Negro Southern League.

John Richey, former batting champion for the 1947 Chicago American Giants, becomes the first African American in the Pacific Coast League since pitcher Jimmy Claxton passed as part Native American in 1916. The San Diego native played for the Padres for two seasons and is commemorated with a bronze bust in Petco Park in 2018.

The New York Rens, led by Sweetwater Clifton's 24 points, lose the World Basketball Championship to the Minneapolis Lakers, led by George Mikan's 40 points, by a score of 75 to 71. This is the last World Basketball tournament that started in 1939.

The New York Rens, relocate to Dayton, Ohio and replace the Detroit Vagabond Kings of the racially integrated National Basketball League (NBL).

Three African American golfers, Theodore "Rags" Rhodes, Bill Spiller and Madison Gunther, try to break the Whites-only policy with a lawsuit against the PGA. The PGA sidesteps the issue by adopting an "invitation only" provision, allowing the golfers to play as non-members.

Sam Lacy is the first African American writer admitted to the Baseball Writers' Association of America (BBWAA).

1949

"One day our descendants will think it incredible that we paid so much attention to things like the amount of melanin in our skin or the shape of our eyes or our gender instead of the unique identities of each of us as complex human beings."
— Franklin Thomas, activist, philanthropist, and former president of the Ford Foundation

Monte Irvin and Hank Thompson become the first African Americans to play with the New York Giants.

Jackie Robinson of the Brooklyn Dodgers becomes the first African American to lead either the American or the National League in batting with a .342 average.

Jackie Robinson, Roy Campanella and Don Newcombe, all of the Brooklyn Dodgers, and Larry Doby of the Cleveland Indians become the first African Americans to play in a white-centric major league All-Star game; the American League wins 11-7 at Ebbets Field.

Jackie Robinson becomes professional baseball's first Most Valuable Player who was Rookie of the Year.

Don Newcombe becomes the first African American pitcher to win the Rookie of the Year Award.

Harold Henson, of San Diego State, becomes the first African American to wrestle in the NCAA tournament.

Wally Triplett from Penn State is the first African American <u>draftee</u> to take the field in an NFL game. Triplett is drafted in the 19th round with the 182nd pick by the Detroit Lions.

George Taliaferro, halfback from Indiana, is the first African American draftee overall. He is selected by the Chicago Bears in the 13th round with the 129th pick, but signs with the Los Angeles Dons of the AAFC.

Fred "Cannonball" Cooper, a running back from Virginia Union University, becomes the first African American professional football player in the deep South when he signs with the Richmond Rebels in the American Football League. Cooper leads the league in rushing and scoring, as the Rebels capture the league title.

Harold Robinson and Hoyt Givens become the first African American football players at Kansas State University, home of the Wildcats. Robinson would earn All-Big 7 Conference honors in 1950.

The Los Angeles Rams sign Paul "Tank" Younger from Grambling State University, the NFL's second player from a predominately Black college. Younger is the first of a record 200-plus players drafted by the NFL who played for Coach Eddie Robinson.

Harrison Dillard appears on the cover of *Newsweek* magazine.

Jumpin' Johnny Wilson becomes the first Negro selected to the College All-Star basketball team, coached by Adolph Rupp. The collegians play George Mikan and the Minneapolis Lakers, losing 94-86, in Chicago.

Zachary M. Clayton, former New York Ren, Harlem Globetrotter and Negro Leagues player, becomes the first African American to receive a boxing referee's license with the state of Pa. Clayton later referees the 1974 Ali-Foreman "Rumble In The Jungle" fight in Kinshasa, Republic of Zaire.

The New York Rens, now based in Dayton, Ohio, and members of the National Basketball League (NBL), play its last game against the Denver Rockets. Coached by "Pop" Gates, its lifetime record over 26 years is 2,318 wins and 381 losses, an 86 winning percentage. Gates is the first African American head coach in the NBL.

1950

"If there is no struggle, there is no progress. Those who profess to favor freedom, and deprecate agitation, are men who want crops without plowing up the group, they want rain without the thunder and lightning." – Frederick Douglass

Althea Gibson becomes the first African American to be accepted for competition in the National Tennis Championship at the U.S. Championships after Alice Marble writes an editorial for the July 1 edition of *American Lawn Tennis* magazine. Marble writes, "Miss Gibson is over a very cunningly wrought barrel, and I can only hope to loosen a few of its staves with one lone opinion. If tennis is a game for ladies and gentlemen, it's also time we acted a little more like gentle people and less like sanctimonious hypocrites." Marble adds that if Gibson is not given the opportunity to compete, "then there is an ineradicable mark against a game to

Colorful Firsts in U.S. Sports

which I have devoted most of my life, and I would be bitterly ashamed." Gibson is inducted into the International Tennis Hall of Fame in 1971.

The Ladies Professional Golf Association is formed and bars members of the Black race from membership. Its 13 founders are: Alice Bauer, Patty Berg, Bettye Danoff, Helen Dettweiler, Marlene Hagge, Helen Hicks, Opal Hill, Betty Jameson, Sally Sessions, Marilynn Smith, Shirley Spork, Louise Suggs, and Babe Zaharias.

Ernie Banks starts his professional baseball career with the Kansas City Monarchs before being drafted into the Korean War by the U.S. Army.

Lorenzo "Piper" Davis becomes the first African American to sign with the Boston Red Sox, the last all-White major league baseball team to integrate in 1959. Davis, 32, is assigned to their Class A affiliate in Scranton, Pa. He never makes the roster of the parent club.

Sam Jethroe, former Cleveland Buckeye outfielder of the Boston Braves, becomes the oldest Rookie of the Year in the re-integrated major leagues at age 33. Jethroe goes on to lead the National League in Stolen Bases with 35 and finishes 27th in the MVP poll. On September 15, the Boston Braves host "Sam Jethroe Night" for their rookie speedster.

Jackie Robinson appears as himself in *The Jackie Robinson Story* film. Ruby Dee plays his wife Rachel.

Jackie Robinson becomes the first African American baseball player to appear on the cover of *Life* magazine. Robinson was on the cover of *Time* magazine in 1947.

Willie Mays joins the Trenton Giants, a New York Giant farm team in the Class B Interstate League and becomes the first Black player and the only African American player in the league. He plays in 81 games and compiles a .353 batting average.

Marion Motley runs for 188 yards with only 11 carries, against the Pittsburgh Steelers. His 17.1 yards per carry is a single-game NFL record. Michael Vick breaks the record in 2002. Motley becomes the first African American to lead the NFL in rushing with 810 yards, and three touchdowns. Motley of the Cleveland Browns is the first African American to participate in an NFL championship game.

Wally Triplett of the Detroit Lions gains 294 yards in four kickoff returns against the Los Angeles Rams, an NFL one-game record of 73.6 yards per return. One run is for 97 yards.

George "Scoop" Taliaferro becomes the first African American quarterback and kicker with the New York Yanks of the NFL. Taliaferro plays in all 12 games under coach Red Strader.

Running backs Buddy Young and Sherman Howard, along with quarterback George Taliaferro become the first African Americans to play for the New York Yanks in the NFL. Taliaferro also appears as a quarterback in 11 games for the Dons.

Bob Mann, an end, becomes the first African American player for the Green Bay Packers in the NFL.

Joe Louis retires from boxing. Louis holds the heavyweight title from 1937 to 1948.

Arthur Dorrington, a dentist, signs with the Atlantic City Seagulls of the Eastern Amateur League to become the first African American to play professional hockey in the U.S.

LaVannes Squires becomes the first African American male basketball player at the University of Kansas. He earns KU's frosh basketball honors in 1950-51 and later plays on the 1952 NCAA championship team coached by Phog Allen.

Harold Robinson, football center, becomes Kansas State University's first African American student-athlete, and the first African American in the Big Seven Conference to be awarded an athletic scholarship.

Duquesne's Chuck Cooper, a second-team All-American, becomes the first African American drafted by an NBA team when he is selected in the second round by the Boston Celtics.

Hank DeZonie from Clark Atlanta University is the first African American to play for the NBA Tri-Cities Blackhawks based in Moline and Rock Island, Ill., and Davenport, Iowa.

Nat "Sweetwater" Clifton is the first African American player for the New York Knicks. Clifton becomes the first former Harlem Globetrotter to sign an NBA contract.

On Halloween Oct. 31, Nov. 1, Nov. 4, and Dec. 3, Earl Lloyd, Chuck Cooper, Nat "Sweetwater" Clifton and Hank DeZonie, respectively, become the first African Americans to play in the National Basketball Association (NBA).

Ed Tucker becomes the first African American basketball player for Stanford University. Upon graduation in 1952, Tucker enters medical school and becomes an obstetrician-gynecologist.

Other African Americans selected in the NBA draft are West Virginia State's Earl Lloyd and North Carolina College's Harold Hunter (both by the Washington Capitols) and Kentucky State's Ed Thompson (by the Fort Wayne Pistons). John McLendon coaches Harold Hunter and Earl Lloyd and takes them to the Washington Capitols for tryouts.

1951

"What Happens to a Dream Deferred?" – Langston Hughes, 1951

Althea Gibson becomes the first African American to play at Wimbledon in England.

In November, Edna Mae Robinson, wife of boxer Sugar Ray Robinson, appears on the cover of the first *Jet* magazine.

Sadie Dixon, called "the female Jackie Robinson" integrates the Bowling Proprietors Association of America (BPAA) bowling tournament.

Gene Wilson becomes the first African American basketball player for the Kansas State University Wildcats.

Solly Walker, guard for St. John's University, becomes the first Black player to play in an integrated college basketball game at the University of Kentucky. Walker hits six of his first seven shots before leaving game due to a body blow, sidelining him for weeks.

Don Barksdale and Davage "Dave" Minor become the first African Americans to play for an NBA team south of the Maxon-Dixon line, the Baltimore Bullets.

Betty Irene Chapman becomes the first African American in professional women's baseball when she joins the Admiral Music Maids, of Des Plaines, Ill., in the National Girls Baseball League, a rival to the All American Girls Professional Baseball League. Chapman is a student at Illinois State Normal College.

Earl Woods, father of Tiger Woods, is the first Black baseball player for the Kansas State University Wildcats. He earns varsity letters in 1952 and 1953.

Judy Johnson becomes the first African American scout in the re-integrated major leagues with the Philadelphia Athletics.

Monte Irvin of the New York Giants becomes the first African American to lead either the American or National League in RBIs with 121.

On June 3, against the St. Louis Cardinals, the New York Giants' Monte Irvin is walked. Willie Mays doubles with Irvin stopping at third base. Hank Thompson is intentionally walked filling the bases. This is the first time in MLB history the bases are loaded with African Americans. With two outs, Dave Koslo (pitcher) strikes out looking. Before 32,564 fans, the Giants win 1-0.

In the playoffs, after an injury to outfielder Don Mueller, the New York Giants employ an all-Black outfield with Hank Thompson, Willie Mays and Monte Irvin. Hank Thompson, normally a third baseman, is sent in to replace Mueller, instead of outfielder Bobby Thomson.

Jackie Robinson appears on the November cover of the *Sports Stars* magazine.

Minnie Miñoso becomes the Chicago White Sox's first Black player and the first Cuban American to lead the American League in Stolen Bases with 31 steals.

Don Newcombe of the Brooklyn Dodgers becomes the first African American pitcher to lead either League in strikeouts with 164 K's. Newcombe also becomes the first African American pitcher to win 20 games (20-9) in the re-integrated major leagues with the National League Brooklyn Dodgers.

Larry Doby becomes the first ball player since 1914 to score four runs without an official at-bat in a game. Doby drew five walks in five plate appearances.

Roy Campanella is named the National League's Most Valuable Player, the first of three MVP awards for Campanella.

Percy Miller makes his debut with the Danville Leafs, the first integrated baseball team in Virginia in the Carolina League. He delivers a two-run single against Durham in the first of his 19 games that season. He is released in February 1952 as not being polished enough. The is a minor league baseball league which operates along the Atlantic Coast of the U.S. It is classified as a Class A-Advanced league.

John Henry Davis becomes the first man to hoist 400 pounds over his head at the National AAU senior championships in Los Angeles.

Hosea Lee Richardson becomes the first Black jockey to get a license to ride in Florida. Richardson, only 16, makes a successful debut riding "Work Done" to second place at Hialeah Park in Miami.

Bernie Custis becomes the first African American regular starter, as quarterback, for a Canadian professional football team, the Hamilton Tiger-Cats of the Interprovincial Rugby Football Union, later known as the Canadian Football League (CFL). He was selected to the IRFU All-Star team.

Duke Slater becomes the only African American elected to the College Football Hall of Fame's inaugural class. Slater is one of five starters on the

Colorful Firsts in U.S. Sports

Rt31921 Iowa team who became lawyers. Slater later moves to Chicago and serves as a Superior Court judge.

John McLendon and three other coaches form the National Athletic Steering Committee to petition the NCAA and the NAIA to give Black schools a chance to play in post season tournaments.

Crystal Ellis becomes the first African American to play basketball for the Bowling Green (Ky) State University Falcons. Ellis later earns his master's and Ph.D. degrees in education from the University.

Joe Bertrand from Chicago, Ill. and Entee Shine from South Bend, Ind. become the first African Americans on Notre Dame's basketball team. Shine plays one season; Bertrand four years.

The *Guinness Book of World Records* lists the Harlem Globetrotters as drawing the largest crowd ever to see a basketball game, when 75,000 fans jam Berlin's Olympic Stadium.

1952

"The Negro, frequently alluded to as 'the white man's burden' carried on strong arms and legs the balance of athletic power in the 1952 Olympic Games. Without the points contributed by Negroes, [the] Soviet Union would have been an easy winner in terms of the unofficial system of scoring. The Olympic Games demonstrated the worth of Negroes as true Americans."

– Edwin B. Henderson

Dick "Night Train" Lane sets an NFL record for most interceptions in a 12-game season with 14.

Don Barksdale becomes the first African American to play in the NBA All-Star game.

Ed Sanders (super heavyweight), Nathan Brooks (flyweight), Charles Adkins (light welterweight), Norvel Lee (light heavyweight) and Floyd Patterson (middleweight) become Olympic African American gold medalists in boxing. Floyd Patterson later becomes the first Olympic gold medalist to win a world professional boxing title.

Archie Moore wins the light heavyweight title. He begins the longest reign of any light heavyweight champion, nine years and one month (December 1952 to February 1962).

Zach Clayton retired professional baseball and basketball player from Philadelphia, becomes the first African American to referee a world heavyweight title fight. Jersey Joe Walcott fights Ezzard Charles in their fourth rematch in Philadelphia. Walcott wins a disputed 15-pound decision.

Jersey Joe Walcott, 37, becomes the oldest man to win the heavyweight championship, and becomes the first athlete to appear on the cover of *Jet* magazine.

New York Yankee general manager George Weiss explains, at a cocktail party, why the Yankees are still an all-White team, five years after Jackie Robinson joins the Brooklyn Dodgers stating, "I will never allow a Black man to wear a Yankee uniform. Box-holders from Westchester (County) don't want that sort of crowd. They would be offended to have to sit with niggers."

Roy Campanella and Jackie Robinson become the first baseball players to appear on the cover of *Jet* magazine.

Marvin "Tex" Williams, a power-hitting second baseman from the Philadelphia Stars and Cleveland Buckeyes, becomes the first Black man to manage a mixed race team when he is appointed manager of the Dorados de Chihuahua (Goldens) in Mexico. Williams takes the helm in late June from Domingo Santana. The Goldens are a Class C team in the Arizona-Texas League, finishing with a record of 57-83. As player/manager, Williams' slash line is .401/.854/1.391.

Kirk Ramsey from Chicago competing in the Atomic League at Garfield Bowl, Chicago, is the first Black bowler to roll a perfect game (300) in American Bowling Congress ABC competition.

The Harlem Globetrotters are the first basketball team to make a complete trip around world, during a tour from April 15 to Oct. 17.

Charles Moore Jr. becomes the first African American to win an Olympic gold medal in the 400-meter hurdles.

Joe Louis, as an amateur, becomes the first African American to play in a PGA sponsored tournament, the San Diego Open.

Former Birmingham Black Baron and Indianapolis Clown third baseman Johnny Britton and former Black Baron pitcher Jimmy Newberry become the first African American players to compete in Japan. They are on loan to the Hankyu Braves of the Japanese Pacific League from the St. Louis Browns' farm system.

Dave Hoskins, former pitcher with the Homestead Grays and the Chicago American Giants, becomes the first African American to appear in a Texas League game with the Dallas Eagles and posts a 22-10 won-lost mark for the season. The right-hander would go on to compile a 9-4 won-lost record during two years with the Cleveland Indians.

A 39-year-old rookie catcher Quincy Trouppe catches relief pitcher "Toothpick Sam" Jones of the Cleveland Indians forming the first African American battery in the American League. Trouppe is also the first African American catcher in the American

League.

Roy Campanella of the Brooklyn Dodgers becomes the African American baseball player on a Wheaties cereal box when featured on the side panel.

Hank Aaron starts his pro baseball career with the Indianapolis Clowns.

Brooklyn Dodger pitcher Joe Black, the National League's Rookie of the Year, becomes the first African American pitcher to win a World Series game.

St. Louis Browns' Satchel Paige, 46, is selected to play in a major league baseball All-Star game.

Larry Doby of the Cleveland Indians becomes the first African American to lead either the American League or National League in home runs. He finishes with 32. Doby also becomes the first African American to lead either the American or National League in slugging percentage, as well, besting all hitters in the American League with a .541 batting average.

Roy Campanella, on June 19, becomes the first African American to catch a no-hitter in the re-integrated major leagues, the first of three career no-hitters. He catches Carl Erskine, as the Dodgers defeat the Chicago Cubs, 5-0.

In January, the PGA tour passes a rule allowing Black golfers to enter a tournament if the sponsor agrees. Bill Spiller becomes one of the first African Americans to play in a major golf tourney.

Paul "Tank" Younger and Dan Towler become the first African Americans to play in the NFL All-Star game, the Pro Bowl.

Running back Dan Towler of the Los Angeles Rams is the first African American named Pro Bowl's Player of the Game.

Clifton Anderson, an end, and running backs Ollie Matson and Wally Triplett become the first African Americans to play for the Chicago Cardinals of the NFL. Anderson is the grandfather of NBA player Kyle Anderson.

Theodore "Ted" Corbitt becomes the first African American to represent the U.S. Olympic team in the marathon at the Helsinki, Finland Olympics. He is the founding president of New York Road Runners and is often called "The Father of American Long Distance Running." Corbitt was in the first class of inductees selected to the National Distance Running Hall of Fame in 1998.

Joie Ray, while not the first African American to race in NASCAR's top series, is the first African American licensed by the American Automobile Association. Joie Ray (Henry J. Ray) becomes the first African American driver to start (at 25th spot) of a NASCAR sanctioned race, when he finished 51st at the Dayton Beach / Highway course.

Arthur B. Brooks from Detroit becomes the first African American accepted as a member of the American Bowling Congress (ABC).

1953

"I am invisible, understand, simply because people refuse to see me." – Ralph Ellison, *Invisible Man*

Joe Perry is the first African American to rush for more than 1,000 yards – 1,018 yards – in a season. In 1962, Cookie Gilchrist becomes the first AFL back to rush for 1,000 yards (1,096 in a 14-game season).

Willie Thrower of the Chicago Bears becomes the first African American quarterback to appear in an NFL game, relieving a slumping George Blanda. He completes three of eight passes for 27 yards. He never plays again.

George "Scoop" Taliaferro becomes the first African American to start an NFL game at quarterback.

Hank Foster joins the Bradley University Bulldogs and becomes the first African American basketball player and track and field hurdler.

Larry Doby is the first athlete featured on the cover of editor Jackie Robinson's new magazine called *Our Sports*. The cover title: "He Can Challenge Ruth's Home Run Record, If -- ."

Roy Campanella becomes the first major league catcher in integrated baseball to hit 20 or more homers in five successive seasons.

Roy Campanella of the Brooklyn Dodgers becomes the first catcher in major league history to hit more than 40 (41) home runs in a season.

The New York Yankees, with Yogi Berra, Mickey Mantle, Phil Rizzuto, Whitey Ford and Johnny Mize, become the last all-White baseball team to win a World Series, when they defeat the Brooklyn Dodgers (4-2) with Joe Black, Jackie Robinson, Roy Campanella and Junior Gilliam.

The city of Birmingham, Ala., bars the Jackie Robinson All-Stars, composed of Black and White players from playing due to a 1944 city ordinance, section 859 which cites "It shall be unlawful for any person in charge of or in control of any room, hall, theater, picture house, auditoriums, yard, court, ballpark, public park or indoor or outdoor place, to which both white persons and negroes (sic) are admitted, to cause, permit or allow mixing of races." In 1950, the city passes Ordinance 798-F to add even more restrictions to prevent racial interaction at baseball, softball, football, basketball or similar games. Robinson's all-star team includes Dodger first

Colorful Firsts in U.S. Sports

baseman Gil Hodges and Indian third baseman Al Rosen.

The Hot Spring Bathers of the Cotton States League (CSL) sign pitching brothers Jim and Leander Tugerson to play only in home games due to segregation sanctions in the deep South. CSL president Al Haraway blocks this loophole in the bylaws. In April, the National Association of Professional Baseball Leagues, an umbrella organization for minor leagues, rules against Haraway and reinstates the Tugersons. Instead, the Tugerson brothers leave the CSL and join the Class D Knoxville Smokies of the Mountain States League. See 1955.

The first woman in professional baseball, Toni Stone, joins the Indianapolis Clowns. She later plays for the Kansas City Monarchs. This season Stone suffers a serious shoulder injury diving for a ground ball in July against the Monarchs, forcing the Indianapolis Clowns to sign Doris Arlene Jackson and Desiree "Boo Boo" Richardson. Stone was rejected by the All-American Girls Professional Baseball League (1943-1954), founded by Philip K. Wrigley, due to its segregation policy.

Quincy Trouppe becomes the first African American scout for the St. Louis Cardinals when signed by new owner August Busch Jr.

The St. Louis Cardinals signs its first African American player, 23-year-old Leonard Tucker from Fresno (Calif.) State College. The first baseman spends nine seasons in the minors and never makes it to the parent club.

The Detroit Tigers signs the club's first African American, Claude Agee. The 18-year-old outfielder is assigned to the Jamestown (N.Y.) Falcons of the Pony League. He plays two seasons in the minor leagues.

Jackie Robinson appears on the February cover of *Inside Baseball* magazine.

The Detroit Lions become the last all-White team to win the NFL championship. They defeat the Cleveland Browns 17-16 at Briggs Stadium in Detroit, Mich.

The Portsmouth Merrimacs become the first team in the Piedmont League to sign African American players: Catchers Claude and Dick Brown; outfielders Bill Louis, James Livingston and Burly Barge; infielders Henry Craighead, Thomas Burt, Eugene "Stank" White; and pitcher Leonard Dunovant. The new team owner Frank Lawrence effectively ended the Virginia-based Piedmont League's 33-year history of racial exclusion. Later, in the season, the Merrimacs signed 45-year-old former Negro League first sacker Buck Leonard. The team, without a major league affiliation, folds after the 1955 season.

The Miami Sun Sox of the Florida International League sign its first two African American players, outfielder Albert "Speed" Baro and third baseman Jonathan "Clyde" Parris. The Sun Sox were a minor league affiliate of the Brooklyn Dodgers.

In Hollywood, Calif., Emmett Ashford is the first African American umpire to work a game, involving contemporary major leagues players, as the umpire-in-chief of a charity contest between the stars of the Pacific Coast League and selected players from major league clubs training in the West. Maxwell Stiles of the *Los Angeles Mirror* reports, "His work was excellent."

William Rhodman from Detroit rolls consecutive games of 223, 233 and 263 in the national tournament at Chicago's Coliseum, becoming the first African American to break into the top standings in an American Bowling Congress tournament.

Leonard Williams, a football player, becomes the first African American athlete at the University of Delaware.

Harold Freeman becomes the first basketball captain at Catholic University in Washington, District of Columbia. He is also the first African American tennis player at the university and wins singles and doubles matches as his team wins its fourth straight Mason-Dixon Conference championship in Baltimore, Md.

Basketball star Walter Dukes of Seton Hall is the first African American to be named First Team All-American. Don Barksdale of UCLA in 1947 was Second Team All-American.

1954

"I think the segregation decision of 1954 probably did more than anything else to awaken the Negro from his apathy to demanding his right to equality." – Thurgood Marshall

Ray Felix, a center for the Baltimore Bullets, is the first African American named NBA Rookie of the Year, for the 1953-54 season.

San Francisco 49er Joe Perry rushes for 1049 yards, to become the first player – Black or White – to rush more than 1,000 yards in back-to-back seasons, following his 1,018 yards in 1953.

The NFL's top three rushers are Black: Joe Perry, John Henry Johnson and Tank Younger. Perry is the first non-drafted NFL player since the draft originated in 1936 to lead the league in rushing.

Joe Perry becomes the first African American to be named NFL's Most Valuable Player.

Horace Gillom of the Cleveland Browns kicks the longest punt (80 yards) in NFL history against the New York Giants. Gillom is credited with inventing the phrase "hang time."

Calvin Jones becomes the first football player, collegiate or professional, to appear on the cover of *Sports Illustrated*.

Fritz Pollard, former Brown University halfback, is named to the College Football Hall of Fame. Frederick Douglass Pollard was the first African American football player at Brown in 1916.

Mal Whitfield, track star, is the first African American to win the James E. Sullivan Award, given each year to the top amateur athlete.

Future St. Louis Cardinals pitcher Bob Gibson is the first African American basketball player at Creighton University. His number 45 is later retired.

Jackie Robinson steals home plate on a rare triple-steal along with teammates Gil Hodges and Sandy Amorós against the Pittsburgh Pirates.

Jackie Robinson appears on the June cover of *Our World* magazine, published from 1946 to 1957.

Mamie "Peanut" Johnson and Connie Morgan join the Indianapolis Clowns, as pitcher and second baseman, respectively. This will be Johnson and Morgan's only year in professional Black baseball. Toni Stone leaves the Clowns and joins the Kansas City Monarchs.

The New York Giants become the first National League baseball team with ebony players to win a World Series, with Monte Irvin, Hank Thompson, Rubén Gómez and Willie Mays. The Cleveland Indians became the first American League team with Black players to a win World Series in 1948.

The Dodgers field the first Black majority team in white-centric major league baseball when they start five African Americans: Jim Gilliam at second, Jackie Robinson at third, Sandy Amorós in left field, Don Newcombe on the mound and Roy Campanella catching. They defeat the Milwaukee Braves, 2-1 in 11 innings at County Stadium.

On April 9, Nat Peeples becomes the first and only African American to take the field in a Southern Association game. Peeples pinch-hits in the fifth inning and plays left field the next evening for the Atlanta Crackers. He goes 0-for-4 with a walk in two games and is gone from the all-White league a week later, demoted to Class A Jacksonville. He never returns to Atlanta, ultimately finishing out his career in the minor leagues.

The Cleveland Indians, in the American League, become the first team to have an all-tan outfield during the regular season with Al Smith, Dave Pope and Larry Doby. In 1951, New York Giants, in the National League, fielded an all-Black outfield in the playoffs.

Theodore "Ted" Corbitt becomes the first African American to win the USA National Marathon Championship.

Under a portable lighting system, the Harlem Globetrotters become the first professional baseball team to play a night game at Wrigley Field. This event is three decades before the Chicago Cubs play its first night game in 1988.

Jackie Moore is the first African American to play for the NBA Milwaukee Hawks.

1955

"We didn't have any of what they called Civil Rights back then.

It was just a matter of survival – existing from day to day." - Rosa Parks

Ray Crowe coaches Indiana's Crispus Attucks to the first state high school basketball title won by an all-Black team in an integrated sport in America. Led by Oscar Robertson, the team also becomes the first Indianapolis school to win the Indiana state basketball championship.

The University of San Francisco Dons basketball team, coached by Phil Woolpert, becomes the first team with three Black starters to win an NCAA championship. The starters were Bill Russell, K. C. Jones and Hal Perry.

Bill Russell of the San Francisco Dons is the first African American to be named MVP of the NCAA Final Four tournament.

Ed Fleming (from Niagara University), Dick Ricketts (Duquesne) and Maurice Stokes (Saint Francis) are the first African Americans to play for the Rochester Royals.

Former Florida A&M basketball star Bob Williams, at 6-foot-6, becomes the first African American on the NBA Minneapolis Lakers.

Jesse Arnelle and Chuck Cooper are the first African Americans to play for the NBA Fort Wayne Pistons.

Earl Lloyd and Jim Tucker for the Syracuse Nationals become the first African Americans to play on an NBA championship team when they defeat the Fort Wayne Pistons.

Waymon Anderson becomes the first African American basketball player for the University of Colorado State Rams.

Colorful Firsts in U.S. Sports

The Hazleton (Pa.) Hawks of the Eastern League become the first professional league franchise to start an all-Black lineup, with Jesse Arnelle, Tom Hemans, Fletcher Johnson, Floyd Lane and Sherman White.

Dick Ricketts from Duquesne University is the first Black to be chosen as the overall number one pick in the NBA draft by the St. Louis Hawks. Ricketts also signs with the baseball St. Louis Cardinals and joins the parent club in 1959.

Hal Greer, as a Marshall Thundering Herd, becomes the first African American to play for a public college in W.Va. In 1976, the Philadelphia 76ers retire its first uniform number, Greer's No. 15.

Julius Pegues from Tulsa, Okla., becomes the first African American basketball player for the University of Pittsburgh Panthers.

Missouri "Big Mo" Arledge from Philander Smith College (Ark.) is the first African American woman named to the All-American team.

Willie Mays, alongside actress Lorraine Day and Leo Durocher, is the first African American baseball player to appear on the cover of *Sports Illustrated*.

Willie Mays leads the National League in home runs with 51. Mays becomes the first African American in the re-integrated major leagues to win a home run title and a batting title, which he won in 1954 with a .345 average.

National Leaguer Sam "Toothpick" Jones of the Chicago Cubs becomes the first Black pitcher to throw a no-hitter in the predominantly White major leagues. He defeats the Pittsburgh Pirates, 4-0, yielding seven walks at Wrigley Field.

Don Newcombe becomes the first African American pitcher to steal home plate after hitting a triple in the 9th inning against the Pittsburgh Pirates.

Don Newcombe becomes the first African American baseball pitcher to appear on the cover of *Sports Illustrated*.

Elston Howard, the first Black New York Yankee, is the only former Negro League player to homer in his first World Series at-bat. He homers off Don Newcombe of the Dodgers in the second inning of Game 1.

Roy Campanella is the first African American to win three MVP awards in baseball.

Bill James becomes the second umpire (after Emmett Ashford in the Pacific Coast League) in professional baseball. James makes his debut in the Pony League at Jamestown, N.Y.

The Pine Bluff (Ark.) Judges of the Cotton States League signs three Black players, outfielder Charles Peppers and infielder from the Memphis Red Sox and pitcher Charles Chatman of the Detroit Stars. The Judges' board of directors announces it will not play the Negroes in Mississippi.

The Cannon Street YMCA All-Stars are the first Black Little League team in South Carolina. When all the White teams withdrew in protest, the Cannon Street team won the state tournament by forfeit and advanced to the Little League World Series in Williamsport, Pa. However the team was declared ineligible because it did not win games on the field. As they watched the first game from the stands the crowd chanted, "Let them play! Let them play!" in support.

The New Orleans Pelicans of the Southern Association (AA) refuse three Negro players assigned by the parent Pittsburgh Pirates club: Bennie Daniels, Román Mejias and R. C. Stevens. General manager Joe Nowak claims, "They don't measure up to Southern Association standards." Black fans boycott the team that averaged 1,700 fans per game. Two seasons later, owners claimed they lost $130,000 and became an affiliate of the New York Yankees. All three players make the Pirates team within a few years.

Isaac Murphy becomes the first jockey voted into the Jockey Hall of Fame at the National Museum of Racing in Saratoga Springs, N.Y.

Former caddy, Gene Smith becomes the first Black golfer to win the Akron Good Park Golf Championship in Ohio. He scores a 73 over an 18-hole course.

Calvin Jones, offensive guard from Iowa University, becomes the first African American to win the Outland Trophy. Jones was the first football player to appear on the cover of *Sports Illustrated* in 1954.

Willie Saucer becomes the first Black quarterback for the University of Evansville Purple Aces.

Charles Bryant and Jon McWilliams, both from the University of Nebraska, are the first Black players to play in the Orange Bowl.

On August 28, Joe Perry of the San Francisco 49ers, becomes the first African American NFL player honored with a day. The 49ers give Perry a TV set and house furniture, but not the car on the field as first believed. He works for Boas Pontiac during the offseason, and the dealership puts the car on the field as advertisement.

Charlie Brackins from Prairie View A&M University is the first Black quarterback employed by the Green Bay Packers. Later in 2013, Seneca Wallace from Iowa State University becomes the Packers' first Black starting quarterback.

Calvin Jones, Iowa's team captain is the first African American to win the Outland Trophy as the best linebacker in college football.

Sugar Ray Robinson becomes the world middleweight champion.

The Supreme Court rules to desegregate public golf courses in Atlanta in the landmark case, *Holmes v. City of Atlanta*. Brothers Alfred "Tup" and Oliver Wendell Holmes challenge the status quo to become the first African Americans to legally play golf at a public facility in Atlanta.

1956

"A little Black girl yearns for the blue eyes of a little White girl, and the horror at the heart of her yearning is exceeded only by the evil of fulfillment." – Toni Morrison, The Bluest Eye

Althea Gibson becomes the first African American female to win the French Open tennis championship, 6-0, and 12-10, in the process becoming the first African American to win a Grand Slam title.

In the All-American City Basketball Tournament in Owensboro, Kentucky, the Ole Miss Rebels lose the opening game and are scheduled to play the Iona College Gaels of N.Y. in the consolation match. Ole Miss coach Bonnie Graham advises officials that if Stanley Hill, a Black guard on the Gaels team, suits up, the game will not be played. The game is forfeited to the Gaels. State legislators praise Ole Miss officials for their "honorable" decision to boycott the game. The 1957 Ole Miss press guide does not list the loss in the team's record book.

Ira Murchison, at 5-foot-2, becomes the shortest sprinter to hold the world record in the 100-meter sprint, with a time of 10.1 seconds.

Ann Gregory becomes the first African American female golfer to play in a U.S. Golf Association national championship, in the Women's Amateur tournament at the Meridian Hills Country Club in Indianapolis.

Sixteen-year-old high school sophomore Willye White becomes the first American female to win a medal (silver) in the long jump at the Melbourne Olympics, with a mark of 19 feet and 11.5 inches.

Dr. Nell Jackson becomes the first African American head coach of the U.S. Olympic Women's Track & Field team.

Aeriwentha "Mae" Faggs Starr becomes the first African American female track and field athlete to represent the U.S. in three consecutive Olympic Games: 1948 London, England; 1952 Helsinki, Finland; and 1956 Melbourne, Australia.

Compton Community College athlete Charles Dumas becomes the first man to break the seven-foot barrier, in the high jump, with a leap of 7 feet, 5/8 inches, at the Olympic trials in Los Angeles.

Milt Campbell becomes the first African American to win the Olympic decathlon.

Jackie Robinson becomes the first baseball player to receive the NAACP's Spingarn Medal, an honor for "the man or woman of African descent and American citizenship who shall have made the highest achievement during the preceding year or years in any honorable field."

Willie Mays becomes the first player to join the 30-30 club, with 36 home runs and 40 stolen bases.

Former 1949 National League Rookie of the Year, Don Newcombe becomes the first player to win the first-ever Cy Young Award and the Most Valuable Player award in the same season.

Don Newcombe becomes the first MVP award winner not selected to the All-Star game the same year.

Roy Campanella catches his second no-hitter of the year and his third career no-hitter to tie a major league record. On 12 May 1956, Campanella caught a no-hitter from Carl Erskine defeating the New York Giants, 3-0. Later that year on September 25, he caught Sal Maglie's no-hitter, beating the Philadelphia Phillies, 5-0.

Buck O'Neil becomes the first Black scout in the white major leagues for the Chicago Cubs.

New Orleans native Osibee J. Jelks becomes the first Black umpire in the Class C Provincial Baseball League.

On August 7, a crowd of 57,000 fans, the largest in minor-league baseball history, watch 50-year-old Satchel Paige of the Miami Marlins beat Columbus in an International League game played in the Orange Bowl.

Bill Russell of the San Francisco Dons is the first African American to be named UPI's Division I Player of the Year.

Bill Russell, K. C. Jones and Carl Cain become the first African Americans named to the U.S. Olympic basketball team.

Willie "The Whale" Naulls from UCLA is the first African American to play for the NBA St. Louis Hawks.

Sidney Williams Jr. becomes the first African American starting quarterback in Big Ten history with the University of Wisconsin Badgers.

Prentice Gautt a running back becomes the University of Oklahoma's first African American athlete. In 1959 he is named MVP of the Orange Bowl.

Colorful Firsts in U.S. Sports

Cornelius Roberts, known as the "Chocolate Rocket," a running back for USC becomes the first Black athlete to compete against the all-white University of Texas Longhorns in Austin, Texas. Despite objections from the university, Roberts rushes for 251 yards on 12 carries, carrying the Trojans to a 44-20 victory. In 1970, the University of Texas allows its first Black player.

Bobby Grier, a fullback and linebacker for the Pittsburgh Panthers is the first African American football player to break the color barrier of the collegiate Sugar Bowl game, which is held in New Orleans, La. Segregationists try to keep Grier from playing because he is Black. Georgia's governor Marvin Griffin publicly threatens the Georgia Tech's president Blake Van Leer to cancel the game. Later in July, the Louisiana state legislature passes Act 579, known as the Athletic Events Bill, which prohibits interracial sports competitions.

Maurice Stokes of the Rochester Royals becomes the first NBA player to lead his team in points (16.6), rebounds (16.3) and assists (4.9), the same season.

Floyd Patterson becomes the first professional African American boxer to appear on the cover of *Sports Illustrated* and the first former Olympian (1952) to win the world heavyweight championship.

The minor league baseball Louisville Colonels of the American Association announce the desegregation of its team. Also for the first time Negroes will be permitted to sit unsegregated in the stands at Parkway Field.

Lenny Moore of the Baltimore Colts is the first African American named Rookie of the Year in the NFL by the *United Press International*.

1957

"Probe the tissue of Negro social life and the Negro reacts to the same illusions that feed the vanity of white men." - E. Franklin Frazier, sociologist

Before the era of Wilt Chamberlain and Bill Russell dominating the boards, Maurice Stokes is the first African American to lead the NBA in rebounding. African Americans will continue to win this category for the next 20 years. Bill Walton (14.4 rpg) breaks the string during the 1976-77 season.

Nat "Sweetwater" Clifton, 34, becomes the oldest first-time NBA All-Star selection. Clifton from Xavier University (La.) is also the first player from an HBCU to play in an NBA All-Star game. Clifton is the first African American to play for the Detroit Pistons.

Billy Lewis becomes the first African American basketball player for the University of Colorado Buffaloes. Lewis later earns his law degree from Howard University.

Tennessee A&I, coached by John McLendon, becomes the first African American college team to win a national title against White competition in any sport, with a 92-73 defeat of Southeastern Oklahoma for the NAIA Division I title.

Govoner Vaughn and Manny Jackson become the first African American basketball players to start and letter for the University of Illinois' basketball team. Jackson later becomes chairman of the Harlem Globetrotter franchise.

Simon Roberts from the University of Iowa wrestling at 147 pounds, captures an NCAA crown placing second in the Big Ten tournament. The following year he wins the conference title, becoming the first Black wrestler to win an NCAA Championship.

Althea Gibson becomes the first African American woman to win the U.S. Tennis Championship, 6-3, 6-2.

Althea Gibson becomes the first Black to win the world's prestigious Wimbledon championship. She defeats American Darlen Hard 6-3, 6-2. Gibson is the first African American woman to appear on the cover of *Sports Illustrated* and the first African American tennis player to appear on the cover of *Time* magazine.

Abner Haynes and Leon King become the first African American collegiate football players in Texas when they join North Texas State College (now University of North Texas) Eagles.

Ollie Matson becomes the first African American NFL player to appear on the cover of *Sports Illustrated*.

Charles Sifford wins the predominantly white Long Beach Open Tournament, a 54-hole event, which includes a $500 bonus for having the lowest round on the final day. Sifford's total winnings are $1,700.

Gary Player from South Africa makes his Masters Tournament debut with an African American caddie named Ernest Nipper.

Chief umpire in the Negro American League Bob Motley graduates from the Al Somers Umpires School in Daytona Beach, Fla. He was the only scholar in the class of 74 to achieve a perfect score on the final examination. Unfortunately, Motley never umpired in either the American or National League.

Jackie Robinson retires from major league baseball. Three league teams, the Phillies, Tigers and the Red Sox, have yet to put an African American on its rosters.

Minnie Miñoso (left field) and Willie Mays (center field) become the first former Negro Leaguers to make major league baseball's first Gold Glove team.

Lowell Perry becomes the first African American assistant coach (receivers coach) in the NFL with the Pittsburgh Steelers.

Willie Wood, a two-way player at USC, at safety and quarterback, becomes the first African American quarterback in the Pacific Coast Conference (PCC) and its successor AAWU, now the Pac-12 Conference.

Jim Brown, of Syracuse, is sought by the baseball New York Yankees and the basketball Syracuse Nationals. Brown signs with the Cleveland Browns for $12,000 with a signing bonus of $3,000. He leads the NFL in rushing his rookie season and is named the *Sporting News'* Rookie of the Year.

Jim Brown is the first African American chosen by the *Associated Press* as NFL Player of the Year.

1958

"Keep on going, keep on pushing, keep on fighting injustice." - Mary Church Terrell

The St. Louis Hawks, led by Bob Pettit, become the last all-White team to win an NBA championship. The Hawks defeat the Boston Celtics 4-2 games.

Wayne Embry is the first African American to play for the Cincinnati Royals.

Althea Gibson becomes the first Black female to win Wimbledon, two years in a row.

Puerto Rican Vic Power (Pellot) of the Cleveland Indians becomes the first non-White player in either league to win the Gold Glove Award at first base.

Ernie Banks of the Chicago Cubs is named the Most Valuable Player in the National League.

Willie Mays appears on the April cover of *Life* magazine.

Buffalo Bisons first baseman Luke Easter wallops an estimated 520-foot home run in an International League game against the Havana Sugar Kings.

Two rookies for the Cleveland Indians, Gary Bell from San Antonio, Texas and a Jim "Mudcat" Grant from Lacoochee, Fla., become the first White & Black roommates in the re-integrated major leagues.

Sugar Ray Robinson becomes the first African American fighter to hold the middleweight title on five separate occasions.

Harry "The Black Panther" Wills dies in N.Y. Critics claim the race barrier prevented Wills from contesting Jack Dempsey's heavyweight crown.

Wendell Smith becomes the first African American to provide radio commentary for a boxing championship match. The middleweight title fight is between Sugar Ray Robinson and Carmen Basilio at Chicago Stadium.

Oscar Robertson becomes the first player to score more than 50 points in an NCAA playoff game. Robertson scores 56, as Cincinnati defeats Arkansas in the Southeast Regional.

Wilt Chamberlain joins the Harlem Globetrotters.

Bill Russell becomes the first NBA player to average more than 20 rebounds (22.7) a game. He is also the first African American recipient of the NBA's Maurice Podoloff Trophy, its Most Valuable Player award.

Jim Brown becomes the first African American to lead the NFL in scoring with 108 points (18 TD, 0 FG, 0 PAT), and the first African American player to win the Jim Thorpe Trophy.

Maurice Kilgore becomes the first African American bowler to appear on national television when he competes in "Beat the Champ" tournament at Chicago's Faetz-Niesen Lanes.

Willie O'Ree, for the Boston Bruins, becomes the first African American in the National Hockey League (NHL) when he joins the Boston Bruins. Legally blind in his right eye, he plays two seasons. O'Ree is later inducted, as a builder, into the Hockey Hall of Fame in 2018 and Canada's Sports Hall of Fame in 2020. In 2021, the Bruins retire his No. 22 jersey, and the following year receives the Congressional Gold Medal from President Joe Biden – the first NHL player to receive this honor.

Phil Reavis, high jumper from Villanova, becomes the first African American track and field athlete to appear on the cover of *Sports Illustrated*.

Rafer Johnson is the first African American to win *Sports Illustrated's* Sportsman of the Year award.

1959

"All I am askin' is for a little respect . . ." – Aretha Franklin

John Thomas becomes the youngest man to set a world record. He leaps 7 feet, 1 ¼ inches in the high jump, one day shy of his 18th birthday.

Colorful Firsts in U.S. Sports

Eroseanna "Rose" Robinson, a high jumper, refuses to stand for the national anthem at the Pan American Games held in Chicago's Wrigley Field, citing the flag represents "war, injustice and hypocrisy." Upon winning the 1958 AAU National Championship, Robinson was named to the U.S. Women's Track and Field team. The predominantly Black team was invited to compete in the Soviet Union at a State Department track meet during the height of the Cold War. Robinson refused to attend, telling *Jet* magazine: "I don't want to be used as a political pawn."

John McLendon's Tennessee A & I basketball team during warmups for the NAIA championships, the Illinois State Normal cheerleaders and band play and sing "Bye Bye Blackbird." McLendon takes his team off the floor and then gives the "talk." The Tigers from Nashville, Tennessee beat the Redbirds, 131-74.

Wilt Chamberlain becomes the first rookie to score at least 40 points (43) on opening night.

Elgin Baylor becomes the first rookie to be named the Most Valuable Player of an NBA All-Star game.

Charlie Neal, Los Angeles Dodgers, becomes the first African American to win the Gold Glove Award at second base.

Charles Sifford is granted "approved tournament player" status by the PGA.

William "Bill" Wright becomes the first African American to win a USGA event, capturing the National Public Links Championship in Denver, Colo.

Robert Ryland, 39, becomes the first African American professional tennis player on the World Pro Tour. Ryland would later coach Arthur Ashe, Serena and Venus Williams.

The American Football League is formed by Texans Lamar Hunt and K.S. "Bud" Adams with listed franchises in New York City, Oakland, Buffalo, Houston, Denver, Los Angeles, Dallas and Boston.

Althea Gibson releases a record album, *Althea Gibson Sings*. She later appears in the film, *The Horse Soldiers*.

Basketball point guard Oscar Robertson of the Cincinnati Bearcats is the first player to be named College Player of the Year. Robertson captures this honor again the following season. In 1998, the award is renamed the Oscar Robertson Trophy.

The Boston Red Sox becomes the last all-White major league team to integrate with a Black athlete when they sign infielder Elijah "Pumpsie" Green.

Sam "Toothpick" Jones of the San Francisco Giants becomes the first African American pitcher to lead the National League in ERA, 2.83, while winning 21 and losing 15 games. Jones becomes the first African American pitcher to pitch a no-hitter (his second, a seven-inning game) on Sept. 26 and also win 20 games in a season. As a Giant, his team defeats the St. Louis Cardinals, 4-0. Jones ends this game with the bases loaded with three walks and then strikes out the side: Dick Groat, Roberto Clemente and Frank Thomas. Note: This was Jones' second no-hitter, the first in 1955. Earlier on June 30, Jones pitched a one-hitter versus Don Drysdale and the Los Angeles Dodgers before 59,312 fans at the LA Coliseum. The lone hit came on a questionable and much debated fielding bobble by shortstop Andre Rodgers. The local scorer, who called the Rodgers error a hit, was Charlie Parks.

Ernie Banks becomes the first player in the National League to win the MVP award two years in a row.

Junior Gilliam is the only man in baseball history to hit a home run in both Negro League (8-20-1950, Comiskey Park) and major league (8-3-1959, Los Angeles Coliseum) All-Star games.

Hank Aaron becomes the first player to win a Gold Glove and lead the league in batting (.355).

John McLendon, of Tennessee A & I, becomes the first African American coach to be selected to coach the National All-Star Team and the first basketball coach to win three consecutive NAIA titles.

1960

"If you can convince the lowest white man he's better than the best colored man, he won't notice you're picking his pocket. Hell, give him somebody to look down on, and he'll empty his pockets for you."

- As told to journalist Bill D. Moyers by President Lyndon B. Johnson

In this decade, Dick "Night Train" Lane tackles wide receivers around the neck. The clothesline tackles, called "Neckties," were subsequently banned by the NFL.

Abner Haynes of the Dallas Texans is the first African American named the American Football League's Most Valuable Player and its Rookie of the Year. Haynes leads the AFL in rushing and becomes the first rookie to amass more than 2,000 all-purpose yards in a season (2,100). Haynes is also named Rookie of the Year by *UPI* and the *Sporting News*.

Lionel Taylor becomes the first African American to lead the American Football League in receiving with 92 receptions and 1,235 yards. Taylor catches 12 TDs.

Halfback Sid Blanks joins the Texas A&I Javelinas and becomes the first Black player in the Lone Star Conference. He is also the first African American to receive a football scholarship to an integrated school in Texas. Blanks later plays for the Houston Oilers and the New England Patriots.

Gene Mingo from Akron (OH) South High School joins the Denver Broncos of the American Football League (AFL) and becomes the first African American placekicker in football. He also recorded the first punt return for a touchdown in the AFL. The versatile Mingo holds the record for the most touchdown passes by a halfback, two.

The African American Students Foundation is created by singer Harry Belafonte, actor Sidney Poitier and baseball player Jackie Robinson, to aid Kenyan students to study in America. One student Barack H. Obama receives a grant to study business administration at the University of Hawaii in Honolulu. Obama Senior meets White American Ann Dunham at the university. They marry and have a son, Barack H. Obama, Junior, who becomes the first Black U.S. president in 2008.

Hank Aaron becomes the first player to win a Gold Glove and lead the league in RBIs (126) in the same year.

Earl Battey becomes the first African American, in either league, to win a Gold Glove Award at catcher.

Ernie Banks of the Chicago Cubs becomes the first African American in either league, to win the Gold Glove Award at shortstop.

At the Rome Olympics, Wilma Rudolph becomes the first American woman to win three gold medals in the same year.

Wilma Rudolph becomes the first American woman to break the 23-second barrier in the 200-meter dash with a time of 22.9 seconds.

Les Carney is the first African American athlete from Ohio University to compete in the Olympics. He wins a silver medal in the 200-meters race. The Lester Carney Track in Kettlewell Stadium at Indian Creek High School, in Wintersville, Ohio, is named in his honor.

Hallow Wilson becomes the first African American wrestler to win an AAU championship, winning the heavyweight title in Greco-Roman.

Althea Gibson tours with the Harlem Globetrotters, playing exhibition tennis.

John McLendon becomes the first African American coach to defeat the U.S. Olympic Team (with Jerry West and Oscar Robertson) with an amateur team, the Cleveland Pipers of the National Industrial Basketball League (NIBL).

Cassius Clay wins a gold medal in the light heavyweight division at the Olympics.

Floyd Patterson becomes the first African American to regain the heavyweight title. Patterson lost his heavyweight title to Ingemar Johansson earlier and regained it nearly a year later when he knocked out Johansson.

Rafer Johnson becomes the first African American to carry the U.S. flag during the Olympic opening ceremony. He becomes the first man to score more than 8,000 (8,063) points in the Decathlon. And becomes the first African American male named Athlete of the Year by *Track & Field News*. Rafer Johnson also appears on the cover of *Time* magazine.

Minnie Miñoso becomes the first Cuban American to lead the American League in hits with 184.

Yankee catcher Elston Howard pioneers the use of the first hinged catcher's mitt that led to the modern one-handed catching technique. Howard would later win Gold Glove awards in 1963 and 1964.

Bill White of the St. Louis Cardinals becomes the first Black National League player to win the Gold Glove Award at first base.

The American League Kansas City Athletics finish in last place with 58 wins – 96 loses and finish 39 games behind the Yankees. The A's became the last major league team to employ an all-white roster for the entire season.

Sgt. Otis Davis becomes the first man to break the 45 second barrier in the 400 meters with 44.9 seconds time in the Rome Olympics.

Bill Russell becomes the first NBA player to gather more than 50 (51) rebounds in a game.

Wilt Chamberlain later breaks Bill Russell's rebounding record with 55 rebounds. Chamberlain becomes the first NBA player to average more than 30 points (37.6) per game. The rookie becomes the first NBA player to score more than 1,000 (1,065) field goals in a season. In the process, he becomes the first NBA player to win the Rookie of the Year and Most Valuable Player awards in the same season.

1961

"To be a Negro in this country and to be relatively conscious is to be in a rage almost all the time."
– James Baldwin, speaking in a 1961 radio interview

Ernie Davis from Syracuse becomes the first African American to win the Heisman Trophy, designated the best player in college football. Davis broke Jim Brown's career rushing record at Syracuse.

Sandy Stephens of the Minnesota Gophers is the first African American quarterback named to the College All-American team.

Colorful Firsts in U.S. Sports

The Pittsburgh Pirates tap Gene Baker the first African American minor league manager within the major leagues' farm system. (Black managers had already been hired by independent teams.) He manages the Batavia Pirates in Class D of the New York-Pennsylvania League. On June 20, he takes over for James Adlam with an 18-24 won-lost record and finishes the season in third place, winning 47 of 82 games. In 1951, Sam Bankhead, managed the Farnham Pirates of Quebec's Provincial League (Class C), but the Farnham club was not affiliated with any major league team at the time.

John Roseboro of the Dodgers becomes the first African American catcher to win a Gold Glove in the National League.

Roberto Clemente becomes the first Puerto Rican to be a National League batting champion with a .351 average.

Washington Senators owner Calvin Griffith moves the team to Minnesota. At a 1978 speaking engagement Griffith shares his reason for the relocation. "I'll tell you why we came to Minnesota. It was when we found out you only had 15,000 blacks here," Griffith said then. "Black people don't go to ballgames, but they'll fill up a rassling ring and put up such a chant it'll scare you to death. We came here because you've got good, hardworking white people here." In 2020, his statue is removed from Target Field. The Twins organization issues this statement: "Our decision to memorialize Calvin Griffith with a statue reflects an ignorance on our part of systemic racism present in 1978, 2010 and today. We apologize for our failure to adequately recognize how the statue was viewed and the pain it caused for many people -- both inside the Twins organization and across Twins Territory. We cannot remove Calvin Griffith from the history of the Minnesota Twins, but we believe removal of this statue is an important and necessary step in our ongoing commitment to provide a Target Field experience where every fan and employee feels safe and welcome."

The Professional Golf Association (PGA) removes the "Caucasians only" clause from its constitution. The vote was unanimous by 87 delegates. Charlie Sifford becomes the first African American to join the PGA Tour.

Connie Hawkins of the Pittsburgh Rens becomes the American Basketball League's (ABL) first Most Valuable Player, receiving 41 of a possible 54 votes.

Connie Hawkins, Bill Bridges and Larry Staverman of the Kansas City Steers, Dan Swartz of the New York Tapers, and Dick Barnett from the Cleveland Pipers are named to the First Team All-Stars of the American Basketball League.

Cleo Hill from Winston-Salem State University is the first player from an HBCU to be drafted No. 1 by the NBA, when selected by the St. Louis Hawks.

Wilt Chamberlain becomes the first NBA player to grab more than 2,000 rebounds (2,149) in a season and the first NBA player to score more than 3,000 (3,033) points in a season.

Wilt Chamberlain becomes the first African American basketball player to appear on the cover of *Sports Illustrated*.

Oscar Robertson becomes the first African American basketball player to appear on the cover of *Time* magazine.

John McLendon becomes the first African American coach to win the National AAU Championship. He also becomes the first African American to coach in the American Basketball League (ABL), with the Cleveland Pipers.

1962

"He was a pilgrim that walked in the lonesome byways toward the high road of Freedom.

He was a sit-inner before sit-ins, a freedom rider before freedom rides." – Dr. Martin Luther King Jr., 1962

Renée Powell becomes the first African American to enter the U.S. Girls' Junior golf tournament. In the junior championship, she surprises many by winning the first round. The *Akron Beacon Journal* calls her the "Queen of the Bantam Golf Show."

Mal Goode becomes the first African American news correspondent when hired by ABC News. He is best known as a journalist for the *Pittsburgh Courier* and later host of local radio broadcast.

Darryl Andre Hill, a wide receiver, becomes the first African American to receive an athletic scholarship to play sports for a major university in the South. The University of Maryland Terrapins are a member of the Atlantic Coast Conference (ACC).

Interior Secretary Stewart Udall issues an ultimatum to Washington Redskins owner George Preston Marshall to sign a Black player. If not, the city-government owned D.C. Stadium (now Robert F. Kennedy Memorial Stadium), will have its 30-year lease rescinded.

The Washington Redskins, owned by George Preston Marshall, become the last NFL team to sign African Americans, wide receiver Bobby Mitchell and fullback Ron Hatcher.

Bobby Mitchell leads the NFL in receptions with 72 catches, as the Redskins finish 5-7-2 in fourth place, under coach Bill McPeak.

R.C. Owens, a 6-foot-3 Baltimore Colts wide receiver, (better known for popularizing the Alley-Oop pass, in which the receiver outjumps the defenders) blocks a 40-yard field goal at the crossbar in a game against the Washington Redskins. At the time, a legal defensive move.

Heisman Trophy winner Ernie Davis, of Syracuse University, is the first African American to be chosen as the first pick, in the first round of the NFL draft by the Washington Redskins. The running back is immediately traded to the Cleveland Browns. Davis is diagnosed with leukemia this year and dies less than a year later at age 23, without ever playing in an NFL game.

Willie Brown from Grambling State University retires from the NFL. He is the first player in NFL history to intercept at least one pass in 16 consecutive seasons.

Cookie Gilchrist becomes the first AFL running back to rush for 1,000 yards (1,096 in a 14-game season). In 1953, Joe Perry, was the first African American player in the NFL to rush for more than 1,000 yards (1,018).

Leon "Daddy Wags" Wagner becomes the first ball player to be named MVP of a major league All-Star game. His American League team wins 9-4 at Wrigley Field.

Buck O'Neil with the Chicago Cubs becomes the first African American from the Negro Leagues to coach in the white major leagues.

Larry Doby and Don Newcombe sign with the Chunichi Dragons to become the first former major leaguers to play in Japan. See 1952, Johnny Britton and Jimmy Newberry.

Boston Red Sox pitcher Earl Wilson is the first African American to throw a no-hitter in the American League.

In his first year of eligibility, Jackie Robinson is the first African American inducted into the National Baseball Hall of Fame in Cooperstown, N.Y. Cleveland Indians pitcher Bob Feller is also inducted this year. After a 1946 exhibition game in San Diego, Feller claimed Robinson, built like a football player, with broad shoulders, was too musclebound to be able to handle inside pitching and would never make it in the re-integrated major leagues.

Jackie Robinson appears on the cover of the *Negro Digest*, a magazine in format like the *Reader's Digest*.

Los Angeles Dodger shortstop Maury Wills is the first major leaguer to steal more than 100 bases (104).

John McLendon becomes the first African American coach to author a book on basketball, *Fast Break Basketball, Fine Points and Fundamentals*. McLendon develops his idea for up-tempo style basketball while at the University of Kansas, under the tutelage of athletic director James Naismith, despite not being allowed to play basketball for the still-segregated Jayhawks. John McLendon is inducted into the NAIA Hall of Fame.

Wade Houston, Eddie Whitehead and Sam Smith become the first African American basketball players at the University of Louisville. In 1989, Houston becomes the first African American head coach in the Southeastern Conference (SEC) with the Tennessee Vols.

Bill Russell becomes the first NBA basketball player to win back-to-back MVP awards.

Wilt Chamberlain becomes the first NBA player to score 100 points in a basketball game and more than 50 points in a playoff game. The Philadelphia Warrior scores 56 points against Syracuse. Chamberlain is also the first NBA player to score more than 4,000 (4,029) points in a season and the first to average more than 50 (50.4) points per game.

San Francisco Warriors' Wilt Chamberlain scores 63 points and the Lakers' Elgin Baylor scores 51 points, to become the first opponents to top 50 in the same game. Baylor later becomes the first player to score more than 60 points in a playoff game. Baylor scores 61 points against the Boston Celtics.

Oscar Robertson becomes the first NBA player to average more than 10 assists (11.4) per game. In process Robertson becomes the first NBA player to average a triple-double in a season. He averages 30.8 points (3rd in the NBA), 11.4 assists and 12.5 rebounds (8th) per game.

1963

"You can kill a man, but you can't kill an idea." – Medgar Evers

A group of African American men meet in New York City to discuss concerns about the cultural and financial obstacles that have limited the achievements of Black men, particularly young men. Among founders of the 100 Black Men of America were David Dinkins, Robert Mangum, Dr. William Hayling, Nathaniel Goldston III, Livingston Wingate, Andrew Hatcher and Jackie Robinson.

Clem Haskins and Dwight Smith become the first Black athletes to integrate the Western Kentucky University (WKU) Hilltoppers basketball program. Haskins later plays in the NBA and serves as an assistant coach on the gold medal winning 1996 Olympic Summer basketball squad.

The Loyola Ramblers (Chicago) become the first major college basketball team to have five Black players on the floor at the same time. They start one White player John Egan and four Black players, Les Hunter, Vic Rouse, Ron Miller and team captain

Colorful Firsts in U.S. Sports

Jerry Harkness. They defeat the Cincinnati Bearcats in overtime to capture the NCAA championship. Earlier in the tournament, despite hate mail from the Klan, the Ramblers faced the all-White Mississippi State Bulldogs against orders from Governor Ross Barnett, banning his Bulldogs from crossing state lines to play the integrated Ramblers. The landmark contest, won by the Ramblers 61-51, is later named the "Game of Change." See 2013.

In Las Vegas for the second Sonny Liston vs. Floyd Patterson fight, it becomes the first million-dollar purse with both fighters receiving $1,434,000 each. Patterson, a 4:1 betting underdog, is knocked down three times and counted out at 2:10 of the first round.

As the first Black player for the Little Rock Arkansas Travelers, a minor league affiliated of the Philadelphia Phillies, Dick Allen makes his debut. Led by White Citizens' Council leader Amis Guthridge, they picketed the ballpark caring signs reading, "Don't Negro-ize baseball" and "Nigger Go Home."

After Maury Wills' base stealing record of 104 steals, baseball institutes a rule change. This year pitchers are required to come to a complete stop (or pause), before delivering the pitch to the plate. The intent is to hold the potential base stealer closer to the bag.

Willie Mays becomes the first Negro Leaguer to win the MVP award at the white-centric major league All-Star game. His National League team wins 5-3.

Zoilo "Zorro" Versailles becomes the first non-White player to win the Gold Glove Award at shortstop in the American League.

The "Old Mongoose" Archie Moore retires with the most knockouts (130) of any light heavyweight champion.

Five months before becoming heavyweight champion, Cassius Clay releases an album, "I Am the Greatest."

L. M. Ellis is the first Black basketball player in the Ohio Valley Conference, when he joins the Austin Peay State University. In 2022, the university retires his jersey, No. 45.

John Austin becomes the first African American basketball player for the Boston College Eagles. Austin is from powerhouse DeMatha High School in Washington, District of Columbia. He later plays for the Baltimore Bullets of the NBA and the New Jersey Americans of the ABA.

Arthur Ashe becomes the first African American named to the U.S. Davis Cup Tennis team. He wins the U.S. Hard Court Championship.

Jake Gaither, coach for Florida A&M Rattlers, creates the Split-Line T formation, later copied by most major college football programs.

Junious "Buck" Buchanan is the first Grambling State University player taken as the overall first pick in the first round by the Dallas Texans of the AFL.

Lloyd C.A. "The Judge" Wells, with the Dallas Texans and later the Kansas City Chiefs, becomes the NFL's African American full-time scout. Wells recruits Jim Kearney, Emmitt Thomas, Buck Buchanan, Willie Lanier and Otis Taylor from HBCUs.

Paul Lowe, running back for the AFL's San Diego Chargers, is the first African American to win the *Associated Press'* Comeback Player of the Year Award.

Cleveland Browns' Jim Brown becomes the first running back with at least 200 carries to average more than six yards per carry (6.4).

After a 13-month battle against acute monocytic leukemia, the most virulent form of blood cancer, former Syracuse running back Ernie Davis succumbs to the disease and dies in a Cleveland hospital. Davis was 23.

Gale Sayers, the Kansas Comet, sets an NCAA record for the longest run from scrimmage with 99 yards against the Nebraska Cornhuskers.

Joe James becomes the first African American wrestler to win a gold medal in the Pan American games.

Wendell Scott becomes the first and only African American driver to win a NASCAR Winston Cup (then the Grand National) race at the Speedway Park in Jacksonville, Fla. The film *Greased Lightning*, starring Richard Pryor, is loosely based on his life.

Tennis star Althea Gibson becomes the first African American member of the Ladies Professional Golf Association (LPGA).

Elston Howard of the New York Yankees becomes the first African American to be named the American League MVP.

Dominican Juan Marichal of the San Francisco Giants becomes the first Latin American-born pitcher to throw a no-hitter, beating the Houston Colt .45s, 1-0.

Bill Russell of the Boston Celtics becomes the first NBA player to win the MVP award three consecutive years. He is also the first player to win the MVP award four times.

Reggie Harding is drafted by the Detroit Pistons in the sixth round with the 48th overall pick, making him the first player ever drafted who did not play in college. Harding graduated in 1960 from Eastern HS in Detroit, before playing for a prep school in Nashville and two seasons in the professional Midwest League in Toledo and Holland, Mich.

1963, The New York Rens, of 1932-33, are named to the Naismith Memorial Basketball Hall of Fame as a team, for its 88 consecutive game winning streak, the longest in professional baseball history.

1964

"I am America. Only, I'm the part you won't recognize. But get used to me.

Black, confident, cocky; my name, not yours;

my religion, not yours; my goals, my own – get used to me!" – Muhammad Ali

A 7-1 underdog, Cassius Clay shocks the world when he knocks out Sonny Liston to win the heavyweight boxing title.

Al Downing is the first African American to lead the American League in strikeouts with 217.

Willie Mays becomes the first African American named captain of a major league team, the San Francisco Giants. He is appointed captain by manager Alvin Dark.

Willie Mays signs with the Giants for $105,000 per year, becoming baseball's highest paid player. Mays becomes the first player to win a Gold Glove and lead the league in homers (47) the same season, demonstrating his all-around talent.

Cuban Tony Oliva becomes the first rookie and non-White player to win a batting title in the American League with a .323 average. The All-Star is named AL Rookie of the Year and finishes fourth in the MVP race.

Norm Bass, former Kansas City A's pitcher from 1961 to 1963, plays one game at defensive back for the Denver Broncos in 1964.

Pete Brown becomes the first African American golfer to win a PGA Tournament – the Waco Turner Open in Burneyville, Okla. He takes home $2,700 in prize money.

Bobby Douglas, Charles Tribble and Robert Pickens become the first Black wrestlers to compete for the U.S. Olympic team in Tokyo, Japan.

Payton Fuller becomes the first African American coach in the Big Ten Conference, when named as the head soccer coach at Michigan State University.

Claude Henry Keystone "Buddy" Young, also known as the "Bronze Bullet," becomes the first Director of Player Relations in the NFL.

John McCluskey becomes the first African American in Ivy League history to start at quarterback. McCluskey leads Harvard to a 6-3 record in 1964 and a 5-2-2 record in 1965.

Charley Taylor, wide receiver for the Washington Redskins becomes the first player named the *Newspaper Enterprise Association's* NFL Rookie of the Year.

In the march magazine of *Ebony*, Olympic gold medalist Mal Whitfield writes an article titled, "Let's Boycott the Olympics" in Tokyo. Whitfield cites "It is time for America to live up to its promises of Liberty, Equality and Justice for all." The boycott did not materialize.

Competing in the Vault, Sid Oglesby from Syracuse University becomes the first Black NCAA event champion.

George Harris becomes the first African American to participate on the U.S. Olympic Judo team in the Tokyo Olympics.

Garfield Smith, a member of Eastern Kentucky University's All-Century team, becomes its first African American basketball player. He is named Ohio Valley Conference's Freshman Center of the Year for the 1964-65 season.

Tommy Woods becomes East Tennessee State University's first African American basketball athlete. ETSU's practice court is named in honor of this two-time All-Ohio Valley Conference selection. Woods later plays for the ABA's Kentucky Colonels.

The Boston Celtics become the first NBA franchise to start five Black players when Willie Naulls replaces the injured Tommy Heinsohn in the starting lineup. Naulls with Bill Russell, K. C. Jones, Sam Jones and Satch Sanders reel off 12 consecutive wins.

The NBA widens the lane to 16 feet from 12 feet to offset Wilt Chamberlain's dominance. The lane was last widened in 1951 to neutralize the presence of George Mikan.

1965

"You're not to be so blind with patriotism that you can't face reality.

Wrong is wrong, no matter who does it or says it." - Malcolm X

Rookie Gale Sayers of the Chicago Bears who scores a record six touchdowns against the San Francisco 49ers, is named Rookie of the Year in the NFL.

Jim Brown of the Cleveland Browns retires. Brown becomes the only NFL player to retire with more touchdowns (106 rushing,

Colorful Firsts in U.S. Sports

20 receiving) than games played (118). He is also the first Black football player to appear on the cover of *Time* magazine.

The American Football League (AFL) All-Star game is scheduled to be played in New Orleans at Tulane Stadium. Black All-Stars including Buck Buchannan, Cookie Gilchrist, Sid Blanks, Bobby Bell, Dick Westmoreland, Frank Buncom, Ernie Warlick, Ernie Ladd, Earl Faison, Dave Grayson and Sherman Plunkett are unable to hail cabs from the airport and denied service in local restaurants. The Black players agree to boycott the game. The All-Star game is moved, one week later, to Rice Stadium in Houston, Texas.

Until 1965 "Fight for Old Dixie" was the rally song for George Preston Marshall's Washington Redskins, the only football team south of the Mason-Dixon line, at the time in 1937.

Warren McVey, a running back from San Antonio, becomes the African American football player for the Houston Cougars.

Burl Toler, a guard from San Francisco University, who never played in the pros, becomes the first African American NFL official. Toler served as a field judge and head linesman. The first African American AFL official is Aaron Wade, in 1966.

Emlen "The Gremlin" Tunnell becomes the first African American coach in the NFL with the New York Giants.

Jerry LeVias becomes the first scholarship athlete at Southern Methodist University (SMU) and the first in the Southwest Conference. Despite death threats, the next season, the 5-foot-9 wide receiver leads SMU to its first Cotton Bowl appearance since Heisman winner Doak Walker suited up for the Mustangs, almost two decades earlier. LeVias would later play for the Houston Oilers and the San Diego Chargers.

Bill Russell becomes the first NBA player to win five MVP awards.

Cisero Murphy becomes the first and only African American to win a World or U.S. National pocket billiard title, the American Billiard Parlor tournament in Burbank, Calif. Murphy is inducted into the Billiard Congress of America Hall of Fame in 1995.

Jim "Mudcat" Grant for the Cleveland Indians becomes the first African American pitcher to win 20 or more games in the American League with 21 victories.

Jackie Robinson joins the ABC-TV baseball broadcast team, becoming the first African American to receive a network broadcasting position. ABC provides the first ever nationwide coverage of baseball every Saturday afternoon.

Satchel Paige of the Kansas City A's becomes the oldest pitcher at 59, to start a major league game, pitching three innings against the Boston Red Sox, giving up one hit to Carl Yastrzemski.

Bob Gibson becomes the first African American pitcher to win a National League Gold Glove for fielding excellence. It is the first of nine Gold Glove awards in a row for Gibson.

Jim "Mudcat" Grant becomes the first African American pitcher, in the American League, to start a World Series when his Minnesota Twins open against the Los Angeles Dodgers. Sandy Koufax sits out the opener because of Yom Kippur. Grant beats Don Drysdale and the Dodgers with a one-hitter for an 8-2 win.

Outfielder Willie Mays of the San Francisco Giants becomes the first Black player to hit 500 home runs, in a 5 to 1 win over Houston. At the age of 34, he becomes the first player to hit 50 or more (52) home runs and win a Gold Glove as an outfielder

In Los Angeles, Maury Wills of the Los Angeles Dodgers and Willie Mays of the San Francisco Giants, exchange lineup cards with umpire Al Barlick. This marks the first time in white-centric major league baseball, the opposing team captains are African Americans.

William "Billy" Jones becomes the first African American athlete in the Atlantic Coast Conference (ACC) as a member of the University of Maryland Terrapins basketball team.

Muhammad Ali knocks out Sonny Liston in the first round of their rematch in Lewiston, Maine with the infamous "phantom punch."

1966

"This system is responsible for making us what we is,
and then it turns around and punish our asses for being the way it made us."

– Claude Brown, *Manchild in the Promised Land*

Texas Western becomes the first NCAA champion to start five African Americans: Harry Flournoy, David Lattin, Bobby Joe Hill, Orsten Artis, and Willie Cager. They upset No. 1 ranked Kentucky's all-White team of Adolph Rupp in the championship game in College Park, Md. For playing an all-Black lineup and beating an all-White team, Haskins reportedly received 40,000 pieces of hate mail and a dozen death threats.

Wilt Chamberlain is the first player to lead the NBA in scoring seven consecutive seasons.

James I. Cash Jr. basketball player for the Texas Christian Horned Frogs becomes the first African American to play in the Southwest Conference (SWC). Dr. Cash later becomes a minority owner of the Boston Celtics. In 2011, Cash's jersey No. 54 is retired by TCU.

Vince Colbert becomes the first African American scholarship athlete at East Carolina University. He letters in baseball and basketball. Colbert later pitches for the Cleveland Indians in the American League.

Lenny Hall plays four minutes of a basketball game for the Florida State Seminoles and becomes its first Black player. He scores two baskets and grabs two rebounds before a knee injury ends his playing career.

An ordained pastor at the age of 15, John Hill Westbrook becomes the first African American to play football in the Southwest Conference, as a running back for the Baylor Bears. In 2009, Baylor University establishes the John Westbrook Award for Courage and Perseverance.

Athens, Texas basketball star Tommy Bowman becomes the first Black scholarship student-athlete at Baylor University, a private university in Waco, Texas.

Norwood Todmann from New York City becomes the first African American scholarship basketball player at Wake Forest. Todmann had played at Power Memorial Academy where the 6-3 guard broke the single-game and single-season scoring records of center Lew Alcindor.

Atoy Wilson becomes the first African American to win a national figure skating title in the men's frosh category of the U.S. National Championships. He is coached by African American Mabel Fairbanks.

Curtis Cokes defeats Manuel Gonzalez in New Orleans to win the vacant world welterweight title. Cokes is the first Harlem Clown basketball player to win a world boxing title.

Emmett Ashford becomes the first African American umpire in the re-integrated major leagues.

Roberto Clemente becomes the first Puerto Rican to receive the MVP award in the National League.

Baltimore Orioles outfielder Frank Robinson wins the MVP award in the American League. He becomes the first player to win the MVP in both leagues, having won the award in the National League with the Cincinnati Reds in 1961. He is also the first African American to win a Triple Crown in the re-integrated major leagues.

Willie Mays appears on the March cover of *Boys' Life* magazine.

Myrtis Dightman becomes the first African American to ride in the National Finals Rodeo.

John McLendon becomes the first African American coach to serve on the U.S. Olympic Committee, responsible for scouting and player performance statistical evaluation.

Coach John McLendon's Kentucky State Thoroughbreds basketball team becomes the first Black college to play outside the U.S (in Iceland & France).

Jackie White is the first African American to officiate an NBA game. He referees a game at the Cleveland Arena between the Chicago Bulls and the Cincinnati Royals.

Lowell Perry becomes the first African American broadcaster in the National Football League, when hired by CBS.

Rommie Loudd becomes the first African American assistant coach in the American Football League for the New England Patriots.

Aaron Wade becomes the first African American official in the American Football League. He is a coach at Centennial High School in Los Angeles, a school that produced Paul Lowe, all-pro running back for the San Diego Chargers.

Jackie Robinson is named general manager of the Continental League's Brooklyn Dodgers Football Club, Inc.

Bill Russell is named head coach of the Boston Celtics, becoming the first African American coach in the NBA and the third (John McLendon was the second in 1962, while Pop Gates was first in 1949) in pro basketball.

Claudius B. Claiborne becomes the first African American basketball player for the Duke Blue Devils. C.B. Claiborne graduated in 1969 with a degree in engineering. He also earned postgraduate degrees from Dartmouth and Virginia Tech. Because of segregation sanctions on the Duke campus, Claiborne spent considerable time in the cafeteria at nearby North Carolina Central University, a historically Black college.

Charlie Scott becomes the first African American player to receive a basketball scholarship from the University of North Carolina at Chapel Hill. The Tar Heel is named first-team All-American twice. Scott would win an Olympic gold medal in 1968, spend a season with the Virginia Squires (ABA), where he would be named Rookie of the Year, and eventually is drafted by the Boston Celtics.

Western Kentucky's Clem Haskins, Houston's Elvin Hayes and Louisville's Wes Unseld become the first African Americans

Colorful Firsts in U.S. Sports

from Southern schools to be named to the first NCAA All-American team.

Clarence "Big House" Gaines coaches Winston-Salem State University to a 32-1 record and the first NCAA Division II championship for an HBCU. The Rams, led by senior Earl Monroe with 41.5 points per game, are the first HBCU to capture a national championship at any level.

1967

"From Muhammad Ali to artists and entertainers who participated in movements, from the women's rights movement to the civil rights movement, this is a noble tradition in our country." – Cory Booker

Muhammad Ali is given draft No. 15-47-42-127. Ali is stripped of his heavyweight title for refusing military induction and sentenced to five years in prison.

Clarence "Big House" Gaines Sr. becomes the first African American to be named NCAA Coach of the Year. Gaines is named CIAA coach of the year eight times: 1953, 1957, 1960, 1961, 1963, 1966, 1970 and 1977.

Al Heartley earns a basketball scholarship as a walk-on at North Carolina State University. Along with Ed Leftwich they become N.C. State's first African American ballers.

Jerry Gaines, a long jumper and hurdler, becomes the first African American student-athlete at Virginia Tech Institute. He later becomes the first Black person inducted into the Virginia Tech Sports Hall of Fame.

John McLendon becomes the first African American head coach of a major college basketball program when hired at Cleveland State University.

Mike Maloy becomes the first American Austrian basketball player for the Davidson (N.C.) College Wildcats. He becomes a three-time All-American and is named Southern Conference Player of the Year in 1969 and 1970.

Considered the most cerebral defensive position in football, Willie Lanier becomes the NFL's first African American starting middle linebacker.

Tommie Smith becomes the first American to hold world records in the 200- and 400-meter races, simultaneously.

San José State sociology professor Dr. Harry Edwards creates the Olympic Committee for Human Rights to address the systemic racism experience by Black athletes. Edwards issues a statement that Black athletes may boycott the 1968 Olympics in Mexico City.

Charlie Sifford becomes the first African American to win a major PGA Tour event, the Greater Hartford Open.

Renée Powell joins the LPGA Tour.

Bubba Smith from Michigan State is the first African American defensive player taken as the first pick, in the first round of the NFL draft. He is chosen by the Baltimore Colts.

Lem Barney of the Detroit Lions becomes the first NFL player to score a touchdown on an interception on the first pass thrown in his direction, versus the Green Bay Packers. Barney is co-leader for the most interceptions that season and becomes the first player named Defensive Rookie of the Year.

Mel Farr of the Detroit Lions becomes the first player named the NFL's Offensive Rookie of the Year.

Emlen Tunnell becomes the first African American elected to the Professional Football Hall of Fame.

Deacon Jones of the Los Angeles Rams becomes the first player to record more than 25 sacks (26) in a season. In 1982, the NFL make "sacks" an official statistic. Jones is infamously known for creating the "head slap."

Lonnie Wright becomes one of the first players to play two professional sports in the same season. Wright played defensive back for the Denver Broncos in 1966-67 and guard for the Denver Rockets (later the Nuggets) from 1967 to 1970.

Former All-American quarterback from Minn., Sandy Stephens becomes infamous by using profanity over the radio during his rookie exhibition game against Denver at Municipal Stadium. Wired for sound, in the heat of battle, as the Chiefs threatened to score, "All right, it's second and two," Stephens barked. "Let's put this (mf) in the end zone." The Chiefs scored on the next play. Stephens is cut before the season starts.

Curtis "The Count" McClinton becomes the first African American to score a TD in the Super Bowl (I), on a seven-yard pass from quarterback Lenny Dawson.

St. Louis Cardinal pitcher Bob Gibson becomes the first African American World Series MVP. Gibson pitches complete games in 1, 4 and 7, striking out 26 Boston Red Sox batters. He only allows three runs and 14 hits in the three games.

By striking out Tony Horton, Don Demeter, Duke Sims on nine pitches, in the second inning, Al Downing of the New York Yankees becomes the first Black pitcher, in the American League, to accomplish this feat. The Yankees defeat the Cleveland Indians, 5-3.

Emmett Ashford becomes the first African American to umpire in the re-integrated major leagues' All-Star game. Ashford works the left field line before 46,309 fans at Anaheim Stadium in Calif.

Perry Eugene Wallace becomes the first African American scholarship basketball player in the Southeastern Conference (SEC) with Vanderbilt University. Wallace graduates with a degree in engineering and later earns his J.D. from Columbia University. A movie about his life *Triumph: The Untold Story of Perry Wallace* debuts in 2017.

Nate Northington becomes the first African American scholarship football player in the Southeastern Conference (SEC) with the University of Kentucky. In 2016, the university unveils a new statue of Northington, Greg Page, Wilbur Hackett and Houston Hogg in recognition of the first four Black football players in the SEC.

Will Allen, known as the Rockville Cyclone, becomes the first African American basketball player at the University of Miami. The 6-foot-6 center ranks number two on the Hurricanes' All-Time rebounding list. Allen later plays for the Miami Floridians of the ABA.

After the dominance of UCLA center Lew Alcindor, the NCAA bans dunking for the upcoming season. The rule is rescinded for the 1976-77 season.

Detroit Piston Dave Bing becomes the first true guard to lead the NBA in total points, 2,142, averaging 27.1 points per game.

Connie Hawkins of the Pittsburgh Pipers becomes the ABA's first Most Valuable Player and the league's first scoring leader, averaging 26.8 points per game.

1968

"My raised right hand stood for the power in Black America. Carlos' raised left hand stood for the unity in Black America. Together they formed an arch of unity and power. The black scarf around my neck stood for Black pride.
The black socks with no shoes stood for Black poverty in racist America.
The totality of our effort was the regaining of Black dignity."
- gold medalist Tommie Smith in an interview with Howard Cosell

Arthur Ashe wins the U.S. Amateur Championships against Davis Cup Teammate Bob Lutz, and in the first US Open of the open era, becomes the first African American male to capture the title and the only player to have won both the amateur and open national championships in the same year.

Arthur Ashe becomes the first Black man to win the U.S. Tennis Championship, 4-6, 6-3, 8-10, 6-0, and 6-4.

Smokin' Joe Frazier is crowned Heavyweight boxing champion when Muhammad Ali is stripped of the title due to his religious convictions as a conscientious objector to the Vietnam war.

From Boys High School in Brooklyn, N.Y., Connie Hawkins, a power forward for the Pittsburgh Pipers, is the first undrafted basketball player selected to an ABA All-Star game.

Irish Catholic Notre Dame University fields an all-Black starting five basketball team, with Austin Carr, Sid Catlett, Collis Jones, Bob Whitmore and Dwight Murphy.

Pittsburgh native Ken Hudson becomes the NBA's second African American referee. Jackie White was the first in 1966.

Chip Dublin, hoopster, is the first African American athlete to play at Jacksonville (Fla.) University.

Jesse Marshall from Tyler (Texas) Junior College becomes the first Black basketball player for Centenary College in Bossier City, La.

Basketball player Greg Andrews becomes the first African American scholarship student-athlete for the University of Chattanooga Mocs.

Earl Lloyd becomes the first African American assistant coach in the NBA with the Detroit Pistons.

Mel Daniels, center for the Minnesota Muskies, becomes rebounding leader and the first Rookie of the Year, in the newly founded ABA.

Bill Russell becomes the first African American coach to win an NBA championship.

On March 18 Wilt Chamberlain, for the Philadelphia 76ers, becomes the only NBA player to record a quintuple-double in the NBA with 53 points, 32 rebounds, 14 assists, 24 blocks and 11 steals against the Los Angeles Lakers.

Wilt Chamberlain becomes the first center to lead the NBA in assist with 702, making him the first player to win NBA scoring, rebounding and assist titles.

John McLendon becomes the first African American basketball coach on the Olympic coaching staff.

Colorful Firsts in U.S. Sports

Charlie Lipscomb becomes the first African American to receive a basketball scholarship at Virginia Tech.

Lester McClain becomes the first African American to play football at the University of Tennessee.

Lee Evans cracks the 44-second barrier in the Olympics, running the 400-meter dash in 43.86 seconds.

Madeline Manning (Mims) becomes the first American woman to win an Olympic gold medal in the 800-meter event.

In the Mexico City Summer Olympics, Bob Beamon leaps 29 feet, 2 ½ inches in the long jump, shattering Ralph Boston's world record by twenty-one and three quarter inches. In the process Beamon breaks the 28- and 29-foot barriers in one jump.

Ralph Boston becomes the first track and field athlete to medal three consecutive times in the Long Jump. Boston won a gold medal in 1960, a silver in 1964 and the bronze in 1968.

At the AAU Track and Field Championships in Sacramento, California, three men break the world record in the 100 meters, Jim Hines, Charlie Greene and Ronnie Ray Smith, with the same time of 9.9 seconds.

Jim Hines becomes the first man to break the sub-10 second barrier in the 100 meters in the Olympics with a 9.95 time in Mexico City.

Tommie Smith becomes the first man to break the sub-20 second barrier in the 200 meters with a 19.83 time in the Mexico City Olympics.

John Carlos and Tommie Smith, in the Mexico City Olympics, after receiving bronze and gold medals in the 200 meters, adorn black gloves and raise their fists to the sky, to protest treatment of Black people in America.

James Kanati Allen becomes the first Black male gymnast to be named to the U.S. Olympic Team.

Wyomia Tyus becomes the first person to win Gold Medals in the 100-meter race, in two consecutive Olympics.

Ron Coleman, who specializes in the triple jump, becomes the University of Florida's first Black scholarship athlete. The university's basketball team would integrate in 1970.

In keeping with current NFL tradition, the Oakland Raiders draft Tennessee State quarterback sensation Eldridge Dickey in the first round as a wide receiver. Dickey becomes the first Black quarterback drafted in the first round by either the American Football or National Football Leagues.

Joe Profit, a running back, becomes the University of Louisiana at Monroe and the Gulf States Conference's (now the Sunbelt Conference) first African American football player. In 1971, he is named the conference's Athlete of the Year.

James I. Cash Jr. becomes Texas Christian University and the Southwest Conference's first African American basketball player. In 2020, the Harvard Business School renames one of its buildings, the Cash House, in honor of the former faculty member. In 2021, TCU installs a statue of Dr. Cash in front of the Ed and Rae Schollmaier Arena.

Marlin Briscoe, for the Denver Broncos, becomes the first African American quarterback to start in the wing-T formation. Briscoe appears in 11 games under Coach Lou Saban.

Homer Jones of the New York Giants becomes the first player to "intentionally" spike a football after a touchdown.

In Super Bowl II, the Grambling State University marching band become the first HBCU to perform the national anthem at the championship game. The "World Famed Tiger Marching Band" would perform again at Super Bowl IX.

Uriah Jones becomes the first African American on a U.S. Olympic Fencing team. He competes in the team foil event. Jones is later inducted into the U.S. Fencing Association Hall of Fame posthumously.

James Kenati Allen, of African American and Native American descent is the first Black gymnast to compete at the Olympic Games. Allen later earns a PhD in physics from the University of Washington.

Dr. Martin Luther King Jr. is assassinated. Baseball players demand, against owners' wishes, that 30 games scheduled for April 8-9 not be played. April 9 is the day of Dr. King's funeral. MLB delays Opening Day until April 10.

Monte Irvin becomes the first African American to receive an executive position in major league baseball, when hired by Commissioner William D. Eckert. The former Newark Eagles star is appointed Assistant Director of Promotion and Public Relations.

New York Yankee catcher Elston Howard invents the weighted donut for baseball bats.

Bob Gibson leads the National League with an ERA of 1.12, while Luis Tiant Jr. leads the American League with a 1.60 ERA. They are the first African American pitchers to win the ERA crown and record the lowest ERAs by pitchers since re-integration (1947) of the major leagues.

Bob Gibson becomes the first pitcher to win a Gold Glove Award, the Cy Young Award and be named MVP in the same season. He also led the National League in strikeouts with 268. Don Newcombe also won the Cy Young and MVP awards in 1956.

1969

Curt Flood is earning $90,000 a year but argues in an interview with Howard Cosell on ABC's Wide World of Sports that "a well-paid slave is, nonetheless, a slave."

St. Louis Cards outfielder Curt Flood, along with Tim McCarver, Joe Hoerner and Byron Browne, are traded to Philadelphia for Dick Allen, Cookie Rojas and Jerry Johnson. Flood challenges baseball's reserve clause, which binds players to the clubs for the life of their careers.

By striking out Len Gabrielson, Paul Popovich, John Miller on nine pitches, in the seventh inning, Bob Gibson of the St. Louis Cardinals, becomes the first Black pitcher, in the National League, to accomplish this feat. The Cardinals defeat the Los Angeles Dodgers, 6-2. See Al Downing, 1967.

Don Wilson of the Houston Astros pitches his second no-hitter. He is the first African American pitcher to have two nine-inning no-hitters to his credit. Toothpick Sam Jones' second no-hitter in 1959, was a seven-inning contest.

Willie Mays becomes the first player to hit 300 home runs, steal 300 bases and win 10 gold gloves (12 awards from 1957 to 1968).

Héctor López from Colon, Panama becomes the first Black man to manage a AAA-level club, the Buffalo Bisons, in the International League. The Bisons are affiliated with the Washington Senators of the American League. Previous Black managers include Gene Baker in 1961, managing Batavia (New York-Pennsylvania League, Class D); Marvin Williams in 1952, managing Chihuahua (Arizona-Texas League, Class C) and Sam Bankhead (1951) managing Farnham (Provincial League, Class C).

Frank White scrapes mortar and seals floors during the construction of Royals (later Kauffman) Stadium, earning the distinction of being the only major league baseball player to literally help build the stadium he would later play in. White is the first graduate of the Royals Baseball Academy to reach the Majors with his debut in 1973.

John McLendon becomes the first African American coach in the American Basketball Association (ABA) when he signs a two-year contract with the Denver (Nuggets) Rockets.

George Reveling joins the coaching staff of Lefty Driesell with the University of Maryland Terrapins, becoming the first Black assistant coach in the Atlantic Coast Conference (ACC).

Gene Knolle becomes the first African American basketball player for the Texas Tech Red Raiders. Knolle, a 6-foot-4, 185-pound forward, currently holds the program record for career-scoring average at 21.5 points per game.

Gale Sayers is the only man to average more than 30 yards on kick returns in a career with a 30.56 average, from 1965 to 1969. Sayers is named *UPI's* Comeback Player of the Year. Sayers retires in 1971.

Johnnie Walton from Elizabeth City State University becomes the first African American quarterback to lead a professional football team to a title, when the Indianapolis Capitols defeat the San Antonio Toros in overtime, 44-38, to capture the Continental Football League championship. Walton later plays in the World Football League (1974-75), the National Football League (1976-79) and the United States Football League (1983-84).

As the overall 192nd pick in the eighth round, James Harris from Grambling University becomes the first Black quarterback for the Buffalo Bills and the first Black QB to start a season-opener in the NFL.

The University of Texas Longhorns, coached by Darrell Royal, become the last all-White team to be named consensus national football champions.

After leading the USC Trojans to an undefeated season, Jimmy Johnson becomes the first Black collegiate quarterback to appear on the cover of *Sports Illustrated*.

Herb Adderley, Green Bay Packers defensive back, becomes the first player to score a touchdown on an interception in the Super Bowl (II) against the Oakland Raiders.

Norman Seabrooks becomes first African American football player for the Citadel Bulldogs in Charleston, S.C.

Honor student Craig Mobley, a 6-foot guard, becomes the first African American basketball player for Clemson University. Mobley appears in only 11 games for the Tigers before devoting time to his academic studies.

Clyde Chesney, a linebacker, becomes North Carolina State University's first African American letterman.

John W. Oswald, president of the University of Kentucky, orders basketball coach Adolph Rupp to begin recruiting Black players. Rupp, three years before his retirement, signs his one and only Black player, Tom Payne.

Henry Harris becomes the first African American scholarship athlete at Auburn University as a basketball player.

Almer Lee from Fort Smith Northside High School becomes the first Black player to letter in basketball at the University of

Colorful Firsts in U.S. Sports

Arkansas.

Wendell Hudson becomes the first African American scholarship athlete in any sport at the University of Alabama, joining the basketball team under coach C.M. Newton. Hudson later becomes head coach of Alabama's women's basketball team in 2008.

Frank Dowsing Jr. defensive back, and Robert Bell, defensive lineman, become the first African American football players at Mississippi State University. See 2017.

Jake Gaither's Florida A&M Rattlers defeat the Spartans of the University of Tampa, 34–28, in the South's first football game between a white college and a historically black college.

Ronnie Hogue becomes the first African American athlete at the University of Georgia (UGA) to earn a full scholarship in any sport. Track star Maxie Foster from Athens, Georgia was the first African American athlete at UGA a year earlier, but he was on a partial scholarship and lived at home.

Charles Steward and Lloyd Wells integrate the track and field team at Louisiana State University, becoming the university's first African Americans in any sport.

Ruth White becomes the youngest woman and the first African American woman to win a national fencing championship.

Tina Sloan Green becomes the first African American woman to compete on the U.S. National Lacrosse team and the U.S. women's national field hockey team from 1969 to 1973. Sloan Green is inducted into the U.S. National Lacrosse Hall of Fame in 1997, the International Women's Sports Hall of Fame in 1999 and the Philadelphia Sports Hall of Fame in 2013.

Lew Alcindor is named Most Outstanding Player of the NCAA tournament for a record third time.

Tom Payne Jr. becomes Adolph Rupp's first-ever African American player at the University of Kentucky. At 7 feet, 2 inches Payne is the tallest player recruited by the Wildcats.

Spencer Haywood, a sophomore at the University of Detroit Mercy, is the first player to file for "hardship," becoming eligible for the NBA draft.

1969-70, Spencer Haywood becomes the first player to win the Scoring Title (30.0), Rebounding Title (19.5), and be selected the Rookie of the Year and Most Valuable Player in the same year with the ABA's Denver Rockets.

1970

"Sam Cunningham did more to integrate Alabama in 60 minutes than Martin Luther King did in 20 years."
- Jerry Claiborne, a Bear Bryant assistant

Quarterback Jimmy Johnson, fullback Sam "The Bam" Cunningham and running back Clarence Davis, of USC, become the first all-Black backfield in Division I football.

The USC Trojans become the first fully integrated team to play in the state of Alabama against Bear Bryant's all-White Crimson Tide of the Southeastern Conference. With a Black quarterback, Jimmy Jones, running back Sam "Bam" Cunningham, plus other African Americans in key positions, the Trojans wallop the Crimson Tide 42 to 21. The game hastens the racial integration of football at Alabama University and in the South.

Eddie McAshan becomes the first Black starting quarterback for the Georgia Tech Yellow Jackets.

D.C. Nobles is the first Black quarterback for the University of Houston Cougars.

The Kansas City Chiefs beat the heavily favored Minnesota Vikings in Super Bowl IV, in the last game before the AFL-NFL merger. The win validates the AFL worthiness for a merger. Thanks to super scout Lloyd Wells, the Chiefs' roster is filled with players from HBCUs; Ceasar Belser (Arkansas AM&N), Buck Buchannan (Grambling), Wendell Hayes (Humboldt State), Robert Holmes (Southern), Jim Kearney (Prairie View A&M), Willie Lanier (Morgan State), Jim Marsalis (Tennessee A&I), Willie Mitchell (Tennessee State), Frank Pitts (Southern), Gloster Richardson (Jackson State), Noland Smith (Tennessee State), Morris Stroud (Clark Atlanta), Otis Taylor (Prairie View A&M) and Emmett Thomas (Bishop).

When the National Football League and the American Football League merge, Hall of Famer and former Baltimore Colts tight-end John Mackey becomes the first president of the National Football League Players Association. Mackey became the lead plaintiff in a court action which led to the overturning of the so-called "Rozelle Rule," which limited a player's ability to act as a free agent. In 1976, the Rozelle Rule was ruled to violate antitrust laws in Mackey v. NFL. Mackey held the presidency until 1973.

Julius Whittier becomes the first Black football player for the University of Texas Longhorns. He plays offensive tackle for UT's National Championship team, and again in 1971, before transitioning to tight end for his senior season in 1972.

Stanley Land, Harrison Davis, Kent Merrit and John Rainey become the University of Virginia's first African Americans to receive football scholarships.

The Buffalo Bills become the first NFL team to have two Black quarterbacks on its roster, James Harris and Marlin Briscoe, although the latter is listed as a wide receiver.

Eddie Wright, a former Boston University hockey player, becomes the first Black coach of an NCAA hockey team at the State University of New York in Buffalo, a Division II. In 2010, the university's volleyball and basketball practice facility was renovated and renamed The Edward L. Wright Practice Facility.

Emmett Ashford becomes the first African American umpire in the re-integrated major leagues' World Series, between the Cincinnati Reds and the Baltimore Orioles. He worked five games, but none behind home plate. The Jackson Five performs the "Star Spangled Banner" before Game 1.

The *Sporting News* names Willie Mays as Player of the Decade for the "cultural decade" of the 1960s.

Hank Aaron becomes the first player, to have more than 3,000 career hits and more than 500 career home runs.

More than 20 future Hall of Famers suit up at Dodger Stadium on March 28, to honor the memory and support the causes of Dr. Martin Luther King Jr. All proceeds from the game go to the Southern Christian Leadership Conference (SCLC) and to the construction of the Dr. Martin Luther King Jr. Center in Atlanta. Joe DiMaggio and Roy Campanella served as managers for the exhibition game. Among the 31,694 fans is Jackie Robinson and Dr. King's widow, Coretta Scott King, who throws out the ceremonial first pitch to Johnny Bench.

Arthur Ashe becomes the first African American tennis player to win the Australian Open championship.

Arrington "Bubble" Klice, a Golden Glove boxing coach for the Gateway Boxing Club, in Kansas City, Mo., takes the first American boxing team to Russia.

After winning the heavyweight championship, Joe Frazier hits the road with a Memphis-style soul revue dubbed "Smokin' Joe & the Knockouts."

Body builder Chris Dickerson is the first African American to be named "Mr. America."

Larry Ellis becomes the first African American coach of any sport in the Ivy League when named head track coach at Princeton University.

Larry Whiteside becomes the first African American beat writer to travel regularly with a baseball team, the Boston Red Sox. He was the fourth African American writer to become a member of the Baseball Writers' Association of America (BBWAA).

Coach John B. McLendon teaches the "Two in the Corner Offense" to North Carolina Coach Dean Smith at a Fellowship of Christian Athletes meeting in Colorado. Smith renames the offense "The Four Corners."

Will Robinson becomes the first African American head coach in NCAA Division I history when he coaches the basketball team at Illinois State University.

Al Drummond becomes the University of Virginia's first African American to receive a scholarship for basketball.

Karl Binns becomes the first African American scholarship basketball player for the Georgia Tech Yellow Jackets.

Coolidge Ball becomes the first African American scholarship basketball player for the University of Mississippi or Ole Miss, where in 1962 James Meredith had become the first African American student at the public university. After two fatalities, President John F. Kennedy sends the National Guard to stop the violence and rioting by Whites opposed to integration.

Forwards Steve Williams and Malcolm Meeks become the first African American basketball players at the University of Florida.

Austin Carr of Notre Dame becomes the first player to score more than 60 points in an NCAA tournament game. Carr scores 61 against Ohio State University in the Southeast Regional. Carr becomes the first player to average more than 50 points a game during the NCAA tournament. Carr averages 52.7 points in three games.

Spencer Haywood becomes the first ABA player to jump to the NBA, leaving the Denver Rockets (Nuggets) for the Seattle SuperSonics.

Willis Reed of the New York Knicks is the first player named the Most Valuable Player in the NBA All-Star game, MVP in the playoffs and MVP of the league, in the same season.

1971

"If you are not a part of the solution, you are a part of the problem." – Eldridge Cleaver, *Soul on Ice*

Irv Cross, former two-time Pro Bowl cornerback, becomes the first African American sports analyst on national TV. His tenure on *CBS Sports* last 23 years.

Bill White becomes the first African American play-by-play announcer for a professional team when hired by the New York Yankees. White joins Phil Rizzuto and Frank Messer in the booth, and the trio lasts for 16 years.

Colorful Firsts in U.S. Sports

Roberto Clemente becomes the first Puerto Rican to receive the World Series MVP award when his Pittsburgh Pirates defeat the Baltimore Orioles, in the best of seven games.

Mel Daniels becomes the first ABA player to win the MVP award twice.

Earl Lloyd becomes the first African American bench coach with the Detroit Pistons. He is fired in 1972 after seven games (two wins, five losses) and replaced by Ray Scott.

John Thompson, no relation to Georgetown coach John Thompson, becomes the first African American to officiate a game between NBA and ABA players, on June 20, at a benefit All-Star game in Indianapolis. Thompson, an ABA referee at the time, was the lead official alongside the NBA's John Parker.

Lew Alcindor and Oscar Robertson of the Milwaukee Bucks appear on the cover of the first issue of *Black Sports* magazine. Founded by Allan P. Barron, it is the first major sports magazine aimed at African Americans. The last issue was published in June 1978.

Collis Temple Jr. from Kentwood, La., is the first African American varsity basketball player at Louisiana State University (LSU). When he joins the team, the U.S. National Guard is called to protect him from alt-right segregationists. Temple later plays for the San Antonio Spurs and two of his sons play basketball for LSU.

Charles Lawrence "Charlie" Davis is named the Atlantic Coast Conference (ACC) men's basketball Player of the Year, becoming the first African American to win the award. The 6-foot-2 guard of the Wake Forest Demon Deacons is later drafted by the Cleveland Cavaliers.

Alan Page is the first African American to win National Football Conference's Player of the Year Award. Page becomes the first defensive player (DT) in NFL history to receive the Most Valuable Player Award. Earning his Juris Doctor in 1978, Page becomes the first African American to serve as an Associate Justice on the Minnesota Supreme Court, in 1992.

Wide receiver Bullet Bob Hayes becomes the first Olympic Gold Medalist (1964, 100 meters) to play for a Super Bowl champion the Dallas Cowboys. Because of his speed, NFL defenses give up playing man-to-man coverage and use zone defenses. Hayes is the first sprinter to run a 9.1 second 100-yard dash and the first to break 6.0 seconds in the 60-yard sprint.

Bill Pickett becomes the first African American selected to the National Rodeo Cowboy Hall of Fame in Oklahoma City, Okla.

Lee Elder becomes the first African American to compete against Whites in South Africa in the South African PGA Open.

Charles Coody and African American caddie Walter "Cricket" Pritchett celebrate victory in the Masters at Augusta National Golf Club.

Cheryl White becomes the first Black female jockey when she rides at the Thistledown Race Track in Cleveland, Ohio.

Althea Gibson is elected to the International Tennis Hall of Fame.

Defensive guard Rich Glover of Nebraska is the first African American named Big Eight Conference Player of the Year.

The Supreme Court overturns the 1967 conviction of Muhammad Ali's draft resistance, based on his Muslim beliefs.

Joe Frazier and Muhammad Ali become the first Black boxers to draw a multimillion dollar gate in their Madison Square Garden bout. Frazier wins the fight on points. The bout grosses $20 million with each fighter receiving $2.5 million.

The Pittsburgh Pirates field an all-Black and Latino starting nine against the Philadelphia Phillies at Three Rivers Stadium. The lineup includes Manny Sanguillén (c), Al Oliver (1b), Rennie Stennett (2b), Dave Cash (3b), Jackie Hernández (ss), Willie Stargell (lf), Gene Clines (cf), Roberto Clemente (rf) and Dock Ellis (p). For the record, the manager Danny Murtaugh's Bucs beat the Phillies 10-7 in front of 11,278 fans.

Satchel Paige becomes the first African American representing the Negro Leagues inducted into the National Baseball Hall of Fame. The Hall creates a controversy with a separate section or wing for the Black players.

Vida Blue becomes the first African American pitcher to win the American League's Cy Young Award. At the all-star break, with a 17-3 won-lost record, he appears on the cover of *Time* magazine. Blue becomes the first African American left-handed pitcher to strike out 300 batters in a season (301).

Oakland A's Vida Blue and Chicago Cubs' Ferguson Jenkins, become the first Black pitchers to win Cy Young Awards in the same year.

Vida Blue (Oakland A's) and Dock Ellis (Pittsburgh Pirates) become the first African American pitchers to start an MLB All-Star game. The American League wins 6-4, as Blue picks up the win and Ellis the loss. Ellis pitches three innings and gives up four hits and four runs, with one walk and two strikeouts. Blue pitches three innings and gives up two hits, three runs, no walks and three strikeouts.

George Braithwaite, a Guyana born immigrant of African ancestry becomes a member of the U.S. Table Tennis team that visits the People's Republic of China in an attempt to improve diplomatic relations between the U.S. and China.

1972

"Light skin, dark skin. High yellow, jet black. What's the big deal?
Why can't we accept each other for what we are?" - James L. Farmer Jr.

Canadian, Alexandra Nicholson becomes the first Black gymnast to win a World Championship with a gold medal on the trampoline, in Stuttgart, Germany. She is the first trampolinist, male or female, to complete a triffis, a triple somersault combined with a twist.

As the first African American student at Duke University Medical School, hematologist Dr. Delano Meriwether runs the 100-yard dash in nine seconds flat at the USA Track & Field Outdoor Championships in Seattle, Wash. Meriweather becomes only the second sprinter, alongside John Carlos, to do so.

The Dallas Chaparrals, citing the need for more White fans, cut two Black all-stars, Donnie Freeman and John Brisker. "Last year, Dallas had only two White players — Gene Phillips and Len Chappell — compared to 10 Black players, and we drew less than 100 fans a game who were colored," said the Chaps' general partner, Joe W. Geary, a Dallas attorney. "A bunch of people want White faces, someone they can identify with," he said. The Chaps' head coach, Babe McCarthy, the dean of A.B.A. coaches, echoed Geary's feelings on the racial issue. Freeman was the Chaps' leading scorer last season with a 24-point average.

Hank Aaron, as an Atlanta Brave, becomes the first player in the re-integrated major leagues to sign for $200K a year.

Chicago White Sox star Dick Allen becomes the first player in baseball's "modern era" to hit two inside-the-park home runs in one game. Both homers were hit off Minnesota Twins pitcher Bert Blyleven in an 8–1 victory at Metropolitan Stadium.

Curt Flood loses his multi-million antitrust suit, Flood v. Kuhn, 407 U.S. 258, against baseball's reserve clause. Flood's attorney, former Supreme Court Justice Arthur Goldberg, asserted that the reserve clause depressed wages and limited players to one team for life. Major League Baseball's counsel, Louis Hoynes, countered that if Flood won his case, "it would be a shambles." On June 19, 1972, the Supreme Court, invoking the principle of stare decisis ("to stand by things decided"). The U.S. Supreme Court votes 5 to 3, one absentee (Justice Lewis Powell recused himself owing to his ownership of stock in Anheuser-Busch, which owned the Cardinals), against Flood's claim that baseball contracts constitute involuntary employment. Professional baseball is considered interstate commerce under the Sherman Antitrust Act. Although his legal challenge failed, it brought about additional solidarity among players as they fought against baseball's reserve clause.

Richard Ewell and Michelle McCladdie become the first African Americans to win the National Pairs Skating Title. They are coached by African American and future U.S. Figure Skating Hall of Famer Mabel Fairbanks.

With a goal towards a level playing field, President Richard M. Nixon signs the Higher Education Act, which contains the Title IX provision that bars gender discrimination in all activities at any college or university receiving federal assistance.

Robert Lewis Douglas (from Saint Kitts), founder and coach of the Renaissance Big Five and the New York Rens, is the first Black man inducted in the Naismith Memorial Basketball Hall of Fame.

Mel Daniels of the Indiana Pacers becomes the first ABA player to score 10,000 points.

Wilt Chamberlain becomes the first player to score 30,000 points in an NBA career.

Wayne Embry with the Milwaukee Bucks is the first African American general manager in the NBA and in pro sports.

Walt Frazier of the New York Knicks becomes the first basketball player with a signature shoe. Puma pays $5,000 to market the red, white and blue shoes with "Clyde" on the side.

Oscar Scott becomes the first African American basketball player for the University of Citadel Bulldogs in Charleston, S.C.

Bob Lanier, six-foot-eleven of the Detroit Pistons beats six-foot-three Boston Celtic Jo Jo White in the first NBA one-on-one tournament for $15,000. The first player to score 20 points must win by four points. Lanier defeats White 21-16.

George Reveling is named head basketball coach at Washington State University, becoming the first Black coach in the Pacific-8 (now Pac-12) Conference. He guides the Cougars to two NCAA tournament appearances during his 11-year tenure.

Alton White from Nova Scotia is the first Black player for the New York Raiders and the Los Angeles Sharks of the World Hockey Association. The rookie becomes the first Black player in history to score a hat-trick in a major hockey professional game, doing so against the Chicago Cougars and the first Black player to surpass 20 goals in a season.

Rich Glover, middle guard from Nebraska University, becomes the first African American to win the Vince Lombardi/Rotary Award. Glover also wins the Outland Trophy for the best college football interior lineman.

Jefferson Street Joe Gilliam from Tennessee State becomes the first Black quarterback for the Pittsburgh Steelers.

Colorful Firsts in U.S. Sports

Condredge Holloway becomes the first Black quarterback in the Southeastern Conference, as a player with the Tennessee Volunteers. Holloway is the only Tennessee student-athlete named to Tennessee's All-Century squads in both baseball and football.

Running back Wilbur Jackson from Carroll High School in Ozark, Ala., becomes the first scholarship football player for Alabama University. In 2007, he is inducted into the Alabama Sports Hall of Fame.

John Mitchell, a two-time Junior College All-American defensive end transfers from Eastern Arizona Junior College to Alabama's Crimson Tide and becomes the first Black player to play in a game for Alabama.

Willie Lanier of the Kansas City Chiefs, becomes the first African American to win the prestigious NFL Man of the Year Award, now named the Walter Payton Man of the Year, in recognition of his service to the community.

When he accepts a position at the University of Arizona, Fred "The Fox" Snowden becomes the first African American head coach at a major white university and the second African American head coach at a Division I school, following Illinois State's Will Robinson. Snowden is the first African American coach to have a major college team finish in a final wire-service Top 20 poll at the 17th position by UPI.

In a private ceremony, Bill Russell's jersey No. 6 is retired. About a dozen former teammates and friends attended. Earlier, his teammate Tom Heinsohn said two White sportswriters from Boston told him they would not vote Russell the league's MVP because he was Black. Considering the racial attitude of Boston, Russell elected to have a private ceremony.

Art Williams becomes the first African American umpire in the National League.

Ferguson Jenkins, a Canadian, becomes the first pitcher to win 20 games in six consecutive seasons.

Minnesota Twin Rod Carew from Panama becomes the first player in MLB to win a batting championship without hitting a home run. Carew's league-leading batting average is .318.

1973

"You learn about equality in history and civics, but you find out life is not really like that." – Arthur Ashe

O.J. Simpson of the Buffalo Bills is the first player to rush for more than 2,000 (2,003) yards in a season. He is named NFL Player of the Year and wins the Jim Thorpe Award. He is the first African American to win the *Sporting News'* Man of the Year award. Simpson becomes the first player to rush for 250 or more yards in a game against the New England Patriots. And he becomes the second running back with at least 200 carries to average more than six yards by per carry (6.0), with Jim Brown the first in 1963.

James Harris becomes the first Black quarterback for the Los Angeles Rams.

Joe Gilliam is the first Black starting quarterback for the Pittsburgh Steelers.

Elmo Wright of the Kansas City Chiefs is credited as the first NFL player to celebrate in the end zone. On 18 November 1973, after catching a touchdown pass thrown by Len Dawson in a 38-14 win over the Houston Oilers, Wright runs in place at a frantic pace, pumping his knees and his arms, stopping long enough to slam the ball to the ground. In 1968, Homer Jones, a wide receiver for the New York Giants, delivered the league's first spike.

Reggie McAfee becomes the first African American to run the mile under four minutes, clocking 3:59.3 at the Big Four Meet in Raleigh, N.C.

Pearl Bailey becomes the first female boxing commentator, when she hosts the heavyweight championship fight in Kingston, Jamaica, between George Foreman and Joe Frazier.

As a member of the Patrick Racing Team, Sumner "Red" Oliver becomes the first official African American mechanic at the Indianapolis 500 raceway.

Lloyd "Butch" Keaser, in Tehran, Iran, becomes the first African American wrestler to win a World Championship gold medal.

Fletcher Carr becomes the first African American coach in the Southeastern Conference, when he is named the wrestling coach at the University of Kentucky.

Marian Washington becomes the first African American coach in the Big Eight (now the Big 12) Conference, when she is named the head women's basketball coach at the University of Kansas. She was later named the school's first and only director of intercollegiate athletics for women's sports in 1974.

On May 8, Cubs' manager Whitey Lockman is ejected in the 11th inning of a game against the San Diego Padres. Coach Ernie Banks fills in as manager for the remainder of the game, which the Cubs win 3-2 in 12 innings. This action predates Frank Robinson's managerial hiring in 1975. See Gene Baker, 1963.

Roberto Clemente becomes the first Puerto Rican to be inducted into the National Baseball Hall of Fame. After his fatal plane crash enroute to Managua, Nicaragua in 1972 the National Baseball Hall of Fame waives its five-year waiting period so that a player who had been deceased for at least six months would be eligible for entry.

In pursuit of Babe Ruth's lifetime home run record, Hank Aaron receives numerous death threats. His daughter Gaile, a student at Fisk University in Nashville, Tenn., receives threatening phone calls and is a target of an abortive kidnapping plot, requiring escorts by FBI agents.

Hank Aaron appears on the September cover of *Guideposts: A Practical Guide to Successful Living* magazine.

Kansas City Kings guard Nate Archibald becomes the first player to lead the NBA in scoring (34.0) and assists (11.4) the same year.

Wilt Chamberlain retires from pro basketball. He plays in 1,045 games, scores 31,419 points and commits 2,075 fouls, but never fouls out of an NBA game.

The NBA starts recording "Steals," probably influenced by guard Walt Frazier's propensity for stealing basketballs. Frazier had outpolled Bill Russell on the All-NBA Defensive team in 1969.

Dock Ellis, Pittsburgh Pirates pitcher, is featured in *Ebony* magazine with hair curlers. Commissioner Bowie Kuhn orders him to cease and desist from wearing rollers and curlers during pre-game workouts. Ellis reluctantly shelves the curlers, after declaring, "They didn't put out any orders about [Yankee star] Joe Pepitone when he wore a hairpiece down to his shoulders."

Dave Winfield becomes the first athlete drafted in three different sports. The San Diego Padres select him as a pitcher with the fourth overall pick in the MLB draft and both the Atlanta Hawks (NBA) and the Utah Stars (ABA) draft him. Although he never played college football, the Minnesota Vikings selected Winfield in the 17th round of the NFL draft. He is one of two players ever to be drafted by three professional sports (the other being Dave Logan in 1976).

The 10 and 5 rule becomes a standard clause in the Collective Bargaining Agreement. It allows any player who is a ten-year major league veteran, including the last five with his current team, to veto a trade to another team. It is known as the Curt Flood Rule.

One of Charlie O. Finley's "innovations" is the "Alert Orange Baseball." Finley contends the ball, painted the color of a construction worker's hat, is easier for both players and fans to see. Pitchers complain that the ball, used in two spring training games in 1973, was slippery and hard to grip, while batters could not pick up the spin of the ball without seeing the seams, which on a normal white ball stands out in red. Finley laid his experiment gracefully to rest but would occasionally give the balls as gifts.

Former big-leaguer Tommie Aaron, the younger brother of Hank Aaron, is hired as manager of the Savannah Braves, on June 15, becoming the first African American manager in Southern League history.

The eight members of the all-Black cheerleading squad for Brown University refuse to stand for the playing of the national anthem before a game against Providence College in Rhode Island. Brown president Donald Hornig defends the act and the freedom to express their beliefs.

Simon Peter Gourdine becomes the first African American vice-president of the NBA.

Ray "Chink" Scott of the Detroit Pistons is the first African American to be named Coach of the Year in the NBA, receiving the Arnold "Red" Auerbach Trophy. Midway through the 1975-76 season, Scott is fired with a 17-25 won-lost record.

1974

"Struggle is a never-ending process. Freedom is never really won. You earn it and win it in every generation."
– Coretta Scott King

Hank Aaron of the Atlanta Braves breaks Babe Ruth's record for lifetime home runs, hitting number 715 off Los Angeles Dodger pitcher Al Downing. Dodgers broadcaster Vin Scully shares the gravity of the moment, "What a marvelous moment for the country and the world. A Black man is getting a standing ovation (53,775 fans) in the Deep South for breaking a record of an all-time baseball (White) idol."

Charley Pride, former Memphis Red Sox pitcher, becomes the first Negro League veteran and first African American to sing the national anthem at the Super Bowl (VIII).

Lee Elder wins the Monsanto Open in Pensacola, Fla., becoming the first African American to qualify for the Masters Tournament. Elder later becomes the first African American golfer to earn $1 million in his career.

Mike Marson, a left wing, becomes the first Black player for the Washington Capitals (NHL), and the only African American, besides sophomore Alton White to skate in the league since Willie O'Ree's retirement in 1961. Marson is also the first Black player to be drafted in an NHL Entry Draft (first introduced in 1963), as a 2nd round, 19th overall pick by the Capitals.

Wilma Rudolph, Ralph Boston, Lee Calhoun, Rafer Johnson, Mal Whitfield, Harrison Dillard and Jesse Owens are the first

Colorful Firsts in U.S. Sports

African Americans inducted into the National Track and Field Hall of Fame.

Lenward Simpson signs with the Detroit Loves and becomes the first African American on a World Team Tennis (WTT) team.

Leo Miles becomes the first African American to officiate a Super Bowl game as head linesman.

Rommie Loudd of the Florida Blazers and Louis R. Lee of the Detroit Wheels become the first African American owners of World Football League (WFL) franchises.

Tommy Reamon, running back for the Florida Blazers, becomes the first player to win the Most Valuable Offensive Player award in the World Football League in its inaugural season. Reamon leads the WFL in rushing yardage, 1,576, in a 20-game season.

Dave Mays and D.C. Nobles are the first Black quarterbacks hired by the Houston Texans of the World Football League.

Joe Gilliam becomes the first Black quarterback to start and win an opening day NFL game, defeating the Baltimore Colts, 30-0. Jefferson Street Joe Gilliam carries the Pittsburgh Steelers to the playoffs under coach Chuck Noll.

Eddie McAshan and Reggie Oliver become the first Black quarterbacks employed by the Jacksonville Sharks of the World Football League.

Matt Reed from Grambling University is the first Black quarterback hired by the Birmingham Americans of the World Football League.

Oakland A's owner Charlie Finley promotes 11-year-old batboy Stanley Burrell to honorary vice-president. Sixteen years later, Burrell records top-selling rap albums, under the name of M.C. Hammer.

Oakland A's owner Charlie Finley hires former Michigan State University sprinter Herb Washington as the first "designated runner" in major league history. Washington has no prior professional baseball experience. He steals 31 bases in 48 attempts and scores 33 runs in 105 ML games.

Don King is the first boxing promoter to offer a $10 million purse with his "Rumble In The Jungle" match between George Foreman and Muhammad Ali in Kinshasa, Republic of Zaire. This fight was refereed by Zach Clayton, a member of the Naismith Memorial Basketball Hall of Fame, and former Negro Baseball League first baseman.

Ben Bluitt becomes Cornell University's first African American basketball head coach.

Nate Thurmond records the first quadruple-double in NBA history. As a Chicago Bull he scores 22 points, gathers 14 rebounds, passes out 13 assists and blocks 12 shots.

Moses Malone becomes the first high school athlete to go directly to the pros from high school. The Utah Stars of the ABA give Malone $565,000 for four years. He scores 19 points, with 11 rebounds, in his first pro game against Dr. J and the New York Nets. (See Reggie Harding, 1963).

1975

"If the First Amendment means anything, it means that the State has no business telling a man, sitting alone in his own house, what books he may read or what films he may watch." – Thurgood Marshall

Irv Cross becomes co-anchor with Brent Musburger, Phyllis George and Jimmy "The Greek" Snyder on *The NFL Today* show. He spends 14 years on this live broadcast.

Washington Bullets center Wes Unseld becomes the first player to win the J. Walter Kennedy Citizenship Award.

Darryl Dawkins (Philadelphia 76ers) and Bill Willoughby (Atlanta Hawks) are the second and third high school basketball players to sign with NBA or ABA teams.

David Thompson becomes the first number one pick by the NBA (Atlanta Hawks) to sign with an ABA team, the Denver Nuggets.

Officials at Gaylord High School in Gaylord, Mich., bans Wilt Chamberlain's book *Wilt*, stating pupils "are more interested in learning how to dribble and shoot" rather than his scores off the court.

K. C. Jones (Washington Bullets) and Al Attles (Golden State Warriors) become the first African Americans to coach NBA All-Star squads. They also square off in the NBA championship to become the first African Americans to take their teams to the finals, doing so seven years after Bill Russell wins the first of two titles as Boston's player/coach. The Warriors sweep the Bullets in four games.

Julius "Dr. J." Erving wins the first ABA Slam Dunk contest. Erving beats out David Thompson in the Denver event.

Lusia Harris of Delta State is the first African American recipient of the KODAK-WBCA All-American award.

Bill Russell, in his first year of eligibility, is voted into the Naismith Memorial Basketball Hall of Fame. He is the first African American player inducted. The five-time NBA MVP awardee refuses induction without an explanation.

Lee Elder is the first professional African American golfer to appear on the cover of *Sports Illustrated*. Bill Russell, basketball center, appeared as a golfer earlier on the 4 August 1969 cover. After his victory in the 1974 Monsanto Open, Lee Elder is the first African American to be eligible to compete in the Masters Tournament at Augusta National.

Charlie Sifford becomes the first African American PGA Seniors Champion.

James Harris from Grambling State University becomes the first African American quarterback to start a playoff game, leading the Los Angeles Rams to a 19-10 victory over the Washington Redskins. Harris becomes the first African American quarterback named Pro Bowl's Player of the Game (MVP) with two fourth-quarter touchdowns.

J.J. Jones is the first Black starting quarterback for the New York Jets, in his only appearance as QB against the San Diego Chargers. He was replaced by Joe Namath.

Johnnie Walton becomes the first Black quarterback for the San Antonio Wings of the World Football League.

Willie Wood becomes the first African American head coach in the modern era with the Philadelphia Bell of the World Football League (WFL).

Archie Griffin, of Ohio State University, becomes the first Division I-A player to rush for over 5,000 yards (5,177) during his collegiate career (1972-75). Griffin also becomes the first person to win consecutive Heisman Trophies.

Franco Harris, running back for the Pittsburgh Steelers, becomes the first African American player to be named Super Bowl MVP, winning the honor in Super Bowl IX against the Minnesota Vikings.

Paul "Tank" Younger becomes the NFL's first African American assistant general manager with the Los Angeles Rams.

Arthur Ashe becomes the first African American to win Wimbledon, 6-1, 6-1, 5-7, and 6-4 over heavy favorite Jimmy Connors. Ashe becomes the first African American to be ranked No. 1 by the U.S. Lawn Tennis Association.

Dorothy Richey, a Tuskegee University grad, becomes the first African American female Athletic Director in the country with Chicago State University in Illinois.

Alice Coachman, the first African American woman to win an Olympic gold medal (high jump in 1948), is inducted into the National Track and Field Hall of Fame in Indianapolis, Ind.

Muhammad Ali fights Chuck Wepner, billed as *Give the White Guy a Break* at the Richfield Coliseum in Summit County, Ohio. Ali is floored in the fight before knocking out Wepner in the 15th round. The fight inspires the 1976 film *Rocky*, which earns $225 million globally and 10 Academy Award nominations, winning three. The film spawns seven sequels.

Muhammad Ali wins by technical knockout (TKO) over Joe Frazier in the 14th round in the "Thrilla in Manila" fight, in Quezon City, Philippines. It is their third and final boxing match.

Panamanian Rennie Stennett, second baseman for the Pittsburgh Pirates, becomes the only player in modern baseball to go 7-for-7 in a nine-inning game when he hits four singles, two doubles and a triple in a 22-0 victory over the Chicago Cubs.

Frank Robinson becomes the first full-time African American manager in the re-integrated major leagues with the Cleveland Indians. He hits a pinch-hit homer in his managerial debut, on Opening Day, to defeat the N.Y. Yankees, 5-3. See Gene Baker, 1963 and Ernie Banks, 1973.

Tom McCraw of the Cleveland Indians switches to the third base coaching box with Dave García, becoming perhaps the first Black man to coach third base in the re-integrated major leagues. The third-base coaching position requires giving signals to batters and critical base running decisions and is seen as a steppingstone to a managerial job.

Luis Tiant Jr. pitches for the Boston Red Sox in the World Series. Twenty-eight years earlier, his father, Luis Senior, pitched in the 1947 Negro World Series for the New York Cubans. They become the first father-and-son combination to pitch in World Series games, albeit in different leagues.

The Seitz decision was a ruling by arbitrator Peter Seitz on December 23, which declared that Major League Baseball players become free agents upon playing one year for their team without a contract, effectively nullifying baseball's reserve clause. The ruling was issued in regard to pitchers Andy Messersmith and Dave McNally.

1976

"Young man, young man, your arm's too short to box with God."
– James Weldon Johnson

Jesse Owens is the first Black athlete presented with the Presidential Medal of Freedom.

Bill Riley, a winger, joins Mike Marson on the Washington Capitals as the third African American hockey player in the NHL.

Julius "Dr. J" Erving becomes the only three-time MVP in the ABA: 1972-73, 1974-75 and 1975-76.

Colorful Firsts in U.S. Sports

The ABA folds, but the New York (later New Jersey) Nets, Denver Nuggets, Indiana Pacers and the San Antonio Spurs join the NBA.

Buffalo Braves Bob McAdoo wins his third straight NBA scoring title. The 6-foot-9 center-forward is the first big man to shoot regularly outside the paint. He shoots better than 50 percent from the floor in half of his 14 NBA seasons, adding a new dimension to the game of basketball.

The dunk is reinstated. The dominance of UCLA center Lew Alcindor had prompted the NCAA to ban dunking in college basketball during the 1967-68 season.

The C.E. Gaines Center, an athletic complex on the Winston-Salem State University campus, is named after Clarence "Big House" Gaines.

Bill Cofield, for the Wisconsin Badgers, becomes the first Black male head basketball coach in the Big Ten Conference.

Edwina Qualls, for the Wisconsin Badgers, becomes the first Black female head basketball coach in the Big Ten Conference.

Tony Dorsett, for Pittsburgh, becomes the first collegiate Division I-A player to rush for more than 6,000 (6,082) yards during his career.

Lem Barney becomes the first NFL player with at least 50 career interceptions and at least 1,000 interception return yards and at least seven touchdowns on interceptions.

Mike Dunn becomes the first Black quarterback for the Duke University football team.

Parnell Dickinson from Mississippi Valley State University Delta Devils becomes the first Black starting quarterback for the Tampa Bay Buccaneers.

Leon Spinks becomes the first Marine to win a gold medal in Olympics boxing history.

The Spinks brothers, Leon and Michael, win Olympic gold medals in boxing.

Tennis players Bruce Foxworth and Roger Guedes lead Hampton University to become the first historically Black college or university to win the NCAA's Division II tennis doubles title.

Bill Lucas, former player for the Atlanta Braves, is named by Braves owner Ted Turner as vice president of player personnel, at the time the highest administrative position in major league baseball. His responsibilities were essentially that of a general manager. (See 1993, Bob Watson, general manager of the Yankees.)

According to biographer Lonnie Wheeler, Henry Aaron was miles ahead of the competition. As Wheeler pointed out, if you were to lay out side by side Aaron's White major league record of 6,856 total bases alongside a highway (90 feet for a single, 180 feet for a double, and so on), he would be 12.3 miles ahead of runner-up Stan Musial, who had 722 fewer total bases and 180 fewer homers.

Glenn Burke, outfielder for the Los Angeles Dodgers, is the first openly gay player in major league baseball.

Allen J. Coage becomes the first African American to medal in Judo, earning the bronze at the Montreal Olympics.

Mamie Rallins, former Tennessee State Tigerbelle hurdler, becomes the first African American woman to coach at Ohio State University.

Lloyd Keaser becomes the first African American to medal at the Montreal Olympics in wrestling, earning a silver in the 149-pound freestyle category.

1977

"Hard work always pays off. Hard work is undefeated."
– Mark Sears, Alabama basketball player

Dusty Baker, of Los Angeles Dodgers, is the first Most Valuable Player named in the National League's Championship Series (NLCS).

Reggie Jackson is the first baseball player to have a candy bar named after him. "Mr. October" becomes the first non-pitcher to win two World Series MVPs for different teams. His first MVP award came as a member of the 1973 Oakland A's, with the second award coming as a New York Yankee.

Frank White of the Kansas City Royals becomes the first African American to the win the Gold Glove Award at second base in the American League.

The first player chosen in the NBA dispersal draft of former ABA players, is not Dr. J., Moses Malone, nor the Ice Man George Gervin, but Artis Gilmore. The Chicago Bulls sign him for $1.1 million.

Cheryl White is the first woman to win the Appaloosa Horse Club's Jockey of the Year award, scoring title. She is a repeat winner in 1983, 1984 and 1985.

Willie Simms becomes the second African American jockey inducted to the National Museum of Racing and Hall of Fame. Simms is credited with introducing the British to the short stirrup style of riding later popularized by Tod Sloan.

Wilma Rudolph's autobiography "Wilma" is made into a movie for TV.

Lusia "Lucy" Harris becomes the first woman to be drafted by the NBA. The 1976 Olympic silver medalist is drafted by the New Orleans Jazz, but never plays.

The NFL outlaws the "head slap" made popular by the retired (1974) Deacon Jones of the Los Angeles Rams, San Diego Chargers and Washington Redskins.

Walter Payton becomes the first player to rush for 275 yards in a game and the youngest (23) to be named NFL's Most Valuable Player. Payton is the first African American chosen by the Pro Football Writers Association as NFL Player of the Year.

Bill Willis, a defensive lineman, becomes the first undrafted African American to be named to the Pro Football Hall of Fame.

Minnesota University's all-time leading passer, Tony Dungy, is not drafted by the NFL. The Pittsburgh Steelers later sign quarterback Dungy as a safety.

Dave Mays is the first Black starting quarterback for the Cleveland Browns.

The Mel Blount Rule or "bump-and-run" bars contact with wide receivers beginning five yards beyond the line of scrimmage. Named after the Pittsburgh Steeler cornerback Mel Blount out of Southern University, this ruling marks a turning point in football in making the passing game more open.

Marques Johnson of UCLA wins the first John R. Wooden Award, given annually to the most outstanding men's and women's college basketball players.

Hank Aaron becomes the first Negro Leaguer to have his uniform number retired twice, when the Milwaukee Brewers and the Atlanta Braves honor him.

1977 to 1987, Edwin Moses starts his winning string of 122 consecutive 400-meter hurdle races.

1978

"To demand freedom is to demand justice. When a man has no protection under the law it is difficult for him to make others recognize him." – James Cone

Jayne Kennedy becomes the first woman to enter the male-dominated world of sports as an announcer on *The NFL Today*.

Franklin Jacobs, only 5-foot-8, sets a world record for the highest clearance over one's head, 23 feet, ¼ inch, clearing the high jump bar at 7 feet, 7 ¼ inches.

Basketball coach John McLendon is inducted into the Central Intercollegiate Athletic Association (CIAA) Hall of Fame.

Minnesota Gopher center Mychal Thompson from Nassau, Bahamas, is the first foreign-born player drafted number one overall by the NBA, when selected by the Portland Trail Blazers.

The tightest race for the NBA scoring title goes down to the final game. George "Ice Man" Gervin, of San Antonio Spurs, scores 63, while David Thompson, of Denver Nuggets, scores 73. The "Ice Man" wins the title with a 27.21 average to beat Thompson's 27.15 average.

Debra Stroman becomes the first African American woman to receive a basketball scholarship at the University of Virginia.

Johnnie Walton becomes the first Black quarterback for the Philadelphia Eagles of the NFL.

After seven pro fights, Leon Spinks fights Muhammad Ali for the heavyweight championship and wins. Spinks is both the fastest to gain and the fastest to lose the heavyweight championship.

Muhammad Ali wins the heavyweight championship for an unprecedented third time by defeating Leon Spinks. The prizefight, held in the Louisiana Superdome, is the first to gross more than $5 million dollars.

Ron LeFlore, Detroit Tigers outfielder, becomes the first non-Hall of Famer to have a TV-movie made about his career, called *One In A Million*.

J.R. Richards of the Houston Astros becomes the first African American right-handed pitcher to strike out 300 batters in a season (303). The next season he strikes out 313 batters.

Joe Morgan becomes the first major leaguer to record 200 career Home Runs and 500 stolen bases.

Larry Doby becomes the first African American manager for the Chicago White Sox.

Doug Williams of Grambling State University is the first African American QB drafted in the first round (17th pick). The Tampa Bay Buccaneers claim they are seeking a foundation for their second-year franchise.

Tony McKegney becomes the first African American hockey player for the Buffalo Sabres.

Colorful Firsts in U.S. Sports

Wendy Hilliard is the African American rhythmic gymnast to represent the U.S. in international competition, including three World Championships (1979, 1981, and 1983). In 1995, Hilliard becomes the first African American president of the Women's Sports Foundation, the leading organization for women's sport issues.

1979

"Human rights are God-given. Civil rights are man-made." – Adam Clayton Powell Jr.

Tony McKegney becomes the first African American hockey player to surpass 20 goals in a single NHL season, while playing for the Buffalo Sabres.

Doug Williams of the Tampa Bay Bucs and Vince Evans of the Chicago Bears become the first African American quarterbacks to face-off in NFL competition. Evans is the first Black starting quarterback for the Bears.

San Diego Padres shortstop Garry Templeton becomes the first National Leaguer with 100 hits from each side of the plate, in a single season, collecting a league leading 211 hits in total. He batts .314 that season.

Outfielder Dave Parker becomes the first ML baseball player to earn a million dollars a year when he signs a five-year, $5 million contract with the Pittsburgh Pirates.

Willie "Pops" Stargell becomes the first player (and the oldest at 39) to win MVPs in the league (shared with Keith Hernandez), the NLCS playoffs and the World Series, all in the same season. Stargell also wins the *Sporting News'* Man of the Year and is Co-winner (with Terry Bradshaw) of *Sport Illustrated's* Sportsman of the Year award.

John McLendon becomes the first coach from a historically Black college to be inducted in the Naismith Memorial Basketball Hall of Fame.

The Alcorn Braves basketball team becomes the first historically Black institution invited to the National Invitation Tournament (NIT). The Braves are led by Davey Whitney, former Kansas City Monarch. His team defeats Mississippi State, 80-78 in the first round, before losing to Indiana, 72-68 in the second round.

Ed "Too Tall" Jones, an NFL All-Star defensive end standing 6-foot-9, retires from the Dallas Cowboys to be become a professional boxer. He labors to six victories before returning to the gridiron. Like Rocky Marciano, "Too Tall" retires undefeated.

An Akron, Ohio grandmother, Edith Burroughs becomes the first Black person to win a professional bowling tournament. She wins the Pabst Blue Ribbon tournament, in Rockford, Ill., taking home the $4000 first place prize.

Lee Elder becomes the first African American to play on a U.S. Ryder Cup team.

Jokester Frank "Fuzzy" Zoeller Jr. becomes just the third player in golf history to win the Masters Tournament in his first appearance. His caddie is African American Jariah "Bubba" Beard.

Brooks Johnson becomes the first African American head coach in Track & Field at Stanford University. He coaches Olympians Esther Stroy, Chandra Cheesborough and Evelyn Ashford.

Willie Jeffries becomes the first African American head football coach in Division I-A when named coach of the Wichita State University (Kansas) Shockers.

David Thompson of the Denver Nuggets is named the Most Valuable Player in the NBA All-Star game. He becomes the only player in pro basketball to be named All-Star MVP in both the NBA and the ABA (in 1976).

Detroit Piston guard Kevin Porter becomes the first player to pass out 1,000 assists (1,099) in a season.

Darryl Dawkins demolishes backboards in at Kansas City's Municipal Auditorium and Philadelphia's Spectrum, prompting the development and implementation of the "Breakaway Rim" in the 1981-82 season. Dawkins from the planet "Lovetron" becomes the first player to name his dunks: The Rim Wrecker, The Gorilla, In Your Face Disgrace, The Look Out Below, Cover Your Head, Dunk You Very Much, Left-Handed-Spine-Chiller-Supreme, The Bun Toaster, The Rump Roaster and the Baby Shaker.

In November, Moses Malone of the Houston Rockets is the first NBA player to be named Player of the Month.

For the week of November 11, Magic Johnson of the Los Angeles Lakers is the first NBA player named Player of the Week.

1979-80, The New York Knicks become the first NBA team with an all-Black roster. The roster includes Bill Cartwright, Jim Clemons, Hollis Copeland, Larry Demic, Mike Glenn, Toby Knight, Joe Meriweather, Earl Monroe, Michael Ray Richardson, Marvin Webster, and Ray Williams. Lacking diversity the Knicks finish in fourth place in the Atlantic Division.

1980

"We cannot solve our problems with the same thinking we used when we created them." – Albert Einstein

Artis Gilmore becomes the first NBA player to record more than 2,000 blocked shots.

Nolan Richardson coaches Western Texas Junior College to the National Junior College Basketball Championship.

Magic Johnson becomes the first rookie to win the MVP award in the NBA finals.

Bill Russell is declared "The Greatest Player in the History of the NBA" by the Professional Basketball Writers Association of America.

Kareem Abdul-Jabbar becomes the first NBA player to win six MVP awards.

Davey Whitney, Alcorn Braves basketball coach, wins a game in the NCAA Tournament. Whitney's Braves become the first team from a historically Black college to win a game in the NIT (1979) and in the NCAA Tournament. The Braves defeat South Alabama, 70-62, before losing to LSU, 98-88 in the second round.

Philadelphia 76er stars Darryl Dawkins and Lloyd "World" Free wear large gold necklaces inscribed "Chocolate Thunder" and "World," respectively. NBA bans the wearing of any type of hand, arm, face, nose, ear, head or neck jewelry during league play, citing a potential safety hazard.

DaVanche "Ron" Galimore from Iowa State University becomes the first gymnast to score a perfect "10" and the first African American member of a U.S. Olympic team. The team was never sent to Moscow because of a U.S. led boycott of the 1980 Summer Olympics. Ron is the son of Willie Galimore, former Chicago Bears halfback.

The first Blacks to participate in the Winter Olympics for the U.S. are Jeff Gadley and 1968 gold medalist 110-meter hurdler Willie Davenport for the four-man bobsled team.

Luci Collins of Creole descent is the first Black gymnast to qualify for the U.S. Women's Olympic team. Because of America's Moscow Olympic boycott, she never competes.

Dickie Bivins becomes the first Black male gymnast to win an individual medal at the World Championships. He wins bronze medals in the Platform Tumbling and Power Tumbling.

The International Women's Sports Hall of Fame, in its first year elects Wilma Rudolph in the Contemporary category, while Althea Gibson receives honors in its Pioneer category.

Tony McKegney, for the Buffalo Sabres, becomes the first African American hockey player to score a goal in Stanley Cup competition - against the New York Islanders.

Kansas City Royals centerfielder Willie Wilson becomes the first American League batter to collect 100 hits from each side of the plate, in a season, with 230 total hits. He is also the first player to record more than 700 (705) at bats in a season.

Maury Wills becomes the first African American manager of the Seattle Mariners.

Rickey Henderson of the Oakland A's steals 100 bases.

Frank White, of Kansas City Royals, is the first player to win the ALCS' Most Valuable Player.

Frank White (2b) and U.L. Washington (ss) of the Kansas City Royals become the first African American double-play combination in American League history.

Vince Evans becomes the first African American quarterback, the second overall, to earn a maximum single-game passing rating of 158.3. Evans of the Chicago Bears completes 18 of 22 passes for 316 yards and throws three touchdowns against the Green Bay Packers.

Earl Campbell of the Houston Oilers becomes the first player to win the NFL's Most Valuable Player Award three years in a row.

Future Pro Bowlers Dwight Stephenson of the Miami Dolphin and Ray Donaldson of the Baltimore Colts become the first African Americans to start at the Center position for an NFL team.

1981

"Malcolm is gone, and Martin is gone, and it is up to all of us to nourish the hope they gave us." – Lena Horne

One hundred- and 200-meter sprinter Evelyn Ashford becomes the first African American female to be named Athlete of the Year by *Track & Field News*.

Lynette Woodard, of Kansas University, is the first African American woman to win the Wade Trophy, presented annually to the best women's basketball player in National Collegiate Athletic Association (NCAA) Division I. The trophy is named after the legendary Lily Margaret Wade, coach of three-time national champion Delta State University. Woodard becomes the first Kansas University woman to have her jersey number retired, No. 31. Upon retiring and before the three-point shot was initiated and women used the smaller basketball, Woodard becomes the all-time career scoring leader in the Association for Intercollegiate Athletes for Women (AIWA) with 3,649 points. Her record is not recognized by the NCAA.

Colorful Firsts in U.S. Sports

Arthur Ashe becomes the first African American to be named Captain of the U.S. Davis Cup team, a position he held until 1985.

Ronnie Barnes, with the New York Giants, becomes the NFL's first Black head athletic trainer. He would later win the National Professional Athletic Trainer of the Year award in 1983 and 1987.

In November, Mark Aguirre of the Dallas Mavericks is the first NBA player named Rookie of the Month.

Calvin Murphy becomes the first NBA player to make more than 95% of his free throws in a season. Murphy of the Houston Rockets compiles a .958 percentage.

Renaldo "Skeets" Nehemiah becomes the first hurdler to break the 13-second barrier in the 110-meter hurdles, with a 12.93 time.

Julius Erving becomes the only player in basketball history to win the MVP award in both the NBA and the ABA. Dr. J. was the MVP in the ABA in 1974, 1975 and 1976; and MVP in the NBA in 1981.

Grant Fuhr, of African-Canadian and European ancestry, becomes the first Black player drafted by the National Hockey League. The goalie, the first Black at that position, is picked in the first round by the world champion Edmonton Oilers.

Valmore James, a left wing, becomes the first Black American to play in the NHL when he debuts with the Buffalo Sabres.

Marcus Allen, of USC, becomes the first collegiate running back to rush for 2,000 (2,342) yards in a season.

A TV movie *Grambling's White Tiger* tells the true story of Jim Gregory, the first White quarterback at Grambling College in 1962.

Vida Blue becomes the first (and only pitcher) to win an All-Star game for both the American and National Leagues, 1971 for the Oakland A's and in 1981 for the San Francisco Giants.

Frank Robinson becomes the first African American manager of the San Francisco Giants. Robinson had previously been manager of the Cleveland Indians from 1975 to 1977.

Calvin Peete becomes the first African American golfer to win the PGA's Driving Accuracy Award with 81.9 rating.

From 1981-83, Calvin Peete becomes the first African American golfer to win "Greens in Regulation," three years in a row, with ratings of 73.1, 72.4 and 71.4.

1982
"Lost time is never found again." – Thelonious Monk

Calvin Peete wins the Greater Milwaukee Open golf tourney, a first for a Black man.

Jackie Robinson becomes the first baseball player to be honored on a U.S. postage stamp.

Rickey Henderson steals a record 130 bases for the Oakland A's.

Charlie Sampson becomes the first African American World Champion Bull Rider by winning the Winston Rodeo Series in Oklahoma City.

After 10 years of professional boxing and annoyed that network announcers often did not refer to him as "Marvelous," Hagler legally changed his name to "Marvelous Marvin Hagler," who reigned as the undisputed middleweight champion from 1980 to 1987.

Playing in the Canadian Football League, Warren Moon becomes the first pro quarterback to throw for 5,000 yards in a season.

Vivian Stringer, coach of Cheyney State, a Division II team, is the first African American woman to take a team to the NCAA basketball tournament. Cheyney State loses the championship game to Louisiana Tech. Stringer is named *Sports Illustrated's* Coach of the Year.

Marian Washington becomes the first African American woman to be the head coach of a U.S. team in international play when she guides the U.S. Select Team to a basketball silver medal in Taiwan.

The first all-Black Division I Consensus All-American team is named: Terry Cummings, DePaul; Quintin Dailey, San Francisco; Eric Floyd, Georgetown; Ralph Sampson, Virginia; and James Worthy, North Carolina.

Cheryl Miller becomes the first high school player, male or female, to be named *Parade* All-American for four straight years, 1978 to 1982.

As a senior Cheryl Miller, for the Polytechnic High School Bears, she set a national record by scoring 105 points in Poly's 179–15 win over the Norte Vista Braves in Riverside, California. On that day, January 26, she becomes the first woman to dunk in a sanctioned league game.

Milwaukee Bucks guard Sidney Moncrief becomes the first player to win the NBA's Defensive Player of the Year award.

Artis Gilmore becomes the first NBA player to record more than 2,500 blocked shots.

1983
"The cost of liberty is less than the price of repression." – W.E.B. Du Bois

Evelyn Ashford becomes the first American woman to break the 11.0 second barrier in the 100-meter dash (10.79).

In Zurich, Switzerland, Calvin Smith becomes the first athlete to run under 10 seconds (9.97) in the 100-meter race, and 20 seconds (19.99) in the 200 meters, on the same day.

Claire Smith, for the New York Yankees, is the first female MLB beat writer, while working for the *Hartford Courant*.

Rickey Henderson steals 108 bases. He becomes the first player to steal more than 100 bases in a season, three times.

Clyde Drexler becomes the first collegiate basketball player to accumulate 1,000 points, 900 rebounds, 300 assists and 250 steals in a career with the Houston Cougars.

Wayman Tisdale becomes the first frosh to be named unanimous All-American.

Nolan Richardson leads the University of Tulsa to the NIT championship.

Calvin Murphy becomes the first player shorter than 6 feet to appear in 1,000 NBA games.

Ralph Sampson, center/forward for the Rockets becomes the NBA's first unanimous Rookie of the Year selection and NBA's first rookie millionaire.

The NBA selects its first all-rookie team: Terry Cummings (San Diego), Clark Kellogg (Indiana), Dominique Wilkins (Atlanta), James Worthy (Los Angeles) and Quintin Dailey (Chicago). Cummings is named Rookie of the Year.

The Eddie G. Robinson Memorial Stadium, a multi-purpose 19,000-seat facility opens at Grambling State University.

Kelvin Bryant of the Philadelphia Stars in the U.S. Football League (USFL) is named its first MVP.

Reggie Collier from the Southern Mississippi Golden Eagles is the first Black quarterback to play for the Birmingham Stallions in the USFL.

Bobby Bell of the Kansas City Chiefs becomes the first outside linebacker inducted in the National Football Hall of Fame in Canton, Ohio.

Billy "White Shoes" Johnson, a wide receiver for the Atlanta Falcons is the first African American to win *Pro Football Weekly's* Comeback Player of the Year award.

Calvin Peete is the first African American member of the U.S. Ryder Cup.

Cheryl White, at the Fresno Fair in California, is the first female jockey to win five races in a single day.

Dianne Durham, 14, becomes the first African American senior National Gymnastic Champion. She takes gold in the vault, uneven bars and the floor routine. Durham is the first American to successfully execute a full-twisting Tsukahara on the vault. The first Tsukahara vault was performed by Mr. Mitsuo Tsukahara of Japan in 1972.

Nelson Vails becomes the first African American cyclist to win a gold medal at the Pan American games.

1984
"I've only just a minute, Only sixty seconds in it. Forced upon me, can't refuse it.
Didn't seek it, didn't choose it, but it's up to me to use it." – Benjamin Mays

Nelson Vails is the first African American to win a silver medal in cycling at the Los Angeles Olympic Games.

Greg Gibson becomes the first African American Greco-Roman wrestler, at 220 pounds, to medal (a silver) at the Los Angeles Olympics.

Carmen Williamson becomes boxing's first African American referee and judge for the Los Angeles Olympics and is presented with an honorary gold medal. Born in 1925, Williamson was a 112-pound amateur flyweight boxer who compiled a 25-14 won-lost record.

Peter Westbrook becomes the first African American to win an Olympic medal in fencing, a bronze.

Greg Gibson becomes the first African American to win an Olympic medal in Greco-Roman wrestling, capturing a silver medal at the Los Angeles games.

Benita Fitzgerald-Mosley, at the Los Angeles Olympic Games, becomes the first Black woman to win a gold medal in the 100-meter hurdles.

With a leap of 56 feet, 7 ½ inches, Al Joyner becomes the first African American in 80 years to win an Olympic gold medal in the triple jump. He is honored with the Jim Thorpe Award, which is given every four years to the best U.S. competitor in an Olympic field event.

Colorful Firsts in U.S. Sports

Goalie Grant Fuhr for the Edmonton Oilers becomes the first African-Canadian hockey player to win a Stanley Cup championship.

Ray Neufield becomes the first African American hockey player for the Hartford Whalers.

Carl Lewis becomes the first African American track star to appear on the cover of *Time* magazine.

Calvin Peete becomes the first African American to win the Vardon Trophy with a 70.56 scoring average. Peete had dropped out of a few tournaments because of illness and those scorecards did not count against his average golf score. The next year, the PGA decides to include all scores regardless of whether the competitor completes the tournament or not. *Golf World* magazine labels the change the Cal Peete Rule.

Edward D. Brown, or "Brown Dick," becomes the first horse trainer inducted to the National Museum of Racing and Hall of Fame. Brown developed Kentucky Derby winners "Ben Brush" and "Plaudit."

Cheryl Miller, of USC, is the first African American woman to win the Naismith Trophy. She would go on to win the trophy three times. She is the first female hoopster to grace the cover of *Sports Illustrated*.

Georgeann Wells, a 6-foot-7 center for the West Virginia Mountaineers, becomes the first woman to dunk in an official game. Wells' dunk occurs against Charleston, en route to a 110-82 victory.

John Thompson becomes the first African American basketball head coach to win the NCAA Division I title, coaching the Georgetown Hoyas to a win over the Houston Cougars.

In January, K. C. Jones of the Boston Celtics is the first African American coach to be named Coach of the Month in the NBA.

Magic Johnson is the first recipient of the IBM Award, based on a computer formula which measures a player's statistical contribution to his team. David Robinson won the award a record five times. The award was discontinued in 2002 with Tim Duncan as the final recipient. Award formula = Player's PTS-FGA+REB+AST+STL+BLK-PF-TO+(team wins x 10) x 250 divided by Team points- FGA+REB+AST+STL+BLK-PF-TO. PTS stands for points, FGA stands for field goal attempts, REB stands for rebounds, AST stands for assists, STL stands for steals, BLK stands for blocks, PF stands for personal fouls, and TO stands for turnovers. The award was given to the player with the highest total.

The USC Women's basketball team are the first female NCAA champions to be invited to the White House, by President Ronald Reagan. The team is led by Cheryl Miller, Cynthia Cooper and the McGee twins Paula and Pamela.

The Iowa State University football stadium is named Cyclone Stadium, and the playing field is named "Jack Trice Field" in honor of the school's first African American athlete, a tackle. Stadium capacity is estimated at 56,800.

Warren Moon from the Washington University Huskies is the first Black starting quarterback for the Houston Oilers.

Marcus Allen becomes the first former Heisman Trophy winner to be named the Super Bowl (XVIII) MVP.

Reggie Collier is the first Black quarterback to play for the Washington Federals in the USFL.

Valerie Brisco-Hooks becomes the first person to record a 200-400-meters double win in the Olympics with times of 21.81 and 48.83 seconds, respectively.

Dwight Gooden is the first rookie pitcher to surpass 250 (276) strikeouts in a season.

Jackie Robinson is posthumously presented with the Presidential Medal of Freedom by President Ronald Reagan, the highest civilian award.

1985

"Racial separation was a creature of the adults; it was not a creature of the children."

– shortstop John Isaac Rivers, the 1955 Cannon Street All-Stars, Charleston, SC

John Thompson, of Georgetown University, is named Coach of the Year by the National Association of Basketball Coaches.

Rookie Patrick Ewing with the New York Knicks is not allowed, by the NBA, to wear a t-shirt under his jersey, as he did with the Georgetown Hoyas to stay warm in cold arenas.

Reggie Collier is the first Black quarterback to play for the Orlando Renegades in the USFL.

Wayman Tisdale becomes the first and only college basketball player to be named consensus All-American by the *Associated Press* in each of his first three years, as an Oklahoma Sooner.

Xavier McDaniel, with the Wichita State Shockers, becomes the first player in college history to lead the NCAA's Division I in rebounding and scoring (27.2) in the same season. He is selected in the first round of the NBA draft by the Seattle SuperSonics.

Diminutive Spud Webb, at 5-foot-7, becomes the first player under six feet to win the NBA Slam Dunk contest.

Lynette Woodard, a 1984 Olympic gold medalist, becomes the first woman to play for the Harlem Globetrotters. She scores seven points in her debut.

Cheryl Miller, of USC, is the first collegiate female basketball player to appear on the cover of *Sports Illustrated* (along with Bruce Dalrymple and Mark Price of Georgia Tech) in the magazine's *College Basketball Special Issue*, 1985-1986.

Randall Cunningham is the first Black starting quarterback for the Philadelphia Eagles.

By winning the NFL's MVP award, running back Marcus Allen earns the distinction of being the only player to win the Heisman Trophy (1981), Maxwell Trophy (1981), Walter Camp Award (1981), NFL Offensive Rookie of the Year (1982), the Super Bowl (1984, 1985), and NFL's MVP (1985).

Lionel James of the San Diego Chargers becomes the first player to gain more than 2500 yards in a season, running for 516 yards, receiving 1027 yards and returning 992 yards for a total of 2,535 yards.

Roger Craig of the San Francisco 49ers becomes the first NFL player to amass more than 1,000 yards rushing and 1,000 yards receiving in the same season. He finishes with 214 carries for 1,050 yards and had a league-best 92 receptions for 1,016 yards.

Eddie Robinson becomes the first Black college coach featured on the cover of *Sports Illustrated*. Entitled "Eddie Robinson Overtakes Bear Bryant with Win No. 324."

Arthur Ashe becomes the first African American male elected to the International Tennis Hall of Fame.

Charlie Williams becomes the first African American umpire in a contemporary major league All-Star game, held at the Hubert H. Humphrey Metrodome in Minneapolis, Minn.

Dwight Gooden becomes the first National League pitcher to strike out 200 or more batters in each of his first two seasons. In the process, Gooden captures the pitcher's Triple Crown with most wins (24), lowest ERA (1.53) and most strikeouts (268).

Alfredo Griffin, Oakland A's, becomes the first Afro-Caribbean to win the Gold Glove at shortstop in the American League.

Dave Parker becomes the first major league player to win the home run derby at the All-Star game. Parker beat out future Hall of Famers Jim Rice, Eddie Murray, Carlton Fisk, Ryne Sandberg and Cal Ripken Jr.

Vince Coleman of the St. Louis Cardinals steals 110 bases and is named NL Rookie of the Year. He is the first rookie to steal more than 100 bases.

Michael Spinks upsets IBF champ Larry Holmes for the heavyweight title. Michael is the first light heavyweight to win the heavyweight crown. Light heavyweights Billy Conn, Bob Foster and Archie Moore failed in earlier attempts. Michael joins his brother Leon as the first siblings to win heavyweight titles. Leon defeated Muhammad Ali in 1978.

1986

"God created Black people and Black people created style." – George C. Wolfe, *The Colored Museum*, 1986

Artis Gilmore becomes the first player to record more than 3,000 blocked shots in his combined ABA and NBA career.

Alvin Robertson, for San Antonio, becomes the first NBA player with more than 300 steals (301) in a season.

Alvin Robertson becomes the first guard to record a quadruple-double (double digits in four statistical categories in a single game) when he registers 20 points, 11 rebounds, 10 assists, and 10 steals while playing for the San Antonio Spurs against the Phoenix Suns on February 18.

Reggie Collier is the first Black quarterback to play for the Dallas Cowboys in the NFL. He appears in four games, attempts 15 passes and completes eight of them. Collier throws for one touchdown and two interceptions.

Bob Watson is named assistant general manager of the Houston Astros.

William "The Refrigerator" Perry, for the Chicago Bears, becomes the first defensive (DT) player to lineup as an offensive player (FB) and score a touchdown in the Super Bowl (XX) against the New England Patriots. The Bears win 46-10.

Walter Payton, Chicago Bears running back, becomes the first African American featured on the front of a Wheaties cereal box.

At Oklahoma, Jamelle Holieway takes over for an injured QB Troy Aikman in his frosh year and leads the Sooners to an 11-1-0 record under Coach Barry Switzer. Oklahoma defeats the Penn State Nittany Lions for the national championship in the Orange Bowl. He becomes the first true frosh quarterback to lead his team to the national title.

Debi Thomas, 18, becomes the first African American to win the World Figure Skating title, in Geneva, Switzerland. Earlier this year, Thomas becomes the first African American to win the U.S. Figure Skating Championship. She is named *Wide World of Sports'* Athlete of the Year.

George Branham III, 24, wins the Brunswick Memorial World Open, defeating Mark Roth in the finals. It is the first time an African American wins a Professional Bowlers Association (PBA) title.

Cheryl Miller is the first basketball player at USC, male or female, to have her jersey number retired, #31.

Colorful Firsts in U.S. Sports

Maurice Cheeks of the Philadelphia 76ers becomes the first NBA player to record 2,000 steals.

Bob Wade, legendary coach from Dunbar High School in Baltimore, becomes the first African American head coach in the Atlantic Coast Conference, (ACC) when he is named basketball coach at the University of Maryland, following the untimely death of All-American forward Len Bias and the resignation of 17-year-veteran coach Lefty Driesell.

Leonard Hamilton becomes the first African American coach in the Big Eight Conference as head coach of the Oklahoma State Cowboys basketball team.

Jackie Joyner-Kersee becomes the first female athlete to break the 7,000 point barrier in the heptathlon with 7,148 points at the Moscow Goodwill Games.

Pam Marshall becomes the first American runner to break the 50-second barrier in the 400 meters. She runs 49.99 in Westwood, Calif.

1987
"But race is the child of racism, not the father." – Ta-Nehisi Coates

On the 40th anniversary of Jackie Robinson's promotion to the Brooklyn Dodgers, his minor league teammate with the Montreal Royals, L.A. Dodgers executive Al Campanis, is fired for racially biased comments. Speaking to Ted Koppel on *Nightline* about the managerial potential of African Americans, Campanis says, "No, I don't believe it's prejudice. I truly believe they (Negroes) may not have some of the necessities to be, let's say, a field manager or perhaps a general manager."

Forty years after his debut with the Brooklyn Dodgers, the Rookie of the Year Award is renamed the Jackie Robinson Award, given to a player from the American and the National League. This is the first MLB award named after a former Negro Leaguer.

The St. Louis Cardinals' Terry Pendleton becomes the first African American player in the National League to win the Gold Glove Award at third base. Though a Black player has now won the award at every position since it was initiated in 1957, neither a Black pitcher nor third baseman has earned the designation in the American League.

Vince Coleman steals more than 100 bases for the third straight season. Coleman steals 110 bases in his rookie year, 1985; 107 bases in 1986 and 109 bases in 1987. He becomes the only player in MLB history to steal 100 or more bases in his first three seasons.

Andre Dawson, outfielder for the Chicago Cubs, becomes the first MVP winner from a last place team.

An independent baseball league, the Empire State League, based in Long Island, N.Y., hires Black managers for all four of its teams. Former major leaguers Paul Blair and George Scott, along with Bernardo Leonard and Brian Flood, nephew of Curt Flood become managers. League games are played at Long Island's Hofstra University. The league folds in 1988 after two weeks of play.

John Thompson of the Georgetown Hoyas is named United Press International's NCAA Coach of the Year.

Phil S. Dixon is the first Black man to issue a U.S. card set about the Negro Leagues. The *Negro League Greats* is a 45 postcard-size, black and white card set.

Tyrone "Muggsy" Bogues (from Wake Forest) at 5-foot-3, the smallest player in NBA history, is the 12th pick by the Charlotte Hornets. Bogues, along with Reggie Lewis (Northwestern, 22nd pick) and Reggie Williams (Georgetown, 4th pick) become the first trio of players from the same high school (Dunbar Poets, Baltimore, Md) to be picked in the first round of the draft in the same year.

Julius Erving becomes the first non-center to score 30,000 points. Dr. J's total includes points from his ABA days.

Charles Barkley, standing 6-foot-5, is the first player under six-foot-six and the shortest player to win an NBA rebounding title. He averages a career-high 14.6 rebounds per game during the 1986–87 season.

Michael Jordan becomes the first NBA player with more than 200 steals (236) and 100 blocked shots (125) in the same season. Jordan also averages a league leading 37.1 points per game.

Jerry Rice of the San Francisco 49ers becomes the first wide receiver to win the scoring title in several years.

Doug Williams is the first Black starting quarterback for the Washington Redskins.

Vince Evans is the first Black starting quarterback for the Oakland Raiders.

Tennessee Vols quarterback Tony Robinson joins the Washington Redskins as a replacement player. He leads the Redskins to a 13-7 victory of the Dallas Cowboys on Monday Night Football. It would be Robinson's only NFL appearance.

Don McPherson, Syracuse quarterback, wins the Maxwell Award and the Davey O'Brien National Quarterback Award.

Teddy Seymour becomes the first African American to sail around the world solo. In his 35-foot fiberglass boat, called the Love Song, Seymour starts sailing from his home port of St. Croix, makes 12 stops, and returns home a year and a half later.

1988

"We've already won! What were the chances of us making it beyond slavery?" – John Lee Hooker

The Civil Rights Restoration Act is passed, applying anti-discrimination laws to entire institutions and putting the "teeth" back in Title IX, a federal law granting females in high schools and colleges the right to equal opportunity in sports.

John Chaney Temple Owls basketball coach is named Coach of the Year by UPI, AP and the U.S. Basketball Writers' Association.

Skater Debi Thomas becomes the first African American female to earn a medal (bronze) in the Winter Olympic Games in Calgary. Thomas is later inducted into the U.S. Figure Skating Hall of Fame in February 2000. In 1997, she graduates from Northwestern Medical School and completes her orthopedic residency program at Charles Drew University in Los Angeles, Calif.

Kenny Monday becomes the first African American wrestler, competing in Seoul, South Korea, to win an Olympic gold medal.

Charles Lakes becomes the second African American gymnast to compete in the Olympics. Kenati Allen, in 1968, was the first. (Ron Galimore is the first African American selected for the Moscow Olympics, but he never competes because of the 1980 boycott.) At the Olympic trials, Lakes finishes first overall. In the Olympics he is the highest ranked American gymnast in the All-Around finals, where he finishes 19th.

Grant Fuhr of the Edmonton Oilers becomes the first Black goalie awarded the Vezina Trophy, given annually to the best goalkeeper by the general managers of NHL clubs.

Tony McKegney becomes the first African American hockey player to score 40 goals in a season, as a St. Louis Blues left wing and surpass 500 NHL career points.

Dirk Graham becomes the first African American captain of an NHL team, the Chicago Blackhawks.

Doug Williams is named MVP of Super Bowl XXII. He is the first African American quarterback to appear in a Super Bowl. Williams throws a record four touchdown passes in the Washington Redskins' 42-10 win over the Denver Broncos. News reporter Butch John asks the dubious question, "How long have you been a Black quarterback?" The intent according to John was, "It's obvious you've been a Black quarterback all your life. When did this really start mattering?"

Johnny Grier becomes the first African American referee in the NFL. Grier served as a field judge in the NFL for seven years before being promoted to referee.

Zina Garrison becomes the first African American to rank in the top 10 on the women's professional tennis tour.

Florence Griffith Joyner, or Flo-Jo, is the first American woman to break the 22-second barrier in the 200-meter dash with a time of 21.34.

Jackie Joyner-Kersee becomes the first woman to crack the 24-foot barrier in the Olympics with a long jump of 24 feet, 3.5 inches. She becomes the only woman to win a gold medal in a multi-event (heptathlon) and in a specialty event (long jump) in the same Olympics. Joyner-Kersee is the first female to win the *Sporting News'* Athlete of the Year award.

Michael Jordan becomes the first NBA player to win the MVP and Defensive Player of the Year awards in the same season.

Michael Jordan becomes the first NBA player to score more than 50 points twice in the same series, against Lenny Wilkens' Cleveland Cavaliers. He also becomes the first pro basketball player to appear on the front of a Wheaties cereal box.

Vivian Stringer, coach for the University of Iowa, wins the Women's Basketball Coaches Association's Coach of the Year Award.

Frank Robinson becomes the first African American manager of the Baltimore Orioles.

Eric Gregg is the home plate umpire for the first night game at Wrigley Field.

On Dr. Martin Luther King Jr's birthday, odds maker Jimmy "The Greek" Snyder responds to reporter Eddie Hotaling's question, about African Americans' alleged superiority in sports, "The slave owner would breed his big Black to his big woman so that he could have a big Black kid. That's where it all started." He adds, "If they take over coaching there's not going to be anything left for the White people." CBS fires Snyder from his $800,000-a-year job.

In college bowl games, 11 teams are led by Black quarterbacks: Terrence Jones (Tulane), Independence Bowl; Major Harris (West Virginia) Sun Bowl; James Jackson (Georgia) Liberty Bowl; Darnell Dickerson (Pittsburgh) Cotton Bowl; Don McPherson (Syracuse) Sugar Bowl; Bobby McAllister (Michigan State) Rose Bowl; Steve Taylor (Nebraska) Fiesta Bowl; Charles Thompson (Oklahoma) Orange Bowl and Demetrius Brown (Michigan) Hall of Fame Bowl.

With championships in the super middleweight and light heavyweight divisions, Sugar Ray Leonard becomes the first boxer to win titles in five divisions, a weight span of 28 pounds. He is also the welterweight (1979), junior middleweight (1981), and middleweight titleholder (1987).

1989

"No life will ever be great until it is dedicated and disciplined." – Peter C.B. Bynoe, NBA owner

Corrinne Tarver, a Georgia Bulldog, becomes the first Black female gymnast to win the NCAA all-around championship.

Andre Ware, of Houston University, becomes the first African American quarterback to win the Heisman Trophy.

Art Shell of the Los Angeles Raiders becomes the first African American head coach in the National Football League. He takes over for Mike Shanahan four games into the season. Later, in 1990, Shell is named Coach of the Year by the Maxwell Football Club, *Pro Football Weekly* and *UPI*.

Rodney Peete from USC becomes the first Black starting quarterback for the Detroit Lions.

Defensive End Reggie White of the Philadelphia Eagles wins the first Drumstick or Turkey Leg Award from John Madden for his play against the Detroit Lions.

Bertram M. Lee and Peter C.B. Bynoe sign an agreement to purchase NBA's Denver Nuggets for $54-$65 million. They become the first African Americans with a minority interest in a professional basketball team. Comsat Video Enterprises, a subsidiary of telecommunications company Comsat Corporation, purchases a majority 67.5 percent stake in the Nuggets, with the remaining 32.5 percent held by Lee and Bynoe. In 1992 Comsat Video assumes 100 percent ownership of the franchise.

For the first time in NBA history, five Blacks are named first team All-Stars; Charles Barkley (76ers), Magic Johnson (Lakers), Michael Jordan (Bulls), Karl Malone (Jazz) and Hakeem Olajuwon (Rockets).

The rock band Red Hot Chili Peppers release "Magic Johnson" the first rock & roll song about an NBA player.

Wade Houston becomes the first African American coach in the Southeastern Conference with the Tennessee Vols. In 1962, Houston was the first of three African Americans on the Louisville Cardinals basketball team. His son, Allan, plays for him at Tennessee and becomes the Vols' all-time leading scorer before enjoying a pro career with the Detroit Pistons and New York Knicks.

William "Pop" Gates of the New York Rens and Washington Bears, becomes the first non-NBA player inducted into the Naismith Memorial Basketball Hall of Fame.

The Wayman Tisdale Award is established by the USBWA to recognize an outstanding frosh collegiate basketball player. Guard Chris Jackson, later known as Mahmoud Abdul-Rauf, of LSU, is the first recipient.

Deion Sanders becomes the first athlete in the pro ranks to hit a home run, with the New York Yankees in the World Series, and score a touchdown (68-yard interception), with the Atlanta Falcons against the Los Angeles Rams, in the same week.

Bo Jackson becomes the first professional football player to win major league baseball's MVP in the All-Star game.

Frank Robinson of the Baltimore Orioles is the first African American named Manager of the Year.

Bill White becomes the first African American President of major league baseball's National League. His term lasted until 1994.

Cito Gaston becomes the first African American manager for the Toronto Blue Jays.

1990

Art Shell of the Los Angeles Raiders is named American Football Conference's Coach of the Year.

Bruce Perkins (from Arizona State) of the Tampa Bay Buccaneers and Derek Loville (Oregon) of the Seattle Seahawks become the first undrafted rookie running backs to start in week one of a season.

David Robinson of the San Antonio Spurs becomes the first NBA rookie to lead a playoff team in scoring. He averages 24.3 points, 12 rebounds and 3.9 blocks per game.

Georgetown basketball coach John Thompson stages a walkout in protest of the National Collegiate Athletic Association's Proposal 42. The NCAA's Proposal 48 sets minimum academic standards for incoming frosh athletes at 700 on the SAT and a 2.0 grade point average. Proposal 42 states that if an athlete does not meet the guidelines of Proposal 48, he or she must sit out the frosh season, leaving only three years of eligibility. Opponents argue Proposal 48's minimum test-score requirements are based on culturally biased standardized tests. The NCAA estimates that nine of every 10 athletes who fail to meet the requirements are Black. Thompson claims that Prop 42 exacerbates the injustice by denying many athletes from low-income families the opportunity to attend college.

Bernadette Locke, at the University of Kentucky, becomes the first Black and female assistant NCAA Division I Men's basketball coach.

Elaine C. Weddington becomes the first Black female assistant general manager in major league baseball with the Boston Red Sox.

Donna Marie Cheek becomes the first African American member of the U.S. Equestrian Team.

Houston University quarterback Andre Ware, the first African American quarterback to win the (1989) Heisman Trophy, is drafted in the seventh round by the Detroit Lions but fails to make the starting grade.

Houston Oilers QB Warren Moon passes for 527 yards against the Kansas City Chiefs. This is the most passing yardage in the NFL since the 1970 merger. The Oilers win 27-10.

Bo Jackson becomes the first athlete to play in the NFL's Pro Bowl and a major league All-Star game (back in 1989).

Ken Griffey Sr., 40, joins the Seattle Mariners and son Junior, 20, to form the first father-and-son combination since the Frank Duncan family appeared for the Monarchs 50 years earlier. Senior plays left field and bats second; Junior plays center and hits third. Both hit first-inning singles against the Kansas City Royals. Later in the year on Sept. 14. they hit back-to-back home runs off of California Angels' Kirk McCaskill, a first for a father-and-son duo.

The Negro Leagues Baseball Museum is founded in Kansas City, Mo., the first institution in America to honor Negro baseball players. It is founded by Horace Peterson, Phil S. Dixon, Bob Motley, Arrington B. Klice, Alfred "Slick" Surratt, John "Buck" O'Neil, Dewitt "Woody" Smallwood and Larry Lester. Treasurer Lester privately funds the museum in its embryonic years and serves as its research director until 1995.

Roseanne Barr sings the national anthem at a San Diego Padres game, by shouting out the lyrics off-key, making obscene gestures, grabbing her crotch and spitting on the pitcher's mound. Padres pitcher Eric Show said, "It's an insult. There are people who died for that song."

The first African Americans named to the International Boxing Hall of Fame are: Joe Gans (inventor of the jab), Jack Johnson, Muhammad Ali, Henry Armstrong, Ezzard Charles, Bob Foster, Joe Frazier, Joe Louis, Sugar Ray Robinson, Sandy Saddler, Jersey Joe Walcott, Archie Moore and Ike Williams.

The NFL withdraws its plans to hold the 1993 Super Bowl in Phoenix due to Arizona's refusal to honor Dr. Martin Luther King Jr.'s birthday as a state holiday.

Bill Pinkney becomes the first Black sailor to single-handedly circle the globe under the five southernmost capes. The 32,000-mile trek starts in Boston to Bermuda and then to the British Virgin Islands, Brazil, Cape Town, South Africa and across the Indian Ocean to Tasmania. Afterwards he sails across the South Pacific around Cape Horn to Uruguay before turning north again to Bermuda. Pinkney was inducted into the National Sailing Hall of Fame in 2021.

Jesse Owens becomes the first African American Olympian on a U.S. postage stamp. The 25-cent stamp is issued in a booklet honoring five Olympic gold medal champions. Owens is posthumously awarded the Congressional Gold Medal.

1991

"I'm sick and tired of being sick and tired." – Fannie Lou Hamer

Hal McRae becomes the first African American manager of the Kansas City Royals.

Willy T. Ribbs becomes the first African American driver to qualify for the Indy 500 with a burst of 217.358 miles per hour, the fastest on the final day of qualifying. A week later at the race, after six laps, Ribbs is forced to drop out due to engine failure.

Dirk Graham, as a Chicago Blackhawk, becomes the first African American to win the Frank J. Selke Trophy, awarded annually to the National Hockey League forward who demonstrates the most skill in the defensive component of the game.

The annual Bayou Classic between the Grambling State University Tigers and the Southern University Jaguars becomes the first black college football game with a national television contract (NBC). The series began in 1932 in Monroe, Louisiana, with the Jaguars victorious 20-0.

Sheryl Swoopes from South Plains Junior College (Texas) is named Junior College Player of the Year.

In the NBA Draft, the University of Nevada Las Vegas is represented by three first-round picks: Larry Johnson (1st pick), Stacey Augmon (9th pick) and Greg Anthony (12th pick). Each of these players chose to wear No. 2 in their rookie season to honor their college coach Jerry Tarkanian, who once wore No. 2.

Magic Johnson and Earl Graves, publisher of *Black Enterprise*, buy a Pepsi Cola bottling plant.

Terdema Ussery II becomes CEO of the Continental Basketball Association (CBA). He is the first African American to operate a professional sports league. Ussery's two-and-a-half-year term was highlighted by a rapid increase in franchise value and overall league-wide financial stability.

1991-92, Wayne Embry, with the Cleveland Cavaliers, is the first African American to be named NBA Executive of the Year by the *Sporting News*. Embry, Cavalier's president/chief operating officer wins the award again in 1999-2000.

Colorful Firsts in U.S. Sports

1992

"A person isn't educated unless he has learned how little he already knows."
– Thomas A. Fleming, national teacher of the year, 1992.

Jackie Joyner-Kersee becomes the first woman to win two Olympic gold medals in multi-event competition at the Barcelona Olympics.

Lighting Ned Mitchell creates the Women's World Basketball Association (WWBA) the first ever spring and summer women's professional basketball league. The original teams included the Kansas Crusaders, Iowa Unicorns, Illinois Knights, Nebraska Xpress, Missouri Mustangs and the Oklahoma Cougars. The league lasts three seasons, 1993 through 1995.

Despite retiring from the NBA, due to testing positive for HIV, Magic Johnson is selected to play in the NBA All-Star game. Johnson wins the MVP award, scoring a game-high 25 points with nine assists.

Lusia Harris-Stewart, three-time national champion with Delta State (Miss.) University and 1977 NBA draftee, is the first female basketball player selected to the Naismith Memorial Basketball Hall of Fame.

Dikembe Mutombo, a Congolese American, is fined several thousand dollars for wagging his index finger at NBA opponents after blocking their shots. The NBA rules that the gesture by the Denver Nugget center is taunting. The four-time NBA Defensive Player of the Year is inducted into the Naismith Memorial Basketball Hall of Fame in 2015. Mutombo's jersey is retired by the Nuggets the following year.

Dr. LeRoy Walker is unanimously elected president of the U.S. Olympic Committee, the first African American to hold the post.

Arthur Ashe, former Wimbledon and US Open champion, tells *USA Today* and *People* magazine, that "being Black is harder than living with AIDS." Ashe contracted AIDS from a tainted blood transfusion during heart surgery in 1988.

Craig Hodges of the Chicago Bulls wears a dashiki to the White House in celebration of the team's championship. He hands President George Bush a letter addressing the issues of racism and opposition of the Persian Gulf War. Hodges is released by the Bulls soon after and never plays in the NBA again. See 1996.

The first John Shippen Memorial Golf Tournament is held in Scotch Plains, N.J., at the Shackamaxon Country Club.

John F. Merchant becomes the first African American to sit on the executive committee of the USGA.

Dominique Dawes, known as "Awesome Dawesome" is the first American-born Black female gymnast on the U.S. Olympic team. Dawes wins a bronze medal in the team competition.

Betty Okino, born in Uganda, Africa, joins Dominique Dawes to become the first Black females to win Olympic gymnastics medals for the U.S. in Barcelona, Spain. Okino creates a move that bears her name, the "Okino," a triple pirouette on one leg on the balance beam. Okino later becomes a television and movie actress.

Randall Cunningham of the Philadelphia Eagles becomes the first African American quarterback named *Pro Football Weekly's* Comeback Player of the Year.

Emmitt Smith becomes the first NFL player to win the league's rushing title and the Super Bowl in the same season.

As manager of the Toronto Blue Jays, Cito Gaston becomes the first African American to win the World Series defeating the Atlanta Braves 4 games to 2.

Ken Griffey Jr. hits a home run in the major league All-Star game. His father Ken recorded a home run in the 1980 major league All-Star game, making them the first son-and-father to homer in All-Star competition.

Ron Simmons becomes the first African American to win the heavyweight World Wrestling Championship (WCW) title. Simmons is a former defensive tackle for the Cleveland Browns (NFL), Ottawa Rough Riders (CFL) and Tampa Bay Bandits (original USFL).

Anita DeFrantz becomes the first African American elected to the executive board on the International Olympic Committee.

Mike Powell leaps 29 feet, 4 ½ inches at the Barcelona Olympics, breaking Bob Beamon's 23-year old world mark (1968) by two inches.

Rod Barnes becomes the first African American head basketball coach at Ole Miss. After inheriting a losing program, the Rebels finish in first place of the Southeastern Conference for the 1996-97 and 1997-98 seasons. Barnes leaves the Rebels after the 1998 season with an 86-81 won-lost record to join the Arizona State Sun Devils.

1993

"After all, democracy takes place when the silenced find a voice, and when we begin to listen to what they have to say." – Lani Guinier

Arthur Ashe is posthumously presented with the Presidential Medal of Freedom by President Bill Clinton, the highest civilian award.

Bill Pickett becomes the first African American cowboy featured on a U.S. postage stamp.

Bo Jackson becomes the first major leaguer to play with an artificial hip. In his return, Jackson homers in the Chicago White Sox opener.

Two-time MLB All-Star Bob Watson is named general manager of the Houston Astros.

Curtis Pride, outfielder for the Montreal Expos, becomes the first deaf African American ball player in the re-integrated major leagues.

Don Baylor becomes the first African American manager of the Colorado Rockies.

Charlie Williams, 49, of the National League becomes the first African American to call balls and strikes in a World Series game. After 13 years as an umpire, he officiates in the marathon fourth game, a four-hour, 14-minute affair that sees the Toronto Blue Jays outlast the Philadelphia Phillies, 15-14.

Joe Louis becomes the first professional boxer to be honored on a U.S. postage stamp.

Quarterback Charlie Ward of Florida State wins the James E. Sullivan Award and the Heisman Trophy.

Manny Jackson becomes the first former Globetrotter to own the team and the first African American to own a major international sports franchise and entertainment organization in America.

The Kansas Crusaders, 10W-5L, become the first Women's Basketball Association (WBA) champion by beating the Nebraska Xpress 100-96. The WBA was originally named the WWBA or the Women's World Basketball Association founded by Lightning Ned Mitchell.

Sarah Campbell, formerly of Central High School in Kansas City and the University of Missouri, becomes the first MVP player in the newly formed Women's Basketball Association (WBA) as a member of the Missouri Mustangs.

Scott Burrell from Connecticut becomes the first basketball player in NCAA Division I-A to top 1500 points, 750 rebounds, 275 assists and 300 steals. Burrell is a first round pick of the NBA's Charlotte Hornets. In 1989, Burrell was a first round pick of the Seattle Mariners in the amateur baseball draft. He becomes the first athlete to be a first-round draftee in two different sports.

Shaquille O'Neal becomes the first NBA player to have a rap album, *Shaq Diesel*, to go platinum.

Dusty Baker of the San Francisco Giants is named Manager of the Year by the AP and the BBWAA. His 103 wins are the most by a rookie manager in National League history.

Emmitt Smith becomes the first running back to win a Super Bowl championship, the NFL's Most Valuable Player award, the NFL rushing crown, and the Super Bowl's Most Valuable Player award in the same season.

Writer Wendell Smith, former travel mate of Jackie Robinson, is the first African American recipient of the Spink Award, first conferred in 1962. Named for J.G. Taylor Spink, founder of *The Sporting News*, the award honors baseball writers for "meritorious contributions to baseball writing" and is presented at the HOF induction ceremonies.

George Branham III becomes the first African American bowler to win a PBA Triple Crown event when he beats Parker Bohn III, 227-214 in the Tournament of Champions.

Sande French becomes the first African American Chair Umpire to preside over a Grand Slam final. She referees the US Open women's singles final in a match between No. 1 Steffi Graft of Germany and Helena Sukova of the Czech Republic. Despite no controversial rulings, French is later demoted by Richard Kaufman of the ITF, for reasons unknown. In 2022, after 36 years of service, she is inducted into the Black Tennis Hall of Fame.

1994

"Of course, the aim of a constitutional democracy is to safeguard the rights of the minority and avoid the tyranny of the majority." – Cornel West

Cecil M. Hollins becomes the only African American Chair Umpire in the world with a gold badge which qualifies him to referee major tennis events.

Berry Gordy of the Motown sound is owner of "Powis Castle" in the Kentucky Derby. The horse finishes eighth.

Colorful Firsts in U.S. Sports

James "Cool Papa" Bell becomes the first former Negro Leaguer to have a street named after him. The first Mississippian to be inducted into the National Baseball Hall of Fame is honored in the city of Jackson.

Alcorn State QB Steve McNair wins the Walter Payton Award as the top player in Division I-AA.

Jeff Blake from East Carolina University becomes the first Black starting quarterback for the Cincinnati Bengals.

Warren Moon becomes the first African American quarterback to play for a Black head coach, Dennis Green, for the Minnesota Vikings. Moon is also the Vikings' first Black starting quarterback.

Deion Sanders becomes the first athlete to play in a Super Bowl (with Dallas Cowboys) and in the World Series (with the 1992 Atlanta Braves and the 1989 N.Y. Yankees).

Olympic decathlon athlete Rafer Johnson's brother James Earl "Jimmy" Johnson is selected to the National Football Hall of Fame. The five-time Pro Bowler was a wide receiver and cornerback for the San Francisco 49ers.

After announcing his intentions to play pro basketball, Florida State quarterback Charlie Ward becomes the first Heisman Trophy winner in 35 years not selected in the NFL draft. Charlie Ward is the first Heisman winner to be selected in the first round (26th pick) in the NBA draft by the New York Knicks.

Grant Fuhr becomes the first Black player to win the William M. Jennings Trophy, awarded to the goalie with a minimum of 25 games played with the fewest goals scored against him.

John Paris Jr. of Nova Scotia becomes the first African American head coach in pro hockey when he accepts the job with the Atlanta Knights of the International Hockey League.

Michael Moorer becomes the first southpaw heavyweight boxing champion when he defeats Evander Holyfield, gaining a majority decision.

George Foreman, 45, knocks out Michael Moorer to become the oldest heavyweight champion in history. Foreman wins the *Associated Press'* Athlete of the Year award.

Rubin "Hurricane" Carter, middleweight, becomes the first boxer to receive a championship belt outside the ring when he was awarded an honorary title after serving nearly 20 years in prison on a wrongful murder conviction.

Oklahoma State shooting guard John Starks is the first undrafted player selected to an NBA All-Star game.

North Carolina's Charlotte Smith, a 6-foot-0 leaper, becomes the second woman to dunk in a basketball game.

Former basketball guard Isiah Lord Thomas buys a nine percent interest in the Toronto Raptors for $11.25 million, becomes the first African American NBA owner.

Nolan Richardson coaches the Arkansas Razorbacks to victory over the Duke Blue Devils to win the NCAA basketball title. He becomes the first coach to win championships in the NJC, NIT and the NCAA.

Hakeem Olajuwon is the first player to win the NBA's Most Valuable Player, Finals MVP, and Defensive Player of the Year in the same season.

Dale Ellis of the Seattle SuperSonics becomes the first player to record 1,000 points on three-point shots.

DeGol Arena, a 3,500-seat multi-purpose facility is named in honor of former Saint Francis and three-time NBA All-Star Maurice Stokes in Loretto, Pa. It is home to the Saint Francis University Red Flash men's and women's basketball and volleyball teams.

1995

"Black people have never had the power to enforce racism, and so this is something that white America is going to have to work out themselves." – Spike Lee

Movie producer Spike Lee and his wife lawyer Tonya Lewis name their first child, a girl, Satchel, after Negro Leagues legend Leroy "Satchel" Paige.

Bob Watson is named general manager of the New York Yankees.

Albert Belle of the Cleveland Indians becomes the first major league player to hit 50 doubles and 50 home runs in the same season.

Josh Gibson, James Cool Papa Bell and Satchel Paige are featured on the front of a Wheaties cereal box.

Plaintiffs Sam and Elsie Jethroe file a class action lawsuit in U.S. District Court for the Western District of Pennsylvania contending that systemic racism prevented Sam Jethroe from gaining the requisite four qualifying years to receive a major league pension. The defendants included MLB Properties, MLB, the Office of the Commissioner of Baseball, MLB Players Association and the MLB Pension Fund. The major leagues moved to dismiss the suit on the grounds that the statute of limitations had expired. The suit was dismissed in October 1996.

In a game at Atlanta-Fulton County Stadium, umpire Charlie Williams calls balls and strikes with his nephew Lenny Webster, catching for the Philadelphia Phillies. The Phillies beat the Braves 3-1. At bat Webster goes 0-for-4. Pitchers for the Braves included John Smoltz (five innings), Brad Woodall (one 2/3), Steve Bedrosian (one), Mike Stanton (one) and Mark Wohlers (1/3). Pitchers for the Phillies included Mike Mimbs (six innings), Gene Harris (one), Norm Charlton (one) and Heathcliff Slocumb (one). The Brave pitchers gave up eight hits, six walks and struck out 11. The Philly pitchers gave up four hits, six walks and struck out six.

Tyrone "Muggsy" Bogues, Charlotte Hornets' guard, wins the first Court Vision Award in the NBA.

Sheryl Swoopes becomes the first woman to have her own signature basketball shoe called Air Swoopes by Nike. She would also have signature models: Air Swoopes II, Air Swoopes Zoom, Air Swoopes IV, Air Tuned Swoopes, Air Swoopes VI and Air Swoopes Premier.

Juwan Howard becomes the first NBA player to leave school early and still earn his degree with his graduating class. The University of Michigan grad majored in communications and minored in business.

Orlando "Hurricane" Antigua becomes the first Latino to play for the Harlem Globetrotters. His parents are of Puerto Rican and Dominican descent. He plays seven seasons with the Globetrotters.

The Sports Network creates the Buck Buchanan Award, presented annually to the most outstanding defensive player in the Division I Football Championship Subdivision (formerly Division I-AA) in college football. Dexter Coakley, a linebacker from Appalachian State University, is the first recipient.

Jim Brown becomes the first man to be inducted into the Halls of Fame for pro football (1971), college football (1995) and lacrosse (1983).

Ray Rhodes in his first season as head coach of the Philadelphia Eagles, becomes the first African American man named Coach of the Year by the *Associated Press* and the *Sporting News*.

Walter Payton becomes the first African American team owner in the Indy Car series. Payton partners with Dale Coyne in preparation for a race in Florida. The car bears Payton's jersey number 34.

Jeff Blake becomes the second African American quarterback, the seventh overall, to earn a maximum single-game passing rating of 158.3. Blake of the Cincinnati Bengals completes 18 of 22 passes for 275 yards and three touchdowns against the Pittsburgh Steelers. Vince Evans of the Chicago Bears was the first Black QB to achieve this rating in 1980.

Cheryl Daniels becomes the first African American to hold the national title in women's professional bowling by winning the U.S. Open Championship.

1996

"I think perhaps education doesn't do us much good unless it is mixed with sweat."

-- Barack Obama, *Dreams from My Father*

The American Basketball League (ABL) is founded. The women league's motto is "Real Basketball." The original teams include the Columbus Quest, Richmond Rage, Atlanta Glory, New England Blizzard, Colorado Xplosion, San José Lasers, Seattle Reign and the Portland Power. The league ceases operations in December 1998.

Allen Iverson, of Georgetown University, becomes the first collegiate basketball player to appear on the cover of *SLAM* magazine.

Alongside model Valeria Mazza in leopard-print bikinis, Tyra Banks becomes the first African American model on the cover of *Sports Illustrated*.

Michael Johnson becomes the first man to win gold medals in the 200 and 400 meters the same year, at the Atlanta Olympics, and the first African American track star on the front of a Wheaties cereal box.

Dominique Dawes becomes the first African American gymnast to win an individual Olympic event medal with her bronze on the floor exercise.

Aquil Hashim Abdullah becomes the first African American (with a Muslim name) to win the U.S. National Rowing Championship.

Jair Lynch is the first African American gymnast to medal (silver) on the parallel bars in the Olympic Games. The Lynch Skill on the horizontal bar, which is a Tkatchev drill with a half turn prior to the catch to a mixed el-grip and swing back up to handstand, is named in his honor.

MaliVai Washington becomes the first African American named to the U.S. Olympic tennis team.

Fred Whitfield becomes the first African American to win the World Championship of Calf Roping.

Colorful Firsts in U.S. Sports

Tyrone Willingham becomes the first African American coach to win a division A-1 bowl game, when his 7-5 Stanford Cardinals defeat the Michigan State Spartans in the Sun Bowl, 38-0.

The Alumni Bowl in Tuskegee, Alabama, is renamed Cleve L. Abbott Memorial Alumni Stadium with an estimated capacity of 10,000. Abbott died in 1955.

Barry Sanders becomes the first player to rush for 1,500 yards three years in a row with an NFL-best 1,553 yards.

Lawrence Taylor of the New York Giants becomes the first player unanimously selected as NFL's Defensive Player of the Year.

Bruce Smith of the Buffalo Bills joins Reggie White as the only two players to record at least 10 sacks in a season, 10 times.

Jerry Rice of the San Francisco 49ers becomes the first NFL receiver to catch 1,000 passes.

Muhammad Ali lights the Olympic torch at the Summer Olympic Games in Atlanta, Ga.

Tiger Woods rallies from five down to defeat Steve Scott in 38 holes at Pumpkin Ridge and becomes the first player to win three straight U.S. Amateur titles.

Roy Jones Jr. becomes the first man to play a pro basketball game (U.S. Basketball League) and fight for the world championship (IBF), as super middleweight, in the same day.

Tim Duncan, a center for Wake Forest Demon Deacons, leads the ACC in scoring, rebounding, field goal percentage, and blocked shots, becoming the first player in conference history to lead in all four categories. He is later named Most Valuable Player of the ACC Tournament.

Dennis Rodman of the Chicago Bulls becomes the first basketball player to make Mr. Blackwell's list of "Worse Dressed Women." Richard Blackwell calls Rodman a "unisex wreck."

Sheryl Swoopes and Rebecca Lobo are the first players to sign contracts with the Women's National Baseball Association (WNBA).

Brent Barry, son of Rick Barry, is the first White player to win an NBA Slam Dunk competition. The six-foot-six Barry from Oregon State representing the Los Angeles Clippers, beats out Michael Finley, Greg Minor, Jerry Stackhouse, Doug Christie and Darrell Armstrong in the finals.

Bob Watson, for the New York Yankees, is the first Black general manager to win a World Series.

Marge Schott, owner of the Cincinnati Reds, in an interview with ESPN states, "Hitler was good at the beginning" and that "he just went too far."

The Wilma Rudolph Courage Award is established Women's Sports Foundation to recognize a female athlete who exhibits extraordinary courage in athletic performance, overcomes adversity and makes significant contributions to sports. Jackie Joyner-Kersee is the first honoree.

1997

"You only know what you see / You don't understand what it takes to be me." – Jay-Z from *Lucky Me*

Yolanda Griffith is selected by the Long Beach Stingrays as the No. 1 pick overall in the American Basketball League draft. Griffith would later win gold medals at the 2000 Sydney and 2004 Athens Olympic Games.

Nikki McCray, a Columbus Quest guard, is voted the American Basketball League's first Most Valuable Player.

Crystal Robinson with the Colorado Xplosion of the women's American Basketball League is named its first Rookie of the Year.

Valerie Still with the Columbus Quest of the women's American Basketball League is named its first ABL Finals MVP.

The first team All-Stars of the American Basketball League are Black: Teresa Edwards (Atlanta Glory), Dawn Staley (Richmond Rage), Natalie Williams (Portland Power), Nikkie McCray (Columbus Quest) and Adrienne Goodson (Richmond Rage).

The Women's National Basketball Association (WNBA) starts play one season after the American Basketball League. The league motto is "Watch Me Work." The original eight teams were the Charlotte Sting, Cleveland Rockers, Houston Comets, New York Liberty, Los Angeles Sparks, Phoenix Mercury, Sacramento Monarchs and the Utah Starzz.

Cheryl Miller becomes the first Black coach and general manager for the Phoenix Mercury of the WNBA.

Tina Thompson, forward from USC, is the first overall pick in the inaugural WNBA collegiate draft, by the Houston Comets.

Denique Graves is the first WNBA player drafted from an HBCU, Howard University in Washington, District of Columbia. She was picked in the second round, 15th overall pick by the Sacramento Monarchs.

Maurice Smith, a Seattle native, defeats UFC heavyweight champion Mark Coleman at UFC 14 in Birmingham to become the first Black title holder. In the process, the world champion kickboxer becomes the first striker to ever defeat a championship wrestler of Coleman's stature.

From 1997 to 2002, the Eddie Robinson Classic kick-starts the football season. In 2002 the NCAA ended the allowance of an extra 12th game, thus effectively ending the Classics.

Barry Sanders of the Detroit Lions becomes the third player to rush for more than 2,000 yards in a season (2,053). Sanders also becomes the third running back with at least 200 carries to average more than six yards per carry (6.1). Jim Brown was the first in 1963; O.J. Simpson, the second in 1973. Sanders also sets an NFL record for most 100-yard games in season with 14 and becomes the first player to post two 80-yard TD runs in the same game. Sanders is the first player to rush for 1,500 yards four years in a row.

Marcus Allen is the first NFL player to gain more than 10,000 (12,243) rushing yards and 5,000 (5,411) receiving yards during his career.

Jason Sehorn starts at right cornerback for the New York Giants. Sehorn is the only White cornerback in the NFL going into the next millennium.

Mel Gray becomes the first NFL player to amass more than 10,000 in kickoff return yards. He retires this year with 10,250 career yards.

Self-proclaimed white supremacist attorney Richard Barrett sues the University of Mississippi over its ban on flagsticks at Ole Miss football games. Barrett contends that the ban interferes with free speech rights by keeping Confederate flags out of the stadium.

Deion Sanders becomes the first athlete to have a pass interception (for 15 return yards in Super Bowl XXIX with the 49ers); and a pass reception (47 yards in Super Bowl XXX with the Cowboys) in Super Bowl competition.

Cornerback Charles Woodson of the University of Michigan becomes the first defensive player to win the Heisman Trophy.

The first Black starting quarterback for the Seattle Seahawks, Warren Moon becomes the NFL's first player over 40 years old to run for a touchdown.

Chris Campbell, a former Olympian wrestler, is named executive director of the U.S. Amateur Boxing, Inc. Campbell is the first African American to hold this post with USA Boxing.

Goaltender Grant Fuhr becomes the first Black player to earn 20 shutouts in a season.

Dee Kantner and African American Violet Palmer become the first female officials in the NBA.

Tyra Banks becomes the first African American model or female athlete to ever have a solo appearance on the cover of *Sports Illustrated*. She had previously appeared with Valeria Mazza on the cover in 1996.

Teresa Weatherspoon becomes the first WNBA player to be named Defensive Player of the Week, averaging 21.5 ppg, 8.5 rpg, and 3.5 apg for the week ending 20 June 1997.

Dale Ellis of the Seattle SuperSonics becomes the first player to record 1,500 points on three-point shots.

Isiah Thomas sells his nine percent stake in the Toronto Raptors to majority owner Allan Slaight. Thomas had tried to buy out Slaight, but Slaight demanded $175 million for his 81% share. According to John Hall of J.P. Morgan, the Raptors are worth about $135 million. Thomas realizes a nifty 15% annualized return on his investment.

Dena Head, 26, is the first and oldest player selected in the WNBA's Elite Draft by the Utah Starzz.

Catcher Josh Gibson becomes the first former Negro League player to appear on the catalogue cover of *Christie's*, a New York auction house.

Tiger Woods becomes the first Thai American golfer to win the prestigious Masters Tournament, setting a course record with 270 strokes, winning by 12 strokes. Fuzzy Zoeller jokingly makes derogatory comments about Tiger Woods' possible ethnic menu of fried chicken, watermelon and collard greens at next year's Masters Tournament dinner. Kmart drops Zoeller as its spokesperson.

Jackie Robinson becomes the first athlete to appear on a Wheaties box, while also on Honey Frosted Wheaties and Crispy Wheaties 'n Raisins. Robinson also becomes the first African American featured on a gold coin by the U.S. Mint. The Mint commemorates Robinson's life by issuing silver $1 and gold $5 coins bearing his likeness.

Jackie Robinson becomes the first athlete to have his jersey number (42) retired in perpetuity. National League President Len Coleman initiates the mandate. The New York Yankees' player Mariano Rivera, who retired after the 2013 season, was the last active player to wear No. 42.

The Cleveland Indians' Albert Belle earns $10 million to become the first player whose salary exceeds that of an entire team, in this case, the Pittsburgh Pirates ($9,071,667).

Arthur Ashe becomes the first African American tennis player on the front of a Wheaties cereal box.

Arthur Ashe and Althea Gibson are remembered at the opening of the new Arthur Ashe Stadium in New York City. The 22,547-seat stadium was dedicated in Ashe's memory and on Gibson's 70th birthday.

Figure skater Mabel Fairbanks becomes the first African American coach inducted to the U.S. Figure Skating Hall of Fame.

Colorful Firsts in U.S. Sports

Myrtis Dightman, becomes the first living African American cowboy inducted into the National Cowboy Hall of Fame in Oklahoma City, Okla.

Florida Marlins catcher Charles Johnson goes the entire season without a fielding error, a record that will never be broken.

Jack Trice Stadium at Iowa State University becomes the first NCAA Division I, and thus far still the only stadium, named for an African American. John G. "Jack" Trice was the first African American athlete for Iowa State College. He died due to injuries suffered during a college football game against the University of Minnesota in Minneapolis on Oct. 6, 1923. Trice died from hemorrhaged lungs and internal bleeding because of the injuries sustained during the game. Many speculated that the injuries were intentionally inflicted by Gopher players. Prior to the re-naming, the venue was named Cyclone Stadium; the playing area was called Jack Trice Field.

Reneé Brown is the first person of color in the WNBA's front office. As Director of Player Personnel, Brown oversees all player recruitment and scouting for the league. Brown would retire in 2016, as WNBA Chief of Basketball Operation and Player Relations.

Ruthie Bolton-Holifield becomes the first to earn Player-of-the-Week honors in the WNBA.

Cynthia Cooper of the Houston Comets is voted the WNBA's first Most Valuable Player and the league's first scoring leader with 22.2 points per game.

Lisa Leslie of the Los Angeles Sparks is the first player to lead the WNBA in rebounds, 266, and the highest average rebounds per game at 9.5.

1998

"White fragility is not weakness per se. In fact, it is a powerful means of white racial control and the protection of white advantage." - Robin DiAngelo, *White Fragility*

Oscar Robertson is honored when the U.S. Basketball Writers Association renames its Player of the Year Award, the "Oscar Robertson Trophy."

Brevin Knight of the Cleveland Cavaliers becomes the first rookie to lead the NBA in steals.

Chamique Holdsclaw of the WNBA's New York Liberty becomes the first female on the cover of *SLAM* magazine.

Lisa Leslie is named USA Basketball Female Athlete of the Year

Natalie Williams is the only woman to lead the ABL in rebounding and scoring in the same year. Williams beats out Yolanda Griffith for the MVP award in the ABL's last year of record. She is the daughter of Robyn Gray and Nate Williams who played eight seasons in the NBA for the Cincinnati Royals, Kansas City Kings, New Orleans Jazz and Golden State Warriors.

Cynthia Cooper is named the MVP of the WNBA for the second consecutive season.

Tracy Reid of the Charlotte Sting wins the WNBA's first Rookie of the Year Award.

Marques Haynes becomes the first Harlem Globetrotter inducted into the Naismith Memorial Basketball Hall of Fame.

Tiger Woods becomes the first Black man to play in the Presidents Cup, a series of men's golf matches between a team representing the U.S. and an International Team representing the rest of the world minus Europe. Europe competes against the U.S. in a similar but considerably older event, the Ryder Cup.

Nike's first African American footwear designer, Wilson Smith III, releases the Women's Air Jordan.

Venus Williams' serve is measured at 125 mph at Wimbledon, the fastest recorded serve by a woman. At the Swisscom Challenge, Williams uncorks a 127 mph serve, a record in women's tennis.

Theodore "Ted" Corbitt, a marathon runner, is inducted into the inaugural class of the National Distance Running Hall of Fame, in Utica, N.Y.

Dirk Graham becomes the first African American head coach in the NHL with the Chicago Blackhawks.

Ansel Williamson becomes the second African American horse trainer inducted to the National Museum of Racing and Hall of Fame. Williamson trained "Aristides," the first Kentucky Derby winner (1875), as well as "Calvin," winner of the Belmont Stakes (1875).

Basketball guard Kobe Bryant, baseball shortstop Alex Rodríguez, football quarterback Kordell Stewart and hockey center Eric Lindros appear on the premier issue of *ESPN The Magazine*.

The Curt Flood Act of 1998 applied antitrust laws to the business of major league baseball, specifically for player employment, ending the antitrust exemption that had protected the sport since the Supreme Court case Federal Baseball Club of Baltimore. Although the Act did not directly create free agency, it overturned the baseball exemption to the Sherman Antitrust Act, allowing players to sue if they believed their employment was affected by unfair practices and directly enabling the free-agency system that later developed. This act did exactly what Flood wanted; it stopped owners from controlling the players' contracts and careers.

Barry Bonds becomes the first major league player to hit 400 home runs and steal 400 bases.

Bernie Williams, New York Yankees outfielder, becomes the first player to win a Gold Glove, a batting title and a World Series ring in the same season.

Terrell Davis for the Denver Broncos rushes for 2,008 yards in 392 attempts, averaging 5.12 yards per carry. He is the fourth player to rush for more than 2,000 yards.

Randall Cunningham, with the Minnesota Vikings, becomes the first African American to lead the NFL in passing with a ranking of 106.0.

Earvin "Magic" Johnson from Cathedral High School in Los Angeles sets a national high school record with eight receiving touchdown catches in one game.

Minnesota Viking defensive end John Randle is fined $5,000 for wearing face paint on Monday Night Football against the Green Bay Packers.

Jerry Rice of the San Francisco 49ers becomes the first non-kicker to score 1,000 points.

Arizona Cardinals fullback Larry Centers becomes the first running back to catch more than 100 passes in a season.

1999

A record six African American quarterbacks are drafted by NFL teams: Akili Smith (Oregon State), Donovan McNabb (Syracuse), Aaron Brooks (Virginia), Michael Bishop (K-State), Shaun King (Tulane), and Daunte Culpepper (Central Florida). McNabb, Smith and Culpepper are taken in the first round, a record. Overall, only four Black QB's had been taken in the first round in the first 63 years of the NFL.

Barry Sanders retires from football. He is the first running back to rush for 1,000 yards in 10 consecutive seasons.

Tony Banks from Michigan State University becomes the first Black starting quarterback for the Baltimore Ravens.

The Green Bay Packers become the first NFL team to hire three Black men at the top three coaching positions. Ray Rhodes is head coach, followed by Sherman Lewis, offensive coordinator, and Emmitt Thomas, defensive coordinator.

Emmitt Smith of the Dallas Cowboys against the Atlanta Falcons becomes the first player to rush for 2,000 yards on Monday Night Football games.

Terrence Wilkins of the Indianapolis Colts becomes the first undrafted rookie to accumulate more than 2,000 yards in a season with 1,134 kickoff, 388 punt, 565 receiving and two rushing yards, for a total of 2,089 yards.

The NFL Man of the Year Award is renamed the Walter Payton NFL Man of the Year Award. It recognizes excellence off the field regarding an NFL player's charity work.

Tiger Woods becomes the first PGA golfer to earn more than $4 million, $5 million, $6 million in prize money in a year. He finished at $6.6 million, shattering the record $2.6 million earned by David Duval the previous year. Woods wins four tournaments in a row and nine overall. He did not miss a cut, and he records the lowest adjusted scoring average (68.43) to win his first Vardon Trophy. The previous record was 68.81 set by Greg Norman in 1994. The accomplishments culminate in Woods being named the first Black recipient of the PGA Player of the Year award.

Allen Iverson, at six feet tall, becomes the shortest player in NBA history to lead the league in scoring with a 26.8 per game average. Iverson is also the first baller to appear on *SLAM* magazine with jewelry -- a necklace, watch, bracelet and ring, in a throwback Philadelphia 76ers jersey.

Sylvia Crawley of the Colorado Xplosion, paces off 10 steps, puts on a blindfold and dunks a basketball during the first ever women's dunk contest during the American Basketball League's second All-Star game.

Angelo Argea, known for his gray afro and as a caddie for Jack Nicklaus, is inducted into the PCA Worldwide Caddie Hall of Fame. Argea's first major victory with Nicklaus was at the PGA Championship in 1975. Their last major victory together was the 1980 U.S. Open at Baltusrol. They would win 40 tournaments together.

Bethune-Cookman College, an HBCU, wins the National Minority College Golf Championship in Port St. Lucie, Fla. The team, which wins by 28 strokes, is composed entirely of White players recruited from abroad. "The rules say your college must be made up of a majority of minorities, not your team," says golf coach Gary Freeman.

Maurice Greene runs the 100-meter dash in 9.79 seconds, in Athens, Greece, to beat Canadian Donovan Bailey's record by 0.05 seconds. He is the first man to break the 9.80 barrier in the 100-meter dash. Greene also becomes the first man to hold the 50-meter, the 60-meter, and the 100-meter records simultaneously.

Colorful Firsts in U.S. Sports

Devean George of Augsburg, Minn., becomes the first player from a Division III school to be drafted in the first round of the NBA draft. George is the 23rd pick of the draft by the Los Angeles Lakers.

Duke University becomes the first college to have four players drafted in the first round of the NBA draft. Elton Brand, No. 1 pick by Chicago; Trajan Langdon, No. 11 pick by Cleveland; Corey Maggette, No. 13 pick by Seattle; and William Avery, No. 14 pick by Minnesota. Despite their wealth of potential pro talent, UConn defeats them in the NCAA championship game, led by Richard Hamilton.

Lusia Harris-Stewart and Cheryl Miller are among the original inductees into the Women's Basketball Hall of Fame in Knoxville, Tenn.

Carolyn Peck, Purdue basketball coach, is named winner of the John & Nellie Wooden Award, Big 10 Coach of the Year and the *Associated Press'* Coach of the Year. This year she becomes the first African American coach to win the NCAA women's basketball championship.

Chamique Holdsclaw becomes the first female basketball player to be named recipient of the James E. Sullivan Memorial Award given annually to the top amateur athlete in the country.

Chamique Holdsclaw is the number one pick in the WNBA draft by the Washington Mystics, as 35 former ABL players are selected. Yolanda Griffith is picked second by Sacramento Monarchs, while Natalie Williams is picked third by the Utah Starzz. Holdsclaw is the WNBA's first Rookie of the Year to have played in its All-Star game.

Yolanda Griffith becomes the first player to win the "Defensive Player on the Year" award in both the ABL and the WNBA. In 1998, Griffith wins the award in the ABL.

Former ABL star Yolanda Griffith is the first WNBA player to be named MVP, Defensive Player of the Year, and Newcomer of the Year, in the same season. Griffith led the league in rebounds (11.3), and steals (2.52), and finished second in scoring (18.8).

Cynthia Cooper becomes the first player to score 1,000 points in the WNBA.

Sheryl Swoopes of the Houston Comets records the first triple-double in WNBA history. Swoopes gets 14 points, 15 rebounds and 10 assists in the Comets win over the Detroit Shock.

Nikki McCray, scoring guard for the Washington Mystics, becomes the first woman to receive a signature shoe with Fila, called the Nikki Delta.

Lisa Leslie scores 13 points and is named MVP of the first WNBA All-Star game. It is played before a sell-out crowd of 18,649, at Madison Square Garden in New York City. Whitney Houston sings the national anthem.

Michael Jordan withdraws his offer to buy 50% of the Charlotte Hornets, when owner George Shinn declines to give Jordan some controlling interests.

Former Detroit Piston guard and Toronto Raptors executive Isiah Thomas buys the CBA (Continental Basketball Association) for $10 million. In 2001, the league is forced into bankruptcy and folds.

The Harlem Globetrotters become the first team to receive the prestigious John W. Bunn Lifetime Achievement Award from the Naismith Memorial Basketball Hall of Fame in Springfield, MA.

Hakeem Olajuwon becomes the first NBA player to reach 2,000 steals and 2,000 blocked shots.

In the Australian Open, Venus Williams is penalized a point while serving to Lindsay Davenport, when beads fall from her braids. Williams notes, "I've never had such treatment before from any other umpire or any other match." Davenport counters, "Well, you can hear them and see them a little bit. Fortunately, you learn to play the ball. I'm not going to say it was a total distraction, but it is a little annoying maybe." The number one seed Davenport defeats fifth seed Williams in the quarterfinals, 6-4 and 6-0.

Venus and Serena Williams compete in the first all-sister final of this century in the Lipton Championship in Key Biscayne, Fla. Venus defeats younger sis Serena 6-4, 4-6, 6-4.

Alexandra Stevenson, 18, becomes the first "qualifier" in Wimbledon history to reach the women's semifinals by defeating Jelena Dokic, 6-3, 1-6, 6-3.

Tennis great Arthur Ashe and Paul Robeson, who earned 12 varsity letters at Rutgers, are among the first 20 electees to the International Scholar-Athlete Hall of Fame in Kingston, R.I.

Laila Ali, 21, daughter of Muhammad, announces her decision to fight professionally. At 5-foot-10 and 160 pounds she will fight in the middleweight class. Ali wins her first fight with a knockout in the first round.

After more than 27 years, the Boston Celtics hold a public ceremony to retire jersey No. 6 of Hall of Fame center Bill Russell. Back in 1972, a private ceremony was held to retire his jersey because of the fear of racial repercussions in predominantly white Boston.

On the 25th anniversary of Hank Aaron breaking Babe Ruth's lifetime home run mark, Commissioner Bud Selig announces the creation of the Hank Aaron Award. The award is a tribute to the best all-around player based on combined number of hits, home runs and RBIs. The honor is the first "official" award named after a former player still living. The initial recipients are Latin Americans Sammy Sosa (Cubs) and Manny Ramirez (Indians).

Fox television features Josh Gibson as an alien in their X-Files series, "The Unnatural" in April. Agents Sculley and Moulder find that he hit 61 home runs in 1947. Fact or fiction, Josh was unlike any slugging species before or after him. As the show reputes, "That Truth is Out There!"

Michael Vick of Virginia Tech becomes the first frosh quarterback to lead the nation in passing, completing 59% of his passes and throwing 12 TDs with five interceptions. His efficiency rating is 180.4. Vick also becomes the first player in Division I history to win a conference's Player of the Year Award (offensive, defensive or special teams) in the same season he is named Rookie of the Year.

Fred Whitfield of Hockley, Texas becomes the first African American to win the All-Around Cowboy World Championships, hosted by the Professional Rodeo Cowboys Association, considered the most prestigious PRCA award for multi-event cowboys. Whitfield wins his fourth calf roping title in the Las Vegas Rodeo.

2000

"If the majority knew of the root of this evil,
then the road to its cure would not be long." – Albert Einstein

Jevon Kearse of the Tennessee Titans, known as "The Freak," becomes the first NFL rookie to record more than 15 sacks (15½) in regular season (1999) and in playoff games (2000).

Tennessee Titans running back Eddie George is the first African American to appear solo on the cover of the *Madden NFL* videogame. George is a four-time pro bowler.

Warren Moon is the first Black starting quarterback in Kansas City Chiefs franchise history.

Jeff Blake becomes the first Black starting quarterback for the New Orleans Saints.

Aaron Gibson from the University of Wisconsin is the first NFL player to weigh over 400 pounds. The six-foot-seven offensive tackle bench presses 475 pounds and has a 31.5 inch vertical jump. Gibson can also dunk a basketball and do the splits.

Marlon St. Julien, an equestrian professional in Thoroughbred horse racing, becomes the first African American jockey to ride in the Kentucky Derby in 79 years, when he rides "Curule" to a seventh-place finish.

Jarome Iginla, the son of a Nigerian immigrant to Canada, is the first Black player in NHL history to be named Player of the Month. Iginla has 10 goals in 12 games for the Calgary Flames in February.

Goaltender Grant Fuhr becomes the first Black player to earn more than 400 NHL wins.

Sean Elliott of the San Antonio Spurs becomes the first professional athlete to return to play after a kidney transplant.

Cynthia Cooper is the first person in WNBA history to score 500, 1,000, 2,000 and 2,500 career points.

Vivian Stringer takes her Rutgers Scarlet Knights to the NCAA Final Four, becoming the first coach in either men's or women's collegiate basketball to take three different schools to the Final Four. In 1972, she took Cheyney State, an historically Black college outside of Philadelphia, to the Final Four. In 1993, she led the University of Iowa Hawkeyes to a Final Four appearance.

Tennessee's Michelle Snow, a 6-foot-5 center, becomes the third woman to dunk in a collegiate game. She repeats the feat in 2001 and 2003. Snow later plays for the WNBA's Houston Comets.

Glenn "Doc" Rivers, coach of the Orlando Magic, becomes the first coach in NBA history to win the Red Auerbach Trophy (Coach of the Year) without his team going to the playoffs. The Magic finish with a surprising 41-41 won-lost record. Rivers gets 60 votes to beat Phil Jackson of the LA Lakers with 53 votes. Other vote-getters include Paul Silas (Charlotte) with three, Jerry Sloan (Utah) with two and Pat Riley (Miami), Scott Skiles (Phoenix) and Butch Carter (Toronto) with one vote each for the award first given in 1963.

Harlem Globetrotter Michael "Wild Thing" Wilson becomes the first human to dunk a basketball on a 12-foot goal. The 6-foot-6 Wilson records the feat at the Ocean Spray NABC Roundball Challenge in Indianapolis, Ind.

Wilt Chamberlain becomes the first former Harlem Globetrotter to have his jersey number retired, #13.

Sam Perkins of the Indiana Pacers wears a do-rag during a preseason game. The NBA identifies the head scarf as a potential safety hazard and bans it.

Rickey Henderson of the Seattle Mariners becomes the third player and first non-slugger to record 2,000 career walks. The other

Colorful Firsts in U.S. Sports

sluggers are Ted Williams and Babe Ruth.

After more than 40 years after the retirement of Jackie Robinson in 1957, the Chicago Cubs hires its first Black manager, Don Baylor. Baylor manages a 65-97 won-lost record for the last place Cubs in the Central Division.

Davey Lopes becomes the Milwaukee Brewers first African American manager.

Jerry Manuel of the Chicago White Sox and Dusty Baker of the San Francisco Giants become the first African American managers from each league to be named Manager of the Year, in the same year. Baker becomes the first African American manager to win the NL award three times.

Ken Williams becomes the first African American general manager in the Chicago White Sox's 100-year history.

Derek Jeter of the New York Yankees becomes the first player to win the All-Star Game MVP and the World Series MVP awards in the same season.

Kim Perrot, No. 10, formerly of the Houston Comets, becomes the first WNBA player to have her jersey retired. The league names its sportsmanship award for her after Perrot dies of lung cancer in 1999. She is the first active WNBA player to die.

The John McLendon Minority Postgraduate Scholarship Program is announced. The scholarships are presented to minority senior students pursuing a graduate degree in athletics administration. The initial six recipients (three men and three women) each received a $5,000 grant. The program is administered by the NACDA (National Association of Collegiate Directors of Athletics) Foundation.

The CIAA (Central Intercollegiate Athletic Association) Hall of Fame, started in 1967, is renamed the John B. McLendon Hall of Fame.

In its 100th year, Tiger Woods by 15 shots becomes the first Black golfer to win the U.S. Open at Pebble Beach Golf Links. He becomes the first golfer to win the U.S. Junior Amateur, U.S. Amateur and the U.S. Open.

Tiger Woods becomes the first Black golfer to win Golf's Triple Crown: The British, U.S. and Canadian Open tournaments. For his accomplishments, he becomes the first athlete to win *Sports Illustrated*'s Sportsman of the Year Award twice, winning also in 1996. For the year, Woods posts a record 67.79 adjusted stroke average, breaking his 1999 record of 68.43.

Venus and Serena Williams become the first sisters to win Wimbledon's doubles crown, beating Ai Sugiyama and Julia Halard-Decugis in straight sets, 6-3, 6-2.

Serena Williams, 17, becomes the first African American to have won the singles (1999), doubles and mixed championships at the US Open.

Venus Williams wins the US Open, defeating Lindsay Davenport. Venus, along with Serena (1999 US Open Champion) become the first sisters to win the tournament.

Barry Larkin becomes the first major league shortstop to record 2,000 hits, 170 homers and 350 steals.

Marion Jones becomes the first woman to win five medals (three gold and two bronze) in the Olympics at the Sydney games.

Alvin & Calvin Harrison become the first twins to win gold medals when they win the 4 x 400 relay with Michael Johnson and Antonio Pettigrew at the Sydney Olympics.

At the Olympic Trials, the Clark Team of baby sister Hazel Clark, sister-in-law Jearl Miles Clark and older sister Joetta Clark sweep the three qualifying positions for the 800 meters event.

For the first time, no player from an HBCU is drafted by an NFL team.

James Hasty is the only NFL player with more than 40 career interceptions and 20 career fumble recoveries with the New York Jets, Kansas City Chiefs and Oakland Raiders.

On October 9, coaches Dennis Green of the Minnesota Vikings and Tony Dungy of the Tampa Bay Buccaneers, with quarterbacks Daunte Culpepper and Shaun King on Monday Night Football, in Minn., become the first teams with African American coaches and African American quarterbacks to face-off. The Vikings win.

Darrell Green of the Washington Redskins becomes the first NFL player over 40 years old to run a sub 4.3 in the 40-yard dash in a record time of 4.24 seconds.

Mike Anderson of the Denver Broncos becomes the first NFL rookie to rush for more 250 yards in a game. Anderson rushes for 251 yards in 37 attempts against the New Orleans Saints.

Terrell Owens of the San Francisco 49ers becomes the first NFL receiver to catch 20 passes in a game. He totals 283 receiving yards against the Chicago Bears.

John Register, with a running prosthesis, wins a silver medal in the long jump at the Sydney Paralympic Games. He also competes in the 100- and 200-meter races.

Anthony Ervin becomes the first U.S. citizen of African descent to medal gold in an individual Olympic swimming event. He wins two medals in the Sydney Olympics: a gold in the 50-meter freestyle, and a silver in the 4x100-meter freestyle relay. Ervin is of Ashkenazi Jewish descent on his mother's side and African American descent on his father's. Ervin has described himself as a "practicing Zen Buddhist." In July 2017 he said: "I'm proud to be a Jew."

Mack Robinson becomes the first Olympic silver medalist (200-meters, 1936 Berlin Olympics) to have a post office named in his honor, the Matthew "Mack" Robinson Post Office in Pasadena, California.

DeWayne Minor becomes the first African American to drive in the Hambletonian at the Meadowlands, N.J., the most prestigious harness race in America.

2001

Tiger Woods wins his second Masters Tournament. In the process he becomes the first golfer to win four consecutive majors, the U.S. Open, British Open, PGA Championship and the Masters.

Tennis star Althea Gibson becomes the first African American female to appear on the front of a Wheaties cereal box.

Jay Sharrers becomes the first Black referee to officiate an NHL game. He worked his first game as an NHL ref when the Philadelphia Flyers faced the visiting Florida Panthers.

Wrestler Toccara Montgomery becomes the first African American woman to win a medal at the World Championships with a silver medal.

Greg Gumbel becomes the first Black *play-by-play* announcer to call a major U.S. sports championship, the Super Bowl. The Baltimore Ravens meet the New York Giants. He also calls the 2004 Super Bowl marred by Janet Jackson's so-called wardrobe malfunction during the halftime show.

Claudia Perry becomes the first female and first Black president of the Society for American Baseball Research's Board of Directors. Ms. Perry appeared on *Jeopardy's Tournament of Champions* (1998), *Million Dollar Masters* (2002) and *Battle of the Decades* (2014). She also appeared on ABC's *500 Questions* (2016) and *Who Wants to Be a Millionaire?* (2018).

Lloyd McClendon with the Pittsburgh Pirates and Hal McRae with the Tampa Bay Devil Rays become those clubs' first African American managers. (Some sources credit Gene Baker as the first Black manager in the American or National leagues, citing a Sept. 21, 1963, game in which he took over as Pirates skipper for two innings after the ejection of Danny Murtaugh.)

Michael Vick from Virginia Tech becomes the first African American quarterback to be the number one overall pick in the NFL draft, when selected by the Atlanta Falcons. He is the first Black starting quarterback for the Atlanta franchise.

Reggie Miller of the Indiana Pacers becomes the first player to score more than 2,000 points with three pointers.

Shaquille O'Neal becomes the first athlete to have an automobile named after him, the Ford Shaq SST Expedition. His name appears on a limited 500 SUVs.

Dime magazine, a "basketball lifestyle" publication covering not only the sport but the off-court lives and lifestyles of its athletes and personalities, makes its debut with Allen Iverson of the Philadelphia 76ers on the cover.

A mourning Allen Iverson, after the fatal shooting of his best friend, Rahsaan Langeford, explains to media why he took a burritos break during a team practice, "We sitting in here -- I'm supposed to be the franchise player, and we in here talking about practice. I mean, listen: We talking about practice. Not a game. Not a game. Not a game. We talking about practice. Not a game. Not the game that I go out there and die for and play every game like it's my last. Not the game. We talking about practice, man."

Two all-Black teams are voted to start the NBA All-Star game. However, due to injuries to Grant Hill, Shaquille O'Neal among others, non-Black players are selected to replace them.

Laila Ali and Jacqueline Frazier-Lyde become the first women featured as the main event for a pay-for-view boxing match. This is the first time in boxing history, daughters of former heavyweight champions will fight.

Kwame Brown becomes the first high school basketball player drafted as the number one overall pick when he is selected by the Washington Wizards. Brown is from Brunswick (Ga.) Glynn Academy.

Lisa Leslie becomes the first WNBA player to be named League MVP, All-Star MVP and Play-off MVP in the same season.

Stephanie Ready is named the first woman to coach in men's professional sports, as assistant coach for the Greenville Groove of the National Basketball Development League (NBDL), the NBA's new minor league.

Warren Moon becomes the first African American quarterback inducted into the Canadian Football Hall of Fame.

Jerry Rice becomes the first NFL player to compile more than 20,000 yards receiving.

Shani Davis, 19, becomes the first African American to make the U.S. Olympic speedskating team. Davis qualifies for the team by winning the 1,000-meter short-track final at the Olympic Trials in Kearns, Utah.

Colorful Firsts in U.S. Sports

2002

"Trying to sneak a fastball past Hank Aaron is like trying to sneak the sunrise past a rooster." – Joe Adcock, teammate

Hank Aaron is presented with the Presidential Medal of Freedom by President George W. Bush, the highest civilian award.

Vonetta Flowers becomes the first African American to win a gold medal at the Winter Olympics. She teams with Jill Bakken to win the women's bobsled competition in Salt Lake City. Soon after, African American men, Randy Jones, Garrett Hines and Bill Schuffenhauer win the silver in the four-man bobsled. Four years later, speedskater Shani Davis would become the first African American athlete to win an individual gold medal.

Dremiel Byers becomes the first African American to win a Greco-Roman world championship gold medal, capturing the title in the heavyweight division in Moscow.

Shenea Booth (with her partner Arthur Davis) becomes the first Black in the Acro Mixed Pairs to win the Sports Acrobatics World Championship in Riesa, Germany. Two years later, the duo returned to defend their title in Liévin, France. They earned the "Most Difficult Skill" award in both world appearances and were inducted into the USAG Hall of Fame in 2009.

Venus Williams becomes the first African American woman to rank World No. 1 since the Women's Tennis Association (WTA) computer rankings began in 1975.

Jarome Iginla becomes the first Black man to win a gold medal at the Winter Olympics and the first Black player to surpass 50 goals in an NHL season. He is also the first Black player to win the NHL's scoring crown, earning the Rocket Richard Trophy. Iginla is also the first Black player to win the Art Ross Trophy and the Lester B. Pearson Award, as the NHL's Most Valuable Player.

Jim Thorpe becomes the second African American golfer to win a senior major when he wins the Countrywide Tradition in Superstition Mountain, Ariz., outside of Phoenix.

Serena Williams defeats older sister Venus in the French Open, 7-5 and 6-3. They become the first sisters to be ranked No. 2 and No. 1, respectively.

The Williams sisters Venus and Serena become the first siblings to compete in the Wimbledon final since 1900. Serena defeats Venus, 7-6 (7-4), 6-3. Sisters Maud and Lillian Watson from London first played their match in 1884.

The NBA Expansion committee approves an expansion franchise for the city of Charlotte to be owned and operation by Robert L. Johnson, former owner of BET. In 2000, Johnson sold BET to Viacom, Inc., for $3 billion.

Sebastian Telfair from Abraham Lincoln High School in Brooklyn, N.Y., and LeBron James from St. Vincent-St. Mary High School in Akron, Ohio, are the first high school basketball players to appear on the cover of *SLAM* magazine.

Jerry Stackhouse wins the first Bob Lanier Community Assist Award for community engagement, philanthropic activity and charity work. This is a monthly award. The winner of the award is presented with a plaque dedicated to NBA Hall of Famer David Robinson.

The U.S. Sports Academy creates the C. Vivian Stringer Coaching Award, presented annually to a woman for outstanding achievement as a coach.

Lisa Leslie, (6-foot-5) of the Los Angeles Sparks, becomes the first WNBA player to dunk in a professional game, playing against the Miami Sol.

The Harlem Globetrotters are inducted into the Naismith Memorial Basketball Hall of Fame as a team. The New York Rens were inducted in 1963.

Renal Brooks-Moon for the San Francisco Giants becomes the first African American woman to serve a major league team as a public-address announcer. She also becomes the first Black woman to perform this function in the World Series against the Anaheim Angels.

Rodney Peete from USC is the first Black starting quarterback for the Carolina Panthers.

Ray Lucas from Rutgers University becomes the first Black starting quarterback for the Miami Dolphins, after an injury to Jay Fiedler.

Jerry Rice, 40, becomes the first NFL player to score 200 career touchdowns.

Three-time pro bowler Daunte Culpepper is the first Black quarterback to appear on the cover of *Madden NFL* sports game.

David Garrard from East Carolina University is the first Black starting quarterback for the Jacksonville Jaguars.

Barry Bonds wins his fifth MVP award by unanimous vote from the Baseball Writers' Association of America (BBWAA). Bonds is the first person to win the award consecutively, twice. In 1992 and 1993, and again in 2001 and 2002.

Tim Raines retires after 24 seasons in the major leagues. He is the only player in league history with at least 100 triples, 150 home runs and 600 stolen bases.

Ulice Payne becomes the first African American president of a major league baseball club, the Milwaukee Brewers, when Bud Selig names him as successor to daughter Wendy Selig-Prieb.

Frank Robinson becomes the first Black manager of the Montreal Expos.

Ken Harvey becomes the first awardee of the Joe Black Trophy, given to the MVP player of the Arizona Fall League (AFL). Harvey receives 15 of 18 votes from AFL managers and coaches.

MLB's Futures Games Most Valuable Player Award presented at its annual All-Star Game is renamed the Larry Doby Award.

Fred Whitfield becomes the first African American to win rodeo's coveted U.S. Smokeless Tobacco Company Cup Series for all-around performance.

Jacqueline Frazier-Lyde beats Suzette Taylor to win the Women's International Boxing Association (WIBA) light heavyweight title. As the daughter of Smokin' Joe Frazier, the two become the first father and daughter to hold boxing titles.

Ozzie Newsome becomes the first Black general manager in the NFL with the Baltimore Ravens.

Annice Canady becomes the first female official to work an NCAA Division I football game.

Michael Vick of the Atlanta Falcons becomes the first quarterback to rush for more than 150 yards in a game, against the Minnesota Vikings, compiling 173 yards on 10 carries. His average of 17.3 yards per carry eclipses running back Marion Motley's 17.09 (11 carries) set in 1950.

Tyrone Willingham becomes the first college football coach to receive the *Sporting News'* Sportsman of the Year award.

As head coach of the San José SaberCats, Darren Arbet is the first African American in the Arena Football League to win the Arena Bowl.

T.J. Ford of the Texas Longhorns becomes the first frosh to lead the NCAA in assists with 8.27 per game average. The 5-foot-10 guard wins the Naismith Award the following year.

2003
"No one can figure out your worth but you." – Pearl Bailey

Roberto Clemente is posthumously presented with the Presidential Medal of Freedom by President George W. Bush, the highest civilian award.

Serena Williams becomes the first African American to capture all four major tennis championships, winning the French, Wimbledon, US Open and Australian Open.

Keeth Smart becomes the first African American fencer to be ranked No. 1 in the world.

Regina Jacobs becomes the first woman to break the 4:00 barrier in the "indoor mile." Jacobs runs a 3:59:98 competing in the 1,500 meters at the Boston Indoor Games.

Teresa Phillips, Tennessee State University athletic director, becomes the first woman to coach a men's Division I college basketball team. Phillips suspends interim coach Hosea Lewis for one game and announces she will coach the Tigers against Austin Peay in Clarksville, Tenn.

Michael Jordan of the Washington Wizards becomes the first NBA player 40 or older to score 40 or more points. Jordan scores 43, hitting 18 of 30 field goals and 7 of 8 free throws against the New Jersey Nets.

Bob Johnson, former owner of Black Entertainment Television (BET), becomes the first African American majority owner of an NBA basketball team, the Charlotte Hornets. According to *Forbes* magazine, he becomes the first African American billionaire in 2001. *Sports Illustrated* names Bob Johnson No. 1 on its list of 101 Most Influential Minorities in Sports.

Amar'e Stoudemire for the Phoenix Suns becomes the first NBA Rookie of the Year to come directly from high school.

Detroit Pistons defensive specialist Ben Wallace, a product of Cuyahoga Community College and Virginia Union, is the first undrafted NBA player selected to its All-Star game, as a starter.

Michelle Carter sets a national high school record in the girls shot put (8 pounds) with a toss of 54 feet, 10 ¾ inches at the Texas state meet in Austin, joining her father, former NFL player Michael Carter, as a national record holder in the event. Michael Carter holds the boys best of 81 feet, 3 ½ inches.

Female wrestler Toccara Montgomery captures the gold medal over Canada's Ohenewa Akuffo in the 72-kg division at the Pan American Games in Santo Domingo, Dominican Republic.

Grant Fuhr becomes the first Black hockey player to be inducted into the National Hockey Hall of Fame.

Barry Bonds becomes the first major league player to hit 500 home runs and steal 500 bases.

Colorful Firsts in U.S. Sports

Jackie Robinson becomes the first Black ball player to posthumously receive the Congressional Gold Medal. It is awarded to persons "who have performed an achievement that has an impact on American history and culture that is likely to be recognized as a major achievement in the recipient's field long after the achievement."

Tiger Woods, after winning the American Express Championship, becomes the first player in PGA Tour history to win at least five tournaments for five years in a row. Ben Hogan, Arnold Palmer and Tom Watson won four times over five consecutive seasons.

Bill Lester of NASCAR fame is the first African American to appear on the Honey Nut Cheerios cereal box.

Announcer Kelly Tilghman and co-host Nick Faldo during a Golf Channel telecast of the Mercedes-Benz Championship, were discussing how players who could possibly challenge the dominant Tiger Woods. Faldo jokingly said perhaps the golfers should "gang up (on Tiger) for a while." The pair laughed a bit before Tilghman declared, "Lynch him in a back alley." Tilghman later apologizes and is suspended for two weeks.

With a win over coach Herman Edwards' New York Jets, Indianapolis Colts coach Tony Dungy becomes the first coach to defeat all 32 NFL teams.

The first NFL Playoff Game featuring two African American head coaches occurs on 4 January. Herman Edwards' New York Jets defeats Tony Dungy's Indianapolis Colts 41-0 in the wild-card round.

Herman Edwards of the New York Jets becomes the first African American NFL coach on the cover of *Sports Illustrated*. The issue entitled "101 Most Influential Minorities in Sports" shows Edwards along with 27 other personalities.

The Fritz Pollard Alliance is founded by attorneys Cyrus Mehri and Johnnie Cochran Jr. The Alliance is a 501(c)(6) membership organization comprised of scouts, coaches, and front office personnel in the NFL as well as other sports professionals committed to equal opportunity in the football industry.

Tony Banks becomes the first Black starting quarterback for the Houston Texans.

Jeff Blake becomes the first Black starting quarterback for the Arizona Cardinals.

The Rooney Rule becomes an NFL policy that requires teams to interview at least one minority candidate for head-coaching jobs when there is a vacancy. In 2009, the Rooney Rule expands to include general manager jobs and equivalent front office positions. The Rooney Rule is named after the late former Pittsburgh Steelers owner and chairman of the league's diversity committee, Dan Rooney.

Steve McNair of the Tennessee Titans becomes the first African American quarterback to lead the NFL in passing and is selected co-MVP of the league.

LaDainian Tomlinson becomes the first NFL player to rush for 1,000 yards and catch 100 passes in a season. In 1998, Arizona Cardinal's fullback Larry Centers caught more than 100 passes in a season.

Myrtis Dightman, Charlie Sampson, and Bill Pickett become the first class of inductees for the National Cowboys of Color Museum and Hall of Fame in Oklahoma City, Okla.

Brittany Hunter, 6-foot-3 from UConn, becomes the first female to participate in the POWERade Jam Fest slam dunk contest, held in conjunction with the McDonald's All-American Games. She failed to complete any dunks.

2004

"People do not necessarily vote in their self-interest. They vote their identity. They vote their values. They vote for who they identify with." – George Lakoff, *Don't Think of an Elephant!*

The 6-foot-3 Naperville (Ill.) Central High School senior, Candace Parker becomes the first female to win the POWERade Jam Fest slam dunk competition held in conjunction with the McDonald's All-American Games. She beats out several male competitors, including Josh Smith, Darius Washington and J.R. Smith.

Shaun Livingston from Peoria (Ill.) Central High School (also of Peoria Richwoods High School) at 6-foot-7, 186 pounds, is the first high school point guard to be drafted into the NBA, by the Los Angeles Clippers with the fourth pick overall.

Dawn Staley is the first WNBA player to bear the U.S. flag at the Olympic Games in Athens, Greece.

Carmelo Anthony of the Denver Nuggets in the western conference and LeBron James of the Cleveland Cavaliers in the eastern conference are the first NBA players to win the Rookie of the Month award in every month of the season, from November through April.

Charlie Sifford becomes the first African American elected to the World Golf Hall of Fame in St. Augustine, Fla. Sifford is already a member of the Northern Ohio PGA Hall of Fame and the North Carolina Sportswriters Hall of Fame.

Natasha Renée Watley, who plays shortstop and first base, is the first African American to play for the USA Softball team in the

Summer Olympics (Athens).

Jackie Joyner-Kersee becomes the first female African American track and field athlete on the cover of a Wheaties cereal box.

Toccara Montgomery becomes the first Black female to wrestle for the U.S. Olympic team.

Maritza Correia, a Puerto Rican of African descent, becomes the first Black woman to make the U.S. Olympic swimming team. She wins a silver medal in the 2004 Athens games in the 4x100-meter freestyle relay.

Aquil Hashim Abdullah becomes the first African American male rower to qualify for the U.S. Olympic squad, teaming with U.S. Navy officer Henry Gantt Nuzum to win double skulls at the Qualified Olympic Small Boat Trials in West Windsor, N.J.

Barry Bonds becomes the first baseball player to record more than 200 walks in a season. He is also the first player to amass more than 100 intentional walks in a season.

Josh Gibson is the first Negro League catcher on the cover of *Sports Collectors Digest*. The magazine had exclusive pricing on Negro League material.

Earl Boykins (5-foot-5, 135 pounds) of the Denver Nuggets becomes the first NBA player less than five and a half feet tall to score more than 30 points in a game. Boykins scores 32 on 11-15 field goals, 2-3 three-point goals, and 8-8 from the free throw line in a 117-109 win over the Detroit Pistons.

A four-time pro bowler Michael Vick becomes the most unstoppable video game foe in *Madden NFL* game history because his speed rating of 95 as a quarterback is astronomical.

Sylvester Croom becomes the first African American head football coach in the Southeastern Conference (SEC) with Mississippi State University. In 2007, he was named SEC Coach of the Year.

Michael "Pinball" Clemons of the Toronto Argonauts is the first Black coach to win the Canadian Football League's Grey Cup.

Scoville Jenkins, 18, becomes the first African American champion to win the USTA National Open Hard Court tennis title.

2005
"If they don't give you a seat at the table, bring a folding chair." – Shirley Chisholm

Muhammad Ali and Frank Robinson are presented with the Presidential Medal of Freedom by President George W. Bush, the highest civilian award.

Chicago Bulls guard Ben Gordon becomes the first rookie to win the NBA's Sixth Man Award.

Amir Johnson, a power forward from Westchester High School in Los Angeles, becomes the last high school player drafted by the NBA. He is selected by the Detroit Pistons in the second round with the 56th overall pick. The NBA institutes a rule prior to the 2006 draft requiring U.S. players to be at least one year removed from their high school graduation to be eligible for the draft.

Sheila Johnson, co-founder of Black Entertainment Television (BET), becomes part-owner of the Lincoln Holdings LLC, which purchases the Washington Mystics from Abe Pollin's Washington Sports & Entertainment. Johnson's stake in Lincoln Holdings is reported to be between 5 and 10 percent. Johnson is believed to be the first African American woman to be a principal shareholder of three professional sports franchises, the Mystics, Washington Wizards and the Washington Capitals.

Arthur Ashe is the first African American male tennis player featured on a U.S. postage stamp.

The Jacksonville Jaguars start the season with three African American quarterbacks: Byron Leftwich, David Garrard and the undrafted Quinn Gray, an NFL first.

Rod Smith from Missouri Southern University becomes the first undrafted NFL player to amass more than 10,000 receiving yards, all with the Denver Broncos, from 1995 to 2006.

Sande French of Albion, Calif., and Cecil Holland of Queens, N.Y., file a lawsuit against the International Tennis Federation and the U.S. Tennis Association in U.S. District Court in Brooklyn, N.Y. Holland, despite attaining "gold badge" status and chairing more than 1,500 professional matches, is never permitted to sit as a chair umpire at the U.S. Open. French has worked more than 1,500 matches and claims that women are only permitted to chair preliminary men's matches due to systemic racism.

In Finland, U.S. Army Staff Sergeant Iris Smith, wins the world wrestling title in the 72 kg/158.5 lb division. Smith, who enjoys dancing and hiking, becomes the first female to win a world gold medal.

Kevin Jackson, who won gold medals at the 1992 Barcelona Olympic games as well as the World Championship games in Varna (1991) and Atlanta (1995) and the Pan American Games in Havana (1991) and Mar del Plata (1995), becomes the first African American inducted into the United World Wrestling Hall of Fame.

James "Bubba" Stewart becomes the first African American to win a major motorsports title, capturing the Mobile Supercross Series and the Toyota Motocross Championship. Stewart rides a Kawasaki KX 450F.

Colorful Firsts in U.S. Sports

Willie Randolph with the New York Mets and Frank Robinson with the Washington Nationals become the clubs' first African American managers.

The Baltimore Orioles are the first major league team to start a season without an African American player since 1959, when Pumpsie Green joined the Boston Red Sox in July.

The Houston Astros are the first World Series team, since the 1953 New York Yankees without an African American on its series roster. Their bench coach Cecil Cooper is Black. During the season, African American outfielders Charles Gipson (19 games) and Charlton Jimerson (one game) played for the Astros.

2006
"The true worth of a race must be measured by the character of its womanhood"
– Mary McLeod Bethune

John "Buck" O'Neil is posthumously presented with the Presidential Medal of Freedom by President George W. Bush, the highest civilian award.

Shani Davis becomes the first African American to win an individual gold medal at the Winter Olympics in the 1,000-meter speed skating event, held in Turin, Italy.

Born in Okinawa, Japan, Sophia Danenberg, 34, becomes the first Black woman to climb to the summit of Mount Everest, the world's tallest mountain.

Candice Dupree, a Temple Owl, is the first WNBA player to compete against her college coach, Dawn Staley. Staley's final WNBA season was Dupree's first. Staley's Houston Comets defeat Dupree's Chicago Sky, 71-60.

Candace Parker, a red-shirted athlete, becomes the first woman to dunk in an NCAA Tournament game, jamming a one-hander on a breakaway early in a Tennessee (102) victory over Army (54). She does another dunk later in the game, finishing with 26 points.

For the first time four non-seniors from the same team, North Carolina University at Chapel Hill, are selected in the first round of the NBA draft. Players include small forward Marvin Williams (2nd pick by Atlanta Hawks), point guard Raymond Felton (5th pick by Charlotte Bobcats), power forward Sean May (13th pick by Charlotte Bobcats) and shooting guard Rashad McCants (14th pick by Minnesota Timberwolves).

Courtney Paris, center for Oklahoma University, becomes the first frosh selected for the *Associated Press'* All-America women's basketball team.

Violet Palmer becomes the first woman to referee an NBA playoff game, when she officiates Game 2 of the first-round series between the Indiana Pacers and New Jersey Nets.

Bryant Gumbel, former NBC's *Today* show host and prime anchor for the 1980 Summer Olympic Games, becomes the NFL Network's first play-by-play commentator.

Warren Moon becomes the first African American quarterback inducted into the Pro Football Hall of Fame in Canton, Ohio. He is also the first player to be inducted in both the NFL Hall of Fame and the Canadian Football Hall of Fame.

Drake University in Des Moines, Iowa, dedicates its football field in honor of the late Johnny Bright, one of the school's greatest athletes and the victim of one of the most notorious acts in college football history. The field will be named "Johnny Bright Field at Drake Stadium." Bright is remembered for an incident on 20 October 1951. Bright's jaw is broken in a game in Stillwater, Okla., by an Oklahoma A&M player in what was perceived as a racially motivated attack.

Oklahoma University paints a solid crimson line on its football field's 38-yard-line from sideline to sideline in its game against the Colorado Buffs. This is in honor of the Sooner's first African American football player, Prentice Gautt, who wore jersey No. 38. Gautt went on to play in the NFL and later a career in athletic administration. He dies in 2005.

NFL quarterback Charlie Batch and former University of Michigan basketball star Antoine "The Judge" Joubert, announce the debut of the Detroit Panthers into the newly formed American Basketball Association franchise. Batch will be the majority owner, while Joubert will be the head coach.

The William "Billy" Walker Stakes at Churchill Downs, of 5 ½ furlongs is named in his honor.

Lisa Leslie becomes the WNBA's first player to score 5,000 career points.

Effa Manley, co-owner of the Newark Eagles, becomes the first woman elected to the National Baseball Hall of Fame, by a Special Committee on Negro Leagues of 12 Negro League historians. The committee was chaired by former Commissioner Fay Vincent.

Johnny Oduya, an African Swedish defenseman whose father was a Luo from Kenya, becomes the first European-trained player of African descent to play in the NHL and make his debut with the New Jersey Devils.

Lewis Hamilton becomes the first Black Englishman driver in Formula 1 after joining McLaren Racing.

Pro Football Hall of Fame running back Emmitt Smith, 37, along with his dancing partner Cheryl Burke, is the first NFL player to win the "Dancing with the Stars" competition in its third season.

Michael Vick of the Atlanta Falcons becomes the first quarterback to rush for more than 1,000 yards (1,039) in the NFL.

Thomas Jones, Chicago Bears, and Julius Jones, Dallas Cowboys, become the first brothers to rush for more than 1,000 yards for different NFL teams in the same season. From Stone Gap, Va., (pop. 4,856) Thomas gains 1,210 yards (4.1 yards per carry), while younger brother Julius gains 1,084 (also 4.1).

Vince Young of the Tennessee Titans becomes the first African American rookie quarterback to play in the Pro Bowl. Dan Marino was the first rookie quarterback.

2007

Taqiy Abdullah-Simmons from Oklahoma University becomes the first Black male gymnast to win the NCAA all-around championship. See Corrinne Tarver.

Lovie Smith coach of the Chicago Bears and Tony Dungy of the Indianapolis Colts become the first African American NFL coaches in the Super Bowl. Smith's Bears defeat the New Orleans Saints, followed by Dungy's Colts defeating the New England Patriots to earn this honor. In the process the Colts defeat the Bears, 29–17, at Dolphin Stadium in Miami Gardens, Fla.

Dallas Cowboy teammates Everson Walls and Ron Springs become the first professional athletes to undergo an organ donation and transplant. Walls donates a kidney to Springs.

Mike Tyson tops ESPN's list of "The Hardest Hitters in Heavyweight History."

John Thompson III, coach of the Georgetown Hoyas basketball team, defeat the North Carolina Tar Heels sending his team to the Final Four in Atlanta, Ga. The win becomes an historic first for a father (John Jr.) and a son to take different Georgetown teams to the Final Four in NCAA history. However, John III's Hoyas lose to Greg Oden and Ohio State University, 67-60 in the semi-finals. The Hoyas finish the season at 30-7.

The Florida Gators become the first college team to have three players drafted among the first 10 picks in the NBA draft. Al Horford is taken 3rd by Atlanta, Corey Brewer is taken 7th by Minnesota and Joakim Noah is taken 9th by Chicago. Horford's father, Tito, played in the NBA. Joakim's parents are Yannick Noah, former professional tennis player, and Cécilia Rodhe, Miss Sweden 1979.

The 1966 Texas Western Miners are inducted into the Naismith Memorial Basketball Hall of Fame. Texas Western, now known as UTEP, is the first team in NCAA history to win a title with a starting lineup of five Black players, beating an all-White Adolph Rupp Kentucky team in the 1966 final. The achievement, regarded as a turning point in the integration of college athletics, was the subject of the film "*Glory Road*." Rupp was inducted into the Hall of Fame in 1969.

Vivian Stringer, coach of Rutgers University, is the first African American coach to take a women's team to the NCAA basketball finals.

CBS Radio fires "shock jock" Don Imus from his radio show after derogatory comments about the Rutgers women's basketball team. A member of the National Broadcaster Hall of Fame and named by *Time* magazine as one of the 25 Most Influential People in America, Imus called the ladies of the team "nappy-headed hos." Several sponsors, including American Express Co., Sprint Nextel Corp., Staples Inc., Procter & Gamble Co., and General Motors Corp. pull ads from Imus' show indefinitely.

Kevin Durant of the Texas Longhorns becomes the first frosh and the first Texas athlete to receive *Associated Press'* College Player of the Year since its inception in 1961.

Gary Neal from the Towson Tigers goes undrafted by the NBA. After spending seasons in Turkey, Spain and Italy, he becomes the first undrafted player selected to the NBA's All-Rookie first team as a San Antonio Spur in 2011 and joins Blake Griffin, John Wall, Landry Fields and DeMarcus Cousins.

Leg tights are added to the list of banned apparel in the NBA. In the previous season, 2005-06, LeBron James (Cavaliers), Kobe Bryant (Lakers), Dwyane Wade (Heat) and White player Jason Williams (Heat) wear full-length hose to keep their sore knees warm. Players must produce a doctor's note for their medical usage.

Ron Washington with the Texas Rangers and Cecil Cooper with the Houston Astros become their teams' first African American managers.

Prince Fielder, for the Milwaukee Brewers, hits 50 home runs. Prince joins his father Cecil Fielder, who hit 51 home runs in

Colorful Firsts in U.S. Sports

1990 with the Detroit Tigers, becoming the first son-father duo to hit 50 or more home runs in a season.

Tony Reagins with the Los Angeles Angels of Anaheim and Michael Hill with the Miami Marlins are named general managers.

In recognition of the 60th anniversary of Jackie Robinson breaking the color barrier, five teams – Dodgers, Astros, Phillies, Pirates and Cardinals – feature all players wearing number 42.

Major league baseball hosts the first Civil Rights Game in tribute to the history of civil rights in the U.S. The St. Louis Cardinals beat the Cleveland Indians, 5 to 1, at AutoZone Park in Memphis, Tenn. The last Civil Rights game is played in 2014 at Minute Maid Park in Houston, Texas.

Chris Young centerfielder for the Arizona Diamondbacks becomes the first rookie major leaguer to hit more than 30 (32) home runs and steal more than 25 (27) bases in the same season.

Venus Williams becomes the lowest ranking player, 31, to become the Wimbledon tennis champion. She defeats Frenchwoman Marion Bartoli. Williams also wins Wimbledon in 2000, 2001 and 2005; and is ranked No. 1 in 2002. Wimbledon, the oldest and most prestigious tennis tournament, announces equal purses for men and women.

2008

"Rosa Parks sat so Martin Luther King could walk. Martin Luther King walked so Obama could run. Obama's running so we all can fly." – Jay-Z

Mike Carey, in his 18th year as an NFL official, becomes the first African American referee in the Super Bowl. Officials are chosen on merit. Carey had been chosen earlier as an alternate.

Jerry Reese with the New York Giants is the NFL's first Black general manager to win a Super Bowl (XLII).

Antonio Bryant, wide receiver for the Tampa Bay Buccaneers, becomes the *Sporting News'* first recipient of its Comeback Player of the Year award.

Coming off a Super Bowl victory in 2007, Tony Dungy becomes the only person to coach a Super Bowl team and write a *New York Times* best seller. Dungy's memoir, *Quiet Strength: The Principles, Practices, and Priorities of a Winning Life*, becomes the first football book to top the best-seller list.

JaVale McGee, with his mother, Pamela McGee, become the first mother-son combo to play in the NBA and the WNBA. McGee, a sophomore, is drafted by the Washington Wizards with the 18th overall pick from the University of Nevada. McGee's parents were both professional basketball players. His father, George Montgomery starred at Illinois and was a second-round draft pick in 1985 by the Portland Trail Blazers. His mother, Pamela, and her twin sister, Paula, were All-Americans who led USC to NCAA National titles in 1983 and 1984.

Tim Howard is named U.S. Soccer Athlete of the Year. He is the most capped goalkeeper of All-Time for the U.S. Men's National Team. Howard is named athlete of the year again in 2014.

Cullen Jones, only the second African American male to make the U.S. Olympic Swim Team, becomes the first African American to hold or share a world record, as a member of the 4x400-meter freestyle relay. Swimming the second leg, he teamed with Michael Phelps, Jason Lezak and Garrett Weber-Gale in a time of 3:08.24.

Brandon Jennings from Oak Hill Academy in Mouth of Wilson, Va. becomes the first high school player to play for a European team, the Lottomatica Roma of the Italian Serie A, rather than play collegiate basketball since the NBA's age restriction rule was implemented. The following year, he is selected 10th overall by the Milwaukee Bucks in the 2009 NBA draft.

Candace Parker of the Los Angeles Sparks becomes the first player to win the WNBA Rookie of the Year Award, the league's Most Valuable Player Award and an Olympic gold medal, in Beijing, in the same season. Parker signs a signature shoe contract with Adidas.

The Detroit Pistons wear a black patch in memory of Will Robinson, a scout who signed Joe Dumars and Dennis Rodman. When Robinson retired in 2003, the Pistons renamed their locker room "Will Robinson Locker Room."

In March, ESPN presents a four-hour documentary entitled *Black Magic*, that portrays the on-and-off-the-court challenges facing Black basketball players at historically African American colleges (HBCUs).

LeBron James becomes the first African American and the third man overall to be on the cover of *Vogue* magazine. He is featured on the March issue with Brazilian model Gisele Bündchen, wife of QB Tom Brady.

Mike Taylor becomes the first player in NBA history to be drafted out of the D-League. Portland acquires the 55th pick from the Phoenix Suns via the Indiana Pacers to select Taylor. However, he is traded to the Los Angeles Clippers on draft night in exchange for a future second-round draft pick and signs with the team on July 15.

Angela James becomes the first African American woman inducted into the International Ice Hockey Federation Hall of Fame.

In the Beijing Olympics, free-style wrestler Randi Miller, competing in the 63-kg weight class, becomes the first African American female to ever medal (a bronze) in the Olympics.

Dusty Baker becomes the Cincinnati Reds' first African American manager.

Serena Williams regains the World No. 1 ranking after five years and one month. This is the longest gap in professional tennis history.

2009

"The darkest places in hell are reserved for those who maintain their neutrality in times of moral crisis." – Dante Alighieri

Ron Cherry, football official from the ACC conference, becomes the first African American referee of a BCS national title game featuring the Oklahoma Sooners against the Florida Gators. Cherry is considered an unpopular referee in this conference.

Pittsburgh Steelers Mike Tomlin becomes the second African American NFL head coach to win a Super Bowl. Tony Dungy was the first in 2007 with the Colts. Tomlin served as defensive backs coach for Dungy in 2001 when they were with the Tampa Bay Bucs.

Josh Freeman from Kansas State University is the first Black regular starting quarterback for the Tampa Bay Buccaneers in his rookie season. QB Parnell Dickinson started one game for the Buccaneers in 1976.

Retired running back Warrick Dunn becomes a minority owner of the Atlanta Falcons. Dunn purchases a 1% minority stake in the Falcons organization for $9 million.

Courtney Paris, center for the University of Oklahoma Sooners, is the first NCAA player to block at least 100 shots in each of her four years in college. Paris is the first player to make All-American teams all four years.

Charlaine Vivian Stringer is the first African American female coach inducted into the Naismith Memorial Basketball Hall of Fame. She is the first coach, male or female, to take three different schools (Cheyney State Wolves, Iowa Hawkeyes and Rutgers Scarlet Knights) to the NCAA's Final Four.

Dwight Howard of the Orlando Magic is the first NBA player to lead the league in blocked shots (231) and total rebounds (1,093) in the same season. He repeats this feat during the 2009-2010 season.

Lisa Leslie becomes the first WNBA player to score 6,000 career points.

Kevin Weekes becomes the first Black TV analyst for NHL games after 14 years as a goaltender in the NHL.

Irv Cross is the first African American to receive the annual Pete Rozelle Radio-Television Award from the Pro Football Hall of Fame for "long-time exceptional contributions to radio and television in pro football."

Dremiel Byers becomes the first Black wrestler, and only the second American, to win three medals at the Greco-Roman World Championships.

Venus and Serena Williams become the first African American women to own part of an NFL franchise when they purchase a minority interest in the Miami Dolphins. Musicians Gloria and Emilio Estefan, and Marc Anthony also bought small shares of the team.

2010

"There's a lot of ways that White women undermine women of color, and Black women in particular." – Robin DiAngelo

Angela James becomes the first African American woman and the second African American goaltender after Grant Fuhr, to be inducted to the Hockey Hall of Fame in Toronto.

Tennessee Volunteer senior Michael Wright becomes the first African American national champion in USA Diving history when he wins the men's one-meter springboard competition, at the USA Diving Winter National Championships in Knoxville, Tenn.

At Petco Park, Cincinnati Red Aroldis Chapman becomes the first human to throw a baseball more than 105 mph, in the eighth inning, against Tony Gwynn Jr.

Winning the 200- and 400-meter runs, Allyson Félix becomes the first person to win two IAAF Diamond League trophies in the same year.

Son of an Army veteran, Edwin Jackson Jr. is the first German-born pitcher to throw a no-hitter in the major leagues. The Arizona Diamondbacks pitcher threw 149 pitches in the no-hitter. This is the highest pitch count in an MLB game since 2005.

Natalie Randolph becomes one of the first female head coaches of a boys' high school football team, at Calvin Coolidge in Washington, District of Columbia. The former wide receiver for the D.C. Divas of the 15-team Independent Women's Football

Colorful Firsts in U.S. Sports

League from 2003 to 2008, has a bachelor's degree in environmental science and a master's in education.

Michael Jordan becomes the first former NBA player to purchase a controlling interest in an NBA team, the Charlotte Bobcats, formerly the Hornets. The league's Board of Governors unanimously approves Jordan's $275 million purchase of the team from Bob Johnson, former president of BET and in 2003 the NBA's first minority majority owner.

The NBA prohibits players, particularly Rajon Rando of the Celtics from wearing headbands upside down as the NBA logo becomes inverted. Richard Hamilton has worn a headband for the better part of the last eight years due in large part to supporting his famous clear facemask. Hamilton is exempt from the ruling as perspiration would leak down into the facemask causing cloudiness and impairing his vision.

Latavious Williams, a small forward, becomes the first high school-to-NBDL (Tulsa 66ers)-to-NBA (Miami Heat) draft choice in history. His draft rights are immediately traded to the Oklahoma City Thunder.

Lady Tiger Seimone Augustus becomes the first female athlete at LSU to have her uniform number (33) retired.

During the 2010–2011 season, Bilquis Abdul-Qaadir for the University of Memphis plays in 34 games and averages 3.9 points per game with 1.3 rebounds per game. She is the first Division I player to wear a hijab. Later in 2015, Bilquis is invited to the White House and was acknowledged by President Barack Obama for being the first Muslim woman to play covered in collegiate basketball. Adbul-Qaadir's journey is told in the documentary Life Without Basketball.

Maya Moore of the WNBA wins the ESPY Award for the Best Female College Athlete.

Dustin Byfuglien, a defensive/right wing for the Chicago Blackhawks, is the first African American to play for a Stanley Cup champion.

USC running back Reggie Bush is stripped of his Heisman Trophy, for allegedly accepting money and gifts from agents. In 2005, he rushes for 2,218 yards and 18 touchdowns. It is the first time in the history of the award that the trophy is returned. 2012 Heisman Trophy winner Johnny Manziel, QB from Texas A&M, announces that he would boycott the Heisman Trophy ceremony until Bush got his trophy back.

Julius Jones of the New Orleans Saints becomes the first NFL player to score a touchdown against the team (Seattle Seahawks) that released him in the same season. See 2006 for note about his brother Thomas Jones.

Troy Smith from Ohio State University is the first Black starting quarterback for the San Francisco 49ers.

Colin Kaepernick of the Nevada Wolf Pack (WAC) becomes the first collegiate football player to pass for 10,000 (10,098) yards and rush for 4,000 (4,112) yards.

Michael Vick of the Philadelphia Eagles becomes the first African American quarterback named *Associated Press'* Comeback Player of the Year.

2011

"White fragility doesn't always manifest in overt ways;
silence and withdrawal are also functions of fragility." – Robin DiAngelo

Bill Russell is presented with the Presidential Medal of Freedom by President Barack Obama, the highest civilian award.

JaVale McGee, in the NBA Slam Dunk Contest, becomes the first player to use three balls at one time in a dunk contest, which is later cited by Guinness World Records as the most basketballs dunked in a single jump. The third ball is passed to him from teammate John Wall.

The WNBA's Maya Moore of the Minnesota Lynx becomes the first woman to sign an endorsement contract with Nike's Jordan Brand. See 1995, Sheryl Swoopes.

On February 17, former NFL player David Duerson commits suicide, requesting his brain be donated to chronic traumatic encephalopathy (CTE) research and further sparking the football safety debate regarding head trauma.

Cam Newton of the Carolina Panthers becomes the first rookie QB to pass for more than 4,000 yards (4,051) and is also the first player to throw more than 400 yards in his NFL debut.

ESPN stops using Hank Williams Jr.'s song "All My Rowdy Friends Are There on Monday Night" on Monday Night Football after he publicly compares President Barack Obama to Adolf Hitler on *Fox and Friends*. Despite songs by Williams that glorify the Confederacy like, "If the South Woulda Won" and "If Heaven Ain't a Lot Like Dixie" he is rehired, in 2017, by ESPN during the first year of Donald Trump's term.

P. K. Subban becomes the first Canadian rookie defenseman to score a hat-trick in a game, which came in an 8–1 victory over the Minnesota Wild.

2012

"I have spent years studying what it means to be White in a society that proclaims race meaningless yet is deeply divided by race." – Robin DiAngelo

In the London Olympics Gabrielle Douglas, the "Flying Squirrel," becomes the first African American to win the gold in the women's gymnastics all-around event that includes floor exercises, the uneven bars, the balance beam and the vault. In addition, she is the first American gymnast to win gold in both the individual and team all-around competition.

At the London Olympic Games, Claressa Shields becomes the first U.S. woman to win a boxing gold medal. The 165-pound Shields wins the Olympic middleweight title by defeating Russian boxer Nadezda Torlopova.

Jarome Iginla becomes the first Black NHL player to surpass 500 goals.

Former Secretary of State Condoleezza Rice and South Carolina financier Darla Moore become the first female members of the Augusta National club, home of the Masters golf tournament. Augusta National, which opened in December 1932 and did not have a Black member until 1990, is believed to have about 300 members.

Magic Johnson buys a 2.3% stake in the Los Angeles Dodgers with a $50 million investment. He is a key investor with the Guggenheim Baseball Management.

Reggie Miller is inducted into the Naismith Memorial Basketball Hall of Fame. Miller and his sister Cheryl (inducted in 1995) will become the only siblings in the Basketball Hall of Fame entering as players. [Note: Brothers Dick and Al McGuire are in the Basketball Hall of Fame as coaches. Paul and Lloyd Waner, and Rube and Willie Foster are the only brothers in the National Baseball Hall of Fame.]

Tiger Woods becomes the first $100 million man on the PGA Tour. Woods finishes third in the Deutsche Bank Championship and makes $544,000, pushing his career total to $100,350,700. Next is Phil Mickelson, who places fourth at TPC Boston and has $66,805,498. Woods has 74 wins, second to Sam Snead. As of 2012, Woods has played 277 times on the PGA Tour, with an average of $362,276.89 per start.

Antron Brown becomes the first African American champion in any NHRA Pro Series when he wins the Top Fuel title in Pomona, Calif.

Robert Griffin III posts the most efficient rookie season in NFL history with a 102.4 QB rating. The mark is the 39th-best overall season by a quarterback in league history and, at 22 years old, RG3 is the youngest player to ever have a season rated 100.0 or better. Despite not playing one game, Griffin's stat line reads 3,200 yards, 20 TD, 5 INT, and a 65.6 completion percentage. Griffin also sets the NFL rookie record for rushing yards by a QB with 815 yards and seven TDs.

Robert Griffin III of the Washington Redskins and Russell Wilson of the Seattle Seahawks are the first Black rookie quarterbacks to face-off in an NFL playoff game.

Russell Wilson of the Seattle Seahawks posts an elite 100.0 QB rating his rookie season, which earned him fourth in the league.

Derrick Coleman, running back for the Minnesota Vikings and later the Seattle Seahawks, is the first deaf offensive player in the NFL.

2013

"It's important for us to also understand that the phrase 'Black Lives Matter' simply refers to the notion that there's a specific vulnerability for African Americans that needs to be addressed. It's not meant to suggest that other lives don't matter. It's to suggest that other folks aren't experiencing this particular vulnerability." — Barack Obama

Ernie Banks is presented with the Presidential Medal of Freedom by President Barack Obama, the highest civilian award.

LaVelle E. Neal III of the *Minneapolis Star Tribune* becomes the first Black reporter to head the Baseball Writers' Association of America (BBWAA).

Denver's Trindon Holliday returns a punt 90 yards for a touchdown in the first quarter and runs back the second-half kickoff for a 104-yard TD versus the Baltimore Ravens. Holliday becomes the first player in NFL post-season history to score on a kick and a punt return in the same game. The Broncos lose 38-35, in two overtimes.

In week 10, Seneca Wallace from Iowa State University becomes the Packers' first Black starting quarterback when Aaron Rodgers suffers a broken collarbone.

Buffalo Bills' Erik Rodriguez "EJ" Manuel Jr. becomes the first rookie QB to defeat a defending Super Bowl champion, the Baltimore Ravens.

Colorful Firsts in U.S. Sports

Theodore "Ted" Corbitt, a marathon runner, is inducted into the inaugural class of the National Black Distance Running Hall of Fame, by the National Black Marathoners Association.

At the World Artistic Gymnastics Championships, 16-year-old Simone Biles performs a double layout with a half-twist (body remains straight and elongated as she flips twice) in the floor exercises. The skill is named the "Biles on the Floor." Moves are named after the first gymnast who completes them in an international competition, according to the International Gymnastics Federation Code of Points. The move must also be above a certain difficulty level.

Nzingha Prescod is the first American female foil fencer to win a Grand Prix title when she wins the gold medal at the Marseille Foil Grand Prix competition in France.

LSU Senior Kimberlyn Duncan, a five-time NCAA champion and a nine-time All-American, is the first female sprinter to win the NCAA indoor and outdoor titles in the 200 meters in consecutive years.

In her rookie season, Brittney Griner of the Phoenix Mercury with a 7-foot-4 wingspan, becomes the first WNBA player to dunk twice in the same game. Previously, Candace Parker dunked twice and Lisa Leslie once in WNBA competition.

Tina Thompson becomes the first WNBA player to compile 7,000 points and 3,000 rebounds in a career. Selected to her ninth all-star appearance, Thompson becomes the first and only player in WNBA history to be named an All-Star in three different decades.

At 5 feet 7 inches, Riquna "Bay Bay" Williams is the first WNBA player to score more than 50 points in a game. She scores 51 points for the Tulsa Shocks (now the Dallas Wings).

Los Angeles Clippers guard Chauncey Billups becomes the first winner of the NBA's new award, the (Jack) Twyman-(Maurice) Stokes Teammate of the Year Award. The award is for a player who displays selfless play and on- and off-court leadership while showing commitment and dedication to his team.

The 1963 Loyola Ramblers, Division I NCAA champions, become the first team inducted into the National Collegiate Basketball Hall of Fame and later honored at the White House by President Barack Obama.

Billy Hamilton of the Cincinnati Reds becomes the first player in the live ball era to steal four bases in his first major league start. Hamilton goes 3-for-4 — his first three major league hits — with two walks and four stolen bases against the Houston Astros. One of his stolen bases leads to a run which broke a 4-4 tie in the 13th inning of a Cincinnati victory.

Retired Detroit Tiger first baseman Tony Clark becomes the first former player to be named executive director of Major League Baseball Players Association. Clark served as deputy executive director and acting executive director of the union before he was appointed executive director in December, upon the death of attorney Michael S. Weiner.

Althea Gibson is the first African American female tennis player featured on a U.S. postage stamp.

P. K. Subban becomes the first African American hockey player to win the James Norris Memorial Trophy as the NHL's top defenseman. The Norris Trophy, originated in 1953, is for the top "defense player who demonstrates throughout the season the greatest all-round ability in the position."

Layshia Clarendon with the Indiana Fever, is the first openly transgender, non-binary player in the WNBA.

Blake Bolden becomes the first African American player taken in the first round of the Canadian Women's Hockey League (CWHL) Draft. She is picked by the Boston Blades as the fifth overall pick.

2014

"Won't it be wonderful when Black history and Native American history and Jewish history and all of U.S. history is taught from one book. Just U.S. history." - Maya Angelou

Charlie Sifford, 92, is presented with the Presidential Medal of Freedom by President Barack Obama, the highest civilian award.

Attorney Michele A. Roberts is named executive director of the National Basketball Players' Association and becomes the first woman to head a major professional sports union in North America. In 2020, she had "Black Lives Matter" painted on NBA courts to promote racial harmony.

Mo'ne Davis becomes the first Little League player, Black or White, to appear on the cover of *Sports Illustrated*. Davis is also the first young lady to earn a win and pitch a shutout in Little League World Series history, as her south Philadelphia Taney Dragons defeat Nashville, 4-0. Davis pitches a two-hitter and strikes out eight in six innings.

In May, President Barack Obama becomes the first sitting president to visit the National Baseball Hall of Fame and Museum in Cooperstown, N.Y.

Cam Newton of the Carolina Panthers becomes the first QB to have more than 10,000 passing yards, and 2,000 rushing yards over his first three seasons.

Mariah Imani Stackhouse becomes the first African American woman golfer to make the Curtis Cup team, for amateurs.

Samarria Brevard becomes the first African American female skateboarder to win the Kimberly Diamond Cup Women's Street Championship in South Africa.

David Brown, 27, becomes the first totally blind athlete to run the 100 meters under 11 seconds with a time of 10.92.

Michael Jordan becomes the first athlete with an estimated net worth of $1 billion, as reported by *Forbes* magazine. Jordan is owner of the Charlotte Hornets.

Future WNBA player Skylar Diggins-Smith from Notre Dame is the first woman signed by Jay Z to a Roc Nation contract, which markets itself as a boutique sports agency.

The Ogwumike sisters, Nneka in 2012 and Chiney in 2014 are the number one overall picks in the WNBA drafts, a first.

Nneka and Chiney Ogwumike, become the first pair of sisters selected to a WNBA All-Star game. And the first sisters to win WNBA Rookie of the Year awards in 2012 and 2014, respectively.

Los Angeles Lakers and Philadelphia Warriors/76ers center Wilt Chamberlain becomes the first NBA player featured on a U.S. postage stamp. The two versions issued are nearly two inches long, or about a third longer than the usual stamp.

The Los Angeles Clippers protest owner Donald Sterling's racist remarks about Black people by wearing their shirts inside-out in order "to obscure any team logo" during their pre-game huddle. Soon after Miami Heat players wear their uniform tops inside-out to show solidarity with the Clippers. LeBron James comments on the situation, "There's no room for Donald Sterling in the NBA." NBA commissioner Adam Silver announces a lifetime ban of Sterling from the league and fines him $2.5 million, the maximum fine allowed by the NBA constitution.

The San Antonio Spurs, led by Coach Gregg Popovich, win the NBA championship with a diversity of talent. The team includes Tony Parker (G) and Boris Diaw (F), both from France; Tiago Splitter (C) from Brazil; Patty Mills (G) from Australia; Manu Ginóbili (G) from Argentina; Marco Belinelli (F) from Italy; and Tim Duncan (C) from Saint Croix in the Virgin Islands. They finished the season with a 62-20 won-loss record (.756) and defeated the Miami Heat in five games.

Russell Wilson of the Seattle Seahawks becomes the first NFL player to pass for more than 300 (313) yards and rush for more than 100 (106) yards in a single game during a 28-26 loss to the St. Louis Rams.

Michael Sam, defensive end from the University of Missouri, is drafted by the St. Louis Rams in the seventh round, the 249th pick of 256 players selected. He becomes the first publicly gay player drafted. Cut during the pre-season by the Rams, Sam signs on with the Montreal Alouettes of the CFL. Coach Jon Gruden calls out Commissioner Roger Goodell, in an email, for pressuring the St. Louis Rams to draft Michael Sam, who was the SEC Co-Defensive Player of the year in 2013.

Jason Collins, center for coach Jason Kidd's Brooklyn Nets, becomes the first openly gay player in the NBA. Collins appears on the cover of *Time's* magazine "Most Influential People."

2015
"If now isn't a good time for the truth, I don't see when we'll get to it." – Nikki Giovanni

TNT sportscaster Ernie Johnson gifts his third Sports Emmy Award to the two daughters of longtime ESPN anchor Stuart Scott, who died recently of cancer at 49. Scott was known for his hip-hop style and catchphrases. He commentary popularized the phrase "booyah" which spread from sports into mainstream culture.

After weeks of protest, University of Missouri president Tim Wolfe resigns when the school's football team, the Tigers, vows to boycott all football-related activities due to unaddressed racial hostility on the campus. The effort is led by #ConcernedStudent1950, named to pay homage to the first year a Black student is admitted to the university. The movement is captured in the documentary, *Field of Vision - Concerned Student 1950*.

Willie Mays is presented with the Presidential Medal of Freedom by President Barack Obama, the highest civilian award.

Wendell Scott is the first African American to be inducted into the NASCAR Hall of Fame.

Sports Illustrated renames its Legacy Award the Muhammad Ali Legacy Award. The first awardee is golfer Jack Nicklaus. The annual honor is bestowed upon one athlete or former athlete that best embodies the ideals of sportsmanship, leadership and philanthropy as vehicles for changing the world.

Katrina Adams becomes president, chairman and CEO of the U.S. Tennis Association (USTA), and the first former professional tennis player, first African American and the youngest person to serve as president in the organization's 135-year history.

Marshawn Lynch, Seattle Seahawks running back, is fined $75,000 by the NFL for not speaking to the media following the NFC Championship game. Later at Super Bowl Media Day, he says, "I'm just here so I won't get fined." Lynch proved prophetic as he was not fined for the now infamous quote.

Claire Smith is the first recipient of the Sam Lacy-Wendell Smith Award, created by the Shirley Povich Center for Sports Journalism. The award is presented annually to a sports journalist or broadcaster who has made significant contributions to racial and gender equality in sports.

In the Beijing World Championships, Allyson Félix becomes the first woman to win world titles in both the 200 and 400 meters.

Shenea Booth, acrobatic gymnast, becomes the first African American female soloist to play a lead character in a Cirque Du Soleil production, by performing as "The Promise" in the classic spectacle Varekai.

Blake Bolden becomes the first African American woman to play in the National Women's Hockey League (NWHL), a subsidiary of the NHL. She plays for the Boston Pride of the NWHL, winners of the inaugural Isobel Cup team championship.

Aroldis Chapman becomes the first player disciplined by major league baseball's new personal conduct policy, which empowers MLB to suspend a player without a final judicial decision from the courts.

Jeffrey Orridge becomes the first African American chief executive of a major North American sports league as the 13th commissioner of the Canadian Football League (CFL).

2016

"There is nothing more powerful than a people, than a nation, steeped in its history.
And there are few things as noble as honoring our ancestors by remembering."

– Lonnie G. Bunch III

Kareem Abdul-Jabbar and Michael Jordan are presented with the Presidential Medal of Freedom by President Barack Obama, the highest civilian award.

Cumberland Posey and John McLendon are inducted to the Naismith Memorial Basketball Hall of Fame. Posey is selected by the Early African American Pioneers Committee, while McLendon is inducted again, this time as a coach. McLendon is the first inductee to be honored as a contributor and coach. Cum Posey is the first man to be inducted into both the National Baseball Hall of Fame and the Naismith Memorial Basketball Hall of Fame.

Blake Bolden becomes the first Black player selected to the NWHL All-Star Game. Her slapshot has been measured at 87 mph.

Ida Keeling, born in Harlem, N.Y., becomes the first woman in history to complete a 100-meter run at the age of 100. Her time of 1:17.33 was witnessed by a crowd of 44,469 at the Penn Relays.

Draymond Green of the Golden State Warriors becomes the first NBA player with more than 1,000 points (1,131), 500 rebounds (769), 500 assists (598), 100 steals (120), 100 blocked shots (113) and 100 three-point field goals (100) in a season. Green finishes seventh in the MVP voting.

Stephen Curry of the Golden State Warriors becomes the first NBA player unanimously voted the MVP, receiving all 131 votes. He leads his Warriors to a record 73-9 won-lost record during the regular season. Curry becomes the first NBA player to average more than 30 points (30.1) while playing less than 35 minutes per game. Curry finishes the regular season with a record 402 three-pointers, making him the first player to score more than 300 and 400 three-point goals in a season, breaking his 2015 record of 286.

Jaylen Brown of the California Golden Bears is drafted by the Boston Celtics as the third pick in the first round. Brown enjoys playing chess and learning foreign languages. The 19-year-old enters the draft without an agent. "He is an extremely intelligent kid," an unnamed NBA assistant general manager said, adding, "He took a graduate school class at Cal in his freshman year. He is a person who is inquisitive about everything. Because he is so smart, it might be intimidating to some teams. He wants to know why you are doing something instead of just doing it. I don't think it's bad, but it's a form of questioning authority. It's not malicious. He just wants to know what is going on. Old-school coaches don't want guys that question stuff."

Pam McGee, a standout athlete at USC, is the first former WNBA mother with kids in the NBA and the WNBA. Her son JaVale debuted in the NBA in 2008 with her daughter Imani joining the WNBA in 2016.

After the deaths of Alton Sterling in Baton Rouge, La., and Philando Castile, outside of St. Paul, Minn., by police officers, the Minnesota Lynx become the first professional team in the U.S. to wear "Black Lives Matter" on the front and the names of Sterling and Castile on the back of their warmup t-shirts.

Andre Shelby becomes the first Black U.S. Paralympic archer at the Rio de Janeiro Olympics. Paralyzed from the chest down from a motorcycle accident, he wins the gold medal.

Simone Manuel becomes the first African American swimmer to win an individual gold medal in an Olympic event, the 100-meter freestyle, in Rio de Janeiro, Brazil. Overall she wins another gold in the 4x100 medley relay and two silver medals in the 50-

meter freestyle and the 4x100 freestyle relay.

Michelle Carter becomes the first American woman to win the gold medal in the shot put. Her father, Michael Carter, is a silver medalist in the 1984 Olympics in Los Angeles. He is a three-time Super Bowl champion with the San Francisco 49ers as a nose tackle. Michelle and her father are Team USA's first father-daughter combination to medal at the Olympic Games.

U.S. women sweep the 100-meter hurdles for the first time in the history of the Olympics. Brianna Rollins is clocked at 12.48 seconds and followed by teammates Nia Ali (12.59) and Kristi Castlin (12.61), who edges Britain's Cindy Ofili (12.63) with a lean at the finish line.

Ibtihaj Muhammad becomes the first Muslim woman to compete for the U.S. in fencing and the first U.S. Olympic athlete to compete in a hijab in the Rio de Janeiro, Brazil, Olympics. The fencing champ also becomes the first female Muslim-American athlete to win an Olympic medal when she takes home the bronze in the team Sabre event at the Summer Games in Rio.

Dalilah Muhammad wins the gold medal in the 400-meter hurdles, running a time of 53.13 seconds and claiming the first ever women's gold in the event for the U.S., at the Rio de Janeiro, Brazil Olympics.

Michael Sam, a consensus All-American and SEC Defensive Player of the Year at the University of Missouri, lobbies against a bill at the Missouri State Capitol that would enable discrimination against the LGBTQ community. Sam was drafted by the St. Louis Rams in the seventh round of 2013 and played on the taxi squads for the Rams and the Dallas Cowboys in 2014.

Josh Freeman is the first Black starting quarterback for the Indianapolis Colts. George Taliaferro had started for the Baltimore Colts back in 1953.

After an injury to backup QB and a suspended Tom Brady, Jacoby Brissett becomes the New England Patriots' first Black starting quarterback.

Claressa Shields becomes the first U.S. boxer to win back-to-back Olympic gold medals, defeating the Netherlands' Nouchka Fontijn.

Kelsey Koelzer is first overall pick in the NWHL draft when selected by the New York Riveters. She makes her first appearance near the end of the 2016-17 season.

2017

"One way that Whites protect their positions when challenged on race is to invoke the discourse of self-defense.

Through this discourse, Whites characterize themselves as victimized, slammed, blamed, and attacked." – Robin DiAngelo

According to Elias Sports, Draymond Green of the Golden State Warriors in a victory over the Memphis Grizzles gathers 12 rebounds, 10 assists and 10 steals to post the first triple-double in NBA history that does not include double-digit points (he scores four points).

Washington Wizards Kelly Oubre Jr. is asked to stop wearing the NBA and Nike sponsored Supreme compression sleeve.

The southeast corner of West 138th Street and Adam Clayton Powell Jr Blvd is named New York Rens Court.

Vince Carter becomes the first 40-year-old player in NBA history to hit six triples in one game.

Upon retirement, Los Angeles Laker Kobe Bryant becomes the only player in NBA history to have multiple numbers, #8 and #24, retired by the same franchise.

The World Series Most Valuable Player Award is renamed the Willie Mays World Series Most Valuable Player. It will be presented by the award's longtime sponsor, Chevrolet. George Springer from the Houston Astros is the first recipient.

Claire Smith is the first woman to receive the Baseball Writers Association of America Career Excellence Award, formerly the J.G. Taylor Spink Award, the highest award given by the Baseball Writers' Association of America (BBWAA).

Oakland A's catcher Bruce Maxwell becomes the first major league baseball player to take a knee to protest police brutality and racial injustice. It takes another three years for anyone else to follow his lead in the big leagues.

Major League Baseball and USA Baseball launch the DREAM Series, a development experience event focusing on the dynamics of pitching and catching for a diverse group of elite high-school athletes, predominantly Black players, during Martin Luther King Jr. holiday weekend. In addition to on-field training, seminars, mentorship, and scout evaluations are provided in this cost-free experience.

David Price's minimalist delivery style of pitching has resulted in what is call the "Price rule" which makes a pitcher specify whether he is working from the stretch or full windup position when a runner is on third. The rule is detailed in this way: If a pitcher takes the rubber and his back foot is parallel to the mound and his other foot is in front, it is assumed he is in the set position and he will stop. This does not matter with no runners on or runners on first and second. But when there is a runner on third, pitchers need to inform the umpires if they are going to stand that way and not stop -- i.e., pitch out of the full windup.

Designer Aleali May becomes the first woman in Jordan Brand history to create a unisex sneaker.

Wayne Simmonds, a Canadian right-winger is the first Black hockey player to be named MVP of the NHL All-Star game.

At the Daytona International Speedway, Brehanna Daniels becomes the first Black woman in a NASCAR Cup Series pit crew at the Coke Zero Sugar 400 annual car race.

Maame Biney becomes the first Black woman to qualify for a U.S. Olympic speedskating team with a victory in the 500 meters in Kearns, Utah. The 17-year-old native of Ghana will be the second Black speedskater on a U.S. Olympic team. Shani Davis was 19 when he made the short track team in 2002. He later switched to long track and won four medals, including two golds.

Carla Williams becomes the Virginia Cavaliers' (UVA) athletic director. She is the first African American woman in the Power Five conferences to hold this position. The Power Five conferences include the Atlantic Coast Conference (ACC), Big Ten Conference, Big 12 Conference, Pac-12 Conference, and the Southeastern Conference (SEC).

Samarria Brevard, known as the "Serena Williams of skateboarding," is the first African American female to medal at the X Games at U.S. Bank Stadium in downtown Minneapolis, Minn.

Former New York Yankee shortstop Derek Jeter and former Chicago Bulls guard Michael Jordan purchase a small interest in the Miami Marlins baseball team.

NBA champions the Golden State Warriors are disinvited by Donald Trump after guard Stephen Curry and teammates said they did not want to go to the White House based on Trump's comments regarding the white supremacist rally in Charlottesville, Va., which resulted in the death of Heather Heyer and several injured spectators.

The NBA moves its All-Star game from Charlotte, North Carolina, to Smoothie King Arena in New Orleans, Louisiana, after a so-called "bathroom bill" that bars transgender people from using the bathroom that matched their gender identity.

The New York Jets make Collette Smith the first Black female coach in the NFL. She coaches the cornerbacks and safeties, reporting to the head defensive backs coach.

Colin Kaepernick appears on the cover of *GQ*, a fashion magazine, as selection for Citizen of the Year.

The New York Giants become the last NFL franchise to start a Black quarterback when Geno Smith from West Virginia University replaces Eli Manning.

Mississippi State University dedicates the Dowsing-Bell Plaza in honor of its first two African American football players, Frank Dowsing Jr. and Robert Bell, in 1969.

Renée Powell is inducted into the PGA of America Hall of Fame. Her father, Bill Powell, is also an inductee, making the pair the only father/daughter honorees.

2018

"All water has a perfect memory and is forever trying to get back to where it was." – Toni Morrison

Alan Page is presented with the Presidential Medal of Freedom, the highest civilian award.

Mookie Betts outfielder for the Boston Red Sox becomes the first MLB player to win the MVP, Silver Slugger, Gold Glove, a batting title and a World Series ring in the same season.

Melissa Harville-Lebron becomes the first African American woman to own a NASCAR team, when her company W.M. Stone Enterprises, Inc., creates E2 Northeast Motorsports. The new team becomes the first multicultural team to race competitively in NASCAR with four Black and Latino drivers. Two drivers are her sons Eric and Enico.

The French Tennis Federation president, Bernard Giudicelli, says that the sleek black catsuit worn by Serena Williams at the French Open goes "too far," adding, "You have to respect the game and the place."

Tamyra Mensah-Stock becomes the first American, male or female, to win back-to-back gold medals at the Golden Ivan Yarygin Grand Prix in Russia.

Cynt Marshall becomes the first Black female CEO of an NBA team when hired by Mark Cuban of the Dallas Mavericks. Marshall spent 36 years at AT&T improving workplace culture and encouraging diversity and inclusion.

Allyson Félix becomes the first sponsored athlete for Athleta, owned by Gap, Inc. When her contract expired with Nike in December 2017, the company offered a pregnant Félix a 70% pay cut in the new contract and failed to explicitly support maternity protections she requested in the contract.

Puma announces a relaunch of its basketball shoe division. Skylar Diggins-Smith, point guard for the Dallas Wings, becomes the first face of the brand's comeback.

Dealing with a kidney stone, at the World Championships, Simone Biles performs a half-twist onto the vaulting table and a front double full somersault off. The skill is named "Biles on the Vault" the second in her name.

In response to LeBron James' comment to ESPN broadcaster Cari Champion that Donald Trump has "The No. 1 job in America, the appointed person is someone who doesn't understand the people," the athlete said, adding that some of the president's comments are "laughable and scary," Laura Ingraham of *Fox News* countered, "It's always unwise to seek political advice from someone who gets paid $100 million a year to bounce a ball," she said. "Keep the political comments to yourselves . . . Shut up and dribble [all the way to the bank]." James provides the hashtag #MoreThanAnAthlete.

Writer Kobe Bryant narrates a six-minute film called *Dear Basketball* and becomes the first professional athlete to win an Academy Award for Best Animated Short Film. In the process, he also becomes the first person to win an Oscar and an Olympic Gold Medal, when as a member of the U.S. Men's basketball teams in 2008 and 2012.

Jordan Greenway, a left wing from Boston University and a 2015 second-round draft pick of the NHL's Minnesota Wild, becomes the first African American to represent Team USA in hockey at the Winter Olympics in Pyeongchang, South Korea. 2018, Greenway also becomes the first player to compete in the Olympic games, an NCAA tournament and the Stanley Cup playoffs within the same season.

2019

"Change will not come if we wait for some other person or . . . some other time.
We are the ones we've been waiting for. We are the change that we seek." -- Barack Obama

Tiger Woods is presented with the Presidential Medal of Freedom, the highest civilian award.

Toni Stone is the first woman from the Negro Leagues to have a Off-Broadway production about her legacy. The Roundabout Theatre Company produces Lydia R. Diamond's *Toni Stone*. April Matthis plays the star athlete.

Ja Morant of Murray State, as a sophomore, becomes the first player in NCAA history to average at least 20 points and 10 assists per game in a single season.

LeBron James becomes the first NBA player to record a triple-double against all 30 teams, starting in 2003.

Erica Wheeler, a guard out of Rutgers, becomes the first undrafted player to be named WNBA All-Star MVP. She scores 25 points in the game.

Kelsey Koelzer is named head coach of the Arcadia University women's ice hockey program, becoming the first Black head coach in NCAA ice hockey history. The Arcadia Knights, located in Glenside, Pa., are in Division III (MAC Commonwealth Conference).

African American hammer thrower Gwen Berry stands on the medal stand wearing bright blue lipstick and a gold medal around her neck. As the end of the national anthem, she bows her head and raises her fist, issuing a silent protest motivated by her personal journey and her belief that, "America can do better."

The USA Triathlon, part of the U.S. Olympic Committee, makes history by electing its first ever African American board member, Dr. Tekemia Dorsey. She serves as its Mideast Region representative.

LSU sophomore JuVaughn Harrison, known as "Mr. Jumps," becomes the first man to win both the high jump (7 feet, 5 ¼ inches) and long jump (26 feet, 11 inches) in the NCAA outdoor championships.

Simone Biles does her double-twisting double-tucked salto backwards dismount off the balance beam during the qualifying round of the gymnastics World Championships in Stuttgart, Germany. The floor routine is valued at a G. This skill is dubbed the "Biles on the Balance Beam" the third in her name. She also completes a triple-twisting double-tucked salto backwards, creating "Biles II on the Floor," a second skill for floor exercises and the fourth in her name.

In the U.S. National Championships, Biles performs a triple-twisting double somersault in her floor routine so complex that on the international A-I scale for difficulty, judges concurred that Biles ought to earn a "J" rating for this move. As a result, the International Gymnastics Federation (FIG or the Fédération Internationale de Gymnastique) update their ranking system to account for the unquestionable difficulty of this move. This move will go into the FIG Women's Artistic Gymnastics Code of Points as the "Biles II." The Biles II is a triple-twisting double-tucked salto backwards.

Nike releases the Air Max 1 Quick Strike sneaker featuring the Betsy Ross flag on the heel. The design drew complaints because the 1776 logo appears to glorify slavery and racism in U.S. history. Nike representative Colin Kaepernick tells *The Wall Street Journal* they should reconsider the design out of concern that it would send the wrong message about race in modern times. Nike pulls the shoes from the marketplace.

Colorful Firsts in U.S. Sports

Penn State basketball coach Pat Chambers tells star freshman Rasir Bolton in January, "I want to be a stress reliever for you. You can talk to me about anything. I need to get some of this pressure off you. I want to loosen the noose that's around your neck." Bolton recounts that Chambers, who is Catholic, said he was making a biblical reference and had intended to say "yoke." After the season, Bolton transfers to Iowa State. Chambers resigns from the basketball program in October.

The NCAA institutes a policy that requires all agents to meet certain prerequisites–including having a bachelor's degree–to serve as an agent for athletes. The ruling is labeled the "Rich Paul Rule" and aimed at Rich Paul who lacks a degree. Paul began his career working with Creative Arts Agency (CAA) in 2006. He left CAA in 2012 to start Klutch Sports, whose clients include Eric Bledsoe, Kentavious Caldwell-Pope, Anthony Davis, Draymond Green, LeBron James, Tyrese Maxey, Jusuf Nurkić, Ben Simmons, John Wall and Trae Young. After backlash from the media, the NCAA later amends its certification process for agents and no longer requires agents to have a bachelor's degree. Rich Paul writes in an op-ed to *The Athletic*: "Requiring a four-year degree accomplishes only one thing -- systematically excluding those who come from a world where college is unrealistic. Does anyone really believe a four-year degree is what separates an ethical person from a con artist?"

Muslim supermodel Halima Aden becomes the first model to wear a hijab and burkini in the *Sports Illustrated* swimsuit issue. Aden, who is Somali-American, grew up in Kenya's Kakuma refugee camp, before moving with her family to the U.S. at the age of seven.

Kalin Bennett, a 6-foot-1 frosh center at Kent State University, becomes the first player with autism to score in a Division I game, finishing with two points in a 97-48 win over Hiram. As the 16th-ranked prospect from Arkansas, Bennett also became the first recruit with autism to sign a letter of intent with a Division I school.

Rapsody in her *Eve* album produces the first rap song about a female tennis player, entitled "Serena" in honor of Serena Williams.

Cori "Coco" Gauff, 15, becomes the youngest woman to qualify for the grass-court Wimbledon tennis tournament. She defeats Venus Williams in the opening round before losing in the fourth round.

Tyreek Hill of the Kansas City Chiefs is fined $10,527 for giving the peace sign during a Thursday Night Football game against the Denver Broncos. The NFL considers this gesture to be taunting.

Zaila Avant-Garde sets a Guinness World Record, in New Orleans, La., with the most bounce juggles, 307, in 30 seconds, using four basketballs.

When University of Alabama defensive tackle Quinnen Williams is the third pick of the 2019 NFL Draft, Nicole Lynn becomes the first Black female agent to represent a first-round draft choice.

Jaren Hall becomes the first African American starting quarterback in Brigham Young University's nearly 100-year history. BYU is owned by the Church of Latter Day Saints (LDS) and its student body is 99% LDS according to its website. BYU lifted the ban on Black people becoming priests and entering their temples in 1978.

2020

"People of color understand what it means to be White more than I ever will." – Robin DiAngelo

In partnership with active and former Major Leagues players and the Major League Baseball Players Association (MLBPA) the Players Alliance is created to change and work to address systemic barriers. Principals include Edwin Jackson (founder and secretary), CC Sabathia (vice-chair), Curtis Sanderson (board chair) and Adam Jones (member).

Former University of Cincinnati baseball players Jordan Ramey and Nathan Moore petition to change the name of Marge Schott Stadium that opened in 2004. Schott owned MLB's Cincinnati Reds from 1984 to 1999. Her racial and ethnic slurs against African American, Jewish and Japanese people prompted a one-year ban from baseball in 1993. After publicly praising Adolf Hitler in a 1996 ESPN interview, Schott was forced to give up day-to-day control of the Reds until 1998. The university's board of trustees voted unanimously to remove Schott's name from both the stadium and a place in the university's archives library.

Running back Kylin Hill declares he will not play for the Mississippi State University Bulldogs unless the state removes a Confederate battle emblem from its flag. In June, the Mississippi legislature votes to the blue cross with 13 white stars from the flag's design. SEC Commissioner Greg Sankey threatens to block future championships events in the state saying, "It is past time for change to be made to the flag of the state of Mississippi." Note, Mississippi State University and Ole Miss stopped flying the Confederate flag in 2016.

Andre Dawson is the recipient of the inaugural Curt Flood Award. The award created by Major League Baseball Players Association commemorates the 50th anniversary of Flood's historic court fight against Major League Baseball's reserve system and celebrates a player who demonstrated selfless devotion to the advancement of players' rights. In 21 major league seasons, Dawson plays for four different teams. He was the National League Rookie of the Year in 1977, the NL MVP in 1987 and an eight-time All-Star.

Tamyra Mensah-Stock wins a gold medal at the Tokyo Olympics and becomes the first Black woman wrestler to win gold.

Jalen Romande Green, a Filipino-American from Napa, California, skips college and becomes the first basketball player to sign with the NBA's G-League, as a bridge between high school and the NBA. He is 6-foot-5 and a student at San Joaquin Memorial in Fresno, Calif. Green is named *Sports Illustrated's* inaugural Boys Basketball Player of the Year.

Andre Ingram is named president of the Interim Executive Committee of Basketball Players Union, of the NBA's G League. In 2018, Ingram scored 19 points in his Los Angeles Laker debut after spending 10 seasons in the G-League. He is from American University.

Converse reveals the Barrier Breaker collection which consists of six total pairs of sneakers, as Converse pays homage to Chuck Cooper, Nat Clifton and Earl Lloyd on two of the brand's most classic silhouettes: the Converse Pro Leather and the Chuck Taylor 70, an updated model of basketball's first performance shoe. Designed with premium materials and a satin finish to symbolize 1950s NBA uniforms, all three editions of the Chuck Taylor in the collection commemorate each barrier-breaking player, as well as their respective first teams. Clifton's blue, orange and white Knicks-themed Chuck features a bottle cap graphic behind the tongue of each shoe as a nod to his nickname, "Sweetwater." Similarly, a cat graphic is printed behind the tongues of the black, green and white shoe, which honors both Lloyd, who was known as "The Big Cat," and the Washington Capitols, a charter member of the NBA for only the 1950-51 season.

The Milwaukee Bucks refuse to take the floor in a playoff game against the Orlando Magic in protest of the police shooting Jacob Blake seven times in his back, in Kenosha, Wis.

To pay respects to the killing of Breonna Taylor, the WNBA is the first professional league to dedicate a season to fight for social justice. A'ja Wilson and other players formed a Social Justice Council and wear warmups with "Say Her Name."

The "Russell Rule," the first of its kind to be adopted by a Division I conference, stipulates that each school in the West Coast Conference (WCC) must include a member of a traditionally underrepresented community in the pool of final candidates for every athletic director, senior administrator, head coach and full-time assistant coach position in the athletic department. Bill Russell, an 11-time NBA Champion, a two-time NCAA Champion and a Presidential Medal of Honor recipient as a life-long advocate for social justice, embraced the opportunity to promote equitable opportunities in college athletics.

Tamara Moore becomes the first African American woman to become a head coach of a men's collegiate basketball program in the U.S., at Mesabi Range College in Virginia, Minn. Moore played six seasons in the WNBA with the Houston Comets, Miami Sol, Minnesota Lynx, New York Liberty, Phoenix Mercury and the Los Angeles Sparks.

Maya Moore of the WNBA is listed in *Time* magazine's 100 Most Influential People of the year.

Washington Mystics point guard Natasha Cloud becomes the first woman to sign an endorsement deal with Converse Shoes.

Nigerian-American Chinenye "Chiney" Ogwumike, a power forward for the Los Angeles Sparks, becomes the first Black woman to host a daily national radio sports-talk show for ESPN.

ESPN host Rachel Nichols expressed frustration that Maria Taylor had been chosen over her to host "NBA Countdown" during the NBA Finals. "I wish Maria Taylor all the success in the world — she covers football, she covers basketball," Nichols said. "If you need to give her more things to do because you are feeling pressure about your crappy longtime record on diversity — which, by the way, I know personally from the female side of it — like, go for it. Just find it somewhere else. You are not going to find it from me or taking my thing away."

Zaila Avant-Garde sets a Guinness World Record, in Baton Rouge, La., with the most bounce juggles, 255, in one minute, using four basketballs.

Zeb Powell is the first African American to win gold in the Winter X games in snowboarding, capturing 1st place in the Men's Knuckle Huck held in Aspen, Colorado.

Seven current and former National Hockey League (NHL) players form the Hockey Diversity Alliance (HDA) group, whose mission is "to eradicate racism and intolerance in hockey." The group appoints San Jose Sharks forward Evander Kane and former NHL player Akim Aliu as co-heads of the organization. The group also includes Detroit Red Wings defenseman Trevor Daley, Minnesota Wild defenseman Matt Dumba, Buffalo Sabres forward Wayne Simmonds, Philadelphia Flyers forward Chris Stewart and former NHL forward Joel Ward. Another goal of the HDA is to promote diversity at all levels of the game. The group will operate independently of the NHL.

The Canada Post unveils a postage stamp in honor of the 1904 Colored Hockey League champions, the Halifax Eurekas, to

Colorful Firsts in U.S. Sports

commemorate the history of Black hockey players in Canada.

Everett Fitzhugh becomes the NHL's first African American play-by-play broadcaster, as the voice of the Seattle Kraken.

Erik Moses is named president of the Nashville Superspeedway and becomes the first Black track president in NASCAR history.

Despite team owner Dan Snyder's adamant resistance to changing the name of his Washington Redskins, the club bows to political pressure and public opinion in becoming the Washington Football Team. Many complained that "Redskins" is racist and offensive to Native Americans. When the NFL reorganized in 1933, the Boston Braves changed its name to Redskins before moving to D.C. in 1937. It is believed that FedEx, which has naming rights to the stadium, also influenced the name change in 2020. In 2022, the football team will become the "Commanders."

Patrick Mahomes, Kansas City Chiefs quarterback, becomes the first half-billion dollar athlete in U.S. sports history. Mahomes signs a 10-year contract extension that with contract incentives is worth a total of $503 million. The contract includes just over $63 million in guaranteed money at the point of signing, and $141 million is guaranteed in the event of injury.

Jason Wright, former No. 31 for the Cardinals, becomes the first African American president of an NFL team, the Washington Football Team, formerly the Washington Redskins. Wright is responsible for leading the organization's business divisions, including operations, finance, sales and marketing.

Jennifer King, a Carolina Panthers intern during the 2017 preseason, joins the Washington Football Team's staff as a full-time assistant coach. King is the first full-time African American female coach in league history and the fourth woman with a full-time assistant job overall. (Collette Smith was the NFL's first Black female coach, serving as an intern with the New York Jets in 2017.) King joins Tampa Bay Buccaneers assistant defensive line coach Lori Locust, Bucs' assistant strength and conditioning coach Maral Javadifar and San Francisco 49ers offensive assistant Katie Sowers as the only women working as full-time NFL coaches.

Former quarterback for the Philadelphia Eagles and the Minnesota Vikings Randall Cunningham is named by coach Jon Gruden as Chaplin of his Las Vegas Raiders. It is believed that no other NFL team has had a former player as its spiritual adviser.

In week 11 on Monday Night Football, the NFL has an all-Black officiating crew for a game between the Los Angeles Rams and the Tampa Bay Buccaneers in Tampa. The crew consists of referee Jerome Boger, umpire Barry Anderson, down judge Julian Mapp, line judge Carl Johnson, side judge Dale Shaw, field judge Anthony Jeffries and back judge Greg Steed. The crew has a combined 89 seasons in the league and has worked six Super Bowls.

Two retired NFL players, Najeh Davenport (running back) and Kevin Henry (defensive lineman), sue the league for discriminating against Black players who submitted claims in a 2013 class-action lawsuit, accusing the league of concealing findings on the dangers of concussion. The players claim the NFL used race-correction in its neurological exams, which prevented the players from being compensated. According to court documents, former players being evaluated for neurocognitive impairment were assumed to have started with worse cognitive function if they were Black. So, if a Black player and a White player received the exact same scores on a battery of thinking and memory tests, the Black player would appear to have suffered less impairment and, the lawsuit claimed, would be less likely to qualify for a payout.

NASCAR bans the Confederate flag from its races and venues, formally severing itself from what is viewed by many citizens as a symbol of slavery and racism. Bubba Wallace, NASCAR's only Black driver, called for the banishment of the flag and said there is "no place" for them in the industry. Wallace drives a car, No. 43, with the hashtag #BlackLivesMatter.

Erik Moses is named president of Nashville Superspeedway, becoming the first African American to hold that title at any NASCAR track. Formerly president of the XFL's DC Defenders, Moses will lead the speedway back from the COVID-19 pandemic in 2021. The 1.33-mile concrete track was built in 2001 by Dover Motorsports and hosted NASCAR and IndyCar events until 2011.

Ashton Washington becomes the first African American woman on the staff of the University of Illinois football program in 130 years. As director of high school relations, she serves to build relationships with prep coaches to help the Illini coaching staff lure recruits. Washington had previously worked for the XFL's Houston Roughnecks as a business and gameday operations specialist.

Tori Miller becomes the first woman to hold the title of general manager in the history of the NBA's G League. She becomes GM of the College Park Skyhawks, affiliate of the Atlanta Hawks. A native of Decatur, Ga., Miller is a University of Miami graduate and spent time as a basketball operations intern for the Phoenix Suns prior to her time in the G League.

Retired outfielder Torii Hunter tells ESPN's "Golic and Wingo" that racially abusive fans at Fenway Park led Hunter to put the Boston Red Sox in the no-trade clause of his contracts. Hunter shares on WEEI-FM's "The Greg Hill Show" that he heard far more racist taunts in Boston than any other city.

Effa Manley, currently the only woman in the National Baseball Hall of Fame, is recipient, posthumously, of SABR's Dorothy Seymour Mills Lifetime Achievement Award for her service as owner of the Newark Eagles.

Major league baseball announces that it will remove former major league baseball Commissioner Kenesaw Mountain Landis' name from the plaques awarded to the American and National League MVPs. The decision comes after a few former MVPs, including Black award winners Barry Larkin and Terry Pendleton, voice displeasure with their plaques being named for Landis, who kept the game segregated during the 24 years he served as commissioner from 1920 until his death in 1944.

After 105 years, the Cleveland Indians move away from a moniker considered racist. In 2019 the team removes the contentious smiling, cartoonish mascot Chief Wahoo logo from its caps and jerseys, but the image is still sold by third-party vendors.

Lonnie Murray becomes the first Black woman to be certified as a player agent by the MLB Player Association. Murray represents Bianca Smith, the first Black woman to coach in professional baseball and represents Bruce Maxwell, Oakland A's catcher, the first MLB player to kneel for the national anthem in protest of police brutality.

Major league baseball announces that the Negro League statistics from 1920 to 1948 will be officially classified as "major league status," marking a long-overdue acknowledgement of Black players who did not have the opportunity to play in the American or National Leagues before 1947.

Umpire Kerwin Danley becomes the first full-time African American crew chief in major league baseball.

LeBron James becomes the first player in NBA history to score at least 10 points in 1,000 consecutive regular season games. James launches "More Than A Vote" a non-profit organization designed to register African Americans to vote, and to stop voter suppression efforts.

Naomi Osaka, winner of the US Open, is named *Associated Press*' Female Athlete of the Year, receiving 18 of 35 first place votes. She is a leading voice in speaking out against racial injustice and police brutality.

Blake Bolden becomes the first Black female pro scout for the Los Angeles Kings in the NHL and the second-ever female pro scout in the NHL.

102 members of the U.S. Congress write a letter to the National Baseball Hall of Fame and Museum, co-signed by Players' unions from the NFL, NHL, NBA, and MLS, asking the Hall of Fame to admit Curt Flood for his pioneering efforts to eliminate the Reserve Clause in MLB.

Toronto Raptors' president, Nigerian-Canadian Masai Ujiri, attempts to enter the court as his Raptors defeat the Golden State Warriors to win the NBA championship, when he is blocked by a San Francisco Bay Area police officer, Alan Strickland. Body cam footage shows the officer shoving Ujiri twice as he attempts to show his access credentials.

Ulysses "Junior" Bridgeman, former Milwaukee Bucks and Los Angeles Clipper player, purchases *Ebony* and *Jet* magazines in U.S. Bankruptcy Court for $14 million. The 12-year NBA veteran is CEO of a Coca-Cola Bottling Company and part-owner of Coca-Cola Canada Bottling Limited. In 2018, Bridgeman attempted to buy *Sports Illustrated* that was sold to Authentic Brands Group for $110 million.

An African American female fishing team, called The Ebony Anglers with Bobbiette Palmer, Gia Peebles, Tiana Davis, Glenda Turner and Lesleigh Mausi win first place in the King Mackerel division of Carteret Community College Foundation's Spanish Mackerel & Dolphin Tournament in Morehead City, N.C.

2021

"No one should fear a history that asks a country to live up to its highest ideals."

- Lonnie G. Bunch III

Maia Chaka becomes the NFL's first African American female referee when officiating a New York Jets game against the Carolina Panthers in Charlotte, N.C. She is a health & physical education teacher in the Virginia Beach public school system and graduate of Norfolk State University, an HBCU.

Zaila Avant-Garde sets a Guinness World Record in Westwego, La. for the most basketballs (6) dribbled simultaneously by a woman. The 14-year-old Avant-Garde later in the year becomes the first African American to win the Scripps National Spelling Bee title at ESPN's *Wide World of Sports* Complex in Orlando, Fla.

Jennifer King becomes the first full-time female African American NFL coach (assistant running backs coach) with the Washington Football Team. She has also coached women's college basketball. King later becomes NFL's first woman named as a position coach when promoted to head running backs coach.

Two-way player at receiver and cornerback, Travis Hunter from Collins Hill High School in Suwanee, Ga., becomes the first five-star recruit to sign with an HBCU school when signing with Jackson State College in Mississippi. He later transfers to the Colorado Buffaloes in the Pac-12 Conference and wins the Heisman Trophy in 2024.

Colorful Firsts in U.S. Sports

New York Jets linebacker Quincy Williams and defensive tackle Quinnen Williams become the first brothers to each record a sack in the same game in a win over the Tennessee Titans.

The NFL is accused of "race norming" in grading the settlements provided to former players for post-concussive syndromes, known as chronic traumatic encephalopathy (CTE). The league's systemic testing scale starts with the assumption that Black athletes have a lower cognitive functioning baseline, resulting in lower payouts than their white counterparts.

Amanda Gorman becomes the first poet to recite a poem at the Super Bowl. At Super Bowl LV at Raymond James Stadium in Tampa, Fla., Gorman reads "Chorus of the Captains" to recognize the three honorary captains: a nurse, a teacher and a Marine veteran.

Renée Montgomery becomes the first former player to become both an owner and executive of a WNBA franchise, the Atlanta Dream. Joining her as investors in the team are real estate investor Larry Gottesdiener and Suzanne Abair, president of Northland Investment Corporation in Massachusetts. The ownership change follows pressure on former Republican Senator Kelly Loeffler to sell her share of the Dream. Loeffler angered WNBA players by opposing the league's racial justice initiatives.

A three-time first-team All-American (2014-18), a three-time SEC Player of The Year and the WNBA's No. 1 draft pick in 2018, and later the league's Rookie of the Year and its MVP (2020), the Olympic gold medalist (2020), A'Ja Wilson is honored with a statue at the Colonial Life Arena on the University of South Carolina campus on MLK Day.

Rich Paul, founder and CEO of Klutch Sports Groups, becomes the first player agent to have a signature shoe, the New Balance 550.

Jalen Green of the G League Ignite is the first player from that league to appear on the cover of *SLAM* magazine, No. 231, also known as the Future issue.

In partnership with the National Basketball Association (NBA) and the International Basketball Federation (FIBA), Africa's new professional basketball league is formed. The Basketball Africa League (BAL) consists of 12 teams from Algeria, Angola, Cameroon, Egypt, Madagascar, Mali, Morocco, Mozambique, Nigeria, Rwanda, Senegal and Tunisia.

Ben Wallace becomes the first undrafted player in NBA history to be inducted into the Naismith Memorial Basketball Hall of Fame.

Former Negro League player Clarence "Fats" Jenkins, captain of the New York Rens, is the first player from the first Black-owned, fully professional African American basketball team inducted into the Naismith Memorial Basketball Hall of Fame.

Iman Shumpert is the first NBA player to win the "Dancing with the Stars" competition. Teaming with dancer Daniella Karagach, they posted two perfect 40 scores in two dances, a cha-cha-cha-foxtrot fusion and a freestyle dance. See Emmitt Smith, 2006.

Portland Trail Blazers forward Carmelo Anthony is named the inaugural winner of the NBA's Kareem Abdul-Jabbar Social Justice Champion award. In July 2020, he partnered with 11-time NBA All-Star Chris Paul of the Phoenix Suns and NBA legend Dwyane Wade to create the Social Change Fund, which aims to address social and economic justice issues facing Black communities and break down the discriminatory barriers to success. Guest editor Anthony of *SLAM's Black Lives Matter* magazine, in 2020, entitled "It Stops Now" provided a platform for the voiceless.

Bianca Smith becomes the first African American female coach in professional baseball when hired as a minor league coach by the Boston Red Sox. A Dartmouth College graduate, Smith obtained a J.D. degree and a MBA in sports management from Case Western Reserve University in 2017.

Dawn Staley of the South Carolina Gamecocks and Adia Barnes of the Arizona Wildcats become the first African American head coaches with teams in the Final Four of the NCAA women's basketball tournament. Staley and Barnes are both former WNBA players. Staley is also the first person to guide an Olympic basketball team to a gold medal as both a player and a coach. As a player in the 1996, 2000 and 2004 Olympics and as a coach in the 2021 Tokyo Olympics.

NCAA basketball champions Baylor and coach Scott Drew refuse a customized Jeep Wrangler wrapped with the school's national championship logo after an insensitive remark made by Ted Teague, general manager of the Allen Samuels dealership in Waco, during a live KWTX-TV interview stating, "Use it to recruit, pull some people out of the hood." Teague immediately apologizes.

The Converse Pro Leather High 'Breaking Down Barriers' pays tribute to Indiana's Crispus Attucks Tigers, who in 1955 became the first all-black high school basketball team to win a state championship. Inspired by the team's letterman's jacket, the vintage hoops shoe features a white felt upper with mismatched Star Chevron branding in yellow and green. The heel tab on the left shoe is embroidered with 'CA 55,' while the Tigers' logo adorns the right.

Betnijah Laney of the New York Liberty, Diamond Deshields of the Phoenix Mercury and Arike Ogunbowale of the Dallas Wings appear on the cover of *WSLAM*, the first all-women issue of *SLAM* magazine.

Champion Timeline

JaVale McGee of the U.S. Basketball team wins gold in the Tokyo Olympics. Thirty-seven years earlier, his mom Pamela of the 1984 Olympic basketball team won a gold medal. Hall of Famer and USC Trojans legend Pamela McGee and JaVale become the first mother and son to win Olympic gold medals.

The International Swimming Federation (FINA) bans swimming caps designed for natural Black hair for use in the Tokyo Olympics. The thickness or density of Black hair does not fit under a traditional swim cap. The caps are made by Black-owned British brand, Soul Cap.

At Guaranteed Field, the Chicago White Sox become the first major league team to fly a flag representing its hometown Chicago American Giants from the Negro Leagues. The American Giants won the Negro World Series in 1926 and 1927.

Major league baseball moves the Atlanta All-Star game to Denver, Colorado, in protest of Georgia's new election rules that disproportionately restricts minority voting rights in urban areas. Governor Brian Kemp adds new identification requirements for absentee ballots, limits use of drop boxes and makes it a misdemeanor for groups to offer food or water to voters waiting in line near polling places.

The Atlanta Board of Education votes unanimously to change the name of the [Nathan Bedford] Forrest Hill Academy to the Hank Aaron New Beginnings Academy. The academy had been named after a Confederate general, a founding figure of the Ku Klux Klan and a Grand Wizard.

LSU senior JuVaughn Harrison, known as "Mr. Jumps," becomes the first man to win both the high jump (7 feet, 6 ½ inches) and long jump (27 feet, 8 ¾ inches) in an NCAA indoor championship.

Allyson Félix starts Saysh, a women-first brand that pioneers a new policy allowing people to swap shoes should their foot size change while pregnant.

Kristen Hayden becomes the first Black woman to win a national diving title when she wins the USA Diving Winter National Championships in Bloomington, Ind. She is also a founding member of the USA Diving's Diversity, Equity and Inclusion Council.

Naomi Osaka, of Haitian and Japanese descent, becomes the first biracial female athlete on the cover of *Sports Illustrated's* Swimsuit issue.

Erin Jackson becomes the first African American woman to win a speedskating title at the ISU Speed Skating World Cup. The 29-year-old athlete wins the women's 500-meter event at the Arena Lodowa in Tomaszów Mazowiecki, Poland, in a time of 37.613 seconds.

Tamyra Mensah-Stock becomes the first African American female wrestler to win an Olympic gold medal. She defeats Nigeria's Blessing Oborududu, 4-1, in the 68-kilogram freestyle wrestling. Mensah-Stock defeated Japan's Sara Dosho, 10-0, in the first round; beat China's Feng Zhao, 10-0, in the quarterfinals; then beat Ukraine's Alla Cherkasova, 10-4, in the semifinal.

Gabrielle Thomas wins a bronze medal in the 200 meters at the Tokyo Olympics. Thomas becomes the first Harvard grad (with neurobiology and global health disciplines) to win an Olympic medal.

Danita Johnson is named president of the D.C. United soccer team, becoming the first Black president in the Major League Soccer (MLS). Johnson also serves as the president and chief operating officer of the WNBA team Los Angeles Sparks.

The Texas chapter of the NAACP and a group of students file a federal civil rights complaint against the University of Texas for its continued use of the school song "The Eyes of Texas," which has racist undertones. The lyrics aren't necessarily racist, but the song's history is. The song was written in 1903 with a history of performances in minstrel shows and musicians in blackface. According to university records the Longhorns took trademark ownership of the phrase "The Eyes of Texas are upon you" in 1936. The complaint says the song creates a hostile campus environment over the "offensive," "disrespectful," and "aggressive" use of the song.

The historical marker to honor Jackie Robinson's birthplace at the Roddenbery Memorial Library in Cairo, Ga., is damaged by gunfire.

The Baseball Writers' Association of America (BBWAA) votes to remove the name of J.G. Taylor Spink, former publisher of the *Sporting News*, from its annual award for meritorious contributions to baseball writing. The BBWAA had 325 of 334 members, or 97%, vote to remove the name following research into racism by Spink. Writer Ryan Fagan explains: "Spink was the publisher of the largest, most powerful baseball publication in the country for nearly half a century, and he used that position to strongly advocate against the integration of the sport." Fagan adds that Spink's *Sporting News* contained "racist language, ugly stereotypes and derogatory portrayals of Negro League players and other Black Americans during Spink's time as publisher, especially in the era before Jackie Robinson made his MLB debut in 1947." The award is renamed the "BBWAA Career Excellence Award."

The Claire Smith Center for Sports Media at Temple University is named in honor of Claire Smith, an alumna. In 2017, Smith was the first woman to receive the Baseball Writers Association of America Career Excellence Award.

HBCU All-Stars LLC announces that the first Historically Black Colleges and Universities (HBCU) All-Star Game, a college basketball showcase highlighting the best HBCU players in the country, will be held at UNO Lakefront Arena in New Orleans in 2022. The game will feature the best talent from the four Historically Black Athletic Conferences pit two teams named in tribute of legendary coaches John McLendon (MEAC & SIAC) and Clarence "Big House" Gaines (SWAC & CIAA). Also playing in the showcase will be players from Tennessee State, Hampton and North Carolina A&T State universities.

The Capital One Arena, the home floor of Georgetown University, is renamed the John Thompson Jr. Court. The Big East Conference also awards the first John Thompson Jr. Award "to recognize significant efforts to fight prejudice and discrimination and advance positive societal change" to Georgetown University.

2022

"Bringing the gifts that my ancestors gave, I am the dream and the hope of the slave.
I rise. I rise. I rise." - Maya Angelou

Simone Biles is presented with the Presidential Medal of Freedom by President Joe Biden, the highest civilian award.

At the U.S. Championships in Tampa, Florida, Konnor McClain (gold), Shilese Jones (silver) and Jordan Chiles (bronze) become the first all-Black trio to medal in the senior-all-around competition.

The Jackie Robinson Museum opens in New York City. It is the city's first museum primarily focused on the Civil Rights Movement.

During the Winter Olympics in Beijing, China, Erin Jackson becomes the first Black woman to win an individual gold medal. The speed skater takes the top spot in the women's 500-meter race with a time of 37.04.

Talitha Diggs wins the 400 meters at the NCAA Indoor Track and Field Championships in Birmingham, Ala. Her mother Joetta Clark Diggs wins the 800 meters NCAA indoor championship in 1983. The pair become the first daughter and mother to win gold medals in an NCAA championship individual event.

Starr Andrews becomes the first U.S. Black figure skater to win an ISU Grand Prix Medal (silver) at Skate Canada.

Candace Parker becomes the first female on the cover of the video game NBA-2K22 in celebration of the 25th anniversary of the WNBA. Parker of the Chicago Sky becomes the first WNBA player to eclipse 6,000 points, 3,000 rebounds and 1,500 assists.

A testament to his durability, Vince Carter is the only player in NBA history to appear in a game in four different decades. Starting in 1998, his career spans 22 seasons with eight teams.

After 50 years of coaching, Vivian Stringer announces her retirement. With 1,055 wins, Stringer is the first Black Division I coach (men's or women's) to reach the 1000-win milestone. Rutgers Scarlet Knights will name the basketball court at Jersey Mike's Arena the "C. Vivian Stringer Court."

Elliot Cadeau of Swedish-Haitian descent is the first American high school athlete (Link Academy, Branson, Mo.) to sign an international Names, Likeness, Image (NIL) deal when he endorses a deal for the Swedish vitamin drink Vitamin Well. Cadeau is also the first high school basketball player to sign with Roc Nation Sports for NIL representation.

The Convocation Center, a multi-purpose sports and entertainment complex on Eastern Michigan University's west campus is renamed the George Gervin GameAbove Center. The following year a commemorative statue by artist Ben Victor is unveiled at EMU.

Seven-time Formula 1 champion Lewis Hamilton is part of a consortium to purchase the Denver Broncos for a record $4.65 billion.

Jaylin Williams is the first player with Vietnamese heritage (Mom was born in Saigon, now Ho Chi Minh City) to be drafted into the NBA. The Oklahoma City Thunder pick him in the second round, the 34th overall pick.

The NBA creates division championship trophies named after African American pioneers of the game. The Pacific Division winner receives the Chuck Cooper Trophy. The Central Division winner receives the Wayne Embry Trophy. The Southwest Division winner receives the Willis Reed Trophy. The Atlantic Division winner receives the Nat "Sweetwater" Clifton Trophy. The Southeast Division winner receives the Earl Lloyd Trophy. The Northwest Division winner receives the Sam Jones Trophy.

Stephen Curry of the Golden State Warriors becomes the first player to win the Kobe Bryant MVP award at the NBA's All-Star Game. The newly designed trophy has an eight-sided base to represent Bryant's No. 8 jersey number. The four-tier trophy has 18 stars around the base to represent Bryant's 18 All-Star selections.

The first ever Magic Johnson Western Conference Finals MVP award is won by Stephen Curry of the Golden State Warriors.

Seattle Storm center Tina Charles becomes the first WNBA player to score 7,000 points and gather 3,500 rebounds.

Milwaukee Bucks guard Jrue Holiday becomes the first player to win the Twyman-Stokes Teammate of the Year Award twice. Holiday also won the award for the 2019-20 season. The award is for a player who displays selfless leadership on and off the court while showing commitment and dedication to his team.

Satchel Paige becomes the first Negro League veteran to be an answer during Jeopardy's "Final Jeopardy." Jackie Kelly, a pension calculation developer from Cary, N.C., tackles "Taking the mound for Cleveland in 1948, he was the first African American to pitch in a World Series." She beats out Ryan Guzzo Purcell, a theatre director from Seattle, Wash., who also had the correct question.

Josh Gibson of the Homestead Grays becomes the first Black man to appear on the cover of *Beckett Vintage Collector* magazine in a Negro League uniform.

After a grade school shooting in Uvalde, Texas, that results in the deaths of 19 young children and two teachers, Jewish manager of the San Francisco Giants Gabe Kapler will skip the national anthem until he feels better about the direction of America regarding gun violence. Unlike Colin Kaepernick's stance against police violence, there are no campaigns to oust Kapler from his job.

Attempting to expand diversity, all 32 NFL teams will be mandated to have a minority offensive assistant coach on staff for the 2022 season. The coach can be a woman or the member of a racial or ethnic minority. With a trend of hiring head coaches from offensive coordinator positions, Pittsburgh Steelers owner Art Rooney II, who serves as chairman of the NFL's diversity committee, said that he hopes the mandate creates a pipeline for minority coaches to rise through the ranks and eventually become head coaches.

Mellody Hobson, co-CEO of Ariel Investments, joins the Walton-Penner ownership group purchasing the NFL's Denver Broncos. The $4.65 billion deal makes Hobson the first Black woman to be part of a new ownership group buying an NFL team. She is later joined by former U.S. Secretary of State Condoleezza Rice, a professional football analyst.

The Las Vegas Raiders name Sandra Douglass Morgan team president, making her the first Black woman to hold the position in NFL history. A native of Las Vegas, Morgan becomes the second Black person named president of an NFL team after the Washington Commanders hired Jason Wright to the position in 2020.

After years of officiating in the SIAC, SWD, Conference-USA and the SEC, and the USFL this past spring, Tra Boger joins his father Jerome (19 years in the NFL) becoming the first African American son-and-father referees in the National Football League.

Jackson State University's football team, coached by Deion Sanders, becomes the first HBCU to host ESPN's "College GameDay". JSU or the "Sonic Boom of the South" faces off against Southern University, the "Human Juke Box," at Smith-Wills Stadium, located at 1200 Cool Papa Bell Drive and home of the Hank Aaron Sports Academy.

The Atlanta Braves become the first baseball team to honor a former Negro League player, Hank Aaron, with the design of their World Series championship rings. The rings are made with 755 diamonds in total to represent the number of career home runs hit by Aaron. There are also 44 emerald cut diamonds on each ring to represent Aaron's retired jersey number. Aaron who died in January of 2021, had played 21 seasons for the Braves franchise.

For the first time since 1950, the World Series features no Black players when the Houston Astros and Philadelphia Phillies face off.

Dusty Baker, manager of the Houston Astros, becomes the first African American manager to win 2,000 major league games when his Astros defeat the Seattle Mariners, 4-0.

The Full Circle Everest climbing team make history as the first all-Black team to stand atop the Mount Everest summit, the highest mountain in the world. The team was led by Philip Henderson, along with Manoah Ainuu, Fred Campbell, James "KG" Kagambi, Thomas Moore, Demond "Dom" Mullins, Eddie Taylor and two women, Abby Dione and Rosemary Saal.

Lester Wright, a 100-year-old World War II veteran, becomes the first African American centenarian to hold the world record in the 100 meters, with a time of 26.34 seconds at the Penn Relays in Philadelphia.

LeBron James of the Los Angeles Lakers becomes the first active NBA player to achieve billionaire status.

The NBA honors the life and legacy of 11-time NBA champion and civil rights pioneer Bill Russell by permanently retiring his No. 6, throughout the league, the first player to be so honored. In addition, all NBA players wear a commemorative patch on the right shoulder of their jerseys, and every NBA court displays a clover-shaped logo with the No. 6 on the sideline near the scorer's table.

Mike Grier is named general manager of the San José Sharks and becomes the first African American general manager in the National Hockey League. Grier's brother, Chris, is the general manager of the NFL's Miami Dolphins.

Konnor McClain captures the U.S. Gymnastic all-around title, in Tampa, Fla., while Shilese Jones and Jordan Chiles come in

Colorful Firsts in U.S. Sports

second and third place. This marks the first time that Black women filled the top three spots in this competition.

Standing 5-foot-9 ¾ Darius Clark becomes the first man to achieve a 50-inch vertical jump from a running start. Clark is a long jumper from Florida State and Texas A&M.

Sara "Lovestyle" Hood, CEO of Sara Belay, Inc., becomes the first Black woman to own a digital sports team. Along with Emmanuel Acho, an NFL analyst and Edward Madongorere, CEO and co-founder of Moon Ultra, Hood is an owner of the Houston Hyenas in SimWin Sports, a sports league in the metaverse that hosts 24/7 fantasy sports and sports betting action featuring NFT players.

2023

"You got to make your own worlds. You got to write yourself in." – Octavia E. Butler

Jalen Hurts of the Philadelphia Eagles and Patrick Mahomes of the Kansas City Chiefs, become the first Black quarterbacks to face off in the Super Bowl, doing so in Glendale, Ariz.

Singer/actress Sheryl Lee Ralph is the first person to sing "Lift Every Voice & Sing" inside a stadium hosting the Super Bowl (LVII, Glendale, Ariz.). The unofficial Black national anthem is usually sung outside or at a remote location at Super Bowl games.

During a pregame broadcast of the Oakland A's game against the Kansas City Royals at Kauffman Stadium announcer Glen Kuiper says: "We had a phenomenal day today, nigger league museum [sic, Negro Leagues Baseball Museum]. And Arthur Bryant's Barbeque." This Freudian slip is reminiscent of a 2010 comment by Mike Greenberg from ESPN's Mike & Mike show when he uttered, "Talking football with you on Martin Luther Coon King Junior Holiday." Greenberg kept his job, Kuiper was suspended and later fired.

The Houston Rockets select Amen XLNC Thompson at No. 4, and the Detroit Pistons select Ausar XLNC Thompson at No. 5. The Thompson twins become the first brothers to be drafted in the top five of the same draft since the 1976 ABA-NBA merger.

The top 10 selections in the NBA Draft are represented by Black agents. Victor Wembanyama is the first pick, and his agent is Bouna Ndiaye. The other picks and their agents: 2) Brandon Miller, agent Wilmer Jackson, 3) Scoot Henderson (Par-Lay Sports and Entertainment), 4) and 5) Amen and Ausar Thompson (father Troy Thompson), 6) Anthony Black (Bill Duffy), 7) Bilal Coulibaly (Bouna Ndiaye), 8) Jarace Walker (Joe Branch, 9) Taylor Hendricks (Raymond Brothers) and 10) Cason Wallace (Marcus Monk).

Attorney Lee A. Hutton III is named commissioner of the Arena Football League. He is the first Black man to lead a professional sports league in the U.S.

The documentary *Black Ice* debuts exposing a history of racism in hockey through the untold stories of Black hockey players, both past and present, in a predominantly white sport. The film examines systemic racism dating back to 1895 and Canada's Colored Hockey League of the Maritimes (CHL), the first all-pro hockey league.

Seimone Augustus becomes the first female athlete in LSU history to have a statue on the school campus; in front of the school's basketball training center next to statues of Bob Pettit, Shaquille O'Neal and Pete Maravich.

At the World Championships in Antwerp, Belgium, Simone Biles (gold), Brazil's Rebeca Andrade (silver) and Shilese Jones (bronze) become the first all-Black trio to medal.

Stephen Curry becomes the first active NBA player to win the American Century Golf Championship which takes place annually in Nevada. He produces a flawless performance which includes a hole-in-one in the second round and an eagle on the final hole. Curry finishes with a final score of 75, beating out Mardy Fish.

Ben Shelton defeats Frances Tiafoe in the US Open quarterfinals. It is the first time that two Black Americans reach the final eight in a grand slam event.

At the U.S. Classic gymnastics, Simone Biles becomes the first woman to perform the Yurchenko half-on with two twists, in competition. The move involves a round-off onto the springboard, followed by a back handspring on the vault. The move becomes the "Biles II on the Vault" skill, and the fifth in her name.

Laulauga Tausaga-Collins is the first Black female discus thrower to win a World Championship in Budapest, Hungary with a toss of more than 227 feet.

Morgan Cato with the Phoenix Suns becomes the first woman of color to hold the title of assistant general manager in the NBA.

Ghalee Waddod Jr. becomes the first athlete, under 10 years old, to sign a six-figure NIL deal with a sports agency. The multi-sport nine-year old talent will be working with Family 4 Life, an agency that represents players from NFL teams, including the New England Patriots, San Francisco 49ers and the New York Giants.

Cage 2WO: Baseball Champions

"There are three things that America will be known for 2,000 years from now when they study this civilization: the Constitution, jazz music, and baseball." - Dr. Gerald Early, Washington University

1855, The *Newark Daily Mercury* reports the first known game between two colored baseball teams, the St. John's and the Union Clubs. The game is played in East Orange, N.J. No score is reported.

1857, Major White League baseball's first <u>recognized</u> African American baseball player, Moses Fleetwood Walker is born in Mt. Pleasant, Ohio.

1859, The *New York Anglo-African* prints the first known box score between two Black teams. The Henson Base Ball Club of Jamaica defeats the Unknowns of Weeksville, 54 to 43, in Jamaica, Long Island.

1860, Brooklyn Excelsiors become the first African American baseball team to tour the U.S.

1867, The National Association of Base Ball Players (NABBP) votes to exclude Black players and their teams from membership, stating "any club which may be composed of one or more colored persons" will be barred. The NABBP reason was "If colored clubs were admitted there would be in all probability some division of feeling, whereas, by excluding them no injury could result to anyone."

1869, The Philadelphia Pythians become the first Black team to defeat an all-White squad, defeating the cross-town rival City Items, 27-17. The *New York Clipper* reports, "The prejudices of race are rapidly disappearing. A week or two ago we chronicled a game between the Pythians (colored) and Olympics (white) clubs of Philadelphia. This affair was a great success, financially and otherwise."

1872, An ideology that would become the motto of the Negro National League, founded by Rube Foster in 1920, was defined by Frederick Douglass at the Colored Men's National Convention in New Orleans, Louisiana. At Mechanics Hall on April 14th, Douglass spoke for the ages: "The Republican Party is the ship, all else is the sea." The delegates add, "Owing our political emancipation in this country to Republican legislation, to which all other parties and political shades of opinion were unjustly and bitterly opposed, we would be blind to our prospects and false to our best interests did we identify ourselves with any other organization."

1878, Cuba forms its first baseball league. It is called the Cuban League and operates until 1961.

1883, A colored women's baseball team from Philadelphia, called the Dolly Vardens start play.

1883, Shep Trusty of the Philadelphia Orions becomes the first player to pitch, catch and hit a home run in the same game. His Orions defeat the hometown Hartville Club, 12 to 10.

1884, Moses Fleetwood Walker, catcher, becomes the first recognized African American to play in the White major leagues with the Toledo Blue Stockings of the American Association.

1885, The *Utica Morning Herald* reports a colored umpire, Jacob Francis from Syracuse, "umpired the game to the complete satisfaction of both teams." The game is between the Syracuse Stars and the Providence Grays of the New York State League.

1885, The Cuban Giants are organized by Frank P. Thompson, head waiter at the Argyle Hotel in Babylon, N.Y., to become the first salaried professional Black team in the U.S. The players earn from $12 to $18 a week.

1886, George Stovey wins 16 of the 49 games won by the Jersey City Skeeters (or Jerseys) in the Eastern League.

1886, Frank Grant, second baseman for the Buffalo Bisons in the International League becomes its first African American player. The next season other African American players Moses Fleetwood Walker, Robert Higgins, William J. Renfroe, George Stovey and Bud Fowler join Grant.

1886, The Southern League of Colored Base Ballists is founded with roughly 19 teams based in Fla., Tenn., Ga., La., Ala. and S.C. The teams are: Athletic Baseball Club - Jacksonville, Fla; Boardways (or Boards) Baseball Club - Savannah, Ga.; Callathumpians Baseball Club - Tallahassee, Fla.; Chattanooga Baseball Club - Chattanooga, Tenn.; Clipper Baseball Club - Jacksonville, Fla.; Daisy Cutter Baseball Club - Fernandina, Fla.; Eclipse Baseball Club - Memphis, Tenn.; Eureka Baseball Club - Memphis, Tenn.; Fox Hunter Baseball Club - Macon, Ga.; Fultons Baseball Club - Charleston, S.C.; Garden Lilies Baseball Club - Palatka, Fla.; Lafayette Baseball Club - Savannah, Ga.; Macedonia Baseball Club - Jacksonville, Fla.; Montgomery Baseball Club - Montgomery, Ala.; Pensacola Baseball Club - Pensacola, Fla.; Roman Cities Baseball Club - LaVilla, Fla.; Tallapoosa Baseball Club - St. Augustine, Fla.; The Georgia Champions' Baseball Club - Atlanta, Ga.; and the Union Baseball Club - New

Colorful Firsts in U.S. Sports

Orleans, La. The league folds in August, naming the Memphis Eclipse as unofficial league champion.

1887, George Stovey signs with Newark of the International League and joins catcher Moses Fleetwood Walker to form the first African American battery in White professional baseball. Stovey wins 33 games against 14 losses for the fourth-place Newark Little Giants. Cap Anson refuses to allow his National League Chicago White Sox to play against the Newark Little Giants because African American pitcher George Stovey is on the roster.

1887, The National Colored Base Ball League (NCBBL) is organized. The original teams are the Boston Resolutes, Philadelphia Pythians, New York Gorhams, Pittsburg[h] Keystones, Baltimore Lord Baltimores, Louisville Falls City, Washington Capitol Citys and the Cincinnati Browns. The Washington and Cincinnati franchises would not play this season. The league folds in May.

1887, *The New York Times* publishes a letter written by several White players entitled "A Color Line in Baseball" on Sept. 12. The letter addresses Chris von der Ahe, a German immigrant and owner of the St. Louis Browns: "Dear Sir, We, the undersigned members of the St. Louis Baseball Club, do not agree to play against negroes (sic) (Cuban Giants) tomorrow. We will cheerfully play against white people at any time, and think, by refusing to play, we are only doing what is right, take everything into consideration and the shape of the team is in at present."

1888, The International League which has eight Black baseball players formally decides to sign no more African Americans as another "Gentlemen's Agreement" is mandated.

1889 to 1946, African American players are excluded from White professional teams by a "Gentlemen's Agreement."

1891, President Benjamin Harrison becomes the first sitting U.S. president to attend an interracial game and witness the New York Big Gorhams (colored) defeat the Cape May team from New Jersey.

1895, The Page Fence Giants out of Adrian, Mich., are organized by John "Bud" Fowler and Grant "Home Run" Johnson. Future Hall of Famer Sol White and ace pitcher George Wilson join the team and they compile a won-lost record of 118-36-2 against all levels of competition, that included two games against the Cincinnati Reds.

1897, Eugene M. Gregory suits for the Harvard freshman baseball team, becoming the first Black ballplayer at the collegiate level.

1899, Danny McClellan pitching the first recorded perfect game by an African American pitcher against the Penn Park Athletic Club of York, Pa., champions of the Tri-State League, is well known in 1903. Recently, Tony Kissel and Wayne Stivers found an earlier no-hitter in 1899. It is pitched by William Selden of the Cuban Giants on July 9 against the Bordentowns, a team in the Middle States League. Selden strikes out three and walks two batters, en route to a 2-0 win. A full account of the game is reported in the *Trenton Daily True American*.

1900, The Cuban League welcomes the addition of an all-Black team from America, the San Francisco B.B.C., which wins the pennant in its first season.

1901, Baltimore Orioles manager John McGraw passes Columbia Giants second baseman off as a Native American named Chief Tokohama. Before the start of the season, Chicago White Sox president Charlie Comiskey exposes the ploy.

1903, Danny McClellan, pitches the first recorded perfect game by an African American pitcher, against the Penn Park Athletic Club of York, Pa., champions of the Tri-State League.

1905, Future heavyweight boxing champion Jack Johnson organizes a semi-pro baseball team called the Johnson's Pets. Johnson plays first base.

1906, William Freihofer, who owns a chain of bakeries in Philadelphia organizes the International League of Independent Professional Base Ball Clubs. The original teams were the Cuban X-Giants, Philadelphia Quaker Giants (later replaced by the Philadelphia Giants), Cuban Stars of Havana, Havana Stars (later replaced by the Wilmington Giants of Delaware) and the Philadelphia Professionals with primarily a White roster. After 40 scheduled games, the Philadelphia Giants are declared winners of the Freihofer Cup.

1907, King Solomon White, captain of the Philadelphia Giants, authors *The History of Colored Base Ball*. The first book written about African Americans in baseball, includes 57 rare images and chapters written by Andrew "Rube" Foster and Grant "Home Run" Johnson, on pitching and batting, respectively.

1909, Pete Hill and Bruce Petway become the first African American players included in the Cabañas Cuban baseball card set.

1910, Leland Giants catcher Bruce Petway, playing for the Havana Reds in Cuba, is reported by the *La Lucha* newspaper, of throwing out American League batting champion Ty Cobb of the Detroit Tigers on several occasions. Cobb vows to never take the field against Black players.

1910, A colored female baseball club, the St. Louis Black Broncos is organized by Conrad Kuebler.

1910, On February 22 the *Altoona Tribune (PA)*, shares editorial thoughts from future Hall of Fame pitcher Cy Young. "The little brown men of Japan are planning an invasion of the U.S. A baseball attack. They are planning to attack the American and National League teams. Among the tribes they will attempt to subdue is the White Sox. Also the Detroit Tigers. The players are students of Kelo (sic, Keio) University. If they succeed, a regular invasion will follow, and we will have unpronounceable names on every club." Young continues, "Baseball belongs to this country. Its supremacy in baseball will never be threatened. And for the very good reason that while some of the athletes of other nations may imitate and even equal our ball players in one department of the game, they cannot excel in all. Take the Japanese athlete. He can't hit worth a hurrah." Young also adds, "A Jap can't pitch. There is one reason for this, of course. That reason is that they can't grip the ball. The hands of the Japs are very small." Young did not forget the Cuban players, "That reason does not hold good with the Cuban. Yet their pitchers are a bad lot. They have no curve ball, and, of course, use little headwork." After Young's death in 1955, the Cy Young Award is created the next season and is given annually to the best pitcher in the American and National Leagues.

1911, Andrew "Rube" Foster, considered the "Father of Black Baseball" organizes the Chicago American Giants.

1916, Alex Pompez's Cuban Stars, with José Méndez and Cristóbal Torriente, become the first Negro League franchise to visit Puerto Rico.

1920, The first Black professional baseball league to survive a full season, the Negro National League of Professional Baseball Clubs, is established by Andrew Rube Foster, J. L. Wilkinson, Tenny Blount, C. I. Taylor and others. The principal stockholders are Willie Foster, Rube Foster, J. L. Wilkinson, Russell Thompson and Walter M. Farmer. The charter teams are the Indianapolis ABCs, Dayton Marcos, Detroit Stars, St. Louis Giants, Kansas City Monarchs, Chicago Giants, Chicago American Giants and the Cuban Stars based in Cincinnati.

1920, The Cuban Stars of the Negro National League put the first all-Latino major league lineup on the field, in a May 9 doubleheader against the Indianapolis ABCs. The lineup in the first game includes, Eufemio Abreu (catcher), Bernardo Baro (centerfield), Valentine Dreke (leftfield), Marcelino Guerra (first base), Mike Herrera (third base), José LeBlanc (pitcher), Cando López (second base), Herman Rios (shortstop), and Faustino Valdés (rightfield).

1921, The Baltimore Black Sox Bloomer Girls baseball team start play.

1923, Earl Brown becomes a member of the Harvard University baseball team.

1923, The Mutual Association of Eastern Colored Clubs, better known as the Eastern Colored League, is created by postal worker Ed Bolden, owner of the Hilldale Athletic Club. Charter members include Hilldale, the Bacharach Giants, the Brooklyn Royal Giants, the Cuban Stars (East), the Lincoln Giants of New York, and the Baltimore Black Sox.

1924, The first Colored World Series is played between the Kansas City Monarchs and the Hilldale Club from Darby, Pa. The Monarchs win the 10-game series, five games to four with one tie. Arguably the most dramatic World Series ever played, as each team reeled off three wins in a row, four games were decided by a single run and five games are won in the final inning.

1925, The Hilldale Club from Darby, Pa. wins the Colored World Series, defeating the Kansas City Monarchs, five games to one, in the best of a nine-game series.

1925, The all-Black Wichita (Kan.) Monrovians of the Colored Western League face off against the local Ku Klux Klan No. 6 team at Wichita's Island Park. To avoid favoritism, the game is officiated by two Irish Catholics. The Monrovians win 10 to 8 with no violence reported by the local newspapers.

1926, The Chicago American Giants defeat the Bacharach Giants to win the Colored World Series, five games to three, in the best of a nine-game series.

1927, The Chicago American Giants repeat as winners of the Colored World Series by beating the Bacharach Giants again, five games to three, in the best of a nine-game series.

1927, The first Negro baseball team to play in Japan, the Philadelphia Royal Giants, owned by Lonnie Goodwin, visits the Far East.

1928, The Chicago American Giants of the Negro National League put numbers on the back of their uniforms. One year before the New York Yankees and the Cleveland Indians do likewise. The earliest photographic evidence of uniform numbers appears in the 1909 *Chicago Daily News*, picturing Cuban pitcher and future Hall of Famer José Méndez in a Cuban Stars uniform with the number "12" on his left sleeve.

1930, The Kansas City Monarchs play its first game under their portable lighting system in Enid, Okla., against the local college. This is six seasons before the first night game is played in the National League at Crosley Field in Cincinnati, Ohio in 1935.

1930, Dexter Park, former home field for the Brooklyn Royal Giants of the Eastern Colored League, in Queens becomes the first ballpark in New York with installed stadium lights. Ebbets Field, home of the Brooklyn Dodgers, will not have a lighting

Colorful Firsts in U.S. Sports

system until 1938.

1930, For the first time in history, two Negro League teams play at Yankee Stadium. The event sponsored by the Brotherhood of Sleeping Car Porters draws 20,000 fans who watch the New York Lincoln Giants and the Baltimore Black Sox split a pair. The Giants win the first game 13-4, with the Black Sox winning the nightcap 5-3. Baltimore's Rap Dixon hits three home runs and the Giants' Chino Smith has two round trippers and a triple.

1932, The *Washington Post* reports the first night baseball game ever played at Griffith Stadium. The Washington Pilots and the Pittsburgh Crawfords of the East-West League play before 4,000 fans under the portable Klieg lighting system. The American League Senators would play its first night game on 28 May 1941.

1932, Gus Greenlee, owner of the Pittsburgh Crawfords, builds Greenlee Park. He installs a permanent overhead lighting system, making it one of the first parks in the country to offer nighttime baseball.

1938, New York Yankee outfielder Jake Powell says in a radio interview on WGN Chicago that as a police officer during the off season, he keeps in shape by "cracking niggers over the head with his nightstick" as he walks his beat in Dayton, Ohio. Powell gets a 10-day suspension by Commissioner Kenesaw Mountain Landis.

1939, The Negro Leagues played two All-Star games, one in New York and the other in Chicago. This was 20 years before the re-integrated major leagues would play two All-Star games in the same season. In 1959, the first major league All-Star game is played at Forbes Field in Pittsburgh and the second game at Los Angeles' Coliseum. In 1942, three East-West All-Star games are scheduled but the third game, in Memphis, is rained out.

1941, Kansas City Monarchs Catcher Frank Duncan Sr. and pitcher Frank Duncan Jr. become the first father and son and the first father-and-son battery, to play for the same team, in the same year. This is 50 years before the Ken Griffey family make ancestral history.

1941, Before the ban on segregated seating was lifted in 1944 at Sportsman's Park in St. Louis, the Kansas City Monarchs, with Satchel Paige on the mound, play the Chicago American Giants before an interracial crowd of 19,178 on the Fourth of July. Average attendance per game for the Cardinals was 8,229 and for the Browns 2,289.

1942, The Kansas City Monarchs sweep the Homestead Grays in four games to capture the Negro League World Series.

1942, The first night East-West All-Star Game in the Negro Leagues is played under the lights at Municipal Stadium in Cleveland, Ohio.

1942, The *Baltimore Afro-American* reports that WWDC 1460 AM radio will broadcast games between the Homestead Grays and the Baltimore Elite Giants on Friday, August 7 and Sunday, August 9.

1943, Alec and Ted Radcliffe become the first brothers to represent the same team, the Chicago American Giants, in the East-West All-Star classic.

1943, The Homestead Grays defeat the Birmingham Black Barons in the Negro World Series, four games to three.

1944, The Homestead Grays repeat as World Champions defeating the Birmingham Black Barons again in the Negro World Series, four games to one.

1944, The St. Louis Cardinals and St. Louis Browns lift its policy of restricting Negroes to the bleachers and pavilion at Sportsman's Park. According to the local press, "Negroes now may purchase seats in the grandstand." Sportsman's Park was the last big league ballpark with a Jim Crow section. The black folks-only right field pavilion was covered by a screen preventing the catch of a home run. In 1927, the screen was removed when the Yankees played the Browns. That season Babe Ruth hit four of his 60 home runs into the pavilion, only 310 feet from home plate.

1945, In a letter to Lee MacPhail, American League President, dated 29 October 1945, Connie Mack, manager and president of the Philadelphia Athletics writes, "It was a great disappointment to me to see that Branch Rickey had signed a negro (sic) for his Montreal Baseball Club. If all Major League Club owners would just let Branch have the negroes (sic), feel that we would all be better off in the long run."

1945, New York Mayor Fiorello La Guardia forms a committee, to study segregation in baseball and, ultimately, pressure the New York teams to sign Black players. Yankee executive Larry MacPhail responds in part, "There are few, if any, negro (sic) players who could qualify for play in the major leagues at this time. A major league player must have something besides natural ability . . . In conclusion: I have no hesitancy in saying that the Yankees have no intention of signing negro (sic) players under contract or reservation to negro (sic) clubs."

1945, The Cleveland Buckeyes defeats the Homestead Grays in four straight games to win the Negro World Series.

1946, The Newark Eagles, owned by Abe and Effa Manley, with Biz Mackey, Monte Irvin, Larry Doby and Leon Day defeat the

Kansas City Monarchs in seven games to capture the Negro World Series title.

1947, The New York Cubans, with Luis Tiant Sr. and Minnie Miñoso, win the Negro World Series by defeating the Cleveland Buckeyes, four games to one.

1948, The U.S. military integrates its service baseball teams.

1948, The Homestead Grays win the last sanctioned Negro World Series defeating Willie Mays and the Birmingham Black Barons, four games to one.

1948 The Cleveland Indians become the first major league (American League) baseball team with Black players to win a World Series, with outfielder Larry Doby and pitcher Satchel Paige.

1948, In the fourth game of the 1948 World Series, Cleveland Indians pitcher Steve Gromek defeats the Boston Braves, 2-1 with the help of Larry Doby's home run. The local Cleveland paper, *The Plain Dealer* snaps a photograph of Doby and Gromek hugging and smiling, in the locker room, to the discontent of many. In his Hall of Fame acceptance speech, Doby fondly remembered that picture: "That was a feeling from within, the human side of two people, one black and one white. That made up for everything I went through. I would always relate back to that whenever I was insulted or rejected from hotels. I'd always think about that picture. It would take away all the negatives."

1949, Jackie Robinson, Roy Campanella and Don Newcombe, all of the Brooklyn Dodgers, and Larry Doby of the Cleveland Indians become the first African Americans to play in a major league All-Star game; the American League wins 11-7 at Ebbets Field.

1951, On June 3, against the St. Louis Cardinals, the New York Giants' Monte Irvin is walked. Willie Mays doubles with Irvin stopping at third base. Hank Thompson is intentionally walked filling the bases. This is the first time in MLB history the bases are loaded with African Americans. With two outs, Dave Koslo (pitcher) strikes out looking. Before 32,564 fans, the Giants win 1-0.

1951, In the playoffs, after an injury to outfielder Don Mueller, the New York Giants employ an all-Black outfield with Hank Thompson, Willie Mays and Monte Irvin. Hank Thompson, normally a third baseman, is sent in to replace Mueller, instead of outfielder Bobby Thomson.

1952, Former Birmingham Black Baron and Indianapolis Clown third baseman Johnny Britton and former Black Baron pitcher Jimmy Newberry become the first African American players to compete in Japan. They are on loan to the Hankyu Braves of the Japanese Pacific League from the St. Louis Browns' farm system.

1952, New York Yankee general manager George Weiss explains, at a cocktail party, why the Yankees are still an all-White team, five years after Jackie Robinson join the Brooklyn Dodgers, "Boxholders from Westchester (County) don't want that sort of crowd. They would be offended to have to sit with niggers."

1953, The New York Yankees, with Yogi Berra, Mickey Mantle, Phil Rizzuto, Whitey Ford and Johnny Mize, become the last all-White baseball team to win a World Series, when they defeat the Brooklyn Dodgers (4-2), with Joe Black, Jackie Robinson, Roy Campanella and Junior Gilliam.

1953, The city of Birmingham, Ala., bars the Jackie Robinson All-Stars, composed of Black and White players from playing due to a 1944 city ordinance, section 859 which cites "It shall be unlawful for any person in charge of or in control of any room, hall, theater, picture house, auditoriums, yard, court, ballpark, public park or indoor or outdoor place, to which both white persons and negroes (sic) are admitted, to cause, permit or allow mixing of races." In 1950, the city passes Ordinance 798-F to add even more restrictions to prevent racial interaction at baseball, softball, football, basketball or similar games. Robinson's all-star team includes Dodger first baseman Gil Hodges and Indian third baseman Al Rosen.

1953, The Hot Spring Bathers of the Cotton States League (CSL) sign pitching brothers Jim and Leander Tugerson to play only in home games due to segregation sanctions in the deep South. CSL president Al Haraway blocks this loophole in the bylaws. In April, the National Association of Professional Baseball Leagues, an umbrella organization for minor leagues, rules against Haraway and reinstates the Tugersons. Instead, the Tugerson brothers leave the CSL and join the Class D Knoxville Smokies of the Mountain States League. See 1955.

1953, The Portsmouth Merrimacs of the Piedmont League become the first league team to sign African American players; catchers Claude and Dick Brown, outfielders Bill Louis, James Livingston and Burly Barge, infielders Henry Craighead, Thomas Burt, Eugene "Stank" White and pitcher Leonard Dunovant. The new team owner Frank Lawrence effectively ended the Virginia-based Piedmont League's 33-year history of racial exclusion. Later, in the season, the Merrimacs signed 45-year-old former Negro League first sacker Buck Leonard. The team, without a major league affiliation, folds after the 1955 season.

1953, The Miami Sun Sox of the Florida International League sign its first two African American players, outfielder Albert "Speed"

Colorful Firsts in U.S. Sports

Baro and third baseman Jonathan "Clyde" Parris. The Sun Sox were a minor league affiliate of the Brooklyn Dodgers.

1954, The Cleveland Indians, in the American League, become the first team to have an all-tan outfield during the regular season with Al Smith, Dave Pope and Larry Doby. In 1951, New York Giants, in the National League, fielded an all-Black outfield in the playoffs.

1954, Mamie "Peanut" Johnson and Connie Morgan join the Indianapolis Clowns, as pitcher and second baseman, respectively. This will be Johnson's and Morgan's only year in professional Black baseball. Toni Stone leaves the Clowns and joins the Kansas City Monarchs.

1954, The New York Giants become the first National League baseball team with ebony players to win a World Series, with Monte Irvin, Hank Thompson, Rubén Gómez, and Willie Mays. The Cleveland Indians became the first American League team with Black players to a win World Series in 1948.

1954, The Dodgers field the first Black majority team in the re-integrated major leagues when they start five African Americans: Jim Gilliam at second, Jackie Robinson at third, Sandy Amorós in left field, Don Newcombe on the mound and Roy Campanella catching. They defeat the Milwaukee Braves, 2-1, in 11 innings at County Stadium.

1954, On April 9, Nat Peeples becomes the first and only African American to take the field in a Southern Association game. Peeples pinch-hits in the fifth inning and plays left field the next evening for the Atlanta Crackers. He goes 0-for-4 with a walk in two games and is gone from the all-White league a week later, demoted to Class A Jacksonville. He never returns to Atlanta, ultimately finishing out his career in the minor leagues.

1954, Under a portable lighting system, the Harlem Globetrotters become the first professional baseball team to play a night game at Wrigley Field. This event is three decades before the Chicago Cubs play its first night game in 1988.

1955, The Cannon Street YMCA All-Stars are the first Black Little League team in South Carolina. When all the White teams withdrew in protest, the Cannon Street team won the state tournament by forfeit and advanced to the Little League World Series in Williamsport, Pa. However the team was declared ineligible because it did not win games on the field. As they watched the first game from the stands the crowd chanted, "Let them play! Let them play!" in support.

1955, The New Orleans Pelicans of the Southern Association (AA) refuse three Negro players assigned by the parent Pittsburgh Pirates club: Bennie Daniels, Román Mejias and R. C. Stevens. General manager Joe Nowak claim, "They don't measure up to Southern Association standards." Black fans boycott the team that averaged 1700 fans per game. Two seasons later, owners claimed they lost $130,000 and become an affiliate of the New York Yankees. All three players make the Pirates team within a few years.

1955, The Pine Bluff (Ark.) Judges of the Cotton States League signs three Black players, outfielder Charles Peppers and infielder Russell Moseley from the Memphis Red Sox and pitcher Charles Chatman of the Detroit Stars. The Judges' board of directors announces it will not play its Negroes in Mississippi.

1955, Bill James becomes the second umpire (after Emmett Ashford in the Pacific Coast League) in professional baseball. James makes his debut in the Pony League at Jamestown, N.Y.

1956, Minnie Miñoso has led the American League in the Hit Batsmen (HBP) category in five of the last six seasons, encouraging the Rules Committee to create a rule, "It is a strike if a legal pitch in flight touches the batter in the strike zone." Despite the ruling, Miñoso continues to lead the league in this dubious category until 1961.

1956, The minor league baseball Louisville Colonels of the American Association announce the desegregation of its team. Also for the first time Negroes will be permitted to sit unsegregated in the stands at Parkway Field.

1959, The Boston Red Sox become the last major league team to play a Black player when they sign infielder Pumpsie Green.

1960, The American League Kansas City Athletics finish in last place with 58 wins – 96 loses and finish 39 games behind the Yankees. The A's became the last major league team to employ an all-white roster for the entire season.

1963, After Maury Wills' base stealing record of 104 steals, baseball institutes a rule change. This year pitchers are required to come to a complete stop (or pause), before delivering the pitch to the plate. The intent is to hold the potential base stealer closer to the bag.

1963, Bill Russell of the Boston Celtics and Earl Wilson of the Boston Red Sox pay homage to Civil Rights leader Medgar Evers assassinated in Jackson, Mississippi. Wilson and Russell circulate among the estimated 1,800 people gathered at the Parkman Bandstand on the Boston Common, to collect funds.

1965, In Los Angeles, Maury Wills of the Dodgers and Willie Mays of the S. F. Giants, exchange lineup cards with umpire Al Barlick. This marks the first time in major league baseball, the opposing team captains are African Americans.

Baseball Champions

1968, Dr. Martin Luther King Jr. is assassinated. Baseball players demand, against owners' wishes, that 30 games scheduled for April 8-9 not be played. April 9 is the day of Dr. King's funeral. MLB delays Opening Day until April 10.

1968, Monte Irvin becomes the first African American to receive an executive position in major league baseball, when hired by Commissioner William D. Eckert. The former Newark Eagles star is appointed Assistant Director of Promotion and Public Relations.

1968, Bob Gibson leads the National League with an ERA of 1.12, while Luis Tiant Jr. leads American League with a 1.60 ERA. They are the first Black pitchers to win the ERA crowns, and they record the lowest ERAs by pitchers since the re-integration (1947) of the white-centric major leagues. The pitching mound is lowered before the next season.

1969, With a rule change, the strike zone is now from armpit to top of the knee, while the pitcher's mound is lowered, five inches, to 10 inches above the ground. These changes are an attempt to aid batters, potentially raising Earned Run Average (ERA) percentages.

1969, St. Louis Cards outfielder Curt Flood, along with Tim McCarver, Joe Hoerner and Byron Browne, are traded to Philadelphia for Dick Allen, Cookie Rojas and Jerry Johnson. Flood challenges baseball's reserve clause, which binds players to the clubs for the life of their careers. He was earning $90,000 a year but argued in an interview with Howard Cosell on ABC's *Wide World of Sports* that "a well-paid slave is, nonetheless, a slave."

1971, The Pittsburgh Pirates field an all-Black and Latino starting nine against the Philadelphia Phillies at Three Rivers Stadium. Lineup includes Manny Sanguillén (c), Al Oliver (1b), Rennie Stennett (2b), Dave Cash (3b), Jackie Hernández (ss), Willie Stargell (lf), Gene Clines (cf), Roberto Clemente (rf) and Dock Ellis (p). For the record, the manager Danny Murtaugh's Bucs beat the Phillies, 10-7, in front of 11,278 fans. Said Pirate Manager Danny Murtaugh of the event, "When it comes to making out the lineup, I'm color blind."

1972, In Flood v. Kuhn, 407 U.S. 258 (1972), a U.S. Supreme Court decision upholds, by a 5–3 margin, the antitrust exemption first granted to Major League Baseball (MLB) in Federal Baseball Club v. National League. It arose from a challenge by St. Louis Cardinals' outfielder Curt Flood when he refused to be traded to the Philadelphia Phillies after the 1969 season. He sought injunctive relief from the reserve clause, which prevented him from negotiating with another team for a year after his contract expired. Named as initial respondents were baseball commissioner Bowie Kuhn, MLB and all of its then-24 member clubs. Although the Court ruled in baseball's favor 5–3, it admitted the original grounds for the antitrust exemption were tenuous at best, that baseball was indeed interstate commerce for purposes of the act and the exemption was an "anomaly" it had explicitly refused to extend to other professional sports or entertainment. That admission set in motion events which ultimately led to an arbitrator's ruling nullifying the reserve clause and opening the door for free agency in baseball and other sports.

1973, On May 8, Cubs' manager Whitey Lockman was ejected in the 11th inning of a game against the San Diego Padres. Coach Ernie Banks fills in as manager for the remainder of the game, which the Cubs win, 3-2, in 12 innings. Technically, if not officially, Banks becomes white MLB's first Black manager, predating Frank Robinson's hiring in 1975.

1974, Oakland A's owner Charlie Finley promotes 11-year-old batboy and rapper Stanley Burrell to honorary vice-president. Sixteen years later, Burrell records top-selling rap albums, under the name of M.C. Hammer.

1974, Oakland A's owner Charlie Finley hires former Michigan State University sprinter Herb Washington as the first "designated runner" in major league history. Washington has no prior professional baseball experience. He steals 31 bases in 48 attempts and scored 33 runs in 105 ML games.

1976, Bill Lucas, former player for the Atlanta Braves, is named by Braves owner Ted Turner as vice president of player personnel, at the time the highest administrative position in major league baseball. His responsibilities were essentially that of a general manager. (See 1993, Bob Watson, general manager of the Yankees.)

1978, Major league baseball initiates the Hal McRae rule. During the 1977 AL Championship Series Kansas City Royal McRae aggressively takes out N.Y. Yankee second baseman Willie Randolph by sliding very wide of second base attempting to break up a double play. The new ruling prohibits runners from targeting fielders.

1981, With Kansas City ahead 7–4 over the Mariners, Amos Otis taps a dribbler down the third base line in the 6th inning. Mariners third baseman Lenny Randle gets down on all fours as the ball rolls along the line, finally going foul. Royals manager Whitey Herzog protests that Randle was blowing the ball foul, while the third baseman argues he was merely pleading with it. Umpire Larry McCoy rules in favor of Herzog and Otis gets a hit. Otis did not score but the Royals win, 8–5.

1985, Dennis "Oil Can" Boyd, son of Negro Leaguer Willie James Boyd, is fined by the Boston Red Sox for having a cocky demeanor and animated fist-pumping and finger-wagging on the mound. Conversely, 10 years earlier, the 1976 A.L. Rookie of the Year, Mark "The Bird" Fidrych of the Detroit Tigers known mostly for talking to the ball, getting on his hands and knees to manicure the pitching mound, was labeled an entertaining "flake" and was never fined.

1987, On the 40th anniversary of Jackie Robinson's promotion to the Brooklyn Dodgers, his minor league teammate with the Montreal Royals, L.A. Dodgers executive Al Campanis, is fired for racially biased comments. Speaking to Ted Koppel on *Nightline* about the managerial potential of African Americans, Campanis says, "No, I don't believe it's prejudice. I truly believe they (Negroes) may not have some of the necessities to be, let's say, a field manager or perhaps a general manager."

1987, An independent baseball league, the Empire State League, based in Long Island, N.Y., hires Black managers for all four of its teams. Hired are former major leaguers Paul Blair and George Scott, along with Bernardo Leonard and Brian Flood, nephew of Curt Flood. League games are played at Long Island's Hofstra University. The league folds in 1988 after two weeks of play.

1987, Phil S. Dixon is the first Black man to issue a U.S. card set about the Negro Leagues. The *Negro League Greats* is a 45 postcard-size, black and white card set.

1989, Bill White becomes the first African American President of major league baseball's National League.

1990, The Negro Leagues Baseball Museum is founded in Kansas City, Mo., the first institution in America to honor Negro baseball players. It is founded by Horace Peterson, Phil S. Dixon, Alfred "Slick" Surratt, John "Buck" O'Neil, Dewitt "Woody" Smallwood and Larry Lester. Treasurer Lester privately funds the museum in its embryonic years and serves as its research director until 1995.

1993, Writer Wendell Smith, former travel mate of Jackie Robinson, is the first African American recipient of the Spink Award, first conferred in 1962. Named for J.G. Taylor Spink, founder of *The Sporting News*, the award honors baseball writers for "meritorious contributions to baseball writing" and is presented at the HOF induction ceremonies.

1996, Bob Watson, for the New York Yankees, is the first Black general manager to win a World Series.

1997, Jackie Robinson becomes the first athlete to have his jersey number (42) retired in perpetuity. National League President Len Coleman initiates the mandate. The New York Yankees' player Mariano Rivera, who retired after the 2013 season, was the last active player to wear No. 42.

1999, On the 25th anniversary of Hank Aaron breaking Babe Ruth's lifetime home run mark, Commissioner Bud Selig announces the creation of the Hank Aaron Award. The award is a tribute to the best all-around player based on combined number of hits, home runs and RBIs. The honor is the first "official" award named after a former player still living. The initial recipients are Latin Americans Sammy Sosa (Cubs) and Manny Ramirez (Indians).

2005, The Baltimore Orioles are the first major league team to start a season without an African American player since 1959, when Pumpsie Green joined the Boston Red Sox in July.

2005, The Houston Astros are the first World Series team, since the 1953 New York Yankees without an African American on its series roster. Their bench coach Cecil Cooper is Black. During the season, African American outfielders Charles Gipson (19 games) and Charlton Jimerson (one game) played for the Astros.

2007, Tony Reagins with the Los Angeles Angels of Anaheim and Michael Hill with the Miami Marlins are named general managers.

2007, In recognition of the 60th anniversary of Jackie Robinson breaking the color barrier, five teams – Dodgers, Astros, Phillies, Pirates and Cardinals – feature all players wearing number 42.

2007, Major league baseball hosts the first Civil Rights Game in tribute to the history of civil rights in the U.S. The St. Louis Cardinals beat the Cleveland Indians, 5 to 1, at AutoZone Park in Memphis, Tenn. The last Civil Rights game is played in 2014 at Minute Maid Park in Houston, Texas.

2017, Oakland A's catcher Bruce Maxwell becomes the first major league baseball player to take a knee to protest police brutality and racial injustice. It takes another three years for anyone else to follow his lead in the big leagues.

2017, Major League Baseball and USA Baseball launch the DREAM Series, a development experience event focusing on the dynamics of pitching and catching for a diverse group of elite high-school athletes, predominantly Black players, during Martin Luther King Jr. holiday weekend. In addition to on-field training, seminars, mentorship, and scout evaluations are provided in this cost-free experience.

2018, The Cleveland Indians announced the retiring and removal of their longtime and controversial logo, Chief Wahoo. Starting in 2019, Chief Wahoo will be gone from all gameday uniforms and will no longer be used by the team at Progressive Field in Cleveland, Ohio. However, fans can still purchase Wahoo merchandise from the team store.

2020, On Opening Day, a stylish MLB/BLM logo is designed on the field's pitching mound, with patches worn on jersey sleeves. African American players Tim Anderson, Josh Bell, Mookie Betts and Jack Flaherty lead this effort in support the Black Lives

Matter movement.

2020, The Baseball Writers' Association of America (BBWAA) vote overwhelmingly to remove former major league baseball Commissioner Kenesaw Mountain Landis' name from the plaques awarded to the American and National League MVPs. The decision comes after a few former MVPs, including Black award winners Barry Larkin and Terry Pendleton, voice displeasure with their plaques being named for Landis, who kept the game segregated during the 24 years he served as commissioner from 1920 until his death in 1944.

2020, The Baseball Writers' Association of America (BBWAA) submits a proposal to remove J.G. Taylor Spink's name from the organization's most prestigious award, which is given to writers for "meritorious contributions to baseball writing" since 1962. Spink, publisher of the *Sporting News* from 1914 to 1962, was the award's first recipient, shortly after his death. The *Sporting News* supports the removing of Spink's name. In the many decades before Jackie Robinson's debut with the Brooklyn Dodgers, the newspaper largely ignored the achievements of Black players and often used its voice to sustain negative stereotypes about them.

2020, After 105 years, the Cleveland Indians move away from a moniker considered racist. In 2019, the team removes the contentious smiling, cartoonish mascot Chief Wahoo logo from its caps and jerseys, but the image is still sold by third-party vendors. A replacement moniker to be announced.

2020, In partnership with active and former Major Leagues players and the Major League Baseball Players Association (MLBPA) the Players Alliance is created to change and work to address systemic barriers. Principals include Edwin Jackson (founder and secretary), CC Sabathia (vice-chair), Curtis Sanderson (board chair) and Adam Jones (member).

2020, Former University of Cincinnati baseball players Jordan Ramey and Nathan Moore petition to change the name of Marge Schott Stadium that opened in 2004. Schott owned MLB's Cincinnati Reds from 1984 to 1999. Her racial and ethnic slurs against African American, Jewish and Japanese people prompted a one-year ban from baseball in 1993. After publicly praising Adolf Hitler in a 1996 ESPN interview, Schott was forced to give up day-to-day control of the Reds until 1998. The university's board of trustees voted unanimously to remove Schott's name from both the stadium and a place in the university's archives library.

2020, Retired outfielder Torii Hunter tells ESPN's "Golic and Wingo" that racially abusive fans at Fenway Park led Hunter to put the Boston Red Sox in the no-trade clause of his contracts. Hunter shares on WEEI-FM's "The Greg Hill Show" that he heard far more racist taunts in Boston than any other city.

2020, Major league baseball announces that the Negro League statistics from 1920 to 1948 will be officially classified as "major league status," marking a long-overdue acknowledgement of Black players who did not have the opportunity to play in the American or National Leagues before 1947.

2021, Major league baseball moves the Atlanta All-Star game to Denver, Colorado, in protest of Georgia's new election rules that disproportionately restricts minority voting rights in urban areas. Governor Brian Kemp adds new identification requirements for absentee ballots, limits use of drop boxes and makes it a misdemeanor for groups to offer food or water to voters waiting in line near polling places.

2021, Tony Humphrey, a 16-year-old junior at Iona Prep, a private school in New Rochelle, N.Y., commits to play baseball at Boston College. Humphrey joins the school's track team and shares with his assistant athletic director, "It never hurts to gain speed." However the educator tells Humphrey that he "gained that speed by running from the police." Soon after Humphrey transfers to a public school near his home in Cortland, N.Y. The assistant AD resigns amid a student walkout.

2021, The historical marker to honor Jackie Robinson's birthplace at the Roddenbery Memorial Library in Cairo, Ga., is damaged by gunfire.

2021, The Atlanta Board of Education votes unanimously to change the name of the [Nathan Bedford] Forrest Hill Academy to the Hank Aaron New Beginnings Academy. The academy had been named after a Confederate general, a founding figure of the Ku Klux Klan and Grand Wizard.

2021, At Guaranteed Field, the Chicago White Sox become the first major league team to fly a flag representing its hometown Chicago American Giants from the Negro Leagues. The American Giants won the Negro World Series in 1926 and 1927.

2022, For the first time since 1950, the World Series features no Black players when the Houston Astros and Philadelphia Phillies face off.

2023, During a pregame broadcast of the Oakland A's game against the Kansas City Royals at Kauffman Stadium announcer Glen Kuiper says: "We had a phenomenal day today, nigger league museum [sic, Negro Leagues Baseball Museum]. And Arthur

Colorful Firsts in U.S. Sports

Bryant's Barbeque." This Freudian slip is reminiscent of a 2010 comment by Mike Greenberg from ESPN's Mike & Mike show when he uttered, "Talking football with you on Martin Luther Coon King Junior Holiday." Greenberg kept his job, Kuiper was suspended and later fired.

Jackie Robinson's last wish

Nine days before his fatal heart attack, Jackie Robinson made his final public appearance before Game 2 of the 1972 World Series, before 53,224 at Cincinnati's Riverfront Stadium to express his final wish.

"I'm extremely proud and pleased to be here this afternoon," Robinson said in a very brief remark after receiving an award of recognition from commissioner Bowie Kuhn, "but must admit, I'm going to be tremendously more pleased and more proud when I look at that third-base coaching line one day and see a Black face managing in baseball."

Since that caffeinated moment in 1972, 46 men have named manager of major league teams without playing a single day in the majors.

Name	Year	Name	Year
Manny Acta	2007	John McLaren	2007
Terry Bevington	1995	Stump Merrill	1990
John Boles	1996	Dave Miley	2003
Dave Bristol	1966	Ray Miller	1985
Daren Brown	2010	Pat Murphy	2015
Terry Collins	1994	Danny Ozark	1973
Tony DeFrancesco	2012	Brian Price	2014
Jim Frey	1980	Mike Quade	2010
Dave Garcia	1977	Vern Rapp	1977
Fredi Gonzalez	2007	Greg Riddoch	1990
John Hart	1989	Jim Riggleman	1992
Trey Hillman	2008	Cal Ripken Sr.	1985
Brandon Hyde	2011	Luis Rojas	2020
Dan Jennings	2015	Bob Schaefer	1991
Kevin Kennedy	1993	Derek Shelton	2020
Jack Krol	1978	Mike Shildt	2018
Karl Kuehl	1976	Buck Showalter	1992
Jim Leyland	1986	Brian Snitker	2016
Nick Leyva	1989	Jayce Tingler	2020
Grady Little	2002	Carlos Tosca	2002
Joe Maddon	1996	Tom Trebelhorn	1986
Oliver Marmol	2022	Dave Trembley	2007
Jack McKeon	1973	Bobby Winkles	1973

HENRY AARON

"A man's ability is limited only by his lack of opportunity."
- Aaron's 1982 Hall of Fame induction speech.

1952, Hank Aaron starts his professional baseball career with the Indianapolis Clowns.

1959, Hank Aaron becomes the first player to win a Gold Glove and lead the league in batting (.355).

1960, Hank Aaron becomes the first player to win a Gold Glove and lead the league in RBIs (126) in the same year.

1970, Hank Aaron becomes the first player, to have more than 3,000 career hits and more than 500 career home runs.

1972, Hank Aaron, as an Atlanta Brave, becomes the first player in the re-integrated major leagues to sign for $200K a year.

1973, In pursuit of Babe Ruth's lifetime home run record, Hank Aaron receives numerous death threats. His daughter Gaile, a student at Fisk University in Nashville, Tenn., receives threatening phone calls and is a target of an abortive kidnapping plot, requiring escorts by FBI agents.

1973, Hank Aaron appears on the September cover of *Guideposts: A Practical Guide to Successful Living* magazine.

1974, Hank Aaron of the Atlanta Braves breaks Babe Ruth's record for lifetime home runs, hitting number 715 off Los Angeles Dodger pitcher Al Downing. Dodgers broadcaster Vin Scully shares the gravity of the moment, "What a marvelous moment for the country and the world. A Black man is getting a standing ovation (53,775 fans) in the Deep South for breaking a record of an all-time baseball (White) idol."

1976, According to biographer Lonnie Wheeler, Henry Aaron was miles ahead of the competition. As Wheeler pointed out, if you were to lay out side by side Aaron's White major league record of 6,856 total bases alongside a highway (90 feet for a single, 180 feet for a double, and so on), he would be 12.3 miles ahead of runner-up Stan Musial, who had 722 fewer total bases and 180 fewer homers.

1977, Hank Aaron becomes the first Negro Leaguer to have his uniform number retired twice, when the Milwaukee Brewers and the Atlanta Braves honor him.

1999, On the 25th anniversary of Hank Aaron breaking Babe Ruth's lifetime home run mark, Commissioner Bud Selig announces the creation of the Hank Aaron Award. The award is a tribute to the best all-around player based on combined number of hits, home runs and RBIs. The honor is the first "official" award named after a former player still living. The initial recipients are Latin Americans Sammy Sosa (Cubs) and Manny Ramirez (Indians).

2002, Hank Aaron is presented with the Presidential Medal of Freedom by President Barack Obama, the highest civilian award.

2022, The Atlanta Braves become the first baseball team to honor a former Negro League player, Hank Aaron, with the design of their World Series championship rings. The rings are made with 755 diamonds in total to represent the number of career home runs hit by Aaron. There are also 44 emerald cut diamonds on each ring to represent Aaron's retired jersey number. Aaron who died in January of 2021, had played 21 seasons for the Braves franchise.

TOMMIE AARON

1973, Former big-leaguer Tommie Aaron, the younger brother of Hank Aaron, is hired as manager of the Savannah Braves, on June 15, becoming the first African American manager in Southern League history.

CLAUDE AGEE

1953, The Detroit Tigers signs the club's first African American, Claude Agee. The 18-year-old outfielder is assigned to the Jamestown (N.Y.) Falcons of the Pony League. He plays two seasons in the minor leagues.

DICK ALLEN

1963, As the first Black player for the Little Rock Arkansas Travelers, a minor league affiliated of the Philadelphia Phillies, Dick Allen makes his debut. Led by White Citizens' Council leader Amis Guthridge, they picketed the ballpark caring signs reading, "Don't Negro-ize baseball" and "Nigger Go Home."

1972, Chicago White Sox star Dick Allen becomes the first player in baseball's "modern era" to hit two inside-the-park home runs in one game. Both homers were hit off Minnesota Twins pitcher Bert Blyleven in an 8–1 victory at Metropolitan Stadium.

FRANK ARMSTRONG

1900, Frank Armstrong becomes Cornell University's first Black graduate. During his final year at Cornell, Armstrong serves as captain of the school's baseball team.

EMMETT ASHFORD

1953, In Hollywood, Calif., Emmett Ashford is the first African American umpire to work a game, involving contemporary major leagues players, as the umpire-in-chief of a charity contest between the stars of the Pacific Coast League and selected players from major league clubs training in the West. Maxwell Stiles of the *Los Angeles Mirror* reports, "His work was excellent."

1966, Emmett Ashford becomes the first African American umpire in the re-integrated major leagues.

1967, Emmett Ashford becomes the first African American to umpire in the re-integrated major leagues' All-Star game. Ashford works the left field line before 46,309 fans at Anaheim Stadium in Calif.

1970, Emmett Ashford becomes the first African American umpire in the re-integrated major leagues' World Series, between the Cincinnati Reds and the Baltimore Orioles. He worked five games, but none behind home plate. The Jackson Five performs the "Star Spangled Banner" before Game 1.

JOHNNIE B. "DUSTY" BAKER

1977, Dusty Baker, of Los Angeles Dodgers, is the first Most Valuable Player named in the National League's Championship Series (NLCS).

1993, Dusty Baker of the San Francisco Giants is named Manager of the Year by the AP and the BBWAA. His 103 wins against only 58 losses are the most by a rookie manager in National League history.

2000, Jerry Manuel of the Chicago White Sox and Dusty Baker of the San Francisco Giants become the first African American managers from each league to be named Manager of the Year, in the same year. Baker becomes the first African American manager to win this NL award three times.

2008, Dusty Baker becomes the Cincinnati Reds' first African American manager.

2022. Dusty Baker, manager of the Houston Astros, becomes the first African American manager to win 2,000 major league games when his Astros defeat the Seattle Mariners, 4-0.

GENE BAKER

1961, The Pittsburgh Pirates tap Gene Baker the first African American minor league manager within the major leagues' farm system. (Black managers had already been hired by independent teams.) He manages the Batavia Pirates in Class D of the New York-Pennsylvania League. On June 20, he takes over for James Adlam with an 18-24 won-lost record and finishes the season in third place, winning 47 of 82 games. In 1951, Sam Bankhead, managed the Farnham Pirates of Quebec's Provincial League (Class C), but the Farnham club was not affiliated with any major league team at the time.

DAN BANKHEAD

1947, Dan Bankhead becomes the first African American pitcher in the re-integrated major leagues, as a member of the Brooklyn Dodgers. He homers in his first plate appearance but does poorly on the mound. In 3 1/3 innings of relief, he gives up 10 hits and six earned runs to the Pittsburgh Pirates.

ERNIE BANKS

"It's a great day for a ballgame; let's play two."

1950, Ernie Banks starts his professional baseball career with the Kansas City Monarchs before being drafted into the Korean War by the U.S. Army.

1958, Ernie Banks of the Chicago Cubs is named the Most Valuable Player in the National League.

1959, Ernie Banks becomes the first player in the National League to win the MVP award two years in a row.

1960, Ernie Banks of the Chicago Cubs becomes the first African American in either league, to win the Gold Glove Award at shortstop.

1973, On May 8, Cubs' manager Whitey Lockman was ejected in the 11th inning of a game against the San Diego Padres. Coach Ernie Banks fills in as manager for the remainder of the game, which the Cubs win, 3-2, in 12 innings. This action predates Frank Robinson's managerial hiring in 1975. See Gene Baker, 1963.

Colorful Firsts in U.S. Sports

2013, Ernie Banks is presented with the Presidential Medal of Freedom by President Barack Obama, the highest civilian award.

EARL BATTEY

1960, Earl Battey, becomes the first African American, in either league, to win a Gold Glove Award at catcher.

DON BAYLOR

1993, Don Baylor becomes the first African American manager of the Colorado Rockies.

2000, After more than 40 years after the retirement of Jackie Robinson in 1957, the Chicago Cubs hires its first Black manager, Don Baylor. Baylor manages a 65-97 won-lost record for the last place Cubs in the Central Division.

JOHN BECKWITH

1928, John Beckwith of the Homestead Grays becomes the first Black player to hit three home runs in a game off an active major league pitcher, Rube Walberg of the Philadelphia Athletics. His Grays defeat the American League All-Stars, 12-10.

JAMES "COOL PAPA" BELL

"I remember one game I got five hits and stole five bases, but none of it was written down because they forgot to bring scorebook to the game that day." Quoted in the 1989 50th Anniversary Hall of Fame Yearbook.

1929, James "Cool Papa" Bell hits three inside-the-park home runs at Aida Park, in Cienfuegos, Cuba.

1940, James "Cool Papa" Bell becomes the first Mexican League player to win the Triple Crown. He leads the circuit in batting average (.437), home runs (12) and RBIs (79), as well as triples (15) and runs scored (119). The fenceless outfields in Mexico aid this speedster.

1994, James "Cool Papa" Bell becomes the first former Negro Leaguer to have a street named after him. The first Mississippian to be inducted into the National Baseball Hall of Fame is honored in the city of Jackson.

1995, Josh Gibson, James Cool Papa Bell and Satchel Paige are featured on the front of a Wheaties cereal box.

ALBERT BELLE

1995, Albert Belle of the Cleveland Indians becomes the first major league player to hit 50 doubles and 50 home runs in the same season.

1997, The Cleveland Indians' Albert Belle earns $10 million to become the first player whose salary exceeds that of an entire team, in this case, the Pittsburgh Pirates ($9,071,667).

MOOKIE BETTS

2018, Mookie Betts outfielder for the Boston Red Sox becomes the first MLB player to win the MVP, Silver Slugger, Gold Glove, a batting title and a World Series ring in the same season.

2020, On Opening Day, a stylish MLB/BLM logo is designed on the field's pitching mound, with patches worn on jersey sleeves. African American players Tim Anderson, Josh Bell, Mookie Betts and Jack Flaherty lead this effort in support the Black Lives Matter movement.

JOE BLACK

"When I was at Morgan State University, I learned what it was to be colored, but also learned that I was somebody."

1952, Brooklyn Dodger pitcher Joe Black, the National League's Rookie of the Year, becomes the first African American pitcher to win a World Series game.

VIDA BLUE

"Charlie Finley has soured my stomach for baseball. He treated me like a damn colored boy."

- *Vida: His Own Story* (1972)

1971, Vida Blue becomes the first African American pitcher to win the American League's Cy Young Award. At the all-star break, with a 17-3 won-lost record, he appears on the cover of Time magazine. Blue becomes the first African American left-handed pitcher to strike out 300 batters in a season (301). Oakland A's Vida Blue and Chicago Cubs' Ferguson Jenkins, become the first Black pitchers to win Cy Young Awards in the same year. Blue (Oakland A's) and Dock Ellis (Pittsburgh Pirates) become the first African American pitchers to start an MLB All-Star game. The American League wins 6-4, as Blue picks up the win and Ellis the loss. Ellis pitches three innings and gives up four hits and four runs, with one walk and two strikeouts. Blue pitches three innings and gives up two hits, three runs, no walks and three strikeouts.

1981, Vida Blue becomes the first (and only pitcher) to win an All-Star game for both the National and Americas Leagues; 1971 for the Oakland A's and in 1981 for the San Francisco Giants.

BARRY BONDS

1998, Barry Bonds becomes the first major league player to hit 400 home runs and steal 400 bases.

2002, Barry Bonds wins his fifth MVP award by unanimous vote from the Baseball Writers' Association of America (BBWAA. Bonds is the first person to win the award consecutively, twice. In 1992 and 1993, and again in 2001 and 2002.

2003, Barry Bonds becomes the first major league player to hit 500 home runs and steal 500 bases.

2004, Barry Bonds becomes the first baseball player to record more than 200 walks in a season. He is also the first player to amass more than 100 intentional walks in a season.

DENNIS "OIL CAN" BOYD

1985, Dennis "Oil Can" Boyd, son of Negro Leaguer Willie James Boyd, is fined by the Boston Red Sox for having a cocky demeanor and animated fist-pumping and finger-wagging on the mound. Conversely, 10 years earlier, the 1976 A.L. Rookie of the Year, Mark "The Bird" Fidrych of the Detroit Tigers known mostly for talking to the ball, getting on his hands and knees to manicure the pitching mound, was labeled an entertaining "flake" and was never fined.

CHET BREWER

1938, Chet Brewer becomes the first African American player to enter the Mexican League.

RENAL BROOKS-MOON

2002, Renal Brooks-Moon for the San Francisco Giants becomes the first African American woman to serve a major league team as a public-address announcer. She also becomes the first Black woman to perform this function in the World Series against the Anaheim Angels.

WILLARD "HOME RUN" BROWN

1947, Willard "Home Run" Brown, an outfielder, joins Hank Thompson in a game against the Boston Red Sox, marking the first time two African Americans appear in the same American League lineup. Willard Brown becomes the first African American ball player to hit a home run in the American League, a pinch-hit, inside-the-park homer in a win over the Detroit Tigers. In the same season, Brown becomes the only baseball player to hit home runs in the Negro Leagues (for the Kansas City Monarchs) and in the American League (St. Louis Browns) in the same season.

GLENN BURKE

1976, Glenn Burke, outfielder for the Los Angeles Dodgers, is the first openly gay player in major league baseball.

ROY CAMPANELLA

"You have to have a lot of the little boy in you to play baseball for a living."

1937, Roy Campanella starts his professional baseball career with the Washington Elite Giants.

1946, Roy Campanella makes his affiliated baseball debut on May 8, with the Nashua Dodgers in the Class B New England League. The future three-time National League MVP goes 3-for-4 with a two-run homer.

1946, Don Newcombe and Roy Campanella form the first all-Black battery to integrate White baseball in the 20th century with the Nashua (NH) Dodgers in the Class B, New England League. Newcombe, whose victory at Pawtucket on the third day of the 1946 season makes him the first African American pitcher to win a game for an integrated professional baseball team.

1948, Roy Campanella makes his Minnesota debut in a Memorial Day twin-bill between the St. Paul Saints and the Minneapolis Millers (with a game in each team's home park). Campanella becomes the first African American player in the American Association, a AAA league. Campy is later joined by pitcher Dan Bankhead from the Memphis Red Sox.

1951, Roy Campanella is named the National League's Most Valuable Player, the first of three MVP awards for Campanella.

1952, Roy Campanella and Jackie Robinson become the first baseball players to appear on the cover of Jet magazine. Campanella is the African American baseball player on a Wheaties cereal box when featured on the side panel.

Colorful Firsts in U.S. Sports

1952, Roy Campanella, on June 19, becomes the first African American to catch a no-hitter in the re-integrated major leagues, the first of three career no-hitters. He catches Carl Erskine, as the Dodgers defeat the Chicago Cubs, 5-0.

1953, Roy Campanella of the Brooklyn Dodgers becomes the first catcher in major league history to hit more than 40 (41) home runs in a season. Campanella also becomes the first major league catcher in integrated baseball to hit 20 or more homers in five successive seasons.

1955, Roy Campanella is the first African American to win three MVP awards in baseball.

1956, Roy Campanella catches his second no-hitter of the year and his third career no-hitter to tie a major league record. On 12 May 1956, Campanella caught a no-hitter from Carl Erskine defeating the New York Giants, 3-0. Later that year on September 25, he caught Sal Maglie's no-hitter, beating the Philadelphia Phillies, 5-0.

ROD CAREW

1972, Minnesota Twin Rod Carew from Panama becomes the first player in MLB to win a batting championship without hitting a home run. Carew's league-leading batting average is .318.

AROLDIS CHAPMAN

2010, At Petco Park, Cincinnati Red Aroldis Chapman becomes the first human to throw a baseball more than 105 mph, in the eighth inning, against Tony Gwynn Jr.

2015, Aroldis Chapman becomes the first player disciplined by major league baseball's new personal conduct policy, which empowers MLB to suspend a player without a final judicial decision from the courts.

BETTY IRENE CHAPMAN

1951, Betty Irene Chapman becomes the first African American in professional women's baseball when she joins the Admiral Music Maids, of Des Plaines, Ill., in the National Girls Baseball League, a rival to the All American Girls Professional Baseball League. Chapman is a student at Illinois State Normal College.

OSCAR CHARLESTON

1920, Oscar Charleston of the Indianapolis ABCs against the Cuban Stars West is the first player to hit for the cycle in the Negro National League, going 4-for-5 with four RBIs.

TONY CLARK

2013, Retired Detroit Tiger first baseman Tony Clark becomes the first former player to be named executive director of Major League Baseball Players Association. Clark served as deputy executive director and acting executive director of the union before he was appointed executive director in December, upon the death of attorney Michael S. Weiner.

JIMMY CLAXTON

1916, The son of an Irish-English mother and an African-French-Native American father, Jimmy Claxton pitches two games for the Oakland Oaks of the Pacific Coast League. Recorded as a mulatto in the 1910 census, Claxton appears on No. 25 of the 143-card set by Zee-Nuts, becoming the first Black player with an American baseball card.

ZACH CLAYTON

1949, Zachary M. Clayton, former New York Ren, Harlem Globetrotter and Negro Leagues player, becomes the first African American to receive a boxing referee's license with the state of Pennsylvania. Clayton later referees the 1974 Ali-Foreman "Rumble In The Jungle" fight in Kinshasa, Republic of Zaire.

1974, Don King is the first boxing promoter to offer a $10 million purse with his "Rumble In The Jungle" match between George Foreman and Muhammad Ali in Kinshasa, Republic of Zaire. This fight was refereed by Zach Clayton, a member of the Naismith Memorial Basketball Hall of Fame, and former Negro Baseball League first baseman.

ROBERTO CLEMENTE

1961, Roberto Clemente becomes the first Puerto Rican to be a National League batting champion with a .351 average.

1966, Roberto Clemente becomes the first Puerto Rican to receive the MVP award in the National League.

1971, Roberto Clemente becomes the first Puerto Rican to receive the World Series MVP award when his Pittsburgh Pirates defeat the Baltimore Orioles, in the best of seven games.

1973, Roberto Clemente becomes the first Puerto Rican to be inducted into the National Baseball Hall of Fame. After his fatal plane crash enroute to Managua, Nicaragua in 1972 the National Baseball Hall of Fame waives its five-year waiting period so that a player who had been deceased for at least six months would be eligible for entry.

2003, Roberto Clemente is posthumously presented with the Presidential Medal of Freedom by President George W. Bush, the highest civilian award.

PANCHO COIMBRE

1941, Francisco "Pancho" Coimbre becomes the first Puerto Rican to play in the East-West All-Star game at Chicago's Comiskey Park.

VINCE COLEMAN

1985, Vince Coleman of the St. Louis Cardinals, steals 110 bases and is named NL Rookie of the Year. He is the first rookie to steal more than 100 bases.

1987, Vince Coleman steals more than 100 bases for the third straight season. Coleman steals 110 bases in his rookie year, 1985: 107 bases in 1986 and 109 bases in 1987. He becomes the only player in MLB history to steal 100 or more bases in his first three seasons.

CECIL COOPER

2007, Ron Washington with the Texas Rangers and Cecil Cooper with the Houston Astros become their teams' first African American managers.

KERWIN DANLEY

2020, Umpire Kerwin Danley becomes the first full-time African American crew chief in major league baseball.

MO'NE DAVIS

2014, Mo'ne Davis becomes the first Little League player, Black or White, to appear on the cover of *Sports Illustrated*. Davis is also the first young lady to earn a win and pitch a shutout in Little League World Series history, as her south Philadelphia Taney Dragons defeat Nashville, 4-0. Davis pitches a two-hitter and strikes out eight in six innings.

LORENZO "PIPER" DAVIS

1950, Lorenzo "Piper" Davis becomes the first African American to sign with the Boston Red Sox, the last all-White major league team to integrate in 1959. Davis, 32, is assigned to their Class A affiliate in Scranton, Pa. He never makes the roster of the parent club.

ANDRE "the HAWK" DAWSON

1987, Andre Dawson, outfielder for the Chicago Cubs, becomes the first MVP winner from a last place team.

2020, Andre Dawson is the recipient of the inaugural Curt Flood Award. The award created by Major League Baseball Players Association commemorates the 50th anniversary of Flood's historic court fight against Major League Baseball's reserve system and celebrates a player who demonstrated selfless devotion to the advancement of players' rights. In 21 major league seasons, Dawson plays for four different teams. He was the National League Rookie of the Year in 1977, the NL MVP in 1987 and an eight-time All-Star.

LEON DAY

1946, Leon Day of the Newark Eagles pitches the only Opening Day no-hitter in Negro league history and the second in major league history, following Cleveland Indian Bob Feller's no-hitter in 1940. Day defeats the Philadelphia Stars, 2-0.

PEDRO DIBUT

1924, Cuban pitcher Pedro Dibut becomes the first player to play in both the Negro Leagues, with the 1923 Cuban Stars and the re-integrated major leagues with the 1924 Cincinnati Reds.

LARRY DOBY

"I knew being accepted was going to be hard, but I knew I was involved in a situation that was going to bring opportunities to other Blacks."

1947, Before the start of the season Cleveland Indians owner Bill Veeck hires Louis Jordan Jones, a Black public relations man, to ". . . prepare the black segment of Cleveland for the arrival of a Black ballplayer, unnamed [Larry Doby]." Jones was a highly visible force in the community who, among other claims to fame, had been singer Lena Horne's first husband. Larry Doby joins the Cleveland Indians, becoming its first African American player.

1949, Larry Doby becomes the first Black player from the American League to participate in the annual All-Star game.

1951, Larry Doby becomes the first ball player since 1914 to score four runs without an official at-bat in a game. Doby drew five walks in five plate appearances.

1952, Larry Doby of the Cleveland Indians becomes the first African American to lead either the American League or National League in home runs. He finishes with 32. Doby also becomes the first African American to lead either the American or National League in slugging percentage, as well, besting all hitters in the American League with a .541 batting average.

1953, Larry Doby is the first athlete featured on the cover of editor Jackie Robinson's new magazine called *Our Sports*. The cover title: "He Can Challenge Ruth's Home Run Record, If -- ."

1954, The Cleveland Indians, in the American League, become the first team to have an all-tan outfield during the regular season with Al Smith, Dave Pope and Larry Doby. In 1951, New York Giants, in the National League, fielded an all-Black outfield in the playoffs.

1962, Larry Doby and Don Newcombe sign with the Chunichi Dragons to become the first former major leaguers to play in Japan.

1978, Larry Doby becomes the first African American manager for the Chicago White Sox.

2002, MLB's Futures Games Most Valuable Player Award presented at its annual All-Star Game is renamed the Larry Doby Award.

AL DOWNING

1964, Al Downing is the first African American to lead the American League in strikeouts with 217.

1967, By striking out Tony Horton, Don Demeter, Duke Sims on nine pitches, in the second inning, Al Downing of the New York Yankees becomes the first Black pitcher, in the American League, to accomplish this feat. The Yankees defeat the Cleveland Indians, 5-3.

FRANK DUNCAN SR. & JR.

1941, Kansas City Monarch Catcher Frank Duncan Sr. and pitcher Frank Duncan Jr. become the first father and son and the first father-and-son battery, to play for the same team, in the same year. This is 50 years before the Ken Griffey family make ancestral history.

GLORIA DYMOND

1948, Outfielders Fabiola Wilson and Gloria "Lovie" Dymond are the first ladies to play for the minor league New Orlean Creoles in a game against the Nashville Cubs in the Negro Southern League.

LUSCIOUS "LUKE" EASTER

"I just hit 'em and forget 'em."

1958, Buffalo Bisons first baseman Luke Easter wallops an estimated 520-foot home run in an International League game against the Havana Sugar Kings.

DOCK ELLIS

1971, Vida Blue (Oakland A's) and Dock Ellis (Pittsburgh Pirates) become the first African American pitchers to start an MLB All-Star game. The American League wins 6-4, as Blue picks up the win and Ellis the loss. Ellis pitches three innings and gives up four hits and four runs, with one walk and two strikeouts. Blue pitches three innings and gives up two hits, three runs, no walks and three strikeouts.

1973, Dock Ellis, Pittsburgh Pirates pitcher, is featured in *Ebony* magazine with hair curlers. Commissioner Bowie Kuhn orders him to cease and desist from wearing rollers and curlers during pre-game workouts. Ellis reluctantly shelves the curlers, after declaring, "They didn't put out any orders about [Yankee star] Joe Pepitone when he wore a hairpiece down to his shoulders."

OSCAR ESTRADA

1924, Cuban pitcher Oscar Estrada with the Cuban Stars of the Eastern Colored League later plays for the 1929 St. Louis Browns, in the white-centric major leagues.

PRINCE FIELDER

2007, Prince Fielder, for the Milwaukee Brewers, hits 50 home runs. Prince joins his father Cecil Fielder, who hit 51 home runs in 1990 with the Detroit Tigers, becoming the first son-father duo to hit 50 or more home runs in a season.

CURT FLOOD

"All the grand work was laid for people who came after me. The Supreme Court decided not to give it to me, so they gave it to two White guys [Andy Messersmith and Dave McNally]. I think that's what they were waiting for."

1969, St. Louis Cards outfielder Curt Flood, along with Tim McCarver, Joe Hoerner and Byron Browne, are traded to Philadelphia for Dick Allen, Cookie Rojas and Jerry Johnson. Flood challenges baseball's reserve clause, which binds players to the clubs for the life of their careers. He was earning $90,000 a year but argued in an interview with Howard Cosell on ABC's *Wide World of Sports* that "a well-paid slave is, nonetheless, a slave."

1972, Curt Flood loses his multi-million antitrust suit, Flood v. Kuhn, 407 U.S. 258, against baseball's reserve clause. Flood's attorney, former Supreme Court Justice Arthur Goldberg, asserted that the reserve clause depressed wages and limited players to one team for life. Major League Baseball's counsel, Louis Hoynes, countered that if Flood won his case, "it would be a shambles." On June 19, 1972, the Supreme Court, invoking the principle of stare decisis ("to stand by things decided"). The U.S. Supreme Court votes 5 to 3, one absentee (Justice Lewis Powell recused himself owing to his ownership of stock in Anheuser-Busch, which owned the Cardinals), against Flood's claim that baseball contracts constitute involuntary employment. Professional baseball is considered interstate commerce under the Sherman Antitrust Act. Although his legal challenge failed, it brought about additional solidarity among players as they fought against baseball's reserve clause.

1973, The 10 and 5 rule becomes a standard clause in the Collective Bargaining Agreement. It allows any player who is a ten-year major league veteran, including the last five with his current team, to veto a trade to another team. It is known as the Curt Flood Rule.

1975, The Seitz decision was a ruling by arbitrator Peter Seitz on December 23, which declared that Major League Baseball players become free agents upon playing one year for their team without a contract, effectively nullifying baseball's reserve clause. The ruling was issued in regard to pitchers Andy Messersmith and Dave McNally.

1997, Just before his death, Curt Flood's legacy was acknowledged in Congress by the Baseball Fans and Communities Protection Act of 1997. Numbered HR 21 (Flood's Cardinals uniform number) and introduced in the House of Representatives on the first day of the 105th Congress by Rep. John Conyers Jr. (D–Michigan), the legislation established federal antitrust law protection for major league baseball players to the same extent as provided for other professional athletes.

1998, The Curt Flood Act of 1998 applied antitrust laws to the business of major league baseball, specifically for player employment, ending the antitrust exemption that had protected the sport since the Supreme Court case Federal Baseball Club of Baltimore. Although the Act did not directly create free agency, it overturned the baseball exemption to the Sherman Antitrust Act, allowing players to sue if they believed their employment was affected by unfair practices and directly enabling the free-agency system that later developed. This act did exactly what Flood wanted; it stopped owners from controlling the players' contracts and careers.

2020, Andre Dawson is the recipient of the inaugural Curt Flood Award. The award created by Major League Baseball Players Association commemorates the 50th anniversary of Flood's historic court fight against Major League Baseball's reserve system and celebrates a player who demonstrated selfless devotion to the advancement of players' rights. In 21 major league seasons, Dawson plays for four different teams. He was the National League Rookie of the Year in 1977, the NL MVP in 1987 and an eight-time All-Star.

2020, 102 members of the U.S. Congress write a letter to the National Baseball Hall of Fame and Museum, co-signed by Players' unions from the NFL, NHL, NBA, and MLS, asking the Hall of Fame to admit Curt Flood for his pioneering efforts to eliminate the Reserve Clause in MLB.

ANDREW "RUBE" FOSTER

"White baseball has never seen anyone quite like Rube Foster. He was Christy Mathewson, John McGraw, Connie Mack, Al Spaulding and Kenesaw Mountain Landis – great pitcher, manager, owner, league organizer, czar all rolled into one."

– John Holway, *The Sporting News* 8 August 1981

1903, Rube Foster of the Cuban X-Giants strikes out 18 Philadelphia Giants to best St. Louis Browns Fred Glade's major league record of 15 whiffs in a game.

1920, The first Black professional baseball league to survive a full season, the Negro National League of Professional Baseball Clubs, is established by Andrew Rube Foster, J. L. Wilkinson, Tenny Blount, C. I. Taylor and others. The principal stockholders are Willie Foster, Rube Foster, J. L. Wilkinson, Russell Thompson and Walter M. Farmer.

WILLIE FOSTER

1920, The first Black professional baseball league to survive a full season, the Negro National League of Professional Baseball Clubs, is established by Andrew Rube Foster, J. L. Wilkinson, Tenny Blount, C. I. Taylor and others. The principal stockholders are Willie Foster, Rube Foster, J .L. Wilkinson, Russell Thompson and Walter M. Farmer.

1926, On the final day of the playoff series in the Negro National League, Willie Foster for the Chicago American Giants wins both games against the Kansas City Monarchs while pitcher Wilber "Bullet" Rogan takes a loss in both games. Their pitch counts are not available.

1933, The Negro Leagues play its first East-West All-Star game in Comiskey Park. Future Hall of Famer Willie Foster pitches the only complete game in major league All-Star history.

JOHN W. "BUD" FOWLER

"My skin is against me. If I had not been quite so black, I might have caught on as a Spaniard or something of that kind. The race prejudice is so strong that my black skin barred me." 13 November 1896 *Buffalo Enquirer*

1878, John W. "Bud" Fowler is the first known African American professional baseball player when he plays for the Live Oaks from Lynn, Mass., of the International Association. He pitches a 3-0 shutout over the Tecumseh of London, Ontario. Fowler was bare-handed infielder and switch hitter. According to the *Bloomingdale Daily Gazette* 2 June 1888, "It is said his judgment is so good when at the bat that he could hit a mosquito."

CITO GASTON

1989, Cito Gaston becomes the first African American manager for the Toronto Blue Jays.

1992, As manager of the Toronto Blue Jays, Cito Gaston becomes the first African American to win the World Series defeating the Atlanta Braves 4 games to 2.

BILL GATEWOOD

1921, Bill Gatewood of the Detroit Stars pitches the first no-hitter in the Negro National League. He shuts out the Cuban Stars from Cincinnati, in a 4-0 win.

BOB GIBSON

"Hitters aren't stupid, but sometimes I think they believe they are smarter than they really are."

- *Ghetto to Glory*

1965, Bob Gibson becomes the first African American pitcher to win a National League Gold Glove for fielding excellence. It is the first of nine Gold Glove awards in a row for Gibson.

1967, St. Louis Cardinal pitcher Bob Gibson becomes the first African American World Series MVP. Gibson pitches complete games in 1, 4 and 7, striking out 26 Boston Red Sox batters. He only allows three runs and 14 hits in the three games.

1968, Bob Gibson leads the National League with an ERA of 1.12, while Luis Tiant Jr. leads American League with a 1.60 ERA. They are the first Black pitchers to win the ERA crowns, and they record the lowest ERAs by pitchers since the re-integration (1947) of the major leagues. The pitching mound is lowered before the next season. Gibson is also the first pitcher to win a Gold Glove Award, the Cy Young Award and be named MVP in the same season. He also led the National League in strikeouts with 268. Don Newcombe also won the Cy Young and MVP awards in 1956.

1969, By striking out Len Gabrielson, Paul Popovich, John Miller on nine pitches, in the seventh inning, Bob Gibson of the St. Louis

Cardinals, becomes the first Black pitcher, in the National League, to accomplish this feat. The Cardinals defeat the Los Angeles Dodgers, 6-2.

JOSH GIBSON

"People I respect tell me . . . Josh Gibson was the greatest ever."
– UCLA basketball coach John Wooden, 10 September 1999, *USA Today*.

1938, Josh Gibson is the first Negro Leaguer to appear on the cover of the NAACP's *The Crisis* magazine.

1995, Josh Gibson, James Cool Papa Bell and Satchel Paige are featured on the front of a *Wheaties* cereal box.

1997, Catcher Josh Gibson becomes the first former Negro League player to appear on the catalogue cover of *Christie's*, a New York auction house.

1999, Fox television features Josh Gibson as an alien in their X-Files series, "The Unnatural" in April. Agents Sculley and Moulder find that he hit 61 home runs in 1947. Fact or fiction, Josh was unlike any slugging species before or after him. As the show reputes, "That Truth is Out There!"

2004, Josh Gibson is the first Negro League catcher on the cover of *Sports Collectors Digest*. The magazine had exclusive pricing on Negro League material.

2022, Josh Gibson of the Homestead Grays becomes the first Black man to appear on the cover of *Beckett Vintage Collector* magazine in a Negro League uniform.

JIM "JUNIOR" GILLIAM

1959, Junior Gilliam is the only man in baseball history to hit a home run in both Negro League (8-20-1950, Comiskey Park) and major league (8-3-1959, Los Angeles Coliseum) All-Star games.

DWIGHT GOODEN

1984, Dwight Gooden is the first rookie pitcher to surpass 250 (276) strikeouts in a season.

1985, Dwight Gooden becomes the first National League pitcher to strike out 200 or more batters in each of his first two seasons. Gooden also captures the pitcher's Triple Crown with most wins (24), lowest ERA (1.53) and most strikeouts (268).

FRANK GRANT

1886, Frank Grant, second baseman for the Buffalo Bisons in the International League becomes its first African American player. The next season other African American players Moses Fleetwood Walker, Robert Higgins, William J. Renfroe, George Stovey and Bud Fowler join Grant.

JIM "MUDCAT" GRANT

1958. Two rookies for the Cleveland Indians, Gary Bell from San Antonio, Texas and a Jim "Mudcat" Grant from Lacoochee, Fla., become the first White & Black roommates in the re-integrated major leagues.

1965, Jim "Mudcat" Grant for the Cleveland Indians becomes the first African American pitcher to win 20 or more games in the American League with 21 victories.

1965, Jim "Mudcat" Grant becomes the first African American pitcher, in the American League, to start a World Series when his Minnesota Twins open against the Los Angeles Dodgers. Sandy Koufax sits out the opener because of Yom Kippur. Grant beats Don Drysdale and the Dodgers with a one-hitter for an 8-2 win.

ELIJAH "PUMPSIE" GREEN

1959, The Boston Red Sox become the last all-White major league team to integrate with a Black athlete when they sign infielder Elijah "Pumpsie" Green.

WILLIE GREEN

1920, Willie Green, third baseman for the Chicago Giants faces pitcher Ed Rile of the Indianapolis ABCs in the first game of the newly formed Negro National League. The ABCs defeat the Giants, 4-2 before an estimated 8,000 fans.

AUGUSTUS "GUS" GREENLEE

1932, Gus Greenlee, owner of the Pittsburgh Crawfords, builds Greenlee Park. He installs a permanent overhead lighting system, making it one of the first parks in the country to offer nighttime baseball.

ERIC GREGG
1988, Eric Gregg is the home plate umpire for the first night game at Wrigley Field.

CLAUDE "RED" GRIER
1926, In the Negro World Series, Claude "Red" Grier for the Bacharach Giants pitches a no-hitter against the Chicago American Giants, the first in Negro League series play. It is the first World Series no-hitter in major league baseball history.

KEN GRIFFEY, SR. & JR.
1990, Ken Griffey Sr. 40, joins the Seattle Mariners and son Junior, 20, to form the first father-and-son combination since the Frank Duncan family appeared for the Monarchs 50 years earlier. Senior plays left field and bats second; Junior plays center and hits third. Both hit first-inning singles against the Kansas City Royals. Later in the year on Sept. 14. they hit back-to-back home runs off of California Angels' Kirk McCaskill, a first for a father-and-son duo.

1992, Ken Griffey Jr. hits a home run in the major league All-Star game. His father Ken recorded a home run in the 1980 major league All-Star game, making them the first son-and-father to homer in All-Star competition.

ALFREDO GRIFFIN
1985, Alfredo Griffin, Oakland A's, becomes the first Afro-Caribbean to win the Gold Glove at shortstop in the American League.

CECIL HALEY
1939, To stop a losing streak, owner Horace Stoneham of the New York Giants hires a 13-year-old Black youth, Cecil Haley as a mascot. Players can rub Cecil's head for good luck. The National League is still without any Black players.

BILLY HAMILTON
2013, Billy Hamilton of the Cincinnati Reds becomes the first player in the live ball era to steal four bases in his first major league start. Hamilton goes 3-for-4 — his first three major league hits — with two walks and four stolen bases against the Houston Astros. One of his stolen bases leads to a run which broke a 4-4 tie in the 13th inning of a Cincinnati victory.

KEN HARVEY
2002, Ken Harvey becomes the first awardee of the Joe Black Trophy, given to the MVP player of the Arizona Fall League (AFL). Harvey receives 15 of 18 votes from AFL managers and coaches.

RICKEY HENDERSON
1980, Rickey Henderson of the Oakland A's steals 100 bases.

1982, Rickey Henderson steals a record 130 bases for the Oakland A's.

1983, Rickey Henderson steals 108 bases. He becomes the first player to steal more than 100 bases in a season, three times.

2000, Rickey Henderson of the Seattle Mariners becomes the third player and first non-slugger to record 2,000 career walks. The other sluggers are Ted Williams and Babe Ruth.

CHICO HERNÁNDEZ
1942, Salvador "Chico" Hernández debuts with the Chicago Cubs as a catcher. In 1945, he joins the Indianapolis Clowns of the Negro American League.

MIKE HERRERA
1920, Cuban Mike Herrera is an infielder for the Cuban Stars of the Negro National League later plays for the Boston Red Sox in the American League in 1925 and 1926. In 1928, he returns to the Eastern Colored League to play for the Cuban Stars.

PETE HILL
1909, Pete Hill and Bruce Petway become the first African American players included in the Cabañas Cuban baseball card set.

1920, Pete Hill of the Detroit Stars hits the first home run in the newly formed Negro National League, against the Cuban Stars from Cincinnati.

DAVE HOSKINS

1952, Dave Hoskins, former pitcher with the Homestead Grays and the Chicago American Giants, becomes the first African American to appear in a Texas League game with the Dallas Eagles and posts a 22-10 won-lost mark for the season. The right-hander would go on to compile a 9-4 record during two years with the Cleveland Indians.

ELSTON HOWARD

"When I finally get a nigger, I get the only one who can't run,"
- New York Yankee manager Casey Stengel in Peter Golenbock's book *Dynasty*.

1955, Elston Howard, the first Black New York Yankee, is the only former Negro League player to homer in his first World Series at-bat. He homers off Don Newcombe of the Dodgers in the second inning of Game 1.

1960, Yankee catcher Elston Howard pioneers the use of the first hinged catcher's mitt that led to the modern one-handed catching technique. Howard would later win Gold Glove awards in 1963 and 1964.

1963, Elston Howard of the New York Yankees becomes the first African American to be named the American League MVP.

1968, Elston Howard, New York Yankee catcher, invents the weighted doughnut for baseball bats.

MONTE IRVIN

"We used to look at each other and say, 'We play the same game with the same rules, the same bat, the same ball, the same field. What the hell does color have to do with it? You don't play with color. You play with talent."

1946, In Game six of the Negro League World Series, against the Kansas City Monarchs, Monte Irvin, for the Newark Eagles, becomes the first player to hit two home runs in a game.

1949, Monte Irvin and Hank Thompson become the first African Americans with the New York Giants.

1951, Monte Irvin of the New York Giants becomes the first African American to lead either the American or National League in RBIs with 121.

1968, Monte Irvin becomes the first African American to receive an executive position in major league baseball, when hired by Commissioner William D. Eckert. The former Newark Eagles star is appointed Assistant Director of Promotion and Public Relations.

VINCENT "BO" JACKSON

"It was clear as day. I saw myself beating the odds, coming back to play again."

1993, Bo Jackson becomes the first major leaguer to play with an artificial hip. In his return, Jackson homers in the Chicago White Sox opener.

EDWIN JACKSON JR.

2010, Son of an Army veteran, Edwin Jackson Jr. is the first German-born pitcher to throw a no-hitter in the major leagues. The Arizona Diamondbacks pitcher threw 149 pitches in the no-hitter. This is the highest pitch count in an MLB game since 2005.

REGGIE JACKSON

"Fans don't boo nobodies."

1977, Reggie Jackson is the first baseball player to have a candy bar named after him.

1977, "Mr. October" becomes the first non-pitcher to win two World Series MVPs for different teams. His first MVP award came as a member of the 1973 Oakland A's, with the second award coming as a New York Yankee.

JIM JEFFRIES

1922, Jim Jeffries from the Indianapolis ABCs becomes the first pitcher to win more than 20 games in a season in the Negro Leagues.

FERGUSON JENKINS

1971, Oakland A's Vida Blue and Chicago Cubs' Ferguson Jenkins, become the first Black pitchers to win Cy Young Awards in the same year.

1972, Ferguson Jenkins, a Canadian, becomes the first pitcher to win 20 games in six consecutive seasons.

Colorful Firsts in U.S. Sports

DEREK JETER
2000, Derek Jeter of the New York Yankees becomes the first player to win the All-Star Game MVP and the World Series MVP awards in the same season.

SAM "THE JET" JETHROE
1950, Sam Jethroe, former Cleveland Buckeye outfielder of the Boston Braves, becomes the oldest Rookie of the Year in the re-integrated major leagues at age 33. Jethroe goes on to lead the National League in Stolen Bases with 35 and finishes 27th in the MVP poll. On September 15, the Boston Braves host "Sam Jethroe Night" for their rookie speedster.

1995, Plaintiffs Sam and Elsie Jethroe file a class action lawsuit in U.S. District Court for the Western District of Pennsylvania contending that systemic racism prevented Sam Jethroe from gaining the requisite four qualifying years to receive a major league pension. The defendants included MLB Properties, MLB, the Office of the Commissioner of Baseball, MLB Players Association and the MLB Pension Fund. The major leagues moved to dismiss the suit on the grounds that the statute of limitations had expired. The suit was dismissed in October 1996.

CHARLES JOHNSON
1997, Florida Marlins catcher Charles Johnson goes the entire season without a fielding error, a record that will never be broken.

JACK JOHNSON
1905, Future heavyweight boxing champion Jack Johnson organizes a semi-pro baseball team called the Johnson's Pets. Johnson plays first base.

JUDY JOHNSON
1951, Judy Johnson becomes the first African American scout in the re-integrated major leagues with the Philadelphia Athletics.

MAMIE JOHNSON
1954, Mamie "Peanut" Johnson and Connie Morgan join the Indianapolis Clowns, as pitcher and second baseman, respectively. This will be Johnson's and Morgan's only year in professional Black baseball.

SAM JONES
1955, National Leaguer Sam "Toothpick" Jones of the Chicago Cubs becomes the first Black pitcher to throw a no-hitter in the predominantly White major leagues. He defeats the Pittsburgh Pirates, 4-0, yielding seven walks at Wrigley Field.

1959, Sam "Toothpick" Jones of the San Francisco Giants becomes the first African American pitcher to lead the National League in ERA, 2.83, while winning 21 and losing 15 games. Jones becomes the first African American pitcher to pitch a no-hitter (his second, a seven-inning game) on Sept. 26 and also win 20 games in a season. As a Giant, his team defeats the St. Louis Cardinals, 4-0. Jones ends this game with the bases loaded with three walks and then strikes out the side: Dick Groat, Roberto Clemente and Frank Thomas. Note: This was Jones' second no-hitter, the first in 1955. Earlier on June 30, Jones pitched a one-hitter versus Don Drysdale and the Los Angeles Dodgers before 59,312 fans at the LA Coliseum. The lone hit came on a questionable and much debated fielding bobble by shortstop Andre Rodgers. The local scorer, who called the Rodgers error a hit, was Charlie Parks.

STUART "SLIM" JONES
1935, Slim Jones of the Philadelphia Stars becomes the first pitcher to hit a home run in East-West All-Star competition, when he slams one off Ray Brown from the Homestead Grays.

NEWT JOSEPH
1924, In the third game, Newt Joseph, third baseman for the Kansas City Monarchs, becomes the first player to hit a home run in the Colored World Series. Joseph hits a two-run homer over the centerfield fence in Baltimore's Maryland Baseball Park, off of Red Ryan of the Hilldale Club.

DOC KOUNTZE
1934, Mabray "Doc" Kountze becomes the first Black sportswriter to receive a Press Pass to Fenway Park.

SAM LACY

"Baseball in its time has given employment to known epileptics, kleptomaniacs, and a generous scattering of saints and sinners. A man who is totally lacking in character has often turned up to be a star in baseball. A man whose skin is white or red or yellow has been acceptable. But a man whose character may be of the highest and whose ability may be Ruthian has been barred completely from the sport because he is colored."

-- Sam Lacy, *Baltimore Afro-American* 10 November 1945

1948, Sam Lacy is the first African American writer admitted to the Baseball Writers' Association of America (BBWAA). Some sources cite writer Wendell Smith as the first in 1947.

2015, Claire Smith is the first recipient of the Sam Lacy-Wendell Smith Award, created by the Shirley Povich Center for Sports Journalism. The award is presented annually to a sports journalist or broadcaster who has made significant contributions to racial and gender equality in sports.

BARRY LARKIN

2000, Barry Larkin becomes the first major league shortstop to record 2,000 hits, 170 homers and 350 steals.

2020, Major league baseball announces that it will remove former major league baseball Commissioner Kenesaw Mountain Landis' name from the plaques awarded to the American and National League MVPs. The decision comes after a few former MVPs, including Black award winners Barry Larkin and Terry Pendleton, voice displeasure with their plaques being named for Landis, who kept the game segregated during the 24 years he served as commissioner from 1920 until his death in 1944.

RON LEFLORE

1978, Ron LeFlore, Detroit Tigers outfielder, becomes the first non-Hall of Famer to have a TV-movie made about his career, called *One In A Million*.

DAVEY LOPES

2000, Davey Lopes becomes the Milwaukee Brewers first African American manager.

HÉCTOR LÓPEZ

1969, Héctor López from Colon, Panama becomes the first Black man to manage a AAA-level club, the Buffalo Bisons, in the International League. The Bisons are affiliated with the Washington Senators of the American League. Previous Black managers include Gene Baker in 1961, managing Batavia (New York-Pennsylvania League, Class D), Marvin Williams in 1952, managing Chihuahua (Arizona-Texas League, Class C) and Sam Bankhead (1951) managing Farnham (Provincial League, Class C).

BILL LUCAS

1976, Bill Lucas former player for the Atlanta Braves is named by Braves owner Ted Turner as vice president of player personnel, at the time the highest administrative position in major league baseball. His responsibilities were essentially that of a general manager. (See 1993, Bob Watson, general manager of the Yankees.)

RALEIGH "BIZ" MACKEY

1927, The first Negro baseball team to play in Japan, the Philadelphia Royal Giants, owned by Lonnie Goodwin, visits the Far East. Catcher and sometimes pitcher Biz Mackey becomes the first player to hit a home run at Jingu Stadium, home of the Yakult Swallos.

EFFA MANLEY

1946, Effa Manley co-owner of the Newark Eagles becomes the first female in the Negro Leagues, whose team wins the World Series.

2006, Effa Manley co-owner of the Newark Eagles becomes the first woman elected to the National Baseball Hall of Fame, by a Special Committee on Negro Leagues of 12 Negro League historians. The committee was chaired by former Commissioner Fay Vincent.

2020, Effa Manley, currently the only woman in the National Baseball Hall of Fame, is recipient, posthumously, of SABR's Dorothy

Colorful Firsts in U.S. Sports

Seymour Mills Lifetime Achievement Award for her service as owner of the Newark Eagles.

JERRY MANUEL

2000, Jerry Manuel of the Chicago White Sox and Dusty Baker of the San Francisco Giants become the first African American managers from each league to be named Manager of the Year, in the same year. Baker becomes the first African American manager to win this NL award three times.

JUAN MARICHAL

1963, Dominican Juan Marichal of the San Francisco Giants becomes the first Latin American-born pitcher to throw a no-hitter, beating the Houston Colt .45s, 1-0.

ARMANDO MARSANS

1911, Cuban Armando Marsans debuts in the white-centric major leagues with the Cincinnati Reds, playing centerfield and first base. He later plays for the St. Louis Browns and the New York Yankees before joining the Cuban Stars of the Eastern Colored League in 1923.

WILLIAM CLARENCE MATTHEWS

1905, Harvard and Boston University scholar William Clarence Matthews is the only known Negro player in professional baseball as a shortstop with Vermont's Northern League. Matthews passes the bar in 1908 and is appointed special assistant to the U.S. district attorney in Boston. He also serves from 1920 to 1923 as legal counsel to Jamaican political activist Marcus Garvey.

BRUCE MAXWELL

2017, Oakland A's catcher Bruce Maxwell becomes the first major league baseball player to take a knee to protest police brutality and racial injustice. It takes another three years for anyone else to follow his lead in the big leagues.

WILLIE "SAY HEY" MAYS

"The Rev. Martin Luther King can't play baseball, so he doesn't try. Now how would I look trying to preach to people. I try to do my best within my abilities, and I think I've helped my people" -- Willie Mays, *Jet* magazine, 1964.

1948, Willie Mays starts his professional baseball career with the Birmingham Black Barons.

1950, Willie Mays joins the Trenton Giants, a New York Giant farm team in the Class B Interstate League and becomes the first Black player and the only African American player in the league. He plays in 81 games and compiles a .353 batting average.

1955, Willie Mays, alongside actress Lorraine Day and Leo Durocher, is the first African American baseball player to appear on the cover of *Sports Illustrated*. Mays also leads the National League in home runs with 51. Mays becomes the first African American in major league history to win a home run title and a batting title, which he won in 1954 with a .345 average.

1956, Willie Mays becomes the first player to join the 30-30 club, with 36 home runs and 40 stolen bases.

1957, Former Negro League players Minnie Miñoso (leftfield) and Willie Mays (centerfield) are named to major league baseball's first Gold Glove team.

1958, Willie Mays appears on the April cover of *Life* magazine.

1963, Willie Mays becomes the first Negro Leaguer to win the MVP award at a major league All-Star game. His National League team wins 5-3.

1964, Willie Mays signs with the Giants for $105,000 per year, becoming baseball's highest paid player. Mays becomes the first African American named captain of a major league team, the San Francisco Giants. He is appointed captain by manager Alvin Dark. Mays is the first player to win a Gold Glove and lead the league in homers (47) the same season, demonstrating his all-around talent.

1965, Outfielder Willie Mays of the San Francisco Giants becomes the first Black player to hit 500 home runs, in a 5 to 1 win over Houston. At the age of 34, he becomes the first player to hit 50 or more (52) home runs and win a Gold Glove as an outfielder.

1965, In Los Angeles, Maury Wills of the Dodgers and Willie Mays of the S. F. Giants, exchange lineup cards with umpire Al Barlick. This marks the first time in major league baseball, the opposing team captains are African Americans.

1966, Willie Mays appears on the March cover of *Boys' Life* magazine.

1969, Willie Mays becomes the first player to hit 300 home runs, steal 300 bases and win 10 gold gloves (12 awards from 1957 to 1968).

1970, The *Sporting News* names Willie Mays as Player of the Decade for the "cultural decade" of the 1960s.

2015, Willie Mays is presented with the Presidential Medal of Freedom by President Barack Obama, the highest civilian award.

2017, The World Series Most Valuable Player Award is renamed the Willie Mays World Series Most Valuable Player. It will be presented by the award's longtime sponsor, Chevrolet. George Springer from the Houston Astros is the first recipient.

DANNY McCLELLAN

1903, Danny McClellan, pitches the first recorded perfect game by an African American pitcher, against the Penn Park Athletic Club of York, Pa., champions of the Tri-State League.

LLOYD McCLENDON

2001, Lloyd McClendon with the Pittsburgh Pirates and Hal McRae with the Tampa Bay Devil Rays become those clubs' first African American managers. (Some sources credit Gene Baker as the first Black manager in the American or National leagues, citing a Sept. 21, 1963, game in which he took over as Pirates skipper for two innings after the ejection of Danny Murtaugh).

TOM McCRAW

1975, Tom McCraw of the Cleveland Indians switches to the third base coaching box with Dave García, becoming perhaps the first Black man to coach third base in the re-integrated major leagues. The third-base coaching position requires giving signals to batters and critical base running decisions and is seen as a steppingstone to a managerial job.

HAL McRAE

1978, Major league baseball initiates the Hal McRae rule. During the 1977 AL Championship Series Kansas City Royal McRae aggressively takes out N.Y. Yankee second baseman Willie Randolph by sliding very wide of second base attempting to break up a double play. The new ruling prohibits runners from targeting fielders.

1991, Hal McRae becomes the first African American manager of the Kansas City Royals.

2001, Lloyd McClendon with the Pittsburgh Pirates and Hal McRae with the Tampa Bay Devil Rays become those clubs' first African American managers. (Some sources credit Gene Baker as the first Black manager in the American or National leagues, citing a Sept. 21, 1963, game in which he took over as Pirates skipper for two innings after the ejection of Danny Murtaugh).

PERCY MILLER

1951, Percy Miller makes his debut with the Danville Leafs, the first integrated baseball team in Virginia in the Carolina League. He delivers a two-run single against Durham in the first of his 19 games that season. He is released in February 1952 as not being polished enough. The Carolina League is a minor league baseball league which operates along the Atlantic Coast of the U.S. It is classified as a Class A-Advanced league.

MINNIE MIÑOSO

1951, Minnie Miñoso becomes the Chicago White Sox's first Black player and the first Cuban American to lead the American League in Stolen Bases with 31 steals.

1957, Former Negro League players Minnie Miñoso (leftfield) and Willie Mays (centerfield) are named to major league baseball's first Gold Glove team.

1960, Minnie Miñoso becomes the first Cuban American to lead the American League in hits with 184.

CONNIE MORGAN

1954, Mamie "Peanut" Johnson and Connie Morgan join the Indianapolis Clowns, as pitcher and second baseman, respectively. This will be Johnson's and Morgan's only year in professional Black baseball.

JOE MORGAN

1978, Joe Morgan becomes the first major leaguer to record 200 career Home Runs and 500 stolen bases.

1990, National Baseball Hall of Fame second baseman Joe Morgan is arrested as a suspect drug courier in Los Angeles International Airport (LAX) by police detective Clayton Searle and William Woessner, a DEA agent. A case of mistaken identity. Morgan files a lawsuit contending he suffered "acute physical and emotional distress and embarrassment" after the incident and expressed concern about damage to his character.

BOB MOTLEY

1957, Chief umpire in the Negro American League Bob Motley graduates from the Al Somers Umpires School in Daytona Beach, Fla. He was the only scholar in the class of 74 to achieve a perfect score on the final examination. Unfortunately, Motley never umpired in either the American or National League.

LONNIE MURRAY

2020, Lonnie Murray becomes the first Black woman to be certified as a player agent by the MLB Player Association. Murray represents Bianca Smith, the first Black woman to coach in professional baseball and represents Bruce Maxwell, Oakland A's catcher, the first MLB player to kneel for the national anthem in protest of police brutality.

EMILIO NAVARRO

1929, Emilio "Milito" Navarro, a shortstop, is the first Puerto Rican to bat more than .300 (.317) in the Negro Leagues as a member of the Cuban Stars of the American Negro League.

CHARLIE NEAL

1959, Charlie Neal, Los Angeles Dodgers, becomes the first African American to win the Gold Glove Award at second base.

DON NEWCOMBE

"He said to me Don, you, Jackie (Robinson), Roy (Campanella), and Larry (Doby) will never know how easy you made it for me to do what I have done in Civil Rights to what you men did on the baseball field." – Dr. Martin L. King Jr., 1968

1946, Don Newcombe and Roy Campanella form the first all-Black battery to integrate White baseball in the 20th century with the Nashua (NH) Dodgers in the Class B, New England League.

1949, Don Newcombe becomes the first African American pitcher to win the Rookie of the Year Award.

1951, Don Newcombe of the Brooklyn Dodgers becomes the first African American pitcher to lead either League in strikeouts with 164 K's. Newcombe also becomes the first African American pitcher to win 20 games (20-9) in the re-integrated major leagues with the National League Brooklyn Dodgers.

1955, Don Newcombe becomes the first African American pitcher to steal home plate after hitting a triple in the 9th inning against the Pittsburgh Pirates. Newcombe also becomes the first African American baseball pitcher to appear on the cover of *Sports Illustrated*.

1956, Former 1949 National League Rookie of the Year Don Newcombe becomes the first player to win the first-ever Cy Young Award and the Most Valuable Player award in the same season. Newcombe becomes the first MVP award winner not selected to the All-Star game the same year.

1962, Larry Doby and Don Newcombe sign with the Chunichi Dragons to become the first former major leaguers to play in Japan.

TONY OLIVIA

1964, Cuban Tony Oliva becomes the first rookie and non-White player to win a batting title in the American League with a .323 average. The All-Star is named AL Rookie of the Year and finishes fourth in the MVP race.

BARACK OBAMA

2014, In May, President Barack Obama becomes the first sitting president to visit the National Baseball Hall of Fame and Museum in Cooperstown, N.Y.

JOHN "BUCK" O'NEIL

1956, Buck O'Neil becomes the first Black scout in the white major leagues for the Chicago Cubs.

1962, Buck O'Neil, with the Chicago Cubs, becomes the first African American from the Negro Leagues to coach in the white major leagues

2006, John "Buck" O'Neil is posthumously presented with the Presidential Medal of Freedom by President George W. Bush, the highest civilian award.

LEROY ROBERT "SATCHEL" PAIGE
"Ain't no man can avoid being born average, but there ain't no man got to be common."

1941, Before the ban on segregated seating was lifted in 1944 at Sportsman's Park in St. Louis, the Kansas City Monarchs, with Satchel Paige on the mound, play the Chicago American Giants before an interracial crowd of 19,178 on the Fourth of July. Average attendance per game for the Cardinals was 8,229 and for the Browns 2,289.

1944, The *New York Amsterdam News* reports that in a game against the New York Cubans, in Ebbets Field, on July 2, Satchel Paige "pulled all his usual tricks, such as loading the bases deliberately and then retiring the side without a run."

1948, Bill Veeck signs 42-year-old Satchel Paige, on his birthday, to a Cleveland Indians' contract. Paige goes 6W-1L for the season. Paige becomes the first African American pitcher in the American League and the first African American to actually pitch in a World Series game. Pitcher Dan Bankhead for the Brooklyn Dodgers was used as a pinch runner in the 1947 World Series.

1952, St. Louis Browns' Satchel Paige, 46, is selected to play in a major league baseball All-Star game.

1956, On August 7, a crowd of 57,000 fans, the largest in minor-league baseball history, watch 50-year-old Satchel Paige of the Miami Marlins beat Columbus in an International League game played in the Orange Bowl.

1965, Satchel Paige of the Kansas City A's becomes the oldest pitcher at 59, to start a major league game, pitching three innings against the Boston Red Sox, giving up one hit to Carl Yastrzemski.

1971, Satchel Paige becomes the first African American representing the Negro Leagues inducted into the National Baseball Hall of Fame. The Hall creates a controversy with a separate section or wing for the Black players.

"This lone Negro will be admitted to Cooperstown's anterooms, but not beyond," Bill Gildea writes in his *Washington Post* article *1st Negro League Inductee Draws Spot in Back of Hall.*" Gildea adds, "He will have gotten out of the bus and into his own little corner of the Hall. To be consistent, the ceremony ought to be held at the back door."

One reason cited was they did not meet the minimum of ten MLB seasons like their White counterparts. Instead of being an honor, the move was viewed by many as another form of segregation. "Technically, you'd have to say he's not in the Hall of Fame," said commissioner Bowie Kuhn at the time, according to the *New York Times*. "But I've often said the Hall of Fame isn't a building but a state of mind. The important thing is how the public views Satchel Paige, and I know how I view him."

The *New York Post* sports columnist Milton Gross rejected Kuhn's dog whistle, writing, "The Hall of Fame is not a state of mind. It is something semi-officially connected with organized baseball that is run by outdated rules which, as Jackie Robinson said the other day, 'can be changed like laws are changed if they are unjust'." With the backdrop of backlash and an upcoming election, the Hall changed its mind in July of that year.

1995, Josh Gibson, James Cool Papa Bell and Satchel Paige are featured on the front of a Wheaties cereal box.

1995, Movie producer Spike Lee and his wife lawyer Tonya Lewis name their first child, a girl, Satchel, after Negro Leagues legend Leroy "Satchel" Paige.

2022, Satchel Paige becomes the first Negro League veteran to be an answer during *Jeopardy's* "Final Jeopardy." Jackie Kelly, a pension calculation developer from Cary, N.C., tackles "*Taking the mound for Cleveland in 1948, he was the first African American to pitch in a World Series.*" She beats out Ryan Guzzo Purcell, a theatre director from Seattle, Wash., who also had the correct question.

DAVE "The COBRA" PARKER
"When the leaves turn brown, I'll be wearing the batting crown."

1979, Outfielder Dave Parker becomes the first ML baseball player to earn a million dollars a year when he signs a five-year, $5 million contract with the Pittsburgh Pirates.

1985, Dave Parker becomes the first major league player to win the home run derby at the All-Star game. Parker beat out future Hall of Famers Jim Rice, Eddie Murray, Carlton Fisk, Ryne Sandberg and Cal Ripken Jr.

ULICE PAYNE

2002, Ulice Payne becomes the first African American president of a major league baseball club, the Milwaukee Brewers, when Bud Selig names him as successor to daughter Wendy Selig-Prieb.

NAT PEEPLES

1954, Nat Peeples becomes the first and only African American to take the field in a Southern Association game. Peeples plays left field goes 0-for-4 with a walk in two games for the Atlanta Crackers. He is gone from the all-White league a week later, demoted to Class A Jacksonville. Peeples never returns to Atlanta, ultimately finishing out his career in the lower minor leagues.

TERRY PENDLETON

1987, The St. Louis Cardinals' Terry Pendleton becomes the first African American player in the National League to win the Gold Glove Award at third base. Though a Black player has now won the award at every position since it was initiated in 1957, neither a Black pitcher nor third baseman has earned the designation in the American League.

2020, Major league baseball announces that it will remove former major league baseball Commissioner Kenesaw Mountain Landis' name from the plaques awarded to the American and National League MVPs. The decision comes after a few former MVPs, including Black award winners Barry Larkin and Terry Pendleton, voice displeasure with their plaques being named for Landis, who kept the game segregated during the 24 years he served as commissioner from 1920 until his death in 1944.

BRUCE PETWAY

1909, Pete Hill and Bruce Petway become the first African American players included in the Cabañas Cuban baseball card set.

1910, Leland Giants catcher Bruce Petway, playing for the Havana Reds in Cuba, is reported by the *La Lucha* newspaper, of throwing out American League batting champion Ty Cobb of the Detroit Tigers on several occasions. Cobb vows to never take the field against Black players.

VIC POWER

1958, Puerto Rican Vic Power (Pellot) of the Cleveland Indians, becomes the first non-White player in either league to win the Gold Glove Award at first base.

DAVID PRICE

2017, David Price's minimalist delivery style of pitching has resulted in what is call the "Price rule" which makes a pitcher specify whether he is working from the stretch or full windup position when a runner is on third. The rule is detailed in this way: If a pitcher takes the rubber and his back foot is parallel to the mound and his other foot is in front, it is assumed he is in the set position and he will stop. This does not matter with no runners on or runners on first and second. But when there is a runner on third, pitchers need to inform the umpires if they are going to stand that way and not stop -- i.e., pitch out of the full windup.

CHARLEY PRIDE

1974, Charley Pride, former Memphis Red Sox pitcher, becomes the first Negro League veteran and first African American to sing the national anthem at the Super Bowl (VIII).

CURTIS PRIDE

1993, Curtis Pride, outfielder for the Montreal Expos, becomes the first deaf African American ball player in the re-integrated major leagues.

ALEC RADCLIFF

1937, The Radcliffe brothers, Chicago American Giants' Alec (3b) and Cincinnati Tigers' Ted (c), become the first siblings to appear in the same East-West All-Star game.

1943, Alec and Ted Radcliffe become the first brothers to represent the same team, the Chicago American Giants, in the East-West all-star classic.

TED RADCLIFFE

1932, Ted Radcliffe of the Pittsburgh Crawfords catches Satchel Paige in the first game of a doubleheader, for a 4-0 win. He pitches the second game and wins 6-0. Radcliffe becomes the first professional baseball player to pitch and catch a game in the same day.

1937, The Radcliffe brothers, Chicago American Giants' Alec (3b) and Cincinnati Tigers' Ted (c), become the first siblings to appear in the same East-West All-Star game.

1943, Alec and Ted Radcliffe become the first brothers to represent the same team, the Chicago American Giants, in the East-West all-star classic.

TIM RAINES

2002, Tim Raines retires after 24 seasons in the major leagues. He is the only player in league history with at least 100 triples, 150 home runs and 600 stolen bases.

WILLIE RANDOLPH

2005, Willie Randolph with the New York Mets and Frank Robinson with the Washington Nationals become the club's first African American managers.

J.R. RICHARDS

1978, J.R. Richards of the Houston Astros becomes the first African American right-handed pitcher to strike out 300 batters in a season (303). The next season he strikes out 313 batters.

JOHN RICHEY

1948, John Richey, former batting champion for the 1947 Chicago American Giants, becomes the first African American in the Pacific Coast League since pitcher Jimmy Claxton passed as part Native American in 1916. The San Diego native played for the Padres for two seasons and is commemorated with a bronze bust in Petco Park in 2018.

FRANK ROBINSON

"He can step on your shoes, but he doesn't mess up your shine." Joe Morgan's view of Robinson as a manager.

1966, Baltimore Orioles outfielder Frank Robinson wins the MVP award in the American League. He becomes the first player to win the MVP in both leagues, having won the award in the National League with the Cincinnati Reds in 1961. He is also the first African American to win a Triple Crown in the re-integrated major leagues.

1975, Frank Robinson becomes the first full-time African American manager in the re-integrated major leagues with the Cleveland Indians. He hits a pinch-hit homer in his managerial debut, on Opening Day, to defeat the N.Y. Yankees, 5-3. See Gene Baker, 1963 and Ernie Banks, 1973.

1981, Frank Robinson becomes the first African American manager of the San Francisco Giants. Robinson had previously been manager of the Cleveland Indians from 1975 to 1977.

1988, Frank Robinson becomes the first African American manager of the Baltimore Orioles.

1989, Frank Robinson of the Baltimore Orioles is the first African American named Manager of the Year.

2002, Frank Robinson becomes the first Black manager of the Montreal Expos.

2005, Willie Randolph with the New York Mets and Frank Robinson with the Washington Nationals become the clubs' first African American managers.

2005, Muhammad Ali and Frank Robinson are presented with the Presidential Medal of Freedom by President George W. Bush, the highest civilian award.

JACKIE ROBINSON

"I cannot stand and sing the anthem. I cannot salute the flag; I know that I am a Black man in a white world."
- *I Never Had It Made* with Alfred Duckett, 1972

1941, Jack Roosevelt Robinson becomes the first athlete to letter in four sports for the UCLA Bruins: baseball, basketball, football and track.

1942, Nate Moreland and Jackie Robinson tryout for manager Jimmy Dykes' Chicago White Sox at its training camp in Pasadena, Calif. The White Sox finish the season in sixth place with a 66-82 won-lost record.

1946, Former All-American UCLA running back and major league infielder with the Kansas City Monarchs, Jackie Robinson makes his minor league debut, as a second baseman, with the Montreal Royals in Canada.

1947, Jackie Robinson, with the Brooklyn Dodgers, becomes the first African American in modern times to play in the re-integrated major leagues and wins the newly created Rookie of the Year Award by the *Sporting News*. Robinson becomes the first African American baseball player to appear on the cover of *Time* magazine.

1947, Jackie Robinson becomes the first African American to lead the National League in Stolen Bases with 29. Black National League players dominate this statistic category for the next 40 years, not winning in 1948 when Richie Ashburn steals 32 bases and in 1952 when Pee Wee Reese steals 30 bases.

Colorful Firsts in U.S. Sports

1949, Jackie Robinson of the Brooklyn Dodgers becomes the first African American to lead either the American or the National League in batting with a .342 average. Robinson becomes professional baseball's first Most Valuable Player who was Rookie of the Year.

1949, Jackie Robinson, Roy Campanella and Don Newcombe, all of the Brooklyn Dodgers, and Larry Doby of the Cleveland Indians become the first African Americans to play in a major league All-Star game; the American League wins 11-7 at Ebbets Field.

1950, Jackie Robinson appears as himself in *The Jackie Robinson Story* film. Ruby Dee plays his wife Rachel.

1950, Jackie Robinson becomes the first African American baseball player to appear on the cover of *Life* magazine.

1951, Jackie Robinson appears on the November cover of the *Sports Stars* magazine.

1952, Roy Campanella and Jackie Robinson become the first baseball players to appear on the cover of *Jet* magazine.

1953, The city of Birmingham, Ala., bars the Jackie Robinson All-Stars, composed of Black and White players from playing due to a 1944 city ordinance, section 859 which cites "It shall be unlawful for any person in charge of or in control of any room, hall, theater, picture house, auditoriums, yard, court, ballpark, public park or indoor or outdoor place, to which both white persons and negroes (sic) are admitted, to cause, permit or allow mixing of races." In 1950, the city passes Ordinance 798-F to add even more restrictions to prevent racial interaction at baseball, softball, football, basketball or similar games. Robinson's all-star team includes Dodger first baseman Gil Hodges and Indian third baseman Al Rosen.

1953, Jackie Robinson appears on the February cover of *Inside Baseball* magazine.

1954, Jackie Robinson appears on the June cover of *Our World* magazine, published from 1946 to 1957.

1954, Jackie Robinson steals home plate on a rare triple-steal along with teammates Gil Hodges and Sandy Amorós against the Pittsburgh Pirates.

1956, Jackie Robinson becomes the first baseball player to receive the NAACP's Spingarn Medal, an honor for "the man or woman of African descent and American citizenship who shall have made the highest achievement during the preceding year or years in any honorable field."

1957, Jackie Robinson retires from major league baseball. Three league teams, Phillies, Tigers and Red Sox have yet to put an African American on its rosters.

1962, In his first year of eligibility, Jackie Robinson is the first African American inducted into the National Baseball Hall of Fame in Cooperstown, N.Y. Cleveland Indians pitcher Bob Feller is also inducted this year. After a 1946 exhibition game in San Diego, Feller claimed Robinson, built like a football player, with broad shoulders, was too musclebound to be able to handle inside pitching and would never make it in the re-integrated major leagues. Jackie Robinson appears on the cover of the *Negro Digest*, a magazine in format like the *Reader's Digest*.

1963, A group of African American men meet in New York City to discuss concerns about the cultural and financial obstacles that have limited the achievements of Black men, particularly young men. Among founders of the 100 Black Men of America were David Dinkins, Robert Mangum, Dr. William Hayling, Nathaniel Goldston III, Livingston Wingate, Andrew Hatcher and Jackie Robinson.

1965, Jackie Robinson joins the ABC-TV baseball broadcast team, becoming the first African American to receive a network broadcasting position. ABC provides the first ever nationwide coverage of baseball every Saturday afternoon.

1966, Jackie Robinson is named manager of the Continental League's Brooklyn Dodgers Football Club, Inc. The announcement on May 2 is made by league Commissioner Saul Rosen and club president Jerry Jacobs.

1972, "There I was, the Black grandson of a slave, the son of a Black sharecropper, part of a historic occasion, a symbolic hero to my people. The air was sparkling. The sunlight was warm. The band struck up the national anthem. The flag billowed in the wind. It should have been a glorious moment for me as the stirring words of the national anthem poured from the stands. Perhaps, it was, but then again, perhaps, the anthem could be called the theme song for a drama called The Noble Experiment. Today, as I look back on that opening game of my first World Series, I must tell you that it was Mr. Rickey's drama and that I was only a principal actor. As I write this twenty years later, I cannot stand and sing the anthem. I cannot salute the flag; I know that I am a Black man in a white world. In 1972, in 1947, at my birth in 1919, I know that I never had it made." Jackie Robinson's *I Never Had It Made* autobiography with Alfred Duckett.

1982, Jackie Robinson becomes the first baseball player to be honored on a U.S. postage stamp.

1984, Jackie Robinson is posthumously presented with the Presidential Medal of Freedom by President Ronald Reagan, the highest civilian award.

1987, Forty years after his debut with the Brooklyn Dodgers, the Rookie of the Year Award is renamed the Jackie Robinson Award, given to a player from the American and the National League. This is the first MLB award named after a former Negro Leaguer.

1997, Jackie Robinson becomes the first athlete to appear on a Wheaties box, while also on Honey Frosted Wheaties and Crispy Wheaties 'n Raisins. Robinson also becomes the first African American featured on a gold coin by the U.S. Mint. The Mint commemorates Robinson's life by issuing silver $1 and gold $5 coins bearing his likeness.

1997, Jackie Robinson becomes the first athlete to have his jersey number (42) retired in perpetuity. National League President Len Coleman initiates the mandate. The New York Yankees' pitcher Mariano Rivera, who retired after the 2013 season, was the last active player to wear No. 42.

2003, Jackie Robinson becomes the first Black ball player to posthumously receive the Congressional Gold Medal. It is awarded to persons "who have performed an achievement that has an impact on American history and culture that is likely to be recognized as a major achievement in the recipient's field long after the achievement."

2007, In recognition of the 60th anniversary of Jackie Robinson breaking the color barrier, five teams – Dodgers, Astros, Phillies, Pirates and Cardinals – feature all players wearing number 42.

2021, The historical marker to honor Jackie Robinson's birthplace at the Roddenbery Memorial Library in Cairo, Ga., is damaged by gunfire.

2022, The Jackie Robinson Museum opens in New York City. It is the city's first museum primarily focused on the Civil Rights Movement.

WILBER "BULLET" ROGAN

"He was the onliest pitcher I ever knew, I ever heard of in my life that was pitching and hitting in the cleanup spot." – Satchel Paige

1926, On the final day of the playoff series in the Negro National League, Willie Foster for the Chicago American Giants wins both games against the Kansas City Monarchs while pitcher Wilber "Bullet" Rogan takes a loss in both games. Their pitch counts are not available.

JOHN ROSEBORO

1961, John Roseboro of the Dodgers becomes the first African American catcher to win a Gold Glove in the National League.

DEION "PRIME TIME" SANDERS

1989, Deion Sanders becomes the first athlete in the pro ranks to hit a home run, with the New York Yankees in the World Series, and score a touchdown (68-yard interception), with the Atlanta Falcons against the Los Angeles Rams, in the same week.

1994, Deion Sanders becomes the first athlete to play in a Super Bowl (with Dallas Cowboys) and in the World Series (with the 1992 Atlanta Braves and the 1989 N.Y. Yankees).

WILLIAM SELDEN

1899, Danny McClellan pitching the first recorded perfect game by an African American pitcher against the Penn Park Athletic Club of York, Pa., champions of the Tri-State League, is well known in 1903. Recently, Tony Kissel and Wayne Stivers found an earlier no-hitter in 1899. It is pitched by William Selden of the Cuban Giants on July 9 against the Bordentowns, a team in the Middle States League. Selden strikes out three and walks two batters, en route to a 2-0 win. A full account of the game is reported in the *Trenton Daily True American*.

BIANCA SMITH

2021, Bianca Smith becomes the first African American female coach in professional baseball when hired as a minor league coach by the Boston Red Sox. A Dartmouth College graduate, Smith obtained a J.D. degree and a MBA in sports management from Case Western Reserve University in 2017.

WENDELL SMITH

"With our noses high and our hands in our pockets, squeezing the same dollar that we hand out to the white players, we walk past their (Negro league) ball parks and go to the major league games.

Nuts – that's what we are. Just plain nuts!" – Wendell Smith, *Pittsburgh Courier* 14 May 1938

1958, Wendell Smith, becomes the first African American to provide radio commentary for a boxing championship match. The middleweight title fight is between Sugar Ray Robinson and Carmen Basilio at Chicago Stadium.

Colorful Firsts in U.S. Sports

1993, Writer Wendell Smith, former travel mate of Jackie Robinson, is the first African American recipient of the Spink Award, first conferred in 1962. Named for J.G. Taylor Spink, founder of *The Sporting News*, the award honors baseball writers for "meritorious contributions to baseball writing" and is presented at the HOF induction ceremonies.

2015, Claire Smith is the first recipient of the Sam Lacy-Wendell Smith Award, created by the Shirley Povich Center for Sports Journalism. The award is presented annually to a sports journalist or broadcaster who has made significant contributions to racial and gender equality in sports.

WILLIE "POPS" STARGELL

1979, Willie "Pops" Stargell becomes the first player (and the oldest at 39) to win MVPs in the league (shared with Keith Hernandez), the NLCS playoffs and the World Series, all in the same season. Stargell also wins the *Sporting News'* Man of the Year award and is Co-winner (with Terry Bradshaw) of *Sport Illustrated's* Sportsman of the Year award.

NORMAN "TURKEY" STEARNES

1932, Chicago American Giants outfielder Turkey Stearnes captures the "Quadruple Crown" in the Negro Southern League, as leader in doubles, triples, home runs and stolen bases. No other player in any league has duplicated this feat.

RENNIE STENNETT

1975, Panamanian Rennie Stennett, second baseman for the Pittsburgh Pirates, becomes the only player in modern baseball to go 7-for-7 in a nine-inning game when he hits four singles, two doubles and a triple in a 22-0 victory over the Chicago Cubs.

TONI STONE

1953, The first woman in professional baseball, Toni Stone, joins the Indianapolis Clowns. She later plays for the Kansas City Monarchs. This season Stone suffers a serious shoulder injury diving for a ground ball in July against the Monarchs, forcing the Indianapolis Clowns to sign Doris Arlene Jackson and Desiree "Boo Boo" Richardson. Stone was rejected by the All-American Girls Professional Baseball League (1943-1954), founded by Philip K. Wrigley, due to its segregation policy.

2019, Toni Stone is the first woman from the Negro Leagues to have a Off-Broadway production about her legacy. The Roundabout Theatre Company produces Lydia R. Diamond's *Toni Stone*. April Matthis plays the star athlete.

GEORGE STOVEY

1886, George Stovey wins 16 of the 49 games won by the Jersey City Skeeters (or Jerseys) in the Eastern League.

1887, George Stovey signs with Newark of the International League and joins catcher Moses Fleetwood Walker to form the first African American battery in White professional baseball. Stovey wins 33 games against 14 losses for the fourth-place Newark Little Giants. Cap Anson refuses to allow his National League Chicago White Stockings to play against the Newark Little Giants because African American pitcher George Stovey is on the roster.

MULE SUTTLES

1933, George "Mule" Suttles of the Chicago American Giants hits the first home run in East-West All-Star competition. Suttles hits a two-run homer off of Sam Streeter of the Pittsburgh Crawfords in the fourth inning.

GARRY TEMPLETON

1979, San Diego Padres shortstop Garry Templeton becomes the first National Leaguer with 100 hits from each side of the plate, in a single season, collecting a league leading 211 hits in total. He batts .314 that season.

HANK THOMPSON

1947, Hank Thompson, a second baseman, becomes the first African American to integrate the St. Louis Browns.

1947, Willard Brown, an outfielder, joins Hank Thompson in a game against the Boston Red Sox, marking the first time two African Americans appear in the same American League lineup.

1949, Monte Irvin and Hank Thompson become the first African Americans to play with the New York Giants.

LUIS TIANT JR.

1968, Bob Gibson leads the National League with an ERA of 1.12, while Luis Tiant Jr. leads American League with a 1.60 ERA. They are the first African American pitchers to win the ERA crown and record the lowest ERAs by pitchers since re-integration

(1947) of the major leagues.

1975, Luis Tiant Jr. pitches for the Boston Red Sox in the World Series. Twenty-eight years earlier, his father, Luis Senior, pitched in the 1947 Negro World Series for the New York Cubans. They become the first father-and-son combination to pitch in World Series games, albeit in different leagues.

JOSÉ TORRES

1926, José "Gacho, Chico" Torres, an outfielder, is the first Puerto Rican to play in the organized Negro Leagues with the Newark Stars of the Eastern Colored League.

CRISTÓBAL TORRIENTE

1923, Cristóbal Torriente of the Chicago American Giants hits for the cycle against the St. Louis Stars in St. Louis, Mo.

QUINCY TROUPPE

1952, A 39-year-old rookie catcher Quincy Trouppe, catches relief pitcher "Toothpick Sam" Jones of the Cleveland Indians forming the first African American battery in the American League. Trouppe is also the first African American catcher in the American League.

1953, Quincy Trouppe becomes the first African American scout for the St. Louis Cardinals when signed by new owner August Busch Jr.

LEN TUCKER

1953, The St. Louis Cardinals signs its first African American player, 23-year-old Leonard Tucker from Fresno (Calif.) State College. The first baseman spends nine seasons in the minors and never makes it to the parent club.

JESUS VELASQUEZ

1917, Shortstop Jesús "El Tigre" Velásquez from Arecibo becomes the first dark-skinned Puerto Rican to play in the U.S.

ZOILO VERSAILLES

1963, Zoilo "Zorro" Versailles becomes the first non-White player to win the Gold Glove Award at shortstop in the American League.

LEON "DADDY WAGS" WAGNER

"I had most of my trouble in Danville, Virginia, in the Carolina League in 1956. I think that's why I hit so many home runs that year, 51 of 'em and 166 RBIs. Insults pushed me to play harder."

1962, Leon "Daddy Wags" Wagner becomes the first ball player to be named MVP of a major league All-Star game. His American League team wins 9-4 at Wrigley Field.

HARRY J. WALKER

1920, The NAACP's *The Crisis* magazine reports that Harry J. Walker, a Negro, is the official announcer for World Series games at Cleveland's League Park. The Cleveland Indians of the American League defeat the Brooklyn Robins of the National League, five games to two.

MOSES FLEETWOOD WALKER

1857, The white major league baseball's first recognized African American baseball player, Moses Fleetwood Walker is born in Mt. Pleasant, Ohio.

1881, Moses Fleetwood Walker, an African American catcher for the Cleveland Whites, is not allowed to play against the Eclipse in Louisville, Ky. In 1884, the Louisville Eclipse and Walker's new team the Toledo Blue Stockings would join the American Association, a designated major league, obliging integrated play on the diamond.

1883, The *Toledo Daily Blade*, March 15, reports that the executive committee of the Northwestern League meets at Toledo's Boody House to consider "a motion … by the representative from the Peoria, Ill., club that no colored player be allowed in the league." This motion is made to ban mulatto Moses Fleetwood Walker from playing. After a hostile discussion, the motion is defeated, allowing Walker to play.

1883, Cap Anson of the Chicago White Stockings refuses to play the Toledo Blue Stockings if Moses Fleetwood Walker takes the

Colorful Firsts in U.S. Sports

field. Anson pouts in the *Toledo Daily Blade*, "We'll play this here game, but won't play never no more with the nigger in."

1884, Moses Fleetwood Walker, catcher, becomes the first recognized African American to play in the white-centric major leagues with the Toledo Blue Stockings of the American Association.

1887, George Stovey signs with Newark of the International League and joins catcher Moses Fleetwood Walker to form the first African American battery in White professional baseball. Stovey wins 33 games against 14 losses for the fourth-place Newark Little Giants.

1891, Moses Fleetwood Walker receives U.S. patent #458,026 for an exploding artillery shell.

1908, Moses Fleetwood Walker authors *Our Home Colony: A Treatise on the Past, Present and Future of the Negro Race in America*. In his writing, Walker expresses defeat and urges Black people to leave the U.S. in search of better opportunities in Africa.

1920, Moses Fleetwood Walker receives U.S. patent #1,328,408 for a film end fastener for motion picture film reels, U.S. patent #1,348,609 for an alarm for motion picture film reels and U.S. patent #1,345,818 for motion picture film reel.

HERB WASHINGTON

1974, Oakland A's owner Charlie Finley hires former Michigan State University sprinter Herb Washington as the first "designated runner" in major league history. Washington has no prior professional baseball experience. He steals 31 bases in 48 attempts and scored 33 runs in 105 ML games.

RON WASHINGTON

2007, Ron Washington with the Texas Rangers and Cecil Cooper with the Houston Astros become their teams' first African American managers.

NATASHA RENÉE WATLEY

2004, Natasha Renée Watley, who plays shortstop and first base, is the first African American to play for the USA Softball team in the Summer Olympics (Athens).

BOB WATSON

1986, Bob Watson is named assistant general manager of the Houston Astros.

1993, Two-time MLB All-Star Bob Watson is named general manager of the Houston Astros.

1995, Bob Watson is named general manager of the New York Yankees.

1996, Bob Watson, for the New York Yankees, is the first Black general manager to win a World Series.

ELAINE C. WEDDINGTON

1990, Elaine C. Weddington, becomes the first Black female assistant general manager with the Boston Red Sox.

WILLIE "The DEVIL" WELLS

1937, Willie Wells returns after five days from a beaning from pitcher Bill Byrd. Wells appears at the plate with a modified construction hat. It is the first known instance of a player donning a "hard" hat -- four years, 1941, before the Brooklyn Dodgers used padded inserts in their headgear.

BILL WHITE

"I had constant trouble with baiters in Burlington-Graham, North Carolina. The more the fans gave it to me, the harder I hit the ball, so they eventually decided to leave me alone, which was a victory over bigotry."

1960, Bill White of the St. Louis Cards becomes the first Black National League player to win the Gold Glove Award at first base.

1971, Bill White becomes the first African American play-by-play announcer for a professional team when hired by the New York Yankees. White joins Phil Rizzuto and Frank Messer in the booth, and the trio lasts for 16 years.

1989, Bill White becomes the first African American President of major league baseball's National League. His term lasted until 1994.

FRANK WHITE

1969, Frank White scrapes mortar and seals floors during the construction of Royals (later Kauffman) Stadium, earning the distinction of being the only major league baseball player to literally help build the stadium he would later play in. White is the first graduate of the Royals Baseball Academy to reach the Majors with his debut in 1973.

1977, Frank White of the Kansas City Royals becomes the first African American to the win the Gold Glove Award at second base in the American League.

1980, Frank White (2b) and U.L. Washington (ss) of the Kansas City Royals become the first African American double-play combination in American League history.

1980, Frank White, of Kansas City Royals, is the first player to win the ALCS' Most Valuable Player.

SOL WHITE

1907, King Solomon White, captain of the Philadelphia Giants, authors *The History of Colored Base Ball*. The first book written about African Americans in baseball, includes chapters by Andrew "Rube" Foster and Grant "Home Run" Johnson, on pitching and batting with 57 rare images.

LARRY WHITESIDE

1970, Larry Whiteside becomes the first African American beat writer to travel regularly with a baseball team, the Boston Red Sox. He was the fourth African American writer to become a member of the Baseball Writers' Association of America (BBWAA).

ALEXANDER McDONALD WILLIAMS

1922, Alexander McDonald Williams, owner of the Pittsburgh Keystones, builds Central Amusement Park. The park is bordered by Humber on the northside, Junilla on the eastside, Hallett on the southside and Chauncey on the westside. It becomes the first Black-owned ballpark in the Negro National League.

ART WILLIAMS

1972, Art Williams becomes the first African American umpire in the National League.

BERNIE WILLIAMS

1998, Bernie Williams, New York Yankees outfielder, becomes the first player to win a Gold Glove, a batting title and a World Series ring in the same season.

CHARLIE WILLIAMS

1985, Charlie Williams becomes the first African American umpire in a major league All-Star game, held at the Hubert H. Humphrey Metrodome in Minneapolis, Minn.

1993, Charlie Williams, 49, of the National League becomes the first African American to call balls and strikes in a World Series game. After 13 years as an umpire, he officiates in the marathon fourth game, a four-hour, 14-minute affair that sees the Toronto Blue Jays outlast the Philadelphia Phillies, 15-14.

1995, In a game at Atlanta-Fulton County Stadium, umpire Charlie Williams calls balls and strikes with his nephew Lenny Webster, catching for the Philadelphia Phillies. The Phillies beat the Braves 3-1. At bat Webster goes 0-for-4. Pitchers for the Braves included John Smoltz (five innings), Brad Woodall (one 2/3), Steve Bedrosian (one), Mike Stanton (one) and Mark Wohlers (1/3). Pitchers for the Phillies included Mike Mimbs (six innings), Gene Harris (one), Norm Charlton (one) and Heathcliff Slocumb (one). The Brave pitchers gave up eight hits, six walks and struck out 11. The Philly pitchers gave up four hits, six walks and struck out six.

KEN WILLIAMS

2000, Ken Williams becomes the first African American general manager in the Chicago White Sox's 100-year history.

MARVIN "TEX" WILLIAMS

1952, Marvin "Tex" Williams, a power-hitting second baseman from the Philadelphia Stars and Cleveland Buckeyes, becomes the first Black man to manage a mixed race team when he is appointed manager of the Dorados de Chihuahua (Goldens) in Mexico. Williams takes the helm in late June from Domingo Santana. The Goldens are a Class C team in the Arizona-Texas League, finishing with a record of 57-83. As player/manager, Williams' slash line is .401/.854/1.391.

MAURY WILLS

1962, Maury Wills is the first major leaguer to steal more than 100 bases (104).

Colorful Firsts in U.S. Sports

1963, After Maury Wills' base stealing record of 104 steals, baseball institutes a rule change. This year pitchers are required to come to a complete stop (or pause), before delivering the pitch to the plate. The intent is to hold the potential base stealer closer to the bag.

1965, In Los Angeles, Maury Wills of the Los Angeles Dodgers and Willie Mays of the San Francisco Giants, exchange lineup cards with umpire Al Barlick. This marks the first time in major league baseball, the opposing team captains are African Americans.

1980, Maury Wills becomes the first African American manager of the Seattle Mariners.

ARTIE WILSON

1948, According to *Howe News Bureau*, Artie Wilson hits .402 for the Birmingham Black Barons of the Negro American League and becomes the last .400 hitter in major league baseball history.

DON WILSON

1962, Boston Red Sox pitcher Earl Wilson is the first African American to throw a no-hitter in the American League.

1969, Don Wilson of the Houston Astros, pitches his second no-hitter. He is the first African American pitcher to have two nine-inning no-hitters to his credit. Toothpick Sam Jones' second no-hitter in 1959, was a seven-inning contest.

EARL WILSON

1962, Earl Wilson is the first African American to throw a no-hitter in the American League.

1963, Bill Russell of the Boston Celtics and Earl Wilson of the Boston Red Sox, pay homage to Civil Rights leader Medgar Evers assassinated in Jackson, Mississippi. Wilson and Russell circulate among the estimated 1,800 people gathered at the Parkman Bandstand on the Boston Common, to collect funds.

FABIOLA WILSON

1948, Outfielders Fabiola Wilson and Gloria "Lovie" Dymond are the first ladies to play for the minor league New Orlean Creoles in a game against the Nashville Cubs in the Negro Southern League.

WILLIE WILSON

1980, Kansas City Royals centerfielder Willie Wilson becomes the first American League batter to collect 100 hits from each side of the plate, in a season, with 230 total hits. He is also the first player to record more than 700 (705) at bats in a season.

DAVE WINFIELD

1973, Dave Winfield becomes the first athlete drafted in three different sports. The San Diego Padres select him as a pitcher with the fourth overall pick in the MLB draft and both the Atlanta Hawks (NBA) and the Utah Stars (ABA) draft him. Although he never played college football, the Minnesota Vikings selected Winfield in the 17th round of the NFL draft. He is one of two players ever to be drafted by three professional sports (the other being Dave Logan in 1976).

NIP WINTERS

1924, Jesse "Nip" Winters of the Hilldale Club pitches the first no-hitter in Eastern Colored League competition. Winters defeats the Harrisburg Giants, 2-0.

1924, In the second game, Nip Winters for the Hilldale Club pitches the first shutout in Negro World Series history. Winters throws a four-hitter in a 11-0 win over the Kansas City Monarchs.

EARL WOODS

1951, Earl Woods, father of Tiger Woods, is the first Black baseball player for the Kansas State University Wildcats. He earns varsity letters in 1952 and 1953.

CHRIS YOUNG

2007, Chris Young, centerfielder for the Arizona Diamondbacks, becomes the first rookie major leaguer to hit more than 30 (32) home runs and steal more than 25 (27) bases in the same season.

Cage 3HREE: Basketball Champions

"White men can't jump? They don't have too. They own the team."
– Paul Mooney, comedian

AMATEUR BASKETBALL TIMELINE

1907, The Smart Set Athletic Club of Brooklyn, managed by J. Hoffman Woods, creates the first independent African American basketball team. Nicknamed the "Grave Diggers" for their tendency to bury opponents, the team would win the first two Colored Basketball World's Championships in 1907-08 and 1908-09.

1907, The Alpha Physical Culture Club of Harlem, founded by Jamaica-born brothers Conrad and Gerald Norman creates the Olympian Athletic League, a Black club basketball league. Better known as the Alpha Big Five, it is America's first all-Black athletic club.

1908, The University of Vermont names its first African American captain of a basketball team, Fenwick Watkins. After graduating from Vermont, Watkins coaches football, basketball, and baseball at Fargo College in Fargo, N.D, where he also leads the athletic program.

1908, The Independent Pleasure Club of Orange, N.J., is created and managed by Nelson Frye. Upon defeating the Alpha Big Five and the Smart Set it is awarded the unofficial 1913 Colored Basketball Championship of New Jersey.

1909, Cumberland Posey Jr. becomes the first colored student-athlete at Penn State. He plays on the freshman and varsity basketball teams and the freshman baseball team in 1910.

1909, Edwin B. Henderson creates the Washington (DC) 12 Streeters basketball team with students from Howard University. Sponsored by the Twelfth Street Colored Y.M.C.A., the team wins the 1909-10 unofficial Colored Basketball World Championship title with an undefeated season.

1910, Cumberland Posey forms an all-Black basketball team, the Monticello Athletic Association in Pittsburgh. The team defeats the Howard University team, 24-19, to claim the 1911-12 Colored Basketball World's Championship.

1910, The Spartan Athletic Club of Brooklyn (N.Y.), perhaps the first all-Black women's basketball team, is organized by President Bernadine Harris. Sister Mary Harris is team captain and manager, with Sidney Jackson coaching. The Spartan Girls were the sister squad to the Smart Set Athletic Club of Brooklyn.

1910, Major Aloysius Hart organizes an all-Black basketball team in Harlem, called the New York All Stars. Their home court is the Manhattan Casino in Harlem. The All Stars are led by Ferdinand Accooe, Charles Scottron and Charles "Mule" Bradford, a baseball pitcher with the Philadelphia Colored Giants of New York.

1913, Will Anthony Madden legally incorporates the St. Christopher Club of New York, Inc., soon to be known as the Incorporators basketball team. The teams defeats Howard University and the Alpha Physical Culture Club of Harlem to claim the unofficial colored championship.

1915, The Pittsburgh Scholastics Basket Ball Club, pre-cursor to the famous Loendi Big Five, is organized by fitness trainer Hunter Johnson. Johnson is credited with training long jumper DeHart Hubbard, a gold medalist in the 1924 Olympics.

1920, The Loendi Big Five, managed by Cumberland Posey win the Colored Basketball World Championships, the first of four consecutive seasons from 1920 to 1923.

1928, Walter Green, of Chicago, starts the Savoy Colts, a women's basketball team, managed by Dick Hudson. Their roster includes guards E. Williams, Blanche Winston, Corrine Robinson, forwards Lula Porter, Virginia Willis, H. Williams and famed Philadelphia tennis star Ora Washington at center.

1929, The Germantown Hornets, in Philadelphia, are formed by the YWCA Branch of Colored Girls and Women. The Hornets basketball team included Ora Washington, Lula Ballard, Louise Penn, Lil Fountainé, Helen Laws and Evelyn Manns.

1930, The Tribune Girls are sponsored by the *Philadelphia Tribune* newspaper. The players come from two Black female basketball teams, the Philadelphia Quick Steppers and the Germantown Hornets. Inez Patterson from the Quick Steppers becomes coach and player of the team. Two tennis players from the YWCA Colored Branch in Germantown, Ora Washington and Lula Ballard become standout hoopsters.

1943, Rudolph "Rocky" Robeson, for the North Carolina College for Negroes (now North Carolina Central University) becomes the first African American hoopster to break a national college record, when he scores 58 points against Shaw University of Raleigh

Colorful Firsts in U.S. Sports

NC to break Stanford forward Hank Luisetti's record of 50 points set in 1938.

1944, John McLendon coaches the first integrated game in the South – North Carolina College of Negroes versus Duke's Navy Medical School, in Durham, N.C. McLendon's Eagles win by a score of 88 to 44. It is the first collegiate basketball contest where Blacks and Whites compete on the same floor. This Sunday morning match has remained a secret for several decades.

1946, John McLendon of North Carolina College co-founds the Central Intercollegiate Athletic Association (CIAA) Tournament with Talmadge Hill (Morgan State), John Burr (Howard University) and Harry Jefferson (Virginia State). The first games are played at Washington District of Columbia's Turner Arena. CIAA tournament becomes a showcase for future NBA players, such as Sam Jones, Earl Monroe, Cleo Hill, Ricky Mahorn, Charles Oakley and Ben Wallace.

1947, After winning the Indiana Intercollegiate Conference basketball title, coach John Wooden of the Indiana State Teacher's College turns down an invitation to play in the National Association of Intercollegiate Basketball (NAIB) due to its policy to banning Black players. Guard Clarence Walker was the Black member of Wooden's team.

1947, The first official basketball game between Black and White collegiate teams is played between Wilberforce University and Bergen College of New Jersey at Madison Square Garden. Wilberforce wins 40-12.

1948, The NAIB (later the NAIA) admits the first African American player, Clarence Walker from coach John Wooden's Indiana State Teachers College team to its tournament. Walker becomes the first African American player to participate in a national college basketball championship at any level.

1951, Solly Walker, guard for St. John's University, becomes the first Black player to play in an integrated college basketball game at the University of Kentucky. Walker hits six of his first seven shots before leaving game due to a body blow, sidelining him for weeks.

1955, The University of San Francisco Dons basketball team, coached by Phil Woolpert, becomes the first team with three Black starters to win an NCAA championship. The starters were Bill Russell, K. C. Jones and Hal Perry.

1956, In the All-American City Basketball Tournament in Owensboro, Kentucky, the Ole Miss Rebels lose the opening game and are scheduled to play the Iona College Gaels of New York in the consolidation match. Ole Miss coach Bonnie Graham advises officials that if Stanley Hill, a Black guard on the Gaels team, suits up, the game will not be played. The game is forfeited to the Gaels. State legislators praise Ole Miss officials for their "honorable" decision to boycott the game. The 1957 Ole Miss press guide does not list the loss in the team's record book.

1963, The Loyola Ramblers (Chicago) become the first major college basketball team to have five Black players on the floor at the same time. They start one White player John Egan and four Black players, Les Hunter, Vic Rouse, Ron Miller and team captain Jerry Harkness. They defeat the Cincinnati Bearcats in overtime to capture the NCAA championship. Earlier in the tournament, despite hate mail from the Klan, the Ramblers faced the all-White Mississippi State Bulldogs against orders from Governor Ross Barnett, banning his Bulldogs from crossing state lines to play the integrated Ramblers. The landmark contest, won by the Ramblers 61-51, is later named the "Game of Change." See 2013.

1966, Texas Western becomes the first NCAA champion to start five African Americans, Harry Flournoy, David Lattin, Bobby Joe Hill, Orsten Artis, and Willie Cager. They upset No. 1 ranked Kentucky's all-White team of Adolph Rupp in the championship game in College Park, Md. For playing an all-Black lineup and beating an all-White team, Haskins reportedly received 40,000 pieces of hate mail and a dozen death threats. The victorious team inspired the 2006 movie *Glory Road*.

1966-67, Western Kentucky's Clem Haskins, Houston's Elvin Hayes and Louisville's Wes Unseld become the first African Americans from Southern schools to be named to the first NCAA All-American team.

1967-68, After the dominance of UCLA center Lew Alcindor, the NCAA bans dunking for the upcoming season. The rule is rescinded for the 1976-77 season.

1968, Irish Catholic Notre Dame University fields an all-Black starting five basketball team, with Austin Carr, Sid Catlett, Collis Jones, Bob Whitmore and Dwight Murphy.

1969, John W. Oswald, president of the University of Kentucky, orders basketball coach Adolph Rupp to begin recruiting Black players. Three years before his retirement, Rupp signs his one and only Black player, Tom Payne.

1970, Coach John B. McLendon teaches the "Two in the Corner Offense" to North Carolina Coach Dean Smith at a Fellowship of Christian Athletes meeting in Colorado. Smith renames the offense "The Four Corners."

1976, The dunk is reinstated. The dominance of UCLA center Lew Alcindor had prompted the NCAA to ban dunking in college basketball during the 1967-68 season.

1979, The Alcorn Braves basketball team becomes the first historically Black institution invited to the National Invitation

Tournament (NIT). The Braves are led by Davey Whitney, former Kansas City Monarch. His team defeats Mississippi State, 80-78 in the first round, before losing to Indiana, 72-68 in the second round.

1982, Vivian Stringer, coach of Cheyney State, a Division II team, is the first African American woman to take a team to the NCAA basketball tournament. Cheyney State loses the championship game to Louisiana Tech. Stringer is named *Sports Illustrated's* Coach of the Year.

1982, The first all-Black Division I Consensus All-American team is named: Terry Cummings, DePaul; Quintin Dailey, San Francisco; Eric Floyd, Georgetown; Ralph Sampson, Virginia; and James Worthy, North Carolina.

1984, The USC Women's basketball team are the first female NCAA champions to be invited to the White House, by President Ronald Reagan. The team is led by Cheryl Miller, Cynthia Cooper and the McGee twins Paula and Pamela.

1989, The Wayman Tisdale Award is established by the USBWA to recognize an outstanding frosh collegiate basketball player. Guard Chris Jackson, later known as Mahmoud Abdul-Rauf, of LSU, is the first recipient.

1990, Georgetown basketball coach John Thompson stages a walkout protesting the National Collegiate Athletic Association's (NCAA) new Proposal 42. The NCAA's Proposal 48 sets minimum academic standards for incoming athletes to earn a 700 on the SAT and achieve a 2.0 grade point average. Proposal 42 adds if an athlete does not meet the guidelines of Proposal 48, he or she must sit out the first season and set a three-year limit on athletic eligibility. Opponents argue Proposal 48's minimum test-score requirements are based on culturally biased standardized tests. The NCAA estimates nine of 10 athletes who fail to meet the requirements are Black. Proposal 42, Thompson claims, exacerbates the injustice by denying many athletes from low-income families the opportunity to attend college.

1994, North Carolina's Charlotte Smith, a 6-foot-0 leaper, becomes the second woman to dunk in a basketball game.

1996-97, The first team All-Stars of the American Basketball League are Black: Teresa Edwards (Atlanta Glory), Dawn Staley (Richmond Rage), Natalie Williams (Portland Power), Nikkie McCray (Columbus Quest) and Adrienne Goodson (Richmond Rage).

1999, Duke University becomes the first college to have four players drafted in the first round of the NBA draft. Elton Brand, No. 1 pick by Chicago; Trajan Langdon, No. 11 pick by Cleveland; Corey Maggett, No. 13 pick by Seattle; and William Avery, No. 14 pick by Minnesota. Despite their wealth of potential pro talent, UConn defeats them in the NCAA championship game.

2006, For the first time four non-seniors from the same team, North Carolina University at Chapel Hill, are selected in the first round of the NBA draft. Players include small forward Marvin Williams (2nd pick by Atlanta Hawks), point guard Raymond Felton (5th pick by Charlotte Bobcats), power forward Sean May (13th pick by Charlotte Bobcats) and shooting guard Rashad McCants (14th pick by Minnesota Timberwolves).

2007, The Florida Gators become the first college team to have three players drafted among the first 10 picks in the NBA draft. Al Horford is taken 3rd by Atlanta, Corey Brewer is taken 7th by Minnesota and Joakim Noah is taken by Chicago. Horford's father, Tito, played in the NBA. Joakim's parents are Yannick Noah, former professional tennis player, and Cécilia Rodhe, Miss Sweden 1978.

2007, The 1966 Texas Western Miners are inducted into the Naismith Memorial Basketball Hall of Fame. Texas Western, now known as UTEP, is the first team in NCAA history to win a title with a starting lineup of five Black players, beating an all-White Adolph Rupp Kentucky team in the 1966 final. The achievement, regarded as a turning point in the integration of college athletics, was the subject of the film "*Glory Road*." Rupp was inducted into the Hall of Fame in 1969.

2009, In July, Ed O'Bannon, a former basketball player for UCLA who was a starter on the 1995 national championship team, and the NCAA Basketball Tournament's Most Outstanding Player of that year, files a lawsuit against the NCAA and the Collegiate Licensing Company, alleging violations of the Sherman Antitrust Act and of actions that deprived him of his right of publicity. He agrees to be the lead plaintiff after seeing his likeness from the 1995 championship team used in the EA Sports title NCAA Basketball 09 without his permission. The game featured an unnamed UCLA player who played O'Bannon's power forward position, while also matching his height, weight, bald head, skin tone, No. 31 jersey, and left-handed shot. In January 2011, Oscar Robertson joined O'Bannon in the class action suit. Bill Russell is also among the 20 former college athletes as plaintiffs.

2013, The 1963 Loyola Ramblers, Division I NCAA champions, become the first team inducted into the National Collegiate Basketball Hall of Fame and later honored at the White House by President Barack Obama.

2015, The city of Indianapolis gives the living members of the 1955 Crispus Attucks state championship basketball team a parade and celebratory ride from the Fieldhouse to Monument Circle that had been previously denied them as the first Black team to win a state championship. Coach Ray Crowe with guard Oscar Robertson won back-to-back championships, 1955 and 1956.

Colorful Firsts in U.S. Sports

2017, The NBA moves its All-Star game from Charlotte, North Carolina, to Smoothie King Arena in New Orleans, Louisiana, after a so-called "bathroom bill" that bars transgender people from using the bathroom that matched their gender identity.

2019, Penn State basketball coach Pat Chambers tells star freshman Rasir Bolton in January: "I want to be a stress reliever for you. You can talk to me about anything. I need to get some of this pressure off you. I want to loosen the noose that's around your neck." Bolton recounts that Chambers, who is Catholic, said he was making a biblical reference and had intended to say "yoke." After the season, Bolton transfers to Iowa State. Chambers resigns from the basketball program in October.

2021, NCAA basketball champions Baylor and coach Scott Drew refuse a customized Jeep Wrangler wrapped with the school's national championship logo after an insensitive remark made by Ted Teague, general manager of the Allen Samuels dealership in Waco, during a live KWTX-TV interview, stating "use it to recruit, pull some people out of the hood." Teague immediately apologizes.

2021, The Converse Pro Leather High 'Breaking Down Barriers' pays tribute to Indiana's Crispus Attucks Tigers, who in 1955 became the first all-black high school basketball team to win a state championship. Inspired by the team's letterman's jacket, the vintage hoops shoe features a white felt upper with mismatched Star Chevron branding in yellow and green. The heel tab on the left shoe is embroidered with 'CA 55,' while the Tigers' logo adorns the right.

PRO BASKETBALL TIMELINE

1902, Harry "Bucky" Lew, a forward with Pawtucketville (Mass.) Athletic Club in New England becomes the first African American professional basketball player.

1906, Harry "Bucky" Lew forms his own basketball team, "Buck Lew's Traveling Five" playing around the New England area.

1922, The Commonwealth Big Five basketball is formed by brothers from the Bronx, Edward and Roderick "Jess" McMahon Sr. The "Commons" become the first all-Black professional team in America. See 1923, New York Rens.

1923, The New York Rens, named after the team's home court, the Renaissance Ballroom and Casino in Harlem, become America's first Black-owned all-Black professional basketball team. They are owned by Robert L. Douglas from St. Kitts, British West Indies.

1925, The colorless American Basketball Association (ABA) is organized and adopts a Jim Crow policy to exclude men of color.

1942, The Chicago Studebakers Champions and the Toledo Jim White Chevrolet of the National Basketball League employ African Americans for the first time in professional basketball. Sonny Boswell, Hillary Brown, Duke Cumberland, Roosie Hudson, Bennie Price and Ted Strong are the barrier breakers for the Studebakers, while Shannie Bennett, Casey Jones, Al Price and Zano West are pioneers for the Toledo team.

1943, Washington Bears (originally the Lichtman Bears) defeat the Oshkosh All-Stars (NBL) in the invitation-only World Professional Basketball Tournament. The undefeated Bears win all 41 games this season.

1946, The Basketball Association of America (BAA) is organized by Walter A. Brown, founder and owner of the Boston Celtics. His league bans African American players. Following its third season, 1948–49, the BAA and the National Basketball League (NBL) merged to create the National Basketball Association (NBA).

1946-47, The NBA outlaws zone defenses to speed up play. Zone defenses were re-instated in the National Basketball Association during the 2001–2002 season.

1949, The New York Rens, now based in Dayton, Ohio, and members of the National Basketball League (NBL), play its last game against the Denver Rockets. Coached by "Pop" Gates, its lifetime record over 26 years is 2,318 wins and 381 losses, an 86 winning percentage. Gates is the first African American head coach in the NBL.

1949, Teams in the National Basketball League (NBL) are merged into the National Basketball Association (NBA). The all-Black Dayton Rens are left out of the merger, creating an all-White NBA until the Washington Capitols, N.Y. Knicks, Boston Celtics and the Tri-Cities Blackhawks signed a Black player for the 1950-51 season.

1950, Duquesne's Chuck Cooper, a second-team All-American, becomes the first African American drafted by an NBA team when he is selected in the second round by the Boston Celtics. Other African Americans selected in the NBA draft are West Virginia State's Earl Lloyd and North Carolina College's Harold Hunter (both by the Washington Capitols) and Kentucky State's Ed Thompson (by the Fort Wayne Pistons).

1950, On Halloween Oct. 31, Nov. 1, Nov. 4, and Dec. 3, Earl Lloyd, Chuck Cooper, Nat "Sweetwater" Clifton and Hank DeZonie, respectively, become the first African Americans to play in the National Basketball Association (NBA).

1955, The Hazleton (Pa.) Hawks of the Eastern League become the first professional league franchise to start an all-Black lineup, with Jesse Arnelle, Tom Hemans, Fletcher Johnson, Floyd Lane and Sherman White.

1957-58, The St. Louis Hawks become the last all-White team to win an NBA championship. The Hawks defeat the Boston Celtics 4-2 games.

1961, The Phoenix Hotel in Lexington, Ky., refuses service in its coffee shop to Black players Bill Russell, Sam Jones, K. C. Jones, Satch Sanders, and Al Butler from the Boston Celtics, along with Woody Sauldsberry and Cleo Hill from the St. Louis Hawks. In turn, these players boycott the exhibition game honoring the homecoming of NBA stars Frank Ramsey and Cliff Hagan.

1962, John McLendon is inducted into the NAIA Hall of Fame.

1963, The New York Rens are named to the Naismith Memorial Basketball Hall of Fame as a team. In 2002, the Harlem Globetrotters are inducted as a team.

1964, The Boston Celtics become the first NBA franchise to start five Black players when Willie Naulls replaced the injured Tommy Heinsohn in the starting lineup. Naulls with Bill Russell, K. C. Jones, Sam Jones and Satch Sanders reel off 12 consecutive wins.

1964-65, The NBA widens the lane to 16 feet from 12 feet to offset Wilt Chamberlain's dominance. The lane was last widened in 1951 to neutralize the presence of 6' 10" George Mikan of the Minneapolis Lakers.

Colorful Firsts in U.S. Sports

1970, An anti-trust lawsuit, Robertson v. National Basketball Association, 556 F.2d 682 (U.S. Court of Appeals for the Second Circuit, argued 7 April 1977) is filed by basketball player Oscar Robertson against the National Basketball Association (NBA). Filed in 1970, the lawsuit was settled in 1976 and resulted in the free agency rules now used in the NBA. Robertson sought through his lawsuit to block any merger of the NBA with the American Basketball Association (ABA), to end the option clause that bound a player to a single NBA team in perpetuity, to end the NBA's college draft binding a player to one team, and to end restrictions on free-agent signings. The suit also sought damages for NBA players for past harm caused by the option clause. Robertson's lawsuit prevented the planned 1970 merger of the National Basketball Association with the American Basketball Association. As president of the NBA players union, Robertson's 1970 suit against the NBA contended the draft, option clause and other rules restricting player movement were violations of antitrust laws. The suit was settled in 1976, when the league agreed to let players become free agents in exchange for their old team's "right of first refusal" to match any offer they might receive.

1971, John Thompson, no relation to Georgetown coach John Thompson, becomes the first African American to officiate a game between NBA and ABA players, on June 20, at a benefit All-Star game in Indianapolis. Thompson, an ABA referee at the time, was the lead official alongside the NBA's John Parker.

1971, Spencer Haywood signs a six-year, $1.5 million contract with the Seattle SuperSonics, ignoring the rule that a player cannot join the NBA until he is four years out of high school. Haywood challenges the decision by commencing an antitrust action against the NBA. As part of his claim against the NBA, Haywood argued that the ruling by the NBA is a "group boycott" and a violation of the Sherman Antitrust Act. The central issue that had to be determined was whether the NBA draft policy was a restraint on trade and therefore was illegal in accordance with the Sherman Act. The U.S. Supreme Court, in Haywood v. National Basketball Association, 401 U.S. 1204 rules, 9–0, against the NBA's requirement that a player may not be drafted by an NBA team unless he has waited four years following his graduation from high school.

1972, The Dallas Chaparrals, citing the need for more White fans, cut two Black all-stars, Donnie Freeman and John Brisker. "Last year, Dallas had only two White players —Gene Phillips and Len Chappell — compared to 10 Black players, and we drew less than 100 fans a game who were colored," said the Chaps' general partner, Joe W. Geary, a Dallas attorney. "A bunch of people want White faces, someone they can identify with," he said. The Chaps' head coach, Babe McCarthy, the dean of A.B.A. coaches, echoed Geary's feelings on the racial issue. Freeman was the Chaps' leading scorer last season with a 24-point average.

1976, The ABA folds, but the New York (later New Jersey) Nets, Denver Nuggets, Indiana Pacers and the San Antonio Spurs join the NBA.

1979, Darryl Dawkins demolishes backboards in at Kansas City's Kemper Arena and Philadelphia's Spectrum, prompting the development and implementation of the "Breakaway Rim" or pressure-release rim for the 1981-82 season. Dawkins from the planet Lovetron, becomes the first player to name his dunks: The Rim Wrecker, The Gorilla, In Your Face Disgrace, The Look Out Below, Cover Your Head, Dunk You Very Much, Left-Handed-Spine-Chiller-Supreme, The Bun Toaster, The Rump Roaster and the Baby Shaker.

1979-80, The New York Knicks become the first NBA team with an all-Black roster. The roster includes Bill Cartwright, Jim Clemons, Hollis Copeland, Larry Demic, Mike Glenn, Toby Knight, Joe Meriweather, Earl Monroe, Michael Ray Richardson, Marvin Webster, and Ray Williams. Lacking diversity the Knicks finish in fourth place in the Atlantic Division.

1983, The NBA selects its first all-rookie team: Terry Cummings (San Diego), Clark Kellogg (Indiana), Dominique Wilkins (Atlanta), James Worthy (Los Angeles) and Quintin Dailey (Chicago). Cummings is named Rookie of the Year.

1989, Bertram M. Lee and Peter C.B. Bynoe sign an agreement to purchase NBA's Denver Nuggets for $54-$65 million. They become the first African Americans with a minority interest in a professional basketball team. Comsat Video Enterprises, a subsidiary of telecommunications company Comsat Corporation, purchases a majority 67.5 percent stake in the Nuggets, with the remaining 32.5 percent held by Lee and Bynoe. In 1992 Comsat Video assumes 100 percent ownership of the franchise.

1989, For the first time in NBA history, five Blacks are named first team All-Stars: Charles Barkley (76ers), Magic Johnson (Lakers), Michael Jordan (Bulls), Karl Malone (Jazz) and Hakeem Olajuwon (Rockets).

1991, In the NBA Draft, the University of Nevada Las Vegas is represented by three first-round picks: Larry Johnson (1st pick), Stacey Augmon (9th pick) and Greg Anthony (12th pick). Each of these players chose to wear No. 2 in their rookie season to honor their college coach Jerry Tarkanian, who once wore No. 2.

1992, Lighting Ned Mitchell creates the Women's World Basketball Association (WWBA) the first ever spring and summer women's professional basketball league. The original teams included the Kansas Crusaders, Iowa Unicorns, Illinois Knights,

Nebraska Xpress, Missouri Mustangs and the Oklahoma Cougars. The league lasts three seasons, 1993 through 1995.

1993, The Kansas Crusaders, 10W-5L, become the first Women's Basketball Association (WBA) champion by beating the Nebraska Xpress 100-96. The WBA was originally named the WWBA or the Women's World Basketball Association founded by Lightning Ned Mitchell.

1994, Former basketball guard Isiah Lord Thomas buys a nine percent interest in the Toronto Raptors for $11.25 million.

1996, The American Basketball League (ABL) is founded. The women league's motto is "Real Basketball." The original teams include the Columbus Quest, Richmond Rage, Atlanta Glory, New England Blizzard, Colorado Xplosion, San José Lasers, Seattle Reign and the Portland Power. The league ceases operations in December 1998.

1996, Sheryl Swoopes and Rebecca Lobo are the first players to sign contracts with the Women's National Baseball Association (WNBA).

1997, The Women's National Basketball Association (WNBA) starts play one season after the American Basketball League. The league motto is "Watch Me Work." The original eight teams were the Charlotte Sting, Cleveland Rockers, Houston Comets, New York Liberty, Los Angeles Sparks, Phoenix Mercury, Sacramento Monarchs and the Utah Starzz.

1997, Dee Kantner and African American Violet Palmer become the first female officials in the NBA.

1999, Lusia Harris-Stewart and Cheryl Miller are among the original inductees into the Women's Basketball Hall of Fame in Knoxville, Tenn.

1999, Duke University becomes the first college to have four players drafted in the first round of the NBA draft. Elton Brand, No. 1 pick by Chicago; Trajan Langdon, No. 11 pick by Cleveland; Corey Maggette, No. 13 pick by Seattle; and William Avery, No. 14 pick by Minnesota. Despite their wealth of potential pro talent, UConn defeats them in the NCAA championship game, led by Richard Hamilton.

2001, Two all-Black teams are voted to start the NBA All-Star game. However, due to injuries to Grant Hill, Shaquille O'Neal among others, non-Blacks are selected in to replace them.

2001, The NBA allows zone defenses for the first time in its history, as possible alternative to stop the dominance of Shaquille O'Neal in the paint.

2002, The NBA Expansion committee approves an expansion franchise for the city of Charlotte to be owned and operation by Robert L. Johnson, former owner of BET. In 2000, Johnson sold BET to Viacom, Inc., for $3 billion.

2003, Bob Johnson, former owner of Black Entertainment Television (BET), becomes the first African American majority owner of an NBA basketball team, the Charlotte Hornets. According to *Forbes* magazine, he becomes the first African American billionaire in 2001. *Sports Illustrated* names Bob Johnson No. 1 on its list of 101 Most Influential Minorities in Sports.

2005, The NBA issues a dress code for the 2005-06 season. Business casual attire is required for team or league activities, including arriving at games, leaving games, conducting interviews and making promotional or other appearances. Players will no longer be able to wear the following: Sleeveless shirts, shorts, T-shirts, chains, pendants or medallions over clothing, sunglasses indoors and headphones (except on the team bus or the plane or in the locker room). Philadelphia 76er guard Allen Iverson is the most outspoken critic of the new dressing standard.

2005, Sheila Johnson, co-founder of Black Entertainment Television (BET), becomes part-owner of the Lincoln Holdings LLC, which purchases the Washington Mystics from Abe Pollin's Washington Sports & Entertainment. Johnson's stake in Lincoln Holdings is reported to be between 5 and 10 percent. Johnson is believed to be the first African American woman to be a principal shareholder of three professional sports franchises, the Mystics, Washington Wizards and the Washington Capitals.

2006, NFL quarterback Charlie Batch and former University of Michigan basketball star Antoine "The Judge" Joubert, announce the debut of the Detroit Panthers into the newly formed American Basketball Association franchise. Batch will be the majority owner, while Joubert will be the head coach.

2006, NBA commissioner David Stern wants to end players overreacting to calls by referees. Players need to curb their enthusiasm when they are whistled for a foul. There is no new rule, but players and coaches were notified by memo with emphasis on a "zero-tolerance policy." Rasheed Wallace, who picked up 16 technical fouls last season, said the passion rule was just "another Sheed Wallace rule."

2007, Leg tights are added to the list of banned apparel in the NBA. In the previous season, 2005-06, LeBron James (Cavaliers), Kobe Bryant (Lakers), Dwyane Wade (Heat) and White player Jason Williams (Heat) wear full-length hose to keep their sore knees warm.

2008, The Detroit Pistons wear a black patch in memory of Will Robinson, a scout who signed Joe Dumars and Dennis Rodman.

Colorful Firsts in U.S. Sports

When Robinson retired in 2003, the Pistons renamed their locker room "Will Robinson Locker Room."

2008, In March, ESPN presents a four-hour documentary entitled *Black Magic*, that portrays the on-and-off-the-court challenges facing Black basketball players at historically African American colleges (HBCUs).

2009, The NBA bans the unique facial accessory wore by Miami Heat guard Dwyane Wade. Originally, he wore a Band-Aid to seal a cut beneath his left eye. Wade later slapped his nickname "Flash" and even the American flag on the Band-Aid after the wound had healed. The ban states that a Band-Aid can be worn for healthcare purposes but should not bear any name or identifications on it.

2010, The NBA prohibits players, particularly Rajon Rando of the Celtics, from wearing headbands upside down as the NBA logo becomes inverted. Richard Hamilton has worn a headband for the better part of the last eight years due in large part to supporting his famous clear facemask. Hamilton is exempt from the ruling as perspiration would leak down into the facemask causing cloudiness and impairing his vision.

2010, Michael Jordan becomes the first former NBA player to purchase a controlling interest in an NBA team, the Charlotte Bobcats, formerly the Hornets. The league's Board of Governors unanimously approves Jordan's $275 million purchase of the team from Bob Johnson, former president of BET and in 2003 the NBA's first minority majority owner.

2012, LeBron James and the Miami Heat players wear hoodies in protest of the shooting death of Trayvon Martin in Sanford, Fla.

2012, Reggie Miller is inducted into the Naismith Memorial Basketball Hall of Fame. Miller and his sister Cheryl Miller (inducted in 1995) will become the only siblings in the Basketball Hall of Fame entering as players. [Note: There are no brothers, as players, in the Naismith Memorial Basketball Hall of Fame. Brothers Dick and Al McGuire are in the Naismith Hall of Fame as coaches. Paul and Lloyd Waner, Rube and Willie Foster are the only brothers in the National Baseball Hall of Fame.]

2013-14, The San Antonio Spurs, led by Coach Gregg Popovich, win the NBA championship with a diversity of talent. The team includes Tony Parker (G) and Boris Diaw (F), both from France; Tiago Splitter (C) from Brazil; Patty Mills (G) from Australia; Manu Ginóbili (G) from Argentina; Marco Belinelli (F) from Italy; and Tim Duncan (C) from Saint Croix in the Virgin Islands. They finished the season with a 62-20 won-loss record (.756) and defeated the Miami Heat in five games.

2014, Los Angeles Clippers protest owner Donald Sterling's racist remarks about Black people by wearing their shirts inside-out in order "to obscure any team logo" during their pre-game huddle. Soon after Miami Heat players wear their uniform tops inside-out to show solidarity with the Clippers. LeBron James comments on the situation, "There's no room for Donald Sterling in the NBA." NBA commissioner Adam Silver announces a lifetime ban of Sterling from the league and fined $2.5 million, the maximum fine allowed by the NBA constitution.

2015, New York City agrees to pay $4 million to Thabo Sefolosha, a 6-foot-6 forward with the Atlanta Hawks, to settle a federal lawsuit in which he accused five police officers of false arrest and using excessive force, breaking his left tibia during an encounter as a bystander outside a Manhattan nightclub. Sefolosha, 32, a Swiss citizen of African heritage, contends that the officers had arrested him arbitrarily and had violated his civil rights, in part because he is Black. He claimed that the injury had shortened his career and had cost him endorsement deals. In 2006, he became the first player from Switzerland to play in the NBA.

2015, Carmelo Anthony of the New York Knicks marches with demonstrators in protest of the death of Freddie Gray from police brutality in his hometown of Baltimore. All six police officers were cleared.

2016, Cum Posey and John McLendon are inducted to the Naismith Memorial Basketball Hall of Fame. Posey selected by the Early African American Pioneers Committee, while McLendon was inducted again, this time as a coach. McLendon is the first inductee to be honored as a contributor and coach. Cumberland Posey is the first man to be inducted into both the National Basketball Hall of Fame and the basketball Hall of Fame.

2016, After the deaths of Alton Sterling in Baton Rouge, La., and Philando Castile, outside of St. Paul, Minn., by police officers, the Minnesota Lynx become the first professional team in the U.S. to wear "Black Lives Matter" on the front and the names of Sterling and Castile on the back of their warmup t-shirts.

2017, Washington Wizards Kelly Oubre Jr. is asked to stop wearing the NBA and Nike sponsored Supreme compression sleeve.

2020, Toronto Raptors' president, Nigerian-Canadian Masai Ujiri, attempts to enter the court as his Raptors defeat the Golden State Warriors to win the NBA championship, when he is blocked by a San Francisco Bay Area police officer, Alan Strickland. Body cam footage shows the officer shoving Ujiri twice as he attempts to show his access credentials.

2020, To pay respects to the late Breonna Taylor, the WNBA is the first professional league to dedicate a season to fight for social justice. A'ja Wilson and other players formed a Social Justice Council and wear warmups with "Say Her Name."

2020, The Milwaukee Bucks refuse to take the floor in a playoff game against the Orlando Magic in protest of the police shooting Jacob Blake seven times in his back, in Kenosha, Wis.

2020, Converse reveals the Barrier Breaker collection which consists of six total pairs of sneakers, as Converse pays homage to Chuck Cooper, Nat Clifton and Earl Lloyd on two of the brand's most classic silhouettes: the Converse Pro Leather and the Chuck Taylor 70, an updated model of basketball's first performance shoe. Designed with premium materials and a satin finish to symbolize 1950s NBA uniforms, all three editions of the Chuck Taylor in the collection commemorate each barrier-breaking player, as well as their respective first teams. Clifton's blue, orange and white Knicks-themed Chuck features a bottle cap graphic behind the tongue of each shoe as a nod to his nickname, "Sweetwater." Similarly, a cat graphic is printed behind the tongues of the black, green and white shoe, which honors both Lloyd, who was known as "The Big Cat," and the Washington Capitols, a charter member of the NBA for only the 1950-51 season.

2021, Portland Trail Blazers forward Carmelo Anthony is named the inaugural winner of the NBA's Kareem Abdul-Jabbar Social Justice Champion award. In July 2020, he partnered with 11-time NBA All-Star Chris Paul of the Phoenix Suns and NBA legend Dwyane Wade to create the Social Change Fund, which aims to address social and economic justice issues facing Black communities and break down the discriminatory barriers to success. Guest editor Anthony of *SLAM's Black Lives Matter* magazine, in 2020, entitled "It Stops Now" provided a platform for the voiceless.

2021, Betnijah Laney of the New York Liberty, Diamond Deshields of the Phoenix Mercury and Arike Ogunbowale of the Dallas Wings appear on the cover of *WSLAM*, the first all-women issue of *SLAM* magazine.

2021, In partnership with the National Basketball Association (NBA) and the International Basketball Federation (FIBA), Africa's new professional basketball league is formed. The Basketball Africa League (BAL) consists of 12 teams from Algeria, Angola, Cameroon, Egypt, Madagascar, Mali, Morocco, Mozambique, Nigeria, Rwanda, Senegal and Tunisia.

2023, The Houston Rockets select Amen XLNC Thompson at No. 4, and the Detroit Pistons select Ausar XLNC Thompson at No. 5. The Thompson twins become the first brothers to be drafted in the top five of the same draft since the 1976 ABA-NBA merger.

2023, The top 10 selections in the NBA Draft are represented by Black agents. Victor Wembanyama is the first pick, and his agent is Bouna Ndiaye. The other picks and their agents: 2) Brandon Miller, agent Wilmer Jackson, 3) Scoot Henderson (Par-Lay Sports and Entertainment), 4) and 5) Amen and Ausar Thompson (father Troy Thompson), 6) Anthony Black (Bill Duffy), 7) Bilal Coulibaly (Bouna Ndiaye), 8) Jarace Walker (Joe Branch, 9) Taylor Hendricks (Raymond Brothers) and 10) Cason Wallace (Marcus Monk).

Colorful Firsts in U.S. Sports

HARLEM GLOBETROTTERS

1926, The Savoy Big Five, based in Chicago, are managed at Wendell Phillips High School by Dick Hudson (fullback for the Minnesota Marines and the Hammond Pros of the NFL). The team includes founder Tommy Brookins, Bobby Anderson, Inman Jackson, Lester Johnson, Joe Lillard (running back of the Chicago Cardinals), Randolph Ramsey and Walter "Toots" Wright. They split a two-game series with George Halas's Chicago Bruins.

1927, The New York Globetrotters play its first game on January 7 in Hinckley, Illinois, before 300 fans.

1928, The Tommy Brookins' Globe Trotters hire Abe Saperstein as a booking agent and play their home games at the Eighth Regiment Armory and the Savoy Ballroom in Chicago.

1929, The first documented game of Abe Saperstein's Harlem Globe Trotters, featuring Runt Pullins, based in Chicago, lose to the Hinckley Merchants by a score of 43-34.

1940, The Harlem Globetrotters defeat George Halas' Chicago Bruins (NBL), 31-29, to capture the World Professional Basketball Championship in Chicago Stadium. Sonny Boswell of the Harlem Globetrotters is named MVP of the World Professional Basketball Tournament.

1942, Reece "Goose" Tatum joins the Harlem Globetrotters and soon drafted into the Army. Bob Karstens becomes the first White player to sign a contract with the Harlem Globetrotters. Karstens is credited with the Magic Ball pregame routine.

1948, The New York Rens, led by Sweetwater Clifton's 24 points, lose the World Basketball Championship to the Minneapolis Lakers, led by George Mikan's 40 points, by a score of 75 to 71. This is the last World Basketball tournament that started in 1939.

1949, Zachary M. Clayton, former New York Ren, Harlem Globetrotter and Negro Leagues player, becomes the first African American to receive a boxing referee's license with the state of Pennsylvania. Clayton later referees the 1974 Ali-Foreman "Rumble In The Jungle" fight in Kinshasa, Republic of Zaire.

1950, Sweetwater Clifton becomes the first former Harlem Globetrotter to sign an NBA contract as a New York Knick.

1951, The *Guinness Book of World Records* lists the Harlem Globetrotters as drawing the largest crowd ever to see a basketball game, when 75,000 fans jam Berlin's Olympic Stadium.

1952, The Harlem Globetrotters are the first basketball team to make a complete trip around world, during a tour from April 15 to Oct. 17.

1954, The Harlem Globetrotters become the first pro baseball team to play a night game at Wrigley Field, when they install portable lights. This event is 33 years, before the Cubs play its first night game.

1957, Govoner Vaughn and Manny Jackson become the first African American basketball players to start and letter for the University of Illinois' basketball team. Jackson later becomes chairman of the Harlem Globetrotter franchise.

1958, Wilt Chamberlain joins the Harlem Globetrotters.

1960, Althea Gibson tours with the Harlem Globetrotters, playing exhibition tennis.

1985, Lynette Woodard, a 1984 Olympic gold medalist, becomes the first woman to play for the Harlem Globetrotters. She scores seven points in her debut.

1993, Manny Jackson becomes the first former Globetrotter to own the team and the first African American to own a major international sports franchise and entertainment organization in America.

1995, Orlando "Hurricane" Antiqua becomes the first Latino to play for the Harlem Globetrotters. His parents are of Puerto Rican and Dominican descent. He plays seven seasons with the Globetrotters.

1998, Marques Haynes becomes the first Harlem Globetrotter inducted into the Naismith Memorial Basketball Hall of Fame.

1999, The Harlem Globetrotters become the first team to receive the prestigious John W. Bunn Lifetime Achievement Award from the Naismith Memorial Basketball Hall of Fame in Springfield, MA.

2000, Wilt Chamberlain becomes the first former Harlem Globetrotter to have his jersey number retired, #13.

2000, Harlem Globetrotter Michael "Wild Thing" Wilson becomes the first human to dunk a basketball on a 12-foot goal. The 6-foot-6 Wilson records the feat at the Ocean Spray NABC Roundball Challenge in Indianapolis, Ind.

2002, The Harlem Globetrotters are inducted into the Naismith Memorial Basketball Hall of Fame as a team. The New York Rens were inducted in 1963.

NEW YORK RENS

"The status quo always favors neutrality which in truth is never neutral at all but supports those who stand against change."
— Michael Eric Dyson, *Tears We Cannot Stop: A Sermon to White America*

1923, The New York Rens, named after the team's home court, the Renaissance Ballroom and Casino in Harlem, become America's first Black-owned all-Black professional basketball team. They are owned by Robert L. Douglas from St. Kitts, British West Indies.

1936, Big Dave DeJernett from integrated Indiana Central University becomes the first African American collegiate athlete to sign with a professional basketball team, the New York Rens.

1939, In Chicago, the New York Rens (Independent) defeat the Oshkosh All-Stars (NBL) in the first World Professional Basketball Tournament, 34-25. Their record for the year was 122 wins against seven defeats. The Harlem Globetrotters take third place.

1939, Clarence "Puggy" Bell of the New York Rens is named MVP of the first World Professional Basketball Tournament.

1943, The Washington Bears, composed almost entirely of former N.Y. Rens, including John Isaacs, Pop Gates, Tarzan Cooper, Dolly and Sonny Woods capture the fifth annual World Professional Basketball Tournament in Chicago, defeating Wisconsin's Oshkosh All-Stars, 43-31.

1948, The New York Rens, led by Sweetwater Clifton's 24 points, lose the World Basketball Championship to the Minneapolis Lakers, led by George Mikan's 40 points, by score of 75 to 71. This is the last World Basketball tournament that started in 1939.

1948, The New York Rens, relocate to Dayton, Ohio and replace the Detroit Vagabond Kings of the racially integrated National Basketball League (NBL).

1949, Zachary M. Clayton, former New York Ren, Harlem Globetrotter and Negro Leagues player, becomes the first African American to receive a boxing referee's license with the state of Pennsylvania. Clayton later referees the 1974 Ali-Foreman "Rumble In The Jungle" fight in Kinshasa, Republic of Zaire.

1949, The New York Rens, now based in Dayton, Ohio, and members of the National Basketball League (NBL), play its last game against the Denver Rockets. Coached by "Pop" Gates, their lifetime record over 26 years is 2,318 wins and 381 losses, an 86 winning percentage. Gates is the first African American head coach in the NBL.

1963, The New York Rens, of 1932-33, are named to the Naismith Memorial Basketball Hall of Fame as a team, for its 88 consecutive game winning streak, the longest in professional baseball history. In 2002, the Harlem Globetrotters are inducted as a team.

1972, Robert Lewis Douglas (from Saint Kitts), founder and coach of the Renaissance Big Five and the New York Rens, is the first Black man inducted in the Naismith Memorial Basketball Hall of Fame.

2017, The southeast corner of West 138th Street and Adam Clayton Powell Jr Blvd is named New York Rens Court.

2021, Former Negro League player Clarence "Fats" Jenkins, captain of the New York Rens, is the first player from the first Black-owned, fully professional African American basketball team inducted into the Naismith Memorial Basketball Hall of Fame.

KAREEM ABDUL-JABBAR
"Your mind is what makes everything else work."

1967-68, After the dominance of UCLA center Lew Alcindor, the NCAA bans dunking for the upcoming season. The rule is rescinded for the 1976-77 season.

1969, Lew Alcindor is named Most Outstanding Player of the NCAA tournament for a record third time.

1971, Lew Alcindor and Oscar Robertson of the Milwaukee Bucks appear on the cover of the first issue of *Black Sports* magazine. Founded by Allan P. Barron, it is the first major sports magazine aimed at African Americans. The last issue was published in June 1978.

1976, The dunk is reinstated. The dominance of UCLA center Lew Alcindor had forced the NCAA to ban dunking in college basketball during the 1967-68 season.

1980, Kareem Abdul-Jabbar becomes the first NBA player to win six MVP awards.

2016, Kareem Abdul-Jabbar and Michael Jordan are presented with the Presidential Medal of Freedom by President Barack Obama, the highest civilian award.

MAHMOUD ABDUL-RAUF

1989, The Wayman Tisdale Award is established by the USBWA to recognize an outstanding frosh collegiate basketball player. Guard Chris Jackson, later known as Mahmoud Abdul-Rauf, of LSU, is the first recipient.

1996, The NBA suspends Mahmoud Abdul-Rauf for his refusal to stand for The Star-Spangled Banner. Abdul-Rauf, born Chris Jackson, claims the flag is a symbol of oppression. Later a compromise is reached allowing Abdul-Rauf to stand during the playing of the anthem, but could close his eyes, look downward and recite an Islamic prayer.

BILQUIS ABDUL-QAADIR

During the 2010–2011 season, Bilquis Abdul-Qaadir for the University of Memphis plays in 34 games and averages 3.9 points per game with 1.3 rebounds per game. She is the first Division I player to wear a hijab. Later in 2015, Bilquis is invited to the White House and was acknowledged by President Barack Obama for being the first Muslim woman to play covered in collegiate basketball. Adbul-Qaadir's journey is told in the documentary *Life Without Basketball*.

MARK AGUIRRE

1981, In November, Mark Aguirre of the Dallas Mavericks is the first NBA player named Rookie of the Month.

WILL ALLEN

1967, Will Allen, known as the Rockville Cyclone, becomes the first African American basketball player at the University of Miami. The 6-foot-6 center ranks number two on the Hurricanes' career rebounding list. Allen later plays for the Miami Floridians of the ABA.

WAYMON ANDERSON

1955, Waymon Anderson becomes the first African American basketball player for the University of Colorado State Rams.

GREG ANDREWS

1968, Basketball player Greg Andrews becomes the first African American scholarship student-athlete for the University of Chattanooga Mocs.

CARMELO ANTHONY

2003-04, Carmelo Anthony of the Denver Nuggets in the western conference and LeBron James of the Cleveland Cavaliers in the eastern conference are the first NBA players to win the Rookie of the Month award in every month of the season, from November through April.

2021, Portland Trail Blazers forward Carmelo Anthony is named the inaugural winner of the NBA's Kareem Abdul-Jabbar Social Justice Champion award. In July 2020, he partnered with 11-time NBA All-Star Chris Paul of the Phoenix Suns and NBA legend Dwyane Wade to create the Social Change Fund, which aims to address social and economic justice issues facing Black communities and break down the discriminatory barriers to success. Guest editor Anthony of *SLAM's Black Lives Matter* magazine, in 2020, entitled "It Stops Now" provided a platform for the voiceless.

ORLANDO "HURRICANE" ANTIQUA

1995, Orlando "Hurricane" Antiqua becomes the first Latino to play for the Harlem Globetrotters. His parents are of Puerto Rican and Dominican descent. He plays seven seasons with the Globetrotters.

NATE "The SKATE" ARCHIBALD

1973, Kansas City Kings guard Nate Archibald, becomes the first player to lead the NBA in scoring (34.0) and assists (11.4) the same year.

BIG MO ARLEDGE

1955, Missouri "Big Mo" Arledge from Philander Smith College (Ark.) is the first African American woman named to the All-American team.

JESSE ARNELLE

1955, Jesse Arnelle and Chuck Cooper are the first African Americans to play for the Fort Wayne Pistons of the NBA.

AL ATTLES

1975, K. C. Jones (Washington Bullets) and Al Attles (Golden State Warriors) become the first African Americans to coach NBA All-Star squads. They also square off in the NBA championship to become the first African Americans to take their teams to the finals, doing so seven years after Bill Russell wins the first of two titles as Boston's player/coach. The Warriors sweep the Bullets in four games.

SIMEONE AUGUSTUS

"The eyes are on the women because the women are doing what's necessary to help our society get to a better place."
– 2016, Minnesota Lynx's "Black Lives Matter" movement.

2010, Lady Tiger Seimone Augustus becomes the first female athlete at LSU to have her uniform number (33) retired.

2023, Seimone Augustus becomes the first female athlete in LSU history to have a statue on the school campus; in front of the school's basketball training center next to statues of Bob Pettit, Shaquille O'Neal and Pete Maravich.

JOHN AUSTIN

1963, John Austin becomes the first African American basketball player for the Boston College Eagles. Austin is from powerhouse DeMatha High School in Washington, District of Columbia. He later plays for the Baltimore Bullets of the NBA and the New Jersey Americans of the ABA.

ZAILA AVANT-GARDE

2019, Zaila Avant-Garde sets a Guinness World Record, in New Orleans, La., with the most bounce juggles, 307, in 30 seconds, using four basketballs.

2020, Zaila Avant-Garde sets a Guinness World Record, in Baton Rouge, La., with the most bounce juggles, 255, in one minute, using four basketballs.

2021, Zaila Avant-Garde sets a Guinness World Record in Westwego, La. for the most basketballs (6) dribbled simultaneously by a woman. The 14-year-old Avant-Garde later in the year becomes the first African American to win the Scripps National Spelling Bee title at ESPN's *Wide World of Sports* Complex in Orlando, Fla.

COOLIDGE BALL

1970, Coolidge Ball becomes the first African American scholarship basketball player for the University of Mississippi or Ole Miss, where in 1962 James Meredith had become the first African American student at the public university. After two fatalities, President John F. Kennedy sends the National Guard to stop the violence and rioting by Whites opposed to integration.

LULA BALLARD

1929, The Germantown Hornets, in Philadelphia, are formed by the YWCA Branch of Colored Girls and Women. The Hornets basketball team included Ora Washington, Lula Ballard, Louise Penn, Lil Fountainé, Helen Laws and Evelyn Manns.

1930, The Tribune Girls are sponsored by the *Philadelphia Tribune* newspaper. The players come from two Black female basketball

Colorful Firsts in U.S. Sports

teams, the Philadelphia Quick Steppers and the Germantown Hornets. Inez Patterson from the Quick Steppers becomes coach and player of the team. Two tennis players from the YWCA Colored Branch in Germantown, Ora Washington and Lula Ballard, become standout hoopsters.

CHARLES BARKLEY

"If I weren't earning more than $3 million a year to dunk a basketball,
most people on the street would run in the other direction if they saw me coming."

1987, Charles Barkley, standing 6-foot-5, is the first player under 6-foot-6 and the shortest player to win an NBA rebounding title. He averages a career-high 14.6 rebounds per game during the 1986–87 season.

DON BARKSDALE

1947, Don Barksdale, of UCLA, becomes the first African American basketball player to be named to the consensus All-American team. He makes the second squad.

1948, Don Barksdale becomes the first African American to play on the U.S. Olympic basketball team.

1951, Don Barksdale and Davage "Dave" Minor become the first African Americans to play for an NBA team south of the Maxon-Dixon line, the Baltimore Bullets.

1952, Don Barksdale becomes the first African American to play in the NBA All-Star game.

ADIA BARNES

2021, Adia Barnes of the Arizona Wildcats and Dawn Staley of the South Carolina Gamecocks become the first African American head coaches with teams in the Final Four of the NCAA women's basketball tournament. Staley and Barnes are both former WNBA players.

RON BARNES

1992, Rod Barnes becomes the first African American head basketball coach at Ole Miss. After inheriting a losing program, the Rebels finish in first place of the Southeastern Conference for the 1996-97 and 1997-98 seasons. Barnes leaves the Rebels after the 1998 season with an 86-81 won-lost record to join the Arizona State Sun Devils.

CHARLIE BATCH

2006, NFL Quarterback Charlie Batch and former University of Michigan basketball star Antoine "The Judge" Joubert, announce the debut of the Detroit Panthers into the newly formed American Basketball Association franchise. Batch will be the majority owner, while Joubert will be the head coach.

ELGIN BAYLOR

1959, Elgin Baylor becomes the first rookie to be named the Most Valuable Player of an NBA All-Star game.

1962, San Francisco Warriors' Wilt Chamberlain scores 63 points and the Lakers' Elgin Baylor scores 51 points, to become the first opponents to top 50 in the same game. Baylor later becomes the first player to score more than 60 points in a playoff game. Baylor scores 61 points against the Boston Celtics.

PUGGY BELL

1939, Clarence "Puggy" Bell of the New York Rens is named MVP of the first World Professional Basketball Tournament.

KALIN BENNETT

2019, Kalin Bennett, a 6-foot-1 frosh center at Kent State University, becomes the first player with autism to score in a Division I game, finishing with two points in a 97-48 win over Hiram. As the 16th-ranked prospect from Arkansas, Bennett also became the first recruit with autism to sign a letter of intent with a Division I school.

JOE BERTRAND

1951, Joe Bertrand from Chicago, Ill. and Entee Shine from South Bend, Ind. become the first African Americans on Notre Dame's basketball team. Shine plays one season; Bertrand four years.

CHAUNCEY BILLUPS
2013, Los Angeles Clippers guard Chauncey Billups becomes the first winner of the NBA's new award, the (Jack) Twyman-(Maurice) Stokes Teammate of the Year Award. The award is for a player who displays selfless play and on- and off-court leadership while showing commitment and dedication to his team.

DAVE BING
1967-68, Detroit Piston Dave Bing becomes the first true guard to lead the NBA in total points, 2,142, averaging 27.1 points per game.

KARL BINNS
1970, Karl Binns becomes the first African American scholarship basketball player for the Georgia Tech Yellow Jackets.

BEN BLUITT
1974, Ben Bluitt becomes Cornell University's first African American head basketball coach.

RUTHIE BOLTON-HOLIFIELD
1997, Ruthie Bolton-Holifield becomes the first ever to earn Player-of-the-Week honors in the WNBA.

SONNY BOSWELL
1940, Sonny Boswell of the Harlem Globetrotters is named MVP of the World Professional Basketball Tournament.

TOMMY BOWMAN
1966, Athens, Texas basketball star Tommy Bowman becomes the first Black scholarship student-athlete at Baylor University, a private university in Waco, Texas.

EARL BOYKINS
2004, Earl Boykins (5-foot-5, 135 pounds) of the Denver Nuggets becomes the first NBA player less than five and a half feet tall to score more than 30 points in a game. Boykins scores 32 on 11-15 field goals, 2-3 three-point goals, and 8-8 from the free throw line in a 117-109 win over the Detroit Pistons.

MUGGSY BOGUES
1987, Tyrone "Muggsy" Bogues (from Wake Forest) at 5-foot-3 the smallest player in NBA history, is the 12th pick by the Charlotte Hornets. Bogues, along with Reggie Lewis (Northwestern, 22nd pick) and Reggie Williams (Georgetown, 4th pick) become the first trio of players from the same high school (Dunbar Poets, Baltimore, Md.) to be picked in the first round of the draft in the same year.
1995, Tyrone "Muggsy" Bogues, Charlotte Hornets' guard, wins the first Court Vision Award in the NBA.

JUNIOR BRIDGEMAN
2020, Ulysses "Junior" Bridgeman, former Milwaukee Bucks and Los Angeles Clipper player, purchases *Ebony* and *Jet* magazines in U.S. Bankruptcy Court for $14 million. The 12-year NBA veteran is CEO of a Coca-Cola Bottling Company and part-owner of Coca-Cola Canada Bottling Limited. In 2018, Bridgeman attempted to buy *Sports Illustrated* that was sold to Authentic Brands Group for $110 million.

BILL BROWN
1946, The Continental Basketball Association is the first professional basketball league to hire Black players. The Hazleton (Pa.) Mountaineers sign Bill Brown, Zach Clayton from the New York Rens and John Isaacs from the Washington Bears.

JAYLEN BROWN
2016, Jaylen Brown of the California Golden Bears is drafted by the Boston Celtics as the third pick in the first round. Brown enjoys playing chess and learning foreign languages. The 19-year-old enters the draft without an agent. "He is an extremely intelligent kid," an unnamed NBA assistant general manager said, adding, "He took a graduate school class at Cal in his freshman year. He is a person who is inquisitive about everything. Because he is so smart, it might be intimidating to some teams. He wants

to know why you are doing something instead of just doing it. I don't think it's bad, but it's a form of questioning authority. It's not malicious. He just wants to know what is going on. Old-school coaches don't want guys that question stuff."

KWAME BROWN

2001, Kwame Brown becomes the first high school basketball player drafted as the number one overall pick when he is selected by the Washington Wizards. Brown is from Brunswick (Ga.) Glynn Academy.

RENÉE BROWN

1997, Renée Brown is the first person of color in the WNBA's front office. As Director of Player Personnel, Brown oversees all player recruitment and scouting for the league. Brown would retire in 2016, as WNBA Chief of Basketball Operation and Player Relations.

KOBE BRYANT

"If you're afraid to fail, then you're probably going to fail."

1998, Basketball guard Kobe Bryant, baseball shortstop Alex Rodríguez, football quarterback Kordell Stewart and hockey center Eric Lindros appear on the premier issue of *ESPN The Magazine*.

2017, Upon retirement, Los Angeles Laker Kobe Bryant becomes the only player in NBA history to have multiple numbers, #8 and #24, retired by the same franchise.

2018, Writer Kobe Bryant narrates a six-minute film called *Dear Basketball* and becomes the first professional athlete to win an Academy Award for Best Animated Short Film. In the process, he also becomes the first person to win an Oscar and an Olympic Gold Medal, when as a member of the U.S. Men's basketball teams in 2008 and 2012.

2022, Stephen Curry of the Golden State Warriors becomes the first player to win the Kobe Bryant MVP award at the NBA's All-Star Game. The newly designed trophy has an eight-sided base to represent Bryant's No. 8 jersey number. The four-tier trophy has 18 stars around the base to represent Bryant's 18 All-Star selections.

SCOTT BURRELL

1993, Scott Burrell from Connecticut, becomes the first basketball player in NCAA Division I-A to top 1500 points, 750 rebounds, 275 assists and 300 steals. Burrell is a first round pick of the NBA's Charlotte Hornets. In 1989, Burrell was a first round pick of the Seattle Mariners in the amateur baseball draft. He becomes the first athlete to be a first-round draftee in two different sports.

ELLIOT CADEAU

2022, Elliot Cadeau of Swedish-Haitian descent is the first American high school athlete (Link Academy, Branson, Mo.) to sign an international Names, Likeness, Image (NIL) deal when he endorses a deal for the Swedish vitamin drink Vitamin Well. Cadeau is also the first high school basketball player to sign with Roc Nation Sports for NIL representation.

SARAH CAMPBELL

1993, Sarah Campbell, formerly of Central High School in Kansas City and the University of Missouri, becomes the first MVP player in the newly formed Women's Basketball Association (WBA) as a member of the Missouri Mustangs.

AUSTIN CARR

1970, Austin Carr of Notre Dame becomes the first player to average more than 50 points a game during the NCAA tournament. Carr averages 52.7 points in three games. Carr is also the first player to score more than 60 points in an NCAA tournament game. Carr scores 61 against Ohio State University in the Southeast Regional.

VINCE CARTER

2017, Vince Carter becomes the first 40-year-old player in NBA history to hit six triples in one game.

2020, A testament to his durability, Vince Carter is the only player in NBA history to appear in a game in four different decades. Starting in 1998, his career spans 22 seasons with eight teams.

JAMES CASH JR.

1966, James I. Cash Jr. basketball player for the Texas Christian Horned Frogs becomes the first African American to play in the

Southwest Conference (SWC). Dr. Cash later becomes a minority owner of the Boston Celtics. In 2011, Cash's jersey No. 54 is retired by TCU. In 2020, the Harvard Business School renames one of its buildings, the Cash House, in honor of the former faculty member. In 2021, TCU installs a statue of Dr. Cash in front of the Ed and Rae Schollmaier Arena.

MORGAN CATO

2023, Morgan Cato with the Phoenix Suns becomes the first woman of color to hold the title of assistant general manager in the NBA.

WILT CHAMBERLAIN
"Everybody pulls for David; nobody roots for Goliath"

1958, Wilt Chamberlain joins the Harlem Globetrotters.

1959, Wilt Chamberlain becomes the first rookie to score at least 40 points (43) on opening night.

1960, Wilt Chamberlain later breaks Bill Russell's rebounding record with 55 rebounds.

1960, Wilt Chamberlain becomes the first NBA player to average more than 30 points (37.6) per game. The rookie becomes the first NBA player to score more than 1,000 (1,065) field goals in a season. In the process, he becomes the first NBA player to win the Rookie of the Year and Most Valuable Player awards in the same season.

1961, Wilt Chamberlain becomes the first NBA player to grab more than 2,000 rebounds (2,149) in a season and score more than 3,000 (3,033) points in a season. Chamberlain becomes the first African American basketball player to appear on the cover of *Sports Illustrated*.

1962, Wilt Chamberlain becomes the first NBA player to score 100 points in a basketball game and more than 50 points in a playoff game. The Philadelphia Warrior scores 56 points against Syracuse. Chamberlain is also the first NBA player to score more than 4,000 (4,029) points in a season and the first to average more than 50 (50.4) points per game.

1962, San Francisco Warriors' Wilt Chamberlain scores 63 points and the Lakers' Elgin Baylor scores 51 points, to become the first opponents to top 50 in the same game.

1964-65, The NBA widens the lane to 16 feet from 12 feet to offset Wilt Chamberlain's dominance. The lane was last widened in 1951 to neutralize the presence of 6' 10" George Mikan of the Minneapolis Lakers.

1966, Wilt Chamberlain is the first player to lead the NBA in scoring seven consecutive seasons.

1968, On March 18 Wilt Chamberlain, for the Philadelphia 76ers, becomes the only NBA player to record a quintuple-double in the NBA with 53 points, 32 rebounds, 14 assists, 24 blocks and 11 steals against the Los Angeles Lakers.

1968, Wilt Chamberlain becomes the first center to lead the NBA in assist with 702, making him the first player to win NBA scoring, rebounding and assist titles.

1972, Wilt Chamberlain becomes the first player to score 30,000 points in an NBA career.

1973, Wilt Chamberlain retires from pro basketball. He plays in 1,045 games, scores 31,419 points and commits 2,075 fouls, but never fouls out of an NBA game.

1975, Gaylord High School in Gaylord, Mich., ban Wilt Chamberlain's book *Wilt*, stating pupils "are more interested in learning how to dribble and shoot" rather than his scores off the court.

2000, Wilt Chamberlain becomes the first former Harlem Globetrotter to have his jersey number retired, #13.

2014, Los Angeles Lakers and Philadelphia Warriors/76ers center Wilt Chamberlain becomes the first NBA player featured on a U.S. postage stamp. The two versions issued are nearly two inches long, or about a third longer than the usual stamp.

JOHN CHANEY

1988, John Chaney Temple Owls basketball coach is named Coach of the Year by UPI, AP and the U.S. Basketball Writers' Association.

TINA CHARLES

2022, Seattle Storm center Tina Charles becomes the first WNBA player to score 7,000 points and gather 3,500 rebounds.

MAURICE CHEEKS

1986, Maurice Cheeks of the Philadelphia 76ers becomes the first NBA player to record 2,000 steals.

Colorful Firsts in U.S. Sports

CLAUDIUS CLAIRBORNE

1966, Claudius B. Claiborne becomes the first African American basketball player for the Duke Blue Devils. C.B. Claiborne graduated in 1969 with a degree in engineering. He also earned postgraduate degrees from Dartmouth and Virginia Tech. Because of segregation sanctions on the Duke campus, Claiborne spent considerable time in the cafeteria at nearby North Carolina Central University, a historically Black college.

LAYSHIA CLARENDON

2013, Layshia Clarendon, with the Indiana Fever, is the first openly transgender, non-binary player in the WNBA.

ZACH CLAYTON

1946, The Continental Basketball Association is the first professional basketball league to hire Black players. The Hazleton (Pa.) Mountaineers sign Bill Brown, Zach Clayton from the New York Rens and John Isaacs from the Washington Bears.

1949, Zachary M. Clayton, former New York Ren, Harlem Globetrotter and Negro Leagues player, becomes the first African American to receive a boxing referee's license with the state of Pennsylvania. Clayton later referees the 1974 Ali-Foreman "Rumble In The Jungle" fight in Kinshasa, Republic of Zaire.

SWEETWATER CLIFTON

1950, Nat "Sweetwater" Clifton is the first African American player for the New York Knicks. Clifton becomes the first former Harlem Globetrotter to sign an NBA contract.

1950, On Halloween Oct. 31, Nov. 1, Nov. 4, and Dec. 3, Earl Lloyd, Chuck Cooper, Nat "Sweetwater" Clifton and Hank DeZonie, respectively, become the first African Americans to play in the National Basketball Association (NBA).

1957, Nat "Sweetwater" Clifton, 34, becomes the oldest first-time NBA All-Star selection. Clifton from Xavier University (La.) is also the first player from an HBCU to play in an NBA All-Star game. Clifton is the first African American to play for the Detroit Pistons.

2022, The NBA creates division championship trophies named after African American pioneers of the game. The Pacific Division winner receives the Chuck Cooper Trophy. The Central Division winner receives the Wayne Embry Trophy. The Southwest Division winner receives the Willis Reed Trophy. The Atlantic Division winner receives the Nat "Sweetwater" Clifton Trophy. The Southeast Division winner receives the Earl Lloyd Trophy. The Northwest Division winner receives the Sam Jones Trophy.

NATASHA CLOUD

2020, Washington Mystics point guard Natasha Cloud becomes the first woman to sign an endorsement deal with Converse Shoes.

BILL COFIELD

1976, Bill Cofield, for the Wisconsin Badgers, becomes the first Black male head basketball coach in the Big Ten Conference.

VINCE COLBERT

1966, Vince Colbert becomes the first African American scholarship athlete at East Carolina University. He letters in baseball and basketball. Colbert later pitches for the Cleveland Indians in the American League.

JASON COLLINS

2014, Jason Collins, center for coach Jason Kidd's Brooklyn Nets, becomes the first openly gay player in the NBA. Collins appears on the cover of *Time's* magazine "Most Influential People."

CHUCK COOPER

1950, Duquesne's Chuck Cooper, a second-team All-American, becomes the first African American drafted by an NBA team when he is selected in the second round by the Boston Celtics. Other African Americans selected in the NBA draft are West Virginia State's Earl Lloyd and North Carolina College's Harold Hunter (both by the Washington Capitols) and Kentucky State's Ed Thompson (by the Fort Wayne Pistons).

1950, On Halloween Oct. 31, Nov. 1, Nov. 4, and Dec. 3, Earl Lloyd, Chuck Cooper, Nat "Sweetwater" Clifton and Hank DeZonie, respectively, become the first African Americans to play in the National Basketball Association (NBA).

1955, Jesse Arnelle and Chuck Cooper are the first African Americans to play for the Fort Wayne Pistons of the NBA.

2022, The NBA creates division championship trophies named after African American pioneers of the game. The Pacific Division winner receives the Chuck Cooper Trophy. The Central Division winner receives the Wayne Embry Trophy. The Southwest Division winner receives the Willis Reed Trophy. The Atlantic Division winner receives the Nat "Sweetwater" Clifton Trophy. The Southeast Division winner receives the Earl Lloyd Trophy. The Northwest Division winner receives the Sam Jones Trophy.

CYNTHIA COOPER

1997, Cynthia Cooper of the Houston Comets is voted the WNBA's first Most Valuable Player and the league's first scoring leader with 22.2 points per game.

1998, Cynthia Cooper is named the MVP of the WNBA for the second consecutive season.

1999, Cynthia Cooper becomes the first player to score 1,000 points in the WNBA.

2000, Cynthia Cooper is the first person in WNBA history to score 500, 1,000, 2,000 and 2,500 career points.

2010, Cynthia Cooper is the first WNBA player inducted into the Naismith Basketball Hall of Fame and Memorial.

SYLVIA CRAWLEY

1999, Sylvia Crawley of the Colorado Xplosion, paces off 10 steps, puts on a blindfold and dunks a basketball during the first ever women's dunk contest during the American Basketball League's second All-Star game.

RAY CROWE

1954-55, Ray Crowe coaches Indiana's Crispus Attucks to the first state high school basketball title won by an all-Black team in an integrated sport in America. Led by Oscar Robertson, the team also becomes the first Indianapolis school to win the Indiana state basketball championship.

2015, The city of Indianapolis gives the living members of the 1955 Crispus Attucks state championship basketball team a parade and celebratory ride from the Fieldhouse to Monument Circle that had been previously denied them as the first Black team to win a state championship. Coach Ray Crowe with guard Oscar Robertson won back-to-back championships, 1955 and 1956.

2021, The Converse Pro Leather High 'Breaking Down Barriers' pays tribute to Indiana's Crispus Attucks Tigers, who in 1955 became the first all-black high school basketball team to win a state championship. Inspired by the team's letterman's jacket, the vintage hoops shoe features a white felt upper with mismatched Star Chevron branding in yellow and green. The heel tab on the left shoe is embroidered with 'CA 55,' while the Tigers' logo adorns the right.

STEPHEN CURRY

"You have to challenge yourself to get better. Good enough is not good enough!"

2016, Stephen Curry of the Golden State Warriors becomes the first NBA player unanimously voted the MVP, receiving all 131 votes. He leads his Warriors to a record 73-9 won-lost record during the regular season. Curry becomes the first NBA player to average more than 30 points (30.1) while playing less than 35 minutes per game. Curry finishes the regular season with a record 402 three-pointers, making him the first player to score more than 300 and 400 three-point goals in a season, breaking his 2015 record of 286.

2022, Stephen Curry of the Golden State Warriors becomes the first player to win the Kobe Bryant MVP award at the NBA's All-Star Game. The newly designed trophy has an eight-sided base to represent Bryant's No. 8 jersey number. The four-tier trophy has 18 stars around the base to represent Bryant's 18 All-Star selections.

2022, The first ever Magic Johnson Western Conference Finals MVP award is won by Stephen Curry of the Golden State Warriors.

MEL DANIELS

1968, Mel Daniels, center for the Minnesota Muskies, becomes rebounding leader and first the Rookie of the Year, in the newly founded ABA.

1971, Mel Daniels becomes the first ABA player to win the MVP award twice.

1972, Mel Daniels of the Indiana Pacers becomes the first ABA player to score 10,000 points.

CHARLIE DAVIS

1971, Charles Lawrence "Charlie" Davis is named the Atlantic Coast Conference (ACC) men's basketball Player of the Year, becoming the first African American to win the award. The 6-foot-2 guard of the Wake Forest Demon Deacons is later drafted by the Cleveland Cavaliers.

DARRYL DAWKINS

1975, Darryl Dawkins (Philadelphia 76ers) and Bill Willoughby (Atlanta Hawks) are the second and third high school basketball players to sign with NBA or ABA teams.

1979, Darryl Dawkins demolishes backboards in at Kansas City's Kemper Arena and Philadelphia's Spectrum, prompting the development and implementation of the "Breakaway Rim" or pressure-release rim for the 1981-82 season. Dawkins from the planet Lovetron becomes the first player to name his dunks: The Rim Wrecker, The Gorilla, In Your Face Disgrace, The Look Out Below, Cover Your Head, Dunk You Very Much, Left-Handed-Spine-Chiller-Supreme, The Bun Toaster, The Rump Roaster and the Baby Shaker.

1980, Philadelphia 76er stars Darryl Dawkins and Lloyd "World" Free wear large gold necklaces inscribed "Chocolate Thunder" and "World," respectively. NBA bans the wearing of any type of hand, arm, face, nose, ear, head or neck jewelry during league play, citing a potential safety hazard.

DAVE DeJERNETT

1936, Big Dave DeJernett from integrated Indiana Central University becomes the first African American collegiate athlete to sign with a professional basketball team, the New York Rens.

DIAMOND DESHIELDS

2022, Betnijah Laney of the New York Liberty, Diamond Deshields of the Phoenix Mercury and Arike Ogunbowale of the Dallas Wings appear on the cover of *WSLAM*, the first all-women issue of *SLAM* magazine.

HANK DeZONIE

1950, Hank DeZonie from Clark Atlanta University is the first African American to play for the NBA Tri-Cities Blackhawks based in Moline and Rock Island, Ill., and Davenport, Iowa.

1950, On Halloween Oct. 31, Nov. 1, Nov. 4, and Dec. 3, Earl Lloyd, Chuck Cooper, Nat "Sweetwater" Clifton and Hank DeZonie, respectively, become the first African Americans to play in the National Basketball Association (NBA).

SKYLAR DIGGINS-SMITH

2014, Future WNBA player Skylar Diggins-Smith from Notre Dame is the first woman signed by Jay Z to a Roc Nation contract, which markets itself as a boutique sports agency.

2018, Puma announces a relaunch of its basketball shoe division. Skylar Diggins-Smith, point guard for the Dallas Wings, becomes the first face of the brand's comeback.

BOB DOUGLAS

1972, Robert Lewis Douglas (from Saint Kitts), founder and coach of the Renaissance Big Five and the New York Rens, is the first Black man inducted in the Naismith Memorial Basketball Hall of Fame.

CLYDE DREXLER

1983, Clyde Drexler becomes the first collegiate basketball player to accumulate 1,000 points, 900 rebounds, 300 assists and 250 steals in a career with the Houston Cougars.

AL DRUMMOND

1970, Al Drummond becomes the University of Virginia's first African American to receive a scholarship for basketball.

CHIP DUBLIN

1968, Chip Dublin, hoopster, is the first African American athlete to play at Jacksonville (Fla.) University.

TIM DUNCAN

1996, Tim Duncan, a center for Wake Forest Demon Deacons, leads the ACC in scoring, rebounding, field goal percentage, and blocked shots, becoming the first player in conference history to lead in all four categories. He is later named Most Valuable Player of the ACC Tournament.

2002, In 1984, Magic Johnson is the first recipient of the IBM Award, based on a computer formula which measures a player's statistical contribution to his team. The award was discontinued in 2002 with Tim Duncan as the final recipient.

2014, The San Antonio Spurs, led by Coach Gregg Popovich, win the NBA championship with a diversity of talent. The team includes Tony Parker (G) and Boris Diaw (F), both from France; Tiago Splitter (C) from Brazil; Patty Mills (G) from Australia; Manu Ginóbili (G) from Argentina; Marco Belinelli (F) from Italy; and Tim Duncan (C) from Saint Croix in the Virgin Islands. They finished the season with a 62-20 won-loss record (.756) and defeated the Miami Heat in five games.

WALTER DUKES

1953, Basketball star Walter Dukes of Seton Hall is the first African American to be named First Team All-American. Don Barksdale of UCLA in 1947 was Second Team All-American.

CANDICE DUPREE

2006, Candice Dupree, a Temple Owl, is the first WNBA player to compete against her college coach, Dawn Staley. Staley's final WNBA season was Dupree's first. Staley's Houston Comets defeat Dupree's Chicago Sky, 71-60.

KEVIN DURANT

2007, Kevin Durant of the Texas Longhorns becomes the first frosh and the first Texas athlete to receive *Associated Press'* College Player of the Year since its inception in 1961.

SEAN ELLIOTT

2000, Sean Elliott of the San Antonio Spurs becomes the first professional athlete to return to play after a kidney transplant.

CRYSTAL ELLIS

1951, Crystal Ellis becomes the first African American to play basketball for the Bowling Green (Ky.) State University Falcons. Ellis later earns his master's and Ph.D. degrees in education from the University.

DALE ELLIS

1994, Dale Ellis of the Seattle SuperSonics becomes the first player to record 1,000 points on three-point shots.

1997, Dale Ellis of the Seattle SuperSonics becomes the first player to record 1,500 points on three-point shots.

L. M. ELLIS

1963, L.M. Ellis is the first Black basketball player in the Ohio Valley Conference, when he joins the Austin Peay State University. In 2022, the university retires his jersey, No. 45.

WAYNE EMBRY

1958, Wayne Embry is the first African American to play for the Cincinnati Royals.

1972, Wayne Embry with the Milwaukee Bucks, is the first African American general manager in the NBA and in pro sports.

1991-92, Wayne Embry, with the Cleveland Cavaliers, is the first African American to be named NBA Executive of the Year by the *Sporting News*. Embry, Cavalier's president/chief operating officer wins the award again in 1999-2000.

2022, The NBA creates division championship trophies named after African American pioneers of the game. The Pacific Division winner receives the Chuck Cooper Trophy. The Central Division winner receives the Wayne Embry Trophy. The Southwest Division winner receives the Willis Reed Trophy. The Atlantic Division winner receives the Nat "Sweetwater" Clifton Trophy. The Southeast Division winner receives the Earl Lloyd Trophy. The Northwest Division winner receives the Sam Jones Trophy.

JULIUS ERVING

"The key to success is to keep growing in all areas of life - mental, emotional, spiritual, as well as physical."

1975, Julius "Dr. J." Erving wins the first ABA Slam Dunk contest. Erving beats out David Thompson in the Denver event.

1976, Julius "Dr. J" Erving, becomes the only three-time MVP in the ABA: 1972-73, 1974-75 and 1975-76.

1981, Julius Erving becomes the only player in basketball history to win the MVP award in both the NBA and the ABA. Dr. J. was the MVP in the ABA in 1974, 1975 and 1976; and MVP in the NBA in 1981.

1987, Julius Erving becomes the first non-center to score 30,000 points. Dr. J's total includes points from his ABA days.

Colorful Firsts in U.S. Sports

PATRICK EWING
1985, Rookie Patrick Ewing with the New York Knicks is not allowed, by the NBA, to wear a t-shirt under his jersey, as he did with the Georgetown Hoyas to stay warm in cold arenas.

RAY FELIX
1954, Ray Felix a center for the Baltimore Bullets is the first African American named NBA Rookie of the Year, for the 1953-54 season.

HONEY FITCH
1934, Harrison "Honey" Fitch becomes University of Connecticut's first African American basketball player. In a game against the U.S. Coast Guard Academy, they had a tradition "that no Negro players be permitted to engage in contests at the Academy." Fitch warms up with the team, but coach John Heldman does not play him.

ED FLEMING
1955, Ed Fleming (from Niagara University), Dick Ricketts (Duquesne) and Maurice Stokes (Saint Francis) are the first African Americans to play for the Rochester Royals.

T. J. FORD
2002, T.J. Ford of the Texas Longhorns becomes the first frosh to lead the NCAA in assists with 8.27 per game average. The 5-foot-10 guard wins the Naismith Award the following year.

HANK FOSTER
1953, Hank Foster joins the Bradley University Bulldogs and becomes the first African American basketball player and track and field hurdler.

WALT FRAZIER
1972, Walt Frazier of the New York Knicks becomes the first basketball player with a signature shoe. Puma pays $5,000 to market the red, white and blue shoes with "Clyde" on the side.

1973, The NBA starts recording "Steals," probably influenced by guard Walt Frazier's propensity for stealing basketballs. Frazier had outpolled Bill Russell on the All-NBA Defensive team in 1969.

WORLD FREE
1980, Philadelphia 76er stars Darryl Dawkins and Lloyd "World" Free wear large gold necklaces inscribed "Chocolate Thunder" and "World," respectively. NBA bans the wearing of any type of hand, arm, face, nose, ear, head or neck jewelry during league play, citing a potential safety hazard.

HAROLD FREEMAN
1953, Harold Freeman becomes the first basketball captain at Catholic University in Washington, District of Columbia. He is also the first African American tennis player at the university and wins singles and doubles matches as his team wins its fourth straight Mason-Dixon Conference championship in Baltimore, Md.

CLARENCE "BIG HOUSE" GAINES
1966-67, Clarence "Big House" Gaines coaches Winston-Salem State University to a 32-1 record and the first NCAA Division II championship for an HBCU. The Rams, led by senior Earl Monroe with 41.5 points per game, are the first HBCU to capture a national championship at any level.

1967, Clarence "Big House" Gaines Sr. becomes the first African American to be named NCAA Coach of the Year. Gaines is named CIAA coach of the year eight times, 1953, 1957, 1960, 1961, 1963, 1966, 1970 and 1977.

1976, The C.E. Gaines Center, an athletic complex on the Winston-Salem State University campus, is named after Clarence "Big House" Gaines.

2021, HBCU All-Stars LLC announces that the first Historically Black Colleges and Universities (HBCU) All-Star Game, a college basketball showcase highlighting the best HBCU players in the country, will be held at UNO Lakefront Arena in New Orleans in 2022. The game will feature the best talent from the four Historically Black Athletic Conferences pit two teams named in tribute of legendary coaches John McLendon (MEAC & SIAC) and Clarence "Big House" Gaines (SWAC & CIAA). Also playing in the showcase will be players from Tennessee State, Hampton and North Carolina A&T State universities.

BILL GARRETT

1947, Bill Garrett becomes the first African American to play on the Indiana University basketball team and also the first to regularly start on a Big Ten Conference team. In 1951, the 6-foot-3 center becomes the third African American drafted into the NBA by the Boston Celtics in the second round, 16th pick.

POP GATES

1939, Pop Gates plays in the first World Professional Basketball (WPB) Tournament. By 1949, he would become the only player to play in all 10 WPB tourneys.

1949, The New York Rens, now based in Dayton, Ohio, and members of the National Basketball League (NBL), play their last game against the Denver Rockets. Coached by "Pop" Gates, their lifetime record over 26 years is 2,318 wins and 381 losses, an 86 winning percentage. Gates becomes the first Black coach in the NBL.

1989, William "Pop" Gates of the New York Rens and Washington Bears, becomes the first non-NBA player inducted into the Naismith Memorial Basketball Hall of Fame.

DEVEAN GEORGE

1999, Devean George of Augsburg, Minn., becomes the first player from a Division III school to be drafted in the first round of the NBA draft. George is the 23rd pick of the draft by the Los Angeles Lakers.

GEORGE GERVIN

1978, The tightest race for the NBA scoring title goes down to the final game. George "Ice Man" Gervin, of San Antonio Spurs, scores 63, while David Thompson, of Denver Nuggets, scores 73. The "Ice Man" wins the title with a 27.21 average to beat Thompson's 27.15 average.

2022, The Convocation Center, a multi-purpose sports and entertainment complex on the Eastern Michigan University's west campus is renamed the George Gervin GameAbove Center. The following year a commemorative statue by artist Ben Victor is unveiled at EMU.

BOB GIBSON

1954, Future St. Louis Cardinals pitcher Bob Gibson is the first African American basketball player at Creighton University. His number 45 is later retired.

ARTIS GILMORE

1977, The first player chosen in the NBA dispersal draft of former ABA players, is not Dr. J., Moses Malone, nor the Ice Man George Gervin, but Artis Gilmore. The Chicago Bulls sign him for $1.1 million.

1980, Artis Gilmore becomes the first NBA player to record more than 2,000 blocked shots.

1982-83, Artis Gilmore becomes the first NBA player to record more than 2,500 blocked shots.

1986, Artis Gilmore becomes the first player to record more than 3,000 blocked shots in his combined ABA and NBA career.

BEN GORDON

2005, Chicago Bulls guard Ben Gordon becomes the first rookie to win the NBA's Sixth Man Award.

SIMON GOURDINE

1973, Simon Peter Gourdine becomes the first African American vice-president of the NBA.

DENIQUE GRAVES

1997, Denique Graves is the first WNBA player drafted from an HBCU, Howard University in Washington, District of Columbia. She was picked in the second round, 15th overall pick by the Sacramento Monarchs.

DRAYMOND GREEN

2016, Draymond Green of the Golden State Warriors becomes the first NBA player with more than 1,000 points (1,131), 500 rebounds (769), 500 assists (598), 100 steals (120), 100 blocked shots (113) and 100 three-point field goals (100) in a season. Green finishes seventh in the MVP voting.

2017, According to Elias Sports, Draymond Green of the Golden State Warriors in a victory over the Memphis Grizzles gathers 12 rebounds, 10 assists and 10 steals to post the first triple-double in NBA history that does not include double-digit points (he scores four points).

JALEN GREEN

2020, Jalen Romande Green, a Filipino-American from Napa, California, skips college and becomes the first basketball player to sign with the NBA's G-League, as a bridge between high school and the NBA. He is 6-foot-5 and a student at San Joaquin Memorial in Fresno, Calif. Green is named *Sports Illustrated's* inaugural Boys Basketball Player of the Year.

2021, Jalen Green of the G League Ignite is the first player from that league to appear on the cover of *SLAM* magazine, No. 231, also known as the Future issue.

HAL GREER

1955, Hal Greer, as a Marshall Thundering Herd, becomes the first African American to play for a public college in W.Va. In 1976, the Philadelphia 76ers retire its first uniform number, Greer's No. 15.

GEORGE GREGORY JR.

1931, George Gregory Jr. captain and center for the Columbia University basketball team from 1928 to 1931, becomes the first African American to gain All-American honors. Despite opposition from the dean, athletic director and the coach, teammates vote him captain.

YOLANDA GRIFFITH

1997, Yolanda Griffith is selected by the Long Beach Stingrays as the No. 1 pick overall in the American Basketball League draft. Griffith would later win gold medals at the 2000 Sydney and 2004 Athens Olympic Games.

1999, Yolanda Griffith becomes the first player to win the "Defensive Player on the Year" award in both the ABL and the WNBA. In 1998, Griffith wins the award in the ABL.

1999, Former ABL star Yolanda Griffith is the first WNBA player to be named MVP, Defensive Player of the Year, and Newcomer of the Year, in the same season. Griffith led the league in rebounds (11.3), and steals (2.52), and finished second in scoring (18.8).

BRITTNEY GRINER

2013, In her rookie season, Brittney Griner of the Phoenix Mercury with a 7-foot-4 wingspan, becomes the first WNBA player to dunk twice in the same game. Previously, Candace Parker dunked twice and Lisa Leslie once in WNBA competition.

LENNY HALL

1966, Lenny Hall plays four minutes of a basketball game for the Florida State Seminoles and becomes its first Black player. He scores two baskets and grabs two rebounds before a knee injury ends his playing career.

LEONARD HAMILTON

1986, Leonard Hamilton becomes the first African American coach in the Big Eight Conference as head coach of the Oklahoma State Cowboys basketball team.

REGGIE HARDING

1963, Reggie Harding is drafted by the Detroit Pistons in the sixth round with the 48th overall pick, making him the first player ever drafted who did not play in college. Harding graduated in 1960 from Eastern HS in Detroit, before playing for a prep school in Nashville and two seasons in the professional Midwest League in Toledo and Holland, Mich.

HENRY HARRIS

1969, Henry Harris becomes the first African American scholarship athlete at Auburn University as a basketball player.

LUCY HARRIS-STEWART

1975, Lusia Harris of Delta State is the first African American recipient of the KODAK-WBCA All-American award.

1977, Lusia "Lucy" Harris becomes the first woman to be drafted by the NBA. The 1976 Olympic silver medalist is drafted by the New Orleans Jazz, but never plays.

1992, Lusia Harris-Stewart, three-time national champion with Delta State (Miss.) University and 1977 NBA draftee, is the first female basketball player selected to the Naismith Memorial Basketball Hall of Fame.

1999, Lusia Harris-Stewart and Cheryl Miller are among the original inductees into the Women's Basketball Hall of Fame in Knoxville, Tenn.

CLEM HASKINS

1963, Clem Haskins and Dwight Smith become the first Black athletes to integrate the Western Kentucky University (WKU) Hilltoppers basketball program. Haskins later plays in the NBA and serves as an assistant coach on the gold medal winning 1996 Olympic Summer basketball squad.

1966-67, Western Kentucky's Clem Haskins, Houston's Elvin Hayes and Louisville's Wes Unseld become the first African Americans from Southern schools to be named to the first NCAA All-American team.

CONNIE HAWKINS

1961, Connie Hawkins of the Pittsburgh Rens becomes the American Basketball League's (ABL) first Most Valuable Player, receiving 41 of a possible 54 votes.

1961, Connie Hawkins, Bill Bridges and Larry Staverman of the Kansas City Steers, Dan Swartz of the New York Tapers, and Dick Barnett from the Cleveland Pipers are named to the First Team All-Stars of the American Basketball League.

1967-68, Connie Hawkins of the Pittsburgh Pipers becomes the ABA's first Most Valuable Player and the league's first scoring leader, averaging 26.8 points per game.

1968, From Boys High School in Brooklyn, N.Y., Connie Hawkins, a power forward for the Pittsburgh Pipers, is the first undrafted basketball player selected to an ABA All-Star game.

ELVIN HAYES

1966-67, Western Kentucky's Clem Haskins, Houston's Elvin Hayes and Louisville's Wes Unseld become the first African Americans from Southern schools to be named to the first NCAA All-American team.

MARQUES HAYNES

1998, Marques Haynes becomes the first Harlem Globetrotter inducted into the Naismith Memorial Basketball Hall of Fame.

SPENCER HAYWOOD

1968, Spencer Haywood is the first high schooler to play on the U.S. Olympic basketball team.

1969, Spencer Haywood, a sophomore at the University of Detroit Mercy, is the first player to file for "hardship," becoming eligible for the NBA draft.

1969-70, Spencer Haywood becomes the first player to win the Scoring Title (30.0), Rebounding Title (19.5), and be selected the Rookie of the Year and Most Valuable Player in the same year with the ABA's Denver Rockets.

1970, Spencer Haywood becomes the first ABA player to jump to the NBA, leaving the Denver Rockets (Nuggets) for the Seattle SuperSonics.

1971, Spencer Haywood signs a six-year, $1.5 million contract with the Seattle SuperSonics, ignoring the rule that a player cannot join the NBA until he is four years out of high school. Haywood challenges the decision by commencing an antitrust action against the NBA. As part of his claim against the NBA, Haywood argued that the ruling by the NBA is a "group boycott" and a violation of the Sherman Antitrust Act. The central issue that had to be determined was whether the NBA draft policy was a restraint on trade and therefore was illegal in accordance with the Sherman Act. The U.S. Supreme Court, in Haywood v. National Basketball Association, 401 U.S. 1204 rules, 9–0, against the NBA's requirement that a player may not be drafted by an NBA team unless he has waited four years following his graduation from high school.

DENA HEAD
1997, Dena Head, 26, is the first and oldest player selected in the WNBA's Elite Draft by the Utah Starzz.

AL HEARTLEY
1967, Al Heartley earns a basketball scholarship as a walk-on at North Carolina State University. Along with Ed Leftwich they become N.C. State's first African American ballers.

EDWIN HENDERSON
1909, Edwin B. Henderson creates the Washington (District of Columbia) 12 Streeters basketball team with students from Howard University. They are sponsored by the Twelfth Street Colored Y.M.C.A. They win the 1909-10 unofficial Colored Basketball World Championship title with an undefeated season.

CLEO HILL
1961, Cleo Hill from Winston-Salem State University is the first player from an HBCU to be drafted No. 1 by the NBA, when selected by the St. Louis Hawks.

CRAIG HODGES
1992, Craig Hodges of the Chicago Bulls wears a dashiki to the White House in celebration of the team's championship. He hands President George Bush a letter addressing the issues of racism and opposition of the Persian Gulf War. Hodges is released by the Bulls soon after and never plays in the NBA again. See 1996.

CHAMIQUE HOLDSCLAW
1998, Chamique Holdsclaw of the WNBA's New York Liberty becomes the first female on the cover of *SLAM* magazine.

1999, Chamique Holdsclaw becomes the first female basketball player to be named recipient of the James E. Sullivan Memorial Award given annually to the top amateur athlete in the country.

1999, Chamique Holdsclaw is the number one pick in the WNBA draft by the Washington Mystics, as 35 former ABL players are selected. Yolanda Griffith is picked second by Sacramento Monarchs, while Natalie Williams is picked third by the Utah Starzz.

1999, Chamique Holdsclaw is the WNBA's first Rookie of the Year to have played in its All-Star game.

JRUE HOLIDAY
2022, Milwaukee Bucks guard Jrue Holiday becomes the first player to win the Twyman-Stokes Teammate of the Year Award twice. Holiday also won the award for the 2019-20 season. The award is for a player who displays selfless leadership on and off the court while showing commitment and dedication to his team.

WADE HOUSTON
1962, Wade Houston, Eddie Whitehead and Sam Smith become the first African American basketball players at the University of Louisville.

1989, Wade Houston becomes the first African American coach in the Southeastern Conference with the Tennessee Vols. His son, Allan, plays for him at Tennessee and becomes the Vols' all-time leading scorer before enjoying a pro career with the Detroit Pistons and New York Knicks.

DWIGHT HOWARD
2009, Dwight Howard of the Orlando Magic is the first NBA player to lead the league in blocked shots (231) and total rebounds (1,093) in the same season. He repeats this feat during the 2009-2010 season.

JUWAN HOWARD
1995, Juwan Howard becomes the first NBA player to leave school early and still earn his degree with his graduating class. The University of Michigan grad majored in communications and minored in business.

WENDELL HUDSON

1969, Wendell Hudson becomes the first African American scholarship athlete in any sport at the University of Alabama, joining the basketball team under coach C.M. Newton. Hudson later becomes head coach of Alabama's women's basketball team in 2008.

BRITTANY HUNTER

2003, Brittany Hunter, 6-foot-3 from UConn, becomes the first female to participate in the POWERade Jam Fest slam dunk contest, held in conjunction with the McDonald's All-American Games. She failed to complete any dunks.

ANDRE INGRAM

2020, Andre Ingram is named president of the Interim Executive Committee of Basketball Players Union, of the NBA's G League. In 2018, Ingram scored 19 points in his Los Angeles Laker debut after spending 10 seasons in the G-League. He is from American University.

JOHN ISAACS

1946, The Continental Basketball Association is the first professional basketball league to hire Black players. The Hazleton (Pa.) Mountaineers sign Bill Brown, Zach Clayton from the New York Rens and John Isaacs from the Washington Bears.

ALLEN "THE ANSWER" IVERSON
"I wasn't a point guard. I was a killer."

1996, Allen Iverson, of Georgetown University, becomes the first collegiate basketball player to appear on the cover of *SLAM* magazine.

1999, Allen Iverson, at six feet tall, becomes the shortest player in NBA history to lead the league in scoring with a 26.8 per game average. Iverson is also the first baller to appear on *SLAM* magazine with jewelry -- a necklace, watch, bracelet and ring, in a throwback Philadelphia 76ers jersey.

2001, *Dime* magazine, a "basketball lifestyle" publication covering not only the sport but the off-court lives and lifestyles of its athletes and personalities, makes its debut with Allen Iverson of the Philadelphia 76ers on the cover.

2001, A mourning Allen Iverson, after the fatal shooting of his best friend, Rahsaan Langeford, explains to media why he took a burritos break during a team practice, "We sitting in here -- I'm supposed to be the franchise player, and we in here talking about practice. I mean, listen: We talking about practice. Not a game. Not a game. Not a game. We talking about practice. Not a game. Not the game that I go out there and die for and play every game like it's my last. Not the game. We talking about practice, man."

2005, The NBA issues a dress code for the 2005-06 season. Business casual attire is required for team or league activities, including arriving at games, leaving games, conducting interviews and making promotional or other appearances. Players will no longer be able to wear the following: Sleeveless shirts, shorts, T-shirts, chains, pendants or medallions over clothing, sunglasses indoors and headphones (except on the team bus or the plane or in the locker room). Philadelphia 76er guard Allen Iverson is the most outspoken critic of the new dressing standard.

LeBRON JAMES
"I like criticism. It makes you strong."

2002, Sebastian Telfair from Abraham Lincoln High School in Brooklyn, N.Y., and LeBron James from St. Vincent-St. Mary High School in Akron, Ohio, are the first high school basketball players to appear on the cover of *SLAM* magazine.

2003-04, Carmelo Anthony of the Denver Nuggets in the western conference and LeBron James of the Cleveland Cavaliers in the eastern conference are the first NBA players to win the Rookie of the Month award in every month of the season, from November through April.

2008, LeBron James becomes the first African American and the third man overall to be on the cover of *Vogue* magazine. He is featured on the March issue with Brazilian model Gisele Bündchen, wife of QB Tom Brady.

2018, In response to LeBron James' comment to ESPN broadcaster Cari Champion that Donald Trump has "The No. 1 job in America, the appointed person is someone who doesn't understand the people," the athlete said, adding that some of the president's comments are "laughable and scary," Laura Ingraham of *Fox News* countered, "It's always unwise to seek political advice

Colorful Firsts in U.S. Sports

from someone who gets paid $100 million a year to bounce a ball," she said. "Keep the political comments to yourselves . . . Shut up and dribble [all the way to the bank]." James provides the hashtag #MoreThanAnAthlete.

2019, LeBron James becomes the first NBA player to record a triple-double against all 30 teams, starting in 2003.

2020, LeBron James becomes the first player in NBA history to score at least 10 points in 1,000 consecutive regular season games. James launches "More Than A Vote" a non-profit organization designed to register African Americans to vote, and to stop voter suppression efforts.

2022, LeBron James of the Los Angeles Lakers becomes the first active NBA player to achieve billionaire status.

FATS JENKINS

2021, Former Negro League player Clarence "Fats" Jenkins, captain of the New York Rens, is the first player from the first Black-owned, fully professional African American basketball team inducted into the Naismith Memorial Basketball Hall of Fame.

BRANDON JENNINGS

2008, Brandon Jennings from Oak Hill Academy in Mouth of Wilson, Va. becomes the first high school player to play for a European team, the Lottomatica Roma of the Italian Serie A, rather than play collegiate basketball since the NBA's age restriction rule was implemented. The following year, he is selected 10th overall by the Milwaukee Bucks in the 2009 NBA draft.

AMIR JOHNSON

2005, Amir Johnson, a power forward from Westchester High School in Los Angeles, becomes the last high school player drafted by the NBA. He is selected by the Detroit Pistons in the second round with the 56th overall pick. The NBA institutes a rule prior to the 2006 draft requiring U.S. players to be at least one year removed from their high school graduation to be eligible for the draft.

BOB JOHNSON

2003, Bob Johnson, former owner of Black Entertainment Television (BET), becomes the first African American majority owner of an NBA basketball team, the Charlotte Hornets. According to *Forbes* magazine, he becomes the first African American billionaire in 2001. *Sports Illustrated* names Bob Johnson No. 1 on its list of 101 Most Influential Minorities in Sports.

HUNTER JOHNSON

1915, The Pittsburgh Scholastics Basket Ball Club, pre-cursor to the famous Loendi Big Five, is organized by fitness trainer Hunter Johnson. Johnson is credited with training long jumper DeHart Hubbard, a gold medalist in the 1924 Olympics.

MAGIC JOHNSON

"In life, winning and losing will both happen. What is never acceptable is quitting."

1979, For the week of November 11, Magic Johnson of the Los Angeles Lakers is the first NBA player named Player of the Week.

1980, Magic Johnson becomes the first rookie to win the MVP award in the NBA finals.

1984, Magic Johnson is the first recipient of the IBM Award, based on a computer formula which measures a player's statistical contribution to his team. David Robinson won the award a record five times. The award was discontinued in 2002 with Tim Duncan as the final recipient. Award formula = Player's PTS-FGA+REB+AST+STL+BLK-PF-TO+(team wins x 10) x 250 divided by Team points- FGA+REB+AST+STL+BLK-PF-TO. PTS stands for points, FGA stands for field goal attempts, REB stands for rebounds, AST stands for assists, STL stands for steals, BLK stands for blocks, PF stands for personal fouls, and TO stands for turnovers. The award was given to the player with the highest total.

1989, The rock band Red Hot Chili Peppers release "Magic Johnson" the first rock & roll song about an NBA player.

1991, Magic Johnson and Earl Graves, publisher of *Black Enterprise*, buy a Pepsi Cola bottling plant.

1992, Despite retiring from the NBA, due to testing positive for HIV, Magic Johnson is selected to play in the NBA All-Star game. Johnson wins the MVP award, scoring a game-high 25 points with nine assists.

1994, Magic Johnson acquires a minority 4.5-percent stake in the Los Angeles Lakers for $10 million. After 16 years he sells his interest.

2012, Magic Johnson buys a 2.3% stake in the Los Angeles Dodgers with a $50 million investment. He is a key investor with the Guggenheim Baseball Management.

2023, Magic Johnson Enterprises, along with a group of others, purchase the Washington DC-based NFL team Washington

Commanders for $6.05 billion.

MARQUES JOHNSON

1977, Marques Johnson of UCLA wins the first John R. Wooden Award, given annually to the most outstanding men's and women's college basketball players.

SHEILA JOHNSON

2005, Sheila Johnson, co-founder of Black Entertainment Television (BET), becomes part-owner of the Lincoln Holdings LLC, which purchases the Washington Mystics from Abe Pollin's Washington Sports & Entertainment. Johnson's stake in Lincoln Holdings is reported to be between 5 and 10 percent. Johnson is believed to be the first African American woman to be a principal shareholder of three professional sports franchises, the Mystics, Washington Wizards and the Washington Capitals.

BENNY JONES

1945, Charles "Benny" Jones becomes the first African American basketball player for the Dayton (Ohio) University Flyers. Jones later becomes business manager for heavyweight boxing champion Ezzard Charles.

BILLY JONES

1965, William "Billy" Jones becomes the first African American athlete in the Atlantic Coast Conference (ACC) as a member of the University of Maryland Terrapins basketball team.

K. C. JONES

1964, The Boston Celtics become the first NBA franchise to start five Black players when Willie Naulls replaced the injured Tommy Heinsohn in the starting lineup. Naulls with Bill Russell, K. C. Jones, Sam Jones and Satch Sanders reel off 12 consecutive wins.

1975, K. C. Jones (Washington Bullets) and Al Attles (Golden State Warriors) become the first African Americans to coach NBA All-Star squads. They also square off in the NBA championship to become the first African Americans to take their teams to the finals, doing so seven years after Bill Russell wins the first of two titles as Boston's player/coach. The Warriors sweep the Bullets in four games.

1984, In January, K. C. Jones of the Boston Celtics is the first African American coach to be named Coach of the Month in the NBA.

ROY JONES JR.

1996, Roy Jones Jr. becomes the first man to play a pro basketball game (U.S. Basketball League) and fight for the world championship (IBF), as super middleweight, in the same day.

SAM JONES

1964, The Boston Celtics become the first NBA franchise to start five Black players when Willie Naulls replaced the injured Tommy Heinsohn in the starting lineup. Naulls with Bill Russell, K. C. Jones, Sam Jones and Satch Sanders reel off 12 consecutive wins.

2022, The NBA creates division championship trophies named after African American pioneers of the game. The Pacific Division winner receives the Chuck Cooper Trophy. The Central Division winner receives the Wayne Embry Trophy. The Southwest Division winner receives the Willis Reed Trophy. The Atlantic Division winner receives the Nat "Sweetwater" Clifton Trophy. The Southeast Division winner receives the Earl Lloyd Trophy. The Northwest Division winner receives the Sam Jones Trophy.

MICHAEL JORDAN

"To be successful you have to be selfish, or else you never achieve.
And once you get to your highest level, then you have to be unselfish."

1987, Michael Jordan becomes the first NBA player with more than 200 steals (236) and 100 blocked shots (125) in the same season. Jordan also averages a league leading 37.1 points per game.

1988, Michael Jordan becomes the first NBA player to score more than 50 points twice in the same series, against Lenny Wilkens' Cleveland Cavaliers. He also becomes the first pro basketball player to appear on the front of a Wheaties cereal box.

1988, Michael Jordan becomes the first NBA player to win the MVP and Defensive Player of the Year awards in the same season.

Colorful Firsts in U.S. Sports

1999, Michael Jordan withdraws his offer to buy 50% of the Charlotte Hornets, when owner George Shinn declines to give Jordan some controlling interests.

2003, Michael Jordan of the Washington Wizards becomes the first NBA player 40 or older to score 40 or more points. Jordan scores 43, hitting 18 of 30 field goals and 7 of 8 free throws against the New Jersey Nets.

2010, Michael Jordan becomes the first former NBA player to purchase a controlling interest in an NBA team, the Charlotte Bobcats, formerly the Hornets. The league's Board of Governors unanimously approves Jordan's $275 million purchase of the team from Bob Johnson, former president of BET and in 2003 the NBA's first minority majority owner.

2014, Michael Jordan becomes the first athlete with an estimated net worth of $1 billion, as reported by *Forbes* magazine. Jordan is owner of the Charlotte Hornets.

2016, Kareem Abdul-Jabbar and Michael Jordan are presented with the Presidential Medal of Freedom by President Barack Obama, the highest civilian award.

DOLLY KING

1937, William "Dolly" King, as a member of the Long Island University basketball team, becomes the first African American to play in the national AAU tournament.

GENE KNOLLE

1969, Gene Knolle becomes the first African American basketball player for the Texas Tech Red Raiders. Knolle, a 6-foot-4, 185-pound forward, currently holds the program record for career-scoring average at 21.5 points per game.

BREVIN KNIGHT

1998, Brevin Knight of the Cleveland Cavaliers becomes the first rookie to lead the NBA in steals.

BETNIJAH LANEY

2022, Betnijah Laney of the New York Liberty, Diamond Deshields of the Phoenix Mercury and Arike Ogunbowale of the Dallas Wings appear on the cover of *WSLAM*, the first all-women issue of *SLAM* magazine.

BOB LANIER

1972, Bob Lanier, six-foot-eleven of the Detroit Pistons beats six-foot-three Boston Celtic Jo Jo White in the first NBA one-on-one tournament for $15,000. The first player to score 20 points must win by four points. Lanier defeats White 21-16.

2002, Jerry Stackhouse wins the first Bob Lanier Community Assist Award for community engagement, philanthropic activity and charity work. This is a monthly award. The winner of the award is presented with a plaque dedicated to NBA Hall of Famer David Robinson.

ALMER LEE

1969, Almer Lee from Fort Smith Northside High School becomes the first Black player to letter in basketball at the University of Arkansas.

ED LEFTWICH

1967, Al Heartley earns a basketball scholarship as a walk-on at North Carolina State University. Along with Ed Leftwich they become N.C. State's first African American ballers.

LISA LESLIE

1997, Lisa Leslie of the Los Angeles Sparks is the first player to lead the WNBA in rebounds, 266, and the highest average rebounds per game at 9.5.

1998, Lisa Leslie is named USA Basketball Female Athlete of the Year

1999, Lisa Leslie scores 13 points, and is named MVP of the first WNBA All-Star game. It is played before a sell-out crowd of 18,649, at Madison Square Garden in New York City. Whitney Houston sings the national anthem.

2001, Lisa Leslie becomes the first WNBA player to be named League MVP, All-Star MVP and Play-off MVP in the same season.

2002, Lisa Leslie, (6-foot-5) of the Los Angeles Sparks, becomes the first WNBA player to dunk in a professional game, playing against the Miami Sol.

2006, Lisa Leslie becomes the WNBA's first player to score 5,000 career points.

2009, Lisa Leslie becomes the first WNBA player to score 6,000 career points.

HARRY "BUCKY" LEW

1902, Harry "Bucky" Lew, a forward with Pawtucketville (Mass.) Athletic Club in New England becomes the first African American professional basketball player.

1906, Harry "Bucky" Lew forms his own basketball team, "Buck Lew's Traveling Five" playing around the New England area.

BILLY LEWIS

1957, Billy Lewis becomes the first African American basketball player for the University of Colorado Buffaloes. Lewis later earns his law degree from Howard University.

REGGIE LEWIS

1987, Muggsy Bogues (Wake Forest) at 5-foot-3 the smallest player in NBA history, is the 12th pick by the Charlotte Hornets. Bogues, along with Reggie Lewis (Northwestern, 22nd pick) and Reggie Williams (Georgetown, 4th pick) become the first trio of players from the same high school (Dunbar Poets, Baltimore, Md.) to be picked in the first round of the same year.

JOE LILLARD

1926, The Savoy Big Five, based in Chicago, are organized at Wendell Phillips High School by Dick Hudson (fullback for the Minnesota Marines and the Hammond Pros of the NFL). The team includes Tommy Brookins, Bobby Anderson, Inman Jackson, Lester Johnson, Joe Lillard (running back of the Chicago Cardinals), Randolph Ramsey and Walter "Toots" Wright. They split a two-game series with George Halas's Chicago Bruins.

CHARLIE LIPSCOMB

1968, Charlie Lipscomb becomes the first African American to receive a basketball scholarship at Virginia Tech.

SHAUN LIVINGSTON

2004, Shaun Livingston from Peoria (Ill.) Central High School (also of Peoria Richwoods High School) at 6-foot-7, 186 pounds, is the first high school point guard to be drafted into the NBA, by the Los Angeles Clippers with the fourth pick overall.

EARL LLOYD

1950, John McLendon coaches Harold Hunter and Earl Lloyd and takes them to the Washington Capitols for tryouts.

1950, Other African Americans selected in the NBA draft are West Virginia State's Earl Lloyd and North Carolina College's Harold Hunter (both by the Washington Capitols) and Kentucky State's Ed Thompson (by the Fort Wayne Pistons).

1950, On Halloween Oct. 31, Nov. 1, Nov. 4, and Dec. 3, Earl Lloyd, Chuck Cooper, Nat "Sweetwater" Clifton and Hank DeZonie, respectively, become the first African Americans to play in the National Basketball Association (NBA).

1955, Earl Lloyd and Jim Tucker for the Syracuse Nationals become the first African Americans to play on an NBA championship team when they defeat the Fort Wayne Pistons.

1968, Earl Lloyd becomes the first African American assistant coach in the NBA with the Detroit Pistons.

1971, Earl Lloyd becomes Detroit Pistons' first African American bench coach. He is fired in 1972 after seven games (two wins, five losses) and replaced by Ray Scott.

2022, The NBA creates division championship trophies named after African American pioneers of the game. The Pacific Division winner receives the Chuck Cooper Trophy. The Central Division winner receives the Wayne Embry Trophy. The Southwest Division winner receives the Willis Reed Trophy. The Atlantic Division winner receives the Nat "Sweetwater" Clifton Trophy. The Southeast Division winner receives the Earl Lloyd Trophy. The Northwest Division winner receives the Sam Jones Trophy.

BERNADETTE LOCKE

1990, Bernadette Locke, at the University of Kentucky, becomes the first Black female assistant coach in Men's NCAA Division I basketball.

MOSES MALONE

"Ain't nobody ever had a jump shot like mine, ain't nobody ever power moves like mine, ain't nobody ever played tough defense like mine and ain't nobody ever had the courage to be a winner like me."

1974, Moses Malone becomes the first high school athlete to go directly to the pros from high school. The Utah Stars of the ABA give Malone $565,000 for four years. He scores 19 points, with 11 rebounds, in his first pro game against Dr. J and the New York Nets. In 1975, Darryl Dawkins (Philadelphia 76ers) and Bill Willoughby (Atlanta Hawks) are the second and third high school basketball players to sign with NBA teams. (See Reggie Harding, 1963).

1979, In November, Moses Malone of the Houston Rockets is the first NBA player to be named Player of the Month.

MIKE MALOY

1967, Mike Maloy becomes the first American Austrian basketball player for the Davidson (NC) College Wildcats. He becomes a three-time All-American and is named Southern Conference Player of the Year in 1969 and 1970.

CYNT MARSHALL

2018, Cynt Marshall becomes the first Black female CEO of an NBA team when hired by Mark Cuban of the Dallas Mavericks. Marshall spent 36 years at AT&T improving workplace culture and encouraging diversity and inclusion.

JESSE MARSHALL

1968, Jesse Marshall from Tyler (Texas) Junior College becomes the first Black basketball player for Centenary College in Bossier City, La.

ALEALI MAY

2017, Designer Aleali May becomes the first woman in Jordan Brand history to create a unisex sneaker.

BOB McADOO

1976, Buffalo Braves Bob McAdoo wins his third straight NBA scoring title. The 6-foot-9 center-forward is the first big man to shoot regularly outside the paint. He shoots better than 50 percent from the floor in half of his 14 NBA seasons, adding a new dimension to the game of basketball.

NIKKI McCRAY

1996-97, Nikki McCray, a Columbus Quest guard, is voted the American Basketball League's first Most Valuable Player.

1999, Nikki McCray, scoring guard for the Washington Mystics, becomes the first woman to receive a signature shoe with Fila, called the Nikki Delta.

XAVIER McDANIEL

1985, Xavier McDaniel, with the Wichita State Shockers, becomes the first player in college history to lead the NCAA's Division I in rebounding and scoring (27.2) in the same season. He is selected in the first round of the NBA draft by the Seattle SuperSonics.

IMANI McGEE

2016, Pam McGee, a standout athlete at USC, is the first former WNBA mother with kids in the NBA and the WNBA. Her son JaVale debuted in the NBA in 2008 with her daughter Imani joining the WNBA in 2016.

PAMELA McGEE

2016, Pam McGee, a standout athlete at USC, is the first former WNBA mother with kids in the NBA and the WNBA. Her son JaVale debuted in the NBA in 2008 with her daughter Imani joining the WNBA in 2016.

JaVALE McGEE

2008, JaVale McGee, with his mother, Pamela McGee, become the first mother-son combo to play in the NBA and the WNBA. McGee, a sophomore, is drafted by the Washington Wizards with the 18th overall pick from the University of Nevada. McGee's parents were both professional basketball players. His father, George Montgomery starred at Illinois and was a second-round draft pick in 1985 by the Portland Trail Blazers. His mother, Pamela, and her twin sister, Paula, were All-Americans who led USC to NCAA National titles in 1983 and 1984.

2011, JaVale McGee, in the NBA Slam Dunk Contest, becomes the first player to use three balls at one time in a dunk contest, which is later cited by Guinness World Records as the most basketballs dunked in a single jump. The third ball is passed to him from teammate John Wall.

2016, Pam McGee, a standout athlete at USC, is the first former WNBA mother with kids in the NBA and the WNBA. Her son JaVale debuted in the NBA in 2008 with her daughter Imani joining the WNBA in 2016.

2021, JaVale McGee of the U.S. Basketball team wins gold in the Tokyo Olympics. Thirty-seven years earlier, his mom Pamela of the 1984 Olympic basketball team won a gold medal. Hall of Famer and USC Trojans legend Pamela McGee and JaVale become the first mother and son to win Olympic gold medals.

JOHN McLENDON

1941, John McLendon begins his basketball coaching career with the North Carolina College (now North Carolina Central University).

1944, John McLendon coaches the first integrated game in the South, North Carolina College of Negroes versus Duke's Navy Medical School, in Durham, N.C. McLendon's Eagles win by a score of 88 to 44. It is the first collegiate basketball contest where Blacks and Whites compete on the same floor. This Sunday morning match has remained a secret for several decades.

1946, John McLendon of North Carolina College co-founds the Central Intercollegiate Athletic Association (CIAA) Tournament with Talmadge Hill (Morgan State), John Burr (Howard University) and Harry Jefferson (Virginia State). The first games are played at Washington District of Columbia's Turner Arena. CIAA tournament becomes a showcase for future NBA players, such as Sam Jones, Earl Monroe, Cleo Hill, Ricky Mahorn, Charles Oakley and Ben Wallace.

1950, John McLendon coaches Harold Hunter and Earl Lloyd and takes them to the Washington Capitols for tryouts.

1951, John McLendon and three other coaches form the National Athletic Steering Committee to petition the NCAA and the NAIA to give Black schools a chance to play in post season tournaments.

1953, Tennessee State University in Nashville, coached by John McLendon, has the first Black basketball team to compete in the national NAIA tournament.

1957, Tennessee A&I, coached by John McLendon, becomes the first African American college team to win a national title against White competition in any sport, with a 92-73 defeat of Southeastern Oklahoma for the NAIA Division I title.

1959, John McLendon's Tennessee A & I basketball team during warmups for the NAIA championships, the Illinois State Normal cheerleaders and band play and sing "Bye Bye Blackbird." McLendon takes his team off the floor and then gives the "talk." The Tigers from Nashville, Tenn. beat the Redbirds, 131-74.

1959, John McLendon, of Tennessee A & I, becomes the first African American coach to be selected to coach the National All-Star Team and the first basketball coach to win three consecutive NAIA titles.

1960, John McLendon becomes the first African American coach to defeat the U.S. Olympic Team (with Jerry West and Oscar Robertson) with an amateur team, the Cleveland Pipers of the National Industrial Basketball League (NIBL).

1961, John McLendon becomes the first African American coach to win the National AAU Championship.

1961-62, John McLendon becomes the first African American to coach in the American Basketball League (ABL), with the Cleveland Pipers.

1962, John McLendon is inducted into the NAIA Hall of Fame.

1962, John McLendon becomes the first African American coach to author a book on basketball, *Fast Break Basketball, Fine Points and Fundamentals*. McLendon develops his idea for up-tempo style basketball while at the University of Kansas, under the tutelage of athletic director James Naismith, despite not being allowed to play basketball for the still-segregated Jayhawks. John McLendon is inducted into the NAIA Hall of Fame.

1966, John McLendon becomes the first African American coach to serve on the U.S. Olympic Committee, responsible for scouting and player performance statistical evaluation.

1966, Coach John McLendon's Kentucky State Thoroughbreds basketball team becomes the first Black college to play outside the U.S (in Iceland & France).

1967, John McLendon becomes the first African American head coach of a major college basketball program when hired at Cleveland State University.

1968, John McLendon becomes the first African American coach on the Olympic coaching staff.

1969, John McLendon becomes the first African American coach in the American Basketball Association (ABA) when he signs a two-year contract with the Denver (Nuggets) Rockets.

Colorful Firsts in U.S. Sports

1970, Coach John B. McLendon teaches the "Two in the Corner Offense" to North Carolina Coach Dean Smith at a Fellowship of Christian Athletes meeting in Colorado. Smith renames the offense "The Four Corners."

1978, Basketball coach John McLendon is inducted into the Central Intercollegiate Athletic Association (CIAA) Hall of Fame.

1979, John McLendon becomes the first coach from a historically Black college to be inducted in the Naismith Memorial Basketball Hall of Fame.

2000, The John McLendon Minority Postgraduate Scholarship Program is announced. The scholarships are presented to minority senior students pursuing a graduate degree in athletics administration. The initial six recipients (three men and three women) each received a $5,000 grant. The program is administered by the NACDA (National Association of Collegiate Directors of Athletics) Foundation.

2000, The CIAA (Central Intercollegiate Athletic Association) Hall of Fame, started in 1967, is renamed the John B. McLendon Hall of Fame.

2016, Cumberland Posey and John McLendon are inducted to the Naismith Memorial Basketball Hall of Fame. Posey is selected by the Early African American Pioneers Committee, while McLendon is inducted again, this time as a coach. McLendon is the first inductee to be honored as a contributor and coach. Cum Posey is the first man to be inducted into both the National Baseball Hall of Fame and the Naismith Memorial Basketball Hall of Fame.

2021, HBCU All-Stars LLC announces that the first Historically Black Colleges & Universities (HBCU) All-Star Game, a college basketball showcase highlighting the best HBCU players in the country, will be held at UNO Lakefront Arena in New Orleans in 2022. The game will feature the best talent from the four Historically Black Athletic Conferences, representing the legendary coaches Team John McLendon (MEAC & SIAC) versus and Team Clarence "Big House" Gaines (SWAC & CIAA) along with Tennessee State, Hampton, and North Carolina A&T State Universities.

MALCOLM MEEKS

1970, Forwards Steve Williams and Malcolm Meeks become the first African American basketball players at the University of Florida.

BUMPS MELVIN

1944, Forward Bill "Bumps" Melvin becomes the first African American on Canisius College's basketball team.

CHERYL MILLER

1982, Cheryl Miller becomes the first high school player, male or female, to be named *Parade* All-American for four straight years, 1978 to 1982.

1982, As a senior Cheryl Miller, for the Polytechnic High School Bears, she set a national record by scoring 105 points in Poly's 179–15 win over the Norte Vista Braves in Riverside, California. On that day, January 26, she becomes the first woman to dunk in a sanctioned league game.

1984, Cheryl Miller, of USC, is the first African American woman to win the Naismith Trophy. She would go on to win the trophy three times. She is the first female hoopster to grace the cover of *Sports Illustrated*.

1985, Cheryl Miller, of USC, is the first collegiate female basketball player to appear on the cover of *Sports Illustrated* (along with Bruce Dalrymple and Mark Price of Georgia Tech) in the magazine's *College Basketball Special Issue*, 1985/1986.

1986, Cheryl Miller is the first basketball player at USC, male or female, to have her jersey number retired, #31.

1997, Cheryl Miller becomes the first Black coach and general manager for the Phoenix Mercury of the WNBA.

1999, Lusia Harris-Stewart and Cheryl Miller are among the original inductees into the Women's Basketball Hall of Fame in Knoxville, Tenn.

2012, Reggie Miller is inducted into the Naismith Memorial Basketball Hall of Fame. Miller and his sister Cheryl (inducted in 1995) will become the only siblings in the Basketball Hall of Fame entering as players. [Note: Brothers Dick and Al McGuire are in the Basketball Hall of Fame as coaches. Paul and Lloyd Waner, and Rube and Willie Foster are the only brothers in the National Baseball Hall of Fame.]

REGGIE MILLER

2001, Reggie Miller of the Indiana Pacers becomes the first player to score more than 2,000 points with three pointers.

2012, Reggie Miller is inducted into the Naismith Memorial Basketball Hall of Fame. Miller and his sister Cheryl (inducted in 1995) will become the only siblings in the Basketball Hall of Fame entering as players. [Note: Brothers Dick and Al McGuire are in the Basketball Hall of Fame as coaches. Paul and Lloyd Waner, and Rube and Willie Foster are the only brothers in the National Baseball Hall of Fame.]

TORI MILLER

2020, Tori Miller becomes the first woman to hold the title of general manager in the history of the NBA's G League. She becomes GM of the College Park Skyhawks, affiliate of the Atlanta Hawks. A native of Decatur, Ga., Miller is a University of Miami graduate and spent time as a basketball operations intern for the Phoenix Suns prior to her time in the G League.

DAVAGE "DAVE" MINOR

1951, Don Barksdale and Davage "Dave" Minor become the first African Americans to play for an NBA team south of the Maxon-Dixon line, the Baltimore Bullets.

NED MITCHELL

1992, Lighting Ned Mitchell creates the Women's World Basketball Association (WWBA) the first ever spring and summer women's professional basketball league. The original teams included the Kansas Crusaders, Iowa Unicorns, Illinois Knights, Nebraska Xpress, Missouri Mustangs and the Oklahoma Cougars. The league lasts three seasons, 1993 through 1995.

CRAIG MOBLEY

1969, Honor student Craig Mobley, a 6-foot guard, becomes the first African American basketball player for Clemson University. Mobley appears in only 11 games for the Tigers before devoting time to his academic studies.

SIDNEY MONCRIEF

1982-83, Milwaukee Bucks guard Sidney Moncrief becomes the first player to win the NBA's Defensive Player of the Year award.

RENÉE MONTGOMERY

2021, Renée Montgomery becomes the first former player to become both an owner and executive of a WNBA franchise, the Atlanta Dream. Joining her as investors in the team are real estate investor Larry Gottesdiener and Suzanne Abair, president of Northland Investment Corporation in Massachusetts. The ownership change follows pressure on former Republican Senator Kelly Loeffler to sell her share of the Dream. Loeffler angered WNBA players by opposing the league's racial justice initiatives.

JACKIE MOORE

1954, Jackie Moore is the first African American to play for the NBA Milwaukee Hawks.

MAYA MOORE

2010, Maya Moore of the WNBA wins the ESPY Award for the Best Female College Athlete.
2011, The WNBA's Maya Moore of the Minnesota Lynx becomes the first woman to sign an endorsement contract with Nike's Jordan Brand. See 1995, Sheryl Swoopes.
2020, Maya Moore of the WNBA is listed in *Time* magazine's 100 Most Influential People of the year.

TAMARA MOORE

2020, Tamara Moore becomes the first African American woman to become a head coach of a men's collegiate basketball program in the U.S., at Mesabi Range College in Virginia, Minn. Moore played six seasons in the WNBA with the Houston Comets, Miami Sol, Minnesota Lynx, New York Liberty, Phoenix Mercury and the Los Angeles Sparks.

JA MORANT

2019, Ja Morant of Murray State, as a sophomore, becomes the first player in NCAA history to average at least 20 points and 10 assists per game in a single season.

CALVIN MURPHY

1981, Calvin Murphy becomes the first NBA player to make more than 95% of his free throws in a season. Murphy of the Houston Rockets compiles a .958 percentage.

Colorful Firsts in U.S. Sports

1983, Calvin Murphy becomes the first player shorter than 6 feet to appear in 1,000 NBA games.

DIKEMBE MUTOMBO

1992, Dikembe Mutombo, a Congolese American, is fined several thousand dollars for wagging his index finger at NBA opponents after blocking their shots. The NBA rules that the gesture by the Denver Nugget center is taunting. The four-time NBA Defensive Player of the Year is inducted into the Naismith Memorial Basketball Hall of Fame in 2015. Mutombo's jersey is retired by the Nuggets the following year.

WILLIE NAULLS

1956, Willie "The Whale" Naulls from UCLA is the first African American to play for the NBA St. Louis Hawks.

1964, The Boston Celtics become the first NBA franchise to start five Black players when Willie Naulls replaces the injured Tommy Heinsohn in the starting lineup. Naulls with Bill Russell, K. C. Jones, Sam Jones and Satch Sanders reel off 12 consecutive wins.

GARY NEAL

2007, Gary Neal from the Towson Tigers goes undrafted by the NBA. After spending seasons in Turkey, Spain and Italy, he becomes the first undrafted player selected to the NBA's All-Rookie first team as a San Antonio Spur in 2011 and joins Blake Griffin, John Wall, Landry Fields and DeMarcus Cousins.

ARIKE OGUNBOWALE

2022, Betnijah Laney of the New York Liberty, Diamond Deshields of the Phoenix Mercury and Arike Ogunbowale of the Dallas Wings appear on the cover of *WSLAM*, the first all-women issue of *SLAM* magazine.

CHINEY OGWUMIKE

2014, The Ogwumike sisters, Nneka in 2012 and Chiney in 2014 are the number one overall picks in the WNBA drafts, a first.

2014, Nneka and Chiney Ogwumike, become the first pair of sisters selected to a WNBA All-Star game. And the first sisters to win WNBA Rookie of the Year awards in 2012 and 2014, respectively.

2020, Chiney Ogwumike became the first Black woman and the first WNBA player to host a national daily radio sports-talk show for ESPN, "Chiney and Golie, Jr."

NNEKA OGWUMIKE

2014, The Ogwumike sisters, Nneka in 2012 and Chiney in 2014 are the number one overall picks in the WNBA drafts, a first.

2014, Nneka and Chiney Ogwumike, become the first pair of sisters selected to a WNBA All-Star game. And the first sisters to win WNBA Rookie of the Year awards in 2012 and 2014, respectively.

HAKEEM OLAJUWON

1994, Hakeem Olajuwon is the first player to win the NBA's Most Valuable Player, Finals MVP, and Defensive Player of the Year in the same season.

1999, Hakeem Olajuwon becomes the first NBA player to reach 2,000 steals and 2,000 blocked shots.

SHAQUILLE O'NEAL

1993, Shaquille O'Neal becomes the first NBA player to have a rap album, *Shaq Diesel*, to go platinum.

2001, The NBA allows zone defenses for the first time in its history, as possible alternative to stop the dominance of Shaquille O'Neal in the paint. O'Neal is also the first athlete to have an automobile named after him, the Ford Shaq SST Expedition. His name appears on a limited 500 SUVs.

EDWINA QUALLS

1976, Edwina Qualls, for the Wisconsin Badgers, becomes the first Black female head basketball coach in the Big Ten Conference.

VIOLET PALMER

1997, Dee Kantner and African American Violet Palmer become the first female officials in the NBA.

2006, Violet Palmer becomes the first woman to referee an NBA playoff game, when she officiates Game 2 of the first-round series between the Indiana Pacers and New Jersey Nets.

CANDACE PARKER

2004, The 6-foot-3 Naperville (Ill.) Central High School senior, Candace Parker becomes the first female to win the POWERade Jam Fest slam dunk competition held in conjunction with the McDonald's All-American Games. She beats out several male competitors, including Josh Smith, Darius Washington, and J.R. Smith.

2006, Candace Parker, a red-shirted athlete, becomes the first woman to dunk in an NCAA Tournament game, jamming a one-hander on a breakaway early in a Tennessee (102) victory over Army (54). She does another dunk later in the game, finishing with 26 points.

2008, Candace Parker of the Los Angeles Sparks becomes the first player to win the WNBA Rookie of the Year Award, the league's Most Valuable Player Award and an Olympic gold medal, in Beijing, in the same season. Parker signs a signature shoe contract with Adidas.

2022, Candace Parker becomes the first female on the cover of the video game NBA-2K22 in celebration of the 25th anniversary of the WNBA. The Chicago Sky star becomes the first WNBA player to eclipse 6,000 points, 3,000 rebounds and 1,500 assists.

COURTNEY PARIS

2006, Courtney Paris, center for Oklahoma University, becomes the first frosh selected for the *Associated Press'* All-America women's basketball team.

2009, Courtney Paris, center for the University of Oklahoma Sooners, is the first NCAA player to block at least 100 shots in each of her four years in college. Paris is the first player to make All-American teams all four years.

RICH PAUL

2021, Rich Paul, founder and CEO of Klutch Sports Groups, becomes the first player agent to have a signature shoe, the New Balance 550.

TOM PAYNE JR.

1969, Tom Payne Jr. becomes Adolph Rupp's first-ever African American player at the University of Kentucky. At 7 feet, 2 inches Payne is the tallest player recruited by the Wildcats.

CAROL PECK

1999, Carolyn Peck, Purdue basketball coach, is named winner of the John & Nellie Wooden Award, Big 10 Coach of the Year and the *Associated Press'* Coach of the Year. This year she becomes the first African American coach to win the NCAA women's basketball championship.

JULIUS PEGUES

1955, Julius Pegues from Tulsa, Okla., becomes the first African American basketball player for the University of Pittsburgh Panthers.

KIM PERROT

2000, Kim Perrot, No. 10, formerly of the Houston Comets, becomes the first WNBA player to have her jersey retired. The league names its sportsmanship award for her after Perrot dies of lung cancer in 1999. She is the first active WNBA player to die.

TERESA PHILLIPS

2003, Teresa Phillips, Tennessee State University athletic director, becomes the first woman to coach a men's Division I college basketball team. Phillips suspends interim coach Hosea Lewis for one game and announces she will coach the Tigers against Austin Peay in Clarksville, Tenn.

KEVIN PORTER

1979, Detroit Piston guard Kevin Porter becomes the first player to pass out 1,000 assists (1,099) in a season.

CUM POSEY

1909, Cumberland Posey Jr. becomes the first colored student-athlete at Penn State. He plays on the freshman and varsity basketball teams and the freshman baseball team in 1910.

1910, Cumberland Posey forms an all-Black basketball team, the Monticello Athletic Association in Pittsburgh. The team defeats the Howard University team, 24-19, to claim the unofficial 1911-12 World's Colored Basketball Championship.

1913, Cumberland Posey Jr. forms a new basketball team, the Loendi Big Five, named after the prestigious Loendi Social Club in Pittsburgh, Pa. The club was known for its social group the FROGS, an acronym for Friendly Rivalry Often Generates Success, the light-skinned elites of Black society.

1920, The Loendi Big Five, managed by Cumberland Posey win the Colored Basketball World Championships, the first of four consecutive seasons from 1920 to 1923.

2016, Cumberland Posey and John McLendon are inducted to the Naismith Memorial Basketball Hall of Fame. Posey is selected by the Early African American Pioneers Committee, while McLendon is inducted again, this time as a coach. McLendon is the first inductee to be honored as a contributor and coach. Cum Posey is the first man to be inducted into both the National Baseball Hall of Fame and the Naismith Memorial Basketball Hall of Fame.

STEPHANIE READY

2001, Stephanie Ready is named the first woman to coach in men's professional sports, as assistant coach for the Greenville Groove of the National Basketball Development League (NBDL), the NBA's new minor league.

WILLIS REED

1970, Willis Reed of the New York Knicks is the first player named the Most Valuable Player in the NBA All-Star game, MVP in the playoffs and MVP of the league, in the same season.

2022, The NBA creates division championship trophies named after African American pioneers of the game. The Pacific Division winner receives the Chuck Cooper Trophy. The Central Division winner receives the Wayne Embry Trophy. The Southwest Division winner receives the Willis Reed Trophy. The Atlantic Division winner receives the Nat "Sweetwater" Clifton Trophy. The Southeast Division winner receives the Earl Lloyd Trophy. The Northwest Division winner receives the Sam Jones Trophy.

TRACY REID

1998, Tracy Reid of the Charlotte Sting wins the WNBA's first Rookie of the Year Award.

GEORGE REVELING

1969, George Reveling joins the coaching staff of Lefty Driesell with the University of Maryland Terrapins, becoming the first Black assistant coach in the Atlantic Coast Conference (ACC).

1972, George Reveling is named head basketball coach at Washington State University, becoming the first Black coach in the Pacific-8 (now Pac-12) Conference. He guides the Cougars to two NCAA tournament appearances during his 11-year tenure.

NOLAN RICHARDSON

1980, Nolan Richardson coaches Western Texas Junior College to the National Junior College Basketball Championship.

1983, Nolan Richardson leads the University of Tulsa to the NIT championship.

1994, Nolan Richardson coaches the Arkansas Razorbacks to victory over the Duke Blue Devils to win the NCAA basketball title. He becomes the first coach to win championships in the NJC, NIT and the NCAA.

DICK RICKETTS

1955, Ed Fleming (from Niagara University), Dick Ricketts (Duquesne) and Maurice Stokes (Saint Francis) are the first African Americans to play for the Rochester Royals.

1955, Dick Ricketts from Duquesne University is the first Black to be chosen as the overall number one pick in the NBA draft by the St. Louis Hawks. Ricketts also signs with the baseball St. Louis Cardinals and joins the parent club in 1959.

DOC RIVERS

2000, Glenn "Doc" Rivers, coach of the Orlando Magic, becomes the first coach in NBA history to win the Red Auerbach Trophy (Coach of the Year) without his team going to the playoffs. The Magic finish with a surprising 41-41 won-lost record. Rivers gets 60 votes to beat Phil Jackson of the Los Angeles Lakers with 53 votes. Other vote-getters include Paul Silas (Charlotte) with three, Jerry Sloan (Utah) with two and Pat Riley (Miami), Scott Skiles (Phoenix) and Butch Carter (Toronto) with one vote each for the award first given in 1963.

MICHELE A. ROBERTS

2014, Attorney Michele A. Roberts is named executive director of the National Basketball Players' Association and becomes the first woman to head a major professional sports union in North America. In 2020, she had "Black Lives Matter" painted on NBA courts to promote racial harmony.

ALVIN ROBERTSON

1986, Alvin Robertson, for San Antonio, becomes the first NBA player with more than 300 steals (301) in a season.

1986, Alvin Robertson becomes the first guard to record a quadruple-double (double digits in four statistical categories in a single game) when he registers 20 points, 11 rebounds, 10 assists, and 10 steals while playing for the San Antonio Spurs against the Phoenix Suns on February 18.

OSCAR ROBERTSON

1958, Oscar Robertson becomes the first player to score more than 50 points in an NCAA playoff game. Robertson scores 56, as Cincinnati defeats Arkansas in the Southeast Regional.

1959, Basketball point guard Oscar Robertson of the Cincinnati Bearcats is the first player to be named College Player of the Year. Robertson captures this honor again the following season. In 1998, the award is renamed the Oscar Robertson Trophy.

1961, Oscar Robertson becomes the first African American basketball player to appear on the cover of *Time* magazine.

1962, Oscar Robertson becomes the first NBA player to average more than 10 assists (11.4) per game.

1962, Oscar Robertson becomes the first NBA player to average a triple-double in a season. He averages 30.8 points (3rd in the NBA), 11.4 assists and 12.5 rebounds (8th) per game.

1965, Oscar Robertson becomes the first African American president of any national sports or entertainment labor union, the National Basketball Players Association (NBPA). He served until his retirement in 1974.

1971, Lew Alcindor and Oscar Robertson of the Milwaukee Bucks appear on the cover of the first issue of *Black Sports* magazine. Founded by Allan P. Barron, it is the first major sports magazine aimed at African Americans. The last issue was published in June 1978.

1998, Oscar Robertson is honored when the U.S. Basketball Writers Association renames its Player of the Year Award, the "Oscar Robertson Trophy."

ROCKY ROBESON

1943, Rudolph "Rocky" Robeson, for the North Carolina College for Negroes (now North Carolina Central University) becomes the first African American hoopster to break a national college record, when he scores 58 points against Shaw University of Raleigh N.C. to break Stanford forward Hank Luisetti's record of 50 points set in 1938.

CRYSTAL ROBINSON

1996-97, Crystal Robinson with the Colorado Xplosion of the women's American Basketball League is named its first Rookie of the Year.

DAVID ROBINSON

1989-90, David Robinson of the San Antonio Spurs becomes the first NBA rookie to lead a playoff team in scoring. He averages 24.3 points, 12 rebounds and 3.9 blocks per game.

2002, Jerry Stackhouse wins the first Bob Lanier Community Assist Award for community engagement, philanthropic activity and charity work. This is a monthly award. The winner of the award is presented with a plaque dedicated to NBA Hall of Famer David Robinson.

WILL ROBINSON

1970, Will Robinson becomes the first African American head coach in NCAA Division I history when he coaches the basketball team at Illinois State University.

Colorful Firsts in U.S. Sports

DENNIS RODMAN

1996, Dennis Rodman of the Chicago Bulls becomes the first basketball player to make Mr. Blackwell's list of "Worse Dressed Women." Richard Blackwell calls Rodman a "unisex wreck."

BILL RUSSELL

"My most prized possession was my library card from the Oakland Public Library."

1955, Bill Russell of the San Francisco Dons is the first African American to be named MVP of the NCAA Final Four tournament.

1956, Bill Russell of the San Francisco Dons is the first African American to be named UPI's Division I Player of the Year. Russell, K. C. Jones and Carl Cain become the first African Americans named to the U.S. Olympic basketball team.

1958, Bill Russell becomes the first NBA player to average more than 20 rebounds (22.7) a game. He is also the first African American recipient of the NBA's Maurice Podoloff Trophy, its Most Valuable Player award.

1960, Bill Russell becomes the first NBA player to sport a goatee and the first NBA player to gather more than 50 (51) rebounds in a game.

1962, Bill Russell becomes the first NBA basketball player to win back-to-back MVP awards.

1963, Bill Russell of the Boston Celtics becomes the first NBA player to win the MVP award three consecutive years. He is also the first player to win the MVP award four times.

1963, Bill Russell of the Boston Celtics and Earl Wilson of the Boston Red Sox, pay homage to Civil Rights leader Medgar Evers assassinated in Jackson, Mississippi. Wilson and Russell circulate among the estimated 1,800 people gathered at the Parkman Bandstand on the Boston Common, to collect funds.

1965, Bill Russell becomes the first NBA player to win five MVP awards.

1966, Bill Russell is named head coach of the Boston Celtics, becoming the first African American coach in the NBA and the third (John McLendon was the second in 1962, while Pop Gates was first in 1949) in pro basketball.

1968, Bill Russell (in his second season) becomes the first Black coach to win an NBA championship.

1972, In a private ceremony, Bill Russell's jersey No. 6 is retired. About a dozen former teammates and friends attend. Earlier, his teammate Tom Heinsohn said two White sportswriters from Boston told him they would not vote Russell the league's MVP because he was Black. Considering the racial attitude of Boston, Russell elected to have a private ceremony.

1975, Bill Russell, in his first year of eligibility, is voted into the Naismith Memorial Basketball Hall of Fame. He is the first African American player inducted. The five-time NBA MVP awardee refuses induction without an explanation.

1980, Bill Russell is declared "The Greatest Player in the History of the NBA" by the Professional Basketball Writers Association of America.

1999, After more than 27 years, the Boston Celtics hold a public ceremony to retire jersey No. 6 of Hall of Fame center Bill Russell. Back in 1972, a private ceremony was held to retire his jersey because of the fear of racial repercussions in predominately White Boston.

2011, Bill Russell is presented with the Presidential Medal of Freedom by President Barack Obama, the highest civilian award.

2020, The "Russell Rule," the first of its kind to be adopted by a Division I conference, stipulates that each school in the West Coast Conference (WCC) must include a member of a traditionally underrepresented community in the pool of final candidates for every athletic director, senior administrator, head coach and full-time assistant coach position in the athletic department. Bill Russell, an 11-time NBA Champion, a two-time NCAA Champion and a Presidential Medal of Honor recipient as a life-long advocate for social justice, embraced the opportunity to promote equitable opportunities in college athletics.

2022, The NBA honors the life and legacy of 11-time NBA champion and civil rights pioneer Bill Russell by permanently retiring his No. 6, throughout the league, the first player to be so honored. In addition, all NBA players wear a commemorative patch on the right shoulder of their jerseys, and every NBA court displays a clover-shaped logo with the No. 6 on the sideline near the scorer's table.

RALPH SAMPSON

1983, Ralph Sampson of the Houston Rockets becomes the NBA's first rookie millionaire and the league's first unanimous Rookie of the Year selection.

SATCH SANDERS
1964, The Boston Celtics become the first NBA franchise to start five Black players when Willie Naulls replaced the injured Tommy Heinsohn in the starting lineup. Naulls with Bill Russell, K. C. Jones, Sam Jones and Satch Sanders reel off 12 consecutive wins.

CHARLIE SCOTT
1966, Charlie Scott becomes the first African American player to receive a basketball scholarship from the University of North Carolina at Chapel Hill. The Tar Heel is named first-team All-American twice. Scott would win an Olympic gold medal in 1968, spend a season with the Virginia Squires (ABA), where he would be named Rookie of the Year, and eventually is drafted by the Boston Celtics.

OSCAR SCOTT
1972, Oscar Scott becomes the first African American basketball player for the University of Citadel Bulldogs in Charleston, S.C.

RAY SCOTT
1973-74, Ray "Chink" Scott of the Detroit Pistons is the first African American to be named Coach of the Year in the NBA, receiving the Arnold "Red" Auerbach Trophy. Midway through the 1975-76 season, Scott is fired with a 17-25 won-lost record.

ENTEE SHINE
1951, Joe Bertrand from Chicago, Ill. and Entee Shine from South Bend, Ind. become the first African Americans on Notre Dame's basketball team. Shine plays one season; Bertrand four years.

IMAN SHUMPERT
2021, Iman Shumpert is the first NBA player to win the "Dancing with the Stars" competition. Teaming with dancer Daniella Karagach, they posted two perfect 40 scores in two dances, a cha-cha-cha-foxtrot fusion and a freestyle dance. See Emmitt Smith, 2006.

GARFIELD SMITH
1964, Garfield Smith, a member of Eastern Kentucky University's All-Century team, becomes its first African American basketball player. He is named Ohio Valley Conference's Freshman Center of the Year for the 1964-65 season.

SAM SMITH
1962, Wade Houston, Eddie Whitehead and Sam Smith become the first African American basketball players at the University of Louisville.

MICHELLE SNOW
2000, Tennessee's Michelle Snow, a 6-foot-5 center, becomes the third woman to dunk in a collegiate game. She repeats the feat in 2001 and 2003. Snow later plays for the WNBA's Houston Comets.

FRED "THE FOX" SNOWDEN
1972, Fred "The Fox" Snowden becomes the first African American head coach at a major White university and the second African American head coach at a Division I school, following Illinois State's Will Robinson, when he accepts a position at the University of Arizona. Snowden is the first African American coach to have a major college team finish in a final wire-service Top 20 poll at the 17th position by UPI.

LaVANNES SQUIRES
1950, LaVannes Squires becomes the first African American male basketball player at the University of Kansas. He earns KU's frosh basketball honors in 1950-51 and later plays on the 1952 NCAA championship team coached by Phog Allen.

JERRY STACKHOUSE
2002, Jerry Stackhouse wins the first Bob Lanier Community Assist Award for community engagement, philanthropic activity and charity work. This is a monthly award. The winner of the award is presented with a plaque dedicated to NBA Hall of Famer

David Robinson.

DAWN STALEY

2004, Dawn Staley is the first WNBA player to bear the U.S. flag at the Olympic Games in Athens, Greece.

2006, Candice Dupree, a Temple Owl, is the first WNBA player to compete against her college coach, Dawn Staley. Staley's final WNBA season was Dupree's first. Staley's Houston Comets defeat Dupree's Chicago Sky, 71-60.

2021, Dawn Staley of the South Carolina Gamecocks and Adia Barnes of the Arizona Wildcats become the first African American head coaches with teams in the Final Four of the NCAA women's basketball tournament. Staley and Barnes are both former WNBA players.

2021, Dawn Staley is the first person to guide an Olympic basketball team to a gold medal as both a player and a coach. As a player in the 1996, 2000 and 2004 Olympics and as a coach in the 2021 Tokyo Olympics.

JOHN STARKS

1994, Oklahoma State shooting guard John Starks is the first undrafted player selected to an NBA All-Star game.

LOWELL STEWARD

1937, Lowell Steward, a childhood friend of Jackie Robinson, becomes the first Black captain of the Santa Barbara State College Gauchos basketball team. He guides the Gauchos to the semifinals of the 1941 NAIA Division I Men's Tournament but is not allowed to play because of his race. Steward later became a member of the Tuskegee Airmen and receives the Distinguished Flying Cross, and the Congressional Gold Medal.

VALERIE STILL

1996-97, Valerie Still with the Columbus Quest of the women's American Basketball League is named its first ABL Finals MVP.

MAURICE STOKES

1955, Ed Fleming (from Niagara University), Dick Ricketts (Duquesne) and Maurice Stokes (Saint Francis) are the first African Americans to play for the Rochester Royals.

1956, Maurice Stokes of the Rochester Royals becomes the first NBA player to lead his team in points (16.6), rebounds (16.3) and assists (4.9), the same season.

1957, Before the era of Wilt Chamberlain and Bill Russell dominating the boards, Maurice Stokes is the first African American to lead the NBA in rebounding. African Americans will continue to win this category for the next 20 years. Bill Walton (14.4 rpg) breaks the string during the 1976-77 season.

1994, DeGol Arena, a 3,500-seat multi-purpose facility is named in honor of former Saint Francis and three-time NBA All-Star Maurice Stokes in Loretto, Pa. It is home to the Saint Francis University Red Flash men's and women's basketball and volleyball teams.

AMAR'E STOUDEMIRE

2003, Amar'e Stoudemire, for the Phoenix Suns, becomes the first NBA Rookie of the Year to come directly from high school.

VIVIAN STRINGER

1982, Vivian Stringer, coach of Cheyney State, a Division II team, is the first African American woman to take a team to the NCAA basketball tournament. Cheyney State loses the championship game to Louisiana Tech. Stringer is named *Sports Illustrated's* Coach of the Year.

1988, Vivian Stringer, coach for the University of Iowa, wins the Women's Basketball Coaches Association's Coach of the Year Award.

2000, Vivian Stringer takes her Rutgers Scarlet Knights to the NCAA Final Four, becoming the first coach in either men's or women's collegiate basketball to take three different schools to the Final Four. In 1972, she took Cheyney State, an historically Black college outside of Philadelphia, to the Final Four. In 1993, she led the University of Iowa Hawkeyes to a Final Four appearance.

2002, The U.S. Sports Academy creates the C. Vivian Stringer Coaching Award, presented annually to a woman for outstanding achievement as a coach.

2007, Vivian Stringer, coach of Rutgers University, is the first African American coach to take a women's team to the NCAA basketball finals.

2007, CBS Radio fires "shock jock" Don Imus from his radio show after derogatory comments about Rutgers women's basketball team. A member of the National Broadcaster Hall of Fame and named by *Time* magazine as one of the 25 Most Influential People in America, Imus called the ladies of the team "nappy-headed hos." Several sponsors, including American Express Co., Sprint Nextel Corp., Staples Inc., Procter & Gamble Co., and General Motors Corp. pull ads from Imus' show indefinitely.

2009, Charlaine Vivian Stringer is the first African American female coach inducted into the Naismith Memorial Basketball Hall of Fame. She is the first coach, male or female, to take three different schools (Cheyney State Wolves, Iowa Hawkeyes and Rutgers Scarlet Knights) to the NCAA's Final Four.

2022, After 50 years of coaching, Vivian Stringer announces her retirement. With 1,055 wins, Stringer is the first Black Division I coach (men's or women's) to reach the 1000-win milestone. Rutgers Scarlet Knights will name the basketball court at Jersey Mike's Arena the "C. Vivian Stringer Court."

DEBRA STROMAN

1978, Debra Stroman becomes the first African American woman to receive a basketball scholarship at the University of Virginia.

SHERYL SWOOPES

1991, Sheryl Swoopes from South Plains Junior College (Texas) is named Junior College Player of the Year.

1995, Sheryl Swoopes becomes the first woman to have her own signature basketball shoe called Air Swoopes by Nike. She would also have signature models: Air Swoopes II, Air Swoopes Zoom, Air Swoopes IV, Air Tuned Swoopes, Air Swoopes VI and Air Swoopes Premier.

1996, Sheryl Swoopes and Rebecca Lobo are the first players to sign contracts with the Women's National Baseball Association (WNBA).

1999, Sheryl Swoopes of the Houston Comets records the first triple-double in WNBA history. Swoopes gets 14 points, 15 rebounds and 10 assists in the Comets win over the Detroit Shock.

MIKE TAYLOR

2008, Mike Taylor becomes the first player in NBA history to be drafted out of the D-League. Portland acquires the 55th pick from the Phoenix Suns via the Indiana Pacers to select Taylor. However, he is traded to the Los Angeles Clippers on draft night in exchange for a future second-round draft pick and signs with the team on July 15.

SEBASTIAN TELFAIR

2002, Sebastian Telfair from Abraham Lincoln High School in Brooklyn, N.Y., and LeBron James from St. Vincent-St. Mary High School in Akron, Ohio, are the first high school basketball players to appear on the cover of *SLAM* magazine.

COLLIS TEMPLE JR.

1971, Collis Temple Jr. from Kentwood, La., is the first African American varsity basketball player at Louisiana State University (LSU). When he joins the team, the U.S. National Guard is called to protect him from alt-right segregationists. Temple later plays for the San Antonio Spurs and two of his sons will play basketball for LSU.

ISIAH THOMAS

"I've always believed no matter how many shots I miss, I'm going to make the next one."

1994, Former basketball guard Isiah Lord Thomas buys a nine percent interest in the Toronto Raptors for $11.25 million, becomes the first African American NBA owner.

1997, Isiah Thomas sells his nine percent stake in the Toronto Raptors to majority owner Allan Slaight. Thomas had tried to buy out Slaight, but Slaight demanded $175 million for his 81% share. According to John Hall of J.P. Morgan, the Raptors are worth about $135 million. Thomas realizes a nifty 15% annualized return on his investment.

1999, Former Detroit Piston guard and Toronto Raptors executive Isiah Thomas buys the CBA (Continental Basketball Association) for $10 million. In 2001, the league is forced into bankruptcy and folds.

AMEN and AUSR THOMPSON

2023, The Houston Rockets select Amen XLNC Thompson at No. 4, and the Detroit Pistons select Ausar XLNC Thompson at No. 5. The Thompson twins become the first brothers to be drafted in the top five of the same draft since the 1976 ABA-NBA merger.

DAVID THOMPSON

1975, David Thompson becomes the first number one pick by the NBA (Atlanta Hawks) to sign with an ABA team, the Denver Nuggets.

1979, David Thompson of the Denver Nuggets is named the Most Valuable Player in the NBA All-Star game. He becomes the only player in pro basketball to be named All-Star MVP in both the NBA and the ABA (in 1976).

JOHN THOMPSON JR. and III

1984, John Thompson becomes the first African American basketball head coach to win the NCAA Division I title, coaching the Georgetown Hoyas to a win over the Houston Cougars.

1985, John Thompson, of Georgetown University, is named Coach of the Year by the National Association of Basketball Coaches.

1987, John Thompson of the Georgetown Hoyas is named United Press International's NCAA Coach of the Year.

1990, Georgetown basketball coach John Thompson stages a walkout in protest of the National Collegiate Athletic Association's Proposal 42. The NCAA's Proposal 48 sets minimum academic standards for incoming frosh athletes at 700 on the SAT and a 2.0 grade point average. Proposal 42 states that if an athlete does not meet the guidelines of Proposal 48, he or she must sit out the frosh season, leaving only three years of eligibility. Opponents argue Proposal 48's minimum test-score requirements are based on culturally biased standardized tests. The NCAA estimates that nine of every 10 athletes who fail to meet the requirements are Black. Thompson claims that Prop 42 exacerbates the injustice by denying many athletes from low-income families the opportunity to attend college.

2007, John Thompson III, coach of the Georgetown Hoyas basketball team, defeat the North Carolina Tar Heels sending his team to the Final Four in Atlanta, Ga. The win becomes an historic first for a father (John Jr.) and a son to take different Georgetown teams to the Final Four in NCAA history. However, John III's Hoyas lose to Greg Oden and Ohio State University, 67-60 in the semi-finals. The Hoyas finish the season at 30-7.

2021, The Capital One Arena, the home floor of Georgetown University, is renamed the John Thompson, Jr. Court. The Big East Conference also awards the first John Thompson Jr. Award "to recognize significant efforts to fight prejudice and discrimination and advance positive societal change" to Georgetown University.

MYCHAL THOMPSON

1978, Minnesota Gopher center Mychal Thompson from Nassau, Bahamas, is the first foreign-born player drafted number one overall by the NBA, when selected by the Portland Trail Blazers. His son Klay later plays in the NBA.

TINA THOMPSON

1997, Tina Thompson, forward from USC, is the first overall pick in the inaugural WNBA collegiate draft, by the Houston Comets.

2013, Tina Thompson becomes the first WNBA player to compile 7,000 points and 3,000 rebounds in a career. Selected to her ninth all-star appearance, Thompson becomes the first and only player in WNBA history to be named an All-Star in three different decades.

NATE THURMOND

1974, Nate Thurmond records the first quadruple-double in NBA history. As a Chicago Bull he scores 22 points, gathers 14 rebounds, passes out 13 assists and blocks 12 shots.

WAYMAN TISDALE

1983, Wayman Tisdale becomes the first frosh to be named unanimous All-American.

1985, Wayman Tisdale becomes the first and only college basketball player to be named consensus All-American by the *Associated Press* in each of his first three years, as an Oklahoma Sooner.

Basketball Champions

NORWOOD TODMANN

1966, Norwood Todmann from New York City becomes the first African American scholarship basketball player at Wake Forest. Todmann had played at Power Memorial Academy where the 6-foot-3 guard broke the single-game and single-season scoring records of center Lew Alcindor.

ED TUCKER

1950, Ed Tucker becomes the first African American basketball player for Stanford University. Upon graduation in 1952, Tucker enters medical school and becomes an obstetrician-gynecologist.

JIM TUCKER

1955, Earl Lloyd and Jim Tucker for the Syracuse Nationals become the first African Americans to play on an NBA championship team when they defeat the Fort Wayne Pistons.

MASAI UJIRI

2020, Toronto Raptors' president, Nigerian-Canadian Masai Ujiri, attempts to enter the court as his Raptors defeat the Golden State Warriors to win the NBA championship, when he is blocked by a San Francisco Bay Area police officer, Alan Strickland. Body cam footage shows the officer shoving Ujiri twice as he attempts to show his access credentials.

WESLEY UNSELD

1966-67, Western Kentucky's Clem Haskins, Houston's Elvin Hayes and Louisville's Wes Unseld become the first African Americans from Southern schools to be named to the first NCAA All-American team.

1975, Washington Bullets center Wes Unseld becomes the first player to win the J. Walter Kennedy Citizenship Award.

TERDEMA USSERY II

1991, Terdema Ussery II becomes CEO of the Continental Basketball Association (CBA). He is the first African American to operate a professional sports league. Ussery's two-and-a-half-year term was highlighted by a rapid increase in franchise value and overall league-wide financial stability.

BOB WADE

1986, Bob Wade, legendary coach from Dunbar High School in Baltimore, becomes the first African American head coach in the Atlantic Coast Conference, (ACC) when he is named basketball coach at the University of Maryland, following the untimely death of All-American forward Len Bias and the resignation of 17-year-veteran coach Lefty Driesell.

CLARENCE WALKER

1948, The NAIB (later the NAIA) admits the first African American player, Clarence Walker from coach John Wooden's Indiana State Teachers College team to its tournament. Walker becomes the first African American player to participate in a national college basketball championship at any level.

SOLLY WALKER

1951, Solly Walker, guard for St. John's University, becomes the first Black player to play in an integrated college basketball game at the University of Kentucky. Walker hits six of his first seven shots before leaving game due to a body blow, sidelining him for weeks.

BEN WALLACE

2003, Detroit Pistons defensive specialist Ben Wallace, a product of Cuyahoga Community College and Virginia Union, is the first undrafted NBA player selected to its All-Star game, as a starter.

2021, Ben Wallace becomes the first undrafted player in NBA history to be inducted into the Naismith Memorial Basketball Hall of Fame.

PERRY WALLACE

1967, Perry Eugene Wallace becomes the first African American scholarship basketball player in the Southeastern Conference (SEC) with Vanderbilt University. Wallace graduates with a degree in engineering and later earns his J.D. from Columbia University.

Colorful Firsts in U.S. Sports

A movie about his life *Triumph: The Untold Story of Perry Wallace* debuts in 2017.

CHARLIE WARD JR.

1994, Florida State quarterback Charlie Ward is the first Heisman winner to be selected in the first round (26th pick) of the NBA draft by the New York Knicks. He plays 11 seasons in the NBA.

MARIAN WASHINGTON

1973, Marian Washington becomes the first African American coach in the Big Eight (now the Big 12) Conference, when she is named the head women's basketball coach at the University of Kansas. She was later named the school's first and only director of intercollegiate athletics for women's sports in 1974.

1982, Marian Washington becomes the first African American woman to be the head coach of a U.S. team in international play when she guides the U.S. Select Team to a basketball silver medal in Taiwan.

ORA MAE WASHINGTON

1928, Walter Green, of Chicago, starts the Savoy Colts, a women's basketball team, managed by Dick Hudson. Their roster includes guards E. Williams, Blanche Winston, Corrine Robinson, forwards Lula Porter, Virginia Willis, H. Williams and famed Philadelphia tennis star Ora Washington at center.

1929, The Germantown Hornets, in Philadelphia, are formed by the YWCA Branch of Colored Girls and Women. The Hornets basketball team included Ora Washington, Lula Ballard, Louise Penn, Lil Fountainé, Helen Laws and Evelyn Manns.

1930, The Tribune Girls are sponsored by the *Philadelphia Tribune* newspaper. The players come from two Black female basketball teams, the Philadelphia Quick Steppers and the Germantown Hornets. Inez Patterson from the Quick Steppers becomes coach and player of the team. Two tennis players from the YWCA Colored Branch in Germantown, Ora Washington and Lula Ballard, become standout hoopsters.

FENWICK WATKINS

1908, The University of Vermont names its first African American captain of a basketball team, Fenwick Watkins. After graduating from Vermont, Watkins coaches football, basketball, and baseball at Fargo College in Fargo, N.D, where he also leads the athletic program.

TERESA WEATHERSPOON

1997, Teresa Weatherspoon becomes the first WNBA player to be named Defensive Player of the Week, averaging 21.5 ppg, 8.5 rpg, and 3.5 apg for the week ending 20 June 1997.

SPUD WEBB

1985, Diminutive Spud Webb, at 5-foot-7, becomes the first player under six feet to win the NBA Slam Dunk contest.

ERICA WHEELER

2019, Erica Wheeler, a guard out of Rutgers, becomes the first undrafted player to be named WNBA All-Star MVP. She scores 25 points in the game.

GEORGEANN WELLS

1984, Georgeann Wells, a 6-foot-7 center for the West Virginia Mountaineers, becomes the first woman to dunk in an official game. Wells' dunk occurs against Charleston, en route to a 110-82 victory.

JACKIE WHITE

1966, Jackie White is the first African American to officiate an NBA game. He referees a game at the Cleveland Arena between the Chicago Bulls and the Cincinnati Royals. In 1968, Pittsburgh native Ken Hudson becomes the NBA's second African American referee.

EDDIE WHITEHEAD

1962, Wade Houston, Eddie Whitehead and Sam Smith become the first African American basketball players at the University of Louisville.

DAVEY WHITNEY

1979, The Alcorn Braves basketball team becomes the first historically Black institution invited to the NIT. The Braves are led by Davey Whitney, former Kansas City Monarch. His team defeats Mississippi State, 80-78 in the first round, before losing to Indiana, 72-68 in the second round.

1980, Davey Whitney, Alcorn Braves basketball coach, wins a game in the NCAA Tournament. Whitney's Braves become the first team from a historically Black college to win a game in the NIT (1979) and in the NCAA Tournament. The Braves defeat South Alabama, 70-62, before losing to LSU, 98-88 in the second round.

LENNY WILKENS

1998, Lenny Wilkens is selected to the Naismith Memorial Basketball Hall of Fame as a coach. Earlier, in 1989, he had been inducted as a player, thus making him the first "professional" to be inducted as both player and coach.

BOB WILLIAMS

1954, Former Florida A&M basketball star Bob Williams, at 6-foot-6, becomes the first African American on the Minneapolis Lakers.

JAYLIN WILLIAMS

2022, Jaylin Williams is the first player with Vietnamese heritage (Mom was born in Saigon, now Ho Chi Minh City) to be drafted into the NBA. The Oklahoma City Thunder pick him in the second round, the 34th overall pick.

LATAVIOUS WILLIAMS

2010, Latavious Williams, a small forward, becomes the first high school-to-NBDL (Tulsa 66ers)-to-NBA (Miami Heat) draft choice in history. His draft rights are immediately traded to the Oklahoma City Thunder.

NATALIE WILLIAMS

1998, Natalie Williams is the only woman to lead the ABL in rebounding and scoring in the same year. Williams beats out Yolanda Griffith for the MVP award in the ABL's last year of record. She is the daughter of Robyn Gray and Nate Williams who played eight seasons in the NBA for the Cincinnati Royals, Kansas City Kings, New Orleans Jazz and Golden State Warriors.

REGGIE WILLIAMS

1987, Muggsy Bogues (Wake Forest) at 5-foot-3 the smallest player in NBA history, is the 12th pick by the Charlotte Hornets. Bogues, along with Reggie Lewis (Northwestern, 22nd pick) and Reggie Williams (Georgetown, 4th pick) become the first trio of players from the same high school (Dunbar Poets, Baltimore, Md.) to be picked in the first round of the same year.

RIQUNA WILLIAMS

2013, At 5 feet 7 inches, Riquna "Bay Bay" Williams is the first WNBA player to score more than 50 points in a game. She scores 51 points for the Tulsa Shocks (now the Dallas Wings).

STEVE WILLIAMS

1970, Forwards Steve Williams and Malcolm Meeks become the first African American basketball players at the University of Florida.

BILL WILLOUGHBY

1975, Darryl Dawkins (Philadelphia 76ers) and Bill Willoughby (Atlanta Hawks) are the second and third high school basketball players to sign with NBA or ABA teams.

A'JA WILSON

2020, To pay respects to the late Breonna Taylor, the WNBA is the first professional league to dedicate a season to fight for social justice. A'ja Wilson and other players formed a Social Justice Council and wear warmups with "Say Her Name."

2021, A three-time first-team All-American (2014-2018), a three-time SEC Player of The Year and the WNBA's No. 1 draft pick in 2018, and later the league's Rookie of the Year and its MVP (2020), the Olympic gold medalist (2020), A'Ja Wilson is honored with a statue at the Colonial Life Arena on the University of South Carolina campus on MLK Day.

Colorful Firsts in U.S. Sports

ARTHUR WILSON
1942, Arthur Wilson is the first African American basketball player at Princeton University.

GENE WILSON
1951, Gene Wilson becomes the first African American basketball player for the Kansas State University Wildcats.

JOHNNY WILSON
1949, Jumpin' Johnny Wilson becomes the first Negro selected to the College All-Star basketball team, coached by Adolph Rupp. The collegians play George Mikan and the Minneapolis Lakers, losing 94-86, in Chicago.

MICHAEL "WILD THING" WILSON
2000, Harlem Globetrotter Michael "Wild Thing" Wilson becomes the first human to dunk a basketball on a 12-foot goal. The 6-foot-6 Wilson records the feat at the Ocean Spray NABC Roundball Challenge in Indianapolis, Ind.

LYNETTE WOODARD
"Records are made to be broken but records are also made to be honored."

1981, Lynette Woodard, of Kansas University, is the first African American woman to win the Wade Trophy, presented annually to the best women's basketball player in National Collegiate Athletic Association (NCAA) Division I. The trophy is named after the legendary Lily Margaret Wade, coach of three-time national champion Delta State University.

1981, Lynette Woodard becomes the first Kansas University woman to have her jersey number retired, No. 31. Upon retiring and before the three-point shot was initiated and women used the smaller basketball, Woodard becomes the all-time career scoring leader in the Association for Intercollegiate Athletes for Women (AIWA) with 3,649 points. Her record is not recognized by the NCAA.

1985, Lynette Woodard, a 1984 Olympian, becomes the first woman to play for the Harlem Globetrotters. She scores seven points in her debut.

TOMMY WOODS
1964, Tommy Woods becomes East Tennessee State University's first African American basketball athlete. ETSU's practice court is named in honor of this two-time All-Ohio Valley Conference selection. Woods later plays for the ABA's Kentucky Colonels.

LONNIE WRIGHT
1967, Lonnie Wright becomes one of the first players to play two professional sports in the same season. Wright played defensive back for the Denver Broncos in 1966-67 and guard for the Denver Rockets (later the Nuggets) from 1967 to 1970.

Cage 4OUR: Boxing Champions

"The failure to see color only benefits white America. A world without color is a world without racial debt."
— Michael Eric Dyson, *Tears We Cannot Stop: A Sermon to White America*

1882, George "Old Chocolate" Godfrey wins the first Colored Heavyweight Championship of America by knocking out Charles Hadley in round six. The referee John L. Sullivan, had refused to fight Godfrey at Bailey's Arena in South Boston, in 1881.

1886, Peter "The Black Prince" Jackson becomes the first African American to win a national boxing crown, when he becomes the Australian Heavyweight champion.

1890, George Dixon claims the World Bantamweight Championship in 1888 and was officially considered the champion after knocking out Nunc Wallace of England in 18 rounds on 27 June 1890. He was a Black Canadian professional boxer and the first Black world boxing champion in any weight class, while also being the first ever Canadian-born boxing champion.

1902, Joe Gans knocks out Frank Erne in the first round to become the first native-born African American to win a world lightweight championship.

1903, Jack Johnson defeats Canadian Tommy Burns, the Great White Hope, in Sydney, Australia to claim the World Heavyweight Championship.

1908, Jack Johnson knocks out Tommy Burns in Sydney, Australia, to become the world's first African American heavyweight champion. The fight lasted 14 rounds before being stopped by the police in front of over 20,000 spectators.

1910, In the "Fight of the Century," former undefeated heavyweight champion James J. Jeffries comes out of retirement to challenge heavyweight champion Jack Johnson, saying "I am going into this fight for the sole purpose of proving that a White man is better than a Negro." Reno, Nevada odds had Jeffries as a 10–7 favorite, but he loses in 15 rounds on a TKO. The outcome of the fight triggers race riots across the country. Many states ban the showing of the Johnson-Jeffries film.

1926, Tiger Flowers becomes the first African American boxer to capture the middleweight title by defeating Harry Greb in New York City.

1940, Jack Wilson, a bantamweight boxer, is the first African American to fight the main event at Hollywood Legion Stadium, when he defeats Tony Chavez.

1941, Joe Louis becomes the first African American to appear on the cover of *Time* magazine.

1944, Staff Sgt. Joe Louis and Sgt. Walker Smith (Sugar Ray Robinson) are jailed at Camp Sibert, Ala., for refusal to observe Jim Crow laws on the post. After participating in a camp show they enter the white section of the bus station to place a phone call for a taxi. There was no phone in the colored section. The camp was commanded by Gen. Haig Shekerjian, an Armenian-American, who ordered their release after several hours.

1950, Joe Louis retires from boxing. Louis holds the heavyweight title from 1937 to 1948.

1951, Jersey Joe Walcott defeats Ezzard Charles to win the heavyweight crown.

1952, Ed Sanders (super heavyweight), Nathan Brooks (flyweight), Charles Adkins (light welterweight), Norvel Lee (light heavyweight) and Floyd Patterson (middleweight) become Olympic African American gold medalists in boxing. Floyd Patterson later becomes the first Olympic gold medalist to win a world professional boxing title.

1952, Zach Clayton of Philadelphia becomes the first African American to referee a world heavyweight title fight. Jersey Joe Walcott fights Ezzard Charles in their fourth rematch in Philadelphia. Walcott wins a disputed 15-pound decision.

1955, Sugar Ray Robinson becomes the world middleweight champion.

1958, Wendell Smith becomes the first African American to provide radio commentary for a boxing championship match. The middleweight title fight is between Sugar Ray Robinson and Carmen Basilio at Chicago Stadium.

1973, Pearl Bailey becomes the first female boxing commentator, when she hosts the heavyweight championship fight in Kingston, Jamaica, between George Foreman and Joe Frazier.

1974, Don King is the first boxing promoter to offer a $10 million purse with his "Rumble In The Jungle" match between George Foreman and Muhammad Ali in Kinshasa, Republic of Zaire. This fight was refereed by Zach Clayton, a member of the Naismith Memorial Basketball Hall of Fame, and former Negro Baseball League first baseman.

1976, Leon Spinks becomes the first Marine to win a gold medal in Olympics boxing history.

1976, The Spinks brothers, Leon and Michael, win Olympic gold medals in boxing.

1984, Carmen Williamson becomes boxing's first African American referee and judge for the Los Angeles Olympics and is presented

Colorful Firsts in U.S. Sports

with an honorary gold medal. Born in 1925, Williamson was a 112-pound amateur flyweight boxer who compiled a 25-14 won-lost record.

1988, Boxer Roy Jones Jr, robbed of the gold, wins a highly controversial silver medal in the Olympics.

1990, The first African Americans named to the International Boxing Hall of Fame are: Joe Gans (inventor of the jab), Jack Johnson, Muhammad Ali, Henry Armstrong, Ezzard Charles, Bob Foster, Joe Frazier, Joe Louis, Sugar Ray Robinson, Sandy Saddler, Jersey Joe Walcott, Archie Moore and Ike Williams.

1996, Muhammad Ali lights the Olympic torch at the Summer Olympic Games in Atlanta, Ga.

1996, Roy Jones Jr. becomes the first man to played a pro basketball game (U.S. Basketball League) and fight for the world championship (IBF), as super middleweight, in the same day.

1997, Maurice Smith, a Seattle native, defeats UFC heavyweight champion Mark Coleman at UFC 14 in Birmingham to become the first Black title holder. In the process, the world champion kickboxer becomes the first striker to ever defeat a championship wrestler of Coleman's stature.

1997, Chris Campbell, a former Olympian wrestler, is named executive director of the U.S. Amateur Boxing, Inc. Campbell is the first African American to hold this post with USA Boxing.

2001, Laila Ali and Jacqueline Frazier-Lyde become the first women featured as the main event for a pay-for-view boxing match. This is the first time in boxing history, daughters of former heavyweight champions will fight.

2002, Jacqueline Frazier-Lyde beats Suzette Taylor to win the Women's International Boxing Association (WIBA) light heavyweight title. As the daughter of Smokin' Joe Frazier, the two become the first father and daughter to hold boxing titles.

2012, At the London Olympic Games in August, Claressa Shields becomes the first U.S. woman to win a boxing gold medal. The 165-pound Shields wins the Olympic middleweight title by defeating Russian boxer Nadezda Torlopova.

LAILI ALI
"Impossible is not a fact, it's an opinion."

1999, Laila Ali, 21, daughter of Muhammad, announces her decision to fight professionally. At 5-foot-10 and 160 pounds she will fight in the middleweight class. Ali wins her first fight with a knockout in the first round.

2001, Laila Ali and Jacqueline Frazier-Lyde become the first women featured as the main event for a pay-for-view boxing match. This is the first time in boxing history, daughters of former heavyweight champions will fight.

MUHAMMAD ALI
"Service to others is the rent you pay for your room in heaven."

1960, Cassius Clay wins a gold medal in the light heavyweight division at the Olympics.

1963, Five months before becoming heavyweight champion, Cassius Clay releases an album, "I Am the Greatest."

1964, A 7-1 underdog, Cassius Clay shocks the world when he knocks out Sonny Liston to win the heavyweight boxing title.

1965, Muhammad Ali knocks out Sonny Liston in the first round of their rematch in Lewiston, Maine with the infamous "phantom punch."

1966, Muhammad Ali, recently converted to the Muslim faith refuses to be drafted into the Army, citing his religious beliefs and how the war effort did not align with his faith. Ali is stripped of his heavyweight title.

1967, Muhammad Ali is given draft No. 15-47-42-127. Ali is stripped of his heavyweight title for refusing military induction and sentenced to five years in prison.

1971, Joe Frazier and Muhammad Ali become the first Black boxers to draw a multimillion dollar gate in their Madison Square Garden bout. Frazier wins the fight on points. The bout grosses $20 million with each fighter receiving $2.5 million.

1971, The Supreme Court overturns the 1967 conviction of Muhammad Ali's draft resistance, based on his Muslim beliefs.

1975, Muhammad Ali fights Chuck Wepner, billed as *Give the White Guy a Break* at the Richfield Coliseum in Summit County, Ohio. Ali is floored in the fight before knocking out Wepner in the 15th round. The fight inspires the 1976 film *Rocky*, which earns $225 million globally and 10 Academy Award nominations, winning three. The film spawns seven sequels.

1975, Muhammad Ali wins by technical knockout (TKO) over Joe Frazier in the 14th round in the "Thrilla in Manila" fight, in Quezon City, Philippines. It is their third and final boxing match.

1978, Muhammad Ali wins the heavyweight championship for an unprecedented third time by defeating Leon Spinks. The prizefight, held in the Louisiana Superdome, is the first to gross more than $5 million dollars.

1996, Muhammad Ali lights the Olympic torch at the Summer Olympic Games in Atlanta, Ga.

2005, Muhammad Ali and Frank Robinson are presented with the Presidential Medal of Freedom by President Geoge W. Bush, the highest civilian award.

2015, *Sports Illustrated* renames its Legacy Award the Muhammad Ali Legacy Award. The first awardee is golfer Jack Nicklaus. The annual honor is bestowed upon one athlete or former athlete that best embodies the ideals of sportsmanship, leadership and philanthropy as vehicles for changing the world.

HENRY ARMSTRONG

1938, Henry "Homicide Hank" Armstrong defeats Lou Ambers at Madison Square Garden to win the lightweight championship, making him the only fighter to hold world championships in three divisions (lightweight, featherweight and welterweight [126 to 147 pounds]), simultaneously.

1938, Henry "Hurricane Henry" Armstrong appears on the cover of *Newsweek* magazine.

AARON BROWN

1904, Aaron Brown becomes the first native-born African American to win the welterweight boxing title.

HURRICANE CARTER

1994, Rubin "Hurricane" Carter, middleweight, becomes the first boxer to receive a championship belt outside the ring when he was awarded an honorary title after serving nearly 20 years in prison on a wrongful murder conviction.

Colorful Firsts in U.S. Sports

ZACH CLAYTON

1952, Zach Clayton retired professional baseball and basketball player from Philadelphia, becomes the first African American to referee a world heavyweight title fight. Jersey Joe Walcott fights Ezzard Charles in their fourth rematch in Philadelphia. Walcott wins a disputed 15-pound decision.

CURTIS COKES

1966, Curtis Cokes defeats Manuel Gonzalez in New Orleans to win the vacant world welterweight title. Cokes is the first Harlem Clown basketball player to win a world boxing title.

GEORGE DIXON

1890, George Dixon claims the World Bantamweight Championship in 1888 and was officially considered the champion after knocking out Nunc Wallace of England in 18 rounds on 27 June 1890. He was a Black Canadian professional boxer and the first Black world boxing champion in any weight class, while also being the first ever Canadian-born boxing champion.

TIGER FLOWERS

1926, Tiger Flowers becomes the first African American boxer to capture the middleweight title by defeating Harry Greb in New York City.

GEORGE FOREMAN

"Being angry and resentful of someone is like letting them live rent-free in your head."

1994, George Foreman, 45, knocks out Michael Moorer to become the oldest heavyweight champion in history. Foreman wins the *Associated Press'* Athlete of the Year award.

JACQUELINE FRAZIER-LYDE

2001, Laila Ali and Jacqueline Frazier-Lyde become the first women featured as the main event for a pay-for-view boxing match. This is the first time in boxing history, daughters of former heavyweight champions will fight.

2002, Jacqueline Frazier-Lyde beats Suzette Taylor to win the Women's International Boxing Association (WIBA) light heavyweight title. As the daughter of Smokin' Joe Frazier, the two become the first father and daughter to hold boxing titles.

JOE FRAZIER

"Champions aren't made in the ring; they are merely recognized there.
What you cheat on in the early light of morning will show up in the ring under the bright lights."

1968, Smokin' Joe Frazier is crowned Heavyweight boxing champion, when Muhammad Ali is stripped of the title due to his religious convictions as a conscientious objector to the Vietnam war.

1970, After winning the heavyweight championship, Joe Frazier hits the road with a Memphis-style soul revue dubbed "Smokin' Joe & the Knockouts."

1971, Joe Frazier and Muhammad Ali become the first Black boxers to draw a multi-million dollar gate in their Madison Square Garden bout. Frazier wins the fight on points. The bout grossed $20 million with each fighter receiving $2.5 million.

JOE GANS

1902, Joe Gans knocks out Frank Erne in the first round to become the first native-born African American to win a world lightweight championship.

GEORGE GODFREY

1882, George "Old Chocolate" Godfrey wins the first Colored Heavyweight Championship of America by knocking out Charles Hadley in round six. The referee John L. Sullivan, had refused to fight Godfrey at Bailey's Arena in South Boston, in 1881.

MARVELOUS MARVIN HAGLER

"It's hard to get up at 6am when you're wearing silk pajamas."

1982, After 10 years of professional boxing and annoyed that network announcers often did not refer to him as "Marvelous," Hagler legally changed his name to "Marvelous Marvin Hagler," who reigned as the undisputed middleweight champion from 1980 to

1987.

PETER JACKSON

1886, Peter "The Black Prince" Jackson becomes the first African American to win a national boxing crown, when he becomes the Australian Heavyweight champion.

JACK JOHNSON

"I am going into this fight for the sole purpose of proving that a White man is better than a Negro."

- James J. Jeffries before the Fight of the Century.

1905, Future heavyweight boxing champion Jack Johnson organizes a semi-pro baseball team called the Johnson's Pets. Johnson plays first base.

1908, Jack Johnson knocks out Tommy Burns in Sydney, Australia, to become the world's first African American heavyweight champion (1908-1915). The fight lasts 14 rounds after being stopped by the police in front of more than 20,000 spectators.

1910, In the "Fight of the Century," former undefeated heavyweight champion James J. Jeffries comes out of retirement to challenge heavyweight champion Jack Johnson. Reno, Nevada odds had Jeffries as a 10–7 favorite, but he losses in 15 rounds on a TKO. The outcome of the fight triggers race riots across the country. Many states ban the showing of the Johnson-Jeffries film.

1922, Jack Johnson, boxing heavyweight champion, receives U.S. patent #1,413,121 for a wrench.

ROY JONES JR.

"I don't believe in luck. Luck is preparation meeting opportunity."

1996, Roy Jones Jr. becomes the first man to play a pro basketball game (U.S. Basketball League) and fight for the world championship (IBF), as super middleweight, in the same day. He was a forward on the North West Florida State Junior College basketball team.

DON KING

"Martin Luther King took us to the mountain top: I want to take us to the bank."

1974, Don King is the first boxing promoter to offer a $10 million purse with his "Rumble In The Jungle" match between George Foreman and Muhammad Ali in Kinshasa, Republic of Zaire. This fight was refereed by Zach Clayton, a member of the Naismith Memorial Basketball Hall of Fame.

BUBBLE KLICE

1970, Arrington "Bubble" Klice, a Golden Glove boxing coach for the Gateway Boxing Club in Kansas City, Mo., takes the first American boxing team to Russia.

SUGAR RAY LEONARD

"You have to know you can win. You have to think you can win. You have to feel you can win."

1988, With championships in the super middleweight and light heavyweight divisions, Sugar Ray Leonard becomes the first boxer to win titles in five divisions, a weight span of 28 pounds. He is also the welterweight (1979), junior middleweight (1981), and middleweight titleholder (1987).

JOHN HENRY LEWIS

1935, John Henry Lewis becomes the first African American boxer to win the light-heavyweight title.

1939, Joe Louis defeats John Henry Lewis to retain his heavyweight championship. This is the first time in boxing history, two Black men fought for the title. Louis is winner by a TKO in the first round.

SONNY LISTON

"Newspapermen ask dumb questions. They look up at the sun and ask if it is shining."

1963, In Las Vegas for the second Sonny Liston vs. Floyd Patterson fight, it becomes the first million-dollar purse with both fighters receiving $1,434,000 each. Patterson, a 4:1 betting underdog, is knocked down three times and counted out at 2:10 of the first round.

Colorful Firsts in U.S. Sports

JOE LOUIS
"Lots of things wrong with America, but Hitler ain't going to fix them."

1935, Joe Louis is the first African American winner of the *Associated Press'* Athlete of the Year.

1936, Joe Louis becomes the first African American voted Fighter of the Year by *Ring* magazine.

1937, Joe Louis defeats James J. Braddock and becomes the heavyweight champion of the world.

1938, Joe Louis defeats German boxer Max Schmeling in a rematch of their 1936 fight. Because of Hitler's disdain for Blacks, the fight becomes a political arena between democracy and Nazism. Louis strikes a blow for democracy, easily defeating Schmeling in the first round.

1939, The National Negro Bowling Association (NNBA) is created by Joe Louis and others, in Detroit, Mich., because of restrictive clauses by the American Bowling Congress (ABC) and the Women's International Bowling Congress (WIBC) of non-Caucasians.

1939, Joe Louis defeats John Henry Lewis to retain his heavyweight championship. This is the first time in boxing history that two African Americans fight for the title. Louis is the winner by a TKO in the first round.

1941, Joe Louis becomes the first African American to appear on the cover of *Time* magazine.

1950, Joe Louis retires from boxing. Louis holds the heavyweight title from 1937 to 1948.

1952, Joe Louis, as an amateur, becomes the first African American to play in a PGA sponsored tournament, the San Diego Open.

1993, Joe Louis becomes the first professional boxer to be honored on a U.S. postage stamp.

ARCHIE MOORE
"I'm like the drunk in the bar who wants just one more for the road."

1952, Archie Moore wins the light heavyweight title. He begins the longest reign of any light heavyweight champion, nine years and one month (December 1952 to February 1962).

1963, The "Old Mongoose" Archie Moore retires with the most knockouts (130) of any light heavyweight champion.

MICHAEL MOORER
"It is over with; I am in the history books."

1994, Michael Moorer becomes the first southpaw heavyweight boxing champion when he defeats Evander Holyfield, gaining a majority decision.

FLOYD PATTERSON
"For if you train hard and responsibly your confidence surges to a maximum."

1956, Floyd Patterson becomes the first professional African American boxer to appear on the cover of *Sports Illustrated*.

1956, Floyd Patterson becomes the first former Olympian (1952) to win the world heavyweight championship.

1960, Floyd Patterson becomes the first African American to regain the heavyweight title. Patterson lost his heavyweight title to Ingemar Johansson earlier and regained it nearly a year later when he knocked out Johansson.

1963, In Las Vegas for the second Sonny Liston vs. Floyd Patterson fight, it becomes the first million-dollar purse with both fighters receiving $1,434,000 each. Patterson, a 4:1 betting underdog, was knocked down three times and counted out at 2:10 of the first round.

SUGAR RAY ROBINSON
"The King, the master, my idol." – Muhammad Ali

1955, Sugar Ray Robinson becomes the world middleweight champion.

1958, Sugar Ray Robinson becomes the first African American fighter to hold the middleweight title on five separate occasions.

CLARESSA SHIELDS

2012, At the London Olympic Games, Claressa Shields becomes the first U.S. woman to win a boxing gold medal. The 165-pound Shields wins the Olympic middleweight title by defeating Russian boxer Nadezda Torlopova.

2016, Claressa Shields becomes the first U.S. boxer to win back-to-back Olympic gold medals, defeating the Netherlands' Nouchka Fontijn.

CHARLES A.C. "THE BLACK THUNDERBOLT" SMITH

1876, Charles A.C. Smith from Macon, Ga. claims the title of the first World Colored Heavyweight Champion. Known as "The Black Thunderbolt" he stood 5-foot-11 and weighed upwards of 230 pounds.

WENDELL SMITH

"Wendell Smith was to sports what Malcolm X and Dr. King were to the Civil Rights Movement." - Author

1958, Wendell Smith becomes the first African American to provide radio commentary for a boxing championship match. The middleweight title fight is between Sugar Ray Robinson and Carmen Basilio at Chicago Stadium.

LEON SPINKS

"I know a lot of people think I'm dumb. Well, at least I ain't no educated fool."

1976, Leon Spinks becomes the first Marine to win a gold medal in Olympics boxing history.

1976, The Spinks brothers, Leon and Michael, win Olympic gold medals in boxing.

1978, After seven pro fights, Leon Spinks fights Muhammad Ali for the heavyweight championship and wins. Spinks is both the fastest to gain and the fastest to lose the heavyweight championship.

MICHAEL SPINKS

1976, The Spinks brothers, Leon and Michael, win Olympic gold medals in boxing.

1985, Michael Spinks upsets IBF champ Larry Holmes for the heavyweight title. Michael is the first light heavyweight to win the heavyweight crown. Light heavyweights Billy Conn, Bob Foster and Archie Moore failed in earlier attempts. Michael joins his brother Leon as the first siblings to win heavyweight titles. Leon defeated Muhammad Ali in 1978.

MIKE TYSON

"There's nothing wrong with being afraid of somebody. Just never be intimidated."

2007, Mike Tyson tops ESPN's list of "The Hardest Hitters in Heavyweight History."

JERSEY JOE WALCOTT

1952, Jersey Joe Walcott, at age 37, becomes the oldest man to win the heavyweight championship, and becomes the first athlete to appear on the cover of *Jet* magazine.

HARRY WILLS

1958, Harry "The Black Panther" Wills dies in N.Y. Critics claim the race barrier prevented Wills from contesting Jack Dempsey's heavyweight crown.

JACK WILSON

1940, Jack Wilson, a bantamweight boxer, is the first African American to fight the main event at Hollywood Legion Stadium, when he defeats Tony Chavez.

Colorful Firsts in U.S. Sports

Cage 5IVE: Football Champions

COLLEGE FOOTBALL TIMELINE

1890, William Henry Lewis and William Tecumseh Sherman Jackson become the first African American players on a White college football team as members of the Amherst squad.

1892, William Henry Lewis, a center from Harvard University, is named the first African American All-American in college football. Lewis later serves 12 years as a football coach at Harvard.

1892, The first collegiate football game is played between two historically Black colleges. In Salisbury, N.C., Livingstone College host Biddle University (now Johnson C. Smith University) from nearby Charlotte. Biddle wins 4-0. The game was played on a snow covered, converted cow pasture. This event is referred to as "The Birth of Black College Football."

1896, William Henry Lewis, former All-American collegian, writes the *Primer of College Football*, the first book of its kind. The volume is published by *Harper & Brothers* and serialized in *Harper's Weekly*. In 1911, he is among the first African Americans to be admitted to the American Bar Association.

1904, Charles W. "Black Cyclone from Wooster" Follis becomes the first professional football player with the Shelby Blues of the Ohio League. Follis, a halfback, and Branch Rickey were teammates on the amateur Shelby Athletic Association in 1902 and 1903.

1905, Bob Marshall from the University of Minnesota is chosen for the Walter Camp's All-American football team.

1906, Charles "Doc" Baker, a halfback, joins the Akron Indians who become the Akron Pros in 1920, a charter member of the American Professional Football Association (later renamed the National Football League in 1922). Raised in the Akron Children's Home, he is known as the second professional African American football player.

1911, Henry McDonald from Haiti becomes the first Black player for the Rochester Jeffersons of the New York Professional Football League. The halfback plays with the team until 1917.

1915, Paul Robeson and Fritz Pollard become the first African American football players at Rutgers and Brown Universities.

1915, Gideon E. "Charlie" Smith, a tackle, becomes the first African American player for the Canton Bulldogs of the Ohio League. Smith plays one game and is the last African American to play professional football exclusively prior to the formation of the National Football League in 1920. Smith becomes professor of physical education and head football coach at Hampton Institute in 1921.

1915, Solomon W. Butler is the first African American to quarterback a team for all four years of college at the University of Dubuque in Iowa. Sol Butler earns 12 varsity letters in football, basketball, baseball and track, and participates in the 1920 Belgium Olympics. In 1926, the all-White New York Giants refuse to play the Canton Bulldogs with Butler as its quarterback.

1916, Fritz Pollard, running back from Brown University, becomes the first African American to play in the Rose Bowl. Pollard is also the first African American football player at Brown. He becomes the first African American, who plays a backfield position, named to the All-American team. See 1892, when William Henry Lewis, a lineman, is selected to the All-American squad.

1918, Fred "Duke" Slater becomes the first African American football player at the University of Iowa.

1921, Football star Frederick Wayman "Duke" Slater from the University of Iowa is named Most Valuable College Player.

1930, Dave Willoughby Myers, an undrafted guard and quarterback from New York University, is the first African American to play for the Staten Island Stapletons in the National Football League (NFL). The next season he plays for the NFL's Brooklyn Dodgers.

1933, The American Association Football League (AAFL) and the Pacific Coast Football League, both minor leagues, open its doors to African American athletes. The AAFL consists of five teams from New York state (Mt. Vernon Cardinals, Brooklyn Bay Parkways, New Rochelle Bulldogs, Staten Island's Stapleton Buffaloes and the White Plains Bears) and three teams from New Jersey (Orange Tornadoes, Paterson Panthers and the Passaic Red Devils). The AAFL operates until 1941, as America enters World War II.

1937, Football coach Eddie Hurt at Morgan State College devises the four-man defensive front, a first. Later, in 1943, his Bears team goes undefeated, untied and unscored upon. Hurt also coached track & field and basketball.

1937, Homer Harris, an end, becomes the first African American captain of a Big Ten Conference football team, with the University of Iowa.

Football Champions

1935, Jerome Heartwell "Brud" Holland, one of 13 children, is the first African American to play football at Cornell University and was chosen as an All American in 1937 and 1938. In 1953, Dr. Holland becomes president of the historically black Delaware State College. In 1965, he becomes a member of the College Football Hall of Fame.

1938, Quarterback Wilmeth Sidat-Singh of Syracuse University, and end Jerome "Brud" Holland, of Cornell University, become the first African Americans invited to play for the College All-Stars against the New York Giants. Because of Sidat-Singh's light complexion and last name, he was thought to be Hindu. Both his parents were African American. After the death of his father, Elias Webb (a pharmacist), his mother, Pauline, married Samuel Sidat-Singh from India who adopted Wilmeth, giving him the family surname.

1939, The *Chicago Defender* reports "We have yet to find another single coach in the history of (college) football that has had the guts to play three of our race at one and have four on the squad." UCLA football starts Jackie Robinson and Kenny Washington in the backfield and Woody Strode at offensive and defensive end. Ray Bartlett is a wide receiver. The Bruins compile a 6–0–4 record (5–0–3 conference), finish in second place in the Pacific Coast Conference.

1940, Leonard Bates, a fullback for New York University, is barred from playing against the University of Missouri, because of its color ban. Seven NYU players object against the Jim Crow policy and are named "The Bates Seven."

1940, Running back Louis Montgomery, Boston College's first African American player, is not allowed to make the trip to the Cotton Bowl due to segregation sanctions. In 1941, he made the trip to the Sugar Bowl in New Orleans but was not allowed to play. In 2012, Boston College retires his No. 21.

1941, Eddie Robinson, Grambling State University football coach, defeats Tillotson College 37-6 for the first of his 400 plus wins.

1944, Ohio State University defensive lineman Bill Willis becomes the first African American to start in a College All-Star football game.

1945, Wally Triplett becomes the first African American football player in Penn State University history. He is also the first African American to start and earn a letter (1946).

1946, Cleveland quarterback Otto Graham sets up over the center with feet parallel, but one foot slightly behind to push off faster to get away from defensive player Bill Willis in practice. Other pro teams soon pick it up and call it the "Bill Willis Step."

1946, Cleveland Abbott becomes the first Black person to be a member of the U.S. Olympic Committee. As head coach of the Tuskegee Golden Tigers, 1923 to 1954, he became the first Black football coach to win 200 games (206-99-27), which included six undefeated seasons. Abbott is a member of least 10 collegiate Halls of Fame.

1947, Buddy Young of the University of Illinois becomes the first African American to score a touchdown in the Rose Bowl.

1947, Chester Pierce, senior tackle for Harvard, becomes the first African American collegian to perform against White players on a Southern collegiate field, Scott Stadium in Charlottesville, Va., against the University of Virginia.

1947, John Edward Brown from North Carolina Central University becomes the first African American football player from a historically Black college to play professional football when he joins the Los Angeles Dons of the AAFC as a center. Tank Younger from Grambling State is usually recognized as the first, in 1949, with the NFL Los Angeles Rams. Marion Motley attends South Carolina State College (now Chaflin University) in 1939 before transferring to the University of Nevada to play varsity football.

1950, Harold Robinson, football center, becomes Kansas State University's first African American student-athlete, and the first African American in the Big Seven Conference to be awarded an athletic scholarship.

1951, Duke Slater becomes the only African American elected to the College Football Hall of Fame's inaugural class. Slater is one of five starters on the 1921 Iowa team who became lawyers. Slater later moves to Chicago and serves as a Superior Court judge.

1953, Leonard Williams, a football player, becomes the first African American athlete at the University of Delaware.

1953, The Detroit Lions become the last all-White team to win the NFL championship. They defeat the Cleveland Browns 17-16 at Briggs Stadium in Detroit, Mich.

1955, Calvin Jones, offensive guard from Iowa University, becomes the first African American to win the Outland Trophy. Jones was the first football player to appear on the cover of *Sports Illustrated* in 1954.

1956, Bobby Grier, a fullback and linebacker for the Pittsburgh Panthers is the first African American football player to break the color barrier of the collegiate Sugar Bowl game, which is held in New Orleans, La. Segregationists try to keep Grier from playing because he is Black. Georgia's governor Marvin Griffin publicly threatens the Georgia Tech's president Blake Van Leer to cancel the game. Later in July, the Louisiana state legislature passes Act 579, known as the Athletic Events Bill, which prohibits interracial sports competitions.

Colorful Firsts in U.S. Sports

1956, Sidney Williams Jr. becomes the first African American starting quarterback in Big Ten history with the University of Wisconsin Badgers.

1960s, Defensive back Dick "Night Train" Lane tackles wide receivers around the neck. The clothesline tackles called "Neckties" are subsequently banned by the NFL.

1960, Freddie "The Hammer" Williamson, a cornerback for the Oakland Raiders and later the Kansas City Chiefs, creates the "hammer" to slow down wide receivers. In 1960, a defensive back could bump the receiver until the quarterback released the football.

1960, Halfback Sid Blanks joins the Texas A&I Javelinas and becomes the first Black player in the Lone Star Conference. He is also the first African American to receive a football scholarship to an integrated school in Texas. Blanks later plays for the Houston Oilers and the New England Patriots.

1961, Secretary of the Interior Stewart Udall warns owner George Preston Marshall to hire Black players or face federal retribution. For the first time in history, the federal government attempts to desegregate a professional sports team. The Washington Redskins were under the threat of civil rights legal action by the Kennedy administration, which would have prevented a segregated team from playing at the new federally-owned D.C. Stadium, managed by the U.S. Department of the Interior. The next season 1962, the Redskins become the final professional American football franchise to integrate, when they draft running back Ernie Davis out of Syracuse.

1961, Sandy Stephens of the Minnesota Gophers is the first Black quarterback named to the College All-American team.

1961, Ernie Davis from Syracuse becomes the first African American to win the Heisman Trophy, designated the best player in college football. Davis broke Jim Brown's career rushing record at Syracuse.

1962, Darryl Andre Hill, a wide receiver, becomes the first African American to receive an athletic scholarship to play sports for a major university in the South. The University of Maryland Terrapins are a member of the Atlantic Coast Conference (ACC).

1963, Jake Gaither, coach for Florida A&M, creates the Split-Line T formation, later copied by most major college football programs.

1964, John McCluskey becomes the first African American in Ivy League history to start at quarterback. McCluskey leads Harvard to a 6-3 record in 1964 and a 5-2-2 record in 1965.

1965, Jerry LeVias becomes the first scholarship athlete at Southern Methodist University (SMU) and the first in the Southwest Conference. Despite death threats, the next season, the 5-foot-9 wide receiver leads SMU to its first Cotton Bowl appearance since Heisman winner Doak Walker suited up for the Mustangs, almost two decades earlier. LeVias would later play for the Houston Oilers and the San Diego Chargers.

1966, Lowell Perry becomes the first African American broadcaster in the National Football League, when hired by CBS.

1966, Rommie Loudd becomes the first African American assistant coach in the American Football League for the New England Patriots.

1966, Aaron Wade becomes the first African American official in the American Football League. He is a coach at Centennial High School in Los Angeles, a school that produced Paul Lowe, all-pro running back for the San Diego Chargers.

1966, Jackie Robinson is named general manager of the Continental League's Brooklyn Dodgers Football Club, Inc. The announcement on May 2 was made by league Commissioner Saul Rosen and club president Jerry Jacobs.

1967, Lonnie Wright becomes one of the first players to play two professional sports in the same season. Wright played defensive back for the Denver Broncos in 1966-67 and guard for the Denver Rockets (later the Nuggets) from 1967 to 1970.

1968, Lester McClain becomes the first African American to play football at the University of Tennessee.

1968, Joe Profit, a running back, becomes the University of Louisiana at Monroe and the Gulf States Conference's (now the Sunbelt Conference) first African American football player. In 1971, he is named the conference's Athlete of the Year.

1969, The University of Texas Longhorns, coached by Darrell Royal, become the last all-White team to be named consensus national football champions.

1969, Jake Gaither's Florida A&M Rattlers defeat the Spartans of the University of Tampa, 34–28, in the South's first football game between a white college and a historically black college.

1969, Clyde Chesney, a linebacker, becomes North Carolina State University's first African American letterman.

1969, Frank Dowsing Jr. defensive back, and Robert Bell, defensive lineman, become the first African American football players at Mississippi State University. See 2017.

1970, Nine members of the Syracuse University football team, remembered erroneously as the "Syracuse 8," make a stand for equality and for more a diverse coaching staff at the school. Gregory Allen, Richard Bulls, John Godbolt, Dana Harrell, John Lobon, Clarence "Bucky" McGill, A. Alif Muhammad, Duane Walker and Ron Womack's demands included increased medical care, equal access to academic support and integration of the team's coaching staff, which had been all White since 1898. "We never were conscious of racism," claimed coach Ben Schwartzwalder. On 20 October 2006, the nine members of the "Syracuse 8" were given the Chancellor's Medal by the university, among the highest honors at the school.

1970, Stanley Land, Harrison Davis, Kent Merrit and John Rainey become the University of Virginia's first African Americans to receive football scholarships.

1970, The USC Trojans become the first fully integrated team to play in the state of Alabama against Bear Bryant's all-White Crimson Tide of the Southeastern Conference. With a Black quarterback, Jimmy Jones, running back Sam "Bam" Cunningham, plus other African Americans in key positions, the Trojans wallop the Crimson Tide 42 to 21. The game hastens the racial integration of football at Alabama University and in the South. Jerry Claiborne, a former Bryant assistant famously said this at the end of the game, "Sam Cunningham did more to integrate Alabama in 60 minutes than Rev. Martin Luther King did in 20 years."

1971, Defensive guard Rich Glover of Nebraska is the first African American named Big Eight Conference Player of the Year.

1972, Rich Glover, middle guard from Nebraska University, becomes the first African American to win the Vince Lombardi/Rotary Award. Glover also wins the Outland Trophy for the best college football interior lineman.

1972, Condredge Holloway becomes the first Black quarterback in the Southeastern Conference, as a player with the Tennessee Volunteers. Holloway is the only Tennessee student-athlete named to Tennessee's All-Century squads in both baseball and football.

1972, Running back Wilbur Jackson from Carroll High School in Ozark, Ala., becomes the first scholarship football player for Alabama University. In 2007, he is inducted into the Alabama Sports Hall of Fame.

1972, John Mitchell, a two-time Junior College All-American defensive end transfers from Eastern Arizona Junior College to Alabama's Crimson Tide and becomes the first Black player to play in a game for Alabama.

1974, Leo Miles becomes the first Black to officiate a Super Bowl game as head linesman.

1976, Mike Dunn becomes the first Black quarterback for the Duke University football team.

1976, Tony Dorsett, for Pittsburgh, becomes the first collegiate Division I-A player to rush for more than 6,000 (6,082) yards during his career.

1979, Willie Jeffries becomes the first African American head football coach in Division I-A when named coach of the Wichita State University (Kansas) Shockers.

1983, The Eddie G. Robinson Memorial Stadium, a multi-purpose 19,000-seat facility opens at Grambling State University.

1984, The Iowa State University football stadium is named Cyclone Stadium, and the playing field is named "Jack Trice Field" in honor of the school's first African American athlete, a tackle. Stadium capacity is estimated at 56,800.

1987, Don McPherson, Syracuse quarterback, wins the Maxwell Award and the Davey O'Brien National Quarterback Award.

1986, At Oklahoma, Jamelle Holieway takes over for an injured QB Troy Aikman in his first year and leads the Sooners to an 11-1-0 record under Coach Barry Switzer. Oklahoma defeats the Penn State Nittany Lions for the national championship in the Orange Bowl. Holieway throws a 71-yard touchdown pass in that game to All-American tight end Keith Jackson as he becomes the first true first-year quarterback to lead his team to the national title.

1986, Leonard Hamilton becomes the first African American coach in the Big Eight Conference as head coach of the Oklahoma State Cowboys basketball team.

1988, In college bowl games, 11 teams are led by Black quarterbacks: Terrence Jones (Tulane), Independence Bowl; Major Harris (West Virginia) Sun Bowl; James Jackson (Georgia) Liberty Bowl; Darnell Dickerson (Pittsburgh) Cotton Bowl; Don McPherson (Syracuse) Sugar Bowl; Bobby McAllister (Michigan State) Rose Bowl; Steve Taylor (Nebraska) Fiesta Bowl; Charles Thompson (Oklahoma) Orange Bowl and Demetrius Brown (Michigan) Hall of Fame Bowl.

1991, The annual Bayou Classic between the Grambling State University Tigers and the Southern University Jaguars becomes the first black college football game with a national television contract (NBC). The series began in 1932 in Monroe, Louisiana, with the Jaguars victorious 20-0.

1996, Tyrone Willingham becomes the first African American coach to win a division A-1 bowl game, when his 7-5 Stanford Cardinals defeat the Michigan State Spartans in the Sun Bowl, 38-0.

1997, Self-proclaimed white supremacist attorney Richard Barrett, sues the University of Mississippi over its ban on flagsticks at Ole Miss football games. Barrett contends that the ban interferes with free speech rights by keeping Confederate flags out of the stadium.

Colorful Firsts in U.S. Sports

1996, The Alumni Bowl in Tuskegee, Alabama, is renamed Cleve L. Abbott Memorial Alumni Stadium with an estimated capacity of 10,000. Abbott died in 1955.

1997, Jack Trice Stadium at Iowa State University becomes the first NCAA Division I, and thus far still the only stadium, named for an African American. John G. "Jack" Trice was the first African American athlete for Iowa State College. He died due to injuries suffered during a college football game against the University of Minnesota in Minneapolis on Oct. 6, 1923. Trice died from hemorrhaged lungs and internal bleeding because of the injuries sustained during the game. Many speculated that the injuries were intentionally inflicted by Gopher players. Prior to the re-naming, the venue was named Cyclone Stadium; the playing area was called Jack Trice Field.

1999, A record six African American quarterbacks are drafted by NFL teams: Akili Smith (Oregon State), Donovan McNabb (Syracuse), Aaron Brooks (Virginia), Michael Bishop (K-State), Shaun King (Tulane), and Daunte Culpepper (Central Florida). McNabb, Smith and Culpepper are taken in the first round, a record. Overall, only four Black QB's had been taken in the first round in the first 63 years of the NFL.

2002, Tyrone Willingham becomes the first college football coach to receive the *Sporting News'* Sportsman of the Year award.

2002, Annice Canady becomes the first female official to work an NCAA Division I football game.

2004, Sylvester Croom becomes the first African American head football coach in the Southeastern Conference (SEC) with Mississippi State University. In 2007, he is named SEC Coach of the Year.

2006, Drake University in Des Moines, Iowa, dedicates its football field in honor of the late Johnny Bright, one of the school's greatest athletes and the victim of one of the most notorious acts in college football history. The field will be named "Johnny Bright Field at Drake Stadium." Bright is remembered for an incident on 20 October 1951. Bright's jaw is broken in a game in Stillwater, Okla., by an Oklahoma A&M player in what was perceived as a racially motivated attack.

2006, Oklahoma University paints a solid crimson line on its football field's 38-yard-line from sideline to sideline in its game against the Colorado Buffs. This is in honor of the Sooner's first Black football player, Prentice Gautt, who wore jersey No. 38. Gautt went on to play in the NFL and later had a career in athletic administration. Gautt died in 2005.

2009, Ron Cherry, football official from the ACC conference, becomes the first African American referee of a BCS national title game featuring the Oklahoma Sooners against the Florida Gators. Cherry is considered an unpopular referee in this conference.

2015, After weeks of protest, University of Missouri president Tim Wolfe resigns when the school's football team, the Tigers, vows to boycott all football-related activities due to unaddressed racial hostility on the campus. The effort is led by #ConcernedStudent1950, named to pay homage to the first year a Black student is admitted to the university. The movement is captured in the documentary, *Field of Vision - Concerned Student 1950*.

2017, Mississippi State University dedicates the Dowsing-Bell Plaza in honor of its first two African American football players, Frank Dowsing Jr. and Robert Bell, in 1969.

2022, Jackson State University's football team, coached by Deion Sanders, becomes the first HBCU to host ESPN's "College GameDay". JSU or the "Sonic Boom of the South" faces off against Southern University, the "Human Juke Box," at Smith-Wills Stadium, located at 1200 Cool Papa Bell Drive and home of the Hank Aaron Sports Academy.

PRO FOOTBALL TIMELINE

1904, Charles "Black Cyclone from Wooster" Follis become the first professional football player with the Blues of the Shelby Athletic Association (Ohio). The Blues were part of the American Professional Football League formed in Ohio of this year.

1916, Fritz Pollard, becomes the first African American named to the All-American team.

1916, Fritz Pollard, running back from Brown University, becomes the first African American to play in the Rose Bowl.

1919, Fritz Pollard joins the Akron Indians (later the Pros) independent football team.

1920, Several professional football players, including Fritz Pollard (with the Akron Pros), and Robert "Rube" Marshall (Rock Island [Ill.] Independents), make their debut in the new American Professional Football Association (APFA), later to become the NFL.

1921, George "Papa Bear" Halas, head coach of the Chicago Staleys, refuses to play the Akron Pros unless they drop quarterback and running back Fritz Pollard from its team.

1922, George Halas, now head coach of the renamed Chicago Bears, refuses to play the Milwaukee Badgers unless they drop African American players Fritz Pollard, Paul Robeson and Duke from the team.

1922, Tackle Duke Slater becomes the first African American lineman in the National Football League as a member of the Rock Island Independents. Slater earns his law degree in 1928 and practices law as a Chicago attorney. In 1948, he is elected to the Cook County Municipal Court, becoming just the second African American judge in Chicago.

1926, Duke Slater signs with the Chicago Cardinals and becomes the first African American to play for a current NFL franchise.

1928, The Chicago Black Hawks, an all-Black team, is organized by Dr. Albert C. Johnson and Fritz Pollard, who also serves as quarterback, running back, and coach. The Black Hawks primarily play against White teams around Chicago.

1933, Ray Kemp with the Pittsburgh Pirates and Joe Lillard with the Chicago Cardinals are last African Americans released from NFL teams leaving the league exclusively white.

1934 to 1945, African American players are banned from the newly re-organized National Football League, which is divided into two divisions and adds three new teams in 1934.

1935, The New York Brown Bombers are created by Herschel "Rip" Day, an African American athletic promoter in Harlem. Fritz Pollard agrees to coach the team. The team lasts until 1942.

1937, Until 1965 "Fight for Old Dixie" was the rally song for George Preston Marshall's Washington Redskins, the only football team south of the Mason-Dixon line, at the time.

1946, An all-Black league, the Virginia Negro Football League is organized. The teams include the Richmond Rams (champions), Norfolk Brown Bombers, Newport News Lighthearts and the Portsmouth Swans.

1946, The Cleveland Browns sign running back Marion Motley and defensive lineman Bill Willis as the AAFC's first African American players.

1946, The Cleveland Browns' Marion Motley and Bill Willis are named to the All-AAFC team in the league's first year of operation.

1946, Cleveland quarterback Otto Graham sets up over the center with feet parallel, but one foot slightly behind to push off faster to get away from defensive player Bill Willis in practice. Other pro teams soon pick it up and call it the "Bill Willis Step."

1946, UCLA products Woody Strode (end) and Kenny Washington (running back) are the first African Americans in the NFL, joining Dan Reeves' newly relocated Los Angeles Rams from Cleveland. Washington is the first Black player to score a rushing touchdown in the NFL.

1946, The All-America Football Conference (AAFC) is organized by Arch Ward, the sports editor of the *Chicago Tribune*. The league would last but four seasons.

1947, Running and defensive back Bert Piggott, receiver Ezzrett "Sugarfoot" Anderson, and center John Brown become AAFC Los Angeles Dons' first African American players.

1947, Running and defensive back Bill Bass becomes AAFC Chicago Rockets' first African American player.

1947, Running back Buddy Young become AAFC New York Yankees' first African American player.

1947, Running back Elmore "Pepper" Harris becomes AAFC Brooklyn Dodgers' first African American player.

1947, Tackle Bob Mike and fullback Joe Perry become AAFC San Francisco 49ers's first Black players.

1948, Running back Joe Perry and tackle Robert Mike become the San Francisco 49ers's (AAFC) first African American players.

1950, Running backs Buddy Young and Sherman Howard, along with quarterback George Taliaferro become the first African

Colorful Firsts in U.S. Sports

Americans to play for the New York Yanks in the NFL.

1951, Bernie Custis becomes the first African American regular starter, as quarterback, for a Canadian professional football team, the Hamilton Tiger-Cats of the Interprovincial Rugby Football Union, later known as the Canadian Football League (CFL). He was selected to the IRFU All-Star team.

1954, The top three NFL rushers are Black, Joe Perry, John Henry Johnson and Tank Younger. Perry is the first non-drafted NFL player (after the draft was originated in 1936) to lead the league in rushing.

1954, Calvin Jones becomes the first football player, collegiate or professional, to appear on the cover of *Sports Illustrated*.

1959, The American Football League is formed by Texans Lamar Hunt and K.S. "Bud" Adams with listed franchises in New York City, Oakland, Buffalo, Houston, Denver, Los Angeles, Dallas and Boston.

1959, The Los Angeles Rams, led by G.M. Pete Rozelle, trade seven players, a 1959 second-round pick and a player to be named later to the Chicago Cardinals for running back Ollie Matson.

1962, Interior Secretary Stewart Udall issues an ultimatum to Washington Redskins owner George Preston Marshall to sign a Black player. If not, the city-government owned D.C. Stadium (now Robert F. Kennedy Memorial Stadium), will have its 30-year lease rescinded.

1962, The Washington Redskins, owned by George Preston Marshall, become the last NFL team to sign African Americans, wide receiver Bobby Mitchell and fullback Ron Hatcher.

1962, Ernie Davis, is the first African American to be chosen as the first pick, in the first round of the NFL draft by the Washington Redskins.

1965, Burl Toler, a guard from San Francisco University, who never played in the pros, becomes the first African American NFL official. Toler served as a field judge and head linesman. The first African American AFL official was Aaron Wade.

1965, The American Football League (AFL) All-Star game is scheduled to be played in New Orleans at Tulane Stadium. Black All-Stars including Buck Buchannan, Cookie Gilchrist, Sid Blanks, Bobby Bell, Dick Westmoreland, Frank Buncom, Ernie Warlick, Ernie Ladd, Earl Faison, Dave Grayson and Sherman Plunkett are unable to hail cabs from the airport and denied service in local restaurants. The Black players agree to boycott the game. The All-Star game is moved, one week later, to Rice Stadium in Houston, Texas.

1968, In Super Bowl II, the Grambling State University marching band become the first HBCU to perform the national anthem at the championship game. The "World Famed Tiger Marching Band" would perform again at Super Bowl IX.

1970, The Kansas City Chiefs beat the heavily favored Minnesota Vikings in Super Bowl IV, in the last game before the AFL-NFL merger. The win validates the AFL worthiness for a merger. Thanks to super scout Lloyd Wells, the Chiefs' roster is filled with players from HBCUs; Ceasar Belser (Arkansas AM&N), Buck Buchannan (Grambling), Wendell Hayes (Humboldt State), Robert Holmes (Southern), Jim Kearney (Prairie View A&M), Willie Lanier (Morgan State), Jim Marsalis (Tennessee A&I), Willie Mitchell (Tennessee State), Frank Pitts (Southern), Gloster Richardson (Jackson State), Noland Smith (Tennessee State), Morris Stroud (Clark Atlanta), Otis Taylor (Prairie View A&M) and Emmett Thomas (Bishop).

1971, Irv Cross, former two-time Pro Bowl cornerback, becomes the first African American sports analyst on national TV. His tenure on *CBS Sports* lasts 23 years.

1974, Leo Miles becomes the first African American to officiate a Super Bowl game as head linesman.

1974, Rommie Loudd of the Florida Blazers and Louis R. Lee of the Detroit Wheels become the first African American owners of World Football League (WFL) franchises.

1975, Irv Cross becomes co-anchor with Brent Musburger, Phyllis George and Jimmy "The Greek" Snyder on *The NFL Today* show. He spends 14 years on this live broadcast.

1975, Willie Wood becomes the first African American head coach in the modern era with the Philadelphia Bell of the World Football League (WFL).

1977, The Mel Blount Rule or "bump-and-run" bars contact with wide receivers beginning five yards beyond the line of scrimmage. Named after the Pittsburgh Steeler cornerback Mel Blount out of Southern University, this ruling marks a turning point in football in making the passing game more open.

1977, The NFL outlaws the "head slap" made popular by the retired (1974) Deacon Jones of the Los Angeles Rams, San Diego Chargers and Washington Redskins.

1978, Jayne Kennedy becomes the first woman to enter the male-dominated world of sports as an announcer on *The NFL Today*.

1979, The NFL rules that tear-away jerseys are illegal. The rule is aimed at Greg "Do-it-to-it" Pruitt of the Cleveland Browns who had several custom-made tear-away jerseys.

1980, Future Pro Bowlers Dwight Stephenson of the Miami Dolphins and Ray Donaldson of the Baltimore Colts, become the first African Americans to start at the Center position for an NFL team.

1981, The Lester Hayes Rule is enforced. The Oakland Raiders cornerback's use of stickum on his fingertips is outlawed. Teammate Fred Biletnikoff, a wide receiver, used the sticky stuff before retiring from the NFL in 1978.

1982, The NFL recognizes "sacks" as an official statistic. This is largely due to the success of defensive end Deacon Jones in his propensity for sacking quarterbacks when he played from 1961 to 1974.

1983, In March, the NFL passes the "Leaping Rule" a few months after Green Bay's Gary Lewis, a 6-foot-5 high-jumping tight end, blocks kicks in four games. In a playoff win over the Cardinals, Lewis blocked a field goal, a PAT and deflected two-field goal attempts, all by racing from about five yards behind the line of scrimmage and leaping. It becomes Rule 12, Section 3, Article 2.

1984, The NFL, in response to celebrations such as a group high-five by the Washington Redskins' "Fun Bunch" and the "Nestea Plunge," where two players flop to the ground, as in the iced tea giant's old commercials, implements a rule banning such celebrations. The NFL rule includes penalties for players who kneel in prayer after scoring.

1988, Johnny Grier becomes the first African American referee in the NFL. Grier served as a field judge in the NFL for seven years before being promoted to referee.

1990, Bruce Perkins (from Arizona State) of the Tampa Bay Buccaneers and Derek Loville (Oregon) of the Seattle Seahawks become the first undrafted rookie running backs to start in week one of a season.

1993, Super Bowl XXVII was originally scheduled to be played at Sun Devil Stadium in Tempe, Ariz., the home of the Phoenix Cardinals. Immediately after the Cardinals relocated from St. Louis, Mo., to the Phoenix, Ariz., area in 1988, the NFL was eager to hold a Super Bowl in this state.

Meanwhile, Martin Luther King Day, the U.S. federal holiday honoring civil rights activist Martin Luther King Jr. was observed for the first time in 1986. However, the holiday was only celebrated in 27 states and the District of Columbia during that first year. Opponents across the nation tried to stop the holiday from being recognized in their own local areas.

In 1986, an Arizona holiday honoring King had been declared by Governor Bruce Babbitt after a bill to create the holiday failed in the state legislature. A year later, newly-elected Governor Evan Mecham rescinded the holiday in 1987 on the grounds that the holiday had been illegally created.

Legislation to create the holiday was passed by the state legislature in 1989, but opponents to the holiday succeeded in forcing the holiday to undergo a ballot initiative. Arizona voters rejected the 1990 initiative to create a King holiday.

The NFL, which has an increasing percentage of African American players, and urged by the NFL Players' Association, votes to snatch Super Bowl XXVII from Arizona, and awarded it instead to the Rose Bowl in Pasadena, Calif. Faced with the boycott, Arizona voters finally approved the King holiday by ballot in 1992, and on 23 March 1993, the NFL awards Super Bowl XXX (1996) to Tempe.

1994, The NFL institutes the two-point conversion option after touchdowns. It is the first scoring change in 75 years of the league.

1997, Jack Trice Stadium at Iowa State University becomes the first NCAA Division I, and thus far still the only stadium, named for an African American. John G. "Jack" Trice was the first African American athlete for Iowa State College. He died due to injuries suffered during a college football game against the University of Minnesota in Minneapolis on Oct. 6, 1923. Trice died from hemorrhaged lungs and internal bleeding because of the injuries sustained during the game. Many speculated that the injuries were intentionally inflicted by Gopher players. Prior to the re-naming, the venue was named Cyclone Stadium; the playing area was called Jack Trice Field.

1997, Barry Sanders of the Detroit Lions becomes the third player to rush for more than 2,000 yards in a season (2,053). Sanders also becomes the third running back with at least 200 carries to average more than six yards per carry (6.1). Jim Brown was the first in 1963; O.J. Simpson, the second in 1973. Sanders also sets an NFL record for most 100-yard games in season with 14 and becomes the first player to post two 80-yard TD runs in the same game. Sanders is the first player to rush for 1,500 yards four years in a row.

1998, Terrell Davis, for the Denver Broncos, rushes for 2008 yards in 392 attempts, averaging 5.12 yards per carry. He is the fourth player to rush for more than 2,000 yards.

1999, The Green Bay Packers become the first NFL team to hire three Black men at the top three coaching positions. Ray Rhodes is head coach, followed by Sherman Lewis, offensive coordinator, and Emmitt Thomas, defensive coordinator.

Colorful Firsts in U.S. Sports

2000, Cris Carter, wide receiver for the Minnesota Vikings, is the first NFL player to receive the renamed Walter Payton Man of the Year Award for 1999. The award honors a player's volunteer and charity work, as well as his excellence on the field.

2000, For the first time, no player from an HBCU is drafted by an NFL team.

2000, On October 9, coaches Dennis Green of the Minnesota Vikings and Tony Dungy of the Tampa Bay Buccaneers, with quarterbacks Daunte Culpepper and Shaun King on Monday Night Football, in Minn., become the first teams with African American coaches and African American quarterbacks to face-off. The Vikings win.

2001, Greg Gumbel becomes the first Black announcer to call a major U.S. sports championship, the Super Bowl. The Baltimore Ravens play the New York Giants. He also calls the 2004 Super Bowl marred by Janet Jackson's so-called wardrobe malfunction during the halftime show.

2002, As head coach of the San José SaberCats, Darren Arbet is the first African American in the Arena Football League to win the Arena Bowl.

2003, The NFL rules that teams are permitted to tackle Dolphins running back Ricky Williams (Edgerrin James and others) by his dreadlocks without fear of penalty. An officiating media tape shows a clip of Williams being tackled by his hair. NFL officiating director Mike Pereira issues a statement making dreadlock tackling legal. Williams, the NFL's leading rusher in 2002, said he had no plans to cut his dreadlocks that he had worn since high school. Williams cut his braids or dreads and retired before the 2004 season.

2003, The Fritz Pollard Alliance is founded by attorneys Cyrus Mehri and Johnnie Cochran Jr. The Alliance is a 501(c)(6) membership organization comprised of scouts, coaches, and front office personnel in the NFL as well as other sports professionals committed to equal opportunity in the football industry.

2003, Herman Edwards, coach of the New York Jets, becomes the first NFL coach on the cover of *Sports Illustrated*. The issue entitled "101 Most Influential Minorities in Sports" shows Edwards along with 27 other personalities.

2003, Popular talk show host Russ Limbaugh is hired by ESPN to do commentary on its Sunday NFL Countdown. Limbaugh comments that Philadelphia Eagles quarterback Donovan McNabb is overrated because the white liberal media wants a Black quarterback to do well. Within 48 hours Limbaugh is forced to resign for his incendiary racist remarks.

2006, Bryant Gumbel, former NBC's *Today* show host and prime anchor for the 1980 Summer Olympic Games, becomes the NFL Network's first play-by-play commentator.

2006, In March, NFL owners vote 29-3 to limit end-zone celebrations. This includes Chad Johnson's practicing his putting stroke with a pylon, Terrell Owens doing sit-ups or signing footballs, or Carolina Panthers' Steve Smith doing a version of "row, row, row your boat" in the end zone. Also banned is Johnson's proposal to a cheerleader on the sideline. However, Johnson's "Riverdance" routine will be allowed because he stays on his feet. Other "allowables" include spiking, dunking or spinning the football after a touchdown. Infractions will incur a 15-yard penalty for unsportsmanlike conduct.

2006, The NFL prohibits teams from penalizing misbehaving players beyond the four-game suspension limit without pay. The previous season, the Philadelphia Eagles suspend wide receiver Terrell Owens for the remainder of the season, costing him $812,000 in salary and beyond the four-game limit established by the players union. The ruling is unofficially known as the Terrell Owens Rule.

2006, Michael Vick of the Atlanta Falcons becomes the first quarterback to rush for more than 1,000 yards in the NFL.

2006, Vince Young becomes the first Black rookie quarterback to play in the Pro Bowl. Dan Marino is the first rookie quarterback to play in the Pro Bowl.

2007, Lovie Smith coach of the Chicago Bears and Tony Dungy of the Indianapolis Colts, become the first African American NFL coaches in the Super Bowl. Smith's Bears defeat the N.O. Saints, first, and then followed by the Dungy's Colts defeating the Boston Patriots to earn this honor.

2007, Tony Dungy, coach of the Indianapolis Colts, becomes the first African American to win a Super Bowl game, defeating the Chicago Bears and Lovie Smith.

2008, Mike Carey, in his 18th year as an NFL official, becomes the first African American referee in the Super Bowl. Officials are chosen on merit. Carey had been chosen earlier as an alternate.

2009, Pittsburgh Steelers Mike Tomlin becomes the second African American NFL head coach to win a Super Bowl. Tony Dungy was the first in 2007 with the Colts. Tomlin served as defensive backs coach for Dungy in 2001 when they were with the Tampa Bay Bucs.

2010, In violation of the NFL's uniform policy, Cincinnati Bengal receiver Chad Ochocinco (formerly Chad Johnson), is fined

$25,000 for wearing gold cleats during a Bengals' 27-21 loss at Pittsburgh on Monday Night Football. Bart Scott, New York Jets linebacker is fined $20,000 for playing without his chin straps snapped – a safety issue – during the Jets' 23-20 overtime victory at Detroit. Minnesota wide receiver Bernard Berrian is fined $5,000 for wearing yellow cleats during the Vikings' 27-24 overtime victory over Arizona.

2011, On February 17, former NFL player David Duerson commits suicide, requesting his brain be donated to chronic traumatic encephalopathy (CTE) research and further sparking the football safety debate regarding head trauma.

2011, ESPN stops using Hank Williams Jr.'s song "All My Rowdy Friends Are There on Monday Night" on Monday Night Football after he publicly compares President Barack Obama to Adolf Hitler on *Fox and Friends*. Despite songs by Williams that glorify the Confederacy like, "If the South Woulda Won" and "If Heaven Ain't a Lot Like Dixie" he is rehired, in 2017, by ESPN during the first year of Donald Trump's term.

2012, Derrick Coleman, running back for the Minnesota Vikings and later the Seattle Seahawks is the first deaf offensive player in the NFL.

2014, Coach Jon Gruden calls out Commissioner Roger Goodell, in an email, for pressuring the St. Louis Rams to draft Michael Sam, a gay player out of Missouri University, who was the SEC Co-Defensive Player of the year in 2013.

2014, Cam Newton of the Carolina Panthers becomes the first QB to have more than 10,000 passing yards, and 2,000 rushing yards over his first three seasons.

2014, Quarterback Robert Griffin III is forced to turn his shirt with the quote "Know Jesus Know Peace" inside out before speaking at a news conference.

2014, Following the police shooting of Michael Brown in the St. Louis suburb of Ferguson, the St. Louis Rams players Tavon Austin, Stedman Bailey, Kenny Britt, Jared Cook and Chris Givens wear "Hands Up, Don't Shoot" t-shirts before a game against the Oakland Raiders.

2014, Wide receiver Andrew Hawkins wears a t-shirt with the inscription, "Justice for Tamir Rice and John Crawford" during his pregame introduction at a Cleveland Browns and Cincinnati Bengals game. The back of the shirt declared the phrase "The Real Battle of Ohio."

2015, William Gay, Pittsburgh Steelers cornerback, is fined for wearing purple cleats to raise awareness about domestic violence.

2015, DeAngelo Williams, Pittsburgh Steelers running back, is fined for wearing "Find the Cure" eye black to raise awareness about breast cancer.

2015, Marshawn Lynch, Seattle Seahawks running back, is fined $75,000 by the NFL for not speaking to the media following the NFC Championship game. Later at Super Bowl Media Day, he says, "I'm just here so I won't get fined." Lynch proved prophetic as he was not fined for the now infamous quote.

2016, The NFL prevents the Dallas Cowboys from wearing a decal on their helmet in honor of five Dallas police officers killed in the line of duty.

2016, The NFL threatens to fine players who wear cleats to commemorate the 15th anniversary of 9/11.

2016, NFL players can wear custom cleats for charity for one week only. The "My Cause, My Cleats" campaign is developed in partnership with *The Players' Tribune*. More than 500 players participate using the hashtag #MyCauseMyCleats.

2016, Colin Kaepernick of the San Francisco 49ers, takes a knee during the national anthem during a preseason game against the Green Bay Packers. Kaepernick objects to the increased cases of police brutality against minorities in America.

2016, Coach Jon Gruden emails Washington team executive Bruce Allen expressing his anger over Colin Kaepernick kneeling during the national anthem. Gruden writes, "They suspend people for taking amino acids they should cut this f------."

2016, Michael Sam, a consensus All-American and SEC Defensive Player of the Year at the University of Missouri, lobbies against a bill at the Missouri State Capitol that would enable discrimination against the LGBTQ community. Sam was drafted by the St. Louis Rams in the seventh round of 2013 and played on the taxi squads for the Rams and the Dallas Cowboys in 2014.

2019, Tyreek Hill of the Kansas City Chiefs is fined $10,527 for giving the peace sign during a Thursday Night Football game against the Denver Broncos. The NFL considers this gesture to be taunting.

2020, The Washington Redskins football team retired the moniker "Redskins" due to public pressure and asking league sponsors Nike, FedEx and Pepsi to cancel contracts. The term "redskin" has been defined as offensive, disparaging, and taboo. Groups like the National Congress of American Indians (NCAI) considered the name a racial slur. Going forward the team will be playing under the banner of the Washington Football Team until a more permanent name is chosen.

Owner Dan Snyder was adamant about never changing the team's moniker. When the NFL reorganized in 1933, the Boston entry changed its name to Redskins from the Braves before moving to District of Columbia in 1937. It is believed that FedEx which has naming rights to the stadium influenced the name drop. In 2022, the football team becomes the "Commanders."

2020, In week 11 on Monday Night Football, the NFL has an all-Black officiating crew for a game between the Los Angeles Rams and the Tampa Bay Buccaneers in Tampa. The crew consist of referee Jerome Boger, umpire Barry Anderson, down judge Julian Mapp, line judge Carl Johnson, side judge Dale Shaw, field judge Anthony Jeffries and back judge Greg Steed. The crew has a combined 89 seasons in the league and has worked six Super Bowls.

2020, Two retired NFL players, Najeh Davenport (running back) and Kevin Henry (defensive lineman), sue the league for allegedly discriminating against Black players who submitted claims in the 2013 class-action lawsuit, accusing the league of concealing findings on the dangers of concussion. The players claim the NFL race-corrected their neurological exams, which prevented them from being compensated. According to court documents, former players being evaluated for neurocognitive impairment were assumed to have started with worse cognitive function if they were Black. So if a Black player and a White player received the exact same scores on a battery of thinking and memory tests, the Black player would appear to have suffered less impairment. And therefore, the lawsuit stated, would be less likely to qualify for a payout.

2021, The NFL is accused of "race norming" in grading the settlements provided to former players for post-concussive syndromes, known as chronic traumatic encephalopathy (CTE). The league's systemic testing scale starts with the assumption that Black athletes have a lower cognitive functioning baseline, resulting in lower payouts than their white counterparts.

2022, Attempting to expand diversity, all 32 NFL teams will be mandated to have a minority offensive assistant coach on staff for the 2022 season. The coach can be a woman or the member of a racial or ethnic minority. With a trend of hiring head coaches from offensive coordinator positions, Pittsburgh Steelers owner Art Rooney II, who serves as chairman of the NFL's diversity committee, said that he hopes the mandate creates a pipeline for minority coaches to rise through the ranks and eventually become head coaches.

2023, Singer/actress Sheryl Lee Ralph is the first person to sing "Lift Every Voice & Sing" inside a stadium hosting the Super Bowl (LVII, Glendale, Ariz.). The unofficial Black national anthem is usually sung outside or at a remote location at Super Bowl games.

2023, Attorney Lee A. Hutton III is named commissioner of the Arena Football League. He is the first Black man to lead a professional sports league in the U.S.

Black/Brown Quarterbacks with a Seasonal Rating of 100 or more points

Player	Rating	Year	Team
Patrick Mahomes - 1	113.8	2018	Kansas City
Lamar Jackson - 1	113.3	2019	Baltimore
Deshaun Watson - 1	112.4	2020	Houston
Daunte Culpepper	110.9	2004	Minnesota
Russell Wilson - 1	110.9	2018	Seattle
Patrick Mahomes - 2	108.2	2020	Kansas City
Russell Wilson - 2	106.3	2019	Seattle
Randall Cunningham (35)	**106.0**	**1998**	**Minnesota - The first**
Dak Prescott - 1	105.9	2023	Dallas
Tua Tagovailoa - 1	105.5	2022	Miami
Patrick Mahomes - 3	105.3	2019	Kansas City
Patrick Mahomes - 4	105.2	2022	Kansas City
Russell Wilson - 3	105.1	2020	Seattle
Dak Prescott - 2	104.9	2016	Dallas
Donovan McNabb	104.7	2004	Philadelphia
Dak Prescott - 3	104.2	2021	Dallas
Deshaun Watson - 2	103.1	2018	Houston
Russell Wilson - 4	103.1	2021	Seattle
Lamar Jackson - 2	102.7	2023	Baltimore
Robert Griffin III	102.4	2012	Washington
Jalen Hurts	101.5	2022	Philadelphia
Russell Wilson - 5	101.2	2013	Seattle
Tua Tagovailoa - 2	101.1	2023	Miami
Geno Smith	100.9	2022	Seattle
C.J. Stroud	100.8	2023	Houston
Kyler Murray	100.6	2021	Arizona
Steve McNair	100.4	2003	Tennessee
Michael Vick	100.2	2010	Philadelphia
Russell Wilson (23) - 6	100.0	2012	Seattle

The NFL passer rating formula ranges on a scale from 0 to 158.3 based on completion percentage, yards per attempt, touchdowns per attempt, and interceptions per attempt.

$$Passer\ Rating = \left(\frac{\left(\frac{COMP}{ATT} - 0.3\right) * 5 + \left(\frac{YARDS}{ATT} - 3\right) * 0.25 + \left(\frac{TD}{ATT}\right) * 20 + 2.375 - \left(\frac{INT}{ATT} * 25\right)}{6} \right) * 100$$

Perfect QB rating of 158.3 for a game:

20 October 1974 – James Harris, Los Angeles Rams 37-14 win over the San Francisco 49ers
7 December 1980 – Vince Evans, Chicago Bears 61-7 win over the Green Bay Packers
10 October 1995 – Jeff Blake, Cincinnati Bengals 27-9 win over the Pittsburgh Steelers
23 September 2007 – Donovan McNabb, Philadelphia Eagles 56-21 win over the Detroit Lions
18 November 2012 – Robert Griffin III, Washington Redskins 31-6 win over the Philadelphia Eagles
28 December 2014 – Geno Smith, New Yorks Jets 37-24 win over the Miami Dolphins
28 October 2018 – Russell Wilson, Seattle Seahawks 28-14 win over the Detroit Lions
8 September 2019 – Lamar Jackson, Baltimore Ravens 59-10 win over the Miami Dolphins
8 September 2019 – Dak Prescott, Dallas Cowboys 35-17 win over the New York Giants - 1
6 October 2019 – Deshaun Watson, Houston Texas 53-32 win over the Atlanta Falcons
10 November 2019 – Lamar Jackson, Baltimore Ravens 49-13 win over the Cincinnati Bengals - 2
31 December 2023 – Lamar Jackson, Baltimore Ravens 56-19 win over the Miami Dolphins - 3

The First Black Starting Quarterbacks for each NFL team

DATE	TEAM	PLAYER	OPPONENT
September 27, 1933	Chicago Cardinals (a)	Joe Lillard	Pittsburgh Pirates
November 22, 1953	Baltimore Colts (b)	George Taliaferro	Los Angeles Rams
October 6, 1968	Denver Broncos	Marlin Briscoe	Cincinnati Bengals
September 14, 1969	Buffalo Bills	**James Harris - 1**	New York Jets
December 3, 1973	Pittsburgh Steelers	Joe Gilliam	Miami Dolphins
October 20, 1974	Los Angeles Rams	**James Harris - 2**	San Francisco 49ers
December 15, 1975	New York Jets	J.J. Jones	San Diego Chargers
October 24, 1976	Tampa Bay Buccaneers	Parnell Dickinson	Miami Dolphins
September 18, 1977	San Diego Chargers (c)	**James Harris - 3**	Oakland Raiders
November 20, 1977	Cleveland Browns	Dave Mays	New York Giants
September 16, 1979	Chicago Bears	**Vince Evans - 1**	Dallas Cowboys
September 2, 1984	Houston Oilers (d)	**Warren Moon - 1**	Los Angeles Raiders
September 15, 1985	Philadelphia Eagles	Randall Cunningham	Los Angeles Rams
December 21, 1986	Dallas Cowboys	Reggie Collier	Chicago Bears
September 20, 1987	Washington Redskins	Doug Williams	Atlanta Falcons
October 4, 1987	Oakland Raiders	**Vince Evans - 2**	Kansas City Chiefs
October 1, 1989	Detroit Lions	**Rodney Peete - 1**	Pittsburgh Steelers
September 4, 1994	Minnesota Vikings	**Warren Moon - 2**	Green Bay Packers
October 30, 1994	Cincinnati Bengals	**Jeff Blake - 1**	Dallas Cowboys
September 7, 1997	Seattle Seahawks	**Warren Moon - 3**	Denver Broncos
October 31, 1999	Baltimore Ravens	**Tony Banks -1**	Buffalo Bills
September 3, 2000	New Orleans Saints	**Jeff Blake - 2**	Detroit Lions
November 26, 2000	Kansas City Chiefs	**Warren Moon - 4**	San Diego Chargers
November 11, 2001	Atlanta Falcons	Michael Vick	Dallas Cowboys
September 8, 2002	Carolina Panthers	**Rodney Peete - 2**	Baltimore Ravens
October 20, 2002	Miami Dolphins	Ray Lucas	Buffalo Bills
December 29, 2002	Jacksonville Jaguars	David Garrard	Indianapolis Colts
September 7, 2003	Arizona Cardinals	**Jeff Blake - 3**	Detroit Lions
November 2, 2003	Houston Texans	**Tony Banks - 2**	Carolina Panthers
October 31, 2010	San Francisco 49ers	Troy Smith	Denver Broncos
November 10, 2013	Green Bay Packers	Seneca Wallace	Philadelphia Eagles
January 3, 2016	Indianapolis Colts	Josh Freeman	Tennessee Titans
September 22, 2016	New England Patriots	Jacoby Brissett	Houston Texans
December 3, 2017	New York Giants	Geno Smith	Oakland Raiders

(a) Became the St. Louis Cardinals in 1960, later the Phoenix Cardinals in 1988 and the Arizona Cardinals in 1994
(b) Became the Indianapolis Colts in 1984
(c) Became the Los Angeles Chargers in 2017
(d) Became the Tennessee Oilers in 1997 and later the Tennessee Titans in 1999

HERB ADDERLEY

1969, Herb Adderley, Green Bay Packers defensive back, becomes the first player to score a touchdown on an interception in the Super Bowl (II) against the Oakland Raiders.

MARCUS ALLEN

1981, Marcus Allen, of USC, becomes the first collegiate running back to rush for 2,000 (2,342) yards in a season.

1984, Marcus Allen becomes the first former Heisman Trophy winner to be named the Super Bowl (XVIII) MVP.

1985, By winning the NFL's MVP award, running back Marcus Allen earns the distinction of being the only player to win the Heisman Trophy (1981), Maxwell Trophy (1981), Walter Camp Award (1981), NFL Offensive Rookie of the Year (1982), the Super Bowl (1984, 1985), and NFL's MVP (1985).

1997, Marcus Allen is the first NFL player to gain more than 10,000 (12,243) rushing yards and 5,000 (5,411) receiving yards during his career.

CLIFTON ANDERSON

1952, Clifton Anderson, an end, and running backs Ollie Matson and Wally Triplett become the first African Americans to play for the Chicago Cardinals of the NFL. Anderson is the grandfather of NBA player Kyle Anderson.

EZZRETT ANDERSON

1947, Running and defensive back Bert Piggott, receiver Ezzrett "Sugarfoot" Anderson, and center John Brown become AAFC Los Angeles Dons' first African American players.

MARK ANDERSON

2000, Mike Anderson of the Denver Broncos becomes the first NFL rookie to rush for more 250 yards in a game. Anderson rushes for 251 yards in 37 attempts against the New Orleans Saints.

DOC BAKER

1906, Charles "Doc" Baker, a halfback, joins the Akron Indians who become the Akron Pros in 1920 and a charter member of the American Professional Football Association (later renamed the National Football League in 1922). Raised in the Akron Children's Home, he is known as the second professional African American football player.

TONY BANKS

1999, Tony Banks from Michigan State University becomes the first Black starting quarterback for the Baltimore Ravens.

2003, Tony Banks becomes the first Black starting quarterback for the Houston Texans.

RONNIE BARNES

1981, Ronnie Barnes, with the New York Giants, becomes the NFL's first Black head athletic trainer. He would later win the National Professional Athletic Trainer of the Year award in 1983 and 1987.

LEM BARNEY

1967, Lem Barney of the Detroit Lions becomes the first NFL player to score a touchdown on an interception on the first pass thrown in his direction, versus the Green Bay Packers. Barney is co-leader for the most interceptions that season and becomes the first player named Defensive Rookie of the Year.

1976, Lem Barney becomes the first NFL player with at least 50 career interceptions and at least 1,000 interception return yards and at least seven touchdowns on interceptions.

BILL BASS

1947, Running and defensive back Bill Bass becomes the AAFC Chicago Rockets' first African American player.

CHARLIE BATCH

2006, NFL quarterback Charlie Batch and former University of Michigan basketball star Antoine "The Judge" Joubert, announce the debut of the Detroit Panthers into the newly formed American Basketball Association franchise. Batch will be the majority owner, while Joubert will be the head coach.

CLEVE ABBOTT

1946, Cleveland Abbott becomes the first Black person to be a member of the U.S. Olympic Committee. As head coach of the Tuskegee Golden Tigers, 1923 to 1954, he became the first Black football coach to win 200 games (206-99-27), which included six undefeated seasons. Abbott is a member of least 10 collegiate Halls of Fame.

1996, The Alumni Bowl in Tuskegee, Alabama, is renamed Cleve L. Abbott Memorial Alumni Stadium with an estimated capacity of 10,000. Abbott died in 1955.

BOBBY BELL

1983, Bobby Bell of the Kansas City Chiefs becomes the first outside linebacker inducted in the National Football Hall of Fame in Canton, Ohio.

JEFF BLAKE

1994, Jeff Blake from East Carolina University becomes the first Black starting quarterback for the Cincinnati Bengals.

1995, Jeff Blake becomes the second African American quarterback, the seventh overall, to earn a maximum single-game passing rating of 158.3. Blake of the Cincinnati Bengals completes 18 of 22 passes for 275 yards and three touchdowns against the Pittsburgh Steelers. Vince Evans of the Chicago Bears was the first Black QB to achieve this rating in 1980.

2000, Jeff Blake becomes the first Black starting quarterback for the New Orleans Saints.

2003, Jeff Blake becomes the first Black starting quarterback for the Arizona Cardinals.

SID BLANKS

1960, Halfback Sid Blanks joins the Texas A&I Javelinas and becomes the first Black player in the Lone Star Conference. He is also the first African American to receive a football scholarship to an integrated school in Texas. Blanks later plays for the Houston Oilers and the New England Patriots.

MEL BLOUNT

1977, The Mel Blount Rule or "bump-and-run" bars contact with wide receivers beginning five yards beyond the line of scrimmage. Named after the Pittsburgh Steeler cornerback Mel Blount out of Southern University, this ruling marks a turning point in football in making the passing game more open.

JEROME AND TRA BOGER

2022, After years of officiating in the SIAC, SWD, Conference-USA and the SEC, and the USFL this past spring, Tra Boger joins his father Jerome (19 years in the NFL) becoming the first African American son-and-father referees in the National Football League.

CHARLIE BRACKINS

1955, Charlie Brackins from Prairie View A&M University is the first Black quarterback employed by the Green Bay Packers. Later in 2013, Seneca Wallace from Iowa State University becomes the Packers' first Black starting quarterback.

JOHNNY BRIGHT

2006, Drake University in Des Moines, Iowa, dedicates its football field in honor of the late Johnny Bright, one of the school's greatest athletes and the victim of one of the most notorious acts in college football history. The field will be named "Johnny Bright Field at Drake Stadium." Bright is remembered for an incident on 20 October 1951. Bright's jaw is broken in a game in Stillwater, Okla., by an Oklahoma A&M player in what was perceived as a racially motivated attack.

MARLIN BRISCOE

"I had no real illusions, but I knew I had shown them I could play.
I thought maybe that would make it a little easier for the next Black player who came through."

1968, Marlin Briscoe, for the Denver Broncos, becomes the first African American quarterback to start in the wing-T formation. Briscoe appears in 11 games under Coach Lou Saban.

1970, The Buffalo Bills become the first NFL team to have two Black quarterbacks on its roster, James Harris and Marlin Briscoe, although the latter is listed as a wide receiver.

JACOBY BRISSETT

2016, After an injury to backup QB Jimmy Garoppolo and a suspended Tom Brady, Jacoby Brissett becomes the New England Patriots' first Black starting quarterback.

JIM BROWN

"A liberal will cut off your leg so he can hand you a crutch."

1957, Jim Brown of Syracuse is sought by the baseball New York Yankees and the basketball Syracuse Nationals. Brown signs with the Cleveland Browns for $12,000 with a signing bonus of $3,000. He leads the NFL in rushing his rookie season and is named the *Sporting News'* Rookie of the Year.

1957, Jim Brown is the first African American chosen by the *Associated Press* as NFL Player of the Year.

1958, Jim Brown becomes the first African American to lead the NFL in scoring with 108 points (18 TD, 0 FG, 0 PAT), and the first African American player to win the Jim Thorpe Trophy.

1963, Cleveland Browns' Jim Brown becomes the first running back with at least 200 carries to average more than six yards per carry (6.4).

1965, Jim Brown of the Cleveland Browns retires. Brown becomes the only NFL player to retire with more touchdowns (106 rushing, 20 receiving) than games played (118). He is also first Black football player to appear on the cover of *Time* magazine.

1995, Jim Brown becomes the first man to be inducted into the Halls of Fame for pro football (1971), college football (1995) and lacrosse (1983).

JOHN EDWARD BROWN

1947, John Edward Brown from North Carolina Central University becomes the first African American football player from a historically Black college to play professional football when he joins the Los Angeles Dons of the AAFC as a center. Tank Younger from Grambling State is usually recognized as the first, in 1949, with the NFL Los Angeles Rams. Marion Motley attends South Carolina State College (now Chaflin University) in 1939 before transferring to the University of Nevada to play varsity football.

WILLIE BROWN

1962, Willie Brown from Grambling State University retires from the NFL. He is the first player in NFL history to intercept at least one pass in 16 consecutive seasons.

ANTONIO BRYANT

2008, Antonio Bryant, wide receiver for the Tampa Bay Buccaneers, becomes the *Sporting News'* first recipient of its Comeback Player of the Year award.

CHARLES BRYANT

1955, Charles Bryant and Jon McWilliams, both from the University of Nebraska, are the first Black players to play in the Orange Bowl.

KELVIN BRYANT

1983, Kelvin Bryant of the Philadelphia Stars in the U.S. Football League (USFL) is named its first MVP.

JUNIOUS "BUCK" BUCHANAN

1963, Buck Buchanan is the first Grambling State player taken as the overall first pick in the first round by the Dallas Texans of the AFL.

1995, The Sports Network creates the Buck Buchanan Award, presented annually to the most outstanding defensive player in the Division I Football Championship Subdivision (formerly Division I-AA) in college football. Dexter Coakley, a linebacker from Appalachian State University, is the first recipient.

Colorful Firsts in U.S. Sports

REGGIE BUSH
"Baseball was my first sport. I wish I would have stayed with it."

2010, USC running back Reggie Bush is stripped of his Heisman Trophy, for allegedly accepting money and gifts from agents. In 2005, he rushes for 2,218 yards and 18 touchdowns. It is the first time in the history of the award that the trophy is returned. 2012 Heisman Trophy winner Johnny Manziel, QB from Texas A&M, announces that he would boycott the Heisman Trophy ceremony until Bush got his trophy back.

SOLOMON BUTLER

1915, Solomon W. Butler is the first African American to quarterback a team for all four years of college at the University of Dubuque in Iowa. Sol Butler earned 12 varsity letters in football, basketball, baseball and track, and participating in the 1920 Belgium Olympics. In 1926, the all-White New York Giants refuse to play the Canton Bulldogs with Butler as its quarterback.

EARL CAMPBELL
"My running style was kind of just head-on, because I couldn't dance."

1980, Earl Campbell of the Houston Oilers becomes the first player to win the NFL's Most Valuable Player Award three years in a row.

ANNICE CANADY

2002, Annice Canady becomes the first female official to work an NCAA Division I football game.

MIKE CAREY

2008, Mike Carey, in his 18th year as an NFL official, becomes the first African American referee in the Super Bowl. Officials are chosen on merit. Carey had been chosen earlier as an alternate.

MICHELLE and MICHAEL CARTER

2003, Michelle Carter sets a national high school record in the girls shot put (8 pounds) with a toss of 54 feet, 10 ¾ inches at the Texas state meet in Austin, joining her father, former NFL player Michael Carter, as a national record holder in the event. Michael Carter stills holds the boys best of 81 feet, 3.5 inches.

LARRY CENTERS

1998, Arizona Cardinals fullback Larry Centers becomes the first running back to catch more than 100 passes in a season.

MAIA CHAKA

2021, Maia Chaka becomes the NFL's first African American female referee when officiating a New York Jets game against the Carolina Panthers in Charlotte, N.C. She is a health & physical education teacher in the Virginia Beach public school system and graduate of Norfolk State University, an HBCU.

RON CHERRY

2009, Ron Cherry, football official from the ACC conference, becomes the first African American referee of a BCS national title game featuring the Oklahoma Sooners against the Florida Gators. Cherry is considered an unpopular referee in this conference.

MICHAEL "PINBALL" CLEMONS

2004, Michael "Pinball" Clemons of the Toronto Argonauts is the first Black coach to win the Canadian Football League's Grey Cup.

DERRICK COLEMAN

2012, Derrick Coleman, running back for the Minnesota Vikings and later the Seattle Seahawks, is the first deaf offensive player in the NFL.

REGGIE COLLIER

1983, Reggie Collier from the Southern Mississippi Golden Eagles is the first Black quarterback to play for the Birmingham Stallions in the USFL.

1984, Reggie Collier is the first Black quarterback to play for the Washington Federals in the USFL.

1985, Reggie Collier is the first Black quarterback to play for the Orlando Renegades in the USFL.

1986, Reggie Collier is the first Black quarterback to play for the Dallas Cowboys in the NFL. He appears in four games, attempts 15 passes and completes eight of them. Collier throws for one touchdown and two interceptions.

FRED "CANNONBALL" COOPER

1949, Fred "Cannonball" Cooper, a running back from Virginia Union University, becomes the first African American professional football player in the deep South when he signs with the Richmond Rebels in the American Football League. Cooper leads the league in rushing and scoring, as the Rebels capture the league title.

ROGER CRAIG

1985, Roger Craig of the San Francisco 49ers becomes the first NFL player to amass more than 1,000 yards rushing and 1,000 yards receiving in the same season. He finishes with 214 carries for 1,050 yards and had a league-best 92 receptions for 1,016 yards.

SYLVESTER CROOM

2004, Sylvester Croom becomes the first African American head football coach in the Southeastern Conference (SEC) with Mississippi State University. In 2007, he was named SEC Coach of the Year.

IRV CROSS

1971, Irv Cross, former two-time Pro Bowl cornerback, becomes the first African American sports analyst on national TV. His tenure on *CBS Sports* lasts 23 years.

1975, Irv Cross becomes co-anchor with Brent Musburger, Phyllis George and Jimmy "The Greek" Snyder on *The NFL Today* show. He spends 14 years on this live broadcast.

2009, Irv Cross is the first African American to receive the annual Pete Rozelle Radio-Television Award from the Pro Football Hall of Fame for "long-time exceptional contributions to radio and television in pro football."

DAUNTE CULPEPPER

1999, A record six African American quarterbacks are drafted by NFL teams: Akili Smith (Oregon State), Donovan McNabb (Syracuse), Aaron Brooks (Virginia), Michael Bishop (K-State), Shaun King (Tulane), and Daunte Culpepper (Central Florida). McNabb, Smith and Culpepper are taken in the first round, a record. Overall, only four Black QB's had been taken in the first round in the first 63 years of the NFL.

2000, On October 9, coaches Dennis Green of the Minnesota Vikings and Tony Dungy of the Tampa Bay Buccaneers, with quarterbacks Daunte Culpepper and Shaun King on Monday Night Football, in Minn., become the first teams with African American coaches and African American quarterbacks to face-off. The Vikings win.

2002, Three-time pro bowler Daunte Culpepper is the first Black quarterback to appear on the cover of *Madden NFL* sports game.

RANDALL CUNNINGHAM

"You can't halfway commit to God."

1985, Randall Cunningham is the first Black starting quarterback for the Philadelphia Eagles.

1992, Randall Cunningham of the Philadelphia Eagles, becomes the first African American quarterback named *Pro Football Weekly's* Comeback Player of the Year.

1998, Randall Cunningham, with the Minnesota Vikings, becomes the first African American to lead the NFL in passing with a ranking of 106.0.

2020, Former quarterback for the Philadelphia Eagles and the Minnesota Vikings, Randall Cunningham is named by coach Jon Gruden as Chaplin of his Las Vegas Raiders. It is believed that no other NFL team has had a former player as its spiritual adviser.

SAM CUNNINGHAM

1970, Quarterback Jimmy Johnson, fullback Sam "The Bam" Cunningham and running back Clarence Davis, of USC, become the first all-Black backfield in Division I football.

Colorful Firsts in U.S. Sports

BERNIE CURTIS

1951, Bernie Custis becomes the first African American regular starter, as quarterback, for a Canadian professional football team, the Hamilton Tiger-Cats of the Interprovincial Rugby Football Union, later known as the Canadian Football League (CFL). He was selected to the IRFU All-Star team.

CLARENCE DAVIS

1970, Quarterback Jimmy Johnson, fullback Sam "The Bam" Cunningham and running back Clarence Davis, of USC, become the first all-Black backfield in Division I football.

ERNIE DAVIS

"The way he carried himself, the way he did not drown in his own tears, the way that he did not hang on his sickness, the way that he functioned as a human being under all of those conditions was tremendous courage," - Jim Brown

1961, Ernie Davis from Syracuse becomes the first African American to win the Heisman Trophy, designated the best player in college football. Davis broke Jim Brown's career rushing record at Syracuse.

1962, Heisman Trophy winner Ernie Davis, of Syracuse University, is the first African American to be chosen as the first pick, in the first round of the NFL draft by the Washington Redskins. The running back is immediately traded to the Cleveland Browns.

1963, After a 13-month battle against acute monocytic leukemia, the most virulent form of blood cancer, former Syracuse running back Ernie Davis succumbs to the disease and dies in a Cleveland hospital. Davis was 23.

TERRELL DAVIS

1998, Terrell Davis, for the Denver Broncos, rushes for 2,008 yards in 392 attempts, averaging 5.12 yards per carry. He is the fourth player to rush for more than 2,000 yards.

GENE DERRICOTTE

1944, Gene Derricotte, a running back and kick return specialist, is the first Black player for the University of Michigan Wolverines football team.

ELDRIDGE DICKEY

1968, In keeping with current NFL tradition, the Oakland Raiders draft Tennessee State quarterback sensation Eldridge Dickey in the first round as a wide receiver. Dickey becomes the first Black quarterback drafted in the first round by either the American Football or National Football Leagues.

PARNELL DICKINSON

1976, Parnell Dickinson from Mississippi Valley State University Delta Devils becomes the first Black starting quarterback for the Tampa Bay Buccaneers.

TONY DORSETT

"I'm a strong believer that you practice like you play, little things make big things happen."

1976, Tony Dorsett for Pittsburgh becomes the first collegiate Division I-A player to rush for more than 6,000 (6,082) yards during his career.

TONY DUNGY

"I don't have the strength or wisdom to get through a single day without guidance and grace from God."

1977, Minnesota University's all-time leading passer, Tony Dungy, is not drafted by the NFL. The Pittsburgh Steelers later sign quarterback Dungy as a safety.

2000, On October 9, coaches Dennis Green of the Minnesota Vikings and Tony Dungy of the Tampa Bay Buccaneers, with quarterbacks Daunte Culpepper and Shaun King on Monday Night Football, become the first teams with Black coaches and Black quarterbacks to face-off.

2003, The first NFL Playoff Game featuring two Black head coaches occurs on 4 January. Herman Edwards' New York Jets defeats Tony Dungy's Indianapolis Colts 41-0 in the wild-card round.

2003, With a win over coach Herman Edwards's New York Jets, Indianapolis Colts coach Tony Dungy becomes the first coach to defeat all 32 NFL teams.

2007, Lovie Smith coach of the Chicago Bears and Tony Dungy of the Indianapolis Colts, become the first African American NFL coaches in the Super Bowl. Smith's Bears defeat the New Orleans Saints, followed by Dungy's Colts defeating the New England Patriots to earn this honor. In the process the Colts defeat the Bears, 29–17, at Dolphin Stadium in Miami Gardens, Fla.

2008, Coming off a Super Bowl victory, Tony Dungy becomes the only person to coach a Super Bowl team and write a *New York Times* best seller. Dungy's memoir, *Quiet Strength: The Principles, Practices, and Priorities of a Winning Life*, becomes the first football book to top the best-seller list.

WARRICK DUNN

2009, Retired running back Warrick Dunn becomes a minority owner of the Atlanta Falcons. Dunn purchases a 1% minority stake in the Falcons organization for $9 million.

HERM EDWARDS
"You play to win the game."

2003, Herman Edwards of the New York Jets becomes the first African American NFL coach on the cover of *Sports Illustrated*. The issue entitled "101 Most Influential Minorities in Sports" shows Edwards along with 27 other personalities.

VINCE EVANS

1979, Doug Williams of the Tampa Bay Bucs and Vince Evans of the Chicago Bears become the first African American quarterbacks to face-off in NFL competition. Evans is the first Black starting quarterback for the Bears.

1980, Vince Evans becomes the first African American quarterback, the second overall, to earn a maximum single-game passing rating of 158.3. Evans of the Chicago Bears completes 18 of 22 passes for 316 yards and throws three touchdowns against the Green Bay Packers.

1987, Vince Evans is the first Black starting quarterback for the Oakland Raiders.

MEL FARR

1967, Mel Farr of the Detroit Lions becomes the first player named the NFL's Offensive Rookie of the Year.

CHARLES FOLLIS

1904, Charles W. "Black Cyclone from Wooster" Follis becomes the first professional football player with the Shelby Blues of the Ohio League. Follis, a halfback, and Branch Rickey were teammates on the amateur Shelby Athletic Association in 1902 and 1903.

JOSH FREEMAN

2009, Josh Freeman from Kansas State University is the first Black regular starting quarterback for the Tampa Bay Buccaneers in his rookie season. QB Parnell Dickinson started one game for the Buccaneers in 1976.

2016, Josh Freeman is the first Black starting quarterback for the Indianapolis Colts. George Taliaferro had started for the Baltimore Colts back in 1953.

JAKE GAITHER
Gaither wanted a player who was "mobile, agile and hostile."

1963, Jake Gaither, coach for Florida A&M Rattlers, creates the Split-Line T formation, later copied by most major college football programs.

1969, Jake Gaither's Florida A&M Rattlers defeat the Spartans of the University of Tampa, 34–28, in the South's first football game between a white college and a historically black college.

DAVID GARRARD

2002, David Garrard from East Carolina University is the first Black starting quarterback for the Jacksonville Jaguars.

2005, The Jacksonville Jaguars start the season with three African American quarterbacks: Byron Leftwich, David Garrard and the undrafted Quinn Gray, an NFL first.

Colorful Firsts in U.S. Sports

PRENTICE GAUTT

2006, Oklahoma University paints a solid crimson line on its football field's 38-yard-line from sideline to sideline in its game against the Colorado Buffs. This is in honor of the Sooner's first African American football player, Prentice Gautt, who wore jersey No. 38. Gautt went on to play in the NFL and later a career in athletic administration. He dies in 2005.

EDDIE GEORGE

2000, Tennessee Titans running back Eddie George is the first African American on the cover of *Madden NFL 2001* sports game, by himself across all platforms. George is a four-time pro bowler.

AARON GIBSON

2000, Aaron Gibson from the University of Wisconsin is the first NFL player to weigh over 400 pounds. The six-foot-seven offensive tackle bench presses 475 pounds and has a 31.5 inch vertical jump. Gibson can also dunk a basketball and do the splits.

COOKIE GILCHRIST

1962, Cookie Gilchrist becomes the first AFL running back to rush for 1,000 yards (1,096 in a 14-game season). In 1953, Joe Perry was the first African American player in the NFL to rush for more than 1,000 yards (1,018).

JOE GILLIAM

"Joe Gilliam threw one of the best spirals I've ever seen." – Terry Bradshaw

1972, Jefferson Street Joe Gilliam from Tennessee State becomes the first Black quarterback for the Pittsburgh Steelers.

1973, Joe Gilliam is the first Black starting quarterback for the Pittsburgh Steelers.

1974, Joe Gilliam becomes the first Black quarterback to start and win an opening day NFL game, defeating the Baltimore Colts, 30-0. Jefferson Street Joe Gilliam carries the Pittsburgh Steelers to the playoffs under coach Chuck Noll.

HORACE GILLOM

1947, Horace Gillom, punter for the Cleveland Browns, records the highest hang time in game history with 5.5 seconds. *Sports Illustrated* writer Dr. Z votes him to the All-Time Browns team in 1999.

1954, Horace Gillom of the Cleveland Browns kicks the longest punt (80 yards) in NFL history against the New York Giants. Gillom is credited with inventing the phrase "hang time."

HOYT GIVENS

1949, Harold Robinson and Hoyt Givens become the first African American football players at Kansas State University, home of the Wildcats. Robinson would earn All-Big 7 Conference honors in 1950.

RICH GLOVER

1971, Defensive guard Rich Glover of Nebraska is the first Black named Big-Eight Conference Player of the Year.

1972, Rich Glover, middle guard from Nebraska University, becomes the first African American to win the Vince Lombardi/Rotary Award. Glover also wins the Outland Trophy for the best college football interior lineman.

MEL GRAY

1997, Mel Gray becomes the first NFL player to amass more than 10,000 in kickoff return yards. He retires this year with 10,250 career yards.

QUINN GRAY

2005, The Jacksonville Jaguars start the season with three African American quarterbacks: Byron Leftwich, David Garrard and the undrafted Quinn Gray, out of Florida A&M, an NFL first.

DARRELL GREEN

2000, Darrell Green of the Washington Redskins becomes the first NFL player over 40 years old to run a sub 4.3 in the 40-yard dash in a record time of 4.24 seconds.

Football Champions

DENNIS GREEN
"The secret of success is to start from scratch and keep on scratching."

2000, On October 9, coaches Dennis Green of the Minnesota Vikings and Tony Dungy of the Tampa Bay Buccaneers, with quarterbacks Daunte Culpepper and Shaun King on Monday Night Football, become the first teams with Black coaches and Black quarterbacks to face-off.

JIM GREGORY

1981, A TV movie *Grambling's White Tiger* tells the true story of Jim Gregory, the first White quarterback at Grambling College in 1962.

BOBBY GRIER

1956, Bobby Grier, a fullback and linebacker for the Pittsburgh Panthers is the first African American football player to break the color barrier of the collegiate Sugar Bowl game, which is held in New Orleans, La. Segregationists try to keep Grier from playing because he is Black. Georgia's governor Marvin Griffin publicly threatens the Georgia Tech's president Blake Van Leer to cancel the game. Later in July, the Louisiana state legislature passes Act 579, known as the Athletic Events Bill, which prohibits interracial sports competitions.

JOHNNY GRIER

1988, Johnny Grier becomes the first African American referee in the NFL. Grier serves as a field judge in the NFL for seven years before being promoted to referee.

ARCHIE GRIFFIN
"In the face of adversity, you find out if you're a fighter or a quitter. It's all about getting up after you've been knocked down."

1975, Archie Griffin of Ohio State University becomes the first Division I-A player to rush for over 5,000 yards (5,177) during his collegiate career (1972-1975). Griffin also becomes the first person to win consecutive Heisman Trophies.

ROBERT GRIFFIN III

2012, Robert Griffin III posts the most efficient rookie season in NFL history with a 102.4 QB rating. The mark is the 39th-best overall season by a quarterback in league history and, at 22 years old, RG3 is the youngest player to ever have a season rated 100.0 or better. Despite not playing one game, Griffin's stat line reads 3,200 yards, 20 TD, 5 INT, and a 65.6 completion percentage. Griffin also sets the NFL rookie record for rushing yards by a QB with 815 yards and seven TDs.

2012, Robert Griffin III of the Washington Redskins and Russell Wilson of the Seattle Seahawks are the first Black rookie quarterbacks to face-off in an NFL playoff game.

2014, Quarterback Robert Griffin III is forced to turn his shirt with the quote "Know Jesus Know Peace" inside out before speaking at a news conference.

MELVIN GROOMES

1948, Melvin Groomes, a halfback, and Bob Mann, an end, become the first African American players for the NFL's Detroit Lions.

JAREN HALL

2019, Jaren Hall becomes the first African American starting quarterback in Brigham Young University's nearly 100-year history. BYU is owned by the Church of Latter Day Saints (LDS) and its student body is 99% LDS according to its website. BYU lifted the ban on Black people becoming priests and entering their temples in 1978.

ELMORE "PEPPER" HARRIS

1947, Running back Elmore "Pepper" Harris becomes the AAFC Brooklyn Dodgers' first African American player.

FRANCO HARRIS
"And so, it's not a thing of how many carries, but were you effective when you did carry."

1975, Franco Harris, running back for the Pittsburgh Steelers, becomes the first African American player to be named Super Bowl MVP, winning the honor in Super Bowl IX against the Minnesota Vikings.

JAMES "SHACK" HARRIS

Early on, I got sacked. On the sideline, one coach came up to me and said, "The offensive line says the reason they missed their blocks was because they couldn't understand your diction."

1969, As the overall 192nd pick in the eighth round, James Harris from Grambling University becomes the first Black quarterback for the Buffalo Bills and the first Black QB to start a season-opener in the NFL.

1970, The Buffalo Bills become the first NFL team to have two Black quarterbacks on its roster, James Harris and Marlin Briscoe, although the latter is listed as a wide receiver.

1973, James Harris becomes the first Black quarterback for the Los Angeles Rams.

1975, James Harris from Grambling State University becomes the first African American quarterback to start a playoff game, leading the Los Angeles Rams to a 19-10 victory over the Washington Redskins.

1975, James Harris becomes the first African American quarterback named Pro Bowl's Player of the Game (MVP) with two fourth-quarter touchdowns.

1977, James Harris becomes the first Black quarterback for the San Diego Chargers.

JAMES HASTY

2000, James Hasty is the only NFL player with more than 40 career interceptions and 20 career fumble recoveries with the New York Jets, Kansas City Chiefs and Oakland Raiders.

RON HATCHER

1962, The Washington Redskins, owned by George Preston Marshall, become the last NFL team to sign African Americans, wide receiver Bobby Mitchell and fullback Ron Hatcher.

"BULLET" BOB HAYES

1964, Bob Hayes is the first sprinter to run the 60-yard dash in less than six seconds (5.9).

1971, Wide receiver Bullet Bob Hayes becomes the first Olympic Gold Medalist (1964, 100 meters) to play for a Super Bowl champion the Dallas Cowboys. Because of his speed, NFL defenses give up playing man-to-man coverage and use zone defenses. Hayes is the first sprinter to run a 9.1 second 100-yard dash.

ABNER HAYNES

1957, Abner Haynes and Leon King become the first African American collegiate football players in Texas when they join North Texas State College (now University of North Texas) Eagles.

1960, Abner Haynes of the Dallas Texans is the first African American named the American Football League's Most Valuable Player and its Rookie of the Year. Haynes leads the AFL in rushing and becomes the first rookie to amass more than 2,000 all-purpose yards in a season (2,100). Haynes is also named Rookie of the Year by *UPI* and the *Sporting News*.

KYLIN HILL

2020, Running back Kylin Hill declares he will not play for the Mississippi State University Bulldogs unless the state removes a Confederate battle emblem from its flag. In June, the Mississippi legislature votes to the blue cross with 13 white stars from the flag's design. SEC Commissioner Greg Sankey threatens to block future championships events in the state saying, "It is past time for change to be made to the flag of the state of Mississippi." Note, Mississippi State University and Ole Miss stopped flying the Confederate flag in 2016.

MELLODY HOBSON

2022, Mellody Hobson, co-CEO of Ariel Investments, joins the Walton-Penner ownership group purchasing the NFL's Denver Broncos. The $4.65 billion deal makes Hobson the first Black woman to be part of a new ownership group buying an NFL team. She is later joined by former U.S. Secretary of State Condoleezza Rice, a professional football analyst.

DENNIE HOGGARD

1948, Wally Triplett and Dennie Hoggard, Jr. become the first African Americans to play in the Cotton Bowl. Triplett catches the tying touchdown in Penn State's 13-13 tie with Southern Methodist University, who discourage the Nittany Lions from bringing

African American players to the game.

JAMELLE HOLIEWAY
"Some people are born on third base and go through life thinking they hit a triple." – Barry Switzer

1986, At Oklahoma, Jamelle Holieway takes over for an injured QB Troy Aikman in his frosh year and leads the Sooners to an 11-1-0 record under Coach Barry Switzer. Oklahoma defeats the Penn State Nittany Lions for the national championship in the Orange Bowl. He becomes the first true frosh quarterback to lead his team to the national title.

BRUD HOLLAND
1935, Jerome Heartwell "Brud" Holland becomes the first African American football player at Cornell University. He achieved gridiron first-team All-American honors in 1937 and 1938. After receiving bachelor's and master's degrees from Cornell, he earned his doctorate from the University of Pennsylvania. Dr. Holland later became president of Delaware State College.

1938, Wilmeth Sidat-Singh of Syracuse and Jerome "Brud" Holland of Cornell become the first African Americans invited to play for the College All-Stars against the New York Giants.

TRINDON HOLLIDAY
2013, Denver's Trindon Holliday returns a punt 90 yards for a touchdown in the first quarter and runs back the second-half kickoff for a 104-yard TD versus the Baltimore Ravens. Holliday becomes the first player in NFL post-season history to score on a kick and a punt return in the same game. The Broncos lose 38-35, in two overtimes.

CONDREDGE HOLLOWAY
1972, Condredge Holloway becomes the first Black quarterback in the Southeastern Conference, as a player with the Tennessee Volunteers. Holloway is the only Tennessee student-athlete named to Tennessee's All-Century squads in both baseball and football.

SHERMAN HOWARD
1950, Running backs Buddy Young and Sherman Howard, along with quarterback George Taliaferro become the first African Americans to play for the New York Yanks in the NFL.

DICK HUDSON
1923, Running back Richard "Dick" Hudson, aka "Super Six," becomes the first African American to play for the Minnesota Marines in the NFL.

TRAVIS HUNTER
2021, Two-way player at receiver and cornerback, Travis Hunter from Collins Hill High School in Suwanee, Ga., becomes the first five-star recruit to sign with an HBCU school when signing with Jackson State College in Mississippi. He later transfers to the Colorado Buffaloes in the Pac-12 Conference and wins the Heisman Trophy in 2024.

EDDIE P. HURT
1937, Football coach Eddie Hurt at Morgan State College devises the four-man defensive front, a first. Later, in 1943, his Bears team goes undefeated, untied and unscored upon. Hurt also coached track & field and basketball.

JALEN HURTS
2023, Jalen Hurts of the Philadelphia Eagles and Patrick Mahomes of the Kansas City Chiefs, become the first Black quarterbacks to face off in the Super Bowl, doing so in Glendale, Ariz.

LEE A. HUTTON III
2023, Attorney Lee A. Hutton III is named commissioner of the Arena Football League. He is the first Black man to lead a professional sports league in the U.S.

LIONEL JAMES
1985, Lionel James of the San Diego Chargers becomes the first player to gain more than 2,500 yards in a season, running for 516

yards, receiving 1,027 yards and returning 992 yards for a total of 2,535 yards.

WILBUR JACKSON

1972, Running back Wilbur Jackson from Carroll High School in Ozark, Alabama becomes the first scholarship football player for Alabama University. In 2007, he is inducted into the Alabama Sports Hall of Fame. See John Mitchell.

WILLIAM TECUMSEH SHERMAN JACKSON

1890, William Henry Lewis and William Tecumseh Sherman Jackson become the first African American players on a White college football team as members of the Amherst squad.

WILLIE JEFFRIES

1979, Willie Jeffries becomes the first Black head football coach in Division I when named coach at Wichita State (Kansas).

GEORGE JEWETT

1890, George Jewett becomes the first African American to play varsity football at the University of Michigan. Jewett was an Ann Arbor High School star in both football and track.

BILLY "WHITE SHOES" JOHNSON

1974, Billy "White Shoes" Johnson of the Houston Oilers does the funky chicken in the end zone after a touchdown. The press labels the act, "sexually suggestive" in nature. The NFL penalizes excessive demonstrative touchdown dances the next year.

1983, Billy "White Shoes" Johnson, a wide receiver for the Atlanta Falcons is the first African American to win *Pro Football Weekly's* Comeback Player of the Year award.

JIMMY JOHNSON

1969, After leading the USC Trojans to an undefeated season, Jimmy Johnson becomes the first Black collegiate quarterback to appear on the cover of *Sports Illustrated*.

1970, Quarterback Jimmy Johnson, fullback Sam "The Bam" Cunningham and running back Clarence Davis, of USC, become the first all-Black backfield in Division I football.

1994, Olympic decathlon athlete Rafer Johnson's brother James Earl "Jimmy" Johnson is selected to the National Football Hall of Fame. The five-time Pro Bowler was a wide receiver and cornerback for the San Francisco 49ers.

MAGIC JOHNSON

1998, Earvin "Magic" Johnson from Cathedral High School in Los Angeles sets a national high school record with eight receiving touchdown catches in one game.

CALVIN JONES

1954, Calvin Jones becomes the first football player, collegiate or professional, to appear on the cover of *Sports Illustrated*.

1955, Iowa's team captain Calvin Jones is the first African American to win the Outland Trophy as the best linebacker in college football.

DEACON JONES

"The head slap was not my invention, but Rembrandt, of course, did not invent painting. The quickness of my hands and the length of my arms was perfect for me. It was the greatest thing I ever did, and when I left the game, they outlawed it."

1967, Deacon Jones of the Los Angeles Rams becomes the first player to record more than 25 sacks (26) in a season. He was nicknamed "the Secretary of Defense."

1977, The NFL outlaws the "head slap" made popular by the retired (1974) Deacon Jones of the Los Angeles Rams, San Diego Chargers and Washington Redskins.

1982, The NFL recognizes "sacks" as an official statistic. This is largely due to the success of defensive end Deacon Jones in his propensity for sacking quarterbacks when he played from 1961 to 1974. He is credited with 173.5 unofficial sacks during 14 seasons.

ED "TOO TALL" JONES

1979, Ed "Too Tall" Jones, an NFL All-Star defensive end standing 6-foot-9, retires from the Dallas Cowboys to be become a professional boxer. He labors to six victories before returning to the gridiron. Like Rocky Marciano, "Too Tall" retires undefeated.

HOMER JONES

1968, Homer Jones of the New York Giants becomes the first player to "intentionally" spike a football after a touchdown.

J.J. JONES

1975, J.J. Jones is the first Black starting quarterback for the New York Jets, in his only appearance as QB against the San Diego Chargers. He was replaced by Joe Namath.

JULIUS and THOMAS JONES

2006, Thomas Jones, Chicago Bears, and Julius Jones, Dallas Cowboys, become the first brothers to rush for more than 1,000 yards for different NFL teams in the same season. From Stone Gap, Va., (pop. 4,856) Thomas gains 1,210 yards (4.1 yards per carry), while younger brother Julius gains 1,084 (also 4.1).

2010, Julius Jones of the New Orleans Saints becomes the first NFL player to score a touchdown against the team (Seattle Seahawks) that released him in the same season.

COLIN KAEPERNICK

"I am not looking for approval. I have to stand up for people that are oppressed.

If they take football away, my endorsements from me, I know that I stood up for what is right."

2010, Colin Kaepernick of the Nevada Wolf Pack (WAC) becomes the first collegiate football player to pass for 10,000 (10,098) yards and rush for 4,000 (4,112) yards.

2016, Colin Kaepernick of the San Francisco 49ers, takes a knee during the national anthem during a preseason game against the Green Bay Packers. Kaepernick objects to the increased cases of police brutality against minorities in America.

2017, Colin Kaepernick appears on the cover of *GQ*, a fashion magazine, as selection for "Citizen of the Year."

2019, Nike releases the Air Max 1 Quick Strike sneaker featuring the Betsy Ross flag on the heel. The design drew complaints because the 1776 logo appears to glorify slavery and racism in U.S. history. Nike representative Colin Kaepernick tells *The Wall Street Journal* they should reconsider the design out of concern that it would send the wrong message about race in modern times. Nike pulls the shoes from the marketplace.

JEVON KEARSE

2000, Jevon Kearse of the Tennessee Titans, known as "The Freak," becomes the first NFL rookie to record more than 15 sacks (15½) in regular season (1999) and in playoff games (2000).

RAY KEMP

1933, Ray Kemp with the Pittsburgh Pirates and Joe Lillard with the Chicago Cardinals are last African Americans released from NFL teams leaving the league exclusively white.

JENNIFER KING

2020, Jennifer King, a Carolina Panthers intern during the 2017 preseason, joins the Washington Football Team's staff as a full-time assistant coach. King is the first full-time African American female coach in league history and the fourth woman with a full-time assistant job overall. (Collette Smith was the NFL's first Black female coach, serving as an intern with the New York Jets in 2017.) King joins Tampa Bay Buccaneers assistant defensive line coach Lori Locust, Bucs' assistant strength and conditioning coach Maral Javadifar and San Francisco 49ers offensive assistant Katie Sowers as the only women working as full-time NFL coaches.

2021, Jennifer King becomes the first full-time female African American NFL coach (assistant running backs coach) with the Washington Football Team. She has also coached women's college basketball. King later becomes NFL's first woman named as a position coach when promoted to head running backs coach.

Colorful Firsts in U.S. Sports

LEON KING

1957, Abner Haynes and Leon King become the first African American collegiate football players in Texas when they join North Texas State College (now University of North Texas) Eagles.

SHAUN KING

1999, A record six African American quarterbacks are drafted by NFL teams: Akili Smith (Oregon State), Donovan McNabb (Syracuse), Aaron Brooks (Virginia), Michael Bishop (K-State), Shaun King (Tulane), and Daunte Culpepper (Central Florida). McNabb, Smith and Culpepper are taken in the first round, a record. Overall, only four Black QB's had been taken in the first round in the first 63 years of the NFL.

2000, On October 9, coaches Dennis Green of the Minnesota Vikings and Tony Dungy of the Tampa Bay Buccaneers, with quarterbacks Daunte Culpepper and Shaun King on Monday Night Football, in Minn., become the first teams with African American coaches and African American quarterbacks to face-off. The Vikings win.

DICK "NIGHTRAIN" LANE

1952, In his rookie year Dick "Night Train" Lane sets an NFL record for most interceptions in a 12-game season with 14.

In the 60's, Dick "Night Train" Lane tackles wide receivers around the neck. The clothesline tackles, called "Neckties," are subsequently banned by the NFL. He was married to jazz singer Dinah Washington.

WILLIE LANIER

1967, Considered the most cerebral defensive position in football, Willie Lanier becomes the NFL's first African American starting middle linebacker.

1972, Willie Lanier of the Kansas City Chiefs becomes the first African American to win the prestigious NFL Man of the Year Award, now named the Walter Payton Man of the Year, in recognition of his service to the community.

BYRON LEFTWICH

2005, The Jacksonville Jaguars start the season with three African American quarterbacks: Byron Leftwich, David Garrard and the undrafted Quinn Gray, an NFL first.

RAY LEWIS

"Bottom line, your body is a temple, and you have to treat it that way. That's how God designed it."

2001, The NFL bans do-rags and bandanas from being worn under football helmets. However, skullcaps are fine as long as they bear the team logo and colors. Team officials say Super Bowl MVP Ray Lewis of the Baltimore Ravens is permitted to wear a covering because of a scalp condition.

WILLIAM HENRY LEWIS

1890, William Henry Lewis and William Tecumseh Sherman Jackson become the first African American players on a White college football team as members of the Amherst squad.

1892, William Henry Lewis, a center from Harvard University, is named the first African American All-American in college football. Lewis later serves 12 years as a football coach at Harvard.

1896, William Henry Lewis, former All-American collegian, writes the *Primer of College Football*, the first book of its kind. The volume is published by *Harper & Brothers* and serialized in *Harper's Weekly*. In 1911 he is among the first African Americans to be admitted to the American Bar Association.

JOE "THE MIDNIGHT EXPRESS" LILLARD

1932, Joe Lillard is the first Black quarterback, and the only person of color, on the Chicago Cardinals of the NFL. Lillard also plays for the Harlem Globetrotters, Chicago Hottentots and Savoy Big Five basketball teams. And a pitcher and outfielder for the Brooklyn Royal Giants, Cincinnati Tigers and Chicago American Giants baseball teams.

1933, Ray Kemp with the Pittsburgh Pirates and Joe Lillard with the Chicago Cardinals are last African Americans released from NFL teams leaving the league exclusively white.

DEREK LOVILLE

1990, Bruce Perkins (from Arizona State) of the Tampa Bay Buccaneers and Derek Loville (Oregon) of the Seattle Seahawks become the first undrafted rookie running backs to start in week one of a season.

PAUL LOWE

1963, Paul Lowe, running back for the AFL's San Diego Chargers, is the first African American to win the *Associated Press'* Comeback Player of the Year Award.

RAY LUCAS

2002, After an injury to Jay Fiedler, Ray Lucas from Rutgers University becomes the first Black starting quarterback for the Miami Dolphins.

MARSHAWN LYNCH

"I ain't got nothing to say. I just wanna play football."

2015, Marshawn Lynch, Seattle Seahawks running back, is fined $75,000 by the NFL for not speaking to the media following the NFC Championship game. At Super Bowl Media Day, he says, "I'm just here so I won't get fined." Lynch proved prophetic as he was not fined for the now infamous quote.

NICOLE LYNN

2019, When University of Alabama defensive tackle Quinnen Williams is the third pick of the 2019 NFL Draft, Nicole Lynn becomes the first Black female agent to represent a first-round draft choice.

JOHN MACKEY

1970, When the National Football League and the American Football League merge, Hall of Famer and former Baltimore Colts tight-end John Mackey becomes the first president of the National Football League Players Association. Mackey became the lead plaintiff in a court action which led to the overturning of the so-called "Rozelle Rule," which limited a player's ability to function as a free agent. In 1976, the Rozelle Rule was ruled to violate antitrust laws in *Mackey v. NFL*. Mackey held the presidency until 1973.

PATRICK MAHOMES

"You can't have a good Thanksgiving meal without a little bit of ketchup on the side."

2020, Patrick Mahomes, Kansas City Chiefs quarterback, becomes the first half-billion dollar athlete in U.S. sports history. Mahomes signs a 10-year contract extension that with contract incentives is worth a total of $503 million. The contract includes just over $63 million in guaranteed money at the point of signing, and $141 million is guaranteed in the event of injury.

2023, Jalen Hurts of the Philadelphia Eagles and Patrick Mahomes of the Kansas City Chiefs, become the first Black quarterbacks to face off in the Super Bowl, doing so in Glendale, Ariz.

BOB MANN

1948, Melvin Groomes, a halfback, and Bob Mann, an end, become the first African American players for the NFL's Detroit Lions.

1950, Bob Mann becomes the first African American player for the Green Bay Packers in the NFL.

EJ MANUEL

2013, Buffalo Bills' Erik Rodriguez "EJ" Manuel Jr. becomes the first rookie QB to defeat a defending Super Bowl champion, the Baltimore Ravens.

OLLIE MATSON

1952, Clifton Anderson, an end, and running backs Ollie Matson and Wally Triplett become the first African Americans to play for the Chicago Cardinals of the NFL.

1957, Ollie Matson becomes the first African American NFL player to appear on the cover of *Sports Illustrated*.

1959, The Los Angeles Rams, led by G.M. Pete Rozelle, trade seven players, a 1959 second-round pick and a player to be named

DAVE MAYS

1974, Dave Mays and D.C. Nobles are the first Black quarterbacks hired by the Houston Texans of the World Football League.

1977, Dave Mays is the first Black starting quarterback for the Cleveland Browns.

EDDIE McASHAN

1970, Eddie McAshan becomes the first Black starting quarterback for the Georgia Tech Yellow Jackets.

1974, Eddie McAshan and Reggie Oliver become the first Black quarterbacks employed by the Jacksonville Sharks of the World Football League.

JOHN McCLUSKEY

1964, John McCluskey becomes the first African American in Ivy League history to start at quarterback. McCluskey leads Harvard to a 6-3 record in 1964 and a 5-2-2 record in 1965.

HENRY McDONALD

1911, Henry McDonald from Haiti becomes the first Black player for the Rochester Jeffersons of the New York Professional Football League. The halfback plays with the team until 1917.

CURTIS McCLINTON

1967, Curtis "The Count" McClinton becomes the first African American to score a TD in the Super Bowl (I), on a seven-yard pass from quarterback Lenny Dawson.

DONOVAN McNABB

"I think in a lot of ways, I handle the leadership role a little different than others. I'm not going to rah-rah or slap you across the helmet or push you. I'm going to talk to you."

1999, A record six African American quarterbacks are drafted by NFL teams: Akili Smith (Oregon State), Donovan McNabb (Syracuse), Aaron Brooks (Virginia), Michael Bishop (K-State), Shaun King (Tulane), and Daunte Culpepper (Central Florida). McNabb, Smith and Culpepper are taken in the first round, a record. Overall, only four Black QB's had been taken in the first round in the first 63 years of the NFL.

2003, Popular talk show host Russ Limbaugh is hired by ESPN to do commentary on its Sunday NFL Countdown. Limbaugh comments that Philadelphia Eagles quarterback Donovan McNabb is overrated because the white liberal media wants a Black quarterback to do well. Within 48 hours Limbaugh is forced to resign for his incendiary racist remarks.

2010, Mike Shanahan, coach of the Washington Redskins, in a game against the Lions in Detroit, trailing 31-25, benches veteran quarterback Donovan McNabb with two minutes left. Replaced by Rex Grossman, who was sacked and fumbled, as the Redskins lose 37-25. When asked by reporters regarding the decision to change quarterbacks, Shanahan replied, "I wasn't sure Donovan (a 12-year veteran) knew our two-minute offense (which is practiced weekly) well enough." Shanahan was pushing the racial coding that Black players are intellectually inferior to their white counterparts. In 2005, McNabb took Andy Reid's Philadelphia Eagles to the Super Bowl.

STEVE McNAIR

1994, Alcorn State QB Steve McNair wins the Walter Payton Award as the top player in Division I-AA.

2003, Steve McNair of the Tennessee Titans becomes the first African American quarterback to lead the NFL in passing and is selected co-MVP of the league.

WARREN McVEY

1965, Warren McVey, a running back from San Antonio, becomes the African American football player for the Houston Cougars.

JON McWILLIAMS

1955, Charles Bryant and Jon McWilliams, both from the University of Nebraska, are the first Black players to play in the Orange Bowl.

ROBERT MIKE

1948, Running back Joe Perry and tackle Robert Mike become San Francisco 49ers's (AAFC) first African American players.

GENE MINGO

1960, Gene Mingo from Akron (OH) South High School joins the Denver Broncos of the American Football League (AFL) and becomes the first African American placekicker in football. He also recorded the first punt return for a touchdown in the AFL. The versatile Mingo holds the record for the most touchdown passes by a halfback, two.

BOBBY MITCHELL

1962, The Washington Redskins, owned by George Preston Marshall, become the last NFL team to sign African Americans, wide receiver Bobby Mitchell and fullback Ron Hatcher.

1962, Bobby Mitchell leads the NFL in receptions with 72 catches, as the Redskins finish 5-7-2 in fourth place, under coach Bill McPeak.

JOHN MITCHELL

1972, John Mitchell, a two-time Junior College All-American defensive end transfers from Eastern Arizona Junior College to Alabama's Crimson Tide and becomes the first Black player to play in a game for Alabama. See Wilbur Jackson.

WARREN MOON

"The CFL made me a more versatile QB because of all the things you had to do once you got on the field. And if I wasn't as versatile as I was, I wouldn't have been as successful in all the different offenses that I was in, in the NFL."

1982, Playing in the Canadian Football League, Warren Moon becomes the first pro quarterback to throw for 5,000 yards in a season.

1984, Warren Moon from the Washington University Huskies is the first Black starting quarterback for the Houston Oilers.

1990, Houston Oilers QB Warren Moon passes for 527 yards against the Kansas City Chiefs. This is the most passing yardage in the NFL since the 1970 merger. The Oilers win 27-10.

1994, Warren Moon becomes the first African American quarterback to play for a Black head coach, Dennis Green, for the Minnesota Vikings. Moon is also the Vikings' first Black starting quarterback.

1997, The first Black starting quarterback for the Seattle Seahawks, Warren Moon becomes the NFL's first player over 40 years old to run for a touchdown.

2000, Warren Moon is the first Black starting quarterback in Kansas City Chiefs franchise history.

2001, Warren Moon becomes the first African American quarterback inducted into the Canadian Football Hall of Fame.

2006, Warren Moon, becomes the first African American quarterback inducted into the Pro Football Hall of Fame in Canton, Ohio. He is also the first player to be inducted in both the NFL Hall of Fame and the Canadian Football Hall of Fame.

LENNY MOORE

1956, Lenny Moore of the Baltimore Colts is the first African American named Rookie of the Year in the NFL by the *United Press International*.

SANDRA DOUGLASS MORGAN

2022, The Las Vegas Raiders name Sandra Douglass Morgan team president, making her the first Black woman to hold the position in NFL history. A native of Las Vegas, Morgan becomes the second Black person named president of an NFL team after the Washington Commanders hired Jason Wright to the position in 2020.

MARION MOTLEY

1946, The Cleveland Browns sign running back Marion Motley and defensive lineman Bill Willis as the AAFC's first African American players. Each player's seasonal salary is $4,000, of which 75% was to be paid semi-monthly. The balance of 25% would be paid after the last game.

1950, Marion Motley runs for 188 yards with only 11 carries, against the Pittsburgh Steelers. His 17.1 yards per carry is a single-game NFL record. Michael Vick breaks the record in 2002. Motley becomes the first African American to lead the NFL in rushing with 810 yards, and three touchdowns. Motley of the Cleveland Browns is the first African American to participate in an NFL championship game.

Colorful Firsts in U.S. Sports

DAVE WILLOUGHBY MYERS

1929, The *New York Daily News* reports that the University of Georgia football team will not play the New York University Violets if quarterback Dave Myers is allowed to take the field. Despite protest from the NAACP, Myers is benched as the Violets beat the Bulldogs 27-19.

1930, Dave Willoughby Myers, an undrafted guard and quarterback from New York University, is the first African American to play for the Staten Island Stapletons in the National Football League (NFL). The next season he plays for the NFL's Brooklyn Dodgers.

JIM NANCE

1966, Jim Nance of the Boston Patriots is the first African American to lead the American Football League in rushing with 1,458.

OZZIE NEWSOME

2002, Ozzie Newsome becomes the first Black general manager in the NFL with the Baltimore Ravens.

CAM NEWTON

"I hate excuses. Excuses are a disease."

2011, Cam Newton of the Carolina Panthers becomes the first rookie QB to pass for more than 4,000 yards (4,051) and is also the first player to throw more than 400 yards in his NFL debut.

2014, Cam Newton of the Carolina Panthers becomes the first QB to have more than 10,000 passing yards, and 2,000 rushing yards over his first three seasons.

D. C. NOBLES

1970, D.C. Nobles is the first Black quarterback for the University of Houston Cougars.

1974, Dave Mays and D.C. Nobles are the first Black quarterbacks hired by the Houston Texans of the World Football League.

NATE NORTHINGTON

1967, Nate Northington becomes the first African American scholarship football player in the Southeastern Conference (SEC) with the University of Kentucky. In 2016, the university unveils a new statue of Northington, Greg Page, Wilbur Hackett and Houston Hogg in recognition of the first four Black football players in the SEC.

REGGIE OLIVER

1974, Reggie Oliver and Eddie McAshan become the first Black quarterbacks employed by the Jacksonville Sharks of the World Football League.

JEFFREY ORRIDGE

2015, Jeffrey Orridge becomes the first African American chief executive of a major North American sports league as the 13th commissioner of the Canadian Football League (CFL).

R. C. OWENS

1962, R.C. Owens, a 6-foot-3 Baltimore Colts wide receiver, (better known for popularizing the Alley-Oop pass, in which the receiver outjumps the defenders) blocks a 40-yard field goal at the crossbar in a game against the Washington Redskins. At the time, a legal defensive move.

TERRELL OWENS

"I love me some me."

2000, Terrell Owens of the San Francisco 49ers becomes the first NFL receiver to catch 20 passes in a game. He totals 283 receiving yards against the Chicago Bears.

2002, The Sharpie Rule is invoked by the NFL. San Francisco 49ers wide receiver Terrell Owens, after scoring a touchdown vs. the Seattle Seahawks on Monday Night Football, pulled out a Sharpie from his sock, autographed the football and handed it to his financial advisor. According to the memo, "A player having any foreign object that is deemed a safety hazard, including a pen, will result in a 15-yard penalty and ejection from the game. Such a penalty can also warrant a fine, congruent with the league's current stance on unsportsmanlike conduct."

ALAN PAGE

1971, Alan Page is the first African American to win National Football Conference's Player of the Year Award.

1971, Alan Page becomes the first defensive player (DT) in NFL history to receive the Most Valuable Player Award. Earning his Juris Doctor in 1978, Page becomes the first African American to serve as an Associate Justice on the Minnesota Supreme Court in 1992.

2018, Alan Page is presented with the Presidential Medal of Freedom, the highest civilian award.

WALTER PAYTON

"When you're good at something, you'll tell everyone. When you're great at something, they'll tell you."

1977, Walter Payton becomes the first player to rush for 275 yards in a game and the youngest (23) to be named NFL's Most Valuable Player.

1977, Walter Payton is the first African American chosen by the Pro Football Writers Association as NFL Player of the Year.

1986, Walter Payton, Chicago Bears running back, becomes the first African American featured on the front of a Wheaties cereal box.

1995, Walter Payton becomes the first African American team owner in the Indy Car series. Payton partners with Dale Coyne in preparation for a race in Florida. The car bears Payton's jersey number 34.

1999, The NFL Man of the Year Award is renamed the Walter Payton NFL Man of the Year Award. It recognizes excellence off the field regarding an NFL player's charity work.

RODNEY PEETE

1989, Rodney Peete becomes the first Black starting quarterback for the Detroit Lions.

2002, Rodney Peete from USC is the first Black starting quarterback for the Carolina Panthers.

BRUCE PERKINS

1990, Bruce Perkins (from Arizona State) of the Tampa Bay Buccaneers and Derek Loville (Oregon) of the Seattle Seahawks become the first undrafted rookie running backs to start in week one of a season.

JOE PERRY

1948, Running back Joe Perry and tackle Robert Mike become San Francisco 49ers's (AAFC) first African American players.

1953, Joe Perry is the first African American to rush for more than 1,000 yards – 1,018 yards – in a season. In 1962, Cookie Gilchrist becomes the first AFL back to rush for 1,000 yards (1,096 in a 14-game season).

1954, San Francisco 49er Joe Perry rushes for 1,049 yards, to become the first player – Black or White – to rush more than 1,000 yards in back-to-back seasons, following his 1,018 yards in 1953.

1954, The NFL's top three rushers are Black: Joe Perry, John Henry Johnson and Tank Younger. Perry is the first non-drafted NFL player since the draft originated in 1936 to lead the league in rushing.

1954, Joe Perry becomes the first African American to be named NFL's Most Valuable Player.

1955, On August 28, Joe Perry of the San Francisco 49ers, becomes the first African American NFL player honored with a day. The 49ers give Perry a TV set and house furniture, but not the car on the field as first believed. He works for Boas Pontiac during the offseason, and the dealership puts the car on the field as advertisement.

LOWELL PERRY

1957, Lowell Perry becomes the first African American assistant coach (receivers coach) in the NFL with the Pittsburgh Steelers.

1966, Lowell Perry becomes the first Black broadcaster in the National Football League, when hired by CBS.

WILLIAM PERRY

1986, William "The Refrigerator" Perry, for the Chicago Bears, becomes the first defensive (DT) player to lineup as an offensive player (FB) and score a touchdown in the Super Bowl (XX) against the New England Patriots. The Bears win 46-10.

Colorful Firsts in U.S. Sports

BERT PIGGOTT

1947, Running and defensive back Bert Piggott, receiver Ezzrett "Sugarfoot" Anderson, and center John Brown become AAFC Los Angeles Dons' first African American players.

FRITZ POLLARD

1915, Paul Robeson and Fritz Pollard become the first Black football players at Rutgers and Brown Universities.

1916, Fritz Pollard, running back from Brown University, becomes the first African American to play in the Rose Bowl. Pollard is also the first African American football player at Brown. He becomes the first African American, who plays a backfield position, named to Walter Camp's All-American team. See 1892, William Henry Lewis, a lineman, was selected to the All-American squad.

1919, Fritz Pollard joins the Akron Pros/Indians independent football team.

1920, Several professional football players Fritz Pollard (with the Akron Pros), and Robert "Rube" Marshall (Rock Island [IL] Independents) make their debut in the new American Professional Football Association (APFA), later to become the NFL.

1921, George "Papa Bear" Halas, head coach of the Chicago Staleys, refuses to play the Akron Pros unless they drop quarterback and running back Fritz Pollard from its team.

1925, Fritz Pollard, a halfback, is the first and only Black player for the Providence Steam Rollers of the NFL.

1928, The Chicago Black Hawks, an all-Black team, is organized by Dr. Albert C. Johnson and Fritz Pollard, who also serves as quarterback, running back, and coach. The Black Hawks generally played against White teams around Chicago.

1935-1942, Herschel "Rip" Day, an African American athletic promoter from Harlem organizes the New York Brown Bombers professional football team. Fritz Pollard is named coach.

1938, The Chicago Brown Bombers organized by Fritz Pollard integrate the Northwest Football League, which lasted two and a half seasons, 1936-1938.

1954, Fritz Pollard, former Brown University halfback, is named to the College Football Hall of Fame. Frederick Douglass Pollard was the first African American football player at Brown in 1916.

2003, The Fritz Pollard Alliance is founded by attorneys Cyrus Mehri and Johnnie Cochran Jr. The Alliance is a 501(c)(6) membership organization comprised of scouts, coaches, and front office personnel in the NFL as well as other sports professionals committed to equal opportunity in the football industry.

GREG PRUITT

1979, The NFL rules that tear-away jerseys are illegal. The rule is aimed at Greg "Do-it-to-it" Pruitt of the Cleveland Browns who had several custom-made tear-away jerseys.

JOHN RANDLE

1998, Minnesota Viking defensive end John Randle is fined $5,000 for wearing face paint on Monday Night Football against the Green Bay Packers.

NATALIE RANDOLPH

2010, Natalie Randolph, becomes one of the first female head coaches of a boys' high school football team, at Calvin Coolidge in Washington, District of Columbia. The former wide receiver for the D.C. Divas of the 15-team Independent Women's Football League from 2003 to 2008, has a bachelor's degree in environmental science and a master's in education.

TOMMY REAMON

1974, Tommy Reamon, running back for the Florida Blazers, becomes the first player to win the Most Valuable Offensive Player award in the World Football League in its inaugural season. Reamon leads the WFL in rushing yardage, 1,576, in a 20-game season.

MATT REED

1974, Matt Reed from Grambling University is the first Black quarterback hired by the Birmingham Americans of the World Football League.

1975, Matt Reed is the first Black quarterback hired by the Birmingham Vulcans of the World Football League.

Football Champions

JERRY REESE
2008, Jerry Reese with the New York Giants is the NFL's first Black general manager to win a Super Bowl (XLII).

RAY RHODES
1995, Ray Rhodes in his first season as head coach of the Philadelphia Eagles, becomes the first African American man named Coach of the Year by the *Associated Press* and the *Sporting News*.

JERRY RICE
"Hard work beats talent when talent doesn't work hard."

1987, Jerry Rice of the San Francisco 49ers becomes the first wide receiver to win the scoring title in several years.
1996, Jerry Rice of the San Francisco 49ers becomes the first NFL receiver to catch 1,000 passes.
1998, Jerry Rice of the San Francisco 49ers becomes the first non-kicker to score 1,000 points.
2001, Jerry Rice becomes the first NFL player to compile more than 20,000 yards receiving.
2002, Jerry Rice, 40, becomes the first NFL player to score 200 career touchdowns.

PAUL ROBESON
"We realize that our future lies chiefly in our own hands.
We know that neither institution nor friends can make a race stand unless it has strength in its own foundation."

1915, Paul Robeson and Fritz Pollard become the first African American football players at Rutgers and Brown Universities.
1922, George Halas, now head coach of the renamed Chicago Bears, refuses to play the Milwaukee Badgers unless they drop African American players Fritz Pollard, Paul Robeson and Duke Slater from the team.
1999, Tennis great Arthur Ashe and Paul Robeson, who earned 12 varsity letters at Rutgers, are among the first 20 electees to the International Scholar-Athlete Hall of Fame in Kingston, R.I.

EDDIE ROBINSON
"The will to win, the desire to succeed, the urge to reach your full potential . . .
these are the keys that will unlock the door to personal excellence."

1941, Eddie Robinson, Grambling State football coach, defeats Tillotson College 37-6 for the first of his 408 wins.
1942, Before male students went off to fight in World War II, causing suspension of the football program for two seasons, Eddie Robinson's Tigers go undefeated, untied and unscored on.
1983, The Eddie G. Robinson Memorial Stadium, a multi-purpose 19,000-seat facility opens at Grambling State University.
1985, Eddie Robinson becomes the first Black college coach featured on the cover of *Sports Illustrated*. Entitled "Eddie Robinson Overtakes Bear Bryant with Win No. 324."
1997 to 2002, The Eddie Robinson Classic kick-starts the football season. In 2002 the NCAA ended the allowance of an extra 12th game, thus effectively ending the Classics.
1998, Super Bowl XXXII, played at Qualcomm Stadium in San Diego, is dedicated to Eddie Robinson. He was accompanied onto the field by Doug Williams and Joe Gibbs to perform the ceremonial coin toss.

HAROLD ROBINSON
1949, Harold Robinson and Hoyt Givens become the first African American football players at Kansas State University, home of the Wildcats. Robinson would earn All-Big 7 Conference honors in 1950.

TONY ROBINSON
1987, Tennessee Vols quarterback Tony Robinson joins the Washington Redskins as a replacement player. He leads the Redskins to a 13-7 victory of the Dallas Cowboys on Monday Night Football. It would be Robinson's only NFL appearance.

MICHAEL SAM
2014, Michael Sam, defensive end from the University of Missouri, is drafted by the St. Louis Rams in the seventh round, the 249th pick of 256 players selected. He becomes the first publicly gay player drafted. Cut during the pre-season by the Rams, Sam signs on with the Montreal Alouettes of the CFL. Coach Jon Gruden calls out Commissioner Roger Goodell, in an email, for

Colorful Firsts in U.S. Sports

pressuring the St. Louis Rams to draft Michael Sam, who was the SEC Co-Defensive Player of the year in 2013.

2016, Michael Sam, a consensus All-American and SEC Defensive Player of the Year at the University of Missouri, lobbies against a bill at the Missouri State Capitol that would enable discrimination against the LGBTQ community. Sam was drafted by the St. Louis Rams in the seventh round of 2013 and played on the taxi squads for the Rams and the Dallas Cowboys in 2014.

BARRY SANDERS
"I really love peace and quiet."

1996, Barry Sanders becomes the first player to rush for 1,500 yards three years in a row with an NFL-best 1,553 yards.

1997, Barry Sanders of the Detroit Lions becomes the third player to rush for more than 2,000 yards in a season (2,053). Sanders also becomes the third running back with at least 200 carries to average more than six yards per carry (6.1). Jim Brown was the first in 1963; O.J. Simpson, the second in 1973. Sanders also sets an NFL record for most 100-yard games in season with 14 and becomes the first player to post two 80-yard TD runs in the same game. Sanders is the first player to rush for 1,500 yards four years in a row.

1999, Barry Sanders retires from football. He is the first running back to rush for 1,000 yards in 10 consecutive seasons.

DEION SANDERS
"I'm married to football; baseball is my girlfriend."

1989, Deion Sanders becomes the first athlete in the pro ranks to hit a home run, with the New York Yankees in the World Series, and score a touchdown (68-yard interception), with the Atlanta Falcons against the Los Angeles Rams, in the same week.

1994, Deion Sanders becomes the first athlete to play in a Super Bowl (with Dallas Cowboys) and in the World Series (with the 1992 Atlanta Braves and the 1989 N.Y. Yankees).

1997, Deion Sanders becomes the first athlete to have a pass interception (for 15 return yards in Super Bowl XXIX with the 49ers); and a pass reception (47 yards in Super Bowl XXX with the Cowboys) in Super Bowl competition.

WILLIE SAUCER

1955, Willie Saucer becomes the first Black quarterback for the University of Evansville Purple Aces.

GALE SAYERS

1963, Gale Sayers, the Kansas Comet, sets an NCAA record for the longest run from scrimmage with 99 yards against the Nebraska Cornhuskers.

1965, Rookie Gale Sayers scores a record six touchdowns against the San Francisco 49ers.

1965, Gale Sayers from the Chicago Bears is named Rookie of the Year in the NFL.

1969, Gale Sayers is the only man to average more than 30 yards on kick returns in a career with a 30.56 average, from 1965 to 1969. Sayers is named *UPI's* Comeback Player of the Year. Sayers retires in 1971.

NORMAN SEABROOKS

1969, Norman Seabrooks becomes first African American football player for the Citadel Bulldogs in Charleston, S.C.

JASON SEHORN

1997, Jason Sehorn starts at right cornerback for the New York Giants. Sehorn is the only White cornerback in the NFL going into the next millennium.

JOHN ANDREW SHELBOURNE

1922, John Andrew Shelbourne, a running back, becomes the second African American player for the Hammond (Ind.) Pros of the NFL.

ART SHELL

1989, Art Shell of the Los Angeles Raiders becomes the first African American head coach in the National Football League. He takes over for Mike Shanahan four games into the season. Later, in 1990, Shell is named Coach of the Year by the Maxwell Football Club, *Pro Football Weekly* and *UPI*.

1990, Art Shell of the Los Angeles Raiders is named American Football Conference's Coach of the Year.

WILMETH SIDAT-SINGH

1936, Wilmeth Sidat-Singh becomes the first African American athlete at Syracuse University. He plays on both basketball and football teams.

1938, Wilmeth Sidat-Singh of Syracuse and Jerome "Brud" Holland of Cornell become the first African Americans invited to play for the College All-Stars against the New York Giants.

O. J. SIMPSON
"I am not Black; I am O. J." – Jay-Z, *The Story of O. J.*

1973, O.J. Simpson of the Buffalo Bills is the first player to rush for more than 2,000 (2,003) yards in a season. He is named NFL Player of the Year and wins the Jim Thorpe Award.

1973, O.J. Simpson is the first African American to win the *Sporting News'* Man of the Year award.

1973, O.J. Simpson becomes the first player to rush for 250 or more yards in a game against the New England Patriots.

1973, O.J. Simpson becomes the second running back with at least 200 carries to average more than six yards by per carry (6.0), with Jim Brown the first in 1963.

1976, O.J. Simpson becomes the only player to rush for more than 250 yards in his career, twice, gaining 273 yards in a game against the Detroit Lions.

DUKE SLATER

1918, Fred "Duke" Slater becomes the first African American football player at the University of Iowa.

1921, Football star Frederick Wayman "Duke" Slater from the University of Iowa is named Most Valuable College Player.

1922, Tackle Duke Slater becomes the first African American lineman in the National Football League as a member of the Rock Island Independents. Slater earns his law degree in 1928 and practices law as a Chicago attorney. In 1948, he is elected to the Cook County Municipal Court, becoming just the second African American judge in Chicago.

1926, Duke Slater signs with the Chicago Cardinals and becomes the first African American to play for a current NFL franchise.

1930, Duke Slater becomes the first lineman, Black or White, to make seven All-Pro teams.

1951, Duke Slater becomes the only African American elected to the College Football Hall of Fame's inaugural class. Slater is one of five starters on the 1921 Iowa team who became lawyers. Slater later moves to Chicago and served as a Superior Court judge.

BRUCE SMITH

1996, Bruce Smith of the Buffalo Bills joins Reggie White as the only two players to record at least 10 sacks in a season, 10 times.

BUBBA SMITH

1967, Charles Aaron "Bubba" Smith from Michigan State is the first African American defensive player taken as the first pick, in the first round of the NFL draft. He is chosen by the Baltimore Colts.

COLLETTE SMITH

2017, The New York Jets make Collette Smith the first Black female coach in the NFL. She coaches the cornerbacks and safeties, reporting to the head defensive backs coach.

EMMITT SMITH

1992, Emmitt Smith becomes the first NFL player to win the league's rushing title and the Super Bowl in the same season.

1993, Emmitt Smith becomes the first running back to win a Super Bowl championship, the NFL's Most Valuable Player award, the NFL rushing crown, and the Super Bowl's Most Valuable Player award in the same season.

1997, The NFL rule book states, "A player cannot remove his helmet at all while on the field of play to use as a weapon or to celebrate, argue, etc." This is an automatic disqualification and is known as the "Emmitt Smith Rule" for his end-zone celebrations.

1999, Emmitt Smith of the Dallas Cowboys against the Atlanta Falcons becomes the first player to rush for 2,000 yards on Monday Night Football games.

2006, Pro Football Hall of Fame running back Emmitt Smith, 37, along with his dancing partner Cheryl Burke, is the first NFL

Colorful Firsts in U.S. Sports

player to win the "Dancing with the Stars" competition in its third season.

GENO SMITH
2017, The New York Giants become the last NFL franchise to start a Black quarterback when Geno Smith from West Virginia University replaces Eli Manning.

GIDEON "CHARLIE" SMITH
1915, Gideon "Charlie" Smith, a tackle, becomes the first African American player for the Canton Bulldogs of the Ohio League. Smith plays one game and is the last African American to play professional football exclusively prior to the formation of the National Football League in 1920. Smith becomes professor of physical education and head football coach at Hampton Institute in 1921.

LOVIE SMITH
"Church on Sunday, football the rest of the week."

2007, Lovie Smith coach of the Chicago Bears and Tony Dungy of the Indianapolis Colts, become the first African American NFL coaches in the Super Bowl. Smith's Bears defeat the New Orleans Saints, followed by Dungy's Colts defeating the New England Patriots to earn this honor. In the process the Colts defeat the Bears, 29–17, at Dolphin Stadium in Miami Gardens, Fla.

NEIL SMITH
1998, The NFL initiates the Neil Smith Rule which prohibits a defensive lineman from flinching on the line, as it may cause an offensive lineman to false start, resulting in a five-yard penalty. Smith wreaked havoc on quarterbacks from 1988 to 2000 and piled up 104.5 sacks.

ROD SMITH
2005, Rod Smith from Missouri Southern University becomes the first undrafted NFL player to amass more than 10,000 receiving yards, all with the Denver Broncos, from 1995 to 2006.

TROY SMITH
2010, Troy Smith from Ohio State University is the first Black starting quarterback for the San Francisco 49ers.

FRED SNOWDEN
1972, When he accepts a position at the University of Arizona, Fred "The Fox" Snowden becomes the first African American head coach at a major white university and the second African American head coach at a Division I school, following Illinois State's Will Robinson. Snowden is the first African American coach to have a major college team finish in a final wire-service Top 20 poll at the 17th position by UPI.

SANDY STEPHENS
1961, Sandy Stephens of the Minnesota Gophers is the first African American quarterback named to the College All-American team.
1967, Former All-American quarterback from Minn., Sandy Stephens becomes infamous by using profanity over the radio during his rookie exhibition game against Denver at Municipal Stadium. Wired for sound, in the heat of battle, as the Chiefs threatened to score, "All right, it's second and two," Stephens barked. "Let's put this (mf) in the end zone." The Chiefs scored on the next play. Stephens is cut before the season starts.

KORDELL STEWART
1998, Basketball guard Kobe Bryant, baseball shortstop Alex Rodríguez, football quarterback Kordell Stewart and hockey center Eric Lindros appear on the premier issue of *ESPN The Magazine*.

WOODY STRODE
1946, UCLA products Woody Strode (end) and Kenny Washington (running back) are the first African Americans in the NFL with the Los Angeles Rams.

GEORGE TALIAFERRO

1949, George Taliaferro, halfback from Indiana, is the first African American draftee overall. He is selected by the Chicago Bears in the 13th round with the 129th pick, but signs with the Los Angeles Dons of the AAFC. Taliaferro also appears as a quarterback in 11 games for the Dons.

1950, Running backs Buddy Young and Sherman Howard, along with quarterback George Taliaferro become the first African Americans to play for the New York Yanks in the NFL.

1950, George "Scoop" Taliaferro becomes the first African American quarterback and kicker with the New York Yanks of the NFL. Taliaferro plays in all 12 games under coach Red Strader.

1953, For the Baltimore Colts, George "Scoop" Taliaferro becomes the first African American to start an NFL game at quarterback.

CHARLEY TAYLOR

1964, Charley Taylor, wide receiver for the Washington Redskins becomes the first player named the *Newspaper Enterprise Association's* NFL Rookie of the Year.

LAWRENCE TAYLOR

1996, Lawrence Taylor of the New York Giants becomes the first player unanimously selected as NFL's Defensive Player of the Year.

LIONEL TAYLOR

"One good thing about staying apart from our White teammates (on the road) was that we really didn't have a bed check or curfew. Nobody from the team wanted to come over to the black part of town."

1960, Denver Bronco Lionel Taylor becomes the first African American to lead the American Football League in receiving with 92 receptions and 1,235 yards. Taylor catches 12 TDs.

WILLIE THROWER

1953, Willie Thrower of the Chicago Bears becomes the first African American quarterback to appear in an NFL game, relieving a slumping George Blanda. He completes three of eight passes for 27 yards. He never plays again.

BURL TOLER

1965, Burl Toler, a guard from San Francisco University, who never played in the pros, becomes the first African American NFL official. Toler served as a field judge and head linesman. The first African American AFL official was Aaron Wade.

MIKE TOMLIN

2009, Pittsburgh Steelers Mike Tomlin becomes the second African American NFL head coach to win a Super Bowl. Tony Dungy was the first in 2007 with the Colts. Tomlin served as defensive backs coach for Dungy in 2001 when they were with the Tampa Bay Bucs.

LaDAINIAN TOMLINSON

2003, LaDainian Tomlinson becomes the first NFL player to rush for 1,000 yards and catch 100 passes in a season. In 1998, Arizona Cardinal's fullback Larry Centers caught more than 100 passes in a season.

DAN TOWLER

1952, Paul "Tank" Younger and Dan Towler become the first African Americans to play in the NFL All-Star game, the Pro Bowl.
1952, Running back Dan Towler of the Los Angeles Rams is the first African American named Pro Bowl's Player of the Game.

JACK TRICE

1997, Jack Trice Stadium at Iowa State University becomes the first NCAA Division I, and thus far still the only stadium, named for an African American. John G. "Jack" Trice was the first African American athlete for Iowa State College. He died due to injuries suffered during a college football game against the University of Minnesota in Minneapolis on Oct. 6, 1923. Trice died from hemorrhaged lungs and internal bleeding because of the injuries sustained during the game. Many speculated that the injuries were intentionally inflicted by Gopher players. Prior to the re-naming, the venue was named Cyclone Stadium; the playing area was called Jack Trice Field.

WALLY TRIPLETT

1945, Wally Triplett becomes the first African American football player in Penn State University history. He is also the first African American to start and earn a letter (1946).

1948, Wally Triplett and Dennie Hoggard, Jr. become the first African Americans to play in the Cotton Bowl. Triplett catches the tying touchdown in Penn State's 13-13 tie with Southern Methodist University, who discourage the Nittany Lions from bringing African American players to the game.

1949, Wally Triplett from Penn State is the first African American <u>draftee</u> to take the field in an NFL game. Triplett is drafted in the 19th round with the 182nd pick by the Detroit Lions.

1950, Wally Triplett of the Detroit Lions gains 294 yards in four kickoff returns against the Los Angeles Rams, an NFL one-game record of 73.6 yards per return. One run is for 97 yards.

1952, Clifton Anderson, an end, and running backs Ollie Matson and Wally Triplett become the first African Americans to play for the Chicago Cardinals of the NFL.

EMLEN TUNNELL

1948, Emlen Tunnell, a defensive back, becomes the first African American to play for the New York Giants of the NFL.

1965, Emlen "The Gremlin" Tunnell becomes the first African American coach in the NFL with the New York Giants.

1967, Emlen Tunnell becomes the first African American elected to the Professional Football Hall of Fame.

MICHAEL VICK

"I stand before you a changed man. Use me as an example of an instrument of change."

1999, Michael Vick of Virginia Tech becomes the first frosh quarterback to lead the nation in passing, completing 59% of his passes and throwing 12 TDs with five interceptions. His efficiency rating is 180.4. Vick also becomes the first player in Division I history to win a conference's Player of the Year Award (offensive, defensive or special teams) in the same season he is named Rookie of the Year.

2001, Michael Vick from Virginia Tech becomes the first African American quarterback to be the number one overall pick in the NFL draft, when selected by the Atlanta Falcons. He is the first Black starting quarterback for the Atlanta franchise.

2002, Michael Vick of the Atlanta Falcons becomes the first quarterback to rush for more than 150 yards in a game, against the Minnesota Vikings, compiling 173 yards on 10 carries. His average of 17.3 yards per carry eclipses running back Marion Motley's 17.09 (11 carries) set in 1950.

2004, A four-time pro bowler Michael Vick becomes the most unstoppable video game foe in *Madden NFL* game history because his speed rating of 95 as a quarterback is astronomical.

2006, Michael Vick of the Atlanta Falcons becomes the first quarterback to rush for more than 1,000 yards (1,039) in the NFL.

2010, Michael Vick of the Philadelphia Eagles becomes the first African American quarterback named *Associated Press'* Comeback Player of the Year.

AARON WADE

1966, Aaron Wade becomes the first African American official in the American Football League. He is a coach at Centennial High School in Los Angeles, a school that produced Paul Lowe, all-pro running back for the San Diego Chargers.

SENECA WALLACE

2013, In week 10, Seneca Wallace from Iowa State University becomes the Packers' first Black starting quarterback when Aaron Rodgers suffers a broken collarbone.

JOHNNIE B. WALTON

1969, Johnnie Walton from Elizabeth City State University becomes the first African American quarterback to lead a professional football team to a title, when the Indianapolis Capitols defeat the San Antonio Toros in overtime, 44-38, to capture the Continental Football League championship. Walton later plays in the World Football League (1974-1975), the National Football League (1976-1979) and the United States Football League (1983-1984).

1975, Johnnie Walton becomes the first Black quarterback for the San Antonio Wings of the World Football League.

1978, Johnnie Walton becomes the first Black quarterback for the Philadelphia Eagles of the NFL.

CHARLIE WARD JR.

1993, Quarterback Charlie Ward of Florida State wins the James E. Sullivan Award and the Heisman Trophy.

1994, After announcing his intentions to play pro basketball, Florida State quarterback Charlie Ward becomes the first Heisman Trophy winner in 35 years not selected in the NFL draft. Charlie Ward is the first Heisman winner to be selected in the first round (26th pick) in the NBA draft by the New York Knicks. He plays 11 seasons in the NBA.

ANDRE WARE

1989, Andre Ware, of Houston University, becomes the first African American quarterback to win the Heisman Trophy.

1990, Houston University quarterback Andre Ware, the first African American quarterback to win the (1989) Heisman Trophy, is drafted in the seventh round by the Detroit Lions but fails to make the starting grade.

ASHTON WASHINGTON

2020, Ashton Washington becomes the first African American woman on the staff of the University of Illinois football program in 130 years. As director of high school relations, she serves to build relationships with prep coaches to help the Illini coaching staff lure recruits. Washington had previously worked for the XFL's Houston Roughnecks as a business and gameday operations specialist.

KENNY WASHINGTON

1939, Running back Kenny Washington of UCLA leads the nation with 1,370 total yards gained. Of the 664 players nominated for All-American by *Liberty Magazine*, Washington is the only player named on every ballot. Washington is not drafted into the lily-white NFL.

1946, UCLA products Woody Strode (end) and Kenny Washington (running back) are the first African Americans in the NFL, joining Dan Reeves' newly relocated Los Angeles Rams from Cleveland. Washington is the first Black player to score a rushing touchdown in the NFL.

LLOYD C.A. "THE JUDGE" WELLS

1963, Lloyd C.A. "The Judge" Wells, with the Dallas Texans and later the Kansas City Chiefs, becomes the NFL's African American full-time scout. Wells recruits Jim Kearney, Emmitt Thomas, Buck Buchanan, Willie Lanier and Otis Taylor from HBCUs.

JOHN WESTBROOK

1966, An ordained pastor at the age of 15, John Hill Westbrook becomes the first African American to play football in the Southwest Conference, as a running back for the Baylor Bears. In 2009, Baylor University establishes the John Westbrook Award for Courage and Perseverance.

REGGIE WHITE

1989, Defensive End Reggie White of the Philadelphia Eagles wins the first Drumstick or Turkey Leg Award from John Madden for his play against the Detroit Lions.

1996, Bruce Smith of the Buffalo Bills joins Reggie White as the only two players to record at least 10 sacks in a season, 10 times.

JULIUS WHITTIER

1970, Julius Whittier becomes the first Black football player for the University of Texas Longhorns. He plays offensive tackle for UT's National Championship team and again in 1971, before transitioning to tight end for his senior season in 1972.

TERRENCE WILKINS

1999, Terrence Wilkins of the Indianapolis Colts becomes the first undrafted rookie to accumulate more than 2,000 yards in a season with 1,134 kickoff, 388 punt, 565 receiving and two rushing yards, for a total of 2,089 yards.

DOUG WILLIAMS

In 1988, news reporter Butch John asks the dubious question, "How long have you been a Black quarterback?" The intent according to John was, "It's obvious you've been a Black quarterback all your life. When did this really start mattering?"

Colorful Firsts in U.S. Sports

1978, Doug Williams of Grambling State University, is the first African American QB drafted in the first round (17th pick). The Tampa Bay Buccaneers claim they are seeking a foundation for their second-year franchise.

1979, Doug Williams of the Tampa Bay Bucs and Vince Evans of the Chicago Bears become the first African American quarterbacks to face-off in NFL competition.

1987, Doug Williams is the first Black starting quarterback for the Washington Redskins.

1988, Doug Williams is named MVP of Super Bowl XXII. He is the first African American quarterback to appear in a Super Bowl. Williams throws a record four touchdown passes in the Washington Redskins' 42-10 win over the Denver Broncos.

JAY "INKY" WILLIAMS

1921, Jay Mayo "Inky" Williams, a wide receiver, becomes the first African American player for the NFL's Hammond (Ind.) Pros and the Canton (Ohio) Bulldogs. Williams is also known for starting the Chicago Record Company, releasing jazz, blues and gospel records on the Black Patti label. In 2004, he was posthumously inducted into the Blues Hall of Fame.

QUINCY and QUINNEN WILLIAMS

2019, When University of Alabama defensive tackle Quinnen Williams is the third pick of the NFL Draft, Nicole Lynn becomes the first Black female agent to represent a first-round draft choice.

2021, New York Jets linebacker Quincy Williams and defensive tackle Quinnen Williams become the first brothers to each record a sack in the same game in a win over the Tennessee Titans.

TYRONE WILLINGHAM

1996, Tyrone Willingham becomes the first African American coach to win a division A-1 bowl game, when his 7-5 Stanford Cardinals defeat the Michigan State Spartans in the Sun Bowl, 38-0.

2002, Tyrone Willingham becomes the first college football coach to receive the *Sporting News'* Sportsman of the Year award.

BILL WILLIS

1944, Bill Willis becomes the first African American to start in a College All-Star game.

1946, The Cleveland Browns sign running back Marion Motley and defensive lineman Bill Willis as the AAFC's first African American players. Each player's seasonal salary is $4,000, of which 75% was to be paid semi-monthly. The balance of 25% would be paid after the last game.

1946, Cleveland quarterback Otto Graham sets up over the center with feet parallel, but one foot slightly behind to push off faster to get away from defensive player Bill Willis in practice. Other pro teams soon pick it up and call it the "Bill Willis Step."

1977, Bill Willis, a defensive lineman, becomes the first undrafted African American to be named to the Pro Football Hall of Fame.

RUSSELL WILSON

2012, Russell Wilson of the Seattle Seahawks posts an elite 100.0 QB rating his rookie season, which earned him fourth in the league.

2012, Robert Griffin III of the Washington Redskins and Russell Wilson of the Seattle Seahawks are the first Black rookie quarterbacks to face-off in an NFL playoff game.

2014, Russell Wilson of the Seattle Seahawks, becomes the first NFL player to pass for more than 300 (313) yards and rush for more than 100 (106) yards in a single game during a 28-26 loss to the St. Louis Rams.

WILLIE WOOD

1957, Willie Wood, a two-way player at USC, at safety and quarterback, becomes the first African American quarterback in the Pacific Coast Conference (PCC) and its successor AAWU, now the Pac-12 Conference.

1975, Willie Wood becomes the first African American head coach in the modern era with the Philadelphia Bell of the World Football League (WFL).

CHARLES WOODSON

1997, Cornerback Charles Woodson of the University of Michigan becomes the first defensive player to win the Heisman Trophy.

ELMO WRIGHT

1973, Elmo Wright of the Kansas City Chiefs is credited as the first NFL player to celebrate in the end zone. On 18 November 1973, after catching a touchdown pass thrown by Len Dawson in a 38-14 win over the Houston Oilers, Wright runs in place at a frantic pace, pumping his knees and his arms, stopping long enough to slam the ball to the ground. In 1968, Homer Jones, a wide receiver for the New York Giants, delivered the league's first spike.

JASON WRIGHT

2020, Jason Wright, former No. 31 for the Cardinals, becomes the first African American president of an NFL team, the Washington Football Team, formerly the Washington Redskins. Wright is responsible for leading the organization's business divisions, including operations, finance, sales and marketing.

BUDDY "BRONZE BULLET" YOUNG

1947, Buddy Young of the University of Illinois becomes the first African American to score a touchdown in the Rose Bowl.

1947, Running back Buddy Young becomes the AAFC New York Yankees' first African American player.

1950, Running backs Buddy Young and Sherman Howard, along with quarterback George Taliaferro become the first African Americans to play for the New York Yanks in the NFL.

1964, Claude Henry Keystone "Buddy" Young, also known as the "Bronze Bullet," becomes the first Director of Player Relations in the NFL.

VINCE YOUNG

2006, Vince Young of the Tennessee Titans becomes the first African American rookie quarterback to play in the Pro Bowl. Dan Marino was the first rookie quarterback.

TANK YOUNGER

1949, The Los Angeles Rams sign Paul "Tank" Younger from Grambling State University, the NFL's second player from a predominately Black college. Younger is the first of a record 200-plus players drafted by the NFL who played for Coach Eddie Robinson. See John Edward Brown.

1952, Paul "Tank" Younger and Dan Towler become the first African Americans to play in the NFL All-Star game, the Pro Bowl.

1975, Paul "Tank" Younger becomes the NFL's first African American assistant general manager with the Los Angeles Rams.

Cage 6IX: Golf Champions

1896, In the second U.S. Open golf tournament, John Shippen becomes the first African American professional golfer to participate. Shippen finishes fifth in the 36-hole event.

1899, African American dentist Dr. George Franklin Grant is issued U.S. patent #638,920 for inventing the golf tee.

1910, Walter Speedy, known as the "Father of African American Golf in Chicago," leads a group suing the city of Chicago for the right to play in a city-sponsored tournament. The Chicago City Amateur Tournament began in 1904 to showcase golf's champion players at Jackson Park. However, tournament organizers excluded African Americans from playing on the public facility.

1913, Golfer John Shippen finishes fourth in the U.S. Open. Because of his light complexion he passes for White in a tournament that excludes African Americans.

1921, The first Black-owned golf course of nine-holes, the Shady Rest Golf & Country Club, is created in Scotch Plains, NJ. The *Pittsburgh Courier* reports the "club house ranks with the best." Activities include golf, tennis, horseback riding and skeet shooting. Notable celebrities at the country club include W.E.B. Du Bois, Count Basie, Ella Fitzgerald, Duke Ellington, Billie Holiday and Cab Calloway. Notables athletes include Ora Washington, Lula Ballard, Althea Gibson, Ted Rhodes, Bill Spiller and Joe Louis, an avid golfer.

1922, Joseph Bartholomew designs the Pontchartrain Golf Course.

1925, The U.S. Colored Golf Association is founded in Washington, District of Columbia. It is renamed the United Golfers Association (UGA) in 1929. Affectionately known as the Chitlin Circuit, the UGA was founded by George Adams and Robert Hawkins. Some members included Pete Brown, Lee Elder, Teddy Rhodes, Bill Spiller and Charlie Sifford. At the time, the Professional Golfers Association (PGA) has an article in its by-laws stating that it is "for members of the Caucasian race." When this by-law is repealed in 1961, the United Golfers Association disbands.

1926, The United Golfers Association (UGA) is founded by Robert Hawkins in Mass. For the next four decades the UGA serves the Black golfing community.

1932, Robert "Pat" Ball files a motion and is granted court injunction allowing him to play in the Philadelphia Public Links Golf Tournament.

1934, The "Caucasian-only" clause is added to the Professional Golfers Association of America's constitution. The discriminatory clause is removed in 1952.

1937, The Pennsylvania Open is the first interracial tournament sponsored by a private organization, Eastern Golf Association.

1937, The Wake Robin Golf Club, Washington, District of Columbia's first Black female golf organization is founded.

1938, The Tuskegee Institute organizes the first intercollegiate golf tournament for African Americans. Alfred Holmes wins the first tournament.

1938, Tuskegee Institute organizes the first intercollegiate golf tournament for Blacks. Alfred Holmes wins the tournament.

1939, Langston Golf Course and Driving Range opens in Washington, District of Columbia. The golf course is named after John Mercer Langston, a Virginia congressman and Howard University Law School dean.

1942, Black golfers are invited to play in the interracial Tam O'Shanter All-American and World Championship tournaments in Chicago.

1946, Bill and Marcella Powell are the first African Americans to design, build and own a golf course. The nine-hole Clearview Golf Course, located in East Canton, Ohio, opens in 1948 to all races. In 1978, the second nine holes are added. The Powells often said, "The only color that matters is the color of the greens."

1947, Thelma Cowans wins the first of four UGA national titles.

1948, Three African American golfers, Theodore "Rags" Rhodes, Bill Spiller and Madison Gunther, try to break the Whites-only policy with a lawsuit against the PGA. The PGA sidesteps the issue by adopting an "invitation only" provision, allowing the golfers to play as non-members.

1950, The Ladies Professional Golf Association is formed and bars members of the Black race from membership. Its 13 founders are: Alice Bauer, Patty Berg, Bettye Danoff, Helen Dettweiler, Marlene Hagge, Helen Hicks, Opal Hill, Betty Jameson, Sally Sessions, Marilynn Smith, Shirley Spork, Louise Suggs, and Babe Zaharias.

1952, Joe Louis, as an amateur, becomes the first African American to play in a PGA sponsored tournament, the San Diego Open.

1952, In January, the PGA tour passes a rule allowing Black golfers to enter a tournament if the sponsor agrees. Bill Spiller becomes one of the first African Americans to play in a major golf tourney.

1955, The Supreme Court rules to desegregate public golf courses in Atlanta in the landmark case, *Holmes v. City of Atlanta*. Brothers Alfred "Tup" and Oliver Wendell Holmes challenge the status quo to become the first African Americans to legally play golf at a public facility in Atlanta.

1956, Ann Gregory becomes the first African American female golfer to play in a U.S. Golf Association national championship, in the Women's Amateur tournament at the Meridian Hills Country Club in Indianapolis.

1957, Gary Player from South Africa makes his Masters Tournament debut with an African American caddie named Ernest Nipper.

1960, Article III, Section I, in The PGA Constitution, in 1960 states: "Male professional golfers of Caucasian race, over the age of eighteen (18) years, residing in North or South America, who can qualify under the terms and conditions, hereinafter specified, shall be eligible for membership."

1961, The Professional Golf Association (PGA) removes the "Caucasians only" clause from its constitution. The vote was unanimous by 87 delegates. Charlie Sifford becomes the first African American to join the PGA Tour.

1964, Pete Brown becomes the first Black golfer to win a PGA Tournament – the Waco Turner Open in Burneyville, Okla.

1971, Lee Elder becomes the first African American to compete against Whites in South Africa in the South African PGA Open.

1971, Charles Coody and African American caddie Walter "Cricket" Pritchett celebrate victory in the Masters at Augusta National Golf Club.

1975, Charlie Sifford is the first African American to win the PGA's Seniors' Championship.

1979, Jokester Frank "Fuzzy" Zoeller Jr. becomes just the third player in golf history to win the Masters Tournament in his first appearance. His caddie is African American Jariah "Bubba" Beard.

1992, John F. Merchant becomes the first African American to sit on the executive committee of the USGA.

1999, Angelo Argea, known for his gray afro and as a caddie for Jack Nicklaus, is inducted into the PCA Worldwide Caddie Hall of Fame. Argea's first major victory with Nicklaus was at the PGA Championship in 1975. Their last major victory together was the 1980 U.S. Open at Baltusrol. They would win 40 tournaments together.

1999, Bethune-Cookman College, an HBCU, wins the National Minority College Golf Championship in Port St. Lucie, Fla. The team, which wins by 28 strokes, is composed entirely of White players recruited from abroad. "The rules say your college must be made up of a majority of minorities, not your team," says golf coach Gary Freeman.

2000, Tiger Woods becomes the first athlete to win *Sports Illustrated's* Sportsman of the Year Award twice. He had previously won in 1996.

2002, Jim Thorpe becomes the second Black golfer to win a senior major when he wins the Countrywide Tradition in Superstition Mountain, Ariz., outside of Phoenix.

2004, Charlie Sifford becomes the first African American elected to the World Golf Hall of Fame in Augustine, Fla. Sifford is already a member of the Northern Ohio PGA Hall of Fame and the North Carolina Sportswriters Hall of Fame.

2012, Former Secretary of State Condoleezza Rice and S.C. financier Darla Moore become the first female members of the Augusta National club, home of the Masters golf tournament. Augusta National, which opened in December 1932 and did not have a Black member until 1990, is believed to have about 300 members.

2017, Renée Powell is inducted into the PGA of America Hall of Fame. Her father, Bill Powell, is also an inductee, making the pair the only father/daughter honorees.

Colorful Firsts in U.S. Sports

PETE BROWN

1964, Pete Brown becomes the first African American golfer to win a PGA Tournament – the Waco Turner Open in Burneyville, Okla. He takes home $2,700 in prize money.

STEPHEN CURRY

2023, Stephen Curry becomes the first active NBA player to win the American Century Golf Championship which takes place annually in Nevada. He produces a flawless performance which includes a hole-in-one in the second round and an eagle on the final hole. Curry finishes with a final score of 75, beating out Mardy Fish.

LEE ELDER

1971, Lee Elder becomes the first African American to compete against Whites in South Africa in the South African PGA Open.

1974, Lee Elder, wins the Monsanto Open in Pensacola, Fla., becoming the first African American to qualify for the Masters Tournament. Elder later becomes the first African American golfer to earn $1 million in his career.

1975, After his victory in the 1974 Monsanto Open, Lee Elder is the first African American to be eligible to compete in the Masters Tournament at Augusta National.

1975, Lee Elder is the first professional African American golfer to appear on the cover of *Sports Illustrated*. Bill Russell, basketball center, appeared as a golfer earlier on the 4 August 1969 cover.

1979, Lee Elder becomes the first African American to play on a U.S. Ryder Cup team.

GEORGE GRANT

1899, African American dentist Dr. George Franklin Grant is issued U.S. patent #638,920 for inventing the golf tee. Grant was only the second African American to graduate from Harvard Dental School and later the first African American professor at Harvard.

ANN GREGORY

1956, Ann Gregory becomes the first African American female golfer to play in a U.S. Golf Association national championship, in the Women's Amateur tournament at the Meridian Hills Country Club in Indianapolis.

CALVIN PEETE

1981, Calvin Peete becomes the first African American golfer to win the PGA's Driving Accuracy Award with 81.9 rating.

1981-1983, Calvin Peete becomes the first African American golfer to win "Greens in Regulation," three years in a row, with ratings of 73.1, 72.4 and 71.4.

1982, Calvin Peete wins the Greater Milwaukee Open golf tourney, the first for a Black man.

1983, Calvin Peete is the first African American member of the U.S. Ryder Cup.

1984, Calvin Peete becomes the first African American to win the Vardon Trophy with a 70.56 scoring average. Peete had dropped out of a few tournaments because of illness and those scorecards did not count against his average golf score. The next year, the PGA decides to include all scores regardless of whether the competitor completes the tournament or not. *Golf World* magazine labels the change the Cal Peete Rule.

BILL POWELL

1946, Bill Powell is the first African American to design, build and own a golf course. The 18-hole course, located in East Canton, Ohio, opened in 1948.

1946, Bill Powell designs and opens Clearview Golf Course in Bayside, N.Y.

2017, Renée Powell is inducted into the PGA of America Hall of Fame. Her father, Bill Powell, is also an inductee, making the pair the only father/daughter honorees.

RENÉE POWELL

1962, Renée Powell becomes the first African American to enter the U.S. Girls' Junior golf tournament. In the junior championship, she surprises many by winning the first round. The *Akron Beacon Journal* calls her the "Queen of the Bantam Golf Show."

1967, Renée Powell joins the LPGA Tour.

2017, Renée Powell is inducted into the PGA of America Hall of Fame. Her father, Bill Powell, is also an inductee, making the pair the only father/daughter honorees.

CONDOLEEZZA RICE

2012, Former Secretary of State Condoleezza Rice and S.C. financier Darla Moore become the first female members of the Augusta National club, home of the Masters golf tournament. The Augusta National, which opened in December 1932 and did not have a Black member until 1990, is believed to have about 300 members.

JOHN SHIPPEN

1896, In the second U.S. Open golf tournament, John Shippen becomes the first African American professional golfer to participate. Shippen finishes fifth in the 36-hole event.

1913, Golfer John Shippen finishes fourth in the U.S. Open. Because of his light complexion he passes for White in a tournament that excluded African Americans.

1992, The first John Shippen Memorial Golf Tournament is held in Scotch Plains, N.J., at the Shackamaxon Country Club.

CHARLIE SIFFORD

1957, Charles Sifford wins the predominantly white Long Beach Open Tournament, a 54-hole event, which includes a $500 bonus for having the lowest round on the final day. Sifford's total winnings are $1,700.

1959, Charles Sifford is granted "approved tournament player" status by the PGA.

1961, The Professional Golf Association (PGA) removes the phrase "Caucasians only" clause from its constitution. The vote was unanimous by 87 delegates. Charlie Sifford becomes the first African American to join the PGA Tour.

1967, Charlie Sifford becomes the first African American to win a major PGA Tour event, the Greater Hartford Open.

1975, Charlie Sifford becomes the first African American PGA Seniors Champion.

2004, Charlie Sifford becomes the first African American elected to the World Golf Hall of Fame in St. Augustine, Fla. Sifford is already a member of the Northern Ohio PGA Hall of Fame and the North Carolina Sportswriters Hall of Fame.

2014, Charlie Sifford, 92, is presented with the Presidential Medal of Freedom by President Barack Obama, the highest civilian award.

GENE SMITH

1955, Former caddy, Gene Smith becomes the first Black golfer to win the Akron Good Park Golf Championship in Ohio. He scores a 73 over an 18-hole course.

BILL SPILLER

1952, In January, the PGA tour passes a rule allowing Black golfers to enter a tournament if the sponsor agrees. Bill Spiller becomes one of the first African Americans to play in a major golf tourney.

MARIAH STACKHOUSE

2014, Mariah Imani Stackhouse becomes the first African American woman golfer to make the Curtis Cup team, for amateurs.

JIM THORPE

2002, Jim Thorpe becomes the second African American golfer to win a senior major when he wins the Countrywide Tradition in Superstition Mountain, Ariz., outside of Phoenix.

TIGER WOODS

1996, Tiger Woods rallies from five down to defeat Steve Scott in 38 holes at Pumpkin Ridge and becomes the first player to win three straight U.S. Amateur titles.

1997, Tiger Woods becomes the first Thai American golfer to win the prestigious Masters Tournament, setting a course record with 270 strokes, winning by 12 strokes.

1997, Fuzzy Zoeller jokingly makes derogatory comments about Tiger Woods' possible ethnic menu of fried chicken, watermelon and collard greens at next year's Masters Tournament dinner. Kmart drops Zoeller as its spokesperson.

1998, Tiger Woods becomes the first Black man to play in the Presidents Cup, a series of men's golf matches between a team representing the U.S. and an International Team representing the rest of the world minus Europe. Europe competes against the U.S. in a similar but considerably older event, the Ryder Cup.

1999, Tiger Woods becomes the first PGA golfer to earn more than $4 million, $5 million, $6 million in prize money in a year. He finished at $6.6 million, shattering the record $2.6 million earned by David Duval the previous year. Woods wins four tournaments in a row and nine overall. He did not miss a cut, and he records the lowest adjusted scoring average (68.43) to win his first Vardon Trophy. The previous record was 68.81 set by Greg Norman in 1994. The accomplishments culminate in Woods being named the first Black recipient of the PGA Player of the Year award.

2000, In its 100th year, Tiger Woods by 15 shots becomes the first Black golfer to win the U.S. Open at Pebble Beach Golf Links. He becomes the first golfer to win the U.S. Junior Amateur, U.S. Amateur and the U.S. Open.

2000, Tiger Woods becomes the first Black golfer to win Golf's Triple Crown: The British, U.S. and Canadian Open tournaments. For his accomplishments, he becomes the first athlete to win *Sports Illustrated*'s Sportsman of the Year Award twice, winning also in 1996. For the year, Woods posts a record 67.79 adjusted stroke average, breaking his 1999 record of 68.43.

2000, Tiger Woods becomes the first Black golfer to win a Grand Slam, when he wins the British Open after previously winning the U.S. Masters in 1997 and the PGA Championship and U.S. Open in 1999. He is the youngest golfer to accomplish this feat.

2000, Tiger Woods becomes the first Black golfer on the cover of *Time* magazine.

2001, Tiger Woods wins his second Masters Tournament. In the process he becomes the first golfer to win four consecutive majors, the U.S. Open, British Open, PGA Championship and the Masters.

2000, Tiger Woods becomes the first athlete to win *Sports Illustrated's* Sportsman of the Year Award twice, previously winning in 1996.

2003, Tiger Woods, after winning the American Express Championship, becomes the first player in PGA Tour history to win at least five tournaments for five years in a row. Ben Hogan, Arnold Palmer and Tom Watson won four times over five consecutive seasons.

2003, Announcer Kelly Tilghman and co-host Nick Faldo during a Golf Channel telecast of the Mercedes-Benz Championship, were discussing how players who could possibly challenge the dominant Tiger Woods. Faldo jokingly said perhaps the golfers should "gang up (on Tiger) for a while." The pair laughed a bit before Tilghman declared, "Lynch him in a back alley." Tilghman later apologizes and is suspended for two weeks.

2012, Tiger Woods becomes the first $100 million man on the PGA Tour. Woods finishes third in the Deutsche Bank Championship and makes $544,000, pushing his career total to $100,350,700. Next is Phil Mickelson, who places fourth at TPC Boston and has $66,805,498. Woods has 74 wins, second to Sam Snead. As of 2012, Woods has played 277 times on the PGA Tour, with an average of $362,276.89 per start.

2019, Tiger Woods is presented with the Presidential Medal of Freedom, the highest civilian award.

BILL WRIGHT

1959, William "Bill" Wright becomes the first African American to win a USGA event, capturing the National Public Links Championship in Denver, Colo. In 2006, Wright is inducted into the African American Golfers Hall of Fame in Riviera Beach, Fla.

Cage S7VEN: Hockey Champions

1895, The Colored Hockey League of the Maritimes (CHL) is founded by four Black Baptist leaders James Borden, James Robinson Johnston, James A.R. Kinney and Henry Sylvester Williams in Halifax, Nova Scotia, Canada. It predates the National Hockey League (NHL) by 32 years. Its rule book is *The Bible*. The *Acadian Recorder* reports the Halifax Stanleys as CHL champions.

1904 is the last year that the Colored Hockey League is considered a professional entity. Some notable teams from the CHL include the Africville Sea-Sides, Amherst Royals, Charlottetown West End Rangers, Dartmouth Jubilees, Dartmouth Victorias, Halifax Diamonds, Halifax Eurekas, Halifax Stanleys, Hammond's Plains Mossbacks, Truro Victorias, and the Truro Sheiks. Many team names reflect the struggle for freedom faced by the players' ancestors and their hope for equality and recognition.

1906, Eddie Martin, with the Halifax Eurekas, in the Colored Hockey League, is the first player to use the slapshot, according to historians George and Darril Fosty.

1946, Manny McIntyre and brothers Herbie and Ossie Carnegie become the first Black hockey players in the Quebec Provincial League when they join the Sherbrooke team.

1948, Herb Carnegie becomes the first African American hockey player to receive a tryout with an NHL team, the New York Rangers. The Rangers only offer him a contract to play in their minor league system. He was posthumously inducted into the Hockey Hall of Fame in the Builder Category in 2022.

1950, Arthur Dorrington a dentist signs with the Atlantic City Seagulls of the Eastern Amateur League, to become the first Black to play organized hockey in the U.S.

1958, Willie O'Ree, for the Boston Bruins, becomes the first African American in the National Hockey League (NHL) when he joins the Boston Bruins. Legally blind in his right eye, he played two seasons. O'Ree is later inducted, as a builder, into the Hockey Hall of Fame in 2018 and Canada's Sports Hall of Fame in 2020. In 2021, the Bruins retire his No. 22 jersey.

1972, Alton White becomes the first African American hockey player in the World Hockey Association when he joins the New York Raiders. Upon joining the Raiders, White becomes the first Black player to surpass 20 goals in a season.

1974, Mike Marson, a left wing, becomes the NHL's second Black player when he is drafted by Washington Capitals, and the only African American in the league since Willie O'Ree's retirement in 1961.

1976, Bill Riley, a winger, joins Mike Marson on the Washington Capitals as the third African American hockey player in the NHL.

1978, Tony McKegney becomes the first Black hockey player for the Buffalo Sabres.

1979, Tony McKegney becomes the first Black hockey player to surpass 20 games in a single NHL season, while playing for the Buffalo Sabres.

1981, Grant Fuhr becomes the first Black player drafted by the National Hockey League. The goalie, the first Black at position, was picked in the first round by the world champion Edmonton Oilers.

1988, Tony McKegney becomes the first African American hockey player to score 40 goals in a season, as a St. Louis Blues left wing and surpass 500 NHL career points.

1991, Dirk Graham, as a Chicago Blackhawk, becomes the first Black player to win the Frank J. Selke Trophy, awarded annually to the National Hockey League forward who demonstrates the most skill in the defensive component of the game.

1994, Grant Fuhr becomes the first Black player to win the William M. Jennings Trophy, awarded to the goalie, with a minimum of 25 games played, with the fewest goals scored against him.

1994, John Paris Jr. of Nova Scotia becomes the first Black head coach in pro hockey when he accepts the job with the Atlanta Knights of the International Hockey League.

1998, Dirk Graham becomes the first Black head coach in the NHL history with the Chicago Blackhawks.

2002, Jarome Iginla is the first Black player win the NHL's scoring crown, earning the Rocket Richard Trophy.

2008, Angela James becomes the first African American woman inducted into the International Ice Hockey Federation Hall of Fame.

2009, Kevin Weekes becomes the first Black TV analyst for NHL games after 14 years as a goaltender in the NHL.

2020, Seven current and former National Hockey League (NHL) players form the Hockey Diversity Alliance (HDA) group, whose mission is "to eradicate racism and intolerance in hockey." The group appoints San Jose Sharks forward Evander Kane and former NHL player Akim Aliu as co-heads of the organization. The group also includes Detroit Red Wings defenseman Trevor Daley, Minnesota Wild defenseman Matt Dumba, Buffalo Sabres forward Wayne Simmonds, Philadelphia Flyers forward Chris Stewart and former NHL forward Joel Ward. Another goal of the HDA is to promote diversity at all levels of the game.

Colorful Firsts in U.S. Sports

The group will operate independently of the NHL.

2020, The Canada Post unveils a postage stamp in honor of the 1904 Colored Hockey League champions, the Halifax Eurekas, to commemorate the history of Black hockey players in Canada.

2023, The documentary *Black Ice* debuts exposing a history of racism in hockey through the untold stories of Black hockey players, both past and present, in a predominantly white sport. The film examines systemic racism dating back to 1895 and Canada's Colored Hockey League of the Maritimes (CHL), the first all-pro hockey league.

BLAKE BOLDEN

2013, Blake Bolden becomes the first African American player taken in the first round of the Canadian Women's Hockey League (CWHL) Draft. She is picked by the Boston Blades as the fifth overall pick.

2015, Blake Bolden becomes the first African American woman to play in the National Women's Hockey League (NWHL), a subsidiary of the NHL. She plays for the Boston Pride of the NWHL, winners of the inaugural Isobel Cup team championship.

2016, Blake Bolden becomes the first Black player selected to the NWHL All-Star Game. Her slapshot has been measured at 87 mph.

2020, Blake Bolden becomes the first Black female pro scout for the Los Angeles Kings in the NHL and the second-ever female pro scout in the NHL.

DUSTIN BYFUGLIEN

2010, Dustin Byfuglien, a defensive/right wing for the Chicago Blackhawks, is the first African American to play for a Stanley Cup champion.

HERB & OSSIE CARNEGIE

1946, Manny McIntyre (left wing) and brothers Herbie (center) and Ossie (right wing) Carnegie become the first Black players for the Sherbrooke Randies of the semi-pro Quebec Provincial League. This first all-Black line in pro hockey is known as "The Black Aces."

1948, Herb Carnegie becomes the first African American hockey player to receive a tryout with an NHL team, the New York Rangers. The Rangers only offer him a contract to play in their minor league system. He was posthumously inducted into the Hockey Hall of Fame in the Builder Category in 2022.

EVERETT FITZHUGH

2020, Everett Fitzhugh becomes the NHL's first African American play-by-play broadcaster, as the voice of the Seattle Kraken.

GRANT FUHR

1981, Grant Fuhr, of African-Canadian and European ancestry, becomes the first Black player drafted by the National Hockey League. The goalie, the first Black at that position, is picked in the first round by the world champion Edmonton Oilers.

1984, Goalie Grant Fuhr for the Edmonton Oilers becomes the first African Canadian hockey player to win a Stanley Cup championship.

1988, Grant Fuhr of the Edmonton Oilers becomes the first Black goalie awarded the Vezina Trophy, given annually to the best goalkeeper by the general managers of NHL clubs.

1994, Grant Fuhr becomes the first Black player to win the William M. Jennings Trophy, awarded to the goalie with a minimum of 25 games played with the fewest goals scored against him.

1997, Goaltender Grant Fuhr becomes the first Black player to earn 20 shutouts in a season.

2000, Goaltender Grant Fuhr becomes the first Black player to earn more than 400 NHL wins.

2003, Grant Fuhr becomes the first Black hockey player to be inducted into the National Hockey Hall of Fame.

HIPPO GALLOWAY

1899, William Hipple "Hippo" Galloway becomes the first African American hockey player with Woodstock of the amateur Central Ontario Hockey Association. Galloway would later play third base for the Cuban Giants and Cuban X-Giants baseball teams.

DIRK GRAHAM

1988, Dirk Graham becomes the first African American captain of an NHL team, the Chicago Blackhawks.

1991, Dirk Graham, as a Chicago Blackhawk, becomes the first African American to win the Frank J. Selke Trophy, awarded annually to the National Hockey League forward who demonstrates the most skill in the defensive component of the game.

1998, Dirk Graham becomes the first African American head coach in the NHL with the Chicago Blackhawks.

Colorful Firsts in U.S. Sports

JORDAN GREENWAY

2018, Jordan Greenway, a left wing from Boston University and a 2015 second-round draft pick of the NHL's Minnesota Wild, becomes the first African American to represent Team USA in hockey at the Winter Olympics in Pyeongchang, South Korea.

2018, Jordan Greenway becomes the first player to compete in the Olympic games, an NCAA tournament and the Stanley Cup playoffs within the same season.

MIKE GRIER

2022, Mike Grier is named general manager of the San José Sharks and becomes the first African American general manager in the National Hockey League. Grier's brother, Chris, is the general manager of the NFL's Miami Dolphins.

JAROME IGINLA

"Any racism towards anybody, it's not acceptable."

2000, Jarome Iginla, the son of a Nigerian immigrant to Canada, is the first African American in NHL history to be named Player of the Month. Iginla has 10 goals in 12 games for the Calgary Flames in February.

2002, Jarome Iginla is the first Black player to win the NHL's scoring crown, earning the Rocket Richard Trophy.

2002, Jarome Iginla becomes the first Black player to win a gold medal at the Winter Olympics.

2002, Jarome Iginla becomes the first Black player to surpass 50 goals in an NHL season. He is also the first Black player to win the Art Ross Trophy and the Lester B. Pearson Award, as the NHL's Most Valuable Player.

2003, Jarome Iginla becomes the first Black captain in NHL history when the talented forward was tabbed to wear the "C" by the Calgary Flames.

2012, Jarome Iginla becomes the first Black NHL player to surpass 500 goals.

ANGELA JAMES

2008, Angela James becomes the first African American woman inducted into the International Ice Hockey Federation Hall of Fame.

2010, Angela James becomes the first African American woman and the second African American goaltender after Grant Fuhr, to be inducted to the Hockey Hall of Fame in Toronto.

VALMORE JAMES

1981, Valmore James, a left wing, becomes the first Black American to play in the NHL when he debuts with the Buffalo Sabres.

KELSEY KOELZER

2016, Kelsey Koelzer is first overall pick in the NWHL draft when selected by the New York Riveters. She makes her first appearance near the end of the 2016-17 season.

2019, Kelsey Koelzer is named head coach of the Arcadia University women's ice hockey program, becoming the first Black head coach in NCAA ice hockey history. The Arcadia Knights, located in Glenside, Pa., are in Division III (MAC Commonwealth Conference).

MIKE MARSON

1974, Mike Marson, a left wing, becomes the first Black player for the Washington Capitals (NHL), and the only African American, besides sophomore Alton White to skate in the league since Willie O'Ree's retirement in 1961. Marson is also the first Black player to be drafted in an NHL Entry Draft (first introduced in 1963), as a 2nd round, 19th overall pick by the Capitals.

EDDIE MARTIN

1906, Eddie Martin, with the Halifax Eurekas, in the Colored Hockey League, is the first player to use the slapshot, according to historians George and Darril Fosty.

MANNY McINTYRE

1946, Manny McIntyre and brothers Herbie and Ossie Carnegie become the first Black players for the Sherbrooke Randies of the semi-pro Quebec Provincial League. This first all-Black line in pro hockey, is known as "The Black Aces." Manny, born as Vincent Churchill McIntyre, becomes the first Black Canadian to sign a professional baseball contract. He joins Quebec's Sherbrooke Canadiens of the Borden League, an affiliate of the St. Louis Cardinals, as a shortstop and appears in 30 games.

TONY McKEGNEY

1978, Tony McKegney becomes the first African American hockey player for the Buffalo Sabres.

1979, Tony McKegney becomes the first African American hockey player to surpass 20 goals in a single NHL season, while playing for the Buffalo Sabres.

1980, Tony McKegney, for the Buffalo Sabres, becomes the first African American hockey player to score a goal in Stanley Cup competition - against the New York Islanders.

1988, Tony McKegney becomes the first African American hockey player to score 40 goals in a season, as a St. Louis Blues left wing and surpass 500 NHL career points.

RAY NEUFIELD

1984, Ray Neufield becomes the first African American hockey player for the Hartford Whalers.

JOHNNY ODUYA

2006, Johnny Oduya, an African Swedish defenseman whose father was a Luo from Kenya, becomes the first European-trained player of African descent to play in the NHL and make his debut with the New Jersey Devils.

WILLIE O'REE

1958, Willie O'Ree, for the Boston Bruins, becomes the first African American in the National Hockey League (NHL) when he joins the Boston Bruins. Legally blind in his right eye, he plays two seasons. O'Ree is later inducted, as a builder, into the Hockey Hall of Fame in 2018 and Canada's Sports Hall of Fame in 2020. In 2021, the Bruins retire his No. 22 jersey, and the following year receives the Congressional Gold Medal from President Joe Biden – the first NHL player to receive this honor.

JOHN PARIS

1994, John Paris Jr. of Nova Scotia becomes the first African American head coach in pro hockey when he accepts the job with the Atlanta Knights of the International Hockey League.

WAYNE SIMMONDS

2017, Wayne Simmonds, a Canadian right-winger is the first Black hockey player to be named MVP of the NHL All-Star game.

JAY SHARRERS

2001, Jay Sharrers becomes the first Black referee to officiate an NHL game. He worked his first game as an NHL ref when the Philadelphia Flyers faced the visiting Florida Panthers.

P. K. SUBBAN

2011, P. K. Subban becomes the first Canadian rookie defenseman to score a hat-trick in a game, which came in an 8–1 victory over the Minnesota Wild.

2013, P. K. Subban becomes the first African American hockey player to win the James Norris Memorial Trophy as the NHL's top defenseman. The Norris Trophy, originated in 1953, is for the top "defense player who demonstrates throughout the season the greatest all-round ability in the position."

KEVIN WEEKES

2009, Kevin Weekes becomes the first Black TV analyst for NHL games after 14 years as a goaltender in the NHL.

ALTON WHITE

1972, Alton White from Nova Scotia is the first Black player for the New York Raiders and the Los Angeles Sharks of the World Hockey Association. The rookie becomes the first Black player in history to score a hat-trick in a major hockey professional game, doing so against the Chicago Cougars and the first Black player to surpass 20 goals in a season.

EDDIE WRIGHT

1970, Eddie Wright, a former Boston University hockey player, becomes the first Black coach of an NCAA hockey team at the State University of New York in Buffalo, a Division II. In 2010, the university's volleyball and basketball practice facility was renovated and renamed The Edward L. Wright Practice Facility.

Colorful Firsts in U.S. Sports

Cage 8IGHT: Horse Racing Champions

"Sport has long been a story that Black Americans used to tell the world something about who they were. During segregation, it revealed their capacity for self-organization, creativity, and resilience. A cultural counterpoint to the often grim experiences encountered at work and in neighborhoods, sport allowed people to revel in their athletic grace and prowess. It fostered cohesion and collective self-esteem during and after the first wave of the Great Migration." – Rob Ruck, University of Pittsburgh

1875, Thirteen of 15 jockeys in the inaugural Kentucky Derby are African Americans. William Lakeland (riding "Ascension") and Cyrus Holloway (on "Enlister") are the only White jockeys. Oliver Lewis rides "Aristides" to the winner's circle. Black jockeys win 15 of the first 28 Derbies.

1875, African American Oliver Lewis becomes the first jockey to win the Kentucky Derby, riding "Aristides" in a winning time of 2:37 ¾.

1877, Billy Walker rides "Baden-Baden" to victory in the Kentucky Derby. Walker also becomes the first African American jockey to win the Dixie Handicap, riding "King Fargo."

1880, George Lewis rides "Fonso" to victory in the Kentucky Derby.

1882, Babe Hurd rides "Apollo" to victory in the Kentucky Derby.

1884, Isaac Murphy, riding "Buchanan," wins his first of three Kentucky Derbies.

1885, Erskine Henderson rides "Joe Cotton" to victory in the Kentucky Derby.

1887, Isaac Lewis rides "Montrose" to victory in the Kentucky Derby.

1889, George "Spider" Anderson becomes the first African American jockey to win the Preakness, riding "Buddhist" to an eight-stride win at the Pimlico Race Course in Baltimore, Md.

1890, Isaac Murphy wins his second Kentucky Derby riding "Riley."

1891, Isaac Murphy wins a third Kentucky Derby, riding "Kingman," and becomes the first jockey to win three Derbies. He is also the first jockey to win back-to-back Derbies.

1892, Fifteen-year-old Alonzo Clayton rides "Azra" to victory in the Kentucky Derby.

1893, Willie Simms rides "Comanche" to first place in the Belmont Stakes.

1894, Willie Simms rides "Henry of Navarre" to first place in the Belmont Stakes.

1894, The Jockey Club is formed to regulate and license all jockeys. One by one, African American jockeys are denied their license renewals. By 1911 all Black jockeys are unemployed. See Marlon St. Julien.

1895, Fifteen-year-old James "Soup" Perkins rides "Halma" to victory in the Phoenix Hotel Stakes. Three days later, Perkins rides "Halma" to victory in the Kentucky Derby. Perkins is America's winningest jockey this year with 192 wins.

1896, Willie Simms rides "Ben Brush" to victory in the Kentucky Derby.

1896, Isaac B. Murphy, jockey, dies of pneumonia at age 36. Murphy won 34.5% of his races, a standard no jockey has since met.

1898, Willie Simms wins his second Kentucky Derby, riding "Plaudit."

1898, Willie Simms is the only African American jockey to win the Preakness, riding "Sly Fox."

1901, Jockey Jimmy Winkfield, riding "His Eminence," wins his first Kentucky Derby.

1902, Jimmy Winkfield, riding "Alan-a-Dale," wins his second consecutive Kentucky Derby. He is the first jockey to win back-to-back Derbies since Isaac Murphy (1890-1891). He also becomes the first African American jockey to win the Crescent City Derby, riding "Lord Quez."

1951, Hosea Lee Richardson becomes the first Black jockey to get a license to ride in Florida. Richardson, only 16, makes a successful debut riding "Work Done" to second place at Hialeah Park in Miami.

1955, Isaac Murphy becomes the first jockey voted into the Jockey Hall of Fame at the National Museum of Racing in Saratoga Springs, N.Y.

1971, Cheryl White becomes the first Black female jockey when she rides at the Thistledown Race Track in Cleveland, Ohio.

2000, Marlon St. Julien, an equestrian professional in Thoroughbred horse racing, becomes the first African American jockey to ride in the Kentucky Derby in 79 years, when he rides Curule to a seventh-place finish.

GEORGE "SPIDER" ANDERSON

1889, George "Spider" Anderson becomes the first African American jockey to win the Preakness, riding "Buddhist" to an eight-stride win at the Pimlico Race Course in Baltimore, Md.

1890, Spider Anderson becomes the first African American jockey to win the Eclipse Stakes, riding "Sallie McClelland."

SHELBY "PIKE" BARNES

1888, Pike Barnes becomes the first African American jockey to win the Flash Stakes, riding "Princess Bowling;" the Futurity Stakes, riding "Proctor Knott;" and the Latonia Oaks, riding "Lavinia Belle." Barnes compiles a record 206 wins this season.

1889, Pike Barnes becomes the first African American jockey to win the Champagne Stakes, riding "June Day." Barnes wins 170 races this year.

1890, Pike Barnes becomes the first African American jockey to win the Ladies' Handicap, riding "Sinaloa II."

1890, Pike Barnes becomes the first African American jockey to win the Belmont Stakes, riding "Burlington."

EDWARD BROWN or BROWN DICK

1870, Ed Brown, or "Brown Dick," becomes the first African American jockey to win the Belmont Stakes, riding "Kingfisher."

1984, Edward D. Brown, or "Brown Dick," becomes the first horse trainer inducted to the National Museum of Racing and Hall of Fame. Brown developed Kentucky Derby winners "Ben Brush" and "Plaudit."

JERRY CHORN

1894, Jerry Chorn becomes the first African American jockey to win the Burns Handicap, riding "Lissak."

ALONZO CLAYTON

1892, Fifteen-year-old Alonzo Clayton rides "Azra" to victory in the Kentucky Derby.

1898, Alonzo Clayton becomes the first African American jockey to win the California Handicap, riding "Traverser."

RALEIGH COLSTON

1870, Raleigh Colston becomes the first African American jockey to win the Kenner Stakes, riding "Enquirer."

BERRY GORDY

1994, Berry Gordy of the Motown sound is owner of "Powis Castle" in the Kentucky Derby. The horse finishes eighth.

ANTHONY HAMILTON

1887, Anthony Hamilton becomes the first African American jockey to win the Gazelle Stakes, riding "Firenze."

1889, Anthony Hamilton becomes the first African American jockey to win the Brooklyn Handicap, riding "Exile."

1890, Anthony Hamilton becomes the first African American jockey to win the Juvenile Stakes, riding "St. Charles" and the Toboggan Handicap, riding "Fides."

1891, Anthony Hamilton becomes the first African American jockey to win the Lawrence Realization, riding "Potomac."

1892, Anthony Hamilton becomes the first African American jockey to win the Grand Trial Stakes, riding "Chiswick."

1896, Anthony Hamilton becomes the first African American jockey to win the Metropolitan Handicap, riding "Counter Tenor."

ABE HAWKINS

1866, Abe Hawkins becomes the first African American jockey to win the Jerome Handicap, riding "Watson" and to win the Travers Stakes, riding "Merrill."

ERSKINE HENDERSON

1885, Erskine Henderson rides "Joe Cotton" to victory in the Kentucky Derby and in the Tennessee Derby.

WILLIE HICKS

1902, Willie Hicks becomes the first African American jockey to win the Matron Stakes, riding "Armenia."

BABE HURD
1882, Babe Hurd rides "Apollo" to victory in the Kentucky Derby.

TOMMY KNIGHT
1903, Tommy Knight becomes the first African American jockey to win the Cincinnati Trophy, riding "Paris."

JIMMY LEE
1908, Jimmy Lee becomes the first African American jockey to win the Great American Stakes, riding "Sir Martin," and the National Stallion Stakes, again riding "Sir Martin."

GEORGE LEWIS
1880, George Lewis rides "Fonso" to victory in the Kentucky Derby.

ISAAC LEWIS
1887, Isaac Lewis rides "Montrose" to victory in the Kentucky Derby. "Montrose" is bred in Kentucky at Col. Milton Young's McGrathiana Stud Farm.

OLIVER LEWIS
1875, African American Oliver Lewis becomes the first jockey to win the Kentucky Derby, riding "Aristides" in a winning time of 2:37 ¾.

DeWAYNE MINOR
2000, DeWayne Minor becomes the first African American to drive in the Hambletonian at the Meadowlands, N.J., the most prestigious harness race in America.

ISAAC MURPHY
1879, Isaac Murphy becomes the first African American jockey to win the Clark Handicap, riding "Falsetto."
1881, Isaac Murphy becomes the first African American jockey to win the Saratoga Cup, riding "Checkmate."
1883, Isaac Murphy becomes the first African American jockey to win the first Latonia Derby, riding "Leonatus."
1884, Isaac Murphy becomes the first Black jockey to win the Latonia Cup riding "Harry Gilmore," and the first to win the American Derby riding "Modesty." Murphy riding "Buchanan," also wins his first of three Kentucky Derbies.
1887, Isaac Murphy becomes the first African American jockey to win the First Special, riding "Volante," also becomes the first African American jockey to win the Hyde Park Stakes, riding the "Emperor of Norfolk."
1888, Isaac Murphy becomes the first African American jockey to win the Dwyer Stakes, riding the "Emperor of Norfolk;" and also wins the Second Special, riding "Kingston;" and the Swift Stakes, again riding the "Emperor of Norfolk."
1890, Isaac Murphy wins his second Kentucky Derby riding "Riley" and is the first African American to win the Tidal Stakes, riding "Burlington" and the first African American jockey to win the Suburban Handicap, riding "Salvator."
1891, Isaac Murphy wins a third Kentucky Derby, riding "Kingman," and becomes the first jockey to win three Derbies. He is also the first jockey to win back-to-back Derbies.
1896, Isaac B. Murphy, jockey, dies of pneumonia at age 36. Murphy won 34.5% of his races, a standard no jockey has since met.
1955, Isaac Murphy becomes the first jockey voted into the Jockey Hall of Fame at the National Museum of Racing in Saratoga Springs, N.Y.

MONK OVERTON
1890, Monk Overton becomes the first African American jockey to win the Chicago Derby, riding "Prince Fonso."

JAMES "SOUP" PERKINS
1895, Fifteen-year-old James "Soup" Perkins rides "Halma" to victory in the Phoenix Hotel Stakes. Three days later, Perkins rides "Halma" to victory in the Kentucky Derby. Perkins is America's winningest jockey this year with 192 wins.

HOSEA LEE RICHARDSON
1951, Hosea Lee Richardson becomes the first Black jockey to get a license to ride in Florida. Richardson, only 16, makes a

Colorful Firsts in U.S. Sports

successful debut riding "Work Done" to second place at Hialeah Park in Miami.

WILLIE SIMMS

1893, Willie Simms rides "Comanche" to first place in the Belmont Stakes.

1894, Willie Simms rides "Henry of Navarre" to first place in the Belmont Stakes.

1896, Willie Simms rides "Ben Brush" to victory in the Kentucky Derby and wins the Wither Stakes, riding "Handspring."

1897, Willie Simms becomes the first African American jockey to win the Brighton Handicap, riding "Ben Brush" and the Tremont Stakes, riding "Handball."

1898, Willie Simms wins his second Kentucky Derby, riding "Plaudit." He is the only African American jockey in horse racing history to win the Preakness, riding "Sly Fox."

1902, Willie Simms becomes the first African American jockey to win at the Annual Champion Stakes, riding "Mid of Harlem."

1977, Willie Simms, becomes the second African American jockey inducted to the National Museum of Racing and Hall of Fame. Simms is credited with introducing the British to the short stirrup style of riding later popularized by Tod Sloan.

MARLON ST. JULIEN

2000, Marlon St. Julien, an equestrian professional in Thoroughbred horse racing, becomes the first African American jockey to ride in the Kentucky Derby in 79 years, when he rides "Curule" to a seventh-place finish.

JOHN "KID" STOVAL

1882, John Stoval becomes the first African American jockey to win the Kentucky Oaks, riding "Katie Creel." He would repeat the next year at the Kentucky Oaks, riding "Vera." Stoval is also the first African American winner of the Spinaway Oaks, riding "Miss Woodford" and the first to win the Alabama Stakes, riding the "Belle of Runnymede."

1883, John Stoval becomes the first African American jockey to win the Clipsetta Stakes, riding "Eva S."

1884, John Stoval becomes the first African American jockey to win the U.S. Hotel Stakes, riding "Kosciusko."

BILLY WALKER

1877, Billy Walker rides "Baden-Baden" to victory in the Kentucky Derby and becomes the first African American jockey to win the Dixie Handicap, riding "King Fargo."

1882, Billy Walker becomes the first African American jockey to win the St. Louis Derby, riding "Monogram."

2020, The William "Billy" Walker Stakes at Churchill Downs, of 5 ½ furlongs is named in his honor.

ED WEST

1885, Ed West becomes the first African American jockey to win the Tennessee Oaks, riding "Ida Hope."

CHERYL WHITE

1971, Cheryl White becomes the first Black female jockey when she rides at the Thistledown Race Track in Cleveland, Ohio.

1977, Cheryl White is the first woman to win the Appaloosa Horse Club's Jockey of the Year award, scoring title. She is a repeat winner in 1983, 1984 and 1985.

1983, Cheryl White, at the Fresno Fair in California, is the first female jockey to win five races in a single day.

TINY WILLIAMS

1885, Tiny Williams becomes the first African American jockey to win the Flatbush Stakes, riding "Charity."

ANSEL WILLIAMSON

1998, Ansel Williamson becomes the second African American horse trainer inducted to the National Museum of Racing and Hall of Fame. Williamson trained "Aristides," the first Kentucky Derby winner (1875), as well as "Calvin," winner of the Belmont Stakes (1875).

JIMMY WINKFIELD

1901, Jockey Jimmy Winkfield, riding "His Eminence" wins his first Kentucky Derby.

1902, Jimmy Winkfield, riding "Alan-a-Dale" wins his second consecutive Kentucky Derby. He is the first jockey to win back-to-back Derbies since Isaac Murphy (1890-1891). He also becomes the first African American jockey to win the Crescent City Derby, riding "Lord Quez."

GEORGE WITHERS

1884, George Withers becomes the first African American jockey to win the Great Western Handicap, riding "Boatman."

MILTON YOUNG

1880, Milton Young is the owner of several Kentucky Derby horses. His horse "Bancroft" finishes 3rd in the 1880 Derby, "Getaway" finishes 5th in the 1881 Derby, "Lost Cause" finishes 13th in the 1882 Derby, "Once Again" finishes 3rd in the 1889 Derby and "Ten Booker" finishes 3rd in the 1885 Derby.

Colorful Firsts in U.S. Sports

Cage 9INE: Olympic Champions

Official Nazi newspaper *Völkischer Beobachter* declared that allowing Black athletes to compete
"is a disgrace and a degradation of the Olympic idea without parallel."
Adding the decreed, "Blacks must be excluded." – 1936, Berlin

1900, Mace Montgomery from Georgetown University becomes the first African American Olympic delegate, as a trainer.

1900, French soccer player Constantin Henriquez de Zubiera becomes the first Black athlete to compete at the modern-day Olympics, which launched four years earlier in 1896. The Haitian-born rugby player was also the first person of color to earn an Olympic gold medal when the French team wins the first Rugby Olympic Tournament.

1904, George Coleman Poage, in St. Louis, Mo., places third in both the 200- and 400-meter hurdles to win Olympic bronze medals. He becomes the first African American to win a medal in the Summer Olympics games.

1908, John Baxter "Doc" Taylor Jr. becomes the first African American to win an Olympic team gold medal, as member of the 4x400-meter relay in London.

1912, Howard Porter Drew becomes the first African American to hold the world record for the 100-yard dash. The media calls him the "Negro Speed Marvel," the "Colored Flyer," the "Negro Dash Man," and the "Crack Colored Sprinter" but the title first given to Drew is one still used today, "World's Fastest Man."

1916, Mabel Fairbanks becomes the first African American and Native American member of the U.S. Professional Skating Association (USPSA). She later coaches Olympians Scott Hamilton, Tai Babilonia, Randy Gardner and Kristi Yamaguchi.

1916, Despite cancellation of the Berlin Olympics, Henry Binga Dismond receives a gold medal for tying Ted Meredith's world record of 47.4 seconds in the 400-meter race. See Archie Williams, 1936.

1924, DeHart Hubbard becomes the first African American to capture an individual gold medal at the Paris Olympics. Hubbard long jumped 24 feet, 5 inches.

1932, Louise Stokes and Tidye Pickett become the first African American women to be on the U.S. Olympic team. However, the track stars remain on the sideline and are not allowed to participate.

1936, Eugene Payton, a hurdler, is the first African American to earn a letter at Southern Illinois University.

1936, John Woodruff becomes the first African American to win the 800-meters race in the Olympics.

1936, Archie Williams becomes the first African American to win the 400 meters race in the Olympics.

1944, Jessie Abbott becomes first women's track coach at Tennessee State University.

1948, Audrey "Mickey" Patterson (Tyler), becomes the first African American female to win an Olympic medal, a bronze in the 200 meters, just days before Alice Coachman wins her gold medal in the high jump.

1948, Alice Coachman (Davis) wins a gold medal in the high jump, clearing 5-foot-6 1/8, becoming the first African American woman to win an Olympic gold medal. She is the only American woman to win a gold medal in track and field this year.

1948, John Davis of Brooklyn, N.Y., becomes the first Black heavyweight lifting champion in the Olympics.

1952, Ed Sanders (super heavyweight), Nathan Brooks (flyweight), Charles Adkins (light welterweight), Norvel Lee (light heavyweight) and Floyd Patterson (middleweight) become Olympic African American gold medalists in boxing. Floyd Patterson later becomes the first Olympic gold medalist to win a world professional boxing title.

1952, Charles Moore Jr. becomes the first African American to win an Olympic gold medal in the 400-meter hurdles.

1952, Theodore "Ted" Corbitt becomes the first African American to represent the U.S. Olympic team in the marathon at the Helsinki, Finland Olympics. He is the founding president of New York Road Runners and is often called "The Father of American Long Distance Running." Corbitt was in the first class of inductees selected to the National Distance Running Hall of Fame in 1998.

1956, Dr. Nell Jackson becomes the first African American head coach of the U.S. Olympic Women's Track & Field team.

1956, Aeriwentha "Mae" Faggs Starr becomes the first African American female track and field athlete to represent the U.S. in three consecutive Olympic Games: 1948 London, England; 1952 Helsinki, Finland; 1956 Melbourne, Australia.

1958, Phil Reavis, high jumper from Villanova, becomes the first African American track and field athlete to appear on the cover of *Sports Illustrated*.

1964, George Harris becomes the first African American to participate on the U.S. Olympic Judo team in the Tokyo Olympics.

Olympic Timeline

1966, John McLendon becomes the first African American coach to serve on the U.S. Olympic Committee, responsible for scouting and player performance statistical evaluation.

1967, Jerry Gaines, a long jumper and hurdler, becomes the first African American student-athlete at Virginia Tech Institute. He later becomes the first Black person inducted into the Virginia Tech Sports Hall of Fame.

1967, San José State sociology professor Dr. Harry Edwards, creates the Olympic Committee for Human Rights to address the systemic racism experience by Black athletes. Edwards issues a statement that Black athletes may boycott the 1968 Olympics in Mexico City.

1968, Tommie Smith, John Carlos, Lee Evans, Larry James, Ron Freeman and other Black athletes protest racism in the U.S. at the Mexico City Olympics, with symbolic gestures on the victory stand.

1968, Ron Coleman, who specializes in the triple jump, becomes the University of Florida's first Black scholarship athlete. The university's basketball team would integrate in 1970.

1968, Uriah Jones becomes the first African American on a U.S. Olympic Fencing team. He competed in the team foil event. Jones is later inducted into the U.S. Fencing Association Hall of Fame posthumously.

1968, James Kenati Allen, of African American and Native American descent is the first Black gymnast to compete at the Olympic Games. Allen later earns a PhD in physics from the University of Washington.

1969, Ronnie Hogue becomes the first African American athlete at the University of Georgia (UGA) to earn a full scholarship in any sport. Track star Maxie Foster from Athens, Georgia was the first African American athlete at UGA a year earlier, but he was on a partial scholarship and lived at home.

1969, Charles Steward and Lloyd Wells integrate the track and field team at Louisiana State University, becoming the university's first African Americans in any sport.

1969, Ruth White becomes the youngest woman and the first African American woman to win a national fencing championship.

1968, Spencer Haywood is the first high schooler to play on the U.S. Olympic basketball team.

1970, Larry Ellis, becomes the first African American coach of any sport in the Ivy League when named head track coach at Princeton University.

1971, Wide receiver Bullet Bob Hayes becomes the first Olympic Gold Medalist (1964, 100 meters) to play for a Super Bowl champion the Dallas Cowboys. Because of his speed, NFL defenses give up playing man-to-man coverage and use zone defenses. Bob Hayes is the first sprinter to run a 9.1 second 100-yard dash and the first to break 6.0 seconds in the 60-yard sprint.

1972, Richard Ewell and Michelle McCladdie become the first African Americans to win the National Pairs Skating Title. They are coached by African American and U.S. Figure Skating Hall of Famer Mabel Fairbanks.

1973, Reggie McAfee becomes the first African American to run the mile under four minutes.

1974, Wilma Rudolph, Ralph Boston, Lee Calhoun, Rafer Johnson, Mal Whitfield, Harrison Dillard and Jesse Owens are the first African Americans inducted into the National Track and Field Hall of Fame.

1976, Leon Spinks becomes the first Marine to win a gold medal in Olympics boxing history.

1976, The Spinks brothers, Leon and Michael, win Olympic gold medals in boxing.

1976, Jesse Owens is presented with the Presidential Medal of Freedom by President Gerald Ford, the highest civilian award.

1976, Allen J. Coage becomes the first African American to medal in Judo, earns the bronze at the Montreal Olympics.

1976, Mamie Rallins, former Tennessee State Tigerbelle hurdler, becomes the first African American woman to coach at Ohio State University.

1976, Lloyd Keaser becomes the first African American to medal at the Montreal Olympics in wrestling, earning a silver in the 149-pound freestyle category.

1977 to 1987, Edwin Moses starts his winning string of 122 consecutive 400-meter hurdle races.

1978, Wendy Hilliard is the African American rhythmic gymnast to represent the U.S. in international competition including three World Championships (1979, 1981, and 1983). In 1995, Hilliard becomes the first African American president of the Women's Sports Foundation, the leading organization for women's sport issues.

1979, Brooks Johnson becomes the first African American head coach in Track & Field at Stanford University. He coaches Olympians Esther Stroy, Chandra Cheesborough and Evelyn Ashford.

1980, DaVanche "Ron" Galimore from Iowa State University becomes the first gymnast to score a perfect "10" and the first African American member of a U.S. Olympic team. The team was never sent to Moscow because of a U.S. led boycott of the 1980 Summer Olympics. Ron is the son of Willie Galimore, former Chicago Bears halfback.

Colorful Firsts in U.S. Sports

1980, The first Blacks to participate in the Winter Olympics for the U.S. are Jeff Gadley and 1968 gold medalist 110-meter hurdler Willie Davenport for the four-man bobsled team.

1980, Luci Collins of Creole descent is the first Black gymnast to qualify for the U.S. Women's Olympic team. Because of America's Moscow Olympic boycott, she never competes.

1980, The International Women's Sports Hall of Fame, in its first year elects Wilma Rudolph in the Contemporary category, while Althea Gibson receives honors in its Pioneer category.

1983, Dianne Durham, 14, becomes the first African American senior National Gymnastic Champion. She takes gold in the vault, uneven bars and the floor routine. Durham is the first American to successfully execute a full-twisting Tsukahara on the vault. The first Tsukahara vault was performed by Mr. Mitsuo Tsukahara of Japan in 1972.

1984, Greg Gibson becomes the first African American Greco-Roman wrestler, at 220 pounds, to medal (a silver) at the Los Angeles Olympics.

1984, Carmen Williamson becomes boxing's first African American referee and judge for the Los Angeles Olympics and is presented with an honorary gold medal. Born in 1925, Williamson was a 112-pound amateur flyweight boxer who compiled a 25-14 won-lost record.

1984, Benita Fitzgerald-Mosley becomes the first Black woman to win a gold medal in the 100-meter hurdles at the Los Angeles Olympic Games.

1984, With a leap of 56 feet, 7 ½ inches, Al Joyner becomes the first African American in 80 years to win an Olympic gold medal in the triple jump. He is honored with the Jim Thorpe Award, which is given every four years to the best U.S. competitor in an Olympic field event.

1984, Peter Westbrook becomes the first African American to win an Olympic medal in fencing, a bronze.

1992, Dr. LeRoy Walker is unanimously elected president of the U.S. Olympic Committee, the first African American to hold the post.

1992, Anita DeFrantz becomes the first African American elected to the executive board on the International Olympic Committee.

1996, The Wilma Rudolph Courage Award is established by the Women's Sports Foundation to recognize a female athlete who exhibits extraordinary courage in athletic performance, overcomes adversity and makes significant contributions to sports. Jackie Joyner-Kersee is the first honoree.

1998, Theodore "Ted" Corbitt, marathon runner is inducted into the inaugural class of the National Distance Running Hall of Fame, in Utica, N.Y.

2003, Female wrestler Toccara Montgomery captures the gold medal over Canada's Ohenewa Akuffo in the 72-kg division at the Pan American Games in Santo Domingo, Dominican Republic.

2016, U.S. women sweep the 100-meter hurdles for the first time in the history of the Olympics. Brianna Rollins is clocked at 12.48 seconds and followed by teammates Nia Ali (12.59) and Kristi Castlin (12.61), who edges Britain's Cindy Ofili (12.63) with a lean at the finish line.

2019, The USA Triathlon, part of the U.S. Olympic Committee, makes history by electing its first ever African American board member, Dr. Tekemia Dorsey. She serves as its Mideast Region representative.

2021, The International Swimming Federation (FINA) bans swimming caps designed for natural Black hair for use in the Tokyo Olympics. The thickness or density of Black hair does not fit under a traditional swim cap. The caps are made by Black-owned British brand, Soul Cap.

2022, The Full Circle Everest climbing team make history as the first all-Black team to stand atop the Mount Everest summit, the highest mountain in the world. The team was led by Philip Henderson, along with Manoah Ainuu, Fred Campbell, James "KG" Kagambi, Thomas Moore, Demond "Dom" Mullins, Eddie Taylor and two women, Abby Dione and Rosemary Saal.

2022, Lester Wright, a 100-year-old World War II veteran, becomes the first African American centenarian to hold the world record in the 100 meters, with a time of 26.34 seconds at the Penn Relays in Philadelphia.

2022, At the U.S. Championships in Tampa, Florida, Konnor McClain (gold), Shilese Jones (silver) and Jordan Chiles (bronze) become the first all-Black trio to medal in the senior-all-around competition.

2023, At the World Championships in Antwerp, Belgium, Simone Biles (gold), Brazil's Rebeca Andrade (silver) and Shilese Jones (bronze) become the first all-Black trio to medal.

AQUIL HASHIM ABDULLAH

1996, Aquil Hashim Abdullah becomes the first African American (with a Muslim name) to win the U.S. National Rowing Championship.

2004, Aquil Hashim Abdullah becomes the first African American male rower to qualify for the U.S. Olympic squad, teaming with U.S. Navy officer Henry Gantt Nuzum to win double skulls at the Qualified Olympic Small Boat Trials in West Windsor, N.J.

TAQIY ABDULLAH-SIMMONS

2007, Taqiy Abdullah-Simmons from Oklahoma University becomes the first Black male gymnast to win the NCAA all-around championship. See Corrinne Tarver.

JAMES KANATI ALLEN

1968, James Kenati Allen, of African American and Native American descent is the first Black gymnast to compete at the Olympic Games. Allen later earns a PhD in physics from the University of Washington.

EVELYN ASHFORD

1981, 100- and 200-meter sprinter Evelyn Ashford becomes the first African American female to be named Athlete of the Year by *Track & Field News*.

1983, Evelyn Ashford becomes the first American woman to break the 11.0 second barrier in the 100-meter dash (10.79).

BOB BEAMON

1968, In the Mexico City Summer Olympics, Bob Beamon leaps 29 feet, 2 ½ inches in the long jump, shattering Ralph Boston's world record by twenty-one and three quarter inches. In the process Beamon breaks the 28- and 29-foot barriers in one jump.

GWEN BERRY

2019, African American hammer thrower Gwen Berry stands on the medal stand wearing bright blue lipstick and a gold medal around her neck. As the end of the national anthem, she bows her head and raises her fist, issuing a silent protest motivated by her personal journey and her belief that, "America can do better."

SIMONE BILES

2013, At the World Artistic Gymnastics Championships, 16-year-old Simone Biles performs a double layout with a half-twist (body remains straight and elongated as she flips twice) in the floor exercises. The skill is named the "Biles on the Floor." Moves are named after the first gymnast who completes them in an international competition, according to the International Gymnastics Federation Code of Points. The move must also be above a certain difficulty level.

2018, Dealing with a kidney stone, at the World Championships, Simone Biles performs a half-twist onto the vaulting table and a front double full somersault off. The skill is named "Biles on the Vault" the second in her name.

2019, Simone Biles does her double-twisting double-tucked salto backwards dismount off the balance beam during the qualifying round of the gymnastics World Championships in Stuttgart, Germany. The floor routine is valued at a G. This skill is dubbed the "Biles on the Balance Beam" the third in her name. She also completes a triple-twisting double-tucked salto backwards, creating "Biles II on the Floor," a second skill for floor exercises and the fourth in her name.

2022, Simone Biles is presented with the Presidential Medal of Freedom by President Joe Biden, the highest civilian award.

2023, At the U.S. Classic gymnastics, Simone Biles becomes the first woman to perform the Yurchenko half-on with two twists, in competition. The move involves a round-off onto the springboard, followed by a back handspring on the vault. The new skill, a triple-twisting double-tucked salto (no hands) backwards vault becomes the "Biles II on the Vault" skill, and the fifth in her name.

MAAME BINEY

2017, Maame Biney becomes the first Black woman to qualify for a U.S. Olympic speedskating team with a victory in the 500 meters in Kearns, Utah. The 17-year-old native of Ghana will be the second Black speedskater on a U.S. Olympic team. Shani

Davis was 19 when he made the short track team in 2002. He later switches to long track and wins four medals, including two golds.

DICKIE BIVINS

1980, Dickie Bivins becomes the first Black male gymnast to win an individual medal at the World Championships. He wins bronze medals in the Platform Tumbling and Power Tumbling.

SHENEA BOOTH

2002, Shenea Booth (with her partner Arthur Davis) becomes the first Black in the Acro Mixed Pairs to win the Sports Acrobatics World Championship in Riesa, Germany. Two years later, the duo returned to defend their title in Liévin, France. They earned the "Most Difficult Skill" award in both world appearances and were inducted into the USAG Hall of Fame in 2009.

2015, Shenea Booth, acrobatic gymnast, becomes the first African American female soloist to play a lead character in a Cirque Du Soleil production, by performing as "The Promise" in the classic spectacle Varekai.

RALPH BOSTON

1968, Ralph Boston becomes the first track and field athlete to medal three consecutive times in the Long Jump. Boston won a gold medal in 1960, a silver in 1964 and the bronze in 1968.

VALERIE BRISCO-HOOKS

1984, Valerie Brisco-Hooks becomes the first person to record a 200-400-meters double win in the Olympics with times of 21.81 and 48.83 seconds, respectively.

DAVID BROWN

2014, David Brown, 27, becomes the first totally blind athlete to run the 100 meters under 11 seconds with a time of 10.92.

MILT CAMPBELL

1956, Milt Campbell becomes the first African American to win the Olympic decathlon.

JOHN CARLOS

1968, John Carlos and Tommie Smith, in the Mexico City Olympics, after receiving bronze and gold medals in the 200 meters, adorn black gloves and raise their fists to the sky, to protest treatment of Black people in America.

LES CARNEY

1960, Les Carney is the first African American athlete from Ohio University to compete in the Olympics. He wins a silver medal in the 200-meters race. The Lester Carney Track in Kettlewell Stadium at Indian Creek High School, in Wintersville, Ohio, is named in his honor.

MICHELLE CARTER

2003, Michelle Carter set a national high school record in the girls shot put (8 pounds) with a toss of 54 feet, 10 ¾ inches at the Texas state meet in Austin, joining her father, former NFL player Michael Carter, as a national record holder in the event. Michael Carter stills holds the boys best of 81 feet 3 ½ inches.

2016, Michelle Carter becomes the first American woman to win the gold medal in the shot put. Her father, Michael Carter, is a silver medalist in the 1984 Olympics in Los Angeles. He is a three-time Super Bowl champion with the San Francisco 49ers as a nose tackle. Michelle and her father are Team USA's first father-daughter combination to medal at the Olympic Games.

SHILESE JONES

2022, At the U.S. Championships in Tampa, Florida, Konnor McClain (gold), Shilese Jones (silver) and Jordan Chiles (bronze) become the first all-Black trio to medal in the senior-all-around competition.

2023, At the World Championships in Antwerp, Belgium, Simone Biles (gold), Brazil's Rebeca Andrade (silver) and Shilese Jones (bronze) become the first all-Black trio to medal.

JOETTA CLARK and TALITHA DIGGS

2000, At the Olympic Trials, the Clark Team of baby sister Hazel Clark, sister-in-law Jearl Miles Clark and older sister Joetta Clark sweep the three qualifying positions for the 800 meters event.

2022, Talitha Diggs wins the 400 meters at the NCAA Indoor Track and Field Championships in Birmingham, Ala. Her mother Joetta Clark Diggs wins the 800 meters NCAA indoor championship in 1983. The pair become the first daughter and mother to win gold medals in an NCAA championship individual event.

ALICE COACHMAN

1948, Alice Coachman (Davis) wins a gold medal in the high jump, clearing 5-foot-6 1/8, becoming the first African American woman to win an Olympic gold medal. She is the only American woman to win a gold medal in track and field this year.

1975, Alice Coachman, the first African American woman to win an Olympic gold medal (high jump in 1948), is inducted into the National Track and Field Hall of Fame in Indianapolis, Ind.

LUCI COLLINS

1980, Luci Collins of Creole descent is the first Black gymnast to qualify for the U.S. Women's Olympic team. Because of America's Moscow Olympic boycott, she never competes.

TED CORBITT

1952, Theodore "Ted" Corbitt becomes the first African American to represent the U.S. Olympic team in the marathon at the Helsinki, Finland Olympics. He is the founding president of New York Road Runners and is often called "The Father of American Long Distance Running." Corbitt was in the first class of inductees selected to the National Distance Running Hall of Fame in 1998.

1954, Theodore "Ted" Corbitt becomes the first African American to win the USA National Marathon Championship.

1998, Theodore "Ted" Corbitt, marathon runner is inducted into the inaugural class of the National Distance Running Hall of Fame, in Utica, N.Y.

2013, Theodore "Ted" Corbitt, marathon runner is inducted into the inaugural class of the National Black Distance Running Hall of Fame, by the National Black Marathoners Association.

MARITZA CORREIA

2004, Maritza Correia, a Puerto Rican of African descent, becomes the first Black woman to make the U.S. Olympic swimming team. She wins a silver medal in the 2004 Athens games in the 4x100-meter freestyle relay.

JOHN DAVIS

1948, John Davis of Brooklyn, N.Y., becomes the first African American heavyweight lifting champion in the Olympics.

1951, John Henry Davis becomes the first man to hoist 400 pounds over his head at the National AAU senior championships in Los Angeles.

OTIS DAVIS

1960, Sgt. Otis Davis becomes the first man to break the 45 second barrier in the 400 meters with 44.9 seconds time in the Rome Olympics.

SHANI DAVIS

2001, Shani Davis, 19, becomes the first African American to make the U.S. Olympic speedskating team. Davis qualifies for the team by winning the 1,000-meter short-track final at the Olympic Trials in Kearns, Utah.

2006, Shani Davis becomes the first African American to win an individual gold medal at the Winter Olympics in the 1,000-meter speed skating event, held in Turin, Italy.

DOMINIQUE DAWES

1992, Dominique Dawes, known as "Awesome Dawesome" is the first American-born Black female gymnast on the U.S. Olympic team. Dawes wins a bronze medal in the team competition.

1996, Dominique Dawes becomes the first African American gymnast to win an individual Olympic event medal with her bronze on the floor exercise.

TALITHA DIGGS

2022, Talitha Diggs wins the 400 meters at the NCAA Indoor Track & Field Championships in Birmingham, Ala. Her mother Joetta Clark Diggs won the bronze medal in the 800 meters indoor championship in 1993. The pair become the first daughter and mother to medal in an NCAA championship individual event.

HARRISON DILLARD

1948, Harrison "Bones" Dillard becomes the first athlete to win both the 100-meter sprint and 100-meter high hurdles in Olympic competition.

1949, Harrison Dillard appears on the cover of *Newsweek* magazine.

GABRIELLE DOUGLAS

2012, In the London Olympics Gabrielle Douglas, the "Flying Squirrel," becomes the first African American to win the gold in the women's gymnastics all-around event that include floor exercises, the uneven bars, the balance beam and the vault. In addition, she is the first American gymnast to win gold in both the individual and team all-around competition.

HOWARD DREW

1912, Howard Porter Drew becomes the first African American to hold the world record for the 100-yard dash. The media calls him the "Negro Speed Marvel, Colored Flyer, Negro Dash Man, and Crack Colored Sprinter" but the title first given to Drew is one still used today, "World's Fastest Man."

CHARLIE DUMAS

1956, Compton Community College athlete Charles Dumas becomes the first man to break the seven-foot barrier, in the high jump, with a leap of 7 feet 5/8 inches at the Olympic trials in Los Angeles.

KIMBERLYN DUNCAN

2013, LSU Senior Kimberlyn Duncan, a five-time NCAA champion and a nine-time All-American, is the first female sprinter to win the NCAA indoor and outdoor titles in the 200 meters in consecutive years.

DIANNE DURHAM

1983, Dianne Durham, 14, becomes the first African American senior National Gymnastic Champion. She takes gold in the vault, uneven bars and the floor routine. Durham is the first American to successfully execute a full-twisting Tsukahara on the vault. The first Tsukahara vault was performed by Mr. Mitsuo Tsukahara of Japan in 1972.

HARRY EDWARDS

1967, San José State sociology professor Dr. Harry Edwards, creates the Olympic Committee for Human Rights to address the systemic racism experience by Black athletes. Edwards issues a statement that Black athletes may boycott the 1968 Olympics in Mexico City.

ANTHONY ERVIN

2000, Anthony Ervin becomes the first U.S. citizen of African descent to medal gold in an individual Olympic swimming event. He wins two medals in the Sydney Olympics: a gold in the 50-meter freestyle, and a silver in the 4x100-meter freestyle relay. Ervin is of Ashkenazi Jewish descent on his mother's side and African American descent on his father's. Ervin has described himself as a "practicing Zen Buddhist." In July 2017 he said: "I'm proud to be a Jew."

LEE EVANS

1968, Lee Evans cracks the 44-second barrier in the Olympics, running the 400-meter dash in 43.86 seconds.

1968, Tommie Smith, John Carlos, Lee Evans, Larry James, Ron Freeman and other Black athletes protest racism in the U.S. at the Mexico City Olympics, with symbolic gestures on the victory stand.

MAE FAGGS

1956, Aeriwentha "Mae" Faggs Starr becomes the first African American female track and field athlete to represent the U.S. in three consecutive Olympic Games: 1948 London, England; 1952 Helsinki, Finland; and 1956 Melbourne, Australia.

MABEL FAIRBANKS

1916, Mabel Fairbanks becomes the first African American member of the U.S. Professional Skating Association (USPSA). She later coaches Olympians Scott Hamilton, Tai Babilonia, Randy Gardner and Kristi Yamaguchi.

1972, Richard Ewell and Michelle McCladdie become the first African Americans to win the National Pairs Skating Title. They are coached by African American and future U.S. Figure Skating Hall of Famer Mabel Fairbanks.

1997, Figure skater Mabel Fairbanks becomes the first African American coach inducted to the U.S. Figure Skating Hall of Fame.

ALLYSON FÉLIX

2010, Winning the 200- and 400-meter runs, Allyson Félix becomes the first person to win two IAAF Diamond League trophies in the same year.

2015, In the Beijing World Championships, Allyson Félix becomes the first woman to win world titles in both the 200 and 400 meters.

2018, Allyson Félix becomes the first sponsored athlete for Athleta, owned by Gap, Inc. When her contract expired with Nike in December 2017, the company offered a pregnant Félix a 70% pay cut in the new contract and failed to explicitly support maternity protections she requested in the contract.

2021, Allyson Félix starts Saysh, a women-first brand that pioneers a new policy allowing people to swap shoes should their foot size change while pregnant.

BENITA FITZGERALD-MOSLEY

1984, Benita Fitzgerald-Mosley, at the Los Angeles Olympic Games, becomes the first Black woman to win a gold medal in the 100-meter hurdles.

FLO-JO

"It's better to look where you are going than to see where you have been."

1988, Florence Griffith Joyner, or Flo-Jo, is the first American woman to break the 22 second barrier in the 200-meter dash with a time of 21.34.

VONETTA FLOWERS

2002, Vonetta Flowers becomes the first African American to win a gold medal at the Winter Olympics. She teams with Jill Bakken to win the women's bobsled competition in Salt Lake City. Soon after, African American men, Randy Jones, Garrett Hines and Bill Schuffenhauer win the silver in the four-man bobsled. Four years later, speedskater Shani Davis would become the first African American athlete to win an individual gold medal.

CHARLIE GREENE

1968, At the AAU Track and Field Championships in Sacramento, California, three men break the world record in the 100 meters, Jim Hines, Charlie Greene and Ronnie Ray Smith, with the same time of 9.9 seconds.

MAURICE GREENE

1999, Maurice Greene runs the 100-meter dash in 9.79 seconds, in Athens, Greece, to beat Canadian Donovan Bailey's record by 0.05 seconds. He is the first man to break the 9.80 barrier in the 100-meter dash. Greene also becomes the first man to hold the 50-meter, the 60-meter, and the 100-meter records simultaneously.

GEORGE HARRIS

1964, George Harris becomes the first African American to participate on the U.S. Olympic Judo team in the Tokyo Olympics.

ALVIN & CALVIN HARRISON

2000, Alvin & Calvin Harrison become the first twins to win gold medals when they win the 4 x 400 relay with Michael Johnson and Antonio Pettigrew at the Sydney Olympics.

JuVAUGHN HARRISON

2019, LSU sophomore JuVaughn Harrison, known as "Mr. Jumps," becomes the first man to win both the high jump (7 feet, 5 ¼ inches) and long jump (26 feet, 11 inches) in the NCAA outdoor championships.

2021, LSU senior JuVaughn Harrison, known as "Mr. Jumps," becomes the first man to win both the high jump (7 feet, 6 ½ inches) and long jump (27 feet, 8 ¾ inches) in an NCAA indoor championship.

BOB HAYES
"It's blood, sweat, sometimes tears."

1964, Bob Hayes is the first sprinter to run the 60-yard dash in less than six seconds (5.9).

1971, Wide receiver Bullet Bob Hayes becomes the first Olympic Gold Medalist (1964, 100 meters) to play for a Super Bowl champion the Dallas Cowboys. Because of his speed, NFL defenses give up playing man-to-man coverage and use zone defenses. Hayes is the first sprinter to run a 9.1 second 100-yard dash.

HAROLD HENSON

1949, Harold Henson of San Diego State becomes the first African American to wrestle in the NCAA tournament.

WENDY HILLIARD

1978, Wendy Hilliard is the African American rhythmic gymnast to represent the U.S. in international competition including three World Championships (1979, 1981, and 1983). In 1995, Hilliard becomes the first African American president of the Women's Sports Foundation, the leading organization for women's sport issues.

JIMMY HINES

1968, At the AAU Track and Field Championships in Sacramento, California, three men break the world record in the 100 meters, Jim Hines, Charlie Greene and Ronnie Ray Smith, with the same time of 9.9 seconds.

1968, Jim Hines becomes the first man to break the sub-10 second barrier in the 100 meters in the Olympics with a 9.95 time in Mexico City.

DEHART HUBBARD

1924, DeHart Hubbard becomes the first African American to capture an individual gold medal at the Paris Olympics. Hubbard long jumps 24 feet, 5 inches.

ERIN JACKSON

2021, Erin Jackson becomes the first African American woman to win a speedskating title at the ISU Speed Skating World Cup. The 29-year-old athlete wins the women's 500-meter event at the Arena Lodowa in Tomaszów Mazowiecki, Poland, in a time of 37.613 seconds.

2022, During the Winter Olympics in Beijing, China, Erin Jackson becomes the first Black woman to win an individual gold medal. The speed skater takes the top spot in the women's 500-meter race with a time of 37.04.

FRANKLIN JACOBS

1978, Franklin Jacobs, only 5-foot-8, sets a world record for the highest clearance over one's head, 23 feet, ¼ inch, clearing the high jump bar at 7 feet, 7 ¼ inches.

REGINA JACOBS

2003, Regina Jacobs becomes the first woman to break the 4:00 barrier in the "indoor mile." Jacobs runs a 3:59:98 competing in the 1,500 meters at the Boston Indoor Games.

EARL JOHNSON

1924, Earl Johnson becomes the first African American long distance runner to medal in the Olympic Games. In Rome, Johnson wins a bronze medal in the 10,000-meter race.

MICHAEL JOHNSON
"The only one who can beat me is me."

1996, Michael Johnson becomes the first man to win gold medals in the 200 and 400 meters the same year at the Atlanta Olympics, and the first African American track star on the front of a Wheaties cereal box.

RAFER JOHNSON

1958, Rafer Johnson is the first African American to win *Sports Illustrated's* Sportsman of the Year award.

1960, Rafer Johnson becomes the first African American to carry the U.S. flag during the Olympic opening ceremony. In the Olympics he becomes the first man to score more than 8,000 (8,063) points in the Decathlon.

1960, Rafer Johnson becomes the first African American male named Athlete of the Year by *Track & Field News*. He later appears on the cover of *Time* magazine.

MARION JONES

2000, Marion Jones becomes the first woman to win five medals (three gold and two bronze) in the Olympics at the Sydney games.

AL JOYNER

1984, With a leap of 56 feet, 7 ½ inches, Al Joyner becomes the first African American in 80 years to win an Olympic gold medal in the triple jump. He is honored with the Jim Thorpe Award, which is given every four years to the best U.S. competitor in an Olympic field event.

JACKIE JOYNER-KERSEE

1986, Jackie Joyner-Kersee becomes the first female athlete to break the 7,000 point barrier in the heptathlon with 7,148 points at the Moscow Goodwill Games.

1988, Jackie Joyner-Kersee becomes the first woman to crack the 24-foot barrier in the Olympics with a long jump of 24 feet, 3.5 inches. She becomes the only woman to win a gold medal in a multi-event (heptathlon) and in a specialty event (long jump) in the same Olympics. Joyner-Kersee is the first female to win the *Sporting News'* Athlete of the Year award.

1992, Jackie Joyner-Kersee becomes the first woman to win two Olympic gold medals in multi-event competition at the Barcelona Olympics.

1996, The Wilma Rudolph Courage Award is established by the Women's Sports Foundation to recognize a female athlete who exhibits extraordinary courage in athletic performance, overcomes adversity and makes significant contributions to sports. Jackie Joyner-Kersee is the first honoree.

2004, Jackie Joyner-Kersee becomes the first female African American track and field athlete on the cover of a Wheaties cereal box.

IDA KEELING

2016, Ida Keeling, born in Harlem, New York, becomes the first woman in history to complete a 100-meter run at the age of 100. Her time of 1:17.33 was witnessed by a crowd of 44,469 at the Penn Relays.

CHARLES LAKES

1988, Charles Lakes, becomes the second African American gymnast to compete in the Olympics. James Kenati Allen, in 1968, was the first. (Ron Galimore is the first African American selected for the Moscow Olympics, but he never competes because of the 1980 boycott.) At the Olympic trials, Lakes finishes first overall. In the Olympics he is the highest ranked American gymnast in the All-Around finals, where he finishes 19th.

CARL LEWIS

1984, Carl Lewis becomes the first African American track star to appear on the cover of *Time* magazine.

JAIR LYNCH

1996, Jair Lynch is the first African American gymnast to medal (silver) on the parallel bars in the Olympic Games. The Lynch Skill on the horizontal bar, which is a Tkatchev drill with a half turn prior to the catch to a mixed el-grip and swing back up to handstand, is named in his honor.

Colorful Firsts in U.S. Sports

MADELINE MANNING
1968, Madeline Manning (Mims), becomes the first American woman to win an Olympic Gold Medal in the 800-meter event.

SIMONE MANUEL
2016, Simone Manuel becomes the first African American swimmer to win an individual gold medal in an Olympic event, the 100-meter freestyle, in Rio de Janeiro, Brazil. Overall she wins another gold in the 4x100 medley relay and two silver medals in the 50-meter freestyle and the 4x100 freestyle relay.

PAM MARSHALL
1986, Pam Marshall becomes the first American runner to break the 50-second barrier in the 400 meters. She runs 49.99 in Westwood, Calif.

MARGARET MATTHEWS
1948, Margaret Matthews (Wilburn) becomes the first female to broad jump more than 20 feet (20 feet, 1 inch).

REGGIE McAFEE
1973, Reggie McAfee becomes the first African American to run the mile under four minutes, clocking 3:59.3 at the Big Four Meet in Raleigh, N.C.

KONNOR McCLAIN
2022, Konnor McClain captures the U.S. Gymnastic all-around title, in Tampa, Fla., while Shilese Jones and Jordan Chiles come in second and third place. This marks the first time that Black women filled the top three spots in this competition.

TAMYRA MENSAH-STOCK
2021, Tamyra Mensah-Stock becomes the first African American female wrestler to win an Olympic gold medal. She defeats Nigeria's Blessing Oborududu, 4-1, in the 68-kilogram freestyle wrestling. Mensah-Stock defeated Japan's Sara Dosho, 10-0, in the first round; beat China's Feng Zhao, 10-0, in the quarterfinals; then beat Ukraine's Alla Cherkasova, 10-4, in the semifinal.

DR. DELANO MERIWETHER
1972, As the first African American student at Duke University Medical School, hematologist Dr. Delano Meriwether runs the 100-yard dash in nine seconds flat at the USA Track & Field Outdoor Championships in Seattle, Wash. Meriweather becomes only the second sprinter, alongside John Carlos, to do so. In 1976, Dr. Meriwether, under President Gerald Ford's administration is tasked to inoculate millions of Americans to tackle the potential swine flu epidemic.

RALPH METCALFE
1934, Ralph Metcalfe, from Marquette University, becomes the first sprinter to win the 200 meter dash in the NCAA Men's Outdoor Track and Field Championship three consecutive years. His times were 20.3 in 1932, 20.4 in 1933 and 20.9 seconds in 1934. In 1971, Illinois House of Representative Metcalfe co-founded the Congressional Black Caucus.

RANDI MILLER
2008, In the Beijing Olympics, free-style wrestler Randi Miller, competing in the 63-kg weight class, becomes the first African American female to ever medal (a bronze) in the Olympics.

CHARLES MOORE JR.
1952, Charles Moore Jr. becomes the first African American to win an Olympic gold medal in the 400-meter hurdles.

EDWIN MOSES
1977 to 1987, Edwin Moses starts his winning string of 122 consecutive 400-meter hurdle races.

DALILAH MUHAMMAD
2016, Dalilah Muhammad wins the gold medal in the 400-meter hurdles, running a time of 53.13 seconds and claiming the first ever women's gold in the event for the U.S., at the Rio de Janeiro, Brazil Olympics.

IBTIHAJ MUHAMMAD
2016, Ibtihaj Muhammad becomes the first Muslim woman to compete for the U.S. in fencing and the first U.S. Olympic athlete to compete in a hijab in the Rio de Janeiro, Brazil, Olympics. The fencing champ also becomes the first female Muslim-American athlete to win an Olympic medal when she takes home the bronze in the team Sabre event at the Summer Games in Rio.

IRA MURCHISON
1956, Ira Murchison, at 5-foot-2, becomes the shortest sprinter to hold the world record in the 100-meter sprint, with a time of 10.1 seconds.

SKEETS NEHEMIAH
1981, Renaldo "Skeets" Nehemiah becomes the first hurdler to break the 13-second barrier in the 110-meter hurdles, with a 12.93 time.

ALEXANDRA NICHOLSON
1972, Canadian, Alexandra Nicholson becomes the first Black gymnast to win a World Championship with a gold medal on the trampoline, in Stuttgart, Germany. She is the first trampolinist, male or female, to complete a triffis, a triple somersault combined with a twist.

BETTY OKINO
1992, Betty Okino, born in Uganda, Africa, joins Dominique Dawes to become the first Black females to win Olympic gymnastics medals for the U.S. in Barcelona, Spain. Okino creates a move that bears her name, the "Okino," a triple pirouette on one leg on the balance beam. Okino later becomes a television and movie actress.

SID OGLESBY
1964, Competing in the Vault, Sid Oglesby from Syracuse University becomes the first Black NCAA event champion.

JESSE OWENS
"We all have dreams. In order to make dreams come into reality, it takes an awful lot of determination, dedication, self-discipline and effort."

1935, At the Big Ten championships in Ann Arbor, Mich., Jesse Owens sets or equals four world records in the same day: 9.4 seconds in the 100-yard dash; 26 feet, 8¼ inches in the long jump; 20.3 seconds in the 200-yard dash and 22.6 seconds in the 200-yard hurdles.

1936, Jesse Owens wins four gold medals at the Berlin Olympics and becomes the first African American on a Wheaties cereal box, back side. His victories helped dispel Nazi-based myths about Aryan supremacy.

1976, Jesse Owens is presented with the Presidential Medal of Freedom by President Gerald Ford, the highest civilian award.

1990, Jesse Owens becomes the first African American Olympian on a U.S. postage stamp. The 25-cent stamp is issued in a booklet honoring five Olympic gold medal champions. Owens is posthumously awarded the Congressional Gold Medal.

MICKEY PATTERSON
1948, Audrey "Mickey" Patterson (Tyler), becomes the first African American female to win an Olympic medal, a bronze in the 200 meters, just days before Alice Coachman wins her gold medal in the high jump.

TIDYE PICKETT
1936, In Berlin, Chicago native Tidye Pickett, 5-foot-2, becomes the first African American woman to compete in the Olympics. She represents the United States in the 80-meter hurdles but fails to medal when she breaks an ankle in the semi-finals. Pickett went on to serve as principal at Cottage Grove Elementary School in East Chicago Heights for 23 years. Upon her retirement in 1980, the school is named in her honor.

GEORGE POAGE
1904, George Coleman Poage, in St. Louis, Mo., places third in both the 200- and 400-meter hurdles to win Olympic bronze medals. He becomes the first African American to win a medal in the Summer Olympics games.

Colorful Firsts in U.S. Sports

MIKE POWELL

1992, Mike Powell leaps 29 feet, 4 ½ inches at the Barcelona Olympics, breaking Bob Beamon's 23-year old world mark (1968) by two inches.

PHIL REAVIS

1958, Phil Reavis, high jumper from Villanova, becomes the first African American track and field athlete to appear on the cover of *Sports Illustrated*.

JOHN REGISTER

2000, John Register, with a running prosthesis, wins a silver medal in the long jump at the Sydney Paralympic Games. He also competes in the 100- and 200-meter races.

SIMON ROBERTS

1957, Simon Roberts from the University of Iowa wrestling at 147 pounds, captures an NCAA crown placing second in the Big Ten tournament. The following year he wins the conference title, becoming the first Black wrestler to win an NCAA Championship.

MACK ROBINSON

2000, Mack Robinson becomes the first Olympic silver medalist (200-meters, 1936 Berlin Olympics) to have a post office named in his honor, the Matthew "Mack" Robinson Post Office in Pasadena, California.

ROSE ROBINSON

1959, Eroseanna "Rose" Robinson, a high jumper, refuses to stand for the national anthem at the Pan American Games held in Chicago's Wrigley Field, citing the flag represents "war, injustice and hypocrisy." Upon winning the 1958 AAU National Championship, Robinson was named to the U.S. Women's Track and Field team. The predominantly Black team was invited to compete in the Soviet Union at a State Department track meet during the height of the Cold War. Robinson refused to attend, telling *Jet* magazine: "I don't want to be used as a political pawn."

WILMA RUDOLPH

"I had a series of childhood illnesses. It started off as scarlet fever, and from there it was polio.
My father was the one who sort of babied me and was sympathetic . . .
My mother was the one who made me work, made me believe that one day it would be possible for me to walk without braces."

1960, At the Rome Olympics, Wilma Rudolph becomes the first American woman to win three gold medals in the same year.

1960, Wilma Rudolph becomes the first American woman to break the 23-second barrier in the 200-meter dash with a time of 22.9 seconds.

1977, Wilma Rudolph's autobiography "Wilma" is made into a movie for TV.

1980, The International Women's Sports Hall of Fame, in its first year elects Wilma Rudolph in the Contemporary category, while Althea Gibson receives honors in its Pioneer category.

1996, The Wilma Rudolph Courage Award is established by the Women's Sports Foundation to recognize a female athlete who exhibits extraordinary courage in athletic performance, overcomes adversity and makes significant contributions to sports. Jackie Joyner-Kersee is the first honoree.

ANDRE SHELBY

2016, Andre Shelby becomes the first Black U.S. Paralympic archer at the Rio de Janeiro Olympics. Paralyzed from the chest down from a motorcycle accident, he wins the gold medal.

CLARESSA SHIELDS

2012, At the London Olympic Games, Claressa Shields becomes the first U.S. woman to win a boxing gold medal. The 165-pound Shields wins the Olympic middleweight title by defeating Russian boxer Nadezda Torlopova.

2016, Claressa Shields becomes the first U.S. boxer to win back-to-back Olympic gold medals, defeating the Netherlands' Nouchka Fontijn.

KEETH SMART
2003, Keeth Smart becomes the first African American fencer to be ranked No. 1 in the world.

CALVIN SMITH
1983, In Zurich, Switzerland, Calvin Smith becomes the first athlete to run under 10 seconds (9.97) in the 100-meter race, and 20 seconds (19.99) in the 200 meters, on the same day.

RONNIE RAY SMITH
1968, At the AAU Track and Field Championships in Sacramento, California, three men break the world record in the 100 meters, Jim Hines, Charlie Greene and Ronnie Ray Smith, with the same time of 9.9 seconds.

TOMMIE SMITH
"Then Peter said, silver and gold have I none; but such as I have I give to thee:
In the name of Jesus Christ of Nazareth rise up and walk." Acts 3:6 is often quoted by Tommie Smith.

1967, Tommie Smith becomes the first American to hold world records in the 200- and 400-meter races, simultaneously.

1968, Tommie Smith becomes the first man to break the sub-20 second barrier in the 200-meters with a 19.83 time in the Mexico City Olympics.

1968, Tommie Smith, John Carlos, Lee Evans, Larry James, Ron Freeman and other Black athletes protest racism in the U.S. at the Mexico City Olympics, with symbolic gestures on the victory stand.

LOUISE STOKES
1936, Louise "The Malden Meteor" Stokes, along with Tidye Pickett become the first African American women selected to the U.S. Olympic team. Stokes, a sprinter, fails to medal. She is honored in the Massachusetts Hall of Black Achievement.

CORRINNE WRIGHT TARVER
1989, Corrinne Tarver, a Georgia Bulldog, becomes the first Black female gymnast to win the NCAA all-around championship.

JOHN "DOC" TAYLOR
1908, John Baxter "Doc" Taylor Jr. becomes the first African American to win an Olympic team gold medal, as member of the 4x400-meters relay in London. This year Taylor completes his degree in veterinary medicine from the University to Pennsylvania.

LAULAUGA TAUSAGA-COLLINS
2023, Laulauga Tausaga-Collins is the first Black female discus thrower to win a World Championship in Budapest, Hungary with a toss of more than 227 feet.

JOHN TERRY
1936, John F. Terry becomes the first African American U.S. Olympic weightlifter. In 1939, he set a world record for the deadlift with 600 pounds, considered enormous for his bodyweight of only 132 pounds.

DEBI THOMAS
1986, Debi Thomas, 18, becomes the first African American to win the World Figure Skating title, in Geneva, Switzerland. Earlier this year, Thomas becomes the first African American to win the U.S. Figure Skating Championship. She is named *Wide World of Sports*' Athlete of the Year.

1988, Skater Debi Thomas becomes the first African American female to earn a medal (bronze) in the Winter Olympic Games in Calgary. Thomas is later inducted into the U.S. Figure Skating Hall of Fame in February 2000. In 1997, she graduates from Northwestern Medical School and completes her orthopedic residency program at Charles Drew University in Los Angeles, Calif.

GABRIELLE THOMAS
2021, Gabrielle Thomas wins a bronze medal in the 200 meters at the Tokyo Olympics. Thomas becomes the first Harvard grad (with neurobiology and global health disciplines) to win an Olympic medal.

Colorful Firsts in U.S. Sports

JOHN THOMAS

1959, John Thomas becomes the youngest man to set a world record. He leaps 7 feet, 1 ¼ inches in the high jump, one day shy of his 18th birthday.

EDDIE TOLAN

1930, Eddie Tolan becomes the first person officially credited with running the 100-yard dash in 9.5 seconds.

1932, Eddie Tolan becomes the first African American sprinter to win gold medals in the Los Angeles Olympics, in both the 100- and 200-meter dashes. He set a world record of 10.3 seconds in the 100-meters and an Olympic record of 21.2 seconds in the 200 meters.

WYOMIA TYUS

1968, Wyomia Tyus becomes the first person to win Gold Medals in the 100-meter race, in two consecutive Olympics.

NELSON VAILS

1983, Nelson Vails becomes the first African American cyclist to win a gold medal at the Pan American games.

1984, Nelson Vails is the first African American to win a silver medal in cycling at the Los Angeles Olympic Games.

HERB WASHINGTON

1972, Herb Washington sets the world record in the 60-yard dash at 5.8 seconds at a track meet in East Lansing, Michigan.

1974, Oakland A's owner Charlie Finley hires former Michigan State University sprinter Herb Washington as the first "designated runner" in major league history. Washington has no prior professional baseball experience. He steals 31 bases in 48 attempts and scored 33 runs in 105 ML games.

MALIVAI WASHINGTON

1996, MaliVai Washington becomes the first African American named to the U.S. Olympic tennis team.

PETER WESTBROOK

1984, Peter Westbrook becomes the first African American to win an Olympic medal in fencing, a bronze.

RUTH WHITE

1969, Ruth White becomes the youngest woman and the first African American woman to win a national fencing championship.

WILLYE WHITE

1956, Sixteen-year-old high school sophomore Willye White becomes the first American female to win a medal (silver) in the long jump at the Melbourne Olympics, with a mark of 19 feet and 11.5 inches.

MAL WHITFIELD

1954, Mal Whitfield, track star, is the first African American to win the James E. Sullivan Award, given each year to the top amateur athlete.

1964, In the march magazine of *Ebony*, Olympic gold medalist Mal Whitfield writes an article titled, "Let's Boycott the Olympics" in Tokyo. Whitfield cites "It is time for America to live up to its promises of Liberty, Equality and Justice for all." The boycott did not materialize.

ARCHIE WILLIAMS

1936, Archie Williams becomes the first African American to win the 400-meters race in the Olympics.

ATOY WILSON

1966, Atoy Wilson becomes the first African American to win a national figure skating title in the men's frosh category of the U.S. National Championships. He was coached by African American Mabel Fairbanks.

JOHN WOODRUFF

1936, John Woodruff becomes the first African American to win the 800-meters race in the Olympics.

MICHAEL WRIGHT

2010, Tennessee Volunteer senior Michael Wright becomes the first African American national champion in USA Diving history when he wins the men's one-meter springboard competition, at the USA Diving Winter National Championships in Knoxville, Tenn.

Cage 10EN: Rodeo Champions

1876, Nat Love or "Deadwood Dick" is the first known African American rodeo champion.

1904, At the Cheyenne Frontier Days in Wyoming, Bill Pickett demonstrates his pioneer bulldogging technique of bringing a steer to its knees by sinking his teeth into the animal's upper lip or nose and releasing both his hands. The event later becomes known as steer-wrestling.

1914, Bill Pickett stars in a silent film called *The Bull-Dogger*, advertising his techniques of steer-wrestling.

1982, Charlie Sampson becomes the first African American World Champion Bull Rider by winning the Winston Rodeo Series in Oklahoma City.

1999, Fred Whitfield of Hockley, Texas becomes the first African American to win the All-Around Cowboy World Championships, hosted by the Professional Rodeo Cowboys Association, considered the most prestigious PRCA award for multi-event cowboys. Whitfield wins his fourth calf roping title in the Las Vegas Rodeo.

2003, Myrtis Dightman, Charlie Sampson, and Bill Pickett become the first class of inductees for the National Cowboys of Color Museum and Hall of Fame in Oklahoma City, Okla.

MYRTIS DIGHTMAN

1966, Myrtis Dightman becomes the first African American to ride in the National Finals Rodeo.

1997, Myrtis Dightman becomes the first living African American cowboy inducted into the National Cowboy Hall of Fame in Oklahoma City, Okla.

2003, Myrtis Dightman, Charlie Sampson, and Bill Pickett become the first class of inductees for the National Cowboys of Color Museum and Hall of Fame in Oklahoma City, Okla.

NAT LOVE

1876, Nat Love or "Deadwood Dick" is the first known Black rodeo champion.

BILL PICKETT

1904, At the Cheyenne Frontier Days in Wyoming, Bill Pickett demonstrates his pioneer bulldogging technique of bringing a steer to its knees by sinking his teeth into the animal's upper lip or nose and releasing both his hands. The event later becomes known as steer-wrestling.

1914, Bill Pickett stars in a silent film called *The Bull-Dogger* advertising his techniques of steer-wrestling.

1932, Rodeo star Bill Pickett dies in a rodeo accident.

1971, Bill Pickett becomes the first African American selected to the National Rodeo Cowboy Hall of Fame in Oklahoma City, Okla.

1993, Bill Pickett becomes the first African American cowboy featured on a U.S. postage stamp.

2003, Myrtis Dightman, Charlie Sampson, and Bill Pickett become the first class of inductees for the National Cowboys of Color Museum and Hall of Fame in Oklahoma City, Okla.

CHARLIE SAMPSON

1982, Charlie Sampson becomes the first African American World Champion Bull Rider by winning the Winston Rodeo Series in Oklahoma City.

FRED WHITFIELD

1996, Fred Whitfield becomes the first African American to win the World Championship of Calf Roping.

1999, Fred Whitfield, of Hockley, Texas, becomes the first African American to win the All-Around Cowboy World Championships, hosted by the Professional Rodeo Cowboys Association, considered the most prestigious PRCA award for multi-event cowboys. Whitfield wins his fourth calf roping title in the Las Vegas Rodeo.

2002, Fred Whitfield becomes the first African American to win rodeo's coveted U.S. Smokeless Tobacco Company Cup Series for all-around performance.

Cage E11VEN: Tennis Champions

"Sports strain to stress to us that we are watching history." – Rowan Ricardo Phillips, Stony Brook University

1890, The Chautauqua Tennis Club of Philadelphia is founded. The African American organization hosts its first interstate tournament in 1898.

1909, Educator Booker T. Washington's son E. Davidson and C.G. Kelly create the first faculty tennis club at Tuskegee Institute.

1914, The Ideal Tennis Club is founded in Harlem, N.Y. Founding members of the Ideal Club are instrumental in the formation of the American Tennis Association (ATA).

1916, The American Tennis Association (ATA) is organized in Washington, District of Columbia, to promote tennis play among African Americans. Organizing officials include Dr. H. S. McCard, Dr. William H. Wright, Dr. B. M. Rhetta, Ralph V. Cook, Dr. Henry Freeman, John F. N. Wilkinson, Tally Holmes and others.

1917, The American Tennis Association (ATA) holds its first tournament. At its first championship in Baltimore at Druid Hill Park, Tally Holmes wins the Men's Singles and Lucy Diggs Slowe wins the Women's Singles. Diggs Stowe becomes the first African American woman to win a major sports title.

1918, The ATA hosts its second tennis tournament in New York City on the Ideal Tennis Courts. Tally Holmes repeats as Men's Singles winner, and Mae Rae wins the Women's Singles event.

1922, The Springfield Tennis Club is organized at St. John's Congregational Church in Springfield, Mass. Practices are held at Forest Park and Pratt Field.

1925, The National Capitol Country Club for African Americans is formed in Washington, District of Columbia. It is known as a semi-social, semi-athletic club, whose membership includes men and women.

1950, Althea Gibson becomes the first African American to be accepted for competition in the National Tennis Championship at the U.S. Championships after Alice Marble writes an editorial for the July 1 edition of *American Lawn Tennis* magazine. Marble writes, "Miss Gibson is over a very cunningly wrought barrel, and I can only hope to loosen a few of its staves with one lone opinion. If tennis is a game for ladies and gentlemen, it's also time we acted a little more like gentle people and less like sanctimonious hypocrites." Marble adds that if Gibson were not given the opportunity to compete, "then there is an ineradicable mark against a game to which I have devoted most of my life, and I would be bitterly ashamed." Gibson is inducted into the International Tennis Hall of Fame in 1971.

1971, George Braithwaite, a Guyana born immigrant of African ancestry becomes a member of the U.S. Table Tennis team that visits the People's Republic of China in an attempt to improve diplomatic relations between the U.S. and China.

1974, Lenward Simpson signs with the Detroit Loves and becomes the first African American on a World Team Tennis (WTT) team.

1976, Tennis players Bruce Foxworth and Roger Guedes lead Hampton University to become the first historically Black college or university to win the NCAA's Division II tennis doubles title.

1992, Arthur Ashe, former Wimbledon and US Open champion, tells *USA Today* and *People* magazine, that "being Black is harder than living with AIDS." Ashe contracted AIDS from a tainted blood transfusion during heart surgery in 1988.

1993, Sande French becomes the first African American Chair Umpire to preside over a Grand Slam final. She referees the US Open women's singles final in a match between No. 1 Steffi Graft of Germany and Helena Sukova of the Czech Republic. Despite no controversial rulings, French is later demoted by Richard Kaufman of the ITF, for reasons unknown.

1994, Cecil M. Hollins becomes the only African American Chair Umpire in the world with a gold badge which qualifies him to referee major tennis events.

1999, Tennis great Arthur Ashe and Paul Robeson, who earned 12 varsity letters at Rutgers, are among the first 20 electees to the International Scholar-Athlete Hall of Fame in Kingston, R.I.

1999, In the Australian Open, Venus Williams is penalized a point while serving to Lindsay Davenport, when beads fall from her braids. Williams notes, "I've never had such treatment before from any other umpire or any other match." Davenport counters, "Well, you can hear them and see them a little bit. Fortunately, you learn to play the ball. I'm not going to say it was a total distraction, but it is a little annoying maybe." The number one seed Davenport defeats fifth seed Williams in the quarterfinals, 6-4 and 6-0.

Colorful Firsts in U.S. Sports

2004, Scoville Jenkins, 18, becomes the first African American champion to win the USTA National Open Hard Court tennis title.

2005, Sande French of Albion, Calif., and Cecil Holland of Queens, N.Y., file a lawsuit against the International Tennis Federation and the U.S. Tennis Association in U.S. District Court in Brooklyn, N.Y. Holland, despite attaining "gold badge" status and chairing more than 1,500 professional matches, is never permitted to sit as a chair umpire at the U.S. Open. French has worked more than 1,500 matches and claims that women are only permitted to chair preliminary men's matches due to systemic racism.

2009, Venus and Serena Williams become the first African American women to own part of an NFL franchise when they purchase a minority interest in the Miami Dolphins. Musicians Gloria and Emilio Estefan, and Marc Anthony also bought small shares of the team.

2015, Video shows white plain-clothes officer James Frascatore wrestling and handcuffing tennis player James Blake, outside of a New York hotel, waiting for a car service to the U.S. Open, without provocation. Four other officers assisted Frascatore in the assault. Blake suffers a cut to his left elbow and bruises to his left leg. The NYPD apologizes to Blake for a case of mistaken identity. As punishment, Frascatore is docked five vacation days. Frascatore later files a defamation of character lawsuit against Blake that is dismissed.

KATRINA ADAMS

2015, Katrina Adams becomes president, chairman and CEO of the U.S. Tennis Association (USTA), and the first former professional tennis player, first African American and the youngest person to serve as president in the organization's 135-year history.

ARTHUR ASHE

When asked which is harder to live with, being Black or having AIDS? "Being Black is! No question about it,"

-- former Wimbledon and US Open champion says in the 8 June 1992 edition of *People* magazine.

"Even now it continues to feel like an extra weight tied around me."

1963, Arthur Ashe becomes the first African American named to the U.S. Davis Cup Tennis team. He wins the U.S. Hard Court Championship.

1968 Arthur Ashe wins the U.S. Amateur Championships against Davis Cup Teammate Bob Lutz, and in the first US Open of the open era, becomes the first African American male to capture the title and the only player to have won both the amateur and open national championships in the same year.

1968, Arthur Ashe becomes the first Black man to win the U.S. Tennis Championship, 4-6, 6-3, 8-10, 6-0, and 6-4.

1970, Arthur Ashe becomes the first African American tennis player to win the Australian Open championship.

1975, Arthur Ashe becomes the first African American to win Wimbledon, 6-1, 6-1, 5-7, and 6-4 over heavy favorite Jimmy Connors.

1975, Arthur Ashe becomes the first African American to be ranked No. 1 by the U.S. Lawn Tennis Association.

1981, Arthur Ashe becomes the first African American to be named Captain of the U.S. Davis Cup team, a position he held until 1985.

1985, Arthur Ashe becomes the first African American male elected to the International Tennis Hall of Fame.

1993, Arthur Ashe is posthumously presented with the Presidential Medal of Freedom by President Bill Clinton, the highest civilian award.

1997, Arthur Ashe becomes the first African American tennis player on the front of a Wheaties cereal box.

1997, Arthur Ashe and Althea Gibson are remembered at the opening of the new Arthur Ashe Stadium in New York City. The 22,547-seat stadium was dedicated in Ashe's memory and on Gibson's 70th birthday.

1999, Tennis great Arthur Ashe and Paul Robeson, who earned 12 varsity letters at Rutgers, are among the first 20 electees to the International Scholar-Athlete Hall of Fame in Kingston, R.I.

2005, Arthur Ashe is the first African American male tennis player featured on a U.S. postage stamp.

LULA BALLARD

1930, The Tribune Girls are sponsored by the *Philadelphia Tribune* newspaper. The players come from two Black female basketball teams, the Philadelphia Quick Steppers and the Germantown Hornets. Inez Patterson from the Quick Steppers becomes coach and player of the team. Two tennis players from the YWCA Colored Branch in Germantown, Ora Washington and Lula Ballard, become standout hoopsters.

SANDE FRENCH

1993, Sande French becomes the first African American Chair Umpire to preside over a Grand Slam final. She referees the US Open women's singles final in a match between No. 1 Steffi Graft of Germany and Helena Sukova of the Czech Republic. Despite no controversial rulings, French is later demoted by Richard Kaufman of the ITF, for reasons unknown.

2005, Sande French of Albion, Calif., and Cecil Holland of Queens, N.Y., files a lawsuit against the International Tennis Federation and the U.S. Tennis Association in U.S. District Court in Brooklyn, N.Y. Holland, despite attaining "gold badge" status and chairing more than 1500 professional matches, he is never permitted to sit as a chair umpire at the US Open. French has worked more than 1500 matches claims that women are only permitted to chair preliminary men's matches due to systemic racism. In 2022, after 36 years of service, she is inducted into the Black Tennis Hall of Fame.

ZINA GARRISON

1988, Zina Garrison becomes the first African American to rank in the top 10 on the women's professional tennis tour.

Colorful Firsts in U.S. Sports

COCO GAUFF

2019, Cori "Coco" Gauff, 15, becomes the youngest woman to qualify for the grass-court Wimbledon tennis tournament. She defeats Venus Williams in the opening round before losing in the fourth round.

ALTHEA GIBSON
"I'm not a Negro tennis player. I'm a tennis player."

1947, Althea Gibson wins the first of 10 straight (all-Black) American Tennis Association (ATA) National Championships, a title that began in 1917.

1950, Althea Gibson becomes the first African American to be accepted for competition in the National Tennis Championship at the U.S. Championships after Alice Marble writes an editorial for the July 1 edition of *American Lawn Tennis* magazine. Marble writes, "Miss Gibson is over a very cunningly wrought barrel, and I can only hope to loosen a few of its staves with one lone opinion. If tennis is a game for ladies and gentlemen, it's also time we acted a little more like gentle people and less like sanctimonious hypocrites." Marble adds that if Gibson is not given the opportunity to compete, "then there is an ineradicable mark against a game to which I have devoted most of my life, and I would be bitterly ashamed." Gibson is inducted into the International Tennis Hall of Fame in 1971.

1951, Althea Gibson becomes the first African American to play at Wimbledon in England.

1956, Althea Gibson becomes the first African American female to win the French Open tennis championship, 6-0, and 12-10, in the process becoming the first African American to win a Grand Slam title.

1957, Althea Gibson becomes the first African American woman to win the U.S. Tennis Championship, 6-3, 6-2.

1957, Althea Gibson becomes the first African American to win the world's prestigious Wimbledon championship. She defeats American Darlen Hard 6-3, 6-2.

1957, Althea Gibson is the first African American woman to appear on the cover of *Sports Illustrated* and the first African American tennis player to appear on the cover of *Time* magazine.

1958, Althea Gibson becomes the first Black female to win Wimbledon, two years in a row.

1959, Althea Gibson releases a record album, *Althea Gibson Sings*. She later appears in the film, *The Horse Soldiers*.

1960, Althea Gibson tours with the Harlem Globetrotters, playing exhibition tennis.

1963, Tennis star Althea Gibson becomes the first African American member of the Ladies Professional Golf Association (LPGA).

1971, Althea Gibson is elected to the International Tennis Hall of Fame.

1997, Arthur Ashe and Althea Gibson are remembered at the opening of the new Arthur Ashe Stadium in New York City. The 22,547-seat stadium was dedicated in Ashe's memory and on Gibson's 70th birthday.

2001, Tennis star Althea Gibson becomes the first African American female to appear on the front of a Wheaties cereal box.

2013, Althea Gibson is the first African American female tennis player featured on a U.S. postage stamp.

TALLY HOLMES

1917, The American Tennis Association (ATA) holds its first tournament. At its first championship in Baltimore at Druid Hill Park, Tally Holmes wins the Men's Singles and Lucy Diggs Slowe wins the Women's Singles. Diggs Stowe becomes the first African American woman to win a major sports title.

NAOMI OSAKA

2020, Naomi Osaka, winner of the US Open, is named *Associated Press'* Female Athlete of the Year, receiving 18 of 35 first place votes. She is a leading voice in speaking out against racial injustice and police brutality.

2021, Naomi Osaka, of Haitian and Japanese descent, becomes the first biracial female athlete on the cover of *Sports Illustrated's* Swimsuit issue.

MAE RAE

1918, The ATA hosts its second tennis tournament in New York City on the Ideal Tennis Courts. Tally Holmes repeats as Men's Singles winner and Mae Rae wins the Women's Singles event.

ROBERT RYLAND

1959, Robert Ryland, 39, becomes the first African American professional tennis player on the World Pro Tour. Ryland would later coach Arthur Ashe, Serena and Venus Williams.

BEN SHELTON
2023, Ben Shelton defeats Frances Tiafoe in the US Open quarterfinals. It is the first time that two Black Americans reach the final eight in a grand slam event.

LUCY DIGGS SLOWE
1917, The American Tennis Association (ATA) holds its first tournament. At its first championship in Baltimore at Druid Hill Park, Tally Holmes wins the Men's Singles and Lucy Diggs Slowe wins the Women's Singles. Diggs Stowe becomes the first African American woman to win a major sports title. Stowe is also one of the founders of the Alpha Kappa Alpha Sorority.

ALEXANDRA STEVENSON
1999, Alexandra Stevenson, 18, becomes the first "qualifier" in Wimbledon history to reach the women's semifinals by defeating Jelena Dokic, 6-3, 1-6, 6-3.

FRANCES TIAFOE
2023, Ben Shelton defeats Frances Tiafoe in the US Open quarterfinals. It is the first time that two Black Americans reach the final eight in a grand slam event.

ORA MAE WASHINGTON
1928, Walter Green, of Chicago, starts the Savoy Colts, a women's basketball team, managed by Dick Hudson. Their roster includes guards E. Williams, Blanche Winston, Corrine Robinson, forwards Lula Porter, Virginia Willis, H. Williams and famed Philadelphia tennis star Ora Washington at center.

1929, The Germantown Hornets, in Philadelphia, are formed by the YWCA Branch of Colored Girls and Women. The Hornets basketball team included Ora Washington, Lula Ballard, Louise Penn, Lil Fountainé, Helen Laws and Evelyn Manns.

1930, The Tribune Girls are sponsored by the *Philadelphia Tribune* newspaper. The players come from two Black female basketball teams, the Philadelphia Quick Steppers and the Germantown Hornets. Inez Patterson from the Quick Steppers becomes coach and player of the team. Two tennis players from the YWCA Colored Branch in Germantown, Ora Washington and Lula Ballard, become standout hoopsters.

1935, Ora Washington becomes the first African American woman to win seven consecutive tennis titles in the ATA (American Tennis Association), from 1929 to 1935, and was undefeated from 1924 to 1936.

SERENA WILLIAMS
"I love who I am, and I encourage other people to love and embrace who they are.
But it definitely wasn't easy. It took me a while."

1999, Venus and Serena Williams compete in the first all-sister final of this century in the Lipton Championship in Key Biscayne, Fla. Venus defeats younger sis Serena 6-4, 4-6, 6-4.

2000, Venus and Serena Williams become the first sisters to win Wimbledon's doubles crown, beating Ai Sugiyama and Julia Halard-Decugis in straight sets, 6-3, 6-2.

2000, Serena Williams, 17, becomes the first African American to have won the singles (1999), doubles and mixed championships at the US Open.

2002, Serena Williams defeats older sister Venus in the French Open, 7-5 and 6-3. They become the first sisters to be ranked No. 2 and No. 1, respectively.

2002, The Williams sisters Venus and Serena become the first siblings to compete in the Wimbledon final since 1900. Serena defeats Venus, 7-6 (7-4), 6-3. Sisters Maud and Lillian Watson from London first played their match in 1884.

2003, Serena Williams becomes the first African American to capture all four major tennis championships, winning the French, Wimbledon, US Open and Australian Open.

2008, Serena Williams regains the World No. 1 ranking after five years and one month. This is the longest gap in professional tennis history.

2009, Venus and Serena Williams become the first African American women to own part of an NFL franchise when they purchase a minority interest in the Miami Dolphins. Musicians Gloria and Emilio Estefan, and Marc Anthony also bought small shares of the team.

2018, The French Tennis Federation president, Bernard Giudicelli, says that the sleek black catsuit worn by Serena Williams at the French Open goes "too far," adding, "You have to respect the game and the place."

2019, Rapsody in her *Eve* album produces the first rap song about a female tennis player, entitled "Serena" in honor of Serena Williams.

VENUS WILLIAMS

1998, Venus Williams' serve is measured at 125 mph at Wimbledon, the fastest recorded serve by a woman. At the Swisscom Challenge, Williams uncorks a 127 mph serve, a record in women's tennis.

1999, Venus and Serena Williams compete in the first all-sister final of this century in the Lipton Championship in Key Biscayne, Fla. Venus defeats younger sis Serena 6-4, 4-6, 6-4.

1999, In the Australian Open, Venus Williams is penalized a point while serving to Lindsay Davenport, when beads fall from her braids. Williams notes, "I've never had such treatment before from any other umpire or any other match." Davenport counters, "Well, you can hear them and see them a little bit. Fortunately, you learn to play the ball. I'm not going to say it was a total distraction, but it is a little annoying maybe." The number one seed Davenport defeats fifth seed Williams in the quarterfinals, 6-4 and 6-0.

2000, Venus and Serena Williams become the first sisters to win Wimbledon's doubles crown, beating Ai Sugiyama and Julia Halard-Decugis in straight sets, 6-3, 6-2.

2000, Venus Williams wins the US Open, defeating Lindsay Davenport. Venus, along with Serena (1999 US Open Champion) become the first sisters to win the tournament.

2002, Venus Williams becomes the first African American woman to rank World No. 1 since the Women's Tennis Association (WTA) computer rankings began in 1975.

2002, The Williams sisters Venus and Serena become the first siblings to compete in the Wimbledon final since 1900. Serena defeats Venus, 7-6 (7-4), 6-3. Sisters Maud and Lillian Watson from London first played their match in 1884.

2007, Venus Williams becomes the lowest ranking player, 31, to become the Wimbledon tennis champion. She defeats Frenchwoman Marion Bartoli. Williams also wins Wimbledon in 2000, 2001 and 2005; and is ranked No. 1 in 2002. Wimbledon, the oldest and most prestigious tennis tournament, announces equal purses for men and women.

2009, Venus and Serena Williams become the first African American women to own part of an NFL franchise when they purchase a minority interest in the Miami Dolphins. Musicians Gloria and Emilio Estefan, and Marc Anthony also bought small shares of the team.

Cage 12ELVE: Other Caged Champions

STARR ANDREWS
2022, Starr Andrews becomes the first U.S. Black figure skater to win an ISU Grand Prix Medal (silver) at Skate Canada.

PEARL BAILEY
1973, Pearl Bailey becomes the first female boxing commentator, when she hosts the heavyweight championship fight in Kingston, Jamaica, between George Foreman and Joe Frazier.

NORM BASS
1964, Norm Bass, former Kansas City A's pitcher from 1961 to 1963, plays one game at defensive back for the Denver Broncos in 1964.

TOM BASS
1893, Saddle horse trainer and equestrian showman, Tom Bass invents the Bass Bit. The horse bit with hinges, prevents pain to the horse's mouth during training. The Bass Bit is still used today.

1899, Tom Bass is credited with developing the American Royal, a rodeo and livestock and horse show, in Kansas City, Mo.

GEORGE BRAITHWAITE
1971, George Braithwaite, a Guyana born immigrant of African ancestry becomes a member of the U.S. Ping Pong team that visits the People's Republic of China in an attempt for better diplomatic relations between the U.S. and China.

GEORGE BRANHAM III
1986, George Branham III, 24, wins the Brunswick Memorial World Open, defeating Mark Roth in the finals. It is the first time an African American wins a Professional Bowlers Association (PBA) title.

1993, George Branham III becomes the first African American bowler to win a PBA Triple Crown event when he beats Parker Bohn III, 227-214 in the Tournament of Champions.

SAMARRIA BREVARD
2014, Samarria Brevard becomes the first African American female skateboarder to win the Kimberly Diamond Cup Women's Street Championship in South Africa.

2017, Samarria Brevard, known as the "Serena Williams of skateboarding," is the first African American female to medal at the X Games at U.S. Bank Stadium in downtown Minneapolis, Minn.

ART BROOKS
1952, Arthur B. Brooks, of Detroit, becomes the African American accepted as a member of the American Bowling Congress.

ANTRON BROWN
2012, Antron Brown becomes the first African American champion in any NHRA Pro Series when he wins the Top Fuel title in Pomona, Calif.

EDITH BURROUGHS
1979, An Akron, Ohio grandmother, Edith Burroughs becomes the first Black person to win a professional bowling tournament. She wins the Pabst Blue Ribbon tournament, in Rockford, Ill., taking home the $4000 first place prize.

DREMIEL BYERS
2002, Dremiel Byers becomes the first African American to win a Greco-Roman world championship gold medal, capturing the title in the heavyweight division in Moscow.

2009, Dremiel Byers becomes the first Black wrestler, and only the second American, to win three medals at the Greco-Roman World Championships.

Colorful Firsts in U.S. Sports

FLETCHER CARR
1973, Fletcher Carr becomes the first African American coach in the Southeastern Conference, when he is named the wrestling coach at the University of Kentucky.

DONNA CHEEK
1990, Donna Marie Cheek becomes the first African American member of the U.S. Equestrian Team.

DARIUS CLARK
2022, Standing 5-foot-9 ¾ Darius Clark becomes the first man to achieve a 50-inch vertical jump from a running start. Clark is a long jumper from Florida State and Texas A&M.

ALLEN COAGE
1976, Allen J. Coage becomes the first African American to medal at the Montreal Olympics in Judo, earning the Bronze.

CURTIS COKES
1966, Curtis Cokes defeats Manuel Gonzalez in New Orleans to win the vacant World Welterweight Title. Cokes is the first Harlem Clown basketball player to win a world boxing title.

SOPHIA DANENBERG
2006, Born in Okinawa, Japan, Sophia Danenberg, 34, becomes the first Black woman to climb to the summit of Mount Everest, the world's tallest mountain.

BREHANNA DANIELS
2017, At the Daytona International Speedway, Brehanna Daniels becomes the first Black woman in a NASCAR Cup Series pit crew at the Coke Zero Sugar 400 annual car race.

CHERYL DANIELS
1995, Cheryl Daniels becomes the first African American to hold the national title in women's professional bowling by winning the U.S. Open Championship.

CHRIS DICKERSON
1970, Body builder Chris Dickerson is the first African American to be named "Mr. America."

MYRTIS DIGHTMAN
"Heroes are not born into greatness; they are not heroes because they come from wealth or power."

1966, Myrtis Dightman becomes the first African American to ride in the National Finals Rodeo.

1997, Myrtis Dightman, becomes the first living Black cowboy inducted into the National Cowboy Hall of Fame in Oklahoma City, Okla.

2003, Myrtis Dightman, Charlie Sampson, and Bill Pickett become the first class of inductees for the National Cowboys of Color Museum and Hall of Fame in Oklahoma City, Okla.

SADIE DIXON-WATERS
1951, Sadie Dixon, called "the female Jackie Robinson" integrates the Bowling Proprietors Association of America (BPAA) bowling tournament.

EBONY ANGLERS
2020, An African American female fishing team, called The Ebony Anglers with Bobbiette Palmer, Gia Peebles, Tiana Davis, Glenda Turner and Lesleigh Mausi win first place in the King Mackerel division of Carteret Community College Foundation's Spanish Mackerel & Dolphin Tournament in Morehead City, N.C.

GREG GIBSON
1984, Greg Gibson becomes the first African American to win an Olympic medal in Greco-Roman wrestling, capturing a silver

medal at the Los Angeles games.

AMANDA GORMAN

2021, Amanda Gorman becomes the first poet to recite a poem at the Super Bowl. At Super Bowl LV at Raymond James Stadium in Tampa, Fla., Gorman reads "Chorus of the Captains" to recognize the three honorary captains: a nurse, a teacher and a Marine veteran.

BRYANT GUMBEL

2006, Bryant Gumbel, former NBC's *Today* show host and prime anchor for the 1980 Summer Olympic Games, becomes the NFL Network's first play-by-play commentator.

GREG GUMBEL

2001, Greg Gumbel becomes the first Black *play-by-play* announcer to call a major U.S. sports championship, the Super Bowl. The Baltimore Ravens meet the New York Giants. He also calls the 2004 Super Bowl marred by Janet Jackson's so-called wardrobe malfunction during the halftime show.

LEWIS HAMILTON

2006, Lewis Hamilton becomes the first Black Englishman driver in Formula 1 after joining McLaren Racing.

2022 Seven-time Formula 1 champion Lewis Hamilton is part of a consortium to purchase the Denver Broncos for a record $4.65 billion.

GEORGE HARRIS

1964, George Harris becomes the first African American to participate on the U.S. Olympic Judo team in the Tokyo Olympics.

FRANK HART

1880, Haiti-American Frank Hart, known as "The Negro Wonder or Black Dan," becomes the first Black world record holder in the 19th century sport of pedestrianism. Born Fred Hichborn, Hart is also the first Black athlete depicted on a sports card, trading card or tobacco-card set, when he appears in Thomas H. Hall's 1880 "Between the Acts & Bravo Cigarettes" card set, N344.

MELISSA HARVILLE-LeBRON

2018, Melissa Harville-Lebron becomes the first African American woman to own a NASCAR team, when her company W.M. Stone Enterprises, Inc., creates E2 Northeast Motorsports. The new team becomes the first multicultural team to race competitively in NASCAR with four Black and Latino drivers. Two drivers are her sons Eric and Enico.

KRISTEN HAYDEN

2021, Kristen Hayden becomes the first Black woman to win a national diving title when she wins the USA Diving Winter National Championships in Bloomington, Ind. She is also a founding member of the USA Diving's Diversity, Equity and Inclusion Council.

WOODY HEDSPATH

1904, In Dayton, Ohio, Woody Hedspath or Headspeth, becomes the first Black cyclist to establish a new "Hour Record." The "Hour Record" is the longest distance cycled in one hour on a bicycle from a stationary start. It is considered one of the most prestigious records in cycling.

HAROLD HENSON

1949, Harold Henson of San Diego State becomes the first African American to wrestle in the NCAA tournament.

MATTHEW HENSON

"I think I'm the first man to sit on top of the world."

1909, Matthew Henson, explorer, becomes the first man to reach the North Pole. He served as Admiral Robert Peary's navigator and craftsman during the Arctic expedition.

Colorful Firsts in U.S. Sports

SARA HOOD

2022, Sara "Lovestyle" Hood, CEO of Sara Belay, Inc., becomes the first Black woman to own a digital sports team. Along with Emmanuel Acho, an NFL analyst and Edward Madongorere, CEO and co-founder of Moon Ultra, Hood is an owner of the Houston Hyenas in SimWin Sports, a sports league in the metaverse that hosts 24/7 fantasy sports and sports betting action featuring NFT players.

TIM HOWARD

2008, Tim Howard is named U.S. Soccer Athlete of the Year. He is the most capped goalkeeper of All-Time for the U.S. Men's National Team. Howard is named athlete of the year again in 2014.

BO JACKSON

"So you have to be more mentally focused in baseball."

1989, Vincent "Bo" Jackson becomes the first professional football player to win major league baseball's MVP in the All-Star game.

1990, Bo Jackson becomes the first athlete to play in the NFL's Pro Bowl and a major league All-Star game (1989).

1991, A hip injury forces Bo Jackson to retire from pro football but stays in pro baseball.

1993, Bo Jackson becomes the first major leaguer to play with an artificial hip, homers in the Chicago White Sox opener.

1995, Bo Jackson retires from major league baseball.

KEVIN JACKSON

2005, Kevin Jackson, who won gold medals at the 1992 Barcelona Olympic games as well as the World Championship games in Varna (1991) and Atlanta (1995) and the Pan American Games in Havana (1991) and Mar del Plata (1995), becomes the first African American inducted into the United World Wrestling Hall of Fame.

MAURICE "ACE" KILGORE

1951, The Allen Supermarket Team from Detroit, Mich., is the first all-Black team to compete in the previously segregated American Bowling Congress (ABC) tournament, held in St. Paul, Minn. The team includes Lafayette Allen, Len Griffin, Maurice Kilgore, Bill Rhodman, and C.W. Williams.

1958, Maurice Kilgore becomes the first African American bowler to appear on national television when he competes in "Beat the Champ" tournament at Chicago's Faetz-Niesen Lanes.

JOE JAMES

1962, Joe James becomes the first African American wrestler to win a gold medal in the Pan American games.

DANITA JOHNSON

2021, Danita Johnson is named president of the D.C. United soccer team, becoming the first Black president in the Major League Soccer (MLS). Johnson also serves as the president and chief operating officer of the WNBA team Los Angeles Sparks.

ROY JONES JR.

"In the ring, I have a gift . . . that gift ain't on the basketball court. That gift ain't at home.
You understand me? That gift is in the ring."

1996, Roy Jones Jr. becomes the first man to played a pro basketball game (U.S. Basketball League) and fight for the world championship (IBF), as super middleweight, in the same day.

LLOYD KEASER

1973, Lloyd "Butch" Keaser, in Tehran, Iran, becomes the first African American wrestler to win a World Championship gold medal.

1976, Lloyd Keaser becomes the first African American to medal at the Montreal Olympics in wrestling, earning a silver in freestyle wrestling in the 149-pound category.

BILL LESTER

2003, Bill Lester of NASCAR fame is the first African American to appear on the Honey Nut Cheerios cereal box.

TAMYRA MENSAH-STOCK
2018, Tamyra Mensah-Stock becomes the first American, male or female, to win back-to-back gold medals at the Golden Ivan Yarygin Grand Prix in Russia.

2020, Tamyra Mensah-Stock wins a gold medal at the Tokyo Olympics, becomes the first Black woman wrestler to win gold.

TOCCARA MONTGOMERY
2001, Wrestler Toccara Montgomery becomes the first African American woman to win a medal at the World Championships with a silver medal.

2004, Toccara Montgomery becomes the first Black female to wrestle for the U.S. Olympic team.

ERIK MOSES
2020, Erik Moses is named president of Nashville Superspeedway, becoming the first African American to hold that title at any NASCAR track. Formerly president of the XFL's DC Defenders, Moses will lead the speedway back from the COVID-19 pandemic in 2021. The 1.33-mile concrete track was built in 2001 by Dover Motorsports and hosted NASCAR and IndyCar events until 2011.

CISERO MURPHY
1965, Cisero Murphy becomes the first and only African American to win a World or U.S. National pocket billiard title, the American Billiard Parlor tournament in Burbank, Calif. Murphy is inducted into the Billiard Congress of America Hall of Fame in 1995.

KENNY MONDAY
1988, Kenny Monday becomes the first African American wrestler, competing in Seoul, South Korea, to win an Olympic gold medal.

SUMNER "RED" OLIVER
1973, As a member of the Patrick Racing Team, Sumner "Red" Oliver becomes the first official African American mechanic at the Indianapolis 500 raceway.

WALTER PAYTON
1995, Walter Payton becomes the first African American team owner in the Indy Car series. Payton partners with Dale Coyne in preparation for a race in Florida. The car bears Payton's jersey number 34.

BILL PINKNEY
1990, Bill Pinkney becomes the first Black sailor to single-handedly circle the globe under the five southernmost capes. The 32,000-mile trek starts in Boston to Bermuda and then to the British Virgin Islands, Brazil, Cape Town, South Africa and across the Indian Ocean to Tasmania. Afterwards he sails across the South Pacific around Cape Horn to Uruguay before turning north again to Bermuda. Pinkney was inducted into the National Sailing Hall of Fame in 2021.

ZEB POWELL
2020, Zeb Powell is the first African American to win gold in the Winter X Games in snowboarding, capturing 1st place in the Men's Knuckle Huck held in Aspen, Colorado.

NZINGHA PRESCOD
2013, Nzingha Prescod is the first American female foil fencer to win a Grand Prix title when she wins the gold medal at the Marseille Foil Grand Prix competition in France.

KIRK RAMSEY
1952, Kirk Ramsey from Chicago, competing in the Atomic League at Garfield Bowl, Chicago, is the first Black bowler to roll a perfect 300 game in American Bowling Congress (ABC) competition.

JOIE RAY
1952, Joie Ray, while not the first African American to race in NASCAR's top series, is the first African American licensed by the American Automobile Association. Joie Ray (Henry J. Ray) becomes the first African American driver to start (at 25th spot)

of a NASCAR sanctioned race, when he finished 51st at the Dayton Beach / Highway course.

WILLIAM RHODMAN

1948, William Rhodman becomes the first bowler to score a perfect 300 game in The Negro Bowling Association (TNBA).

1951, The Allen Supermarket Team from Detroit, Mich. is the first all-Black team to compete in the previously segregated American Bowling Congress (ABC) tournament, held in St. Paul, Minn. The team includes Lafayette Allen, Len Griffin, Maurice Kilgore, William Rhodman, and C.W. Williams.

1953, William Rhodman from Detroit rolls consecutive games of 223, 233 and 263 in the national tournament at Chicago's Coliseum, becoming the first African American to break into the top standings in an American Bowling Congress tournament.

WILLY T. RIBBS

"The way I approached my entire racing career is to do it right."

1991, Willy T. Ribbs becomes the first African American driver to qualify for the Indy 500 with a burst of 217.358 miles per hour, the fastest on the final day of qualifying. A week later at the race, after six laps, Ribbs is forced to drop out due to engine failure.

DEION "PRIME TIME" SANDERS

"If you look good, you feel good. If you feel good, you play good. If you play good, they pay good."

1989, Deion Sanders becomes the first athlete in the pro ranks to hit a home run, with the New York Yankees in the World Series, and score a touchdown (68-yard interception), with the Atlanta Falcons against the Los Angeles Rams, in the same week.

1994, Deion Sanders becomes the first athlete to play in a Super Bowl (with Dallas Cowboys) and in the World Series (with the 1992 Atlanta Braves and the 1989 N.Y. Yankees).

1997, Deion Sanders becomes the first athlete to have a pass interception (15 yards in Super Bowl XXIX with the 49ers); and a pass reception (47 yards in Super Bowl XXX with the Cowboys) in Super Bowl competition.

WENDELL SCOTT

1963, Wendell Scott becomes the first and only African American driver to win a NASCAR Winston Cup (then the Grand National) race at the Speedway Park in Jacksonville, Fla. The film *Greased Lightning*, starring Richard Pryor, is loosely based on his life.

2015, Wendell Scott is the first African American to be inducted into the NASCAR Hall of Fame.

TEDDY SEYMOUR

1987, Teddy Seymour becomes the first African American to sail around the world solo. In his 35-foot fiberglass boat, called the Love Song, Seymour starts sailing from his home port of St. Croix, makes 12 stops, and returns home a year and a half later.

RON SIMMONS

1992, Ron Simmons becomes the first African American to win the heavyweight World Wrestling Championship (WCW) title. Simmons is a former defensive tackle for the Cleveland Browns (NFL), Ottawa Rough Riders (CFL) and Tampa Bay Bandits (original USFL).

VIRO SMALL

1870, Viro "Black Sam" Small makes his wrestling debut at Owney's Bastille in New York, making him the first known African American wrestler in the U.S.

CLAIRE SMITH

"I had to prove, day in, and day out, what I wasn't. I wasn't weak. I wasn't a quitter."

1983, Claire Smith, for the New York Yankees, is the first female MLB beat writer, while working for the *Hartford Courant*.

2015, Claire Smith is the first recipient of the Sam Lacy-Wendell Smith Award, created by the Shirley Povich Center for Sports Journalism. The award is presented annually to a sports journalist or broadcaster who has made significant contributions to racial and gender equality in sports.

2017, Claire Smith is the first woman to receive the Baseball Writers Association of America Career Excellence Award, formerly the J.G. Taylor Spink Award, the highest award given by the Baseball Writers' Association of America (BBWAA).

2021, The Claire Smith Center for Sports Media at Temple University is named in honor of Claire Smith, an alumna.

2025, William C. Rhoden, sports columnist for ESPN's AndScape and former *New York Times* columnist; Michael Wilbon, co-host of ESPN's "Pardon The Interruption" and former *Washington Post* columnist; and Claire Smith, the first female to cover Major League Baseball for the *Hartford Courant*, will be the three inductees into the Black Sportswriters Hall of Fame, at North Carolina A&T, founded by Rob Parker, the first Black sports columnist at the *Detroit Free Press*. The "Original Six" of pioneer sportswriters and editors – including Sam Lacy, Larry Whiteside, Wendell Smith, Bryan Burwell, Thom Greer and Ralph Wiley – will be honored posthumously at the Hall of Fame.

IRIS SMITH

2005, In Finland, U.S. Army Staff Sergeant Iris Smith, wins the world wrestling title in the 72 kg/158.5 lb division. Smith, who enjoys dancing and hiking, becomes the first female to win a world gold medal.

MAURICE SMITH

1997, Maurice Smith, Seattle native, defeats UFC heavyweight champion Mark Coleman at UFC 14 in Birmingham to become the first Black title holder. In the process, the world champion kickboxer becomes the first striker to ever defeat a championship wrestler of Coleman's stature.

WENDELL SMITH

1958, Wendell Smith becomes the first African American to provide radio commentary for a boxing championship match. It is a middleweight title fight is between Sugar Ray Robinson and Carmen Basilio at Chicago Stadium.

1993, Writer Wendell Smith, former travel mate of Jackie Robinson, is the first African American recipient of the Spink Award, first conferred in 1962. Named for J.G. Taylor Spink, founder of *The Sporting News*, the award honors baseball writers for "meritorious contributions to baseball writing" and is presented at the HOF induction ceremonies.

BUBBA STEWART

2005, James "Bubba" Stewart becomes the first African American to win a major motorsports title, capturing the Mobile Supercross Series and the Toyota Motocross Championship. Stewart rides a Kawasaki KX 450F.

MAJOR "BLACK CYCLONE" TAYLOR

"In closing I wish to say that while I was sorely beset by a number of White riders in my racing days, I have also enjoyed the friendship of countless thousands of White men whom I class as among my closest friends."

1895, Major Taylor wins his first significant cycling competition, when he becomes the only rider to finish a 75-mile road race near Indianapolis.

1896, After setting an unofficial world record in the one-fifth of a mile race and beating the one-mile time on the Capital City Track in Indianapolis, cyclist Major Taylor is banned from this venue.

1898, Major Taylor is declared national cycling champion with 121 total points from 21 first-place victories, 13 second-place berths and 11 third-place showings. Taylor uses the Sager chainless bicycle, and in the process becomes the first Black athlete sponsored by the Sager Gear Company of Rochester, New York.

1899, Major Taylor wins the world one-mile sprint championship in Montreal, Canada, defeating Boston rival Tom Butler. Taylor becomes the first African American world champion athlete.

1900, Major Taylor becomes the U.S. Sprint champion in bicycle racing for the second consecutive year.

1908, Major Taylor, in Paris, sets world records in the Quarter Mile (25.4 seconds) and in the Half Mile (42.2 seconds) in cycling competition.

1928, Cyclist Major Taylor self-publishes his autobiography "The Fastest Bicycle Rider in the World."

BUBBA WALLACE

2020, NASCAR bans the Confederate flag from its races and venues, formally severing itself from what is viewed by many citizens as a symbol of slavery and racism. Bubba Wallace, NASCAR's only Black driver, called for the banishment of the flag and said there is "no place" for them in the industry. Wallace drives a car, No. 43, with the hashtag #BlackLivesMatter.

CHARLIE WARD

1994, After announcing his intentions to play pro basketball, Florida State quarterback Charlie Ward becomes the first Heisman Trophy winner in 35 years not selected in the NFL draft.

1994, Charlie Ward becomes the first Heisman winner to be selected in the first round (26th pick) of the NBA draft by the New York Knicks.

CHARLIE WIGGINS

1924, The annual Gold and Glory Sweepstakes, a 100-mile race on a one-mile dirt track at the Indiana State Fairgrounds is started by mechanic and race-car driver Charlie "the Negro Speed King" Wiggins. The inaugural event draws approximately 12,000 fans.

1934, Charlie Wiggins, posing as a janitor to circumvent Jim Crow laws, is hired by Indy car driver Bill Cummings to tune his car. Cummings wins the Indianapolis 500 and sets a track record.

HALLOW WILSON

1960, Hallow Wilson becomes the first African American wrestler to win an AAU championship, winning the heavyweight title in Greco-Roman.

LESTER WRIGHT

2022, Lester Wright, a 100-year-old World War II veteran, becomes the first African American centenarian to hold the world record in the 100 meters, with a time of 26.34 seconds at the Penn Relays in Philadelphia.

LONNIE WRIGHT

1967, Lonnie Wright becomes one of the first players to play two professionals sports in the same season. Wright played defensive back for the Denver Broncos in 1966-67 and with the Denver Nuggets from 1967 to 1970.

Cage 13HIRTEEN: Roadblocks, Rules & Protests

"Don't nobody bring me no bad news." – Mable King, a.k.a. Evillene, The Wiz

1867, The National Association of Base Ball Players (NABBP) vote to exclude Black players and their teams from membership, stating "Any club which may be composed of one or more colored persons" will be barred. The NABBP reason was "If colored clubs were admitted there would be in all probability some division of feeling, whereas, by excluding them no injury could result to anyone."

1887, George Stovey signs with Newark of the International League and joins catcher Moses Fleetwood Walker to form the first African American battery in White professional baseball. Stovey wins 33 games against 14 losses for the fourth-place Newark Little Giants. Cap Anson refuses to allow his National League Chicago White Sox to play against the Newark Little Giants because African American pitcher George Stovey is on the roster.

1887, *The New York Times* publishes a letter written by several White players entitled "A Color Line in Baseball" on Sept. 12. The letter addresses Chris von der Ahe, a German immigrant and owner of the St. Louis Browns: "Dear Sir, We, the undersigned members of the St. Louis Baseball Club, do not agree to play against negroes (sic) (Cuban Giants) tomorrow. We will cheerfully play against white people at any time, and think, by refusing to play, we are only doing what is right, take everything into consideration and the shape of the team is in at present."

1888, The International League which has eight Black baseball players formally decides to sign no more African Americans as another "Gentlemen's Agreement" is mandated.

1889 to 1946, African American players are excluded from White professional teams by a "Gentlemen's Agreement."

1908, Moses Fleetwood Walker authors *Our Home Colony: A Treatise on the Past, Present and Future of the Negro Race in America*. In his writing, Walker expresses defeat and urges Black people to leave the U.S. in search of better opportunities in Africa.

1910, On February 22 the *Altoona Tribune (PA)*, shares editorial thoughts from future Hall of Fame pitcher Cy Young. "The little brown men of Japan are planning an invasion of the U.S. A baseball attack. They are planning to attack the American and National League teams. Among the tribes they will attempt to subdue is the White Sox. Also the Detroit Tigers. The players are students of Kelo (sic, Keio) University. If they succeed, a regular invasion will follow, and we will have unpronounceable names on every club." Young continues, "Baseball belongs to this country. Its supremacy in baseball will never be threatened. And for the very good reason that while some of the athletes of other nations may imitate and even equal our ball players in one department of the game, they cannot excel in all. Take the Japanese athlete. He can't hit worth a hurrah." Young also adds, "A Jap can't pitch. There is one reason for this, of course. That reason is that they can't grip the ball. The hands of the Japs are very small." Young did not forget the Cuban players, "That reason does not hold good with the Cuban. Yet their pitchers are a bad lot. They have no curve ball, and, of course, use little headwork." After Young's death in 1955, the Cy Young Award is created the next season and is given annually to the best pitcher in the American and National Leagues.

1913, Golfer John Shippen finishes fourth in the U.S. Open. Because of his light complexion he passes for White in a tournament that excludes African Americans.

1922, George Halas, now head coach of the renamed Chicago Bears, refuses to play the Milwaukee Badgers unless they drop African American players Fritz Pollard, Paul Robeson and Duke Slater from the team.

1925, The U.S. Colored Golf Association is founded in Washington, District of Columbia. It is renamed the United Golfers Association (UGA) in 1929. Affectionately known as the Chitlin Circuit, the UGA was founded by George Adams and Robert Hawkins. Some members included Pete Brown, Lee Elder, Teddy Rhodes, Bill Spiller and Charlie Sifford. At the time, the Professional Golfers Association (PGA) had an article in its by-laws stating that it was "for members of the Caucasian race." When this by-law is repealed in 1961, the United Golfers Association disbands.

1929, The *New York Daily News* reports that the University of Georgia football team will not play the New York University Violets if quarterback Dave Myers is allowed to take the field. Despite protest from the NAACP, Myers is benched as the Violets beat the Bulldogs 27-19.

1933, Ray Kemp with the Pittsburgh Pirates and Joe Lillard with the Chicago Cardinals are last African Americans released from NFL teams leaving the league exclusively white.

1934 to 1945, Black players are banned from the National Football League (NFL).

Colorful Firsts in U.S. Sports

1934, The "Caucasian-only" clause is added to the Professional Golfers Association of America's constitution. The discriminatory clause is removed in 1952.

1934, Harrison "Honey" Fitch becomes University of Connecticut's first African American basketball player. In a game against the U.S. Coast Guard Academy, due to a tradition "that no Negro players be permitted to engage in contests at the Academy." Fitch warms up with the team, but coach John Heldman does not play him.

1937, Until 1965 "Fight for Old Dixie" was the rally song for George Preston Marshall's Washington Redskins, the only football team south of the Mason-Dixon line at the time.

1937, Willie Wells returns five days after a beaning from spitball pitcher Bill Byrd. Wells appears at the plate wearing a coal miner's helmet with the spotlight. It is the first known instance of a player donning a "hard hat" four years before the Brooklyn Dodgers put on padded inserts in their headgear in 1941. Charlie Muse, traveling secretary for the Pittsburgh Pirates, is credited as the inventor of the batting helmet. In 1952, the Pirates became the first white MLB team to wear hard helmets.

1937, President Rafael "El Jefe" Trujillo creates an All-Star team, the Ciudad Trujillo, to beat his political rival's team the Estrellas de Oriente for dictatorial rule of Santo Domingo, the capital of the Dominican Republic. Dictator Trujillo incarcerates Satchel Paige, Josh Gibson, Cool Papa Bell and other stars the night before the championship game to avoid midnight carousing. Before armed soldiers, El Presidente's team wins 6-5.

1938, New York Yankee outfielder Jake Powell says in a radio interview on WGN Chicago that as a police officer during the off season, he keeps in shape by "cracking niggers over the head with his nightstick" as he walks his beat in Dayton, Ohio. Powell gets a 10-day suspension by Commissioner Kenesaw Mountain Landis.

1939, The *Chicago Defender* reports "We have yet to find another single coach in the history of (college) football that has had the guts to play three of our race at one and have four on the squad." UCLA football starts Jackie Robinson and Kenny Washington in the backfield and Woody Strode at offensive and defensive end. Ray Bartlett is a wide receiver. The Bruins compile a 6–0–4 record (5–0–3 conference), finish in second place in the Pacific Coast Conference.

1939, Running back Kenny Washington of UCLA leads the nation with 1,370 total yards gained. Of the 664 players nominated for All-American by *Liberty Magazine*, Washington is the only player named on every ballot. Washington is not drafted into the lily-white NFL.

1939, To stop a losing streak, owner Horace Stoneham of the New York Giants hires a 13-year-old Black youth, Cecil Haley as a mascot. Players can rub Cecil's head for good luck. The National League is still without any Black players.

1940, Leonard Bates, a fullback for New York University, is barred from playing against the University of Missouri, because of its color ban. Seven NYU players object against the Jim Crow policy and are named "The Bates Seven."

1940, Running back Louis Montgomery, Boston College's first African American player, is not allowed to make the trip to the Cotton Bowl due to segregation sanctions. In 1941, he made the trip to the Sugar Bowl in New Orleans but is not allowed to play. In 2012, Boston College retires his No. 21.

1941, On the Fourth of July, Sportsman's Park in St. Louis hosts its first Negro League baseball game. The Kansas City Monarchs, with Satchel Paige on the mound, play the Chicago American Giants before an interracial crowd of 19,178 fans.

1944, The St. Louis Cardinals and St. Louis Browns lift its policy of restricting Negroes to the bleachers and pavilion at Sportsman's Park. According to the local press, "Negroes now may purchase seats in the grandstand." Sportsman's Park is the last major league ballpark with a Jim Crow section. The black folks-only right field pavilion was covered by a screen preventing the catch of a home run. In 1927, the screen was removed when the Yankees played the Browns. That season Babe Ruth hit four of his 60 home runs into the pavilion, only 310 feet from home plate.

1944, Staff Sgt. Joe Louis and Sgt. Walker Smith (Sugar Ray Robinson) are jailed at Camp Sibert, Ala., for refusal to observe Jim Crow laws on the post. After participating in a camp show they enter the white section of the bus station to place a phone call for a taxi. There was no phone in the colored section. The camp was commanded by Gen. Haig Shekerjian, an Armenian-American, who ordered their release after several hours.

1945, In a letter to Lee MacPhail, American League President, dated 29 October 1945, Connie Mack, manager and president of the Philadelphia Athletics writes, "It was a great disappointment to me to see that Branch Rickey had signed a negro (sic) for his Montreal Baseball Club. If all Major League Club owners would just let Branch have the negroes (sic), feel that we would all be better off in the long run."

1945, New York Mayor Fiorello La Guardia forms a committee, to study segregation in baseball and, ultimately, pressure the New York teams to sign Black players. Yankee executive Larry MacPhail responds in part, "There are few, if any, negro (sic) players who could qualify for play in the major leagues at this time. A major league player must have something besides natural ability ... In conclusion: I have no hesitancy in saying that the Yankees have no intention of signing negro (sic) players under contract or reservation to negro (sic) clubs."

1946, The Cleveland Browns sign running back Marion Motley and defensive lineman Bill Willis as the AAFC's first African American players.

1946, Cleveland quarterback Otto Graham sets up over the center with feet parallel, but one foot slightly behind to push off faster to get away from defensive player Bill Willis in practice. Other pro teams soon pick it up and call it the "Bill Willis Step."

1946, UCLA products Woody Strode (end) and Kenny Washington (running back) are the first African Americans in the NFL with the Los Angeles Rams.

1946, The Basketball Association of America (BAA) is organized by Walter A. Brown, founder and owner of the Boston Celtics. His league bans African American players. Following its third season, 1948–49, the BAA and the National Basketball League (NBL) merged to create the National Basketball Association (NBA).

1946-47, The NBA outlaws zone defenses to speed up play. Zone defenses are re-instated in the National Basketball Association during the 2001–2002 season.

1947, After winning the Indiana Intercollegiate Conference basketball title, coach John Wooden of the Indiana State Teacher's College turns down an invitation to play in the National Association of Intercollegiate Basketball (NAIB) due to its policy to banning Black players. Guard Clarence Walker was the Black member of Wooden's team.

1948, The U.S. military integrates its service baseball teams.

1948, Three Black golfers, Theodore "Rags" Rhodes, Bill Spiller and Madison Gunther, try to break the Whites-only policy with a lawsuit against the PGA. The PGA sidesteps the issue by adopting an "invitation only" provision, allowing the golfers to play as non-members.

1949, Teams in the National Basketball League (NBL) are merged into the National Basketball Association (NBA). The all-Black Dayton Rens are left out of the merger, creating an all-White NBA until the Washington Capitols, N.Y. Knicks, Boston Celtics and the Tri-Cities Blackhawks signed a Black player for the 1950-51 season.

1950, Althea Gibson becomes the first African American to be accepted for competition in the National Tennis Championship at the U.S. Championships after Alice Marble writes an editorial for the July 1 edition of *American Lawn Tennis* magazine. Marble writes, "Miss Gibson is over a very cunningly wrought barrel, and I can only hope to loosen a few of its staves with one lone opinion. If tennis is a game for ladies and gentlemen, it's also time we acted a little more like gentle people and less like sanctimonious hypocrites." Marble adds that if Gibson is not given the opportunity to compete, "then there is an ineradicable mark against a game to which I have devoted most of my life, and I would be bitterly ashamed." Gibson is inducted into the International Tennis Hall of Fame in 1971.

1950, Branch Rickey purchases Sam Jethroe's contract for $5,000 from the Negro American League's Cleveland Buckeyes. Jethroe, known as "Jet," stole 89 bases at Triple-A Montreal in 1949, but Rickey did not promote him. According to Jules Tygiel's book, *Baseball's Great Experiment*, Rickey said that five Black players on the Dodgers would have been "too many." He sold Jethroe to the Boston Braves for $150,000 and several players.

1952, In January, the PGA tour passes a rule allowing Black golfers to enter a tournament if the sponsor agrees. Bill Spiller becomes one of the first African Americans to play in a major golf tourney.

1952, New York Yankee general manager George Weiss explains, at a cocktail party, why the Yankees are still an all-White team, five years after Jackie Robinson joins the Brooklyn Dodgers stating, "I will never allow a Black man to wear a Yankee uniform. Boxholders from Westchester (County) don't want that sort of crowd. They would be offended to have to sit with niggers."

1953, The New York Yankees become the last all-White baseball team to win a World Series, when they defeat the Brooklyn Dodgers (4-2), with Joe Black, Jackie Robinson, Roy Campanella and Junior Gilliam.

1953, The city of Birmingham, Ala., bars the Jackie Robinson All-Stars, composed of Black and White players from playing due to a 1944 city ordinance, section 859 which cites "It shall be unlawful for any person in charge of or in control of any room, hall, theater, picture house, auditoriums, yard, court, ballpark, public park or indoor or outdoor place, to which both white persons and negroes (sic) are admitted, to cause, permit or allow mixing of races." In 1950, the city passes Ordinance 798-F to add even more restrictions to prevent racial interaction at baseball, softball, football, basketball or similar games. Robinson's all-star team includes Dodger first baseman Gil Hodges and Indian third baseman Al Rosen.

1953, The Hot Spring Bathers of the Cotton States League (CSL) sign pitching brothers Jim and Leander Tugerson to play only in home games due to segregation sanctions in the deep South. CSL president Al Haraway blocks this loophole in the bylaws. In April, the National Association of Professional Baseball Leagues, an umbrella organization for minor leagues, rules against Haraway and reinstates the Tugersons. Instead, the Tugerson brothers leave the CSL and join the Class D Knoxville Smokies of the Mountain States League. See 1955.

1953, The Portsmouth Merrimacs become the first team in the Piedmont League to sign African American players: Catchers Claude and Dick Brown; outfielders Bill Louis, James Livingston and Burly Barge; infielders Henry Craighead, Thomas Burt, Eugene "Stank" White; and pitcher Leonard Dunovant. The new team owner Frank Lawrence effectively ended the Virginia-based Piedmont League's 33-year history of racial exclusion. Later, in the season, the Merrimacs signed 45-year-old former Negro League first sacker Buck Leonard. The team, without a major league affiliation, folds after the 1955 season.

1955, The Pine Bluff (Ark.) Judges of the Cotton States League, signs three Black players, outfielder Charles Peppers and infielder Russell Moseley from the Memphis Red Sox and pitcher Charles Chatman of the Detroit Stars. The Judges' board of directors announces it will not play its Negroes in Mississippi.

1955, The Cannon Street YMCA All-Stars are the first Black Little League team in South Carolina. When all the White teams withdrew in protest, the Cannon Street team won the state tournament by forfeit and advanced to the Little League World Series in Williamsport, Pa. However the team was declared ineligible because it did not win games on the field. As they watched the first game from the stands the crowd chanted, "Let them play! Let them play!" in support.

1955, The New Orleans Pelicans of the Southern Association (AA) refuse three Negro players assigned by the parent Pittsburgh Pirates club: Bennie Daniels, Román Mejias and R. C. Stevens. General manager Joe Nowak claims, "They don't measure up to Southern Association standards." Black fans boycott the team that averaged 1,700 fans per game. Two seasons later, owners claimed they lost $130,000 and became an affiliate of the New York Yankees. All three players make the Pirates team within a few years.

1955, The Supreme Court rules to desegregate public golf courses in Atlanta in the landmark case, *Holmes v. City of Atlanta*. Brothers Alfred "Tup" and Oliver Wendell Holmes challenge the status quo to become the first African Americans to legally play golf at a public facility in Atlanta.

1956, Minnie Miñoso has led the American League in the Hit Batsmen (HBP) category in five of the last six seasons, encouraging the Rules Committee to create a rule, "It is a strike if a legal pitch in flight touches the batter in the strike zone." Despite the ruling, Miñoso continues to lead the league in this dubious category until 1961.

1956, Bobby Grier, a fullback and linebacker for the Pittsburgh Panthers is the first African American football player to break the color barrier of the collegiate Sugar Bowl game, which is held in New Orleans, La. Segregationists try to keep Grier from playing because he is Black. Georgia's governor Marvin Griffin publicly threatens the Georgia Tech's president Blake Van Leer to cancel the game. Later in July, the Louisiana state legislature passes Act 579, known as the Athletic Events Bill, which prohibits interracial sports competitions.

1956, In the All-American City Basketball Tournament in Owensboro, Kentucky, the Ole Miss Rebels lose the opening game and are scheduled to play the Iona College Gaels of New York in the consolidation match. Ole Miss coach Bonnie Graham advises officials that if Stanley Hill, a Black guard on the Gaels team, suits up, the game will not be played. The game is forfeited to the Gaels. State legislators praise Ole Miss officials for their "honorable" decision to boycott the game. The 1957 Ole Miss press guide does not list the loss in the team's record book.

1957, Jackie Robinson retires from major league baseball. Three league teams, the Phillies, Tigers and the Red Sox, have yet to put an African American on its rosters.

1958, Two rookies for the Cleveland Indians, Gary Bell from San Antonio, Texas and Jim "Mudcat" Grant from Lacoochee, Fla., become the first White & Black roommates in the re-integrated major leagues.

1959, Eroseanna "Rose" Robinson, a high jumper, refuses to stand for the national anthem at the Pan American Games held in Chicago's Wrigley Field, citing the flag represents "war, injustice and hypocrisy." Upon winning the 1958 AAU National Championship, Robinson was named to the U.S. Women's Track and Field team. The predominantly Black team was invited to compete in the Soviet Union at a State Department track meet during the height of the Cold War. Robinson refused to attend, telling *Jet* magazine: "I don't want to be used as a political pawn."

1959, John McLendon's Tennessee A & I basketball team during warmups for the NAIA championships, the Illinois State Normal cheerleaders and band play and sing "Bye Bye Blackbird." McLendon takes his team off the floor and then gives the "talk." The Tigers from Nashville, Tennessee beat the Redbirds, 131-74.

1960, The African American Students Foundation is created by singer Harry Belafonte, actor Sidney Poitier and baseball player Jackie Robinson, to aid Kenyan students to study in America. One student Barack H. Obama receives a grant to study business administration at the University of Hawaii in Honolulu. Obama Senior meets White American Ann Dunham at the university. They marry and have a son, Barack H. Obama, Junior, who becomes the first Black U.S. president in 2008.

1960, The American League Kansas City Athletics finish in last place with 58 wins – 96 loses and finish 39 games behind the Yankees. The A's became the last major league team to employ an all-white roster for the entire season.

1960, Yankee catcher Elston Howard pioneers the use of the first hinged catcher's mitt that led to the modern one-handed catching technique. Howard would later win Gold Glove awards in 1963 and 1964.

1960s, Defensive back Dick "Night Train" Lane tackles wide receivers around the neck. The clothesline tackles called "Neckties" are subsequently banned by the NFL.

1960, Freddie "The Hammer" Williamson, a cornerback for the Oakland Raiders and later the Kansas City Chiefs, creates the "hammer" to slow down wide receivers. In 1960, a defensive back could bump the receiver until the quarterback released the football.

1960, Article III, Section I, in The PGA Constitution, in 1960 states: "Male professional golfers of Caucasian race, over the age of eighteen (18) years, residing in North or South America, who can qualify under the terms and conditions, hereinafter specified, shall be eligible for membership."

1961, The Professional Golf Association of America (PGA) removes the phrase "Caucasians only" clause from its constitution. The vote was unanimous by 87 delegates. Charlie Sifford becomes the first African American to join the PGA Tour.

1961, The Phoenix Hotel in Lexington, Ky., refuses service in its coffee shop to Black players Bill Russell, Sam Jones, K. C. Jones, Satch Sanders, and Al Butler from the Boston Celtics, along with Woody Sauldsberry and Cleo Hill from the St. Louis Hawks. In turn, these players boycott the exhibition game honoring the homecoming of NBA stars Frank Ramsey and Cliff Hagan.

1961, Washington Senators owner Calvin Griffith moves the team to Minnesota. At a 1978 speaking engagement Griffith shares his reason for the relocation. "I'll tell you why we came to Minnesota. It was when we found out you only had 15,000 blacks here," Griffith said then. "Black people don't go to ballgames, but they'll fill up a rassling ring and put up such a chant it'll scare you to death. We came here because you've got good, hardworking white people here." In 2020, his statue is removed from Target Field. The Twins organization issues this statement: "Our decision to memorialize Calvin Griffith with a statue reflects an ignorance on our part of systemic racism present in 1978, 2010 and today. We apologize for our failure to adequately recognize how the statue was viewed and the pain it caused for many people -- both inside the Twins organization and across Twins Territory. We cannot remove Calvin Griffith from the history of the Minnesota Twins, but we believe removal of this statue is an important and necessary step in our ongoing commitment to provide a Target Field experience where every fan and employee feels safe and welcome."

1961, Secretary of the Interior Stewart Udall warns owner George Preston Marshall to hire Black players or face federal retribution. For the first time in history, the federal government attempts to desegregate a professional sports team. The Washington Redskins were under the threat of civil rights legal action by the Kennedy administration, which would have prevented a segregated team from playing at the new federally-owned D.C. Stadium, managed by the U.S. Department of the Interior. The next season 1962, the Redskins become the final professional American football franchise to integrate, when they draft running back Ernie Davis out of Syracuse.

1962, R.C. Owens, a 6-foot-3 Baltimore Colts wide receiver, (better known for popularizing the Alley-Oop pass, in which the receiver outjumps the defenders) blocks a 40-yard field goal at the crossbar in a game against the Washington Redskins. At the time, a legal defensive move.

1963, The Loyola Ramblers (Chicago) become the first major college basketball team to have five Black players on the floor at the same time. They start one White player John Egan and four Black players, Les Hunter, Vic Rouse, Ron Miller and team captain Jerry Harkness. They defeat the Cincinnati Bearcats in overtime to capture the NCAA championship.

Earlier in the tournament, despite hate mail from the Klan, the Ramblers faced the all-White Mississippi State Bulldogs against orders from Governor Ross Barnett, banning his Bulldogs from crossing state lines to play the integrated Ramblers. The landmark contest, won by the Ramblers 61-51, is later named the "Game of Change." See 2013.

1963, As the first Black player for the Little Rock Arkansas Travelers, a minor league affiliated of the Philadelphia Phillies, Dick Allen makes his debut. Led by White Citizens' Council leader Amis Guthridge, they picketed the ballpark caring signs reading, "Don't Negro-ize baseball" and "Nigger Go Home."

1963, Bill Russell of the Boston Celtics and Earl Wilson of the Boston Red Sox, pay homage to Civil Rights leader Medgar Evers

Colorful Firsts in U.S. Sports

assassinated in Jackson, Mississippi. Wilson and Russell circulate among the estimated 1,800 people gathered at the Parkman Bandstand on the Boston Common, to collect funds.

1963, After Maury Wills' base stealing record of 102 steals, baseball institutes a rule change. This year pitchers are required to come to a complete stop (or pause), before delivering the pitch to the plate. The intent is to hold the potential base stealer closer to the bag.

1964-65, The NBA widens the lane to 16 feet from 12 feet to offset Wilt Chamberlain's dominance. The lane was last widened in 1951 to neutralize the dominance of George Mikan.

1964, In the march magazine of *Ebony*, Olympic gold medalist Mal Whitfield writes an article titled, "Let's Boycott the Olympics" in Tokyo. Whitfield cites "It is time for America to live up to its promises of Liberty, Equality and Justice for all." The boycott did not materialize.

1965, Oscar Robertson becomes the first African American president of any national sports or entertainment labor union, the National Basketball Players Association (NBPA). He served until his retirement in 1974.

1965, The American Football League (AFL) All-Star game is scheduled to be played in New Orleans at Tulane Stadium. Black All-Stars including Buck Buchannan, Cookie Gilchrist, Sid Blanks, Bobby Bell, Dick Westmoreland, Frank Buncom, Ernie Warlick, Ernie Ladd, Earl Faison, Dave Grayson and Sherman Plunkett are unable to hail cabs from the airport and denied service in local restaurants. The Black players agree to boycott the game. The All-Star game is moved, one week later, to Rice Stadium in Houston, Texas.

1966, Muhammad Ali, recently converted to the Muslim faith refuses to be drafted into the Army, citing his religious beliefs and how the war effort did not align with his faith. Ali is stripped of his heavyweight title.

1966, Texas Western becomes the first NCAA champion to start five African Americans: Harry Flournoy, David Lattin, Bobby Joe Hill, Orsten Artis, and Willie Cager. They upset No. 1 ranked Kentucky's all-White team of Adolph Rupp in the championship game in College Park, Md. For playing an all-Black lineup and beating an all-White team, Haskins reportedly received 40,000 pieces of hate mail and a dozen death threats. The victorious team inspired the 2006 movie *Glory Road*.

1966, Claudius B. Claiborne becomes the first African American basketball player for the Duke Blue Devils. C.B. Claiborne graduated in 1969 with a degree in engineering. He also earned postgraduate degrees from Dartmouth and Virginia Tech. Because of segregation sanctions on the Duke campus, Claiborne spent considerable time in the cafeteria at nearby North Carolina Central University, a historically Black college.

1967, Deacon Jones of the Los Angeles Rams becomes the first player to record more than 25 sacks (26) in a season. In 1982, the NFL make "sacks" an official statistic. Jones is infamously known for creating the "head slap." See 1977.

1967, Former All-American Quarterback from Minn., Sandy Stephens becomes infamous by using profanity over the radio during his rookie exhibition game against Denver at Municipal Stadium. Wired for sound, in the heat of battle, as the Chiefs threatened to score, "All right, it's second and two," Stephens barked. "Let's put this (mf) in the end zone." The Chiefs scored on the next play. Stephens is cut before the season starts.

1967, San José State sociology professor Dr. Harry Edwards, creates the Olympic Committee for Human Rights to address the systemic racism experience by Black athletes. Edwards issues a statement that Black athletes may boycott the 1968 Olympics in Mexico City.

1967, Muhammad Ali is given draft No. 15-47-42-127. Ali is stripped of his heavyweight title for refusing military induction and sentenced to five years in prison.

1968, Smokin' Joe Frazier is crowned Heavyweight boxing champion, when Muhammad Ali is stripped of the title due to his religious convictions as a conscientious objector to the Vietnam war.

1967-68, Lew Alcindor (later Kareem Abdul-Jabbar) dominates college basketball with a variety of dunks in his sophomore year, his first year of varsity play. The NCAA bans dunking at the start of Alcindor's junior year. They cite "safety concerns and damaged equipment" as the reason for the ban. The rule is rescinded for the 1976-77 season.

1968, Lew Alcindor joins the Muslim faith and changes his name to Kareem Abdul-Jabbar. He boycotts the Olympic Games in protest of how African Americans are treated in the U.S.

1968, John Carlos and Tommie Smith, in the Mexico City Olympics, after receiving bronze and gold medals in the 200 meters, adorn black gloves and raise their fists to the sky, to protest treatment of Black people in America. Upon returning his medal Tommie Smith in an interview with Howard Cosell expresses: "My raised right hand stood for the power in Black America. Carlos' raised left hand stood for unity in Black America. Together they formed an arch of unity and power. The black scarf around my neck stood for Black pride. The black socks with no shoes stood for Black poverty in racist America. The totality of our effort was the regaining of Black dignity."

1968, In keeping with current NFL tradition, the Oakland Raiders draft Tennessee State quarterback sensation Eldridge Dickey in the first round as a wide receiver.

1968, Dr. Martin Luther King Jr. is assassinated. Baseball players demand, against owners' wishes, that 30 games scheduled for April 8-9 not be played. April 9 is the day of Dr. King's funeral. MLB delays Opening Day until April 10.

1968, New York Yankee catcher Elston Howard invents the weighted doughnut for baseball bats.

1968, Bob Gibson leads the National League with an ERA of 1.12, while Luis Tiant Jr. leads the American League with a 1.60 ERA. They are the first Black pitchers to win the ERA crowns, and they record the lowest ERAs by pitchers since the integration (1947) of the re-integrated major leagues. The pitching mound is lowered before the next season.

1969, John W. Oswald, president of the University of Kentucky, orders basketball coach Adolph Rupp to begin recruiting Black players. Three years before his retirement, Rupp signs his one and only Black player, Tom Payne.

1969, With a rule change, the strike zone is now from armpit to top of the knee, while the pitcher's mound is lowered, five inches, to 10 inches above the ground. These changes are an attempt to aid batters, potentially raising Earned Run Average (ERA) percentages.

1969, St. Louis Cards outfielder Curt Flood, along with Tim McCarver, Joe Hoerner and Byron Browne, are traded to Philadelphia for Dick Allen, Cookie Rojas and Jerry Johnson. Flood challenges baseball's reserve clause, which binds players to the clubs for the life of their careers. He was earning $90,000 a year but argued in an interview with Howard Cosell on ABC's *Wide World of Sports* that "a well-paid slave is, nonetheless, a slave."

1970, More than 20 future Hall of Famers suit up at Dodger Stadium on March 28, to honor the memory and support the causes of Dr. Martin Luther King Jr. All proceeds from the game go to the Southern Christian Leadership Conference (SCLC) and to the construction of the Dr. Martin Luther King Jr. Center in Atlanta. Joe DiMaggio and Roy Campanella served as managers for the exhibition game. Among the 31,694 fans is Jackie Robinson and Dr. King's widow, Coretta Scott King, who throws out the ceremonial first pitch to Johnny Bench.

1970, An anti-trust lawsuit, Robertson v. National Basketball Association, 556 F.2d 682 (U.S. Court of Appeals for the Second Circuit, argued 7 April 1977) is filed by basketball player Oscar Robertson against the National Basketball Association (NBA). Filed in 1970, the lawsuit was settled in 1976 and resulted in the free agency rules now used in the NBA. Robertson sought through his lawsuit to block any merger of the NBA with the American Basketball Association (ABA), to end the option clause that bound a player to a single NBA team in perpetuity, to end the NBA's college draft binding a player to one team, and to end restrictions on free-agent signings.

The suit also sought damages for NBA players for past harm caused by the option clause. Robertson's lawsuit prevented the planned 1970 merger of the National Basketball Association with the American Basketball Association. As president of the NBA players union, Robertson's 1970 suit against the NBA contended the draft, option clause and other rules restricting player movement were violations of antitrust laws. The suit was settled in 1976, when the league agreed to let players become free agents in exchange for their old team's "right of first refusal" to match any offer they might receive.

1970, When the National Football League and the American Football League merge, Hall of Famer and former Baltimore Colts tight-end John Mackey becomes the first president of the National Football League Players Association. Mackey became the lead plaintiff in a court action which led to the overturning of the so-called "Rozelle Rule," which limited a player's ability to act as a free agent. In 1976, the Rozelle Rule was ruled to violate antitrust laws in *Mackey v. NFL*. Mackey held the presidency until 1973.

1970, Coolidge Ball becomes the first African American scholarship basketball player for the University of Mississippi or Ole Miss, where in 1962 James Meredith had become the first African American student at the public university. After two fatalities, President John F. Kennedy sends the National Guard to stop the violence and rioting by Whites opposed to integration.

1970, The USC Trojans become the first fully integrated team to play in the state of Alabama against Bear Bryant's all-White Crimson Tide of the Southeastern Conference. With a Black quarterback, Jimmy Jones, running back Sam "Bam" Cunningham, plus other African Americans in key positions, the Trojans wallop the Crimson Tide 42 to 21. The game hastens the racial integration of football at Alabama University and in the South. Jerry Claiborne, a former Bryant assistant famously said this at the end of the game, "Sam Cunningham did more to integrate Alabama in 60 minutes than Martin Luther King did in 20 years."

1970, Nine members of the Syracuse University football team, remembered erroneously as the "Syracuse 8," make a stand for equality and for more a diverse coaching staff at the school. Gregory Allen, Richard Bulls, John Godbolt, Dana Harrell, John Lobon, Clarence "Bucky" McGill, A. Alif Muhammad, Duane Walker and Ron Womack's demands included increased medical care, equal access to academic support and integration of the team's coaching staff, which had been all White since 1898. "We never were conscious of racism," claimed coach Ben Schwartzwalder. On 20 October 2006, the nine members of the "Syracuse 8" were given the Chancellor's Medal by the university, among the highest honors at the school.

1971, Collis Temple Jr. from Kentwood, La., is the first African American varsity basketball player at Louisiana State University (LSU). When he joins the team, the U.S. National Guard is called to protect him from alt-right segregationists. Temple later plays for the San Antonio Spurs and two of his sons will play basketball for LSU.

1971, The Supreme Court overturns the 1967 conviction of Muhammad Ali's draft evasion, based on his Muslim beliefs.

1971, Bullet Bob Hayes becomes the first Olympic Gold Medalist (1964, 100 meters) to play for a Super Bowl Champion. Hayes plays wide receiver for the Dallas Cowboys. Because of his speed, NFL defenses had to give up playing man-to-man coverage and convert to zone defenses. Bob Hayes was the first sprinter to run a 9.1 second 100-yard dash and the first to break 6.0 seconds in the 60-yard sprint.

1971, Spencer Haywood signs a six-year, $1.5 million contract with the Seattle SuperSonics, ignoring the rule that a player cannot join the NBA until he is four years out of high school. Haywood challenges the decision by commencing an antitrust action against the NBA. As part of his claim against the NBA, Haywood argued that the ruling by the NBA is a "group boycott" and a violation of the Sherman Antitrust Act. The central issue that had to be determined was whether the NBA draft policy was a restraint on trade and therefore was illegal in accordance with the Sherman Act. The U.S. Supreme Court, in Haywood v. National Basketball Association, 401 U.S. 1204 rules, 9–0, against the NBA's requirement that a player may not be drafted by an NBA team unless he has waited four years following his graduation from high school.

1971, Satchel Paige becomes the first African American representing the Negro Leagues inducted into the National Baseball Hall of Fame. The Hall creates a controversy with a separate section or wing for the Black players.

"This lone Negro will be admitted to Cooperstown's anterooms, but not beyond," Bill Gildea writes in his *Washington Post* article *1st Negro League Inductee Draws Spot in Back of Hall*." Gildea adds, "He will have gotten out of the bus and into his own little corner of the Hall. To be consistent, the ceremony ought to be held at the back door."

One reason cited was they did not meet the minimum of ten MLB seasons like their White counterparts. Instead of being an honor, the move was viewed by many as another form of segregation. "Technically, you'd have to say he's not in the Hall of Fame," said commissioner Bowie Kuhn at the time, according to the *New York Times*. "But I've often said the Hall of Fame isn't a building but a state of mind. The important thing is how the public views Satchel Paige, and I know how I view him."

The *New York Post* sports columnist Milton Gross rejected Kuhn's dog whistle, writing, "The Hall of Fame is not a state of mind. It is something semi-officially connected with organized baseball that is run by outdated rules which, as Jackie Robinson said the other day, 'can be changed like laws are changed if they are unjust'." With the backdrop of backlash and an upcoming election, the Hall changed its mind in July of that year.

1972, The Dallas Chaparrals, citing the need for more White fans, cut two Black all-stars, Donnie Freeman and John Brisker. "Last year, Dallas had only two White players —Gene Phillips and Len Chappell — compared to 10 Black players, and we drew less than 100 fans a game who were colored," said the Chaps' general partner, Joe W. Geary, a Dallas attorney. "A bunch of people want White faces, someone they can identify with," he said. The Chaps' head coach, Babe McCarthy, the dean of A.B.A. coaches, echoed Geary's feelings on the racial issue. Freeman was the Chaps' leading scorer last season with a 24-point average.

1972, "There I was, the Black grandson of a slave, the son of a Black sharecropper, part of a historic occasion, a symbolic hero to my people. The air was sparkling. The sunlight was warm. The band struck up the national anthem. The flag billowed in the wind. It should have been a glorious moment for me as the stirring words of the national anthem poured from the stands. Perhaps, it was, but then again, perhaps, the anthem could be called the theme song for a drama called The Noble Experiment. Today, as I look back on that opening game of my first World Series, I must tell you that it was Mr. Rickey's drama and that I was only a principal actor. As I write this twenty years later, I cannot stand and sing the anthem. I cannot salute the flag; I know that I am a Black man in a white world. In 1972, in 1947, at my birth in 1919, I know that I never had it made." Jackie Robinson's *I Never Had It Made* autobiography with Alfred Duckett.

1972, In Flood v. Kuhn, 407 U.S. 258 (1972), a U.S. Supreme Court decision upholds, by a 5–3 margin, the antitrust exemption first granted to Major League Baseball (MLB) in Federal Baseball Club v. National League. It arose from a challenge by St. Louis Cardinals' outfielder Curt Flood when he refused to be traded to the Philadelphia Phillies after the 1969 season. He sought injunctive relief from the reserve clause, which prevented him from negotiating with another team for a year after his contract expired. Named as initial respondents were baseball commissioner Bowie Kuhn, MLB and all of its then-24 member clubs. Although the Court ruled in baseball's favor 5–3, it admitted the original grounds for the antitrust exemption were tenuous at best, that baseball was indeed interstate commerce for purposes of the act and the exemption was an "anomaly" it had explicitly refused to extend to other professional sports or entertainment. That admission set in motion events which ultimately led to an arbitrator's ruling nullifying the reserve clause and opening the door for free agency in baseball and other sports.

1973, The 10 and 5 rule becomes a standard clause in the Collective Bargaining Agreement. It allows any player who is a ten-year major league veteran, including the last five with his current team, to veto a trade to another team. It is known as the Curt Flood Rule.

1973, The eight members of the all-Black cheerleading squad for Brown University refuse to stand for the playing of the national anthem before a game against Providence College in Rhode Island. Brown president Donald Hornig defends the act and the freedom to express their beliefs.

1973, Dock Ellis, Pittsburgh Pirates pitcher, is featured in *Ebony* magazine with hair curlers. Commissioner Bowie Kuhn orders him to cease and desist from wearing rollers and curlers during pre-game workouts. Ellis reluctantly shelves the curlers, after declaring, "They didn't put out any orders about [Yankee star] Joe Pepitone when he wore a hairpiece down to his shoulders."

1973, In pursuit of Babe Ruth's lifetime home run record, Hank Aaron receives numerous death threats. His daughter Gaile, a student at Fisk University in Nashville, Tenn., receives threatening phone calls and is a target of an abortive kidnapping plot, requiring escorts by FBI agents.

1973, The 10 and 5 rule becomes a standard clause in the Collective Bargaining Agreement. It allows any player who is a ten-year major league veteran, including the last five with his current team, to veto a trade to another team. It is known as the Curt Flood Rule.

1974, Hank Aaron of the Atlanta Braves breaks Babe Ruth's record for lifetime home runs, hitting number 715 off Los Angeles Dodger pitcher Al Downing. Dodgers' broadcaster Vin Scully shares the gravity of the moment, "What a marvelous moment for the country and the world. A Black man is getting a standing ovation (53,775 fans) in the Deep South for breaking a record of an all-time baseball (White) idol."

1974, Billy "White Shoes" Johnson of the Houston Oilers does the funky chicken in the end zone after a touchdown. The press labels the act, "sexually suggestive" in nature. The NFL penalizes excessive demonstrative touchdown dances the next year.

1975, Officials at Gaylord High School in Gaylord, Mich., bans Wilt Chamberlain's book *Wilt*, stating pupils "are more interested in learning how to dribble and shoot" rather than his scores off the court.

1975, The Seitz decision was a ruling by arbitrator Peter Seitz on December 23, which declared that Major League Baseball players become free agents upon playing one year for their team without a contract, effectively nullifying baseball's reserve clause. The ruling was issued in regard to pitchers Andy Messersmith and Dave McNally.

1977, Minnesota University's all-time leading passer, Tony Dungy, is not drafted by the NFL. The Pittsburgh Steelers later sign quarterback Dungy as a safety.

1977, The Mel Blount Rule or "bump-and-run" bars contact with wide receivers beginning five yards beyond the line of scrimmage. Named after the Pittsburgh Steeler cornerback Mel Blount out of Southern University, this ruling marks a turning point in football in making the passing game more open.

1977, The NFL outlaws the "head slap" made popular by the retired (1973) Deacon Jones of the Los Angeles Rams.

1978, Major league baseball initiates the Hal McRae rule. During the 1977 AL Championship Series Kansas City Royal McRae aggressively takes out N.Y. Yankee second baseman Willie Randolph by sliding very wide of second base attempting to break up a double play. The new ruling prohibits runners from targeting fielders.

1979, Darryl Dawkins demolishes backboards in at Kansas City's Kemper Arena and Philadelphia's Spectrum, prompting the development and implementation of the "Breakaway Rim" or pressure-release rim for the 1981-82 season. Dawkins from the planet Lovetron becomes the first player to name his dunks; The Rim Wrecker, The Gorilla, In Your Face Disgrace, The Look Out Below, Cover Your Head, Dunk You Very Much, Left-Handed-Spine-Chiller-Supreme, The Bun Toaster, The Rump Roaster and the Baby Shaker.

1979, The NFL rules that tear-away jerseys are illegal. The rule is aimed at Greg "Do-it-to-it" Pruitt of the Cleveland Browns who had several custom-made tear-away jerseys.

1980, Philadelphia 76er stars Darryl Dawkins and Lloyd "World" Free, wear large gold necklaces inscribed "Chocolate Thunder"

Colorful Firsts in U.S. Sports

and "World," respectively. NBA bans the wearing of any type of hand, arm, face, nose, ear, head, or neck jewelry during league play, citing a potential safety hazard.

1981, With Kansas City ahead 7–4 over the Mariners, Amos Otis taps a dribbler down the third base line in the 6th inning. Mariners third baseman Lenny Randle gets down on all fours as the ball rolls along the line, finally going foul. Royals manager Whitey Herzog protests that Randle was blowing the ball foul, while the third baseman argues he was merely pleading with it. Umpire Larry McCoy rules in favor of Herzog and Otis gets a hit. Otis did not score but the Royals win, 8–5.

1981, The Lester Hayes Rule is enforced. The Oakland Raiders cornerback's use of stickum on his fingertips is outlawed. Teammate Fred Biletnikoff, a wide receiver, used the sticky stuff before retiring from the NFL in 1978.

1982, The NFL recognizes "sacks" as an official statistic. This is largely due to the success of defensive end Deacon Jones in his propensity for sacking quarterbacks when he played from 1961 to 1974.

1982, When coaching Georgetown University to the NCAA's Final Four tournament, George Thompson is asked during a press conference who he felt about being the first Black coach to reach the Final Four. "I resent the hell out of that question," Thompson said, "because it implies that I'm the first Black coach capable of reaching the Final Four. I'm Not. There have been plenty of men who came before me who were just as capable, if not more capable. I'm just the first one to get the opportunity who was lucky enough to make it here. They didn't have the same opportunity."

1983, In March, the NFL passes the "Leaping Rule" a few months after Green Bay's Gary Lewis, a 6-foot-5 high-jumping tight end, blocks kicks in four games. In a playoff win over the Cardinals, Lewis blocked a field goal, a PAT and deflected two-field goal attempts, all by racing from about five yards behind the line of scrimmage and leaping. It becomes Rule 12, Section 3, Article 2.

1984, Calvin Peete becomes the first African American to win the Vardon Trophy with a 70.56 scoring average. Peete had dropped out of a few tournaments because of illness and those scorecards did not count against his average golf score. The next year, the PGA decides to include all scores regardless of whether the competitor completes the tournament or not. *Golf World* magazine labels the change the Cal Peete Rule.

1984, The NFL, in response to celebrations such as a group high-five by the Washington Redskins' "Fun Bunch" and the "Nestea Plunge," where two players flop to the ground, as in the iced tea giant's old commercials, implements a rule banning such celebrations. The NFL rule includes penalties for players who kneel in prayer after scoring.

1985, Dennis "Oil Can" Boyd, son of Negro Leaguer Willie James Boyd, is fined by the Boston Red Sox for having a cocky demeanor and animated fist-pumping and finger-wagging on the mound. Conversely, 10 years earlier, the 1976 A.L. Rookie of the Year, Mark "The Bird" Fidrych of the Detroit Tigers known mostly for talking to the ball, getting on his hands and knees to manicure the pitching mound, was labeled an entertaining "flake" and was never fined.

1985, Rookie Patrick Ewing with the New York Knicks is not allowed, by the NBA, to wear a t-shirt under his jersey, as he did with the Georgetown Hoyas to stay warm in cold arenas.

1987, On the 40th anniversary of Jackie Robinson's promotion to the Brooklyn Dodgers, his minor league teammate with the Montreal Royals, L.A. Dodgers executive Al Campanis, is fired for racially biased comments. Speaking to Ted Koppel on *Nightline* about the managerial potential of African Americans, Campanis says, "No, I don't believe it's prejudice. I truly believe they (Negroes) may not have some of the necessities to be, let's say, a field manager or perhaps a general manager."

1988, News reporter Butch John asks the dubious question, "How long have you been a Black quarterback?" The intent according to John was, "It's obvious you've been a Black quarterback all your life. When did this really start mattering?"

1988, The Civil Rights Restoration Act is passed, applying anti-discrimination laws to entire institutions and putting the "teeth" back in Title IX, a federal law granting females in high schools and colleges the right to equal opportunity in sports.

1988, On Dr. Martin Luther King Jr's birthday, odds maker Jimmy "The Greek" Snyder responds to reporter Eddie Hotaling's question, about African Americans' alleged superiority in sports, "The slave owner would breed his big Black to his big woman so that he could have a big Black kid. That's where it all started." He adds, "If they take over coaching there's not going to be anything left for the White people." CBS fires Snyder from his $800,000-a-year job.

1989, The Wayman Tisdale Award is established by the USBWA to recognize an outstanding frosh collegiate basketball player. Guard Chris Jackson, later known as Mahmoud Abdul-Rauf, of LSU, is the first recipient.

1990, The NFL withdraws its plans to hold the 1993 Super Bowl in Phoenix due to Arizona's refusal to honor Dr. Martin Luther King Jr.'s birthday as a state holiday.

1990, National Baseball Hall of Fame second baseman Joe Morgan is arrested as a suspect drug courier in Los Angeles International

Airport (LAX) by police detective Clayton Searle and William Woessner, a DEA agent. A case of mistaken identity. Morgan files a lawsuit contending he suffered "acute physical and emotional distress and embarrassment" after the incident and expressed concern about damage to his character.

1990, Roseanne Barr sings the national anthem at a San Diego Padres game, by shouting out the lyrics off-key, making obscene gestures, grabbing her crotch and spitting on the pitcher's mound. Padres pitcher Eric Show said, "It's an insult. There are people who died for that song."

1990, Georgetown basketball coach John Thompson stages a walkout in protest of the National Collegiate Athletic Association's Proposal 42. The NCAA's Proposal 48 sets minimum academic standards for incoming frosh athletes at 700 on the SAT and a 2.0 grade point average. Proposal 42 states that if an athlete does not meet the guidelines of Proposal 48, he or she must sit out the frosh season, leaving only three years of eligibility. Opponents argue Proposal 48's minimum test-score requirements are based on culturally biased standardized tests. The NCAA estimates that nine of every 10 athletes who fail to meet the requirements are Black. Thompson claims that Prop 42 exacerbates the injustice by denying many athletes from low-income families the opportunity to attend college.

1992, Dikembe Mutombo, a Congolese American, is fined several thousand dollars for wagging his index finger at NBA opponents after blocking their shots. The NBA rules that the gesture by the Denver Nugget center is taunting. The four-time NBA Defensive Player of the Year is inducted into the Naismith Memorial Basketball Hall of Fame in 2015. Mutombo's jersey is retired by the Nuggets the following year.

1992, Arthur Ashe, former Wimbledon and US Open champion, tells *USA Today* and *People* magazine, that "being Black is harder than living with AIDS." Ashe CONTRACTED AIDS from a tainted blood transfusion during heart surgery in 1988.

1992, Craig Hodges of the Chicago Bulls wears a dashiki to the White House in celebration of the team's championship. He hands President George H.W. Bush a letter addressing the issues of racism and opposition of the Persian Gulf War. Hodges is released by the Bulls soon after and never plays in the NBA again. See 1996.

1993, Super Bowl XXVII was originally scheduled to be played at Sun Devil Stadium in Tempe, Ariz., the home of the Phoenix Cardinals. Immediately after the Cardinals relocated from St. Louis, Mo., to the Phoenix, Ariz. area in 1988, the NFL was eager to hold a Super Bowl in this state.

Meanwhile, Martin Luther King Day, the U.S. federal holiday honoring civil rights activist Martin Luther King Jr. was observed for the first time in 1986. However, the holiday was only celebrated in 27 states and the District of Columbia during that first year. Opponents across the nation tried to stop the holiday from being recognized in their own local areas.

In 1986, an Arizona holiday honoring King had been declared by Governor Bruce Babbitt after a bill to create the holiday failed in the state legislature. A year later, newly-elected Governor Evan Mecham rescinded the holiday in 1987 on the grounds that the holiday had been illegally created.

Legislation to create the holiday was passed by the state legislature in 1989, but opponents to the holiday succeeded in forcing the holiday to undergo a ballot initiative. Arizona voters rejected the 1990 initiative to create a King holiday.

The NFL, which has an increasing percentage of African American players, and urged by the NFL Players' Association, votes to snatch Super Bowl XXVII from Arizona, and awarded it instead to the Rose Bowl in Pasadena, Calif. Faced with the boycott, Arizona voters finally approved the King holiday by ballot in 1992, and on 23 March 1993, the NFL awards Super Bowl XXX (1996) to Tempe.

1995, Eugene E. Parker negotiates a $35 million contract between Deion Sanders and the Dallas Cowboys. Sanders' contract includes a $13 million signing bonus which prompts the NFL to institute the "Deion Rule." This ruling prevents rookies from receiving a huge, up-front signing bonus and deferring more salary than bonus beyond the next three seasons in order to fit under the salary cap. The largest signing bonus at the time was to Cowboys' quarterback Troy Aikman at $7 million.

1995, Plaintiffs Sam and Elsie Jethroe file a class action lawsuit in U.S. District Court for the Western District of Pennsylvania contending that systemic racism prevented Sam Jethroe from gaining the requisite four qualifying years to receive a major league pension. The defendants included MLB Properties, MLB, the Office of the Commissioner of Baseball, MLB Players Association and the MLB Pension Fund. The major leagues moved to dismiss the suit on the grounds that the statute of limitations had expired. The suit was dismissed in October 1996.

1996, Marge Schott, owner of the Cincinnati Reds, in an interview with ESPN states, "Hitler was good at the beginning" and that "he just went too far."

1996, Craig Hodges files a $40 million lawsuit against the NBA and its 29 teams, claiming they blackballed him for his association

Colorful Firsts in U.S. Sports

with minister Louis Farrakhan. After the 1992 NBA Championship, Hodges wears a dashiki and delivers a hand-written letter to President George H.W. Bush expressing his thoughts on the office's treatment of the minorities and poverty. After the 1992 season, Hodges is waived by the Chicago Bulls.

1996, The NBA suspends Mahmoud Abdul-Rauf for his refusal to stand for The Star-Spangled Banner. Abdul-Rauf, born Chris Jackson, claims the flag is a symbol of oppression. Later a compromise is reached allowing Abdul-Rauf to stand during the playing of the anthem, but could close his eyes, look downward and recite an Islamic prayer.

1997, Self-proclaimed white supremacist attorney Richard Barrett, sues the University of Mississippi over its ban on flagsticks at Ole Miss football games. Barrett contends that the ban interferes with free speech rights by keeping Confederate flags out of the stadium.

1997, Fuzzy Zoeller jokingly makes derogatory comments about Tiger Woods' possible ethnic menu of fried chicken, watermelon and collard greens at next year's Masters Tournament dinner. Kmart drops Zoeller as its spokesperson.

1997, Jack Trice Stadium at Iowa State University becomes the first NCAA Division I, and thus far still the only stadium, named for an African American. John G. "Jack" Trice was the first African American athlete for Iowa State College. He died due to injuries suffered during a college football game against the University of Minnesota in Minneapolis on Oct. 6, 1923. Trice died from hemorrhaged lungs and internal bleeding because of the injuries sustained during the game. Many speculated that the injuries were intentionally inflicted by Gopher players. Prior to the re-naming, the venue was named Cyclone Stadium; the playing area was called Jack Trice Field.

1997, Just before his death, Curt Flood's legacy was acknowledged in Congress by the Baseball Fans and Communities Protection Act of 1997. Numbered HR 21 (Flood's Cardinals uniform number) and introduced in the House of Representatives on the first day of the 105th Congress by Rep. John Conyers Jr. (D–Michigan), the legislation established federal antitrust law protection for major league baseball players to the same extent as provided for other professional athletes.

1997, The NFL rule book states, "A player cannot remove his helmet at all while on the field of play to use as a weapon or to celebrate, argue, etc." This is an automatic disqualification and is known as the "Emmitt Smith Rule" for his end-zone celebrations.

1998, Minnesota Vikings defensive end John Randle is fined $5,000 for wearing excessive face paint on Monday Night Football against the Green Bay Packers.

1998, The NFL initiates the Neil Smith Rule which prohibits a defensive lineman from flinching on the line, as it may cause an offensive lineman to false start, resulting in a five-yard penalty. Smith wreaked havoc on quarterbacks from 1988 to 2000 and piled up 104.5 sacks.

1998, The Curt Flood Act of 1998 applied antitrust laws to the business of major league baseball, specifically for player employment, ending the antitrust exemption that had protected the sport since the Supreme Court case Federal Baseball Club of Baltimore. Although the Act did not directly create free agency, it overturned the baseball exemption to the Sherman Antitrust Act, allowing players to sue if they believed their employment was affected by unfair practices and directly enabling the free-agency system that later developed. This act did exactly what Flood wanted; it stopped owners from controlling the players' contracts and careers.

1999, The NFL fines Brett Favre for drawing a finger menacingly across his throat. Favre's gesture was directed at Detroit Lions cornerback Robert Bailey. New Orleans Saints defensive lineman Willie Whitehead is also fined $10 grand for using this gesture a week later against the St. Louis Rams. The ruling is called the "O.J." rule.

1999, After more than 27 years, the Boston Celtics hold a public ceremony to retire jersey No. 6 of Hall of Fame center Bill Russell. Back in 1972, a private ceremony was held to retire his jersey because of the fear of racial repercussions in predominately White Boston.

1999, In the Australian Open, Venus Williams is penalized a point while serving to Lindsay Davenport, when beads fall from her braids. Williams notes, "I've never had such treatment before from any other umpire or any other match." Davenport counters, "Well, you can hear them and see them a little bit. Fortunately, you learn to play the ball. I'm not going to say it was a total distraction, but it is a little annoying maybe." The number one seed Davenport defeats fifth seed Williams in the quarterfinals, 6-4 and 6-0.

2000, Sam Perkins of the Indiana Pacers wears a do-rag during a preseason game. The NBA identifies the head scarf as a potential safety hazard and bans it.

2001, A mourning Allen Iverson, after the fatal shooting of his best friend, Rahsaan Langeford, explains to media why he took a burritos break during a team practice, "We sitting in here -- I'm supposed to be the franchise player, and we in here talking about practice. I mean, listen: We talking about practice. Not a game. Not a game. Not a game. We talking about practice. Not a game. Not the game that I go out there and die for and play every game like it's my last. Not the game. We talking about practice, man."

2001, The NFL bans do-rags and bandanas from being worn under football helmets. However, skullcaps are fine as long as they bear the team logo and colors. Team officials say Super Bowl MVP Ray Lewis of the Baltimore Ravens is permitted to wear a covering because of a scalp condition.

2001, The NBA allows zone defenses for the first time in its history, as possible alternative to stop the dominance of Shaquille O'Neal in the paint.

2002, The Sharpie Rule is invoked by the NFL. San Francisco 49ers wide receiver Terrell Owens, after scoring a touchdown vs. the Seattle Seahawks on Monday Night Football, pulled out a Sharpie from his sock, autographed the football and handed it to his financial advisor. According to the memo, "A player having any foreign object that is deemed a safety hazard, including a pen, will result in a 15-yard penalty and ejection from the game. Such a penalty can also warrant a fine, congruent with the league's current stance on unsportsmanlike conduct."

2003, The NFL rules that teams are permitted to tackle Dolphins running back Ricky Williams (Edgerrin James and others) by his dreadlocks without fear of penalty. An officiating media tape shows a clip of Williams being tackled by his hair. NFL officiating director Mike Pereira issues a statement making dreadlock tackling legal. Williams, the NFL's leading rusher in 2002, said he had no plans to cut his dreadlocks that he had worn since high school. Williams cut his braids or dreads and retires before the 2004 season.

2003, Announcer Kelly Tilghman and co-host Nick Faldo during a Golf Channel telecast of the Mercedes-Benz Championship, were discussing how players who could possibly challenge the dominant Tiger Woods. Faldo jokingly said perhaps the golfers should "gang up (on Tiger) for a while." The pair laughed a bit before Tilghman declared, "Lynch him in a back alley." Tilghman later apologizes and is suspended for two weeks.

2003, Popular talk show host Russ Limbaugh is hired by ESPN to do commentary on its Sunday NFL Countdown. Limbaugh comments that Philadelphia Eagles quarterback Donovan McNabb is overrated because the white liberal media wants a Black quarterback to do well. Within 48 hours Limbaugh is forced to resign for his incendiary racist remarks.

2003, The Rooney Rule becomes an NFL policy that requires teams to interview at least one minority candidate for head-coaching jobs when there is a vacancy. In 2009, the Rooney Rule expands to include general manager jobs and equivalent front office positions. The Rooney Rule is named after the late former Pittsburgh Steelers owner and chairman of the league's diversity committee, Dan Rooney.

2005, The NBA issues a dress code for the 2005-06 season. Business casual attire is required for team or league activities, including arriving at games, leaving games, conducting interviews and making promotional or other appearances. Players will no longer be able to wear the following: Sleeveless shirts, shorts, T-shirts, chains, pendants or medallions over clothing, sunglasses indoors and headphones (except on the team bus or the plane or in the locker room). Philadelphia 76er guard Allen Iverson is the most outspoken critic of the new dressing standard.

2005, Sande French of Albion, Calif., and Cecil Holland of Queens, N.Y., file a lawsuit against the International Tennis Federation and the U.S. Tennis Association in U.S. District Court in Brooklyn, N.Y. Holland, despite attaining "gold badge" status and chairing more than 1500 professional matches, he is never permitted to sit as a chair umpire at the US Open. French has worked more than 1500 matches claims that women are only permitted to chair preliminary men's matches due to systemic racism.

2006, Drake University in Des Moines, Iowa, dedicates its football field in honor of the late Johnny Bright, one of the school's greatest athletes and the victim of one of the most notorious acts in college football history. The field will be named "Johnny Bright Field at Drake Stadium." Bright is remembered for an incident on 20 October 1951. Bright's jaw is broken in a game in Stillwater, Okla., by an Oklahoma A&M player in what was perceived as a racially motivated attack.

2006, Oklahoma University paints a solid crimson line on its football field's 38-yard-line from sideline to sideline in its game against the Colorado Buffs. This is in honor of the Sooner's first African American football player, Prentice Gautt, who wore jersey No. 38. Gautt went on to play in the NFL and later a career in athletic administration. He dies in 2005.

2006, In March, NFL owners vote 29-3 to limit end-zone celebrations. This includes Chad Johnson's practicing his putting stroke with a pylon, Terrell Owens doing sit-ups or signing footballs, or Carolina Panthers' Steve Smith doing a version of "row, row, row your boat" in the end zone. Also banned is Johnson's proposal to a cheerleader on the sideline. However, Johnson's

Colorful Firsts in U.S. Sports

"Riverdance" routine will be allowed because he stays on his feet. Other "allowables" include spiking, dunking or spinning the football after a touchdown. Infractions will incur a 15-yard penalty for unsportsmanlike conduct.

2006, The NFL prohibits teams from penalizing misbehaving players beyond the four-game suspension limit without pay. The previous season, the Philadelphia Eagles suspend wide receiver Terrell Owens for the remainder of the season, costing him $812,000 in salary and beyond the four-game limit established by the players union. The ruling is unofficially known as the Terrell Owens Rule.

2006, NBA commissioner David Stern wants to end players overreacting to calls by referees. Players need to curb their enthusiasm when they are whistled for a foul. There is no new rule, but players and coaches were notified by memo with emphasis on a "zero-tolerance policy." Rasheed Wallace, who picked up 16 technical fouls last season, said the passion rule was just "another Sheed Wallace rule."

2007, Major league baseball hosts the first Civil Rights Game in tribute to the history of civil rights in the U.S. The St. Louis Cardinals beat the Cleveland Indians, 5 to 1, at AutoZone Park in Memphis, Tenn. The last Civil Rights game is played in 2014 at Minute Maid Park in Houston, Texas.

2007, CBS Radio fires "shock jock" Don Imus from his radio show after derogatory comments about Rutgers women's basketball team. A member of the National Broadcaster Hall of Fame and named by *Time* magazine as one of the 25 Most Influential People in America, Imus called the ladies of the team "nappy-headed hos." Several sponsors, including American Express Co., Sprint Nextel Corp., Staples Inc., Procter & Gamble Co., and General Motors Corp. pull ads from Imus' show indefinitely.

2007, Leg tights are added to the list of banned apparel in the NBA. In the previous season, 2005-06, LeBron James (Cavaliers), Kobe Bryant (Lakers), Dwyane Wade (Heat) and White player Jason Williams (Heat) wear full-length hose to keep their sore knees warm.

2008, In March, ESPN presents a four-hour documentary entitled *Black Magic*, which portrays the on-and-off-the-court challenges facing Black basketball players at historically African American colleges (HBCUs).

2009, The NBA bans the unique facial accessory wore by Miami Heat guard Dwyane Wade. Originally, he wore a Band-Aid to seal a cut beneath his left eye. Wade later slapped his nickname "Flash" and even the American flag on the Band-Aid after the wound had healed. The ban states that a Band-Aid can be worn for healthcare purposes but should not bear any name or identifications on it.

2009, In July, Ed O'Bannon, a former basketball player for UCLA who was a starter on the 1995 national championship team, and the NCAA Basketball Tournament's Most Outstanding Player of that year, files a lawsuit against the NCAA and the Collegiate Licensing Company, alleging violations of the Sherman Antitrust Act and of actions that deprived him of his right of publicity. He agrees to be the lead plaintiff after seeing his likeness from the 1995 championship team used in the EA Sports title NCAA Basketball 09 without his permission. The game featured an unnamed UCLA player who played O'Bannon's power forward position, while also matching his height, weight, bald head, skin tone, No. 31 jersey, and left-handed shot. In January 2011, Oscar Robertson joined O'Bannon in the class action suit. Bill Russell is also among the 20 former college athletes as plaintiffs.

On 8 August 2014, U.S. District Court for the Northern District of California Judge Claudia Wilken rules that the NCAA's long-held practice of barring payments to athletes violated antitrust laws. She ordered that schools should be allowed to offer full cost-of-attendance scholarships to athletes, covering cost-of-living expenses that were not currently part of NCAA scholarships. Wilken also ruled that colleges be permitted to place as much as $5,000 into a trust for each athlete per year of eligibility.

The NCAA subsequently appealed the ruling, arguing that Judge Wilken did not properly consider NCAA v. Board of Regents of the University of Oklahoma. In that case, the NCAA was denied control of college football television rights. The Supreme Court denied the NCAA's appeal. The NCAA was also ordered to pay the plaintiffs $42.2 million in fees and costs.

2010, In violation of the NFL's uniform policy, Cincinnati Bengal receiver Chad Ochocinco (formerly Chad Johnson), is fined $25,000 for wearing gold cleats during a Bengals' 27-21 loss at Pittsburgh on Monday Night Football. Bart Scott, New York Jets linebacker is fined $20,000 for playing without his chin straps snapped – a safety issue – during the Jets' 23-20 overtime victory at Detroit. Minnesota wide receiver Bernard Berrian is fined $5,000 for wearing yellow cleats during the Vikings' 27-24 overtime victory over Arizona.

2010, Mike Shanahan, coach of the Washington Redskins, in a game against the Lions in Detroit, trailing 31-25, benches veteran quarterback Donovan McNabb with two minutes left. Replaced by Rex Grossman, who was sacked and fumbled, as the Redskins lose 37-25. When asked by reporters regarding the decision to change quarterbacks, Shanahan replied, "I wasn't sure Donovan (a 12-year veteran) knew our two-minute offense (which is practiced weekly) well enough." Shanahan was pushing the racial coding that Black players are intellectually inferior to their white counterparts. In 2005, McNabb took Andy Reid's Philadelphia Eagles to the Super Bowl.

2010, The NBA prohibits players, particularly Rajon Rando of the Celtics, from wearing headbands upside down as the NBA logo becomes inverted. Richard Hamilton has worn a headband for the better part of the last eight years due in large part to supporting his famous clear facemask. Hamilton is exempt from the ruling as perspiration would leak down into the facemask causing cloudiness and impairing his vision.

2011, ESPN stops using Hank Williams Jr.'s song "All My Rowdy Friends Are There on Monday Night" on Monday Night Football after he publicly compares President Barack Obama to Adolf Hitler on *Fox and Friends*. Despite songs by Williams that glorify the Confederacy like, "If the South Woulda Won" and "If Heaven Ain't a Lot Like Dixie" he is rehired, in 2017, by ESPN during the first year of Donald Trump's term.

2012, LeBron James and the Miami Heat players wear hoodies in protest of the shooting death of Trayvon Martin in Sanford, Fla.

2014, Following the police shooting of Michael Brown in the St. Louis suburb of Ferguson, the St. Louis Rams players Tavon Austin, Stedman Bailey, Kenny Britt, Jared Cook and Chris Givens wear "Hands Up, Don't Shoot" t-shirts before a game against the Oakland Raiders.

2014, Wide receiver Andrew Hawkins wears a t-shirt with the inscription, "Justice for Tamir Rice and John Crawford" during his pregame introduction at a Cleveland Browns and Cincinnati Bengals game. The back of the shirt declared the phrase "The Real Battle of Ohio."

2014, Los Angeles Clippers protest owner Donald Sterling's racist remarks about Black people by wearing their shirts inside-out in order "to obscure any team logo" during their pre-game huddle. Soon after Miami Heat players wear their uniform tops inside-out to show solidarity with the Clippers. LeBron James comments on the situation, "There's no room for Donald Sterling in the NBA." NBA commissioner Adam Silver announces a lifetime ban of Sterling from the league and fines him $2.5 million, the maximum fine allowed by the NBA constitution.

2014, Quarterback Robert Griffin III is forced to turn his shirt with the quote "Know Jesus Know Peace" inside out before speaking at a news conference.

2014, Coach Jon Gruden also calls out Commissioner Roger Goodell, in an email, for pressuring the St. Louis Rams to draft Michael Sam, a gay player out of Missouri University, who was the SEC Co-Defensive Player of the year in 2013.

2015, After weeks of protest, University of Missouri president Tim Wolfe resigns when the school's football team, the Tigers, vows to boycott all football-related activities due to unaddressed racial hostility on the campus. The effort is led by #ConcernedStudent1950, named to pay homage to the first year a Black student is admitted to the university. The movement is captured in the documentary, *Field of Vision - Concerned Student 1950*.

2015, William Gay, Pittsburgh Steelers cornerback, is fined for wearing purple cleats to raise awareness about domestic violence.

2015, DeAngelo Williams, Pittsburgh Steelers running back, is fined for wearing "Find the Cure" eye black to raise awareness about breast cancer.

2015, Marshawn Lynch, Seattle Seahawks running back, is fined $75,000 by the NFL for not speaking to the media following the NFC Championship game. At Super Bowl Media Day, he says, "I'm just here so I won't get fined." Lynch proved prophetic as he was not fined for the now infamous quote.

2015, The city of Indianapolis gives the living members of the 1955 Crispus Attucks state championship basketball team a parade and celebratory ride from the Fieldhouse to Monument Circle that had been previously denied them as the first Black team to win a state championship. Coach Ray Crowe with guard Oscar Robertson won back-to-back championships, 1955 and 1956.

2015, New York City agrees to pay $4 million to Thabo Sefolosha, a 6-foot-6 forward with the Atlanta Hawks, to settle a federal lawsuit in which he accused five police officers of false arrest and using excessive force, breaking his left tibia during an encounter as a bystander outside a Manhattan nightclub. Sefolosha, 32, a Swiss citizen of African heritage, contends that the officers had arrested him arbitrarily and had violated his civil rights, in part because he is Black. He claimed that the injury had shortened his career and had cost him endorsement deals. In 2006, he became the first player from Switzerland to play in the NBA.

2015, Video shows white plain-clothes officer James Frascatore wrestling and handcuffing tennis player James Blake, outside of a New York hotel, without provocation. Blake suffers a cut to his left elbow and bruises to his left leg. The NYPD apologizes to Blake for a case of mistaken identity. Frascatore later files a defamation of character lawsuit against Blake that is dismissed.

2015, Carmelo Anthony of the New York Knicks marches with demonstrators in protest of the death of Freddie Gray from police

Colorful Firsts in U.S. Sports

brutality in his hometown of Baltimore. All six police officers were cleared.

2016, NFL players can wear custom cleats for charity for one week only. The "My Cause, My Cleats" campaign is developed in partnership with *The Players' Tribune*. More than 500 players participate using the hashtag #MyCauseMyCleats.

2016, Colin Kaepernick of the San Francisco 49ers, takes a knee during the national anthem during a preseason game against the Green Bay Packers. Kaepernick objects to the increased cases of police brutality against minorities in America.

2016, Coach Jon Gruden emails Washington team executive Bruce Allen expressing his anger over Colin Kaepernick kneeling during the national anthem. Gruden writes, "They suspend people for taking amino acids they should cut this f------."

2016, Michael Sam, a consensus All-American and SEC Defensive Player of the Year at the University of Missouri, lobbies against a bill at the Missouri State Capitol that would enable discrimination against the LGBTQ community. Sam was drafted by the St. Louis Rams in the seventh round of 2013 and played on the taxi squads for the Rams and the Dallas Cowboys in 2014.

2016, The NFL prevents the Dallas Cowboys from wearing a decal on their helmet in honor of five Dallas police officers killed in the line of duty.

2016, The NFL threatens to fine players who wear cleats to commemorate the 15th anniversary of 9/11.

2016, After the deaths of Alton Sterling in Baton Rouge, La., and Philando Castile, outside of St. Paul, Minn., by police officers, the Minnesota Lynx become the first professional team in the U.S. to wear "Black Lives Matter" on the front and the names of Sterling and Castile on the back of their warmup t-shirts.

2016, Jaylen Brown of the California Golden Bears is drafted by the Boston Celtics as the third pick in the first round. Brown enjoys playing chess and learning foreign languages. The 19-year-old enters the draft without an agent. "He is an extremely intelligent kid," an unnamed NBA assistant general manager said, adding, "He took a graduate school class at Cal in his freshman year. He is a person who is inquisitive about everything. Because he is so smart, it might be intimidating to some teams. He wants to know why you are doing something instead of just doing it. I don't think it's bad, but it's a form of questioning authority. It's not malicious. He just wants to know what is going on. Old-school coaches don't want guys that question stuff."

2017, Washington Wizards Kelly Oubre Jr. is asked to stop wearing the NBA and Nike sponsored Supreme compression sleeve.

2017, NBA champions the Golden State Warriors are disinvited by Donald Trump after guard Stephen Curry and teammates said they did not want to go to the White House based on Trump's comments regarding the white supremacist rally in Charlottesville, Va., which resulted in the death of Heather Heyer and several injured spectators.

2017, The NBA moves its All-Star game from Charlotte, North Carolina, to Smoothie King Arena in New Orleans, Louisiana, after a so-called "bathroom bill" that bars transgender people from using the bathroom that matched their gender identity.

2017, Bruce Maxwell becomes the first major league baseball player to take a knee to protest police brutality and racial injustice. It takes another three years for anyone else to follow his lead in the big leagues.

2017, David Price's minimalist delivery style of pitching has resulted in what is call the "Price rule" which makes a pitcher specify whether he is working from the stretch or full windup position when a runner is on third. The rule is detailed in this way: If a pitcher takes the rubber and his back foot is parallel to the mound and his other foot is in front, it is assumed he is in the set position and he will stop. This does not matter with no runners on or runners on first and second. But when there is a runner on third, pitchers need to inform the umpires if they are going to stand that way and not stop -- i.e., pitch out of the full windup.

2018, The French Tennis Federation president, Bernard Giudicelli, said that the sleek black catsuit worn by Serena Williams at the French Open went "too far," adding: "You have to respect the game and the place."

2018, Allyson Félix becomes the first sponsored athlete for Athleta, owned by Gap, Inc. When her contract expired with Nike in December 2017, the company offered a pregnant Félix a 70% pay cut in the new contract and failed to explicitly support maternity protections she requested in the contract.

2018, The Cleveland Indians announced the retiring and removal of their longtime and controversial logo, Chief Wahoo. Starting in 2019, Chief Wahoo will be gone from all gameday uniforms and will no longer be used by the team at Progressive Field in Cleveland, Ohio. However, fans can still purchase Wahoo merchandise from the team store.

2018, In response to LeBron James' comment to ESPN broadcaster Cari Champion that Donald Trump has "The No. 1 job in America, the appointed person is someone who doesn't understand the people," the athlete said, adding that some of the president's comments are "laughable and scary," Laura Ingraham of *Fox News* countered, "It's always unwise to seek political advice from someone who gets paid $100 million a year to bounce a ball," she said. "Keep the political comments to yourselves . . . Shut up and dribble [all the way to the bank]." James provides the hashtag #MoreThanAnAthlete.

2019, Tyreek Hill of the Kansas City Chiefs is fined $10,527 for giving the peace sign during a Thursday Night Football game against the Denver Broncos. The NFL considers this gesture to be taunting.

2019, Penn State basketball coach Pat Chambers tells star freshman Rasir Bolton in January, "I want to be a stress reliever for you. You can talk to me about anything. I need to get some of this pressure off you. I want to loosen the noose that's around your neck." Bolton recounts that Chambers, who is Catholic, said he was making a biblical reference and had intended to say "yoke." After the season, Bolton transfers to Iowa State. Chambers resigns from the basketball program in October.

2019, The NCAA institutes a policy that requires all agents to meet certain prerequisites–including having a bachelor's degree–to serve as an agent for athletes. The ruling is labeled the "Rich Paul Rule" and aimed at Rich Paul who lacks a degree. Paul began his career working with Creative Arts Agency (CAA) in 2006. He left CAA in 2012 to start Klutch Sports, whose clients include Eric Bledsoe, Kentavious Caldwell-Pope, Anthony Davis, Draymond Green, LeBron James, Tyrese Maxey, Jusuf Nurkić, Ben Simmons, John Wall and Trae Young. After backlash from the media, the NCAA later amends its certification process for agents and no longer requires agents to have a bachelor's degree.

Rich Paul writes in an op-ed to *The Athletic*: "Requiring a four-year degree accomplishes only one thing -- systematically excluding those who come from a world where college is unrealistic. Does anyone really believe a four-year degree is what separates an ethical person from a con artist?"

2019, African American hammer thrower Gwen Berry stands on the medal stand wearing bright blue lipstick and a gold medal around her neck. As the end of the national anthem, she bows her head and raises her fist, issuing a silent protest motivated by her personal journey and her belief that, "America can do better."

2019, Jaren Hall becomes the first African American starting quarterback in Brigham Young University's nearly 100-year history. BYU is owned by the Church of Latter Day Saints (LDS) and its student body is 99% LDS according to its website. BYU lifted the ban on Black people becoming priests and entering their temples in 1978.

2019, Nike releases the Air Max 1 Quick Strike sneaker featuring the Betsy Ross flag on the heel. The design drew complaints because the 1776 logo appears to glorify slavery and racism in U.S. history. Nike representative Colin Kaepernick tells *The Wall Street Journal* they should reconsider the design out of concern that it would send the wrong message about race in modern times. Nike pulls the shoes from the marketplace.

2020, On Opening Day, a stylish MLB/BLM logo is designed on the field's pitching mound, with patches worn on jersey sleeves. African American players Tim Anderson, Josh Bell, Mookie Betts and Jack Flaherty lead this effort in support the Black Lives Matter movement.

2020, Toronto Raptors' president, Nigerian-Canadian Masai Ujiri, attempts to enter the court as his Raptors defeat the Golden State Warriors to win the NBA championship, when he is blocked by a San Francisco Bay Area police officer, Alan Strickland. Body cam footage shows the officer shoving Ujiri twice as he attempts to show his access credentials.

2020, To pay respects to the late Breonna Taylor, the WNBA is the first professional league to dedicate a season to fight for social justice. A'ja Wilson and other players formed a Social Justice Council and wear warmups with "Say Her Name."

2020, The Milwaukee Bucks refuse to take the floor in a playoff game against the Orlando Magic in protest of the police shooting Jacob Blake seven times in his back, in Kenosha, Wis.

2020, The "Russell Rule," the first of its kind to be adopted by a Division I conference, stipulates that each school in the West Coast Conference (WCC) must include a member of a traditionally underrepresented community in the pool of final candidates for every athletic director, senior administrator, head coach and full-time assistant coach position in the athletic department. Bill Russell, an 11-time NBA Champion, a two-time NCAA Champion and a Presidential Medal of Honor recipient as a life-long advocate for social justice, embraced the opportunity to promote equitable opportunities in college athletics.

2020, Despite team owner Dan Snyder's adamant resistance to changing the name of his Washington Redskins, the club bows to political pressure and public opinion in becoming the Washington Football Team. Many complained that "Redskins" is racist and offensive to Native Americans. When the NFL reorganized in 1933, the Boston Braves changed its name to Redskins before moving to D.C. in 1937. It is believed that FedEx, which has naming rights to the stadium, also influenced the name change in 2020. In 2022, the football team will become the "Commanders."

2020, NASCAR bans the Confederate flag from its races and venues, formally severing itself from what is viewed by many citizens as a symbol of slavery and racism. Bubba Wallace, NASCAR's only Black driver, called for the banishment of the flag and said there is "no place" for them in the industry. Wallace drives a car, No. 43, with the hashtag #BlackLivesMatter.

2020, Seven current and former National Hockey League (NHL) players form the Hockey Diversity Alliance (HDA) group, whose mission is "to eradicate racism and intolerance in hockey." The group appoints San Jose Sharks forward Evander Kane and

Colorful Firsts in U.S. Sports

former NHL player Akim Aliu as co-heads of the organization. The group also includes Detroit Red Wings defenseman Trevor Daley, Minnesota Wild defenseman Matt Dumba, Buffalo Sabres forward Wayne Simmonds, Philadelphia Flyers forward Chris Stewart and former NHL forward Joel Ward. Another goal of the HDA is to promote diversity at all levels of the game. The group will operate independently of the NHL.

2020, LeBron James becomes the first player in NBA history to score at least 10 points in 1,000 consecutive regular season games. James launches "More Than A Vote" a non-profit organization designed to register African Americans to vote, and also to stop voter suppression efforts.

2020, ESPN host Rachel Nichols expressed frustration that Maria Taylor had been chosen over her to host "NBA Countdown" during the NBA Finals. "I wish Maria Taylor all the success in the world — she covers football, she covers basketball," Nichols said. "If you need to give her more things to do because you are feeling pressure about your crappy longtime record on diversity — which, by the way, I know personally from the female side of it — like, go for it. Just find it somewhere else. You are not going to find it from me or taking my thing away."

2020, Two retired NFL players, Najeh Davenport (running back) and Kevin Henry (defensive lineman), sue the league for allegedly discriminating against Black players who submitted claims in the 2013 class-action lawsuit, accusing the league of concealing findings on the dangers of concussion. The players claim the NFL race-corrected their neurological exams, which prevented them from being compensated. According to court documents, former players being evaluated for neurocognitive impairment were assumed to have started with worse cognitive function if they were Black. So if a Black player and a White player received the exact same scores on a battery of thinking and memory tests, the Black player would appear to have suffered less impairment. And therefore, the lawsuit stated, would be less likely to qualify for a payout.

2020, Former University of Cincinnati baseball players Jordan Ramey and Nathan Moore petition to change the name of Marge Schott Stadium that opened in 2004. Schott owned MLB's Cincinnati Reds from 1984 to 1999. Her racial and ethnic slurs against African American, Jewish and Japanese people prompted a one-year ban from baseball in 1993. After publicly praising Adolf Hitler in a 1996 ESPN interview, Schott was forced to give up day-to-day control of the Reds until 1998. The university's board of trustees voted unanimously to remove Schott's name from both the stadium and a place in the university's archives library.

2020, Retired outfielder Torii Hunter tells ESPN's "Golic and Wingo" that racially abusive fans at Fenway Park led Hunter to put the Boston Red Sox in the no-trade clause of his contracts. Hunter shares on WEEI-FM's "The Greg Hill Show" that he heard far more racist taunts in Boston than any other city.

2020, After 105 years, the Cleveland Indians move away from a moniker considered racist. In 2019 the team removes the contentious smiling, cartoonish mascot Chief Wahoo logo from its caps and jerseys, but the image is still sold by third-party vendors.

2020, The Baseball Writers' Association of America (BBWAA) vote overwhelmingly to remove former Major League Baseball Commissioner Kenesaw Mountain Landis' name from the plaques awarded to the American and National League MVPs. The decision comes after a few former MVPs, including Black award winners Barry Larkin and Terry Pendleton, voice displeasure with their plaques being named for Landis, who kept the game segregated during the 24 years he served as commissioner from 1920 until his death in 1944.

2020, The Baseball Writers' Association of America (BBWAA) submits a proposal to remove J.G. Taylor Spink's name from the organization's most prestigious award, which is given to writers for "meritorious contributions to baseball writing" since 1962. Spink, publisher of the *Sporting News* from 1914 to 1962, was the award's first recipient, shortly after his death. The *Sporting News* supports the removing of Spink's name. In the many decades before Jackie Robinson's debut with the Brooklyn Dodgers, the newspaper largely ignored the achievements of Black players and often used its voice to sustain negative stereotypes about them.

2020, Washington Senators owner Calvin Griffith moves the team to Minnesota. At a 1978 speaking engagement Griffith shares his reason for the relocation. "I'll tell you why we came to Minnesota. It was when we found out you only had 15,000 blacks here," Griffith said then. "Black people don't go to ballgames, but they'll fill up a rassling ring and put up such a chant it'll scare you to death. We came here because you've got good, hardworking white people here." In 2020, his statue is removed from Target Field. The Twins organization issues this statement: "Our decision to memorialize Calvin Griffith with a statue reflects an ignorance on our part of systemic racism present in 1978, 2010 and today. We apologize for our failure to adequately recognize how the statue was viewed and the pain it caused for many people -- both inside the Twins organization and across Twins Territory. We cannot remove Calvin Griffith from the history of the Minnesota Twins, but we believe removal of this statue is an important and necessary step in our ongoing commitment to provide a Target Field experience where every fan and employee feels safe and welcome."

2020, In partnership with active and former Major Leagues players and the Major League Baseball Players Association (MLBPA) the Players Alliance is created to change and work to address systemic barriers. Principals include Edwin Jackson (founder and secretary), CC Sabathia (vice-chair), Curtis Sanderson (board chair) and Adam Jones (member).

2020, 102 members of the U.S. Congress write a letter to the National Baseball Hall of Fame and Museum, co-signed by Players' unions from the NFL, NHL, NBA, and MLS, asking the Hall of Fame to admit Curt Flood for his pioneering efforts to eliminate the Reserve Clause in MLB.

2020, Running back Kylin Hill declares he will not play for the Mississippi State University Bulldogs unless the state removes a Confederate battle emblem from its flag. In June, the Mississippi legislature votes to the blue cross with 13 white stars from the flag's design. SEC Commissioner Greg Sankey threatens to block future championships events in the state saying, "It is past time for change to be made to the flag of the state of Mississippi." Note, Mississippi State University and Ole Miss stopped flying the Confederate flag in 2016.

2021, The NFL is accused of "race norming" in grading the settlements provided to former players for post-concussive syndromes, known as chronic traumatic encephalopathy (CTE). The league's systemic testing scale starts with the assumption that Black athletes have a lower cognitive functioning baseline, resulting in lower payouts than their white counterparts.

2021, Major league baseball moves the Atlanta All-Star game to Denver, Colorado, in protest of Georgia's new election rules that disproportionately restricts minority voting rights in urban areas. Governor Brian Kemp adds new identification requirements for absentee ballots, limits use of drop boxes and makes it a misdemeanor for groups to offer food or water to voters waiting in line near polling places.

2021, The Atlanta Board of Education votes unanimously to change the name of the [Nathan Bedford] Forrest Hill Academy to the Hank Aaron New Beginnings Academy. The academy had been named after a Confederate general, a founding figure of the Ku Klux Klan and Grand Wizard.

2021, Portland Trail Blazers forward Carmelo Anthony is named the inaugural winner of the NBA's Kareem Abdul-Jabbar Social Justice Champion award. In July 2020, he partnered with 11-time NBA All-Star Chris Paul of the Phoenix Suns and NBA legend Dwyane Wade to create the Social Change Fund, which aims to address social and economic justice issues facing Black communities and break down the discriminatory barriers to success. Guest editor Anthony of *SLAM's Black Lives Matter* magazine, in 2020, entitled "It Stops Now" provides a platform for the voiceless.

2021, The Texas chapter of the NAACP and a group of students file a federal civil rights complaint against the University of Texas for its continued use of the school song "The Eyes of Texas," which has racist undertones. The lyrics aren't necessarily racist, but the song's history is. The song was written in 1903 with a history of performances in minstrel shows and musicians in blackface. According to university records the Longhorns took trademark ownership of the phrase "The Eyes of Texas are upon you" in 1936. The complaint says the song creates a hostile campus environment over the "offensive," "disrespectful," and "aggressive" use of the song.

2021, NCAA basketball champions Baylor and coach Scott Drew refuse a customized Jeep Wrangler wrapped with the school's national championship logo after an insensitive remark made by Ted Teague, general manager of the Allen Samuels dealership in Waco, during a live KWTX-TV interview stating, "Use it to recruit, pull some people out of the hood." Teague immediately apologizes.

2021, The Baseball Writers' Association of America (BBWAA) votes to remove the name of J.G. Taylor Spink, former publisher of the *Sporting News*, from its annual award for meritorious contributions to baseball writing. The BBWAA had 325 of 334 members, or 97%, vote to remove the name following research into racism by Spink. Writer Ryan Fagan explains: "Spink was the publisher of the largest, most powerful baseball publication in the country for nearly half a century, and he used that position to strongly advocate against the integration of the sport." Fagan adds that Spink's *Sporting News* contained "racist language, ugly stereotypes and derogatory portrayals of Negro League players and other Black Americans during Spink's time as publisher, especially in the era before Jackie Robinson made his MLB debut in 1947." The award is renamed the "BBWAA Career Excellence Award."

2021, The International Swimming Federation (FINA) bans swimming caps designed for natural Black hair for use in the Tokyo Olympics. The thickness or density of Black hair does not fit under a traditional swim cap. The caps are made by Black-owned British brand, Soul Cap.

Colorful Firsts in U.S. Sports

2021, The historical marker to honor Jackie Robinson's birthplace at the Roddenbery Memorial Library in Cairo, Ga., is damaged by gunfire. The marker read:

Birthplace of Jackie Robinson: First African American in Modern-Day Major League Baseball

Robinson was born 13 miles south of Cairo on January 31, 1919, before he and his family moved to California in 1920. After attending U.C.L.A., serving in the U.S. Army, and playing in the Negro American Baseball and International Leagues, Robinson played for the Brooklyn Dodgers in 1947, breaking Major League Baseball's color barrier. Adding to his many athletic accomplishments, he served as special assistant to New York Governor Nelson Rockefeller, established the first African American Modern Bank/Freedom National Bank, and provided housing for the underprivileged through his construction firm. Robinson died in 1972. His birthplace burned in 1996, but the chimney still stands.

Re-erected in 2021 by the Georgia Historical Society, The Jackie Robinson Cairo Memorial Institute, Inc., and Major League Baseball.

2021, Tony Humphrey, a 16-year-old junior at Iona Prep, a private school in New Rochelle, N.Y., commits to play baseball at Boston College. Humphrey joins the school's track team and shares with his assistant athletic director, "It never hurts to gain speed." However the educator tells Humphrey that he "gained that speed by running from the police." Soon after Humphrey transfers to a public school near his home in Cortland, N.Y. The assistant AD resigns amid a student walkout.

2022, Attempting to expand diversity, all 32 NFL teams will be mandated to have a minority offensive assistant coach on staff for the 2022 season. The coach can be a woman or the member of a racial or ethnic minority. With a trend of hiring head coaches from offensive coordinator positions, Pittsburgh Steelers owner Art Rooney II, who serves as chairman of the NFL's diversity committee, said that he hopes the mandate creates a pipeline for minority coaches to rise through the ranks and eventually become head coaches.

2022, After a grade school shooting in Uvalde, Texas, that results in the deaths of 19 young children and two teachers, Jewish manager of the San Francisco Giants Gabe Kapler will skip the national anthem until he feels better about the direction of America regarding gun violence. Unlike Colin Kaepernick's stance against police violence, there are no campaigns to oust Kapler from his job.

2023, During a pregame broadcast of the Oakland A's game against the Kansas City Royals at Kauffman Stadium announcer Glen Kuiper says: "We had a phenomenal day today, nigger league museum [sic, Negro Leagues Baseball Museum]. And Arthur Bryant's Barbeque." This Freudian slip is reminiscent of a 2010 comment by Mike Greenberg from ESPN's Mike & Mike show when he uttered, "Talking football with you on Martin Luther Coon King Junior Holiday." Greenberg kept his job, Kuiper was suspended and later fired.

Afterword

As a teenager in 1963, I was captivated by A. S. "Doc" Young's new book *Negro Firsts in Sports*. The hurricane in my brain often asked, "What other historical 'firsts' had been achieved beyond Doc's excellent thesis?" Sixty years later, my discoveries found the competition sparked with glory but also soaked with vengeance. As a youth I got the scoop, if you tell the truth, you are always bullet proof. You will not find the truth for some calendar-type entries in search engines like Goober, Bang or Wahoo, but they did happen!

Back in 1857, in the infamous Dred Scott decision, Supreme Court Chief Justice Roger Brooke Taney ruled that African Americans were an inferior class of humans and had no rights in which the White man was bound to respect. Taney wrote that the Founders' words in the Declaration of Independence, "all men were created equal," were never intended to apply to Black folks. The ideology of white supremacy made abuse of Black people moral and socially acceptable. Sadly, snippets of Taney's creed continue today in some minds of the ruling majority, as Lady Liberty passes the torch to little Jimmy Crow.

Let's add a thought from a father-figure like Hank Aaron, "A man's ability is limited only by his lack of opportunity." Under clouds of cigar smoke, opportunities were limited by those in seniority and authority as they whiskey around the truth. Lies, more lies, and alibis forced us to realize that guilty lips know no truth! This lack of accountability of embedded racist policies goes beyond the playing fields, as their attitudes become life-like tattoos. Hopefully, my treatise will offend their greedy ambitions for ascendancy, as athletes with fleeced locks continue to pound their bronze chests victoriously in overcoming these stoic attitudes and synthetic barriers.

Whether these barrier breakers are on a prayerful knee or raising a fisted salute, they can be viewed as unpatriotic, uppity, aggressive, disrespectful, belligerent, un-American, and unappreciative of the opportunities afforded by the apartheid sympathizers. The inclusion of Black excellence can sometimes be threatening. Gladiatorially, fans learn diversity creates competition and competition eliminates mediocrity. In the process, the caste system of privilege pushes the caged athlete to become more resilient, adaptable, innovative, and creative, forging both the will and the skills for survival and exponential greatness.

The first 11 chapters cover major sports along with cross references by individual pioneers. Chapter 12 is a catch-all for minor sports and lesser known caged champions other than No. 42, who, along with Larry Doby, et al, dismantled apartheid in America's most popular sports institution at the time, baseball.

Chapter 13 is an add-on tax. A "Black Tax" that weighs the hardships of every athlete of color. Colored athletes that are criminalized, marginalized or chastened for just walking or driving to their field of dream as they are quarantined from the collective mainstream. This chapter testifies to the monstrosities of white supremacy, while showcasing the resiliency of minority athletes in fighting systemic racism, micro aggressions and implicit bias, as their dreams grow bigger than their fears.

Let your curiosity become your philosophy to learn more about their journeys. An intense curiosity with a calm core in addressing how to share this joyful noise in a spirited way. Let your sentimental heart have a renaissance of faith in recognizing these social change agents.

Today let's "Lift Every Voice & Sing" in praise of these champions until earth and heaven ring. Blessingly assured, this is my story, and this is my song, praising sports all-the-day long.

I close with words from 17th century Irish philosopher Edmund Burke, "The only thing necessary for evil to triumph is for good men to do nothing." I pledge allegiance to do my part. Will you?

Bibliography

"If a race has no history, if it has no worthwhile tradition, it becomes a negligible factor in the thought of the world, and it stands in danger of being exterminated." – Carter Godwin Woodson

Adelson, Bruce. *Brushing Back Jim Crow: The Integration of Minor-League Baseball in the American South*. Virginia: The University Press of Virginia, 1999.

Anthony, Carmelo. *SLAM: Black Lives Matter* magazine. "It Stops Now." SLAM Media, New York, N.Y., 2020.

Ashe, Jr., Arthur R. *A Hard Road to Glory: A History of the African-American Athlete, 1916-1918* and *1919-1945*. New York: Warner Books, 1998.

Baker, Mark Allen. *The World Colored Heavyweight Championship, 1876-1937*. Jefferson, NC: McFarland & Company, Inc., Publishers, 2020.

Baseball-Reference.com at https://www.baseball-reference.com/

Basketball-Reference.com at https://www.basketball-reference.com/

Black Fives Foundation at https://www.blackfives.org/

Bradley, Robert. *Compendium of Professional Basketball*. Tempe, Ariz.: Xaler Press, 1999.

Bryant, Howard. *The Heritage: Black Athletes, a Divided America, and the Politics of Patriotism*. Boston, Mass., Beacon Press, 2018.

Bryant, Howard. *Full Dissidence: Notes from an Uneven Playing Field*. Boston, Mass., Beacon Press, 2020

Bunch III, Lonnie G. and Louie Robinson. *The Black Olympians: 1904-1984*. California Afro-American Museum, 1984.

Carrington, Jr., Arthur A. *Black Tennis: An Archival Collection*: Self-published.1890-1962. 2009.

Carroll, John M. *Fritz Pollard and the Brown Bombers*. The *Coffin Corner*: Volume 12, Number 1, 1990.

Chalk, Ocania. *Black College Sport*. New York, N.Y.: Dodd, Mead and Co., 1976.

Chalk, Ocania. *Pioneers of Black Sport*. New York, N.Y.: Dodd, Mead and Co., 1975.

Charlton, James. *The Baseball Chronology: The Complete History of the Most Important Events in the Game of Baseball*. New York, N.Y.: Macmillan Publishing Company, 1991.

Cobb, Jelani and David Remnick. *The Matter of Black Lives: Writing from The New Yorker*. New York, N.Y., HarperCollins, 2021.

Cowan, Tom and Jack Maguire. *Timelines of African-American History: 500 Years of Black Achievement*. New York, N.Y.: Perigee Books, 1994.

Davis, Lenwood and Belinda S. Daniels. *Black Athletes in the U.S*. Conn.: Greenwood Press, 1981.

Dawkins, Marvin P. and Graham C. Kinloch. *African American Golfers During the Jim Crow Era*. Westport, Conn.: Praeger Publishers, 2000.

Demas, Lane. *Integrating the Gridiron: Black Civil Rights and American College Football*. Piscataway, NJ: Rutgers University Press, 2010.

Dolin, Nick and Chris Dolin and David Check. *Basketball Stars*. New York, N.Y.: Black Dog & Leventhal Publishers, Inc., 1997

Downey, Bill. *Tom Bass: Black Horseman*. St. Louis, Mo.: Saddle and Bridle, Inc., 1975.

Draper, Deborah Riley with Travis Thrasher. *Olympic Pride, American Prejudice: The Untold Story of 18 African Americans Who Defied Jim Crow and Adolf Hitler to Compete in the 1936 Berlin Olympics*. Atria Books, an imprint of Simon & Schuster, Inc., 2020.

Dreier, Peter and Robert Elias. *Baseball Rebels: The Players, People, and Social Movements That Shook Up the Game and Changed America*. Lincoln, Neb.: University of Nebraska Press, 2022.

Early, Gerald L. *A Level Playing Field: African American Athletes and the Republic of Sports*. Boston, Mass.: Harvard University Press, 2011.

Edwards, Dr. Harry. *The Revolt of the Black Athlete*. New York, N.Y.: MacMillan Publishing Company, 1985.

Essington, Amy. *The Integration of the Pacific Coast League: Race and Baseball on the West Coast*. Lincoln, Neb.: University of Nebraska Press, 2018.

Bibliography

Feinstein, John. *Raise A Fist, Take A Knee: Race and the Illusion of Progress in Modern Sports*. New York, N.Y.: Little, Brown and Company, 2021.

Fink, Rob. *Football at Historically Black Colleges and Universities in Texas*. College Station: Texas A&M University Press, 2019.

Football-Reference.com at https://www.pro-football-reference.com/

Fosty, George and Darril Fosty. *Black Ice: The Lost History of the Colored Hockey League of the Maritimes, 1895-1925*. New York City, N.Y.: Stryker-Indigo Publishing Company, Inc., 2004.

George, Nelson. *Elevating the Game: The History & Aesthetics of Black Men in Basketball*. N.Y.: HarperCollins Publishers, Inc., 1992.

Green, Ben. *Spinning the Globe: The Rise, Fall and Return to Greatness of the Harlem Globetrotters*. N.Y.: Amistad, imprint of HarperCollins Books, 2005.

Gould, Todd. *For Gold & Glory: Charlie Wiggins and the African-American Racing Car Circuit*. Bloomington, Ind.: Indiana University Press, 2002.

Grundy, Pamela and Susan Shackelford. *Shattering the Glass: The Remarkable History of Women's Basketball*. N.Y.: The New Press, 2005.

Gruver, Ed. *The American Football League: A Year-by-Year History, 1960-1969*. Jefferson, N.C.: McFarland & Company, Inc., Publishers, 1997.

Harley, Sharon. *The Timetables of African-American History: A Chronology of the Most Important People and Events in Africa-American History*. New York, N.Y.: Simon & Schuster, 1995.

Harris, Cecil. *Breaking the Ice: The Black Experience in Professional Hockey*. Toronto, Ontario, Canada, Insomniac Press, 2003.

Harris, Cecil and Larryette Kyle-DeBose. *Charging the Net: A History of Blacks in Tennis, from Althea Gibson and Arthur Ashe to the Williams Sisters*. Chicago, Ill.: Ivan R. Dee Publisher, 2007.

Henderson, Edwin B. *The Negro in Sports*. Washington, District of Columbia: Associated Publishers Inc., 1949.

Hoberman, John. *Darwin's Athletes: How Sports Has Damaged Black America and Preserved the Myth of Race*. New York, N.Y.: Houghton Mifflin Company, 1997.

Hornsby, Jr., Alton. *Chronology of African-American History: Significant Events and People from 1619 to the Present*. Detroit, Washington District of Columbia, London: Gale Research, 1991.

Hurd, Michael. *The Pride and the Passion: The Long, Hard Evolution of Black College Football*. ESPN College Football Encyclopedia: The Complete History of the Game. New York: ESPN Books, 2005.

Hurd, Michael. *Black College Football, 1892-1992: One Hundred Years of History, Education, & Pride*. Schiffer Pub Ltd, United Kingdom, 2000.

Jacobs, Barry. *Across the Line: Profiles in Basketball Courage, Tales of the First Black Players in the ACC and SEC*. Guilford, Conn., 2008.

Jacobus, Robert D. *Black Man in the Huddle: Stories from the Integration of Texas Football*. College Station: Texas A&M University Press, 2019.

Johnson, Martenzie @10zJohnson. *The First Black Quarterback for Each NFL Team – and how he lasted*. https://andscape.com/features/first-black-starting-quarterback-for-each-nfl-team-geno-smith/

Katz, Milton S. *Breaking Through: John B. McLendon, Basketball Legend and Civil Rights Pioneer*. Fayetteville, Ark.: The University of Arkansas Press, 2007.

Kelly-Gangi, Carol. *Essential Black Wisdom: Quotes of Inspiration and Strength*. N.Y.: Fall River Press, 2018.

Kimbro, Dennis. *Think and Grow Rich: A Black Choice*. N.Y.: Fawcett Book, 1993.

Kuska, Bob. *Hot Potato: How Washington and New York Gave Birth to Black Basketball and Changed America's Game Forever*. Va.: University of Virginia Press, 2004.

Johnson, Claude. *The Black Fives: The Epic Story of Basketball's Forgotten Era*. New York, N.Y.: Abram Press, 2021.

Lacy, Sam with Moses J. Newson. *Fighting For Fairness: The Life Story of Hall of Fame Sportswriter Sam Lacy*. Centreville, Md.: Tidewater Publishers, 1998.

Lamb, Chris. *Stolen Dreams: The 1955 Cannon Street All-Stars and Little League Baseball's Civil War*. Lincoln, Neb.: University of Nebraska Press, 2022.

Colorful Firsts in U.S. Sports

Lapchick, Richard. *100 Pioneers: African-Americans Who Broke Color Barriers in Sport*. W. Va.: Fitness Information Technology, 2008.

Lapchick, Richard. *Smashing Barriers: Race and Sports in the New Millennium*. Lanham, Md.: Madison Books, 1991.

Leonard, David J. *Playing While White: Privilege and Power On and Off the Field*. Seattle, Wash.: University of Washington Press, 2017.

Luke, Bob. *Integrating the Orioles: Baseball and Race in Baltimore*. Jefferson, N.C.: McFarland & Company Inc., Publishers, 2016.

Maher, Tod. *Wiffle: The World Football League Chronicle*. Professional Football Researchers Association, 1990.

Marc, David. *Leveling the Playing Field: The Story of the Syracuse 8*. Syracuse, N.Y.: Syracuse University Press, 2015.

Martin, Charles H. *Benching Jim Crow: The Rise and Fall of the Color Line in Southern College Sports, 1890-1980*. Urbana, Chicago and Springfield, Ill.: University of Illinois Press, 2010.

Miller, Jeff. *Going Long: The Wild 10-Year Saga of the Renegade American Football League in the Words of Those Who Lived It*. New York, N.Y.: McGraw-Hill, 2003.

Moffi, Larry and Jonathan Kronstadt. *Crossing the Line: Black Major Leagues, 1947-1959*. Jefferson, N.C.: McFarland & Company Inc., Publishers, 1994.

Moore, Louis. *We Will Win the Day: the Civil Rights Movement, the Black Athlete, and the Quest for Equality*. Lexington, Ky.: The University Press of Kentucky, 2021.

Mura, David. *The Stories Whiteness Tells Itself: Racial Myths and our American Narratives*. Minneapolis, Minn.: University of Minnesota Pres, 2022.

Negro Leaguers in Puerto Rico website by Jorge Colón Delgado and Thomas E. Van Hyning. https://negroleaguerspuertorico.com/

Nelson, Murry R. *Abe Saperstein and the American Basketball League, 1960-1963*. Jefferson, N.C.: McFarland & Company Inc., Publishers, 2013.

Nemec, David. *Great Baseball Feats, Facts & Firsts*. N.C.: Plume, 1987.

Northington, Nathaniel. *0* . Lexington, KY: The University Press of Kentucky, 2013.

Orr, Jack. *The Black Athlete: His Story in American History*. New York, N.Y.: Pyramid Books, 1970.

Overmyer, James E. *Cum Posey of the Homestead Grays: A Biography of the Negro Leagues Owner and Hall of Famer*. Jefferson, N.C.: McFarland & Company, Inc., Publishers, 2020.

Peterson, Robert W. *Pigskin: The Early Years of Pro Football*. New York, NY: Oxford University Press, 1997.

Rayl, Susan J. *The New York Renaissance Professional Black Basketball Team, 1923-1950*. PhD dissertation, Pennsylvania State University, 1996.

Rhoden, William C. *Forty Million Dollar Slaves: The Rise, Fall, and Redemption of the Black Athlete*. New York, N.Y.: Crown Publishing, 2006.

Rhoden, William C. *Third and a Mile: From Fritz Pollard to Michael Vick – an Oral History of the Trials, Tears and Triumphs of the Black Quarterback*. New York, N.Y.: ESPN Books, 2007.

Ross, Charles K. *Outside the Lines: African Americans and the Integration of the National Football League*. New York, N.Y.: New York University Press, 1999.

Runstedtler, Theresa. *Black Ball: Kareem Abdul-Jabbar, Spencer Haywood, and the Generation that Save the Soul of the NBA*. New York, N.Y.: Bold Type Books, 2023.

Sapp, Erin Grayson. *Moving the Chains: The Civil Rights Protest That Saved the Saints and Transformed New Orleans*. Baton Rouge, Louisiana: Louisiana State University Press, 2023.

Saunders, James Robert and Monica Renae Saunders. *Black Winning Jockeys in the Kentucky Derby*. Jefferson, N.C.: McFarland & Company Inc., Publishers, 2003.

Schleppi, John. *The World Tournament of Professional Basketball and the College All-Star Game*. Haworth, N.J.: Saint Johann Press, 2008.

Seamheads at https://www.seamheads.com/NegroLgs/

Sinnette, Calvin H. *Forbidden Fairways: African Americans and the Game of Golf*. Baltimore, Md.: Black Classic Press, 1998.

Smith, Jessie Carney. *Black Firsts: 4,000 Ground-Breaking and Pioneering Historical Events*. Canton, Mich.: Visible Ink Press, 2003.

Bibliography

Smith, Thomas G. *Outside the Pale: The Exclusion of Blacks from the National Football League, 1934-1946*. The Coffin Corner: Volume 11, Number 4, 1989.

Solomon, Burt. *The Baseball Timeline: The Day-By-Day History of Baseball from Valley Forge to the Present Day*. New York, N.Y.: Stonesong Press, 1997.

Swaine, Rick. *The Integration of Major League Baseball: A Team by Team History*. Jefferson, N.C.: McFarland & Company Inc., Publishers, 2009.

Thomas, Etan. *We Matter: Athletes and Activism*. Brooklyn, N.Y.: Akashic Books, 2018.

Whitted, Fred. *Black College Sports Encyclopedia*. Fayetteville, N.C.: Resources 2000, 2008.

Wiley, Ralph. *Classic Wiley: A Lifetime of Punchers, Player s, Punks & Prophets*. New York, N.Y.: Hyperion, 2005.

Wiggins, David K. *Clio and the Black Athlete in America: Myths, Heroes and Realities*. Quest 32 (1980): 217-225.

Wiggins, David K. *From Plantation to Playing Field: Historical Writings on the Black Athlete in American Sport*. Research Quarterly for Exercise and Sport 57 (June 1982): 101-116.

Wright, Marshall D. *The International League: Year-by-Year Statistics, 1884-1953*. Jefferson, N.C.: McFarland & Company, Inc., 1998.

Yoder, Matt. *Your White Guy Code Word Power Rankings*. Awful Announcing, January 8, 2014

Young, A.S. "Doc". *Negro Firsts in Sports*. Chicago, Ill.: Johnson Publishing Co., Inc., 1963.

Index

#

#ConcernedStudent1950, 99, 210, 309

1

10 and 5 rule
    Baseball's Collective Bargaining Agreement, 61, 131, 303

5

50-inch vertical jump
    Darius Clark, 112, 288

A

Aaron, Hank, 37, 44, 45, 57, 59, 61, 65, 85, 109, 111, 120, 121, 124, 210, 303, 313, 315
    Gaile Aaron, 61, 124, 303
Aaron, Henry, 64, 124
Aaron, Tommie, 61, 124
Abbott, Cleve, 207, 210, 220
Abbott, Jessie, 28, 264
Abdul-Jabbar, Kareem, 67, 108, 159, 162, 300, 313
    Lew Alcindor, 51, 53, 56, 64, 152, 162, 195, 300
Abdullah, Aquil Hashim, 79, 91, 267
Abdullah-Simmons, Taqiy, 93, 267
Abdul-Qaadir, Bilquis, 96, 162
Abdul-Rauf, Mahmoud
    Chris Jackson, 74, 153, 162, 304, 306
Abreu, Eufemio, 20, 115
Accooe, Ferdinand, 18, 151
Adam Clayton Powell Jr Blvd, 101, 161
Adams, K.S. "Bud", 44, 212
Adams, Katrina, 99, 283
Adcock, Joe, 88
Adderley, Herb, 55, 219
Aden, Halima, 104
Adkins, Charles, 36, 199, 264
Admiral Music Maids, 35, 128
African American Students Foundation, 45, 299
Africville Sea-Sides (CHL), 16, 253
Agee, Claude, 38, 124
Aguirre, Mark, 68, 162
Aida Park, 23, 126
Aikman, Troy, 71, 209, 229, 305
Ailey, Alvin, 13
Ainuu, Manoah, 111, 266
Akron Indians, 16, 206, 219
Akron Pros, 16, 19, 20, 206, 211, 219, 238
Al Somers Umpires School, 42, 140
Alabama Sports Hall of Fame, 60, 209, 230
Ali, Laila, 84, 87, 200, 201, 202
Ali, Muhammad, 50, 52, 53, 58, 62, 63, 65, 71, 75, 80, 99, 128, 199, 200, 201, 202, 203, 205, 300, 302
    Cassius Clay, 45, 48, 49, 201
Ali, Nia, 101, 266
Alighieri, Dante, 95
Aliu, Akim, 105, 253, 312
All-America Football Conference (AAFC), 29, 211
All-American Girls Professional Baseball League, 38, 146
Allen, Bruce, 215, 310
Allen, Dick "Richie", 59, 124
Allen, James Kanati, 54
Allen, James Kenati, 54, 265, 267
Allen, Lafayette, 290, 292
Allen, Marcus, 68, 70, 219
Allen, Phog, 34, 191
Allen, Richie Dick, 55, 119, 131, 301
Allen, Will "Rockville Cyclone", 53, 162
Allen, Willie, 53
Alpha Big Five, 16, 17, 151
Alpha Physical Culture Club of Harlem, 16, 18, 151
Ambers, Lou, 26, 201
American Association, 10, 11, 24, 32, 113, 127, 147, 148, 206
American Association Football League, 24, 206
American Basketball Association (ABA), 22, 55, 92, 155, 156, 157, 164, 183, 219, 301
American Basketball League, 46, 79, 80, 157, 174, 175, 182, 183, 318
American Bowling Congress (ABC), 27, 36, 37, 38, 204, 287, 291, 292
American Football League, 33, 44, 45, 50, 51, 56, 208, 212, 223, 228, 233, 235, 236, 243, 244, 300, 301, 317, 318
American Lawn Tennis magazine, 33, 281, 284, 297
American Professional Football Association, 16, 20, 206, 211, 219, 238
American Tennis Association (ATA), 18, 19, 25, 31, 281, 284, 285
Amherst (CHL), 253
Amherst College, 13, 206, 230, 232
Amherst Royals (CHL), 16, 253
Amorós, Sandy, 39, 118, 144
Anaheim Angels, 88, 127
Anderson, Barry, 106, 216
Anderson, Bobby, 22, 160, 181
Anderson, Clifton, 37, 219, 233, 244
Anderson, Ezzrett "Sugarfoot", 30, 211, 219, 238
Anderson, George "Spider", 12, 259, 260
Anderson, Kyle, 37, 219
Anderson, Marian, 11
Anderson, Mike, 86, 219
Anderson, Spider, 13, 260
Anderson, Tim, 120, 126, 311
Anderson, Waymon, 39, 162
Andrews, Greg, 53, 162
Andrews, Starr, 110, 287
Angelou, Maya, 12, 98, 110
Anson, Cap, 11, 12, 114, 146, 147, 295
Anthony, Carmelo, 108, 158, 159, 162, 309, 313
Anthony, Greg, 75, 156
Antiqua, Orlando "Hurricane", 79, 160, 163

Index

Appalachian State University, 79, 221
Arbet, Darren, 89, 214
Arcadia Knights, 103, 256
Arcadia University, 103, 256
Archibald, Nate, 61, 163
Arena Football League, 89, 112, 214, 216, 229
Argea, Angelo, 83, 249
Argyle Hotel, 11, 113
Arizona Cardinals, 83, 90, 220, 222
Arizona Diamondbacks, 94, 95, 135, 150
Arledge, Missouri "Big Mo", 40, 163
Armstrong, Frank, 15, 125
Armstrong, Henry, 26, 75, 200, 201
Arnelle, Jesse, 39, 40, 155, 163, 168
Art Ross Trophy, 88, 256
Artis, Orsten, 50, 152, 300
Ashburn, Richie, 31, 143
Ashe, Arthur, 44, 48, 53, 57, 63, 71, 76, 81, 84, 91, 239, 281, 283, 284, 285, 305, 317
Ashford, Emmett, 38, 40, 51, 53, 57, 118, 125
Ashford, Evelyn, 66, 67, 69, 265, 267
Associated Press, 25, 48, 78, 84, 92, 93, 96, 107, 171, 187, 202, 204, 233, 244, 284
Associated Press' Athlete of the Year, 25, 78, 202, 204
Association for Intercollegiate Athletes for Women (AIWA), 67, 198
Athletic Baseball Club - Jacksonville, FL, 11, 113
Atlanta Braves, 59, 61, 64, 65, 76, 78, 111, 119, 124, 132, 137, 145, 240, 292, 303
Atlanta Falcons, 69, 74, 83, 87, 89, 93, 95, 145, 214, 217, 218, 225, 230, 240, 241, 244, 292
Atlanta Glory, 79, 157
Atlanta Hawks, 61, 62, 92, 106, 150, 153, 158, 170, 182, 185, 194, 197, 309
Atlantic City Seagulls, 34, 253
Atlantic Coast Conference, 46, 50, 55, 58, 72, 102, 169, 179, 188, 195, 208
Attles, Al, 62, 163, 179
Auburn University, 55, 175
Augmon, Stacey, 75, 156
Augustus, Seimone, 96, 112, 163
Austin Peay State University, 48, 171
Austin, John, 48, 163
Austin, Tavon, 215, 309
Australian Open, 84, 281, 286, 306
Australian Open tennis, 57, 89, 283, 285
AutoZone Park, 94, 120, 308
Avant-Garde, Zaila, 104, 105, 107, 163
Avery, William, 84, 153, 157

B

Babbitt, Governor Bruce, 213, 305
Babilonia, Tai, 19, 264, 271
Bacharach Giants, 21, 22, 115, 134
Bailey, Pearl, 60, 89, 199, 287
Bailey, Robert, 306
Bailey, Stedman, 215, 309
Baker, Charles "Doc", 16, 206, 219
Baker, Dusty, 64, 77, 86, 95, 111, 125, 138
Baker, Gene, 60, 63, 125, 143

Bakken, Jill, 88, 271
Baldwin, James, 27, 45
Ball, Coolidge, 57, 163, 301
Ball, Robert "Pat", 24, 248
Ballard, Lula, 20, 23, 151, 163, 164, 196, 248, 283, 285
Baltimore Afro-American, 26, 116
Baltimore Black Sox, 20, 21, 23, 115, 116
Baltimore Black Sox Bloomer Girls, 20, 115
Baltimore Bullets, 35, 38, 48, 163, 164, 172
Baltimore Colts, 42, 46, 52, 62, 67, 101, 213, 225, 226, 235, 236, 241, 299
Baltimore Elite Giants, 116
Baltimore Lord Baltimores, 12, 114
Baltimore Orioles, 15, 51, 57, 73, 74, 92, 114, 120, 125, 143
Baltimore Ravens, 83, 87, 89, 97, 214, 217, 218, 219, 229, 232, 233, 236, 289, 307
Bankhead, Dan, 31, 32, 125, 127, 141
Bankhead, Sam, 46, 125
Banks, Ernie, 34, 43, 44, 45, 60, 63, 119, 125, 143
Banks, Tony, 83, 90, 219
Banks, Tyra, 79, 81
Banneker, Benjamin, 9
Barge, Burly, 38, 117, 298
Barkley, Charles, 72, 74, 156, 164
Barksdale, Don, 31, 32, 35, 36, 38, 164, 171, 185
Barnes, Adia, 108, 164, 192
Barnes, Pike, 12, 13, 260
Barnes, Rod, 76, 164
Barnes, Ronnie, 68, 219
Barnett, Dick, 46, 175
Barnett, Governor Ross, 48, 152, 299
Barney, Lem, 52, 64, 219
Baro, Albert "Speed", 38, 118
Baro, Bernardo, 20, 115
Barr, Roseanne, 75, 305
Barrett, Richard, 81, 209, 306
Barron, Allan P., 58, 162, 189
Barry, Brent, 80
Bartholomew, Joseph, 21, 248
Bartlett, Ray, 27, 207, 296
Baseball Fans and Communities Protection Act of 1997
    Curt Flood case, 131, 306
Baseball Writers' Association of America, 88, 97, 121, 127, 312, 313
Baseball Writers' Association of America (BBWAA), 33, 57, 101, 109, 137, 149, 293
Basie, Count, 20, 248
Basketball Africa League (BAL), 108, 159
Basketball Association of America (BAA), 30, 155, 297
Bass, Bill, 31, 211, 219
Bass, Tom
    The Bass Bit, 13, 15, 287, 316
Batavia Pirates, 46, 125
Batch, Charlie, 92, 157, 164, 219
Battey, Earl, 45, 126
Bauer, Alice, 34, 248
Baylor University, 51, 165, 245
Baylor, Don, 77, 86, 126
Baylor, Elgin, 44, 47, 164, 167
Bayou Classic, 75, 209
Beamon, Bob, 54, 76, 267, 276

321

Emancipation Index

Beard, Jariah "Bubba", 66, 249
Beavers, Louise, 19
Beckett Vintage Collector magazine, 111, 133
Beckwith, John, 23, 126
Belafonte, Harry, 45, 299
Belinelli, Marco, 99, 158, 171
Bell, Bobby, 50, 69, 212, 220, 300
Bell, Clarence "Puggy", 27, 161, 164
Bell, James "Cool Papa", 23, 27, 78, 126, 133, 141
Bell, Josh, 120, 126, 311
Belle, Albert, 78, 81, 126
Bennett, Kalin, 104, 164
Bennett, Shannie, 155
Berg, Patty, 34, 248
Bergen College of New Jersey, 31, 152
Berra, Yogi, 37, 117
Berry, Gwen, 103, 267, 311
Bertrand, Joe, 36, 164, 191
Bethune, Mary McLeod, 92
Bethune-Cookman College, 83, 249
Betsy Ross flag, 103, 231, 311
Betts, Mookie, 102, 120, 126, 311
Between the Acts & Bravo Cigarettes, 10, 289
Bias, Len, 72, 195
Biddle University, 206
Biden, President Joe, 43, 257
Big Ten Conference, 26, 31, 49, 102, 173, 206
Biles II on the Floor, 103, 267
Biles II on the Vault, 112, 267
Biles on the Balance Beam, 103, 267
Biles on the Floor, 98, 267
Biles on the Vault, 103, 267
Biles, Simone, 98, 103, 112, 267
Biletnikoff, Fred, 213, 304
Billups, Chauncey, 98, 165
Biney, Maame, 102, 267
Bing, Dave, 53, 165
Binns, Karl, 57, 165
Birmingham Americans, 62, 238
Birmingham Black Barons, 29, 32, 36, 116, 117, 138, 150
Birmingham Stallions, 69, 222
Birmingham Vulcans, 238
Birth of Black College Football, 206
Bishop, Michael, 83, 210, 223, 232, 234
Bivins, Dickie, 67, 268
Black Enterprise, 75, 178
Black Lives Matter, 97, 108, 121, 126, 159, 162, 311, 313, 316
Black Magic documentary, 94, 158, 308
Black Quarterbacks, 19, 20, 23, 24, 26, 29, 34, 35, 37, 40, 41, 43, 45, 49, 52, 54, 55, 56, 57, 59, 60, 62, 63, 64, 65, 66, 67, 68, 69, 70, 71, 72, 73, 74, 75, 76, 77, 78, 79, 81, 83, 85, 86, 87, 88, 89, 90, 91, 92, 93, 95, 96, 97, 101, 102, 104, 106, 206, 207, 208, 209, 210, 211, 212, 213, 214, 215, 219, 220, 221, 222, 223, 224, 225, 226, 227, 228, 229, 230, 231, 232, 233, 234, 235, 236, 237, 238, 239, 240, 242, 243, 244, 245, 246, 247, 294, 297, 299, 300, 301, 304, 305, 306, 307, 308, 309, 311, 317, 318
Black Sports magazine, 58, 162, 189
Black Sportswriters Hall of Fame
   Rob Parker, 293
Black, Anthony, 112, 159
Black, Joe, 37, 89, 117, 126, 134, 297

Blair, Paul, 72, 120
Blake, James, 282, 309
Blake, Jeff, 78, 79, 85, 90, 220
Blanda, George, 37, 243
Blanks, Sid, 44, 50, 208, 212, 220, 300
Bloomingdale Daily Gazette, 132
Blount, Mel, 65, 212, 220, 303
Blount, Tenny, 20, 115, 132
Blue, Vida, 58, 68, 126, 127, 130, 135
Bluitt, Ben, 62, 165
Blyleven, Bert, 59, 124
Boardways (or Boards) Baseball Club - Savannah, GA, 11, 113
Bob Lanier Community Assist Award, 88, 180, 189, 191
Boger, Jerome, 106, 216
Boger, Tra, 111, 220
Bogues, Tyrone "Muggsy", 72, 79, 165
Bolden, Blake, 98, 100, 107, 255
Bolden, Ed, 21, 115
Bolton, Rasir, 104, 154, 311
Bolton-Holifield, Ruthie, 82, 165
Bonds, Barry, 83, 88, 89, 91, 127
Booker, Cory, 52
Booth, Shenea, 88, 100, 268
Borden League, 30, 256
Borden, James (CHL), 14, 253
Bordentowns, 14, 114, 145
Boston Blades, 98, 255
Boston Braves, 34, 136, 297
Boston Celtics, 30, 31, 34, 43, 47, 48, 51, 59, 70, 84, 100, 118, 150, 155, 164, 165, 167, 168, 173, 179, 180, 190, 191, 297, 299, 306, 310
Boston College, 27, 48, 121, 163, 207, 296, 314
Boston Red Sox, 31, 34, 44, 47, 50, 52, 57, 63, 74, 92, 102, 106, 108, 118, 119, 120, 121, 126, 127, 129, 132, 133, 141, 145, 146, 147, 148, 149, 150, 190, 299, 304, 312
Boston Resolutes, 12, 114
Boston, Ralph, 54, 61, 265, 267, 268
Boswell, Sonny, 27, 155, 160, 165
Bowling Green (KY) State University, 36, 171
Bowman, Tommy, 51, 165
Boyd, Dennis "Oil Can", 119, 127, 304
Boyd, Willie James, 119, 127, 304
Boykins, Earl, 91, 165
Boys' Life magazine, 51, 138
Brackins, Charlie, 40, 220
Braddock, James J., 26, 204
Bradford, Charles "Mule", 18, 151
Bradley (IL) University, 37, 172
Bradshaw, Terry, 66, 146
Brady, Tom, 94, 101, 177, 221
Braithwaite, George, 58, 281, 287
Branch, Joe, 112, 159
Brand, Elton, 84, 153, 157
Branham III, George, 71, 77, 287
Braun, Carol Moseley, 15
Brazile, Donna, 9
Breakaway Rim, 66, 156, 170, 303
Brevard, Samarria, 99, 102, 287
Brewer, Chet, 26, 127
Brewer, Corey, 93, 153
Bridgeman, Junior, 107, 165

Bridges, Bill, 46, 175
Briggs Stadium, 38, 207
Brigham Young University, 104, 227, 311
Bright, Johnny, 92, 210, 220, 307
Briscoe, Marlin, 54, 57, 220, 221, 228
Brisco-Hooks, Valerie, 70, 268
Brisker, John, 59, 156, 302
Brissett, Jacoby, 101, 221
Britt, Kenny, 215, 309
Britton, Johnny, 36, 117
Brookins, Tommy, 160, 181
   Savoy Big Five founder, 22
Brooklyn Bay Parkways, 24, 206
Brooklyn Dodgers, 12, 23, 26, 31, 32, 33, 35, 36, 37, 38, 51, 72, 115, 117, 118, 121, 125, 128, 140, 141, 143, 144, 148, 208, 211, 227, 296, 297, 312
Brooklyn Excelsiors, 9, 113
Brooklyn Robins, 20, 147
Brooklyn Royal Giants, 21, 23, 24, 115, 232
Brooks, Aaron, 83, 210, 223, 232, 234
Brooks, Arthur B., 37, 287
Brooks, Nathan, 36, 199, 264
Brooks-Moon, Renal, 88, 127
Brotherhood of Sleeping Car Porters, 23, 116
Brown University, 19, 39, 61, 206, 211, 238, 303
Brown, Aaron, 15, 201
Brown, Antron, 97, 287
Brown, Bill, 30, 165, 168, 177
Brown, Claude, 50
Brown, David, 99, 268
Brown, Demetrius, 73, 209
Brown, Earl, 21, 115
Brown, Edward D. "Brown Dick", 9, 70, 260
Brown, Hillary, 155
Brown, Jaylen, 100, 165, 310
Brown, Jim, 43, 45, 48, 49, 50, 60, 79, 81, 208, 213, 221, 224, 240, 241
Brown, John, 211, 219, 238
Brown, John Edward, 30, 31, 207, 221
Brown, Kwame, 87, 166
Brown, Ray, 25, 136
Brown, Reneé, 82
Brown, Walter A., 30, 155, 297
Brown, Walter S., 12
Brown, Willard "Home Run", 31, 127, 146
Brown, Willie, 47, 221
Browne, Byron, 55, 119, 131, 301
Bryant, Antonio, 94, 221
Bryant, Bear, 56, 209, 301
Bryant, Charles, 40, 221, 234
Bryant, Kelvin, 69, 221
Bryant, Kobe, 82, 93, 110, 157, 166, 169, 242, 308
Buchanan, Buck, 48, 79, 221, 245
Buck Buchanan Award, 79, 221
Buck Lew's Traveling Five, 16, 155, 181
Buffalo Bills, 55, 57, 60, 80, 97, 221, 228, 233, 241, 245
Buffalo Bisons, 11, 43, 113, 130, 133
Buffalo Braves, 64, 182
Buffalo Enquirer, 132
Buffalo Sabres, 65, 66, 67, 105, 253, 257, 312
Bunch III, Lonnie G., 100, 107

Burke, Glenn, 64, 127
Burns, Tommy, 17, 199, 203
Burr, John, 30, 152, 183
Burrell, Scott, 77, 166
Burroughs, Edith, 66, 287
Burt, Thomas, 38, 117, 298
Burwell, Bryan, 293
Busch, Jr., August, 38, 147
Bush, President George, 76, 176
Bush, President George H. W., 305
Bush, Reggie, 96, 222
Butler, Octavia E., 112
Butler, Solomon W., 19, 206, 222
Butler, Tom, 15, 293
Byers, Dremiel, 88, 95, 287
Byfuglien, Dustin, 96, 255
Bynoe, Peter C.B., 74, 156
Byrd, Bill, 26, 148, 296

C

Cabañas Cuban baseball card set, 17, 114, 134, 142
Cadeau, Elliot, 110, 166
Cager, Willie, 50, 152, 300
Calgary Flames, 85, 256
Calhoun, Lee, 61, 265
Callathumpians Baseball Club - Tallahassee, FL, 11, 113
Calloway, Cab, 20, 248
Camp Sibert, Alabama, 28, 199, 296
Campanella, Roy, 26, 30, 32, 33, 35, 36, 37, 39, 40, 41, 57, 117, 118, 127, 128, 140, 144, 297, 301
Campanis, Al, 72, 120, 304
Campbell, Chris, 81, 200
Campbell, Earl, 67, 222
Campbell, Fred, 111, 266
Campbell, Milt, 41, 268
Campbell, Sarah, 77, 166
Canadian Football Hall of Fame, 87, 92, 235
Canady, Annice, 89, 210, 222
Canisius College (Buffalo, NY), 29, 184
Cannon Street YMCA All-Stars, 40, 118, 298
Canton (Ohio) Bulldogs, 19, 20, 206, 222, 242, 246
Capital City Track (Indianapolis), 14, 293
Carew, Rod, 60, 128
Carey, Mike, 94, 214, 222
Carlos, John, 54, 59, 265, 268, 270, 274, 277, 300
Carnegie, Herb, 32, 253, 255
Carnegie, Herbie & Ossie, 30, 253, 255, 256
Carney, Les, 45, 268
Carolina League, 35, 139
Carolina Panthers, 88, 96, 98, 106, 107, 214, 215, 222, 231, 236, 237, 307
Carr, Austin, 53, 57, 152, 166
Carr, Fletcher, 60, 288
Carter, Cris, 214
Carter, Michael, 89, 101, 222, 268
Carter, Michelle, 89, 101, 222, 268
Carter, Rubin "Hurricane", 78, 201
Carter, Vince, 101, 110, 166
Cartwright, Bill, 66, 156
Cash, Dave, 58, 119

Emancipation Index

Cash, Jr., James I., 51, 54, 166
Caste, 31
Castlin, Kristi, 101, 266
Catholic (District of Columbia) University, 38, 172
Catlett, Sid, 53, 152
CBS Sports, 57, 212, 223
Centenary (LA) College, 53, 182
Centers, Larry, 83, 90, 222, 243
Chaflin University, 31, 207, 221
Chaka, Maia, 107, 222
Chamberlain, Wilt, 42, 43, 44, 45, 46, 47, 49, 50, 53, 59, 61, 62, 155, 164, 167, 192, 300, 303
Chambers, Pat, 104, 154, 311
Champion, Cari, 103, 177, 310
Chaney, John, 73, 167
Chapman, Aroldis, 95, 100, 128
Chapman, Betty Irene, 35, 128
Chappell, Len, 59, 156, 302
Charles, Ezzard, 29, 36, 75, 179, 199, 200, 202
Charles, Tina, 111, 167
Charlotte Bobcats, 92, 96, 153, 158, 180
Charlotte Hornets, 72, 77, 84, 89, 99, 157, 165, 166, 178, 180, 181, 197
Charlotte Sting, 80, 82, 157, 188
Charlottetown West End Rangers (CHL), 16, 253
Chatman, Charles, 40, 118, 298
Chattanooga Baseball Club - Chattanooga, TN, 11, 113
Chautauqua Tennis Club of Philadelphia, 13, 281
Chavez, Tony, 27, 199, 205
Cheek, Donna Marie, 75, 288
Cheeks, Maurice, 72, 167
Cheesborough, Chandra, 66, 265
Cherry, Ron, 95, 210, 222
Chesney, Clyde, 55, 208
Cheyney State, 68, 85, 95, 153, 192, 193
Chicago American Giants, 18, 20, 22, 23, 24, 26, 28, 32, 36, 109, 115, 116, 121, 132, 134, 135, 141, 142, 143, 145, 146, 147, 232, 296
Chicago Bears, 21, 33, 37, 49, 66, 67, 71, 86, 93, 211, 214, 225, 231, 236, 237, 239, 240, 242, 243, 246, 265, 295
Chicago Black Hawks, 23, 211, 238
Chicago Blackhawks (NHL), 73, 82, 96, 253, 255
Chicago Brown Bombers, 26, 238
Chicago Bruins
    George Halas, 22, 27, 160, 181
Chicago Bruins (NBL), 27, 160
Chicago Bulls, 51, 62, 64, 76, 80, 91, 102, 173, 176, 190, 194, 196, 305, 306
Chicago Cardinals, 22, 24, 37, 160, 181, 211, 212, 219, 231, 232, 233, 234, 241, 244, 295
Chicago City Amateur Golf Tournament, 17, 248
Chicago Cougars, 59, 257
Chicago Cubs, 37, 39, 40, 41, 43, 45, 47, 58, 63, 72, 86, 118, 125, 126, 128, 129, 135, 136, 140, 146
Chicago Giants, 20, 133
Chicago Hottentots, 24, 232
Chicago Rockets, 31
Chicago State University, 63
Chicago Studebakers, 155
Chicago Tribune, 29, 211, 219, 238
Chicago White Sox, 12, 15, 35, 65, 77, 86, 114, 125, 130, 135, 138, 139, 143, 146, 149, 290, 295
Chicago White Stockings, 11, 147
Chief Wahoo, 107, 120, 121, 310, 312
Chiles, Jordan, 110, 111, 266, 268, 274
Chisholm, Shirley, 91
Chorn, Jerry, 14, 260
Christie's auction house, 81, 133
Chunichi Dragons, 47, 130, 140
Churchill Downs, 92, 262
CIAA, 30, 52, 65, 86, 110, 152, 172, 173, 183, 184
Cincinnati Bearcats, 44, 48, 152, 189, 299
Cincinnati Bengals, 78, 79, 215, 220, 309
Cincinnati Browns, 12, 114
Cincinnati Reds, 14, 18, 51, 57, 95, 98, 104, 114, 121, 125, 129, 134, 138, 143, 312
Cincinnati Royals, 43, 51, 82, 171, 196, 197
Cincinnati Tigers, 24, 26, 142, 232
Civil Rights Game, 94, 120, 308
Civil Rights Restoration Act, 73, 304
Claiborne, Claudius B., 51, 168, 300
Claiborne, Jerry, 56, 209, 301
Clarendon, Layshia, 98, 168
Clark Atlanta University, 34, 170
Clark, Darius, 112, 288
Clark, Hazel, 86, 269
Clark, Jearl Miles, 86, 269
Clark, Joetta, 86, 110, 269, 270
Clark, Septima, 14
Clark, Tony, 98, 128
Clarke, John Henrik, 25
Claxton, Jimmy, 19, 32, 128, 143
Clayton, Alonzo, 13, 14, 259, 260
Clayton, Zach, 30, 33, 36, 62, 128, 160, 161, 165, 168, 177, 199, 202, 203
Clearview Golf Course, 30, 248, 250
Cleaver, Eldridge, 57
Clemente, Roberto, 44, 46, 51, 58, 60, 119, 128, 129, 136
Clemons, Jim, 66, 156
Clemons, Michael "Pinball", 91, 222
Clemson University, 55, 185
Cleveland Browns, 29, 31, 34, 38, 43, 47, 48, 49, 65, 76, 207, 211, 212, 215, 221, 224, 226, 234, 235, 238, 246, 292, 297, 303, 309
Cleveland Buckeyes, 29, 31, 116, 117, 297
Cleveland Cavaliers, 58, 73, 75, 82, 169, 171, 179, 180
Cleveland Indians, 20, 23, 31, 32, 33, 36, 37, 39, 43, 47, 50, 51, 52, 63, 68, 78, 94, 107, 115, 117, 118, 120, 121, 126, 130, 133, 135, 139, 141, 142, 143, 144, 147, 168, 298, 308, 310, 312
Cleveland Pipers, 45, 46, 175, 183
Cleveland Rockers, 80, 157
Cleveland State University, 52, 183
Clifton Trophy, Nat "Sweetwater", 110, 168, 169, 171, 179, 181, 188
Clifton, Nat "Sweetwater", 32, 34, 160, 161
Clines, Gene, 58, 119
Clipper Baseball Club - Jacksonville, FL, 11, 113
Cloud, Natasha, 105, 168
Coachman, Alice, 32, 63, 264, 269, 275
Coage, Allen J., 64, 265, 288
Coakley, Dexter, 79, 221
Coates, Ta-Nehisi, 9, 10, 15, 72
Cobb, Ty, 17, 114, 142

324

Cochran, Jr., Johnnie, 90, 214, 238
Cofield, Bill, 64, 168
Coimbre, Francisco "Pancho", 28, 129
Cokes, Curtis, 51, 202, 288
Colbert, Vince, 51, 168
Coleman, Derrick, 97, 215, 222
Coleman, Len, 81, 120, 145
Coleman, Mark, 80, 200, 293
Coleman, Ron, 54, 265
Coleman, Vince, 71, 72, 129
College All-Star football game, 29, 198, 207, 246, 318
College Football Hall of Fame, 35, 207, 241
Collier, Reggie, 69, 70, 71, 222, 223
Collins, Jason, 99, 168
Collins, Luci, 67, 266, 269
Colorado Buffaloes, 42, 107, 181, 229
Colorado Rockies, 77, 126
Colorado Xplosion, 79, 157
Colored Basketball World Championship, 17, 151, 176
Colored Branch of the Young Women's Christian Association, 19
Colored Hockey League of the Maritimes (CHL), 14, 16, 253, 317
Colored Men's National Convention, 10, 113
Colored World Series, 21, 22, 115, 136
Colston, Raleigh, 9, 260
Columbia Giants, 15, 114
Columbia University, 24, 53, 174, 195
Columbus Quest, 79, 80, 157, 182
Comiskey Park, 24, 28, 44, 58, 129, 132, 133
Comiskey, Charlie, 15, 114
Commonwealth Big Five, 21, 155
Cone, James, 65
Confederacy
    Confederate, 96, 215, 309
Confederate
    Confederacy, 81, 104, 106, 109, 121, 209, 228, 293, 306, 311, 313
Congressional Gold Medal, 26, 43, 90, 145, 192, 257
Continental Basketball Association, 30, 75, 84, 165, 168, 177, 193, 195
Converse, 105, 108, 154, 159, 168, 169
Conyers Jr., Representative John
    Curt Flood case, 131, 306
Coody, Charles, 58, 249
Cook, Jared, 215, 309
Cooper Trophy, Chuck, 110, 168, 169, 171, 179, 181, 188
Cooper, Chuck, 30, 34, 39, 155, 163, 168, 170, 181
Cooper, Cynthia, 70, 82, 84, 153, 169
Cooper, Elzie, 24
Cooper, Fred "Cannonball", 33, 223
Cooper. Cecil, 92, 93, 120, 129, 148
Copeland, Hollis, 66, 156
Corbitt, Theodore "Ted", 37, 39, 82, 98, 264, 266, 269
Cornell University, 15, 25, 62, 125, 165, 207, 229
Correia, Maritza, 91, 269
Cosell, Howard, 53, 55, 119, 131, 300, 301
Cotton Bowl, 27, 32, 50, 73, 207, 208, 209, 228, 244, 296
Cotton States League, 38, 40, 117, 118, 297, 298
Coulibaly, Bilal, 112, 159
Craig, Roger, 71, 223
Craighead, Henry, 38, 117, 298
Crawford, John, 5, 215, 309

Crawley, Sylvia, 83, 169
Creighton University, 39, 173
Crisis magazine, 20, 26, 133, 147
Crispus Attucks Tigers, 108, 154, 169
Croom, Sylvester, 91, 210, 223
Crosley Field, 23, 115
Cross, Irv, 57, 62, 95, 212, 223
Crowe, Ray, 39, 153, 169, 309
CTE (chronic traumatic encephalopathy, 96, 108, 215, 216, 313
Cuban Giants, 11, 12, 14, 15, 113, 114, 145, 255, 295
Cuban League, 10, 15, 113, 114
Cuban Stars, 16, 18, 19, 20, 21, 23, 114, 115, 128, 129, 132, 134, 138, 140
Cuban X-Giants, 15, 16, 114, 132, 255
Cuban, Mark, 102, 182
Culpepper, Daunte, 83, 86, 88, 210, 214, 217, 223, 224, 227, 232, 234
Cumberland, Duke, 155
Cummings, Bill, 25, 294
Cummings, Terry, 68, 69, 153, 156
Cunningham, Randall, 71, 76, 83, 106, 223
Cunningham, Sam, 56, 209, 223, 224, 230, 301
Curry, Stephen, 100, 102, 110, 166, 169, 310
Curt Flood Act of 1998, 82, 131, 306
Curt Flood Rule, 61, 131, 303
Custis, Bernie, 35, 212, 224

D

Dailey, Quintin, 68, 69, 153, 156
Daisy Cutter Baseball Club - Fernandina, FL, 11, 113
Dallas Chaparrals, 59, 156, 302
Dallas Cowboys, 58, 66, 71, 72, 78, 83, 93, 101, 145, 215, 223, 228, 231, 239, 240, 241, 265, 272, 292, 302, 305, 310
Dallas Eagles, 36, 135
Dallas Mavericks, 68, 102, 162, 182
Dallas Texans, 44, 48, 221, 228
Dallas Wings, 98, 102, 108, 159, 170, 180, 186, 197
Dancing with the Stars, 93, 108, 191, 242
Danenberg, Sophia, 92, 288
Daniels, Bennie, 40, 118, 298
Daniels, Brehanna, 102, 288
Daniels, Cheryl, 79, 288
Daniels, Mel, 53, 58, 59, 169
Danley, Kerwin, 107, 129
Danoff, Bettye, 34, 248
Danville (VA) Leafs, 35, 139
Dartmouth Jubilees (CHL), 16, 253
Dartmouth Victorias (CHL), 16, 253
Davenport, Najeh, 106, 216, 312
Davenport, Willie, 67, 266
Davidson (NC) College, 52, 182
Davis, Charles Lawrence "Charlie", 58, 169
Davis, Clarence, 56, 223, 224, 230
Davis, Ernie, 45, 47, 48, 208, 212, 224, 299
Davis, Harrison, 56, 209
Davis, John Henry, 32, 35, 264, 269
Davis, Lorenzo "Piper", 34, 129
Davis, Mo'ne, 98, 129
Davis, Sergeant Otis, 45, 269
Davis, Shani, 87, 88, 92, 102, 268, 269, 271

Emancipation Index

Davis, Terrell, 83, 213, 224
Davis, Tiana, 107, 288
Davis, Willie, 26
Dawes, Dominique, 76, 79, 269, 275
Dawkins, Darryl, 62, 66, 67, 156, 170, 172, 182, 197, 303
Dawson, Andre, 72, 104, 129, 131
Dawson, Len, 52, 60, 234, 247
Day, Herschel "Rip", 25, 211, 238
Day, Leon, 30, 116, 129
Day, Lorraine, 40, 138
Dayton (Ohio) University, 29, 179
Daytona International Speedway, 102, 288
Dear Basketball
   Kobe Bryant, Oscar, 103, 166
DeBois, W.E.B., 20
DeFrantz, Anita, 76, 266
DeJernett, Dave, 25, 161, 170
del Plata, Mar, 91, 290
Delaware State College, 25, 207, 229
DeMatha High School (District of Columbia), 48, 163
Demeter, Don, 52, 130
Demic, Larry, 66, 156
Denver Broncos, 49, 52, 54, 73, 83, 86, 91, 104, 110, 111, 198, 208, 213, 215, 218, 219, 220, 224, 228, 242, 246, 287, 289, 294, 311
Denver Nuggets, 62, 64, 65, 66, 74, 91, 156, 165, 173, 194, 294
Denver Rockets, 33, 52, 56, 57, 155, 161, 173, 175, 198, 208
Derricotte, Gene, 29, 224
Detroit Lions, 32, 33, 34, 38, 52, 74, 75, 81, 207, 213, 219, 225, 227, 233, 237, 240, 241, 244, 245, 306
Detroit Loves, 62, 281
Detroit Panthers, 92, 157, 164, 219
Detroit Pistons, 42, 48, 53, 58, 59, 61, 66, 74, 84, 89, 91, 94, 112, 157, 159, 165, 168, 174, 176, 178, 180, 181, 187, 191, 193, 194, 195
Detroit Shock, 84, 193
Detroit Stars, 20, 40, 118, 132, 134, 298
Detroit Tigers, 17, 31, 38, 65, 114, 115, 120, 124, 127, 137, 142, 295, 304
Detroit Vagabond Kings, 33, 161
Dettweiler, Helen, 34, 248
Dexter Park, 23, 115
DeZonie, Hank, 34, 170
Diamond, Lydia R., 103, 146
DiAngelo, Robin, 82, 95, 96, 97, 101, 104
Diaw, Boris, 99, 158, 171
Dibut, Pedro, 129
Dickerson, Chris, 57, 288
Dickerson, Darnell, 73, 209
Dickey, Eldridge, 54, 224, 301
Dickinson, Parnell, 64, 95, 224, 225
Diggins, Skylar, 99, 102, 170
Diggs, Talitha, 110, 269, 270
Dightman, Myrtis, 51, 82, 90, 280, 288
Dillard, Harrison, 33, 61, 265, 270
Dillard, Harrison, 32
DiMaggio, Joe, 57, 301
Dime magazine, 87, 177
Dione, Abby, 111, 266
Disabilities
   Blindness, 43, 99, 119, 253, 257, 268
   Deafness, 77, 97, 142, 215, 222
   Prosthesis, 86, 276
Dismond, Henry Binga, 19, 264
Distinguished Flying Cross, 26, 192
Dixon, George, 13, 199, 202
Dixon, Herbert "Rap", 23, 116
Dixon, Phil S., 72, 75, 120
Dixon, Sadie, 35, 288
Doby, Larry, 30, 31, 32, 33, 35, 37, 39, 47, 65, 116, 117, 118, 130, 140, 144
Dodson, Nell, 26, 32
Dolly Vardens, 11, 113
Don't Think of an Elephant!, 90
Donaldson, Ray, 67, 213
Dorados de Chihuahua, 36, 149
Dorrington, Arthur, 34, 253
Dorsett, Tony, 64, 209, 224
Dorsey, Dr. Tekemia, 103, 266
Douglas, Gabrielle, 97, 270
Douglas, Robert Lewis, 21, 59, 155, 161, 170
Douglass, Frederick, 10, 11, 33, 39, 113, 238
Downing, Al, 49, 52, 61, 124, 130, 303
Dowsing-Bell Plaza
   Frank Dowsing, Jr., 56, 102, 208, 210
   Robert Bell, 56, 102, 208, 210
Dr. Martin Luther King Jr. Center, 57, 301
Drake University, 92, 210, 220, 307
DREAM Series, 101, 120
Dreams from My Father, 79
Dreke, Valentine, 20, 115
Drew, Howard Porter, 18, 264, 270
Drew, Scott, 108, 154, 313
Drexler, Clyde, 69, 170
Driesell, Lefty, 55, 72, 188, 195
Drummond, Al, 57, 170
Du Bois, W.E.B., 15, 17, 69, 248
Dublin, Chip, 53, 170
Duckett, Alfred, 143, 144, 302
Duerson, David, 96, 215
Duffy, Bill, 112, 159
Duke University, 51, 59, 64, 78, 84, 153, 157, 168, 188, 209, 274, 300
Duke University Medical School, 59, 152, 274
Dumas, Charles, 41, 270
Dunbar Poets, Baltimore, MD, 72, 165, 181, 197
Duncan, Frank, Sr., and Frank, Jr.,, 28, 75, 116, 130, 134
Duncan, Kimberlyn, 98, 270
Duncan, Tim, 99, 158, 171
Dungy, Tony, 65, 86, 90, 93, 94, 95, 214, 223, 224, 225, 227, 232, 242, 243, 303
Dunham, Ann, 45, 299
Dunn, Mike, 64, 209
Dunn, Warrick, 95, 225
Dunovant, Leonard, 38, 117, 298
Durant, Kevin, 93, 171
Durham, Dianne, 69, 266, 270
Durocher, Leo, 40, 138
Dymond, Gloria "Lovie", 32, 130, 150
Dyson, Michael Eric, 199

E

Early, Gerald, 113
East Carolina University, 51, 78, 88, 168, 220, 225
East Tennessee State, 49
East Tennessee State University, 198
Eastern Amateur (Hockey) League, 34, 253
Eastern Colored League, 18, 21, 22, 23, 115, 138, 147, 150
Eastern Golf Association, 26, 248
Eastern League, 11, 40, 113, 146, 155
East-West All-Star, 2, 24, 25, 26, 27, 28, 116, 129, 132, 136, 142, 146
Ebbets Field, 23, 33, 115, 117, 144
Ebony Anglers, 107, 288
Ebony magazine, 49, 61, 107, 130, 165, 278, 300, 303
Eclipse Baseball Club - Memphis, TN, 11, 113
Eddie G. Robinson Memorial Stadium, 69, 209, 239
Edmonton Oilers, 68, 70, 73, 253, 255
Edwards, Dr. Harry, 52, 265, 270, 300
Edwards, Herman, 90, 214, 224, 225
Edwards, Teresa, 80, 153
Egan, John, 47, 152, 299
Einstein, Albert, 66, 85
Elder, Lee, 58, 61, 63, 66, 248, 249, 250, 295
Elizabeth City State University, 55, 244
Ellington, Duke, 20, 248
Elliott, Sean, 85, 171
Ellis, Crystal, 36, 171
Ellis, Dale, 78, 81, 171
Ellis, Dock, 58, 61, 119, 126, 130, 303
Ellis, L. M., 48
Ellis, Larry, 57, 265
Ellison, Ralph, 37
Embry Trophy, Wayne, 110, 168, 169, 171, 179, 181, 188
Embry, Wayne, 43, 59, 75, 171
Empire State League, 72, 120
ERA
    Earned Run Average, 54, 71, 119, 132, 133, 146, 301
Erskine, Carl, 37, 41, 128
Ervin, Anthony, 86, 270
Erving, Julius "Dr. J.", 62, 63, 64, 68, 72, 171, 173, 182
ESPN, 80, 82, 93, 94, 96, 99, 103, 104, 105, 106, 107, 111, 112, 121, 122, 158, 163, 166, 177, 186, 205, 210, 214, 215, 234, 242, 305, 307, 308, 309, 310, 312, 314, 318
ESPN The Magazine, 82, 166, 242
Estrada, Oscar, 21, 131
Eureka Baseball Club - Memphis, TN, 11, 113
Evans, Lee, 54, 265, 270, 277
Evans, Vince, 66, 67, 72, 225, 246
Evers, Medgar, 5, 47, 118, 150, 190, 299
Ewell, Richard, 59, 265, 271
Ewing, Patrick, 70, 172, 304

F

Fagan, Ryan, 109, 313
Fairbanks, Mabel, 19, 51, 59, 81, 264, 265, 271, 278
Family 4 Life, 112
Farmer, Jr., James L., 59
Farmer, Walter M., 20, 115, 132
Farnham Pirates, 46, 125
Farr, Mel, 52, 225
Farrakhan, Louis, 306
Favre, Brett, 306
FedEx, 106, 215, 216, 311
Félix, Allyson, 95, 100, 102, 109, 271, 310
Felix, Ray, 38, 172
Feller, Bob, 30, 47, 129, 144
Felton, Raymond, 92, 153
Fenway Park, 25, 106, 121, 136, 312
Fidrych, Mark "The Bird", 120, 127, 304
Field of Vision - Concerned Student 1950, 99
Fielder, Cecil, 93, 131
Fielder, Prince, 93, 131
Fight of the Century, 17, 199, 203
Fila
    Nikki Delta, 84, 182
Finch, Atticus, 21
Finley, Charlie, 61, 62, 119, 126, 148, 278
Fitch, Harrison "Honey", 25, 172, 296
Fitzgerald, Ella, 19, 20, 248
Fitzgerald-Mosley, Benita, 69, 266, 271
Fitzhugh, Everett, 106, 255
Flaherty, Jack, 120, 126, 311
Fleming, Ed, 39, 172, 188, 192
Fleming, Thomas A.
    National Teacher of the Year, 76
Flood v. Kuhn, 59, 119, 131, 302
Flood, Brian, 72, 120
Flood, Curt, 55, 59, 72, 104, 119, 120, 129, 131, 301, 302
Florida A&M Rattlers, 39, 48, 56, 197, 208, 225, 226
Florida Blazers, 62, 212, 238
Florida Marlins, 82, 136
Florida Panthers, 87, 257
Florida State University, 51, 174
Flournoy, Harry, 50, 152, 300
Flowers, Tiger, 22, 199, 202
Flowers, Vonetta, 88, 271
Floyd, Eric, 68, 153
Follis, Charles W. "Black Cyclone from Wooster", 16, 206, 225
Forbes Field, 27, 116
Forbes magazine, 89, 99, 157, 178, 180
Ford, President Gerald, 63, 265, 275
Ford, T J., 89, 172
Ford, Whitey, 37, 117
Foreman, George, 60, 62, 78, 128, 199, 202, 203, 287
Fort Smith Northside High School, 55, 180
Fort Wayne Pistons, 34, 39, 155, 163, 168, 181, 195
Foster, Bob, 71, 75, 200, 205
Foster, Hank, 37, 172
Foster, Maxie, 56, 265
Foster, Rube, vii, 15, 16, 18, 20, 114, 115, 132
Foster, Willie, 20, 22, 24, 97, 115, 132, 145, 158, 184, 185
Fosty, George and Darril, 16, 253, 256, 317
Fountainé, Lil, 23, 151, 163, 196, 285
Fowler, John W. "Bud", 10, 11, 14, 113, 114, 132, 133
Fox Hunter Baseball Club - Macon, GA, 11, 113
Foxworth, Bruce, 64, 281
Francis, Jacob, 11, 113
Franklin, Aretha, 43
Frascatore, James, 282, 309
Frazier, E. Franklin, 42

Emancipation Index

Frazier, Joe, 53, 57, 58, 60, 63, 75, 89, 199, 200, 201, 202, 287, 300
    Smokin' Joe & the Knockouts, 57, 202
Frazier, Walt, 59, 61, 172
Frazier-Lyde, Jacqueline, 87, 200, 201, 202
Free, Lloyd "World", 67, 170, 172, 303
Freeman, Donnie, 59, 156, 302
Freeman, Gary, 83, 249
Freeman, Harold, 38, 172
Freeman, Josh, 95, 101, 225
Freeman, Ron, 265, 270, 277
Freihofer, William, 16, 114
French Open, 41, 88, 102, 284, 285, 286, 310
French, Sande, 77, 91, 281, 282, 283, 307
Fresno (CA) State College, 38, 147
FROGS, 18, 188
Fuhr, Grant, 68, 70, 73, 78, 81, 85, 89, 95, 253, 255, 256
Full Circle Everest climbing team, 111, 266
Fultons Baseball Club - Charleston, SC, 11, 113

G

Gabrielson, Len, 55, 132
Gadley, Jeff, 67, 266
Gaines, Clarence "Big House", 52, 64, 110, 172, 173, 184
Gaines, Jerry, 52, 265
Gaither, Jake, 48, 208, 225
Galimore, DaVanche "Ron", 67, 265
Galimore, Willie, 67, 265
Galloway, William Hipple "Hippo", 15, 255
Game of Change, 48, 152, 299
Gans, Joe, 15, 75, 199, 200, 202
García, Dave, 63, 139
Garden Lilies Baseball Club - Palatka, FL, 12, 113
Gardner, Randy, 19, 264, 271
Garoppolo, Jimmy, 221
Garrard, David, 88, 91, 225, 226, 232
Garrett, Bill, 31, 173
Garrison, Zina, 73, 283
Gaston, Cito, 74, 76, 132
Gates, William "Pop", 27, 33, 74, 155, 161, 173
Gateway Boxing Club, 57, 203
Gatewood, Bill, 20, 132
Gauff, Coco, 104, 284
Gautt, Prentice, 41, 92, 210, 226, 307
Gay, William, 215, 309
Gaylord High School (Michigan), 62, 167, 303
Geary, Joe W., 59, 156, 302
Gentlemen's Agreement, 114, 295
George Gervin GameAbove Center, 110, 173
George, Devean, 84, 173
George, Eddie, 85, 226
George, Phyllis, 62, 212, 223
Georgetown University, 15, 70, 79, 110, 177, 194, 264, 304
Georgia Institute of Technology, 42, 56, 57, 71, 165, 184, 207, 227, 234, 298
Germantown Hornets, 23, 151, 163, 164, 196, 283, 285
Gervin, George "Ice Man", 64, 65, 173
Gibson, Aaron, 85, 226
Gibson, Althea, 20, 31, 33, 35, 41, 42, 43, 44, 45, 48, 58, 67, 81, 87, 98, 160, 248, 266, 276, 281, 283, 284, 297, 317
Gibson, Bob, 39, 50, 52, 54, 55, 119, 132, 146, 173, 301

Gibson, Greg, 69, 266, 288
Gibson, Josh, 78, 81, 91, 111, 126, 133, 141, 296
Gilchrist, Carlton "Cookie", 37, 47, 50, 212, 226, 237, 300
Gildea, Bill, 141, 302
Gilliam, Joe, 59, 60, 62, 226
Gilliam, Junior, 37, 39, 44, 117, 118, 133, 297
Gillom, Horace, 31, 38, 226
Gilmore, Artis, 64, 66, 68, 71, 173
Ginóbili, Manu, 99, 158, 171
Giovanni, Nikki, 28, 99
Giudicelli, Bernard, 102, 286, 310
Givens, Chris, 215, 309
Givens, Hoyt, 33, 226, 239
Glade, Fred, 15, 132
Glenn, Mike, 66, 156
Glover, Rich, 58, 59, 209, 226
Godfrey, George "Old Chocolate", 11, 199, 202
Gold and Glory Sweepstakes, 22, 294
Gold Glove Winners, 43, 44, 45, 46, 48, 49, 50, 54, 64, 71, 72, 83, 102, 124, 125, 126, 132, 134, 135, 138, 139, 140, 142, 145, 147, 148, 149, 299
Gold Medals, 15, 17, 19, 22, 24, 25, 32, 36, 45, 47, 48, 51, 54, 60, 63, 64, 69, 73, 75, 76, 79, 80, 86, 88, 89, 91, 92, 94, 97, 100, 101, 102, 105, 108, 109, 110, 174, 175, 183, 187, 191, 192, 199, 200, 201, 204, 205, 256, 264, 265, 266, 268, 269, 271, 272, 273, 274, 275, 276, 277, 278, 287, 290, 291, 293, 300
Goldberg, Supreme Court Justice Arthur
    Curt Flood case, 59, 131
Golden Glove Boxing, 57, 203
Golden State Warriors, 82, 100, 101, 102, 107, 110, 158, 166, 169, 174, 195, 197, 310, 311
Golf World magazine, 70, 250, 304
Gómez, Rubén, 39, 118
Goode, Mal, 46
Goodell, Roger, 99, 215, 239, 309
Gooden, Dwight, 70, 71, 133
Goodson, Adrienne, 80, 153
Goodwin, Lonnie, 115
Gordon, Ben, 91, 173
Gordy, Berry, 77, 260
Gorman, Amanda, 108, 289
Gourdine, Simon Peter, 61, 173
GQ magazine, 102, 231
    Citizen of the Year, 102, 231
Graham, Bonnie, 41, 152, 298
Graham, Dirk, 73, 75, 82, 253, 255
Graham, Otto, 29, 207, 211, 246, 297
Grambling State University, 28, 31, 33, 47, 48, 54, 55, 62, 63, 65, 207, 212, 221, 228, 238, 239, 246, 247
Grant, Charlie
    Chief Tokohama, 15
Grant, Dr. George, 14
Grant, Frank, 11, 113, 133
Grant, Mudcat, 43, 50, 133, 298
Graves, Denique, 80, 173
Graves, Earl, 75, 178
Gray, Mel, 81, 226
Gray, Quinn, 91, 225, 226, 232
Greb, Harry, 22, 199, 202
Green Bay Packers, 34, 40, 52, 55, 67, 83, 213, 215, 219, 220, 225, 231, 233, 238, 306, 310

Index

Green, Darrell, 86, 226
Green, Dennis, 78, 86, 214, 223, 224, 227, 232, 235
Green, Draymond, 100, 101, 104, 174, 311
Green, Jalen Romande, 105, 108, 174
Green, Pumpsie, 44, 92, 118, 120, 133
Green, Tina Sloan, 56
Green, Walter
    Savoy Colts, 23, 151, 196, 285
Green, Willie, 20, 133
Greenberg, Mike, 112, 122, 314
Greene, Charlie, 54, 271, 272, 277
Greene, Maurice, 83, 271
Greenlee Park, 24, 116, 133
Greenlee, Gus, 24, 116, 133
Greenway, Jordan, 103, 256
Greer, Hal, 40, 174
Greer, Thom, 293
Gregg, Eric, 73, 134
Gregory, Ann, 41, 249, 250
Gregory, Eugene M., 14, 114
Gregory, Jim, 68, 227
Gregory, Jr., George, 24, 174
Grey Cup, 91, 222
Grier, Bobby, 42, 207, 227, 298
Grier, Claude "Red", 22, 134
Grier, Johnny, 73, 213, 227
Grier, Mike, 111, 256
Griffey, Ken, Sr., and Ken, Jr.,, 28, 75, 76, 116, 130, 134
Griffin III, Robert, 97, 215, 217, 227, 246, 309
Griffin, Archie, 63, 227
Griffin, Len, 290, 292
Griffin, Marvin
    Georgia Governor, 42, 207, 227, 298
Griffith Stadium, 24, 116
Griffith, Calvin, 46, 299, 312
Griffith, Yolanda, 80, 82, 84, 174, 176, 197
Griner, Brittney, 98, 174
Gromek, Steve, 32, 117
Groomes, Melvin, 32, 227, 233
Gross, Milton, 141, 302
Gruden, Jon, 99, 106, 215, 223, 239, 309, 310
Guaranteed Field, 109, 121
Guedes, Roger, 64, 281
Guerra, Marcelino, 20, 115
Guideposts magazine, 61, 124
Guinier, Lani, 77
Guinness Book of World Records, 36, 104, 105, 107, 160, 163, 183
Gumbel, Bryant, 92, 214, 289
Gumbel, Greg, 87, 214, 289
Gunther, Madison, 33, 248, 297
Guthridge, Amis
    White Citizens' Council, 48, 124, 299
Gwynn, Jr., Tony, 95, 128

H

Hackett, Wilbur, 53, 236
Hadley, Charles, 11, 199, 202
Hagge, Marlene, 34, 248
Hagler, Marvelous Marvin, 68, 202
Halas, George "Papa Bear", 20, 21, 211, 238, 239

Haley, Cecil, 27, 134, 296
Halifax Diamonds (CHL), 16, 253
Halifax Eurekas (CHL), 16, 105, 253, 254
Halifax Stanleys (CHL), 14, 16, 253
Hall, Jaren, 104, 227, 311
Hall, Lenny, 51, 174
Hambletonian, 87, 261
Hamer, Fannie Lou, 75
Hamilton Tiger-Cats, 35, 212, 224
Hamilton, Anthony, 12, 13, 14, 260
Hamilton, Billy, 98, 134
Hamilton, Leonard, 72, 174, 209
Hamilton, Lewis, 93, 110, 289
Hamilton, Richard, 84, 96, 157, 158, 309
Hamilton, Scott, 19, 264, 271
Hammond (IN) Pros, 20, 21, 240, 246
Hammond's Plains Mossbacks (CHL), 16, 253
Hampton University, 19, 64, 110, 173, 184, 206, 242, 281
Hankyu Braves, 36, 117
Haraway, Al, 38, 117, 298
Harding, Reggie, 48, 62, 174, 182
Harkness, Jerry, 48, 152, 299
Harlem Clowns, 51, 202, 288
Harlem Globetrotters, 22, 24, 27, 28, 36, 39, 43, 45, 70, 79, 84, 88,
    118, 155, 160, 161, 163, 165, 167, 198, 232, 284, 317
Harper's Weekly, 14, 206, 232
Harris, Bernadine, 18, 151
Harris, Elmore "Pepper", 31, 211, 227
Harris, Franco, 63, 227
Harris, George
    Judo, 49, 264, 271, 289
Harris, Henry, 55, 175
Harris, Homer, 26, 206
Harris, James, 55, 57, 60, 63, 221, 228
Harris, Lusia "Lucy", 62, 65, 76, 84, 157, 175, 184
Harris, Major, 73, 209
Harris, Mary, 18, 151
Harrisburg Giants, 21, 150
Harrison, Alvin & Calvin, 86, 271
Harrison, JuVaughn, 103, 109, 272
Harrison, President Benjamin, 13, 114
Hart, Frank "The Negro Wonder", 10, 289
Hart, Major Aloysius, 18, 151
Hartford Whalers, 70, 257
Harvard University, 13, 21, 115, 206, 232, 316
Harvey, Ken, 89, 134
Harville-Lebron, Melissa, 102, 289
Haskins, Clem, 47, 51, 152, 175, 195
Hasty, James, 86, 228
Hatcher, Ron, 46, 212, 228, 235
Havana Reds, 17, 114, 142
Havana Stars, 16, 114
Hawkins, Abe, 9, 260
Hawkins, Andrew, 215, 309
Hawkins, Connie, 46, 53, 175
Hawkins, Robert, 22, 248, 295
Hayden, Kristen, 109, 289
Hayes, Bullet Bob, 58, 228, 265, 272, 302
Hayes, Elvin, 51, 152, 175, 195
Haynes, Abner, 42, 44, 228, 232
Haynes, Marques, 82, 160, 175

Emancipation Index

Haywood, Spencer, 56, 57, 156, 175, 265, 302
Hazleton (PA) Hawks, 40, 155
Hazleton (PA) Mountaineers, 30, 165, 168, 177
HBCUs, 42, 46, 52, 54, 80, 83, 86, 107, 110, 111, 168, 172, 173, 176, 184, 210, 212, 214, 222, 249
Head, Dena, 81, 176
Heartley, Al, 52, 176, 180
Hedspath, Woody, 16, 289
Heinsohn, Tom, 60, 190
Heinsohn, Tommy, 49, 155, 179, 186, 191
Heisman Trophy, 45, 47, 63, 70, 74, 75, 77, 78, 81, 208, 219, 224, 227, 245, 246, 294
Heldman, John, 25, 172, 296
Hemans, Tom, 40, 155
Henderson, Edwin B., 17, 36, 151, 176
Henderson, Erskine, 11, 259, 260
Henderson, Philip, 111, 266
Henderson, Rickey, 67, 68, 69, 85, 134
Henderson, Scoot, 112, 159
Hendricks, Taylor, 112, 159
Hendrix, Jimi, 28
Henriquez de Zubiera, Constantin, 15, 264
Henry, Kevin, 106, 216, 312
Henson Base Ball Club of Jamaica, 9, 113
Henson, Harold, 33, 272, 289
Henson, Matthew, 17, 289
Hernández, Chico, 28, 134
Hernández, Jackie, 58, 119
Hernandez, Keith, 66, 146
Herrera, Mike, 20, 115
Herzog, Whitey, 119, 304
Heyer, Heather, 102, 310
Hicks, Helen, 34, 248
Hicks, Willie, 15, 260
Higgins, Robert, 11, 113, 133
Hill, Bobby Joe, 50, 152, 300
Hill, Cleo, 30, 46, 152, 155, 176, 183, 299
Hill, Darryl Andre, 46, 208
Hill, Grant, 87, 157
Hill, Kylin, 104, 228, 313
Hill, Michael, 94, 120
Hill, Opal, 34, 248
Hill, Pete, 17, 20, 114, 134, 142
Hill, Stanley, 41, 152, 298
Hill, Talmadge, 30, 152, 183
Hill, Tyreek, 104, 215, 310
Hilldale Club, 21, 22, 115, 136, 150
Hilliard, Wendy, 66, 265, 272
Hines, Jim, 54, 272
hitler, adolf, 96, 104, 121, 215, 309, 312, 316
hitler, adolph, 26, 80, 204, 305
Hobson, Mellody, 111, 228
Hockey Diversity Alliance, 105, 253, 311
Hodges, Craig, 76, 176, 305
Hodges, Gil, 38, 39, 117, 144, 297
Hoerner, Joe, 55, 119, 131, 301
Hogg, Houston, 53, 236
Hoggard, Dennie, 32, 228, 244
Hogue, Ronnie, 56, 265
Holdsclaw, Chamique, 82, 84, 176
Holiday, Billie, 20, 248

Holiday, Jrue, 111, 176
Holieway, Jamelle, 71, 209, 229
Holland, Cecil, 91, 282, 283, 307
Holland, Jerome Heartwell "Brud", 25, 26, 229
Holliday, Trindon, 97, 229
Hollins, Cecil, 77, 281
Holloway, Condredge, 60, 209, 229
Holloway, Cyrus, 10, 259
Hollywood Legion Stadium, 27, 199, 205
Holmes et al. vs. Atlanta, 41, 249, 298
Holmes, Alfred, 26, 248
Holmes, Alfred "Tup", 41, 249, 298
Holmes, Larry, 71, 205
Holmes, Oliver Wendell, 41, 249, 298
Holmes, Tally, 19, 281, 284, 285
Holyfield, Evander, 78, 204
Homestead Grays, 23, 25, 28, 29, 32, 36, 111, 116, 117, 126, 133, 135, 136, 318
Honey Nut Cheerios, 90, 290
Hood, Sara "Lovestyle", 112, 290
Hooker, John Lee, 73
Horford, Al, 93, 153
Horne, Lena, 31, 67, 130
Hornig, Donald, 61, 303
Horton, Tony, 52, 130
Hoskins, Dave, 36, 135
Hot Spring Bathers (CSL), 38, 117, 297
Hour Record (cycling), 16, 289
Houston Astros, 55, 65, 71, 77, 92, 93, 98, 101, 111, 120, 121, 125, 129, 134, 139, 143, 148, 150
Houston Colt .45s, 48, 138
Houston Comets, 80, 82, 84, 85, 86, 105, 157, 169, 185, 187, 191, 193, 194
Houston Cougars, 50, 56, 69, 70, 170, 194, 234, 236
Houston Hyenas, 112, 290
Houston Oilers, 45, 50, 60, 67, 70, 75, 208, 220, 222, 230, 235, 247, 303
Houston Rockets, 66, 68, 112, 159, 182, 185, 190, 194
Houston Roughnecks, 106, 245
Houston Texans, 90, 219
Houston, Wade, 47, 74, 176, 191, 196
Houston, Whitney, 84, 180
Howard University, 17, 18, 27, 30, 42, 80, 151, 152, 173, 176, 181, 183, 188, 248
Howard, Dwight, 95, 176
Howard, Elston, 40, 45, 48, 54, 135, 299, 301
Howard, Juwan, 79, 176
Howard, Tim, 94, 290
Howe News Bureau, 32, 150
Hoynes, Attorney Louis
    Curt Flood case, 59, 131
Hubbard, DeHart, 19, 22, 151, 178, 264, 272
Hudson, Dick
    Savoy Colts, 22, 23, 151, 160, 181, 196, 285
Hudson, Ken, 53, 196
Hudson, Richard "Dick", 21, 229
Hudson, Roosie, 155
Hudson, Wendell, 56, 177
Hughes, Langston, 35
Human Juke Box, 111, 210
Humphrey, Tony, 121, 314

Hunt, Lamar, 44, 212
Hunter, Brittany, 90, 177
Hunter, Harold, 34, 155, 168, 181, 183
Hunter, Les, 47, 152, 299
Hunter, Torii, 106, 121, 312
Hunter, Travis, 107, 229
Hurd, Babe, 10, 259, 261
Hurston, Zora Neale, 13
Hurt, Eddie, 206, 229
Hurt, Eddie P., 26
Hurts, Jalen, 112, 229, 233
Hutton III, Lee A., 112, 216, 229

I

Ideal Tennis Club (Harlem), 18, 281
Ifill, Gwen, 9
Iginla, Jarome, 85, 88, 97, 253, 256
Illinois Knights, 76, 156, 185
Illinois State Normal University, 35, 44, 128, 183, 298
Illinois State University, 57, 189
Imus, Don, 93, 193, 308
Independent Pleasure Club of Orange, 17, 151
Indiana Central University, 25, 161, 170
Indiana Pacers, 59, 64, 87, 92, 94, 156, 169, 184, 187, 193
Indiana State Teachers College, 32, 152, 195
Indiana University, 31, 173, 317
Indianapolis 500, 25, 60, 291, 294
Indianapolis ABCs, 20, 21, 115, 128, 133, 135
Indianapolis Capitols, 55, 244
Indianapolis Clowns, 36, 37, 38, 39, 117, 118, 124, 136, 139, 146
Indianapolis Colts, 83, 90, 93, 101, 214, 224, 225, 242, 245
Ingraham, Laura, 103, 177, 310
Ingram, Andre, 105, 177
Inside Baseball magazine, 38, 144
International League, 11, 12, 16, 38, 41, 43, 113, 114, 117, 130, 133, 141, 146, 148, 295, 319
International Tennis Hall of Fame, 34, 58, 71, 281, 283, 284, 297
Invisible Man, 37
Iona College Gaels of N.Y., 41
Iowa State University, 40, 67, 70, 82, 97, 209, 210, 213, 220, 243, 244, 265, 306
Iowa Unicorns, 76, 156, 185
Irvin, Monte, 30, 33, 35, 39, 54, 116, 117, 118, 119, 135, 146
Isaacs, John, 30, 165, 168, 177
Iverson, Allen, 79, 83, 87, 157, 177, 307

J

Jackson Five, 57, 125
Jackson State College, 107, 229
Jackson, Bo, 74, 75, 77, 135, 290
Jackson, Chris
  See Abdul-Rauf, Mahmoud, 74, 153, 162, 304, 306
Jackson, Doris Arlene, 38, 146
Jackson, Dr. Nell, 41, 264
Jackson, Edwin, 95, 104, 121, 135, 313
Jackson, Erin, 109, 110, 272
Jackson, Inman, 22, 160, 181
Jackson, James, 73, 209
Jackson, Janet, 87, 214, 289

Jackson, Jr., Edwin, 95, 135
Jackson, Keith, 209
Jackson, Kevin, 91, 290
Jackson, Lamar, 217
Jackson, Manny, 42, 77, 160
Jackson, Peter "The Black Prince", 12, 199, 203
Jackson, Reggie, 64, 135
Jackson, Sidney, 18, 151
Jackson, Wilbur, 60, 209, 230, 235
Jackson, William Tecumseh Sherman, 13, 206, 230, 232
Jackson, Wilmer, 112, 159
Jacksonville (FL) University, 53, 170
Jacksonville Jaguars, 88, 91, 225, 226, 232
Jacksonville Sharks, 62, 234, 236
Jacobs, Franklin, 65, 272
Jacobs, Regina, 89, 272
James E. Sullivan Award, 39, 77, 245, 278
James, Angela, 95, 253, 256
James, Bill, 40, 118
James, Edgerrin, 214, 307
James, Joe, 48, 290
James, Larry, 265, 270, 277
James, LeBron, 88, 93, 94, 99, 103, 104, 107, 111, 157, 158, 177, 178, 193, 308, 309, 310, 311, 312
James, Lionel, 71, 229
James, Valmore, 68, 256
Jameson, Betty, 34, 248
Jamestown (NY) Falcons, 38, 124
Japan, 17, 22, 36, 47, 49, 69, 92, 109, 115, 117, 130, 137, 140, 266, 270, 274, 288, 295
Japanese Pacific League, 36, 117
Javadifar, Maral, 106, 231
Jay-Z, 80, 94
Jefferson, Harry, 30, 152, 183
Jeffries, Anthony, 106, 216
Jeffries, James J., 17, 199, 203
Jeffries, Jim, 135
Jeffries, Willie, 66, 209, 230
Jelks, Osibee J., 41
Jenkins, Clarence "Fats", 108, 161, 178
Jenkins, Ferguson, 58, 60, 126, 135
Jenkins, Scoville, 91, 282
Jennings, Brandon, 94, 178
Jeopardy
  Game Show, 87, 111, 141
Jersey City Skeeters, 11, 113, 146
Jet magazine, 35, 36, 107, 127, 144, 165, 205, 297
Jeter, Derek, 86, 102, 136
Jethroe, Sam "The Jet", 34, 136, 297
Jethroe, Sam and Elsie, 78, 136, 305
Jim Crow sanctions, 22, 25, 28, 29, 116, 155, 199, 207, 294, 296, 316, 318
Jockey Hall of Fame, 40, 259, 261
Johansson, Ingemar, 45, 204
John R. Wooden Award, 65, 179
John Thompson, 70
Johnson C. Smith University, 206
Johnson, Amir, 91, 178
Johnson, Billy "White Shoes", 69, 230, 303
Johnson, Bob, 89, 96, 157, 158, 178, 180
Johnson, Brooks, 66, 265

Emancipation Index

Johnson, Carl, 106, 216
Johnson, Charles, 82, 136
Johnson, Danita, 109, 290
Johnson, Dr. Albert C.
   Chicago Black Hawks, 23, 211, 238
Johnson, Earl, 22, 272
Johnson, Earvin "Magic", 83, 230
Johnson, Ernie, 99
Johnson, Fletcher, 40, 155
Johnson, Grant "Home Run", 14, 16, 114, 149
Johnson, Hunter, 19, 151, 178
Johnson, Jack, 16, 17, 21, 75, 114, 136, 199, 200, 203
Johnson, James Earl "Jimmy", 78, 230
Johnson, James Weldon, 18, 63
Johnson, Jerry, 55, 119, 131, 301
Johnson, Jimmy, 55, 56, 223, 224, 230
Johnson, John Henry, 38, 212, 237
Johnson, Larry, 75, 156
Johnson, Lester, 22, 160, 181
Johnson, Magic, 66, 67, 74, 75, 76, 110, 156, 169, 178
Johnson, Mamie "Peanut", 39, 118, 136, 139
Johnson, Marques, 65, 179
Johnson, Michael, 79, 86, 271, 273
Johnson, President Lyndon B., 44
Johnson, Rafer, 43, 45, 61, 78, 230, 265, 273
Johnson, Robert L., 88, 157
Johnson, Sheila, 91, 157, 179
Johnson, William "Judy", 35, 136
Johnston, James Robinson (CHL), 14, 253
Jones Trophy, Sam, 110, 168, 169, 171, 179, 181, 188
Jones, Adam, 104, 121, 313
Jones, Billy, 50, 179
Jones, Calvin, 39, 40, 207, 212, 230
Jones, Casey, 155
Jones, Charles "Benny", 29, 179
Jones, Collis, 53, 152
Jones, Cullen, 94
Jones, Deacon, 52, 65, 212, 213, 230, 300, 303, 304
Jones, Ed "Too Tall", 66, 231
Jones, Homer, 54, 60, 231, 247
Jones, J. J., 63, 231
Jones, Jr., Roy, 80, 179, 200, 203, 290
Jones, Julius, 93, 96, 231
Jones, K. C., 39, 41, 62, 70, 152, 155, 163, 179, 190, 299
Jones, Louis Jordan, 31, 130
Jones, Marion, 86, 273
Jones, Sam, 30, 36, 40, 44, 49, 136, 147, 152, 155, 179, 183, 186, 191, 299
Jones, Shilese, 110, 111, 112, 266, 268, 274
Jones, Stuart "Slim", 25, 136
Jones, Terrence, 73, 209
Jones, Thomas, 93, 96, 231
Jones, Uriah, 54, 265
Jordan, Michael, 72, 73, 74, 84, 89, 96, 99, 102, 156, 158, 179, 180
Joseph, Newt, 21, 136
Joubert, Antoine "The Judge", 92, 157, 164, 219
Joyner, Al, 69, 266, 273
Joyner, Florence Griffith, 73, 271
Joyner-Kersee, Jackie, 72, 73, 76, 80, 91, 266, 273, 276

K

Kaepernick, Colin, 96, 102, 103, 111, 215, 231, 310, 311, 314
Kagambi, James "KG", 111, 266
Kane, Evander, 105, 253, 311
Kansas City Athletics, 45, 118, 299
Kansas City Chiefs, 60, 69, 75, 85, 104, 106, 208, 215, 220, 232, 233, 235, 247, 299, 310
Kansas City Kings, 61, 82, 163, 197
Kansas City Monarchs, 2, 21, 22, 23, 28, 30, 31, 34, 38, 39, 66, 115, 116, 117, 118, 125, 127, 130, 132, 136, 143, 145, 146, 150, 153, 197
Kansas City Royals, 64, 67, 75, 112, 121, 134, 139, 149, 150, 314
Kansas City Steers, 46, 175
Kansas Crusaders, 76, 77, 156, 157, 185
Kansas State University, 33, 34, 35, 95, 150, 198, 207, 225, 226, 239
Kantner, Dee, 81, 157, 186
Kapler, Gabe, 111, 314
Karagach, Daniella, 108, 191
Kaufman, Richard, 77, 281, 283
Kearney, Jim, 48, 245
Kearse, Jevon, 85, 231
Keaser, Lloyd, 60, 64, 265, 290
Keio University, 17, 115, 295
Kellogg, Clark, 69, 156
Kelly, C.G., 17, 281
Kelly, Jackie, 111, 141
Kemp, Governor Brian, 109, 121, 313
Kemp, Ray, 24, 211, 231, 232, 295
Kennedy, Jayne, 65, 212
Kennedy, President John F., 57, 163, 301
Kentucky Derby, 10, 11, 12, 13, 14, 15, 70, 82, 85, 259, 260, 261, 262
Kentucky State University, 34, 51, 155, 168, 181, 183
Kilgore, Maurice, 43, 290, 292
King, Coretta Scott, 57, 61, 301
King, Don, 62, 128, 199, 203
King, Jennifer, 106, 107, 231
King, Jr., Dr. Martin Luther, 54, 73, 75, 119, 213, 301, 304, 305
King, Jr., Martin Luther, 46, 57, 73, 75, 101, 120, 301, 304
King, Mable, 295
King, Shaun, 83, 86, 210, 214, 223, 224, 227, 232, 234
King, William "Dolly", 26, 180
Kinney, James A.R. (CHL), 14, 253
Kinshasa, Republic of Zaire, 33, 62, 128, 160, 161, 168, 199, 203
Kissel, Tony, 14, 114, 145
Klice, Arrington "Bubble", 57, 203
Klutch Sports Groups, 108, 187
Knight, Brevin, 82, 180
Knight, Toby, 66, 156
Knight, Tommy, 15, 261
Knolle, Gene, 55, 180
Knoxville Smokies, 38, 117, 298
Koelzer, Kelsey, 101, 103, 256
Koppel, Ted, 72, 120, 304
Koslo, Dave, 35, 117
Kountze, Mabray "Doc", 25, 136
Ku Klux Klan, 22, 109, 115, 121, 313
Kuebler, Conrad, 17, 114
Kuhn, Bowie, 61, 119, 123, 130, 141, 302, 303

Index

Kuiper, Glen, 112, 121, 314

L

La Guardia, Fiorello, 29, 116, 296
Lacy, Sam, viii, 29, 33, 100, 137, 146, 292, 317
Ladies Professional Golf Association, 34, 48, 248, 284
Lafayette Baseball Club - Savannah, GA, 12, 113
Lakeland, William, 10, 259
Lakes, Charles, 73, 273
Lakoff, George, 90
Land, Stanley, 56, 209
Landis, Kenesaw Mountain, 26, 107, 116, 121, 137, 142, 296, 312
Lane, Dick "Night Train" Lane, 36, 44, 208, 232, 299
Lane, Floyd, 40, 155
Laney, Betnijah, 108, 159, 170, 180, 186
Langdon, Trajan, 84, 153, 157
Langeford, Rahsaan, 87, 177, 306
Langston Golf Course and Driving Range, 27, 248
Langston, John Mercer, 27, 248
Lanier, Bob, 180
Lanier, Willie, 48, 52, 56, 60, 212, 232, 245
Larkin, Barry, 86, 107, 121, 137, 142, 312
Las Vegas Raiders, 106, 111, 223, 235
Last all-White teams, 34, 37, 38, 43, 44, 55, 117, 129, 133, 155, 207, 208, 297
Lattin, David, 50, 152, 300
Lawrence, Frank, 38, 117, 298
League Park (Cleveland), 20, 147
LeBlanc, José, 20, 115
Lee, Almer, 55, 180
Lee, Bertram M., 74, 156
Lee, Jimmy, 17, 261
Lee, Louis R., 62, 212
Lee, Norvel, 36, 199, 264
Lee, Spike, 78, 141
LeFlore, Ron, 65, 137
Leonard, Bernardo, 72, 120
Leonard, Sugar Ray, 73, 203
Leonard, Walter "Buck", 38, 117, 298
Leslie, Lisa, 82, 84, 87, 88, 92, 95, 98, 174, 180, 181
Lester B. Pearson Award, 88, 256
Lester Hayes Rule, 213, 304
Lester, Bill, 90, 290
Lester, Larry, 75, 120
LeVias, Jerry, 50, 208
Lew, Harry "Bucky", 15, 16, 155, 181
Lewis, Carl, 70, 273
Lewis, Gary "Leaping Rule", 304
Lewis, George, 10, 259, 261
Lewis, Isaac, 12, 259, 261
Lewis, John Henry, 25, 27, 203, 204
Lewis, Oliver, 10, 259, 261
Lewis, Reggie, 72, 165, 181, 197
Lewis, Sherman, 83, 213
Lewis, William Henry, 13, 14, 19, 206, 230, 232, 238
Liberty Magazine, 27, 245, 296
Lichtman Bears, 28, 155
Life magazine, 34, 43, 138, 144
Lift Every Voice & Sing, 112, 216, 315
Lillard, Joe, 22, 24, 160, 181, 211, 231, 232, 295

Limbaugh, Russ, 214, 234, 307
Lincoln Giants, 21, 23, 115, 116
Lipscomb, Charlie, 54, 181
Liston, Sonny, 48, 49, 50, 201, 203, 204
Little Rock Arkansas Travelers, 48, 124, 299
Livingston, James, 38, 117, 298
Livingston, Shaun, 90, 181
Livingstone College, 206
Lloyd Trophy, Earl, 110, 168, 169, 171, 179, 181, 188
Lloyd, Earl, 34, 39, 53, 58, 155, 168, 170, 181, 183, 195
Lobo, Rebecca, 80, 157, 193
Locke, Alain, 22
Locke, Bernadette, 74, 181
Lockman, Whitey, 60, 119, 125
Locust, Lori, 106, 231
Loeffler, Kelly, 108, 185
Loendi Big Five, 18, 19, 20, 151, 178, 188
Logan, Dave, 61, 150
Long Beach Stingrays, 80, 174
Long Island University, 26, 180
Lopes, Davey, 86, 137
López, Cando, 20, 115
Los Angeles Angels, 94, 120
Los Angeles Clippers, 80, 90, 94, 98, 99, 158, 165, 181, 193, 309
Los Angeles Dodgers, 44, 50, 55, 64, 125, 127, 133, 136, 140
Los Angeles Dons, 30, 31, 33, 207, 211, 219, 221, 238, 243
Los Angeles Kings, 107, 255
Los Angeles Lakers, 66, 84, 99, 111, 167, 173, 178
Los Angeles Raiders, 74, 240
Los Angeles Rams, 30, 31, 33, 34, 37, 52, 60, 63, 65, 106, 207, 211, 212, 216, 221, 228, 230, 233, 242, 243, 244, 245, 247, 297, 300, 303
Los Angeles Sparks, 80, 82, 88, 94, 105, 109, 157, 180, 185, 187, 290
Los Angeles' Coliseum, 27, 116
Loudd, Rommie, 51, 62, 208, 212
Louis, Bill, 38, 117, 298
Louis, Joe, 20, 25, 26, 27, 28, 34, 36, 75, 77, 199, 200, 203, 204, 248, 296
Louisiana State University, 56, 58, 193, 265, 302
Louisville Colonels, 42, 118
Louisville Falls City, 12, 114
Love, Nat "Deadwood Dick", 10, 280
Loville, Derek, 74, 213, 233, 237
Lowe, Paul, 48, 51, 208, 233, 244
Loyola (Chicago) Ramblers, 47, 98, 152, 153, 299
LPGA, 48, 52, 250, 284
Lucas, Bill, 64, 119, 137
Lucas, Ray, 88, 233
Lucky Me, 80
Luisetti, Hank, 28, 152, 189
Lutz, Bob, 53, 283
Lynch, Jair, 79, 273
Lynch, Marshawn, 99, 215, 233, 309
Lynn, Nicole, 104, 233, 246

M

M.C. Hammer
  Stanley Burrell, 62, 119
Mabley, Jackie "Moms", 24

Emancipation Index

Macedonia Baseball Club - Jacksonville, FL, 12, 113
Mack, Connie, 29, 116, 296
Mackey v. NFL, 56, 233, 301
Mackey, Biz, 22, 116, 137
Mackey, John, 56, 233, 301
MacPhail, Larry, 29, 116, 296
MacPhail, Lee, 29, 116, 296
Madden NFL, 85, 88, 91, 223, 226, 244
Madden, John, 74, 245
Madden, Will Anthony, 18, 151
Madison Square Garden, 26, 31, 58, 84, 152, 180, 201, 202
Maggette, Corey, 84, 157
Magic Johnson Enterprises, 178
Mahomes, Patrick, 106, 233
Major League Baseball Players Association, 98, 104, 121, 128, 129, 131, 313
Makeba, Mariam, 23
Malcolm X, 20, 49
Malone, Karl, 74, 156
Malone, Moses, 62, 64, 66, 173, 182
Maloy, Mike, 52, 182
Manchild in the Promised Land, 50
Mandela, Nelson, 9
Manhattan Casino in Harlem, 18, 151
Manley, Effa, 30, 92, 106, 137
Mann, Bob, 32, 34, 227, 233
Manning, Eli, 102, 242
Manning, Madeline, 54, 274
Mantle, Mickey, 37, 117
Manuel Jr., E. J., 97
Manuel, Jerry, 86, 125, 138
Manuel, Simone, 100, 274
Manziel, Johnny, 96, 222
Mapp, Julian, 106, 216
Marble, Alice, 33, 281, 284, 297
Marciano, Rocky, 66, 231
Marichal, Juan, 48, 138
Marsans, Armando, 18, 138
Marseille Foil Grand Prix, 98, 291
Marshall, Bob, 16, 206
Marshall, Cynt, 102, 182
Marshall, George Preston, 46, 50, 208, 211, 212, 228, 235, 296, 299
Marshall, Jesse, 53, 182
Marshall, Pam, 72, 274
Marshall, Thurgood, 17, 38, 62
Marson, Mike, 61, 63, 253, 256
Martin Luther King Day, 213, 305
Martin, Eddie (CHL), 16, 253, 256
Masters Tournament, 42, 61, 63, 66, 81, 87, 249, 250, 251, 252, 306
Matson, Ollie, 37, 42, 212, 219, 233, 234, 244
Matthews, Margaret, 32, 274
Matthews, William Clarence, 16, 138
Matthis, April, 103, 146
Mausi, Lesleigh, 107, 288
Maxwell, Bruce, 101, 107, 120, 138, 140, 310
Maxwell, Sherman "Jocko", 23
May, Aleali, 102, 182
May, Sean, 92, 153
Mays, Benjamin, 69

Mays, Dave, 65, 234
Mays, Willie, 32, 34, 35, 39, 40, 41, 42, 43, 48, 49, 50, 51, 55, 57, 101, 117, 118, 138, 139, 150
Mazza, Valeria, 79, 81
McAdoo, Bob, 64, 182
McAfee, Reggie, 60, 265, 274
McAllister, Bobby, 73, 209
McAshan, Eddie, 56, 62, 234, 236
McCants, Rashad, 92, 153
McCarthy, Babe, 59, 156, 302
McCarver, Tim, 55, 119, 131, 301
McCladdie, Michelle, 59, 265, 271
McClain, Konnor, 110, 111, 266, 268, 274
McClain, Lester, 54, 208
McClellan, Danny, 14, 15, 114, 139, 145
McClendon, Lloyd, 87, 139
McClinton, Curtis "The Count", 52, 234
McCluskey, John, 49, 208, 234
McCoy, Larry, 119
McCoy, Umpire Larry, 304
McCraw, Tom, 63, 139
McCray, Nikki, 80, 84, 182
McDaniel, Xavier, 70, 182
McDevitt, Daniel J., 21
McDonald, Henry, 18, 206, 234
McGee, JaVale, 94, 96, 109, 182, 183
McGee, Pamela, 94, 100, 109, 182, 183
McGee, Pamela and Paula, 70, 153
McGraw, John, 15, 114
McIntyre, Manny, 30, 253, 255, 256
McKegney, Tony, 65, 66, 67, 73, 253, 257
McLendon, John, 28, 30, 34, 36, 42, 44, 45, 46, 47, 51, 52, 53, 55, 57, 65, 66, 86, 100, 110, 152, 155, 158, 173, 181, 183, 184, 188, 265
McMahon, Edward and Roderick "Jess", 21, 155
McNabb, Donovan, 83, 210, 214, 217, 223, 232, 234, 307, 308
McNair, Steve, 78, 90, 234
McNally, Dave, 63, 131, 303
McPherson, Don, 72, 73, 209
McRae, Hal, 75, 87, 119, 139, 303
McVey, Warren, 50, 234
McWilliams, Jon, 40, 221, 234
Mecham, Governor Evan, 213, 305
Meeks, Malcolm, 57, 184, 197
Mehri, Cyrus, 90, 214, 238
Mejias, Roman, 40, 118, 298
Melvin, Bill "Bumps", 29, 184
Memphis Grizzles, 101, 174
Memphis Red Sox, 32, 40, 61, 118, 127, 142, 298
Méndez, José, 19, 115
Mensah-Stock, Tamyra, 102, 105, 109, 274, 291
Merchant, John F., 76, 249
Meredith, James, 57, 163, 301
Meredith, Ted, 19, 264
Meriweather, Joe, 66, 156
Meriwether, Dr. Delano, 59, 274
Merrit, Kent, 56, 209
Messer, Frank, 57, 148
Messersmith, Andy, 63, 131, 303
Metcalfe, Ralph, 24, 274
Mexican League, 26, 27, 126, 127

Miami Dolphins, 67, 88, 95, 111, 213, 233, 256, 282, 285, 286
Miami Floridians, 53, 162
Miami Heat, 96, 99, 158, 197, 308, 309
Miami Marlins, 41, 94, 102, 120, 141
Miami Sun Sox, 38, 117
Michigan State University, 49, 52, 62, 73, 80, 83, 119, 148, 209, 219, 241, 246, 278
Middle States League, 14, 114, 145
Mikan, George, 32, 33, 49, 155, 160, 161, 167, 198, 300
Mike, Robert, 32, 211, 235, 237
Miles, Leo, 62, 209, 212
Miller, Brandon, 112, 159
Miller, Cheryl, 68, 70, 71, 80, 84, 153, 157, 158, 175, 184
Miller, John, 55, 132
Miller, Percy, 35, 139
Miller, Randi, 95, 274
Miller, Reggie, 87, 97, 158, 184
Miller, Ron, 47, 152, 299
Miller, Tori, 106, 185
Mills, Patty, 99, 158, 171
Milwaukee Badgers, 21, 211, 239, 295
Milwaukee Braves, 39, 118
Milwaukee Brewers, 65, 86, 89, 124, 137, 141
Milwaukee Bucks, 58, 59, 68, 94, 105, 107, 111, 159, 162, 165, 171, 176, 178, 185, 189, 311
Milwaukee Hawks, 39, 185
Mingo, Gene, 45, 235
Minneapolis College Women's Club, 32
Minneapolis Lakers, 32, 33, 39, 160, 161, 197, 198
Minneapolis Millers, 32, 127
Minneapolis Star Tribune, 97
Minnesota Gophers, 45, 208, 242
Minnesota Lynx, 96, 100, 105, 158, 163, 185, 310
Minnesota Marines, 21, 22, 160, 181, 229
Minnesota Timberwolves, 92, 153
Minnesota Twins, 46, 50, 59, 124, 133, 299, 312
Minnesota Vikings, 61, 63, 78, 86, 89, 97, 106, 150, 214, 215, 222, 223, 224, 227, 232, 235, 244, 306
Minnesota Wild, 96, 103, 105, 253, 256, 257, 312
Minor, Davage "Dave", 35, 164, 185
Minor, DeWayne, 87, 261
Miñoso, Orestes "Minnie", 31, 35, 42, 45, 117, 118, 138, 139, 298
Minute Maid Park, 94, 120, 308
Mississippi State Bulldogs, 48, 56, 66, 91, 102, 152, 153, 197, 208, 210, 223, 299
Mississippi Valley State University, 64, 224
Missouri Mustangs, 76, 77, 157, 166, 185
Missouri Southern University, 91, 242
Mitchell, Bobby, 46, 212, 228, 235
Mitchell, John, 60, 209, 230, 235
Mitchell, Lighting Ned, 76, 156, 185
Mitchell, Lightning Ned, 77, 157
Mize, Johnny, 37, 117
Mobley, Craig, 55, 185
Moncrief, Sidney, 68, 185
Monday, Kenny, 73, 291
Monk, Marcus, 112, 159
Monk, Thelonious, 68
Monroe, Earl, 30, 52, 66, 152, 156, 172, 183
Montgomery Baseball Club - Montgomery, AL, 12, 113
Montgomery, George, 94, 182

Montgomery, Louis, 27, 207, 296
Montgomery, Mace, 15, 264
Montgomery, Renée, 108, 185
Montgomery, Toccara, 87, 89, 91, 266, 291
Monticello Athletic Association (Pittsburgh), 18, 151, 188
Montreal Alouettes, 99, 239
Montreal Royals, 12, 30, 143
Moon, Warren, 68, 70, 75, 78, 85, 87, 92, 235
Mooney, Paul, 21, 151
Moore, Archie, 36, 48, 71, 75, 200, 204, 205
Moore, Darla, 97, 249, 251
Moore, Jackie, 39, 185
Moore, Jr., Charles, 36, 264, 274
Moore, Maya, 96, 105, 185
Moore, Nathan, 104, 121, 312
Moore, Tamara, 105, 185
Moore, Thomas, 111, 266
Moorer, Michael, 78, 202, 204
Morant, Ja, 103, 185
Moreland, Nate, 143
Morgan State, 30, 152, 183
Morgan State College, 26, 206, 229
Morgan State College (University), 26
Morgan, Connie, 39, 118, 136, 139
Morgan, Joe, 65, 139, 143, 304
Morgan, Sandra Douglass, 111, 235
Morrison, Toni, 24, 41, 102
Moseley, Russell, 118, 298
Moses, Edwin, 65, 265, 274
Moses, Erik, 106, 291
Most Valuable College Player, 20, 206, 241
Motley, Bob, 42, 75, 140
Motley, Marion, 29, 31, 34, 89, 207, 211, 221, 235, 244, 246, 297
Mountain States League, 38, 117, 298
Moyers, Bill D., 44
Mr. October, 64, 135
Mt. Vernon Cardinals, 24, 206
Mueller, Don, 35, 117
Muhammad, Dalilah, 101, 274
Muhammad, Ibtihaj, 101, 275
Mullins, Demond "Dom", 111, 266
Municipal Stadium in Cleveland, 116
Murchison, Ira, 41, 275
Murphy, Calvin, 68, 69, 185, 186
Murphy, Cisero, 50, 291
Murphy, Dwight, 53, 152
Murphy, Isaac, 10, 11, 12, 13, 14, 15, 40, 259, 261, 263
Murray, Kyler, 217
Murray, Lonnie, 107, 140
Murtaugh, Danny, 58, 119
Musburger, Brent, 62, 212, 223
Muse, Charlie, 26, 296
Mutombo, Dikembe, 76, 186, 305
Mutual Association of Eastern Colored Clubs, 21, 115
MVP
    Most Valuable Player, 27, 30, 34, 35, 39, 40, 41, 44, 47, 48, 49, 50, 51, 52, 54, 57, 58, 60, 62, 63, 64, 66, 67, 68, 69, 70, 72, 73, 74, 76, 77, 78, 82, 84, 86, 87, 88, 89, 90, 100, 102, 103, 105, 110, 125, 126, 127, 128, 129, 131, 132, 134, 135, 136, 138, 140, 143, 147, 160, 161, 162, 164, 165, 166, 169, 171, 174, 178, 180, 186, 188, 190, 194, 196, 197, 219, 221, 227,

228, 232, 234, 246, 257, 290, 307
Myers, Dave, 23
Myers, Dave Willoughby, 23, 206, 236, 295

N

Naismith, James, 47, 183
Namath, Joe, 63, 231
NASCAR, 37, 48, 90, 99, 102, 106, 289, 290, 291, 292, 293, 311
Nashua Dodgers, 30, 127
Nashville Cubs, 32, 130, 150
National Anthem, 44, 54, 61, 84, 107, 111, 140, 142, 180, 212, 215, 231, 276, 298, 303, 310, 314
National Association of Base Ball Players (NABBP), 9, 113, 295
National Athletic Steering Committee, 36, 183
National Basketball Association, 30, 34, 108, 155, 156, 157, 159, 168, 170, 175, 181, 297, 301, 302
National Basketball League, 33, 155, 161, 173, 297
National Basketball League (NBL), 33, 161
National Bowling Association, 27
National Capitol Country Club for African Americans, 22, 281
National Colored Base Ball League (NCBBL), 12, 114
National Cowboys of Color Museum and Hall of Fame, 90, 280, 288
National Football League, 16, 19, 21, 23, 24, 51, 55, 74, 111, 206, 208, 211, 219, 220, 236, 237, 240, 241, 242, 244, 295, 318, 319
   New York Yanks, 34, 212, 229, 243, 247
National Girls Baseball League, 35, 128
National Industrial Basketball League, 45, 183
National Negro Bowling Association, 27, 204
National Rodeo Cowboy Hall of Fame, 58, 280
National Sailing Hall of Fame, 75, 291
National Tennis Championship, 33, 281, 284, 297
Native Son, 27
Naulls, Willie, 41, 49, 155, 179, 186, 191
Navarro, Emilio "Milito", 23, 140
Ndiaye, Bouna, 112, 159
Neal III, LaVelle E., 97
Neal, Charlie, 44, 140
Neal, Gary, 93, 186
Nebraska Xpress, 76, 77, 157, 185
Neckties
   Night Train Lane, 44, 208, 232, 299
Negro Digest, 47, 144
Negro History Bulletin, 26
Negro National League, 20, 22, 23, 115, 132, 133, 134, 145
Negro World Series, 63, 147
Nehemiah, Renaldo "Skeets", 68, 275
Neil Smith Rule, 242, 306
Neufield, Ray, 70, 257
New England Blizzard, 79, 157
New England Patriots, 45, 51, 60, 71, 93, 101, 208, 220, 221, 225, 237, 241, 242
New Jersey Americans, 48, 163
New Jersey Devils, 93
New Orlean Creoles, 32, 130, 150
New Orleans Jazz, 65, 82, 175, 197
New Orleans Pelicans, 40, 118, 298
New Orleans Saints, 85, 86, 93, 96, 219, 220, 225, 231, 242, 306
New Rochelle Bulldogs, 24, 206
New York All Stars, 18, 151
New York Brown Bombers, 25, 211, 238

New York Clipper, 9, 113
New York Cubans, 31, 63, 117, 147
New York Giants, 19, 26, 27, 32, 33, 35, 38, 39, 41, 50, 54, 60, 68, 80, 81, 87, 94, 102, 112, 117, 118, 128, 130, 134, 135, 146, 206, 207, 214, 217, 218, 219, 222, 226, 229, 231, 239, 240, 241, 242, 243, 244, 247, 289, 296
New York Gorhams, 12, 114
New York Islanders, 67, 257
New York Jets, 63, 90, 106, 107, 108, 214, 215, 222, 224, 225, 231, 246, 308
New York Knicks, 34, 57, 59, 66, 70, 74, 78, 156, 158, 168, 172, 176, 188, 196, 245, 294, 304, 309
New York Liberty, 80, 82, 105, 108, 157, 159, 170, 176, 180, 185, 186
New York Mets, 92, 143
New York Nets, 62, 182
New York Professional Football League, 18, 206, 234
New York Raiders, 253
New York Rangers, 32, 253, 255
New York Rens, 21, 25, 27, 30, 32, 33, 49, 59, 74, 88, 108, 155, 160, 161, 164, 165, 168, 170, 173, 177, 178
New York Rens Court, 101, 161
New York Riveters, 101, 256
New York State League, 11, 113
New York Tapers, 46, 175
New York Times, 12, 94, 114, 141, 225, 295, 302
New York University, 23, 206, 207, 236, 296, 318
New York Yankee, 26, 36, 40, 54, 64, 102, 116, 117, 135, 296, 297, 301
New York Yankees, 18, 23, 31, 37, 40, 43, 48, 52, 57, 69, 78, 80, 81, 83, 86, 92, 115, 117, 118, 120, 130, 135, 136, 138, 145, 148, 149, 211, 221, 247, 292, 297, 298
Newark Daily Mercury, 9, 113
Newark Eagles, 23, 30, 54, 92, 106, 116, 119, 129, 135, 137, 138
Newark Little Giants, 12, 114, 146, 148, 295
Newark Stars, 22, 147
Newberry, Jimmy, 36, 117
Newcombe, Don, 30, 33, 35, 39, 40, 41, 47, 54, 117, 118, 127, 130, 132, 135, 140, 144
Newport News Lighthearts, 29, 211
Newsome, Ozzie, 89, 236
Newsweek, 26, 33, 201, 270
Newton, C.M., 56, 177
Newton, Cam, 96, 98, 215, 236
NHL All-Star game, 102, 257
Nichols, Rachel, 105, 312
Nicholson, Alexandra, 59, 275
Nicklaus, Jack, 83, 99, 201, 249
Nigger Heaven, 22
NIL
   Name, Image, Likeness, 112
Nixon, President Richard M., 59
Noah, Joakim, 93, 153
Noah, Yannick, 93, 153
Nobles, D.C., 56, 236
No-hitters, 14, 20, 21, 22, 30, 37, 40, 41, 44, 47, 48, 55, 95, 114, 128, 129, 132, 134, 135, 136, 138, 145, 150
Noll, Chuck, 62, 226
Norfolk Brown Bombers, 29, 211
Norman, Conrad and Gerald, 16, 151
Norris Trophy, 98, 257

Index

Norris, Michele, 9
North Carolina A&T, 110, 173, 184, 293
North Carolina A&T State University, 110, 173, 184
North Carolina Central University, 28, 31, 51, 151, 168, 183, 189, 207, 221, 300
North Carolina College for Negroes, 28, 30, 34, 151, 152, 155, 168, 181, 183, 189
North Carolina Sportswriters Hall of Fame, 90, 249, 251
North Carolina State University, 52, 55, 176, 180, 208
Northern Illinois University, 24
Northington, Nate, 53, 236
Northwest Football League, 26, 238
Notre Dame University, 36, 53, 57, 99, 152, 164, 166, 170, 191
Nuzum, Henry Gantt, 91, 267

O

O'Neal, Shaquille, 87, 157, 186, 307
O'Neil, Buck, 41, 47, 75, 92, 120, 140
O'Ree, Willie, 43, 61, 253, 256, 257
O'Shanter, Tam All-American and World Championship, 248
Oakland Athletics, 58, 62, 67, 68, 71, 107, 119, 126, 127, 134, 135, 140
Oakland Oaks, 19, 128
Oakland Raiders, 54, 55, 72, 86, 208, 213, 215, 219, 224, 225, 228, 299, 301, 304, 309
Obama, President Barack, 45, 79, 96, 97, 98, 103, 140, 153, 162, 180, 215, 299, 309
O'Bannon, Ed, 153, 308
Oduya, Johnny, 92, 257
Ogunbowale, Arike, 108, 159, 170, 180, 186
Ogwumike sisters, Nneka and Chiney, 99, 186
Ogwumike, Chiney, 99, 105, 186
Ohio State University, 29, 63, 64, 93, 96, 166, 194, 207, 227, 242, 265
Ohio University, 45, 268
Ohio Valley Conference, 48, 49, 171, 191, 198
Okino, Betty, 76, 275
Oklahoma City Thunder, 96, 110, 197
Oklahoma Cougars, 76, 157, 185
Olajuwon, Hakeem, 74, 78, 84, 156, 186
Oliver, Al, 58, 119
Oliver, Reggie, 62, 234, 236
Oliver, Sumner "Red", 60, 291
Olympian Athletic League, 16, 151
Olympic Committee for Human Rights, 52, 265, 270, 300
Olympics, 15, 16, 17, 22, 24, 25, 32, 36, 37, 41, 45, 47, 49, 51, 52, 53, 54, 58, 63, 64, 65, 67, 69, 73, 75, 76, 78, 79, 80, 86, 87, 91, 92, 94, 97, 100, 101, 102, 103, 108, 109, 160, 164, 174, 175, 183, 187, 190, 191, 192, 199, 200, 201, 204, 205, 214, 228, 230,264, 265, 266, 267, 268, 269, 270, 271, 272, 273, 274, 275, 276, 277, 278, 288, 289, 290, 291, 300, 302, 316
O'Neal, Shaquille, 77, 112, 163, 186
Orange (NJ) Tornadoes, 24, 206
Orange Bowl, 40, 41, 71, 73, 141, 209, 221, 229, 234
Orlando Magic, 85, 95, 105, 159, 176, 188, 311
Orlando Renegades, 70, 223
Orridge, Jeffrey, 100, 236
Osaka, Naomi, 107, 109, 284
Oshkosh All-Stars (NBL), 27, 28, 155, 161
Oswald, John W., 55, 152, 301

Otis, Amos, 119, 304
Ottawa Rough Riders, 76, 292
Oubre, Jr., Kelly, 101, 158, 310
Our Sports magazine, 37, 130
Our World magazine, 39, 144
Outland Trophy, 40, 59, 207, 209, 226, 230
Overton, Monk, 13, 261
Owens, Jesse, 25, 61, 63, 75, 265, 275
Owens, R.C., 46, 236, 299
Owens, Terrell, 86, 214, 236, 307, 308

P

Pacific Coast Football League, 24, 206
Pacific Coast League, 19, 32, 38, 40, 118, 125, 128, 143, 316
Page Fence Giants, 14, 114
Page, Alan, 58, 102, 237
Page, Greg, 53, 236
Paige, Satchel, 24, 29, 32, 37, 41, 50, 58, 78, 111, 117, 126, 133, 141, 142, 296, 302
Palmer, Bobbiette, 107, 288
Palmer, Violet, 81, 92, 157, 186
Paris, Courtney, 92, 95, 187
Paris, Jr., John, 78, 253, 257
Parker, Candace, 90, 92, 94, 98, 110, 174, 187
Parker, Dave, 66, 71, 141
Parker, Tony, 99, 158, 171
Parks, Rosa, 18, 39, 94
Parkway Field
 Louisville, KY, 42, 118
Par-Lay Sports and Entertainment, 112, 159
Parris, Jonathan, 38, 118
Passaic (NJ) Red Devils, 24, 206
Paterson (NJ) Panthers, 24, 206
Patterson, Audrey "Mickey", 32, 264, 275
Patterson, Floyd, 36, 42, 45, 199, 204, 264
Patterson, Inez, 23, 151, 164, 196, 283, 285
Paul, Rich, 104, 108, 187, 311
Payne, Tom, 55, 56, 152, 187, 301
Payne, Ulice, 89, 141
Payton, Eugene, 25, 264
Payton, Walter, 60, 65, 71, 78, 79, 214, 232, 234, 237, 291
Peary, Admiral Robert, 17, 289
Peck, Carolyn, 84, 187
Peebles, Gia, 107, 288
Peeples, Nat, 39, 118, 141
Peete, Calvin, 68, 69, 70, 250, 304
Peete, Rodney, 74, 88, 237
Pegues, Julius, 40, 187
Pendleton, Terry, 107, 121, 137, 142, 312
Penn State, 17, 29, 32, 33, 71, 104, 151, 154, 187, 207, 209, 228, 229, 244, 311
Pennsylvania Open (Golf), 26, 248
Pensacola Baseball Club - Pensacola, FL, 12, 113
Pensions, 78, 136, 305
Pepitone, Joe, 61, 130, 303
Peppers, Charles, 40, 118, 298
Pereira, Mike, 214, 307
Perfect 300 Game, 291
Perfect Game, 15, 36, 114, 139
Perkins, Bruce, 74, 213, 233, 237

Emancipation Index

Perkins, James "Soup", 14, 259, 261
Perkins, Sam, 85, 306
Perrot, Kim, 86, 187
Perry, Claudia, 87
Perry, Hal, 39, 152
Perry, Joe, 32, 37, 38, 40, 47, 211, 212, 226, 235, 237
Perry, Lowell, 43, 51, 208, 237
Perry, William "The Refrigerator", 71, 237
Peterson, Horace, 75, 120
Pettit, Bob, 43, 112, 163
Petway, Bruce, 17, 114, 134, 142
PGA, 24, 33, 36, 37, 44, 46, 49, 52, 58, 63, 68, 70, 83, 87, 90, 97, 102, 204, 248, 249, 250, 251, 252, 295, 297, 299, 304
Philadelphia 76ers, 40, 62, 72, 167, 170, 174, 182, 197
Philadelphia Athletics, 23, 29, 35, 116, 126, 136, 296
Philadelphia Bell, 63, 212, 246
Philadelphia Colored Giants of New York, 18, 151
Philadelphia Eagles, 65, 71, 74, 76, 79, 96, 106, 214, 223, 234, 239, 244, 245, 307, 308, 309
Philadelphia Flyers, 87, 105, 253, 257, 312
Philadelphia Giants, 15, 16, 114, 132, 149
Philadelphia Orions, 11, 113
Philadelphia Phillies, 41, 48, 58, 77, 79, 111, 119, 121, 124, 128, 149, 299, 302
Philadelphia Public Links Golf Tournament, 24, 248
Philadelphia Pythians, 9, 12, 113, 114
Philadelphia Quaker Giants, 16, 114
Philadelphia Quick Steppers, 23, 151, 164, 196, 283, 285
Philadelphia Royal Giants, 22, 115, 137
Philadelphia Stars, 25, 30, 69, 129, 136, 221
Philadelphia Taney Dragons, 98, 129
Philadelphia Warriors, 47, 167
Philander Smith College, 40, 163
Phillips, Gene, 59, 156, 302
Phillips, Rowan Ricardo, 281
Phillips, Teresa, 89, 187
Phoenix Cardinals, 213, 305
Phoenix Mercury, 80, 98, 105, 108, 157, 159, 170, 174, 180, 184, 185, 186
Phoenix Suns, 89, 94, 106, 108, 159, 162, 185, 192, 193, 313
Pickett, Bill, 16, 18, 58, 77, 90, 280, 288
Pickett, Tidye, 24, 25, 264, 275, 277
Piedmont League, 117
Pierce, Chester, 31, 207
Piggott, Bert, 30, 211, 219, 238
Pinkney, Bill, 75, 291
Pittsburg[h] Keystones, 12, 114
Pittsburgh Courier, 20, 145, 248
Pittsburgh Crawfords, 24, 116, 133, 142, 146
Pittsburgh Keystones, 21, 149
Pittsburgh Panthers, 40, 42, 187, 207, 227, 298
Pittsburgh Pipers, 53, 175
Pittsburgh Pirates, 31, 40, 46, 58, 61, 63, 118, 125, 129, 144, 298
  NFL, 24, 26, 39, 66, 87, 119, 125, 126, 130, 136, 139, 140, 141, 146, 211, 231, 232, 295, 296, 303
Pittsburgh Scholastics Basketball Club, 19, 151, 178
Pittsburgh Steelers, 34, 43, 59, 60, 62, 63, 65, 79, 90, 95, 111, 214, 215, 216, 220, 224, 226, 227, 235, 237, 243, 303, 307, 309, 314
Planet Lovetron
  Darryl Dawkins, 156, 170, 303
Players Alliance, 104, 121, 313

Poage, George Coleman, 16, 264, 275
Poitier, Sidney, 45, 299
Pollard, Fritz, 19, 20, 21, 23, 25, 26, 39, 90, 206, 211, 214, 238, 239, 295, 316, 318
Pompez, Alex, 19, 115
Pontchartrain Golf Course, 21, 248
Pony League, 38, 40, 118, 124
Pope, Dave, 39, 118, 130
Popovich, Gregg, 99, 158, 171
Popovich, Paul, 55, 132
Porter, Kevin, 66, 187
Portland Power, 79, 80, 153, 157
Portland Trail Blazers, 65, 94, 108, 159, 162, 182, 194, 313
Portsmouth (VA) Merrimacs, 38, 117, 298
Portsmouth Swans, 29, 211
Posey, Cumberland, 17, 18, 20, 100, 151, 158, 184, 187, 188, 318
Postage Stamps, 68, 75, 77, 91, 98, 99, 105, 144, 167, 204, 254, 275, 280, 283, 284
Powell Jr., Adam Clayton, 66
Powell, Bill, 102, 249, 250, 251
Powell, Bill and Marcella, 30, 248
Powell, Jake, 26, 116, 296
Powell, Mike, 76, 276
Powell, Renée, 46, 52, 102, 249, 250, 251
Powell, Supreme Court Justice Lewis
  Curt Flood case, 59, 131
Powell, Zeb, 105, 291
Power Memorial High School (NY), 51, 195
Preakness, 12, 14, 259, 260, 262
Prescod, Nzingha, 98, 291
Prescott, Dak, 217
Presidential Medal of Freedom, 70, 77, 89, 91, 92, 96, 98, 99, 100, 102, 103, 110, 124, 126, 129, 139, 140, 143, 144, 190, 201, 237, 251, 252, 265, 267, 275, 283
Presidents Cup, 82, 251
Price, Al, 155
Price, Bennie, 155
Price, David, 101, 142, 310
Price, Leontyne, 22
Pride, Charley, 61, 142
Pride, Curtis, 77, 142
Princeton University, 57, 198, 265
Pritchett, Walter "Cricket", 58, 249
Pro Bowl's Player of the Game, 37, 63, 228, 243
Professional Golfers Association (PGA), 22, 248, 295, 296
Profit, Joe, 54, 208
Providence College, 61, 303
Providence Grays, 11, 113
Providence Steam Rollers (NFL), 22, 238
Purcell, Ryan Guzzo, 111, 141

Q

Qualls, Edwina, 64, 186
Quebec Provincial League, 30, 253

R

Radcliffe, Alex and Ted, 26, 142
Radcliffe, Ted, 24, 28, 116, 142
Rae, Mae, 19, 281, 284

Raines, Tim, 88, 143
Rainey, John, 56, 209
Rallins, Mamie, 64, 265
Ralph, Sheryl Lee, 112, 216
Ramey, Jordan, 104, 121, 312
Ramirez, Manny, 85, 120, 124
Ramsey, Kirk, 36, 291
Ramsey, Randolph, 22, 160, 181
Randle, John, 83, 238, 306
Randle, Lenny, 119, 304
Rando, Rajon, 96, 158, 309
Randolph, Natalie, 95, 238
Randolph, Willie, 92, 119, 139, 143, 303
Rapsody, 104, 286
Ray, Joie, 37, 291
Ready, Stephanie, 87, 188
Reagan, President Ronald, 70, 153
Reagins, Tony, 94, 120
Reamon, Tommy, 62, 238
Reavis, Phil, 43, 264, 276
Red Hot Chili Peppers, 74, 178
Reed Trophy, Willis, 110, 168, 169, 171, 179, 181, 188
Reed, Matt, 62, 238
Reed, Willis, 57, 188
Reese, Jerry, 94, 239
Reese, Pee Wee, 31, 143
Reeves, Dan, 30, 211, 245
Register, John, 86, 276
Reid, Tracy, 82, 188
Renaissance Big Five, 59, 161, 170
Renfroe, William J., 11, 113, 133
Reveling, George, 55, 59, 188
Rhoden, William C., 293
Rhodes, Ray, 79, 83, 213, 239
Rhodes, Teddy, 20, 33, 248, 295, 297
Rhodman, William, 32, 38, 290, 292
Ribbs, Willy T., 75, 292
Rice, Condoleezza, 97, 111, 228, 249, 251
Rice, Jerry, 72, 80, 83, 87, 88, 239
Rice, Tamir, 7, 215, 309
Rich Paul Rule, 104, 311
Richards, J.R., 65, 143
Richardson, Desiree "Boo Boo", 38, 146
Richardson, Hosea Lee, 35, 259, 261
Richardson, Michael Ray, 66, 156
Richardson, Nolan, 67, 69, 78, 188
Richey, Dorothy, 63
Richey, John, 32, 143
Richmond Rage, 79, 157
Richmond Rams, 29, 211
Richmond Rebels, 33, 223
Ricketts, Dick, 39, 40, 172, 188, 192
Rickey, Branch, 16, 29, 116, 206, 225, 296, 297
Rile, Ed, 20, 133
Riley, Bill, 63, 253
Ring magazine, 25, 204
Rios, Herman, 20, 115
Rivera, Mariano, 81, 120, 145
Rivers, Glenn "Doc", 85, 188
Rivers, John
    Cannon Street All-Stars, 70

Rizzuto, Phil, 37, 57, 117, 148
Roberts, Michele A., 98, 189
Robertson, Alvin, 71, 189
Robertson, Oscar, 39, 43, 44, 45, 46, 47, 82, 153, 156, 169, 183, 189, 300, 301, 308, 309
Robeson, Paul, 19, 21, 84, 206, 211, 238, 239, 281, 283, 295
Robeson, Rudolph "Rocky", 28, 151, 189
Robinson, Crystal, 80, 189
Robinson, David, 88, 180, 192
Robinson, Eddie, 28, 33, 207, 239, 247
Robinson, Edna Mae, 35
Robinson, Eroseanna "Rose", 44, 276, 298
Robinson, Frank, 51, 60, 63, 68, 73, 74, 89, 92, 119, 125, 143
Robinson, Harold, 33, 34, 207, 226, 239
Robinson, Jackie, 12, 26, 28, 30, 31, 33, 34, 36, 37, 39, 41, 42, 45, 47, 50, 51, 68, 72, 77, 81, 86, 90, 94, 109, 117, 118, 120, 121, 126, 127, 141, 143, 144, 145, 146, 192, 208, 293, 297, 298, 299, 302, 304, 312, 313, 314
Robinson, Mack, 87, 276
Robinson, Sugar Ray, 28, 35, 41, 43, 75, 145, 199, 200, 204, 205, 293, 296
Robinson, Will, 57, 60, 94, 157, 158, 189, 191, 242
Rochester Jeffersons, 18, 206, 234
Rochester Royals, 39, 42, 172, 188, 192
Rock Island Independents, 21, 211, 241
Rocket Richard Trophy, 88, 253, 256
Rocky the movie, 63, 201
Roddenbery Memorial Library, 109, 121, 145, 314
Rodgers, Aaron, 97, 244
Rodhe, Cécilia, 93, 153
Rodman, Dennis, 80, 94, 157, 190
Rogan, Wilber "Bullet", 22, 132, 145
Rojas, Cookie, 55, 119, 131, 301
Rollins, Brianna, 101, 266
Roman Cities Baseball Club - LaVilla, FL, 12, 113
Rookie of the Year, 31, 33, 34, 37, 38, 41, 42, 43, 44, 45, 49, 51, 52, 53, 56, 69, 71, 72, 82, 84, 85, 89, 94, 105, 120, 126, 127, 129, 131, 136, 140, 143, 144, 156, 167, 169, 172, 175, 176, 187, 188, 190, 191, 192, 219, 221, 225, 228, 235, 240, 243, 244, 304
Rooney Rule, 90, 307
Rooney, Art, 111, 216, 314
Rose Bowl, 19, 30, 73, 206, 207, 209, 211, 213, 238, 247, 305
Roseboro, John, 46, 145
Rosen, Al, 38, 117, 144, 297
Rouse, Vic, 47, 152, 299
Royal, Darrell, 55, 208
Rozelle Rule, 56, 233, 301
Ruck, Rob, 259
Rudolph, Wilma, 45, 61, 65, 67, 80, 265, 266, 273, 276
Rumble In The Jungle, 33, 62, 128, 160, 161, 168, 199, 203
Rupp, Adolph, 33, 50, 55, 56, 93, 152, 153, 187, 198, 300, 301
Russell Rule, 105, 190, 311
Russell, Bill, 39, 41, 42, 43, 45, 47, 48, 50, 51, 53, 60, 61, 62, 63, 67, 84, 118, 150, 152, 153, 155, 163, 167, 172, 179, 190, 192, 250, 299, 306, 308
Russell, Nipsey, 23
Ruth, Babe, 61, 85, 86, 120, 124, 134, 303
Ryan, Red, 21, 136
Ryder Cup, 82, 252
Ryland, Robert, 44, 284

Emancipation Index

S

Saal, Rosemary, 111, 266
Saban, Lou, 54, 220
Sabathia, C.C., 104, 121, 313
Sacramento Monarchs, 80, 84, 157, 173, 176
Saddler, Sandy, 75, 200
Salley, John, 25
Sam, Michael, 99, 101, 215, 239, 240, 309, 310
Sampson, Charlie, 68, 90, 280, 288
Sampson, Ralph, 68, 69, 153, 190
San Antonio Spurs, 58, 64, 65, 71, 85, 99, 156, 158, 171, 173, 189, 193, 302
San Antonio Toros, 55, 244
San Antonio Wings, 63, 244
San Diego Chargers, 48, 50, 51, 63, 71, 208, 228, 229, 231, 233, 244
San Diego Open, 36, 248
San Diego Padres, 60, 61, 66, 75, 119, 125, 146, 150, 305
San Diego State, 33, 272, 289
San Francisco 49ers, 32, 40, 49, 71, 72, 78, 80, 86, 96, 101, 106, 211, 215, 223, 230, 231, 235, 236, 237, 239, 240, 242, 268, 307, 310
San Francisco B.B.C., 15, 114
San Francisco Dons, 39, 41, 152, 190
San Francisco Giants, 44, 49, 68, 73, 77, 86, 88, 111, 125, 127, 134, 136, 138, 143, 314
San José Lasers, 79, 157
San José Sharks, 111, 256
Sanders, Barry, 80, 81, 83, 213, 240
Sanders, Deion, 74, 78, 81, 111, 145, 210, 240, 292, 305
Sanders, Ed, 36, 199, 264
Sanders, Satch, 49, 155, 179, 186, 191, 299
Sanderson, Curtis, 104, 121, 313
Sanguillén, Manny, 58, 119
Sankey, Greg, 104, 228, 313
Santa Barbara State College Gauchos, 26, 192
Saucer, Willie, 40, 240
Sauldsberry, Woody, 155, 299
Savannah Braves, 61, 124
Savoy Big Five
   (basketball team), 22, 24, 160, 181, 232
Savoy Colts, 23, 151, 196, 285
Sayers, Gale, 48, 49, 55, 240
Schmeling, Max, 26, 204
Schott. Marge, 104, 121, 312
Scott Stadium in Charlottesville, Virginia, 31, 207
Scott, Charlie, 51, 191
Scott, George, 72, 120
Scott, Oscar, 59, 191
Scott, Ray, 58, 61, 181, 191
Scott, Stuart, 99
Scott, Wendell, 48, 99, 292
Scottron, Charles, 18, 151
Scully, Vin, 61, 124, 303
Seabrooks, Norman, 55, 240
Searle, Clayton, 139, 305
Sears, Mark, 64
Seattle Kraken (NHL), 106, 255
Seattle Mariners, 67, 75, 77, 85, 111, 125, 134, 150, 166
Seattle Reign, 79, 157

Seattle Seahawks, 74, 81, 96, 97, 99, 213, 215, 222, 227, 231, 233, 235, 236, 237, 246, 307, 309
Seattle SuperSonics, 57, 70, 78, 81, 156, 171, 175, 182, 302
Sefolosha, Thabo, 158, 309
Sehorn, Jason, 81, 240
Seitz, Peter
   Curt Flood case, 63, 131, 303
Selden, William, 14, 114, 145
Selig, Bud, 85, 89, 120, 124, 141
Sessions, Sally, 34, 248
Seymour, Teddy, 72, 292
Shady Rest Golf & Country Club, 20, 248
Shanahan, Mike, 74, 234, 240, 308
Sharrers, Jay, 87, 257
Shaw University, 28, 151, 189
Shaw, Dale, 106, 216
Shekerjian, General Haig, 28, 199, 296
Shelbourne, John Andrew, 21, 240
Shelby Blues
   Ohio League, 16, 206, 225
Shelby, Andre, 100, 276
Shell, Art, 74, 240
Sherbrooke Canadians, 30, 256
Sherbrooke Randies, 30, 255, 256
Sherman Antitrust Act, 59, 82, 131, 153, 156, 175, 302, 306, 308
Shields, Claressa, 97, 101, 200, 204, 276
Shine, Entee, 36, 164, 191
Shinn, George, 84, 180
Shippen, John, 14, 18, 76, 248, 251, 295
Show, Eric, 75, 305
Shumpert, Iman, 108, 191
Sidat-Singh, Wilmeth, 25, 26, 207, 229, 241
Sifford, Charles, 42, 44, 46, 52, 63, 90, 248, 249, 251, 295, 299
Silver Slugger, 102, 126
Simmonds, Wayne, 102, 105, 253, 257, 312
Simmons, Ron, 76, 292
Simms, Willie, 13, 14, 15, 65, 259, 262
Simpson, Lenward, 62, 281
Simpson, O. J., 60, 81, 213, 240, 241
Sims, Duke, 52, 130
SLAM magazine, 79, 82, 88, 108, 159, 170, 174, 176, 177, 180, 186, 193
SLAM's Black Lives Matter magazine, 108, 159, 162, 313
Slater, Duke, 19, 20, 21, 22, 23, 35, 36, 206, 207, 211, 239, 241, 295
Slater, Fred "Duke", 21
Sloan, Tod, 65, 262
Small, Viro "Black Sam", 9, 292
Smallwood, Dewitt "Woody", 75, 120
Smart Set Athletic Club of Brooklyn, 16, 17, 18, 151
Smart, Keeth, 89, 277
Smith III, Wilson, 82
Smith, Akili, 83, 210, 223, 232, 234
Smith, Al, 39, 118, 130
Smith, Bianca, 107, 108, 140, 145
Smith, Bruce, 80, 241, 245
Smith, Bubba, 52, 241
Smith, Calvin, 69, 277
Smith, Charles A.C. "The Black Thunderbolt", 10, 205
Smith, Charlotte, 78, 153
Smith, Chino, 23, 116

Index

Smith, Claire, 100, 101, 109, 137, 146, 292, 293
Smith, Coach Dean, 57, 152, 184
Smith, Collette, 106, 231
Smith, Dwight, 47, 175
Smith, Emmitt, 76, 77, 83, 93, 241, 306
Smith, Gene
    golfer, 40, 251
Smith, Geno, 102, 217, 218, 242
Smith, Gideon "Charlie", 19, 242
Smith, Iris, 91, 293
Smith, Lovie, 93, 214, 225, 242
Smith, Marilynn, 34, 248
Smith, Maurice, 80, 200, 293
Smith, Rod, 91, 242
Smith, Ronnie Ray, 54, 271, 272, 277
Smith, Sam, 47, 176, 191, 196
Smith, Tommie, 52, 54, 265, 268, 270, 277, 300
Smith, Troy, 96, 242
Smith, Wendell, 43, 77, 100, 120, 137, 145, 146, 199, 205, 292, 293
Snow, Michelle, 85, 191
Snowden, Fred "The Fox", 60, 191, 242
Snyder, Dan, 106, 215, 311
Snyder, Jimmy, 62, 73, 212, 223, 304
Social Change Fund
    NBA players, 108, 159, 162, 313
Sonic Boom of the South, 111, 210
Sosa, Sammy, 85, 120, 124
Soul on Ice, 57
Souls of Black Folk, 15
South Carolina State College, 31, 207, 221
Southeastern Conference (SEC), 47, 53, 56, 60, 74, 76, 91, 102, 164, 176, 195, 209, 210, 223, 229, 236, 288, 301
Southern Association BB League, 40, 118, 141, 298
Southern Illinois University, 25, 264
Southern League of Colored Base Ballists, 11, 113
Southern Methodist University, 32, 50, 208, 228, 244
Southern University, 65, 75, 111, 209, 210, 212, 220, 303
Southwest Conference (SWC), 50, 51, 54, 167, 208, 245
Sowers, Katie, 106, 231
Spartan Athletic Club of Brooklyn (NY) [basketball], 18, 151
Spaulding, Albert Goodwill, 132
Speedy, Walter, 17, 248
Spiller, Bill, 20, 33, 37, 248, 251, 295, 297
Spingarn Medal (NAACP), 41, 144
Spink Award, 77, 101, 120, 146, 293
Spinks, Leon, 64, 65, 199, 201, 205, 265
Spinks, Michael, 71, 205
Splitter, Tiago, 99, 158, 171
Spork, Shirley, 34, 248
Sport Illustrated's Sportsman of the Year, 66, 146
Sporting Life, 12, 14
Sports Collectors Digest magazine, 91, 133
Sports Illustrated, 31, 39, 40, 42, 43, 46, 55, 63, 68, 70, 71, 79, 81, 86, 89, 90, 98, 99, 104, 105, 107, 109, 129, 138, 140, 153, 157, 165, 167, 174, 178, 184, 192, 201, 204, 207, 212, 214, 225, 226, 230, 233, 249, 250, 252, 264, 273, 276, 284
Sports Stars magazine, 35, 144
Sportsman's Park (St. Louis, MO), 29, 116, 296
Springfield Tennis Club (MA), 21, 281
Springs, Ron, 93
Squires, LaVannes, 34, 191

St. Christopher Club of New York, 18, 151
St. John's University, 35, 152, 195
St. Julien, Marlon, 13, 85, 259, 262
St. Louis Black Broncos, 17, 114
St. Louis Blues, 73, 253, 257
St. Louis Browns, 15, 18, 29, 31, 36, 37, 116, 117, 127, 132, 138, 141, 146, 296
St. Louis Cardinals, 29, 30, 35, 38, 39, 40, 44, 45, 55, 71, 94, 116, 117, 119, 120, 129, 133, 136, 147, 173, 188, 256, 296, 302, 308
St. Louis Hawks, 40, 41, 43, 46, 155, 176, 186, 188, 299
St. Louis Rams, 99, 101, 215, 239, 240, 246, 306, 309, 310
St. Paul Saints, 32, 127
Stackhouse, Jerry, 80, 88, 180, 191
Stackhouse, Mariah Imani, 99, 251
Staley, Dawn, 108, 164, 192
Stanford University, 34, 66, 195, 265
Stanley Cup, 67, 70, 96, 255, 257
Stapleton Buffaloes, 24, 206
Stargell, Willie, 58, 66, 119, 146
Starks, John, 78, 192
Starr, "Mae" Faggs, 41, 264, 271
Staten Island Stapletons, 23, 206, 236
Staverman, Larry, 46, 175
Stearnes, Norman "Turkey", 24, 146
Steed, Greg, 106, 216
Steinbeck, John, 16
Stengel, Casey, 135
Stennett, Rennie, 58, 63, 119, 146
Stephens, Sandy, 45, 52, 208, 242, 300
Stephenson, Dwight, 67, 213
Sterling, Donald, 99, 158, 309
Stern, David, 157, 308
Stevens, R. C., 40, 118, 298
Stevenson, Alexandra, 84, 285
Steward, Charles, 56, 265
Steward, Lowell, 26, 192
Stewart, James "Bubba", 91, 293
Stewart, Kordell, 82, 166, 242
Stiles, Maxwell, 38, 125
Still, Valerie, 80, 192
Stivers, Wayne, 2, 14, 114, 145
Stokes, Louise, 24, 25, 264, 277
Stokes, Maurice, 39, 42, 78, 172, 188, 192
Stone, Toni, 38, 39, 118, 146
Stoneham, Horace, 27, 134, 296
Stoudemire, Amar'e, 89, 192
Stoval, John, 11, 262
Stovey, George, 11, 12, 113, 114, 133, 146, 148, 295
Stowe, Lucy Diggs, 19, 281, 284, 285
Streeter, Sam, 24, 146
Strickland, Alan, 107, 158, 195, 311
Stringer, Vivian, 68, 73, 85, 88, 93, 95, 110, 153, 192, 193
Strode, Woody, 27, 29, 207, 211, 242, 245, 296, 297
Stroman, Debra, 65, 193
Strong, Ted, 155
Stroud, C.J., 217
Stroy, Esther, 66, 265
Subban, P. K., 96, 98, 257
Sugar Bowl, 27, 42, 73, 207, 209, 227, 296, 298
Suggs, Louise, 34, 248
Sullivan, John L., 11, 199, 202

Emancipation Index

Super Bowl, 52, 54, 55, 58, 61, 62, 63, 70, 71, 73, 75, 76, 77, 78, 81, 93, 94, 95, 97, 99, 101, 108, 142, 145, 209, 212, 213, 214, 215, 219, 222, 225, 227, 228, 232, 233, 234, 237, 240, 241, 242, 243, 246, 265, 268, 272, 289, 292, 302, 304, 305, 307, 309
Surratt, Alfred "Slick", 75, 120
Suttles, George "Mule", 24, 146
Swartz, Dan, 46, 175
Switzer, Barry, 71, 209, 229
Swoopes, Sheryl, 75, 79, 80, 84, 96, 157, 185, 193
Syracuse 8, 208, 301, 318
Syracuse Nationals, 39, 43, 181, 195, 221
Syracuse Stars, 11, 12, 113
Syracuse University, 25, 47, 207, 208, 224, 229, 241, 301

T

Tagovailoa, Tua, 217
Taliaferro, George, 33, 34, 37, 101, 211, 225, 229, 243, 247
Tallapoosa Baseball Club - St. Augustine, FL, 12, 113
Tampa Bay Bandits, 76, 292
Tampa Bay Buccaneers, 64, 65, 74, 86, 94, 95, 106, 213, 214, 216, 221, 223, 224, 225, 227, 231, 232, 233, 237, 246
Tampa Bay Devil Rays, 87, 139
Target Field, 46, 299, 312
Tarkanian, Jerry, 75, 156
Tarver, Corrinne, 74, 93, 267, 277
Tatum, Reece "Goose", 28, 160
Tausaga-Collins, Laulauga, 112, 277
Taylor, C. I., 20, 115, 132
Taylor, Eddie, 111, 266
Taylor, John Baxter "Doc", 17, 264, 277
Taylor, Lawrence, 80, 243
Taylor, Lionel, 44, 243
Taylor, Major, 14, 15, 17, 23, 293
Taylor, Maria, 105, 312
Taylor, Mike, 94, 193
Taylor, Otis, 48, 245
Taylor, Steve, 73, 209
Taylor, Suzette, 89, 200, 202
Teague, Ted
    Allen Samuels dealership, 108, 154, 313
Telfair, Sebastian, 88, 177, 193
Temple, Jr., Collis, 58, 193, 302
Templeton, Garry, 66, 146
Tennessee A & I, 44, 183
Tennessee State, 54, 59, 64
Tennessee State University, 28, 89, 110, 173, 183, 184, 187, 224, 226, 264, 265, 301
Tennessee Titans, 85, 90, 93, 108, 226, 231, 234, 246, 247
Terrell, Mary Church, 43
Terry, John F., 25, 277
Texas A&I Javelinas, 44, 208, 220
Texas Christian Horned Frogs, 51, 166
Texas Rangers, 93, 129, 148
Texas Tech Red Raiders, 55, 180
Texas Western University (UTEP), 50, 93, 152, 153, 300
The Bluest Eye, 41
The Colored Museum, 71
The Eyes of Texas, 109, 313
The Georgia Champions' Baseball Club - Atlanta, GA, 12, 113
The Greg Hill Show, 106, 121, 312

The Horse Soldiers, 44, 284
The Plain Dealer, 32, 117
The Sporting News, 18, 31, 43, 44, 57, 60, 66, 73, 75, 77, 79, 89, 94, 109, 120, 121, 139, 143, 146, 171, 210, 221, 228, 239, 241, 246, 273, 293, 312, 313
Thomas, Debi, 71, 73, 277
Thomas, Emmitt, 48, 83, 213, 245
Thomas, Franklin
    Ford Foundation, 33
Thomas, Gabrielle, 109, 277
Thomas, Isiah, 78, 81, 84, 157, 193
Thomas, John, 43, 278
Thompson, Amen XLNC, 112, 159, 194
Thompson, Ausar XLNC, 159
Thompson, Ausar XLNC, 112
Thompson, Charles, 73, 209
Thompson, David, 62, 65, 66, 171, 173, 194
Thompson, Ed, 34, 155, 168, 181
Thompson, Frank P., 11, 113
Thompson, George, 304
Thompson, Hank, 31, 33, 35, 39, 117, 118, 127, 135, 146
Thompson, John, 58, 70, 72, 74, 93, 110, 153, 156, 194, 305
Thompson, Mychal, 65, 194
Thompson, Russell, 20, 115, 132
Thompson, Tina, 80, 98, 194
Thompson, Troy, 159
Thomson, Bobby, 35, 117
Thorn, John, 30
Thorpe, Jim, 43, 60, 69, 88, 221, 241, 249, 251, 266, 273
Three Rivers Stadium, 58, 119
Thrower, Willie, 37, 243
Thurmond, Nate, 62, 194
Tiant, Jr., Luis, 54, 63, 119, 132, 146, 147, 301
Tiant, Sr., Luis, 31, 63, 117, 147
Tiger Woods
    Earl Woods, 150
Tilghman, Kelly, 90, 252, 307
Time magazine, 28, 31, 34, 42, 45, 46, 50, 58, 70, 93, 105, 126, 143, 185, 189, 193, 199, 204, 221, 252, 273, 284, 308
Tisdale, Wayman, 69, 70, 74, 153, 162, 194, 304
To Kill A Mockingbird, 21
Todmann, Norwood, 51, 195
Tolan, Eddie, 23, 24, 278
Toledo Blue Stockings, 10, 11, 113, 147, 148
Toledo Daily Blade, 11, 147, 148
Toledo Jim White Chevrolet, 155
Tomlin, Mike, 95, 214, 243
Tomlinson, LaDainian, 90, 243
Toronto Argonauts, 91, 222
Toronto Blue Jays, 74, 76, 77, 132, 149
Toronto Raptors, 78, 81, 84, 107, 157, 158, 193, 195, 311
Torres, José "Gacho, Chico", 22, 147
Torriente, Cristóbal, 19, 115, 147
Towler, Dan, 37, 243, 247
Track & Field News, 45, 67, 267, 273
transgender, 98, 102, 154, 168, 310
Trenton Giants, 34, 138
Tribune Girls (Philadelphia), 23, 151, 163, 196, 283, 285
Trice, Jack, 70, 82, 209, 210, 213, 243, 244, 306
Tri-Cities Blackhawks, 34, 155, 170, 297
Triplett, Wally, 29, 32, 33, 34, 37, 207, 219, 228, 233, 244

Index

Trouppe, Quincy, 36, 38, 147
Trujillo, Rafael "El Jefe", 296
Truman, President Harry S., 29
trump, donald, 96, 102, 103, 177, 215, 309, 310
Truro Sheiks (CHL), 16, 253
Truro Victorias (CHL), 16, 253
Trusty, Shep, 11, 113
Truth, Sojourner, 11
Tsukahara, Mitsuo, 69, 266, 270
Tucker, Ed, 34, 195
Tucker, Jim, 39, 181, 195
Tucker, Leonard, 38, 147
Tugerson, Jim and Leander, 38, 117, 297
Tulsa Shocks, 98, 197
Tunnell, Emlen, 32, 52, 244
Turkey Leg Award, 74, 245
Turner, Glenda, 107, 288
Turner, Ted, 64, 119, 137
Tuskegee Airmen, 26, 192
Tuskegee Institute, 17, 26, 248, 281
Tutu, Desmond, 10
Tyson, Mike, 93
Tyus, Wyomia, 54, 278

U

U.S. Coast Guard Academy, 25, 172, 296
U.S. Davis Cup Tennis, 48, 283
U.S. Golf Association, 41, 249, 250
U.S. military integrates, 31, 117, 297
U.S. Open, 79, 91, 282, 288
U.S. Open (golf), 14, 18, 83, 86, 87, 248, 249, 251, 252, 295
U.S. Ryder Cup, 66, 69, 250
U.S. Soccer Athlete of the Year, 94, 290
UCLA, 27, 28, 29, 30, 31, 38, 41, 53, 64, 65, 133, 143, 152, 153, 162, 164, 171, 179, 186, 211, 242, 245, 296, 297, 308
Udall, Secretary Stewart, 46
Udall, Stewart
    Secretary of the Interior, 212
Udall, Stewart
    Secretary of the Interior, 208
Udall, Stewart
    Secretary of the Interior, 299
Ujiri, Masai, 107, 158, 195, 311
Union Baseball Club - New Orleans, LA, 12, 114
United Golfers Association (UGA), 22, 248, 295
United Press International, 41, 44, 55, 60, 73, 74, 167, 190, 191, 228, 240, 242
United States Colored Golf Association, 22, 248, 295
United States Football League, 55, 69, 221, 244
United States Lawn Tennis Association, 63, 283
United States National Guard, 58, 193, 302
United States Professional Skating Association (USPSA), 19, 264, 271
University of Alabama, 56, 104, 177, 233, 246
University of Arkansas, 56, 180
University of Citadel, 59, 191
University of Colorado State, 39, 162
University of Connecticut, 25, 172, 296
University of Delaware, 38, 207
University of Detroit Mercy, 56, 175

University of Florida, 54, 57, 184, 197, 265
University of Georgia, 56, 265
University of Houston, 56, 236
University of Illinois, 30, 42, 106, 160, 207, 245, 247, 318
University of Iowa, 26
University of Kansas, 34, 47, 60, 183, 191, 196
University of Louisiana, 54, 208
University of Maryland, 46, 50, 55, 72, 179, 188, 195, 208
University of Miami, 53, 106, 162, 185
University of Michigan, 13, 29, 79, 81, 92, 157, 164, 176, 219, 224, 230, 246
University of Mississippi, 57, 81, 163, 209, 301, 306
University of Nevada, 31, 75, 94, 156, 182, 207, 221
University of North Carolina, 51, 191
University of Pennsylvania, 25, 229
University of Pittsburgh, 40, 187
University of Southern California, 43, 55, 56, 68, 70, 71, 74, 80, 88, 94, 109, 153, 182, 183, 184, 194, 209, 219, 223, 224, 230, 237, 246, 301
University of Tennessee, 54, 208
University of Tennessee at Chattanooga, 53, 162
University of Texas, 55, 109, 208, 313
University of Tulsa, 69, 188
University of Villanova, 43, 264, 276
University of Virginia, 31, 56, 57, 65, 170, 193, 207, 209, 317
University of Washington, 54, 265, 267, 318
Unknowns of Weeksville, 9, 113
Unseld, Wes, 51, 62, 152, 175, 195
US Open (tennis), 53, 76, 77, 86, 89, 107, 112, 281, 283, 284, 285, 286, 305, 307
USA Baseball, 101, 120
USA National Marathon, 39, 269
USAG Hall of Fame, 88, 268
Ussery II, Terdema, 75, 195
Utah Stars, 61, 62, 150, 182
Utah Starzz, 80, 81, 84, 157, 176
Utica Morning Herald, 11, 113

V

Vails, Nelson, 69, 278
Valdés, Faustino, 20, 115
Vanderbilt University, 53, 195, 236
Vardon Trophy, 70, 83, 250, 252, 304
Vechten, Carl Van, 22
Veeck, Bill, 31, 32, 130, 141
Velásquez, Jesús "El Tigre", 19, 147
Versailles, Zoilo "Zorro", 48, 147
Vick, Michael, 34, 85, 87, 89, 91, 93, 96, 214, 235, 244, 318
Victor, Ben
    sculptor, 110, 173
Vincent, Fay, 92, 137
Virginia Negro Football League, 29, 211
Virginia Squires, 51, 191
Virginia State, 30, 34, 152, 155, 168, 181, 183
Virginia Tech Institute, 51, 52, 54, 85, 87, 168, 181, 244, 265, 300
Virginia Union University, 33, 223
Vogue magazine, 94, 177

Emancipation Index

W

Waddod Jr., Ghalee, 112
Wade, Aaron, 50, 51, 208, 212, 243, 244
Wade, Bob, 72, 195
Wade, Dwyane, 93, 108, 157, 158, 159, 162, 308, 313
Wade, Lily Margaret
   Wade Trophy, 67, 198
Wagner, Leon "Daddy Wags", 47, 147
Wake Forest University, 51, 58, 72, 165, 169, 181, 195, 197
Wake Robin Golf Club, 26, 248
Walberg, Rube, 23, 126
Walcott, Jersey Joe, 36, 75, 199, 200, 202, 205
Walker, Alice, 28
Walker, Billy, 10, 11, 92, 259, 262
Walker, Clarence, 32, 152, 195, 297
Walker, Doak, 50, 208
Walker, Dr. LeRoy, 76, 266
Walker, Harry J., 20, 147
Walker, Jarace, 112, 159
Walker, Maggie L., 15
Walker, Moses Fleetwood, vii, 9, 10, 11, 12, 13, 17, 20, 113, 114, 133, 146, 147, 148, 295
Walker, Solly, 35, 152, 195
Wall Street Journal, 103, 231, 311
Wallace, Ben, 30, 89, 108, 152, 183, 195
Wallace, Bubba, 106, 293, 311
Wallace, Cason, 112, 159
Wallace, Nunc, 13, 199, 202
Wallace, Perry Eugene, 53, 195
Wallace, Seneca, 40, 97, 220, 244
Walls, Everson, 93
Walter Camp Award, 71, 219
Walter Camp's All-American football team, 16, 19, 206, 238
Walter Payton Man of the Year, 60, 214, 232
Walton, Johnnie, 55, 65, 244, 245
Ward, Arch, 29, 211
Ward, Charlie, 77, 78, 196, 245, 294
Ware, Andre, 74, 75, 245
Washington (DC) 12 Streeters, 17, 151, 176
Washington Bears, 28, 30, 74, 155, 165, 168, 173, 177
Washington Bullets, 62, 195
Washington Capitals, 61, 63, 91, 157, 179, 253, 256
Washington Capitol Citys, 12, 114
Washington Capitols, 34, 105, 155, 159, 168, 181, 183, 297
Washington Commanders, 111, 179, 235
Washington Elite Giants, 26, 127
Washington Federals, 70, 223
Washington Football Team, 106, 107, 215, 231, 247
Washington Mystics, 84, 91, 105, 157, 168, 176, 179, 182
Washington Nationals, 92, 143
Washington Pilots, 24, 116
Washington Post, 24, 116, 141, 302
Washington Redskins, 46, 47, 49, 63, 72, 73, 86, 97, 106, 208, 212, 213, 215, 224, 226, 227, 228, 234, 235, 236, 239, 243, 246, 247, 299, 304, 308
Washington Senators, 46, 55, 137, 299, 312
Washington State University, 59, 188
Washington Wizards, 87, 89, 91, 94, 101, 157, 158, 166, 179, 180, 182, 310
Washington, Ashton, 106, 245

Washington, E. Davidson, 17, 281
Washington, Herb, 62, 119, 148, 278
Washington, Kenny, 27, 29, 207, 211, 242, 245, 296, 297
Washington, MaliVai, 79, 278
Washington, Marian, 60, 68, 196
Washington, Ora, 20, 23, 25, 151, 163, 164, 196, 248, 283, 285
Washington, Ron, 93, 129, 148
Washington, U. L., 67, 149
Watkins, Fenwick, 17, 151, 196
Watley, Natasha Renée, 90, 148
Watson, Bob, 64, 71, 77, 78, 80, 119, 120, 137, 148
Watson, Deshaun, 217
Weatherspoon, Teresa, 81, 196
Webb, Spud, 70, 196
Webster, Marvin
   The Human Eraser, 66, 156
Weddington, Elaine C., 74, 148
Weekes, Kevin, 95, 253, 257
Weiner, Michael S., 98, 128
Weiss, George, 36, 117, 297
Wells, Georgeann, 70, 196
Wells, Lloyd, 48, 56, 245, 265
Wells, Willie "The Devil", 26, 148, 296
Wembanyama, Victor, 112, 159
Wepner, Chuck, 63, 201
West Virginia University, 102, 242
West, Cornel, 77
West, Ed, 11, 262
West, Jerry, 45, 183
West, Zano, 155
Westbrook, John Hill, 51, 245
Westbrook, Peter, 69, 266, 278
Western Kentucky University, 47, 175
Western Texas Junior College, 67, 188
Wheaties cereal box, 25, 37, 71, 73, 78, 79, 81, 87, 91, 126, 127, 133, 141, 145, 179, 237, 273, 275, 283, 284
Wheeler, Erica, 103, 196
Wheeler, Lonnie, 64, 124
White Fragility, 82
White Plains Bears, 24, 206
White, Alton, 59, 61, 253, 256, 257
White, Bill, 45, 57, 74, 120, 148
White, Cheryl, 58, 64, 69, 259, 262
White, Eugene "Stank", 38, 117, 298
White, Frank, 55, 64, 67, 148, 149
White, Jackie, 51, 53, 196
White, Jo Jo, 180
White, King Solomon, 14, 16, 114
White, Reggie, 74, 80, 241, 245
White, Ruth, 56, 265, 278
White, Sherman, 40, 155
White, Willye, 41, 278
Whitehead, Eddie, 47, 176, 191, 196
Whitehead, Willie, 306
Whiteside, Larry, 57, 149, 293
Whitfield, Fred, 79, 85, 89, 280
Whitfield, Mal, 39, 49, 61, 265, 278, 300
Whitmore, Bob, 53, 152
Whitney, Davey, 66, 67, 153, 197
Whittier, Julius, 56, 245
Wichita (KS) Monrovians, 22, 115

Index

Wichita State University, 66, 209
Wide World of Sports, 55, 71, 107, 119, 131, 163, 277, 301
Wiggins, Charlie "the Negro Speed King", 22, 25, 294, 317
Wilberforce University, 31, 152
Wilbon, Michael, 293
Wiley, Ralph, 293
Wilken, Judge Claudia, 308
Wilkerson, Isabel, 19, 28, 31
Wilkins, Dominique, 69, 156
Wilkins, Terrence, 83, 245
Wilkinson, J. L., 20, 115, 132
Williams, Alexander McDonald, 21, 149
Williams, Archie, 19, 25, 264, 278
Williams, Art, 60, 149
Williams, Bob, 39, 197
Williams, C.W., 290, 292
Williams, Carla, 102
Williams, Charlie, 71, 77, 149
Williams, DeAngelo, 215, 309
Williams, Doug, 65, 66, 72, 73, 225, 246
Williams, Henry Sylvester (CHL), 14, 253
Williams, Ike, 75, 200
Williams, Jay Mayo "Inky", 20, 246
Williams, Jaylin, 110, 197
Williams, Jr., Hank, 96, 215, 309
Williams, Ken, 86, 149
Williams, Latavious, 96, 197
Williams, Leonard, 38, 207
Williams, Marvin, 36, 92, 149, 153
Williams, Marvin "Tex", 55, 137
Williams, Natalie, 80, 82, 84, 153, 176, 197
Williams, Quincy, 108, 246
Williams, Quinnen, 104, 108, 233, 246
Williams, Ray, 66, 156
Williams, Reggie, 72, 165, 181, 197
Williams, Ricky, 214, 307
Williams, Riquna "Bay Bay", 98, 197
Williams, Serena, 84, 86, 88, 89, 95, 102, 282, 285, 286, 287, 310
Williams, Serena and Venus, 44, 285
Williams, Steve, 57, 184, 197
Williams, Tiny, 11, 262
Williams, Venus, 82, 84, 86, 88, 94, 104, 281, 284, 286, 306
Williamson, Ansel, 82, 262
Williamson, Carmen, 69, 199, 266
Williamson, Freddie "The Hammer", 208, 299
Willingham, Tyrone, 80, 89, 209, 210, 246
Willis, Bill, 29, 65, 207, 211, 235, 246, 297
Willoughby, Bill, 62, 170, 182, 197
Wills, Maury, 47, 48, 50, 67, 118, 138, 149, 150, 300
Wilson, A'Ja, 108, 197
Wilson, Arthur, 198
Wilson, Atoy, 51, 278
Wilson, Don, 55, 150
Wilson, Earl, 47, 118, 150, 190, 299
Wilson, Fabiola, 32, 130, 150
Wilson, Flip, 24
Wilson, Gene, 35, 198
Wilson, George, 14, 114
Wilson, Hallow, 45, 294
Wilson, Jack, 27, 199, 205
Wilson, Jumpin' Johnny, 33, 198
Wilson, Michael "Wild Thing", 85, 160, 198
Wilson, Russell, 97, 99, 217, 227, 246
Wilson, Willie, 67, 150
Wimbledon, 35, 42, 43, 63, 76, 82, 84, 86, 88, 89, 94, 104, 281, 283, 284, 285, 286, 305
Winfield, Dave, 61, 150
Winkfield, Jimmy, 15, 259, 262, 263
Winston-Salem State University, 46, 52, 64, 69, 71, 172, 176, 209, 239
Winter X Games, 291
Winters, Jesse "Nip", 21, 150
Withers, George, 11, 263
WNBA, 80, 81, 82, 84, 85, 86, 87, 88, 90, 92, 94, 95, 96, 98, 99, 100, 103, 105, 108, 109, 110, 111, 157, 158, 164, 165, 166, 167, 168, 169, 170, 171, 173, 174, 176, 180, 181, 182, 183, 184, 185, 187, 188, 191, 192, 193, 194, 196, 197, 290, 311
Woessner, William, 139, 305
Wolfe, George C., 71
Wolfe, Tim, 99, 210, 309
Women's International Bowling Congress, 27, 204
Women's National Basketball Association (WNBA), 157
Women's Sports Foundation, 66, 80, 265, 266, 272, 273, 276
Women's World Basketball Association (WWBA), 76, 156, 185
Wood, Willie, 43, 63, 212, 246
Woodard, Lynette, 67, 70, 160, 198
Wooden, John, 32, 152, 195
Woodruff, John, 25, 264, 278
Woods, J. Hoffman, 16, 151
Woods, Tiger, 35, 80, 81, 82, 83, 86, 87, 90, 97, 103, 150, 249, 251, 252, 306, 307
Woods, Tiger
   Earl Woods, 35
Woodson, Carter G., 26
Woodson, Charles, 81, 246
Woolpert, Phil, 39, 152
World Football League, 55, 62, 63, 212, 234, 236, 238, 244, 246, 318
World Football League (WFL), 63
World Hockey Association, 59, 253, 257
World Professional Basketball Tournament, 27, 28, 155, 160, 161, 164, 165, 173
World Series, 20, 21, 22, 23, 28, 29, 30, 31, 32, 37, 39, 40, 50, 52, 57, 58, 63, 64, 66, 74, 76, 77, 78, 80, 83, 86, 88, 92, 98, 101, 102, 111, 115, 116, 117, 118, 120, 123, 124, 125, 126, 127, 129, 132, 133, 134, 135, 136, 137, 139, 141, 144, 145, 146, 147, 148, 149, 150, 240, 292, 297, 302
World Team Tennis (WTT), 62, 281
Worthy, James, 68, 69, 153, 156
Wright, Eddie, 57, 257
Wright, Elmo, 60, 247
Wright, Jason, 106, 111, 235, 247
Wright, Lester, 111, 266, 294
Wright, Lonnie, 52, 198, 208, 294
Wright, Michael, 95, 279
Wright, Richard, 27
Wright, Walter "Toots", 22, 160, 181
Wright, William "Bill", 44, 252
Wrigley Field, 39, 40, 44, 47, 118, 136, 147, 160, 276, 298
Wrigley, Philip K., 38, 146
WSLAM magazine, 108, 159, 170, 180, 186

Emancipation Index

X

X-Files series
    The Unnatural, *85, 133*

Y

Yamaguchi, Kristi, 19, 264, 271
Yankee Stadium, 23, 116
Young, Buddy, 30, 31, 34, 207, 211, 229, 243, 247
Young, Chris, 94, 150
Young, Cy, 17, 18, 41, 54, 58, 115, 126, 132, 135, 140, 295
Young, Milton, 10, 12, 261, 263
Young, Vince, 93, 214, 247
Younger, Paul "Tank", 31, 33, 37, 38, 63, 207, 212, 221, 237, 243, 247

Z

Zaharias, Babe, 34, 248
Zee-Nuts, 19, 128
Zoeller, Fuzzy, 66, 81, 249, 251, 306

www.ingramcontent.com/pod-product-compliance
Lightning Source LLC
Chambersburg PA
CBHW080454110426
42742CB00017B/2888